Everyone's an Author

WITH READINGS

SECOND EDITION

ANDREA LUNSFORD
STANFORD UNIVERSITY

MICHAL BRODY
SONOMA STATE UNIVERSITY

LISA EDE
OREGON STATE UNIVERSITY

BEVERLY J. MOSS
THE OHIO STATE UNIVERSITY

CAROLE CLARK PAPPER
HOFSTRA UNIVERSITY

KEITH WALTERS
PORTLAND STATE UNIVERSITY

W. W. NORTON AND COMPANY
New York • London

W. W. Norton & Company has been independent since its founding in 1923, when William Warder Norton and Mary D. Herter Norton first published lectures delivered at the People's Institute, the adult education division of New York City's Cooper Union. The firm soon expanded its program beyond the Institute, publishing books by celebrated academics from America and abroad. By midcentury, the two major pillars of Norton's publishing program—trade books and college texts—were firmly established. In the 1950s, the Norton family transferred control of the company to its employees, and today—with a staff of four hundred and a comparable number of trade, college, and professional titles published each year—W. W. Norton & Company stands as the largest and oldest publishing house owned wholly by its employees.

Editor: Marilyn Moller
Associate Editor: Tenyia Lee
Assistant Editor: Claire Wallace
Managing Editor, College: Marian Johnson
Managing Editor, College Digital Media: Kim Yi
Production Manager: Jane Searle
Media Editor: Erica Wnek
Media Project Editor: Cooper Wilhelm
Marketing Manager, Composition: Megan Zwilling
Design Director: Rubina Yeh
Designer: Jo Anne Metsch
Cover Design: Doyle Partners
Photo Editor: Ted Szczepanski
Permissions: Elizabeth Trammell
Composition and Layout: Carole Desnoes
Manufacturing: RRD Crawfordsville

Permission to use copyrighted material is included at the back of this book.

Library of Congress Cataloging-in-Publication Data
Names: Lunsford, Andrea A., 1942- author. | Brody, Michal, author. | Ede, Lisa S., 1947- author. | Moss, Beverly J., author. | Papper, Carole Clark, author. | Walters, Keith, 1952- author.
Title: Everyone's an author with readings / Andrea Lunsford ; Michal Brody ; Lisa Ede ; Beverly J. Moss ; Carole Clark Papper ; Keith Walters.
Description: Second Edition. | New York : W.W. Norton & Company, [2017] | Includes bibliographical references and index.
Identifiers: LCCN 2015044578 | **ISBN 9780393265293** (pbk.)
Subjects: LCSH: English language--Rhetoric. | Report writing. | Authorship. | College readers.
Classification: LCC PE1408 .L874 2016 | DDC 808/.0427--dc23 LC record available at http://lccn.loc.gov/2015044578

W. W. Norton & Company, Inc., 500 Fifth Avenue, New York, NY 10110
wwnorton.com

W. W. Norton & Company Ltd., Castle House, 75/76 Wells Street, London W1T 3QT

1 2 3 4 5 6 7 8 9

For our students, authors all.

Preface

S EVERYONE AN AUTHOR? In the first edition of this book, we answered that question with an emphatic "yes!" and hoped teachers and students would agree. We're happy to say they did, embracing what is now even more obvious than it was during the years we spent drafting that first edition: that writers today have important things to say and want—indeed demand—to be heard, and that anyone with access to a computer can publish their writing, can in fact become an *author*. So we are thrilled that our book has found a large and enthusiastic audience.

As we began work on the second edition, we went back to our title, which has come to have many levels of meaning for us. Two key words: "author" and "everyone." Certainly "author" informs our book throughout, from the Introduction that shows students the many ways they are already authors to the final chapter that offers advice on ways of publishing their writing. Indeed, every chapter in the book assumes that students are capable of creating and producing knowledge and of sharing that knowledge with others, of being *authors*. And we know that this focus has struck a chord with teachers and students across the country; in fact, we now meet students who talk comfortably about their role as authors, something we surely didn't see a decade or even five years ago.

And then we thought about the other key word in our title: "everyone." And like good rhetoricians, we thought about the primary audience for this book: our students. Have we reached every one of them? When they read what we say or imply about college students, will they see themselves, their friends, their communities? Will our book interest them? Will the examples and readings we've chosen inspire them to write? Have we, in other words, written a book for *everyone*? We went on to ask ourselves just who this "everyone" is: as it turns out, it's a very expansive group, including students in community and two-year colleges, in historically black colleges and universities, in Hispanic-serving and Tribal colleges, in dual enrollment classes, on regional campuses of large state universities, in private liberal arts schools, in research one universities. Students from many different communities, from all socioeconomic backgrounds, with a wide range of abilities and ableness. In short, anyone who has something to say—and that's EVERYONE.

But let's back up for a moment and ask another question: what led us to pursue this goal of inviting every student to take on the responsibility of authorship? When we began teaching (we won't even say how many years ago that was), our students wrote traditional academic essays by hand—or sometimes typed them on typewriters. But that was then. Those were the days when writing was something students were assigned, rather than something they did every single day and night. When "text" was a noun, not a verb. When tweets were sounds birds made. When blogs didn't even exist. The writing scene has changed radically. Now students write, text, tweet, and post to everything from *Facebook* to *Blackboard* to *Instagram* at home, in the library, on the bus, while walking down the street. Writing is ubiquitous—they barely even notice it.

What students are learning to write has changed as well. Instead of "essays," students today engage a range of genres: position papers, analyses of all kinds, reports, narratives—and more. In addition, they work across media, embedding images and even audio and video in what they write. They do research, not just for assigned "research papers" but for pretty much everything they write. And they write and research not just to report or analyze but to join conversations. With the click of a mouse they can respond to a *Washington Post* blog, publishing their views alongside those of the *Post* writer. They can create posters for the We Are the 99% *Facebook* page, post a review of a novel on *Amazon*, contribute to a wiki, submit a poem or story to their college literary magazine, assemble a digital portfolio to use in applying for jobs or internships. The work of these students speaks clearly to a sea change in literacy and to a major premise of this book: if you have access to a computer, you can publish what you write. Today, everyone can be an author.

We began to get a hint of this shift nearly a decade ago. In a 2009 article in *Seed* magazine, researchers Denis Pelli and Charles Bigelow argue that while "nearly universal literacy is a defining characteristic of today's modern civilization, nearly universal authorship will shape tomorrow's."[1]

---

1. Denis G. Pelli and Charles Bigelow, "A Writing Revolution," *Seedmagazine.com*, 20 Oct. 2009, Web, 3 Jan. 2012.

Authors per year

Authors per year
(as % of world pop.)

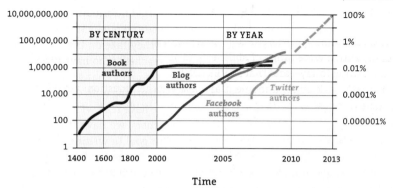

Number of authors who published in each year for various media since 1400 by century (left) and by year (right). *Source*: Denis G. Pelli and Charles Bigelow, "A Writing Revolution," *Seedmagazine.com*, 20 Oct. 2009, Web, 3 Jan. 2012.

They go on to offer a graph of the history of "authorship" from 1400 projected through 2013, noting that while we've seen steep rises in authorship before (especially around 1500 and 1800), the current rise is more precipitous by far.

Tracking another shift, rhetorician Deborah Brandt suggests that now that a majority of Americans make their living in the so-called information economy, where writing is part of what they do during their workday, it could be said that "writing is . . . eclipsing reading as the literate skill of consequence."[2] Pelli and Bigelow put this shift more starkly, saying, "As readers, we consume. As authors, we create."

Today's authors are certainly creators, in the broadest sense. Protestors are using *Twitter* to organize and demonstrate on behalf of pressing social and political issues around the world. Fans create websites for those who follow certain bands, TV shows, sports teams. As this book goes to press, U.S. presidential candidates are using *Facebook* and *Twitter* to broadcast their messages, raise money, and mobilize voters.

Clearly, we are experiencing a major transition in what it means to be a writer. Such a massive shift brings challenges as well as opportunities. Many worry, for example, about the dangers the internet poses to our privacy. As authors, we also understand that being a *productive* author brings

2. Deborah Brandt, "Writing at Work," Hunter College, New York, 12 Nov. 2011, Lecture.

certain responsibilities: working fairly and generously with others, taking seriously the challenges of writing with authority, standing behind the texts we create, being scrupulous about where we get information and how we use it, and using available technologies in wise and productive ways.

This book aims to guide student writers as they take on the responsibilities, challenges, and joys of authorship. As teachers who have been active participants in the literacy revolution brought on by changes in modes and technologies of communication, we've been learning with our students how best to engage such changes. As scholars, we have read widely in what many refer to as the "new literacies"; as researchers, we have studied the changing scene of writing with excitement. Our goal in writing this textbook has been to take some of the best ideas animating the field of rhetoric and writing and make them accessible to and usable by students and teachers—and to invite *everyone* to become authors.

As Beverly Moss put it in a recent presentation, one challenge in writing any composition textbook is to find a balance between meeting students where they are and where they come from—and yet at the same time challenging them to move out of their comfort zones: to embrace the unfamiliar, to see themselves as meaning makers and see writing in whatever medium as an opportunity to create, to inform, to entertain, to move, to connect with others—including those who are not like them, who maybe do not speak the same language or hail from the same communities. With each page that we write, we try to achieve that balance. Every one of our students has important things to say, and we aim to help them do just that.

Highlights

- *On the genres college students need to write:* arguments, analyses, narratives, reports, reviews—a *new* chapter on proposals—and *new* guidance in visual analysis, literacy narratives, profiles, and literature reviews. Chapter 10 gives students help "Choosing Genres" when the choice is theirs.

- *On the need for rhetoric.* From Chapter 1 on "Thinking Rhetorically" to Chapter 5 on "Writing and Rhetoric as a Field of Study" to the many prompts throughout the book that help students think about their own rhetorical situations and choices, this book makes them aware of the importance of rhetoric.

- **On academic writing.** We've tried to demystify academic writing—and to show students how to enter academic conversations. Chapter 4 offers advice on "Meeting the Demands of Academic Writing," and we've added *new* guidance on writing visual analyses, literature reviews, literacy narratives, and other common college assignments.

- **On argument.** Chapter 11 covers "Arguing a Position," Chapter 17 covers "Analyzing and Constructing Arguments" (with *new* coverage of Classical, Toulmin, Rogerian, and Invitational approaches), and Chapter 18 offers "Strategies for Supporting an Argument."

- **On reading.** Chapter 3 offers guidelines on "Reading Rhetorically": to read not only with careful attention but also with careful *intention*— to listen, engage, and then respond. And it offers strategies for reading texts of all kinds—written in words or images, on-screen or off-.

- **On research.** The challenge today's students face is not gathering data, but making sense of massive amounts of information and using it effectively in support of their own arguments. Chapters 19–28 cover all stages of research, from finding and evaluating sources to citing and documenting them. Chapter 20, on "Finding Sources," has been reorganized to combine print and online sources in a way that better aligns with how students today search for information, and *new* examples guide students through annotating, summarizing, and synthesizing the sources they find.

- **On writing in multiple modes.** Chapter 34 provides practical advice on writing illustrated essays, blogs, wikis, audio and video essays, and posters, and Chapter 35 covers oral presentations—both *new* to this edition. The companion *Tumblr* site provides a regularly updated source of multimodal readings.

- **On social media.** We've tried to bridge the gap between the writing students do on social media sites and the writing they do in college. We reject the notion that *Google* is making us stupid; in fact, we find that student writers are adept at crafting messages that will reach their intended audiences *because* they do so every day on *Facebook* and other such sites. Chapter 30 shows how the rhetorical strategies they use instinctively in social media are used in academic writing—and also how social media is now used in academia.

- *On style.* We pay attention to style, with guidelines that will help students think carefully and creatively about the stylistic choices open to them. Chapter 29 defines style as a matter of appropriateness, and Chapter 31 covers "How to Write Good Sentences."

- *On social justice.* Minimum wages, affordable housing, Black Lives Matter: many of the examples in this book demonstrate how people from various walks of life use writing in ways that strive to help create "a more perfect union," a society that is more just and equitable for all its members. We don't always agree on how to go about reaching those goals, and that's why rhetoric and civic discourse matter.

- *Many new examples about topics students will relate to.* From a description of how Steph Curry shoots a basketball and a rhetorical analysis of what makes Pharrell's "Happy" so catchy to a blog post from a student NASCAR driver and a visual analysis of the *New Yorker*'s Bert and Ernie cover, we hope that all students will find examples and images that will make them smile—and inspire them to read and write.

- *An anthology of 32 readings—and more readings posted weekly on Tumblr.* Marginal links refer readers from the rhetoric to examples in the readings—and vice versa. You can center your course on either the rhetoric or the readings, and the links will help you draw from the other part as need be.

- *Menus, directories, documentation templates, and a glossary / index* make the book easy to use—and to understand.

Everyone's an Author is available in two versions, with and without an anthology of readings. Readings are arranged alphabetically by author, with menus indexing the readings by genre and theme. And the book is formatted as two books in one, rhetoric in front and readings in the back. You can therefore center your course on either the rhetoric or the readings, since links in the margins will help you draw from the other part as you wish to.

What's Online

As an ebook. Both versions of *Everyone's an Author* are available as ebooks and include all the readings and images found in the print books. At a fraction of the price of the print books, the ebooks allow students to access the entire book, search, highlight, bookmark, take and share notes with ease, and click on online examples—and can be viewed and synched on all computers and mobile devices.

Everyonesanauthor.tumblr.com adds essays, videos, audio clips, speeches, infographics, and more. Searchable by genres, themes, and chapters in the book, the site is updated with new readings weekly. Each item is introduced with a brief contextual note and followed by questions that prompt students to analyze, reflect on, and respond to the text. A "comments" button lets students post comments and share texts with others. The site also includes clusters of texts, conversations on topics being widely discussed. Find a chapter-by-chapter menu of the online examples in this book by clicking "Links from the Book." See you and your students at everyonesanauthor.tumblr.com!

Norton/write. Find a library of model student papers; more than 1,000 online exercises and quizzes; research and plagiarism tutorials; documentation guidelines for MLA, APA, *Chicago*, and CSE styles; MLA citation drills, and more—all just a click away. Free and open, no password required. Access the site at wwnorton.com/write.

Coursepacks are available for free and in a variety of formats, including *Blackboard, Desire2Learn, Moodle, Canvas,* and *Angel*. Coursepacks work within your existing learning management system, so there's no new system to learn, and access is free and easy. The *Everyone's an Author* coursepack includes the "Think Beyond Words" exercises that prompt students to analyze interesting online examples of multimodal writing; the "Reflect" exercises found throughout the book; model student papers; quizzes and exercises on grammar and research; documentation guidelines; revision worksheets, and more. Coursepacks are ready to use, right from the start—but are also easy to customize, using the system you already know and understand. Download the coursepack at wwnorton.com/instructors.

Author videos. Andrea Lunsford, Lisa Ede, Beverly Moss, Carole Clark Papper, and Keith Walters answer questions they're often asked by other instructors: about fostering collaboration, teaching multimodal writing, taking advantage of the writing center, teaching classes that include both L1 and L2 students, and more. View the videos at wwnorton.com/instructors.

Go to wwnorton.com/instructors to find all of the resources described here. Select "Composition," and then choose *Everyone's an Author 2e* to get started.

The Guide to Teaching *Everyone's an Author*

Available in a tabbed three-ring binder that will also hold your own class notes, this guide offers practical advice and activities from Lisa Ede for teaching all the chapters and readings in the book, including a new chapter by Michal Brody on how to use the companion *Tumblr* site with your students. In addition, it offers detailed advice from Richard Bullock, Andrea Lunsford, Maureen Daly Goggin, and others about teaching writing more generally: how to create a syllabus, respond to student writing, help students whose primary language isn't English, and more. Order a print copy or access the online version at wwnorton.com/instructors.

Acknowledgments

We are profoundly grateful to the many people who have helped bring *Everyone's an Author* into existence. Indeed, this text provides a perfect example of what an eighteenth-century German encyclopedia meant when it defined *book* as "the work of many hands." Certainly this one is the work of many hands, and among those hands none have been more instrumental than those of Marilyn Moller: the breadth of her vision is matched by her meticulous attention to detail, keen sense of style and design, and ability to get more work done than anyone we have ever known. Throughout the process of composing this text, she has set the bar high for us, and we've tried hard to reach it. And our deep gratitude goes to Tenyia Lee, whose astute judgment and analytical eye have guided us through this edition. A big thank you as well to Marian Johnson for making time to read and respond to many of the chapters in the first edition—and especially for stepping in at the eleventh hour of this second edition to make it happen! Thanks also to John Elliott, whose careful and graceful line editing helped shape the first edition.

We are similarly grateful to many others who contributed their talents to this book, especially Carole Desnoes and Jane Searle, for all they did to produce this book in record time (no small undertaking). Thanks as well to Elizabeth Trammell for her work clearing the many text permissions and to Ted Szczepanski and Elyse Rieder for their work finding and clearing permissions for the many images. Last but certainly not least, we thank Claire Wallace for undertaking countless tasks large and small with energy and unprecedented efficiency.

The design of this book is something we are particularly proud of, and for that we offer very special thanks to several amazing designers. Stephen Doyle created the spectacular cover that embodies a key message of our book: that we live in a world made of words and images. Carin Berger created the illuminated alphabet, also made of text, that opens every chapter. JoAnne Metsch did the lovely interior design. And Debra Morton-Hoyt, Rubina Yeh, Michael Wood, and Tiani Kennedy oversaw the whole thing as well as adding their own elegant—and whimsical!—touches inside and out. Best thanks to all of them.

Everyone's an Author is more than just a print book, and we thank Erica Wnek, Kim Yi, Mateus Teixeira, Ava Bramson, and Cooper Wilhelm for creating and producing the superb ebook and instructors' site. And we again want to thank Cliff Landesman for his work in creating the fantastic *Tumblr* site.

Special thanks to the fabled Norton Travelers, who have worked so hard to introduce teachers across the country to what *Everyone's an Author* can offer them. And a big thank you to Megan Zwilling, Maureen Connelly, Lib Triplett, and Doug Day for helping us keep our eye on our audience: teachers and students at colleges where rhetorics of this kind are assigned. Finally, we are grateful to Roby Harrington, Julia Reidhead, and Steve Dunn, who have given their unwavering support to this project for more than a decade now. We are fortunate indeed to have had the talent and hard work of this distinguished Norton team.

An astute and extremely helpful group of reviewers has helped us more than we can say: we have depended on their good pedagogical sense and advice in revising every chapter of this book. Special thanks to Stevens Amidon, Indiana University-Purdue Fort Wayne; Georgana Atkins, University of Mississippi; Kristen Belcher, University of Colorado, Denver; Samantha Bell, Johnson County Community College; Dawn Bergeron, St. Johns River State College; Cassandra Bishop, Southern Illinois University; Erin Breaux, South Louisiana Community College; Ellie Bunting, Edison State College; Maggie Callahan, Louisiana State University; Laura Chartier, University of Alaska, Anchorage; Tera Joy Cole, Idaho State University; Anne-Marie Deitering, Oregon State University; Debra Dew, Valparaiso University; Robyn DeWall, Idaho State University; Patrick Dolan Jr., University of Iowa; Maryam El-Shall, Jamestown Community College; Lindsay Ferrara, Fairfield University; Maureen Fitzpatrick, Johnson County Community College; Kitty Flowers, University of Indianapolis; Robin Gallaher, Northwest Missouri State University; Tara Hembrough, Southern Illinois University; Samuel Head, Idaho

State University; Emma Howes, Coastal Carolina University; Joyce Inman, University of Southern Mississippi; Michelle S. Lee, Daytona State College; Sonja Lynch, Wartburg College; Chelsea Murdock, University of Kansas; Jessie Nixon, University of Alaska, Anchorage; Thomas Reynolds, Northwestern State University; Matthew Schmeer, Johnson County Community College; John Sherrill, Purdue University; Mary Lourdes Silva, Ithaca College; Marc Simoes, California State University, Long Beach; Susan Smith, Georgia Southern University; Tracie Smith, University of Indianapolis; Paulette Swartzfager, Rochester Institute of Technology; Jason Tham, St. Cloud State University; Tom Thompson, The Citadel; Verne Underwood, Rogue Community College; Jennifer Vala, Georgia State University; Emily Ward, Idaho State University; and Lauren Woolbright, Clemson University.

We'd also like to thank those reviewers who helped us to shape the first edition: Edward Baldwin, College of Southern Nevada; Michelle Ballif, University of Georgia; Larry Beason, University of South Alabama, Mobile; Kevin Boyle, College of Southern Nevada; Elizabeth Brockman, Central Michigan University; Stephen Brown, University of Nevada, Las Vegas; Vicki Byard, Northeastern Illinois University; Beth Daniell, Kennesaw State University; Nancy DeJoy, Michigan State University; Ronda Dively, Southern Illinois University, Carbondale; Douglas Downs, Montana State University; Suellynn Duffey, University of Missouri, St. Louis; Anne Dvorak, Longview Community College; Patricia Ericsson, Washington State University; Frank Farmer, University of Kansas; Casie Fedukovich, North Carolina State University; Lauren Fitzgerald, Yeshiva University; Diana Grumbles, Southern Methodist University; Ann Guess, Alvin Community College; Michael Harker, Georgia State University; Charlotte Hogg, Texas Christian University; Melissa Ianetta, University of Delaware; Jordynn Jack, University of North Carolina, Chapel Hill; Sara Jameson, Oregon State University; David A. Jolliffe, University of Arkansas; Ann Jurecic, Rutgers University; Connie Kendall, University of Cincinnati; William Lalicker, West Chester University; Phillip Marzluf, Kansas State University; Richard Matzen, Woodbury University; Moriah McCracken, The University of Texas, Pan American; Mary Pat McQueeney, Johnson County Community College; Clyde Moneyhun, Boise State University; Whitney Myers, Texas Wesleyan University; Carroll Ferguson Nardone, Sam Houston State University; Rolf Norgaard, University of Colorado, Boulder; Katherine Durham Oldmixon, Huston-Tillotson University; Matthew Oliver, Old Dominion University; Gary Olson, Idaho State University; Paula Patch, Elon University; Scott Payne, University of Central Arkansas; Mary Jo Reiff, University of Kansas; Albert Rouzie, Ohio

University; Alison Russell, Xavier University; Kathleen J. Ryan, University of Montana; Emily Robins Sharpe, Penn State University; Eddie Singleton, The Ohio State University; Allison Smith, Middle Tennessee State University; Deborah Coxwell Teague, Florida State University; Rex Veeder, St. Cloud State University; Matthew Wiles, University of Louisville; and Mary Wright, Christopher Newport University.

Collectively, we have taught for over 150 years: that's a lot of classes, a lot of students—and we are grateful for every single one of them. We owe some of the best moments of our lives to them—and in our most challenging moments, they have inspired us to carry on. In *Everyone's an Author*, we are particularly grateful to the student writers whose work adds so much to this text: Ade Adegboyega, Rutgers University; Crystal Aymelek, Portland State University; Amanda Baker, The Ohio State University; Carrie Barker, Kirkwood Community College; Ryan Joy, Portland State University; Julia Landauer, Stanford University; Larry Lehna, University of Michigan, Dearborn; Melanie Luken, The Ohio State University; Mitchell Oliver, Georgia State University; David Pasini, The Ohio State University; Walter Przybylowski, Rutgers University; Melissa Rubin, Hofstra University; Anya Schulz, University of California, Berkeley; Katryn Sheppard, Portland State University; Katherine Spriggs, Stanford University; Shuqiao Song, Stanford University; Saurabh Vaish, Hofstra University; and Kameron Wiles, Ball State University.

Each of us also has special debts of gratitude. Andrea Lunsford thanks her students and colleagues at the Bread Loaf Graduate School of English and in the Program in Writing and Rhetoric at Stanford, along with her sisters Ellen Ashdown and Liz Middleton, editor and friend Carolyn Lengel, friends and life supporters Shirley Brice Heath, Betty Bailey, Cheryl Glenn, and Jackie Royster; and especially—and forever—her grandnieces Audrey and Lila Ashdown, who are already budding authors.

Michal Brody would like to thank her two wonderful families in California and Yucatan who so graciously support (and endure) her crazy and restless transnational life. Her conversations—both the actual and the imagined—with each and all of those loved ones provide the constant impetus to reach for both the texture and depth of experience and the clarity with which to express it. She also thanks her students in both countries, who remind her every day that we are all teachers, all learners.

Lisa Ede thanks her husband, Greg Pfarr, for his support, for his commitment to his own art, and for their year-round vegetable garden. Thanks as well to her siblings, who have stuck together through thick and thin: Leni

Ede Smith, Andrew Ede, Sara Ede Rowkamp, Jeffrey Ede, Michele Ede Smith, Laurie Ede Drake, Robert Ede, and Julie Ede Campbell. She also thanks her colleagues in the Oregon State School of Writing, Literature, and Film for their encouragement and support. Special thanks go to the school's director, Anita Helle, and to their amazing administrative staff: Ann Leen, Aurora Terhune, and Felicia Phillips.

Beverly Moss thanks her parents, Harry and Sarah Moss, for their love, encouragement, and confidence in her when her own wavered. In addition, she thanks her Ohio State and Bread Loaf students, who inspire her and teach her so much about teaching. She also wants to express gratitude to her colleagues in Rhetoric, Composition, and Literacy at Ohio State for their incredible support. Finally, she thanks two of her own former English teachers, Dorothy Bratton and Jackie Royster, for the way they modeled excellence inside and outside the classroom.

Carole Clark Papper would like to thank her husband, Bob, and wonderful children—Dana, Matt, Zack, and Kate—without whose loving support little would happen and nothing would matter. In addition, she is grateful to the Hofstra University Writing Center faculty and tutors, whose dedication and commitment to students always inspire.

Keith Walters thanks his partner of thirty years, Jonathan Tamez, for sharing a love of life, language, travel, flowers, and beauty. He is also grateful to his students in Tunisia, South Carolina, Texas, and Oregon, who have challenged him to find ways of talking about what good writing is and how to do it.

Finally, we thank those who have taught us—who first helped us learn to hold a pencil and print our names, who inspired a love of language and of reading and writing, who encouraged us to take chances in writing our lives as best we could, who prodded and pushed when we needed it, and who most of all set brilliant examples for us to follow. One person who taught almost all of us—about rhetoric, about writing, and about life—was Edward P. J. Corbett. We remember him with love and with gratitude

—Andrea Lunsford, Michal Brody, Lisa Ede,
Beverly Moss, Carole Clark Papper, Keith Walters

CONTENTS

PART III   Genres of Writing   105

15 Writing a Review / "Two Thumbs Up"   297

16 Making a Proposal / "Here's What I Recommend"   340

Is Everyone an Author?

E'VE CHOSEN A PROVOCATIVE TITLE for this book, so it's fair to ask if we've gotten it right, if everyone is an author. Let's take just a few examples that can help to make the point:

- A student creates a *Facebook* page, which immediately finds a large audience of other interested students.

- A visitor to the United States sends an email to a few friends and family members in Slovakia—and they begin forwarding it. The message circles the globe in a day.

- A professor assigns students in her class to work together to write a number of entries for *Wikipedia*, and they are surprised to find how quickly their entries are revised by others.

- An airline executive writes a letter of apology for unconscionable delays in service and publishes the letter in newspapers, where millions will read it.

- A small group of high school students who are keen on cooking post their recipe for Crazy Candy Cookies on their *Cook's Corner* blog and are overwhelmed with the number of responses to their invention.

- Five women nominated for the Academy Award for Best Actress prepare acceptance speeches: one of them will deliver the speech live before an international audience.

- You get your next assignment in your college writing class and set out to do the research necessary to complete it. When you're finished, you turn in your twelve-page argument to your instructor and classmates for their responses—and you also post it on your webpage under "What I'm Writing Now."

All of these examples represent important messages written by people who probably do not consider themselves authors. Yet they illustrate what we mean when we say that today "everyone's an author." Once upon a time, the ability to compose a message that reached wide and varied audiences was restricted to a small group; now, however, this opportunity is available to anyone with access to the internet.

The word *author* has a long history, but it is most associated with the rise of print and the ability of a writer to claim what he or she has written as property. The first copyright act, in the early eighteenth century, ruled that authors held the primary rights to their work. And while anyone could potentially be a writer, an author was someone whose work had been published. That rough definition worked pretty well until recently, when traditional copyright laws began to show the strain of their 300-year history, most notably with the simple and easy file sharing that the internet makes possible.

In fact, the web has blurred the distinction between writers and authors, offering anyone with access to a computer the opportunity to publish what they write. Whether or not you own a computer, if you have access to one (at school, at a library), you can publish what you write and thus make what you say available to readers around the world.

Think for a minute about the impact of blogs, which first appeared in 1997. When this book was first published, there were more than 156 million public blogs, and as this new edition goes to press, there are more than 250 million blogs on *Tumblr* and *Wordpress* alone. Add to blogs the rise of *Facebook*, *Twitter*, *YouTube*, *Instagram*, and other social networking sites for even more evidence to support our claim: today, everyone's an author. Moreover, twenty-first-century authors just don't fit the image of the Romantic writer, alone in a garret, struggling to bring forth something unique. Rather, today's authors are part of a huge, often global, conversation; they build on what others have thought and written, they create mash-ups and remixes, and they practice teamwork at almost every turn. They are authoring for the digital age.

Redefining Writing

If the definition of *author* has changed in recent years, so has our understanding of the definition, nature, and scope of *writing*.

Writing, for example, now includes much more than words, as images and graphics take on an important part of the job of conveying meaning. In addition, writing can now include sound, video, and other media. Perhaps more important, writing now often contains many voices, as information from the web is incorporated into the texts we write with increasing ease. Finally, as we noted above, writing today is almost always part of a larger conversation. Rather than rising mysteriously from the depths of a writer's original thoughts, a stereotype made popular during the Romantic period, writing almost always responds to some other written piece or to other ideas. If "no man [or woman] is an island, entire of itself," then the same holds true for writing.

Writing now is also often highly collaborative. You work with a team to produce an illustrated report, the basis of which is used by members of the team to make a key presentation to management; you and a classmate carry out an experiment, argue over and write up the results together, and present your findings to the class; a business class project calls on you and others in your group to divide up the work along lines of expertise and then to pool your efforts in meeting the assignment. In all of these cases, writing is also performative—it performs an action or, in the words of many students we have talked with, it "makes something happen in the world."

Perhaps most notable, this expanded sense of writing challenges us to think very carefully about what our writing is for and whom it can and might reach. Email provides a good case in point. In the aftermath of the September 11 attacks, Tamim Ansary, a writer who was born in Afghanistan, found himself stunned by the number of people calling for bombing Afghanistan "back to the Stone Age." He sent an email to a few friends expressing his horror at the events, his condemnation of Osama bin Laden and the Taliban, and his hope that those in the United States would not act on the basis of gross stereotyping. The few dozen friends to whom Ansary wrote hit their forward buttons. Within days, the letter had circled the globe more than once, and Ansary's words were published by the Africa News Service, the *Philippine Daily Inquirer*, the *Evening Standard* in London, the *San Francisco Chronicle* and many other papers in the United States, as well as on many websites.

Authors whose messages can be instantly transported around the world need to consider those who will receive those messages. As the example of Tamim Ansary shows, no longer can writers assume that they write only to a specified audience or that they can easily control the dissemination of their messages. We now live not only in a city, a state, and a country but in a global community as well—and we write, intentionally or not, to speakers of many languages, to members of many cultures, to believers of many creeds.

Everyone's a Researcher

Since all writing responds to the ideas and words of others, it usually draws on some kind of research. Think for a moment of how often you carry out research. We're guessing that a little reflection will turn up lots of examples: you may find yourself digging up information on the pricing of new cars, searching *Craigslist* or the want ads for a good job, comparing two new smartphones, looking up statistics on a favorite sports figure, or searching for a recipe for tabbouleh. All of these everyday activities involve research. In addition, many of your most important life decisions involve research— what colleges to apply to, what jobs to pursue, where to live, and more. Once you begin to think about research in this broad way—as a form of inquiry related to important decisions—you'll probably find that research is something you do almost every day. Moreover, you'll see the ways in which the research you do adds to your credibility—giving you the authority that goes along with being an author.

But research today is very different from the research of only a few decades ago. Take the example of the concordance, an alphabetized listing of every instance of all topics and words in a work. Before the computer age, concordances were done by hand: the first full concordance to the works of Shakespeare took decades of eye-straining, painstaking research, counting, and sorting. Some scholars spent years, even whole careers, developing concordances that then served as major resources for other scholars. As soon as Shakespeare's plays and poems were in digital form—voilà!—a concordance could be produced automatically and accessed by writers with the click of a mouse.

To take a more recent example, first-year college students just twenty years ago had no access to the internet. Just think of how easy it is now to check temperatures around the world, track a news story, or keep up to the minute on stock prices. These are items that you can *Google*, but you may also have many expensive subscription databases available to you through your school's library. It's not too much of an exaggeration to say that the world is literally at your fingertips.

What has *not* changed is the need to carry out research with great care, to read all sources with a critical eye, and to evaluate sources before depending on them for an important decision or using them in your own work. What also has not changed is the sheer thrill research can bring: while much research work can seem plodding and even repetitious, the excitement of discovering materials you didn't know existed, of analyzing information in a new way, or of tracing a question through one particular historical period brings its own reward. Moreover, your research adds to what philosopher Kenneth Burke calls "the conversation of humankind," as you build on what others have done and begin to make significant contributions of your own to the world's accumulated knowledge.

Everyone's a Student

More than 2,000 years ago, the Roman writer Quintilian set out a plan for education, beginning with birth and ending only with old age and death. Surprisingly enough, Quintilian's recommendation for a lifelong education has never been more relevant than it is in the twenty-first century, as knowledge is increasing and changing so fast that most people must continue to be active learners long after they graduate from college. This explosion of knowledge also puts great demands on communication. As a result, one of your biggest challenges will be learning how to learn and how to communicate what you have learned across wider distances, to larger and increasingly diverse sets of audiences, and using an expanding range of media and genres.

When did you first decide to attend college, and what paths did you take to achieve that goal? Chances are greater today than at any time in our past that you may have taken time off to work before beginning college, or that you returned to college for new training when your job changed, or that you are attending college while working part-time or even full-time. These characteristics of college students are not new, but they are increasingly important, indicating that the path to college is not as straightforward as it was once thought to be. In addition, college is now clearly a part of a process of lifetime learning: you are likely to hold a number of positions—and each new position will call for new learning.

Citizens today need more years of education and more advanced skills than ever before: even entry-level jobs now call for a college diploma. But what you'll need isn't just a college education. Instead, you'll need an education that puts you in a position to take responsibility for your own learning and to take a direct, hands-on approach to that learning. Most of us learn best by *doing* what we're trying to learn rather than just being told about it. What does this change mean in practice? First, it means you will be doing much more writing, speaking, and researching than ever before. You may, for instance, conduct research on an economic trend and then use that research to create a theory capable of accounting for the trend; you may join a research group in an electrical engineering class that designs, tests, and implements a new system; you may be a member of a writing class that works to build a website for the local fire department, writes brochures for a nonprofit agency, or makes presentations before municipal boards. In each case, you will be doing what you are studying, whether it is economics, engineering, or writing.

Without a doubt, the challenges and opportunities for students today are immense. The chapters that follow try to keep these challenges and opportunities in the foreground, offering you concrete ways to think about yourself as a writer—and yes, as an author; to think carefully about the rhetorical situations you face and about the many and varied audiences for your work; and to expand your writing repertoire to include new genres, new media, and new ways of producing and communicating knowledge.

PART I

The Need for Rhetoric and Writing

CLOSE YOUR EYES and imagine a world without any form of language—no spoken or written words, no drawings, no mathematical formulas, no music—no way, that is, to communicate or express yourself. It's pretty hard to imagine such a world, and with good reason. For better or worse, we seem to be hardwired to communicate, to long to express ourselves to others. That's why philosopher Kenneth Burke says that people are, at their essence, "symbol-using animals" who have a basic need to communicate.

We can look across history and find early attempts to create systems of communication. Think, for instance, of the

Horses in prehistoric art: Uffington White Horse, Oxfordshire, England (approx. 3,000 years old); Chauvet Cave, near Vallon-Pont-d'Arc, France (approx. 30,000 years old); rock paintings, Bhimbetka, India (approx. 30,000 years old).

chalk horses of England, huge figures carved into trenches that were then filled with white chalk some 3,000 years ago. What do they say? Do they act as maps or road signs? Do they celebrate, or commemorate, or tell a story? Whatever their original intent, they echo the need to communicate to us from millennia away.

Cave paintings, many of them hauntingly beautiful, have been discovered across Europe, some thought to be 30,000 years old. Such communicative art—all early forms of writing—has been discovered in many other places, from Africa to Australia to South America to Asia.

While these carvings and paintings have been interpreted in many different ways, they all attest to the human desire to leave messages. And we don't need to look far to find other very early attempts to communicate— from makeshift drums and whistles to early pictographic languages to the symbols associated with the earliest astronomers.

As languages and other symbolic forms of communication like our own alphabet evolved, so did a need for ways to interpret and organize these forms and to use them in effective and meaningful ways. And out of these needs grew rhetoric—the art, theory, and practice of communication. In discussing rhetoric, Aristotle says we need to understand this art for two main reasons: first, in order to express our own ideas and thoughts, and second, to protect ourselves from those who would try to manipulate or harm us. Language, then, can be used for good or ill, to provide information that may help someone—or to deliberately mislead.

We believe the need for understanding rhetoric may be greater today than at any time in our history. At first glance, it may look as if communication has never been easier. We can send messages in a nanosecond, reaching people in all parts of the world with ease. We can broadcast our thoughts, hopes, and dreams—and invectives—in emails, blogs, status updates, tweets, text messages, and a plethora of other ways.

So far, perhaps, so good. But consider the story of the Tower of Babel, told in different ways in both the Qur'an and the Bible. When the people sought to build a tower that would reach to the heavens, God responded to their hubris by creating so many languages that communication became impossible and the tower had to be abandoned. As with the languages in Babel, the means of communication are proliferating today, bringing with them the potential for miscommunication. From the struggle to sift through the amount of information created in a day—more than was previously created in several lifetimes—to the difficulty of trying to communicate across vast differences in languages and cultures, we face challenges that our parents and grandparents never did.

Pieter Brueghel the Elder, *Tower of Babel*, 1563.

"The need for rhetoric" translated from English to Japanese.

In a time when new (and sometimes confusing) forms of communication are available, many of us are looking for help with making our messages known. *Google Translate* and *Bing Translator,* for example, are attempts to offer instant translation of texts from one language to another.

Such new technologies and tools can certainly help us as we move into twenty-first-century global villages. But they are not likely to reduce the need for an art and a theory that can inform the conversations we have there—that can encourage thoughtfulness, empathy, and responsible use of such technologies. Rhetoric responds to this need. Along with writing, which we define broadly to include speaking and drawing and performing as well as the literal inscription of words, rhetoric offers you solid ground on which to build both your education and your communicative ability and style. The chapters that follow will introduce you more fully to rhetoric and writing—and engage you in acquiring and using their powers.

ONE

Thinking Rhetorically

The only real alternative to war is rhetoric.

—WAYNE BOOTH

ROFESSOR WAYNE BOOTH made this statement at a national conference of scholars and teachers of writing held only months after 9/11, and it quickly drew a range of responses. Just what did Booth mean by this stark statement? How could rhetoric—the art and practice of persuasion—act as a counter to war?

A noted critic and scholar, Booth explored these questions throughout his long career, identifying rhetoric as an ethical art that begins with deep and intense listening and that searches for mutual understanding and common ground as an alternative to violence and war. Put another way, two of the most potent tools we have for persuasion are language—and violence: when words fail us, violence often wins the day. Booth sees the careful, persistent, and ethical use of language as our best approach to keeping violence and war at bay.

During the summer of 2014, Booth's words echoed again, as Israel and Hamas faced off in another armed conflict that raged for months, leaving thousands dead and resolving nothing. Meanwhile, in the United States, people across the country protested the killings of Michael Brown in Ferguson, Missouri; Eric Garner in Staten Island, New York; and other African American men, all at the hands of police officers. At marches and sit-ins, protesters held up signs saying "Black Lives Matter" and "I can't breathe," echoing Eric Garner's last words after being wrestled to the

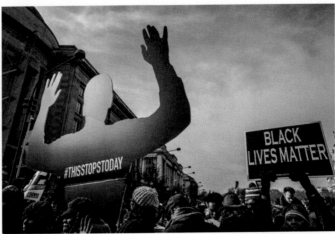

Protestors use posters, raised fists, and more to communicate their positions.

We didn't burn
down buildings. . . .
You can do a lot
with a pen and pad.
—ICE CUBE

ground in a chokehold. Protestors took to social media as well, using these dramatic and memorable statements as rhetorical strategies that captured and held the attention of millions of Americans.

So how can you go about developing your own careful, ethical use of language? Our short answer: by learning to think and act rhetorically, that is, by developing habits of mind that begin with listening and searching for understanding before you decide what you yourself think, and by thinking hard about your own beliefs before trying to persuade others to listen to and act on what you say.

Learning to think rhetorically can serve you well as you negotiate the complexities of life in today's world. In many everyday situations, you'll need to communicate successfully with others in order to get things done, and done in a responsible and ethical way. On the job, for example, you may need to bring coworkers to consensus on how best to raise productivity when there is little, if any, money for raises. Or in your college community, you may find yourself negotiating difficult waters.

When a group of students became aware of how little the temporary workers on their campus were paid, for example, they met with the workers and listened to gather information about the issue. They then mounted a campaign using flyers, newsletters, speeches, and sit-ins—in other words, using the available means of persuasion—to win attention and convince

Students use posters and conversation to protest the low wages paid to campus workers.

the administration to raise the workers' pay. These students were think-ing and acting rhetorically, and doing so responsibly and ethically. Note that these students, like the protesters in Ferguson, worked together, both with the workers and with each other. In other words, none of us can manage such actions all by ourselves; we need to engage in conversation with others and listen hard to what they say. Perhaps that's what philosopher Kenneth Burke had in mind when he created his famous "parlor" metaphor:

> Imagine that you enter a parlor. You come late. When you arrive, others have long preceded you, and they are engaged in a heated discussion, a discussion too heated for them to pause and tell you exactly what it is about. . . . You listen for a while, until you decide that you have caught the tenor of the argument; then you put in your oar.
>
> —KENNETH BURKE, *The Philosophy of Literary Form*

In this parable, each of us is the person arriving late to a room full of ani-mated conversation; we don't understand what is going on. Yet instead of butting in or trying to take over, we listen closely until we catch on to what people are saying. Then we join in, using language and rhetorical strategies to engage with others as we add our own voices to the conversation.

This book aims to teach you to *think and act rhetorically*—to listen carefully and then to "put in your oar," join conversations about important issues, and develop strong critical and ethical habits of mind that will help you engage with others in responsible ways. This chapter will help you develop the habit of thinking rhetorically.

First, Listen

Thinking rhetorically begins with listening, with being willing to hear the words of others in an open and understanding way. It means paying attention to what others say before and even *as a way* of making your own contributions to a conversation. Think of the times you are grateful to others for listening closely to you: when you're talking through a conflict with a family member, for instance, or even when you're trying to explain to a salesperson what it is you're looking for. On those occasions, you want the person you're addressing to really *listen* to what you say.

> We have two ears and one mouth so we may listen more and talk less.
>
> —EPICTETUS

This is a kind of listening that rhetorician Krista Ratcliffe dubs "rhetorical listening," opening yourself to the thoughts of others and making the effort not only to hear their words but to take those words in and fully understand what people are saying. It means paying attention to what others say as a way of establishing good will and acknowledging the importance of their views. And yes, it means taking seriously and engaging with views that differ, sometimes radically, from your own.

Rhetorical listening is what middle school teacher Julia Blount asked for in a *Facebook* post following the 2015 riots in Baltimore after the death of Freddie Gray, who suffered fatal spinal injuries while in police custody:

> Every comment or post I have read today voicing some version of disdain for the people of Baltimore—"I can't understand" or "They're destroying their own community"—tells me that many of you are not listening. I am not asking you to condone or agree with violence. I just need you to listen. . . . If you are not listening, not exposing yourself to unfamiliar perspectives . . . not engaging in conversation, then you are perpetuating white privilege. . . . It is exactly your ability to *not* hear, to ignore the situation, that is a mark of your privilege.
>
> —JULIA BLOUNT, "Dear White *Facebook* Friends: I Need You to Respect What Black America Is Feeling Right Now"

Hear What Others Are Saying—and Think about Why

When you enter any conversation, whether academic, professional, or personal, take the time to understand what is being said rather than rushing to a conclusion or a judgment. Listen carefully to what others are saying and consider what motivates them: where are they coming from?

Developing such habits of mind will be useful to you almost every day, whether you are participating in a class discussion, negotiating with friends over what movie is most worth seeing, or studying a local ballot issue to decide how you'll vote. In each case, thinking rhetorically means being flexible and fair, able to hear and consider varying—and sometimes conflicting—points of view.

In ancient Rome, Cicero argued that considering alternative points of view and counterarguments was key to making a successful argument, and it is just as important today. Even when you disagree with a point of view—perhaps especially when you disagree with it—allow yourself to see the issue from the viewpoint of its advocates before you reject their positions. You may be skeptical that hydrogen fuel will be the solution to global warming—but don't reject the idea until you have thought hard about others' perspectives and carefully considered alternative solutions.

Thinking hard about others' views also includes considering the larger context and how it shapes what they are saying. This aspect of rhetorical thinking goes beyond the kind of reading you probably learned to do in high school literature classes, where you looked very closely at a particular text and interpreted it on its own terms, without looking at secondary sources. When you think rhetorically, you go one step further and put that close analysis into a larger context—historical, political, or cultural, for example—to recognize and consider where the analysis is "coming from."

In analyzing the issue of gay marriage, for instance, you would not merely consider your own thinking or do a close reading of texts that address the issue. In addition, you would look at the whole debate in context by considering its historical development over time, thinking about the broader political agendas of both those who advocate for and those who oppose gay marriage, asking what economic ramifications adopting—or rejecting—gay marriage might have, examining the role of religion in the debate, and so on. In short, you would try to see the issue from as many different perspectives and in as broad a context as possible before you formulate your own stance. When you write, you draw on these sources—what others have said about the issue—to support your own position and to help you consider counterarguments to it.

See how carefully Brent Staples considers the positions and reasoning that he is opposing on p. 1065.

REFLECT. *Go to* everyonesanauthor.tumblr.com *and read "The 'Other Side'*
Is Not Dumb" by blogger Sean Blanda, who warns that many of us gravitate on social media to those who think like we do, which often leads to the belief that we are right and that those with other worldviews are "dumb." He argues that we need to "make an honest effort to understand those who are not like us" and to remember that "we might be wrong." Look at some of your own recent posts. How many different perspectives do you see represented? What might you do to listen—and think—more rhetorically?

What Do You Think—and Why?

Examining all points of view on any issue will engage you in some tough thinking about your own stance—literally, where you are coming from on an issue—and why you think as you do. Such self-scrutiny can eventually clarify your stance or perhaps even change your mind; in either case, you stand to gain. Just as you need to think hard about the motivations of others, it's important to examine your own motivations in detail, asking yourself what influences in your life lead you to think as you do or to take certain positions. Then you can reconsider your positions and reflect on how they relate to those of others, including your audience—those you wish to engage in conversation or debate.

In your college assignments, you probably have multiple motivations and purposes, one of which is to convince your instructor that you are a serious and hardworking student. But think about additional purposes as well: What could you learn from doing the assignment? How can doing it help you attain goals you have?

Examining your own stance and motivation is equally important outside the classroom. Suppose you are urging fellow members of a campus group to lobby for a rigorous set of procedures to deal with accusations of sexual harassment. On one level, you're alarmed by the statistics showing a steep increase in cases of rape on college campuses and you want to do something about it. But when you think a bit more, you might find that you have additional motivations. Perhaps you've long wanted to become a leader of this group and see this as an issue that can help you to do so. You may have just seen *The Hunting Ground*, a documentary about rape on U.S. college campuses, and found it deeply upsetting—and persuasive. Or maybe a close friend has been a victim of sexual harassment. These realizations shouldn't necessarily change your mind about what action you want your group to take, but examining what you think and why will help you to challenge your own position—and to make sure that it is fair and appropriate.

Do Your Homework

Rhetorical thinking calls on you to do some homework, to find out every-thing you can about what's been said about your topic, to **ANALYZE** what you find, and then to **SYNTHESIZE** that information to inform your own ideas. To put it another way, you want your own thinking to be aware and deeply informed, to reflect more than just your own opinion.

To take an everyday example, you should do some pretty serious think-ing when deciding on a major purchase, such as a new car. You'll want to begin by considering the purchase in the larger context of your life. What motivates you to buy a car? Do you need one for work? Do you want it in part as a status symbol? Are you concerned about the environment and want to switch to an electric vehicle? Who besides you might be affected by this decision? A thoughtful analysis of the context and your specific motiva-tions and purposes can guide you in drawing up a preliminary list of cars to consider.

Then you'll need to do some research, checking out product reviews and reports on safety records, efficiency, cost, and so on. Sometimes it can be hard to evaluate such sources: how much should you trust the mileage sta-tistics provided by the carmaker, for example, or one particular reviewer's evaluation? For this reason, you should consult multiple sources and check them against one another.

You will also want to consider your findings in light of your priorities. Cost, for instance, may not be as high on your priority list as fuel efficiency. Such careful thinking will help you come to a sound decision, and then to explain it to others. If your parents, for instance, are helping you buy the car, you'll want to consider what their responses to your decision will be, antici-pating questions they may ask and how to respond.

Doing your homework also means taking an analytic approach, focus-ing on *how* various rhetorical strategies work to persuade you. You may have been won over by a funny car commercial you saw on Super Bowl Sunday. So what made that advertisement so memorable? To answer that question, you'll need to study the ad closely, determining just what qualities—a clev-er script? memorable music? celebrity actors? cute animals? a provocative

TAKE A LOOK at the 2011 Super Bowl Chrysler ad at <u>everyonesanauthor.tumblr.com</u>.
*You'll see many scenes from Detroit, and hear a voiceover say, "What does this city
know about luxury? What does a town that's been to hell and back know about the
finer things in life? I'll tell you, more than most." What kind of rhetorical thinking did
the ad writers do? Who was their target audience, and how did they go about appealing
to them? This was an award-winning ad—but how successful do you think it was as an
ad? In other words, do you think it sold a lot of cars? If you were looking to buy a car,
what would this ad tell you about Chryslers—and what would you have to find out
from other sources?*

message?—made the ad so persuasive. Once you've determined that, you'll
want to consider whether the car will actually live up to the advertiser's
promises. This is the kind of analysis and research you will do when you
engage in rhetorical thinking.

Give Credit

As part of engaging with what others have thought and said, you'll want to
give credit where credit is due. Acknowledging the work of others will help
build your own **ETHOS**, or character, showing that you have not only done
your homework but that you want to credit those who have influenced you.

The great physicist Isaac Newton famously and graciously gave credit when he wrote to his rival Robert Hooke in 1676, saying:

> What Descartes did was a good step. You have added much in several ways, and especially in taking the colours of thin plates into philosophical consideration. If I have seen a little further it is by standing on the shoulders of giants.   —ISAAC NEWTON, letter to Robert Hooke

In this letter, Newton acknowledges the work of Descartes as well as of Hooke before saying, with a fair amount of modesty, that his own advancements were made possible by their work. In doing so, he is thinking—and acting—rhetorically.

You can give credit informally, as Newton did in this letter, or you can do so formally with a full citation. Which method you choose will depend on your purpose and context. Academic writing, for instance, usually calls for formal citations, but if you are writing for a personal blog, you might embed a link that connects to another's work—or give an informal shout-out to a friend who contributed to your thinking. In each case, you'll want to be specific about what ideas or words you've drawn from others, as Newton does in referring to Hooke's consideration of the colors of thin plates. Such care in crediting your sources contributes to your credibility—and is an important part of ethical, careful rhetorical thinking.

Be Imaginative

Remember that intuition and imagination can often lead to great insights. While you want to think carefully and analytically, don't be afraid to take chances. A little imagination can lead you to new ideas about a topic you're studying and about how to approach the topic in a way that will interest others. Such insights and intuitions can often pay off big-time. One student athlete we know was interested in how the mass media covered the Olympics, and he began doing research on the coverage in *Sports Illustrated* from different periods. So far, so good: he was gathering information and would be able to write an essay showing that the magazine had been a major promoter of the Olympics.

While looking through old issues of *Sports Illustrated*, however, he kept feeling that something he was seeing in the early issues was different from current issues of the magazine . . . something that felt important to him though he couldn't quite articulate it. This hunch led him to make an imaginative leap, to study that difference even though it was outside of the topic he had set out to examine. Excited that he was on to something, he returned to his chronological examination of the magazine. On closer inspection, he found that over the decades of its Olympics coverage, *Sports Illustrated* had slowly but surely moved from focusing on teams to depicting *only* individual stars.

This discovery led him to make an argument he would never have made had he not followed his creative hunch—that the evolution of sports from a focus on the team to a focus on individual stars is perfectly captured in the pages of *Sports Illustrated*. It also helped him write a much more interesting—and more persuasive—essay, one that captured the attention not only of his instructor and classmates but of a local sports newsmagazine, which reprinted his essay. Like this student, you can benefit by using your imagination and listening to your intuition. You could stumble upon something exciting.

Two *Sports Illustrated* covers depicting hockey players in the Winter Olympics. The cover on the left, from 1980, showcases the U.S. team's "miracle on ice" victory win over the heavily favored USSR team. The one on the right, from 2010, pictures Canada's superstar Sidney "Sid the Kid" Crosby, who scored the game-winning shot in the gold medal game against the United States.

Put In Your Oar

So rhetorical thinking offers a way of entering any situation with a tool kit of strategies that will help you understand it and "put in your oar." When you think rhetorically, you ask yourself certain questions:

- How do you want to come across to your audience?
- What can you do to represent yourself as knowledgeable and credible?
- What can you do to show respect both for your audience and for those whose work and thinking you engage with?
- How can you show that you have your audience's best interests at heart?

This kind of rhetorical thinking will help ensure that your words will be listened to and taken seriously.

We can find examples of such a rhetorical approach in all fields of study. Take, for instance, the landmark essay by James Watson and Francis Crick on the discovery of DNA, published in *Nature* in 1953. This essay shows Watson and Crick to be thinking rhetorically throughout, acutely aware of their audience (major scientists throughout the world) as well as of competitors who were simultaneously working on the same issue.

Here is Wayne Booth's analysis of Watson and Crick's use of rhetoric:

In [Watson and Crick's] report, what do we find? Actually scores of *rhetorical* choices that they made to strengthen the appeal of their scientific claim. (Biographies and autobiographies have by now revealed that they did a lot of conscientious revising, not of the data but of the mode of presentation; and their lives were filled, before and after the triumph, with a great deal of rhetoric-charged conflict.) We could easily compose a dozen different versions of their report, all proclaiming the same scientific results. But most alternatives would prove less engaging to the intended audience. They open, for example, with

"*We wish to suggest* a structure" that has "*novel* features which are of *considerable* biological *interest*." *(My italics, of course)*

Why didn't they say, instead: "We shall here demonstrate a *startling, totally new structure* that will *shatter* everyone's conception of the biological world"? Well, obviously their rhetorical choice presents an ethos much

The original sketch showing the structure of DNA that appeared in Watson and Crick's article.

more attractive to most cautious readers than does my exaggerated alternative. A bit later they say

> "We have made the *usual chemical assumptions,* namely . . ."

Why didn't they say, *"As we all know"*? Both expressions acknowledge reliance on warrants, commonplaces within a given rhetorical domain. But their version sounds more thoughtful and authoritative, especially with the word "chemical." Referring to Pauling and Corey, they say

> "They *kindly* have made their manuscript available."

Okay, guys, drop the rhetoric and just cut that word "kindly." What has that got to do with your scientific case? Well, it obviously strengthens the authors' ethos: we are nice guys dealing trustfully with other nice guys, in a rhetorical community.

And on they go, with *"In our opinion"* (rather than "We proclaim" or "We insist" or "We have miraculously discovered": again ethos—we're not dogmatic); and Fraser's *"suggested"* structure is *"rather ill-defined"* (rather than "his structure is stupid" or "obviously faulty"—we *are* nice guys, right?).

And on to scores of other such choices.

—WAYNE BOOTH, *The Rhetoric of Rhetoric*

Booth shows in each instance how Watson and Crick's exquisite understanding of their rhetorical situation—especially of their audience and of the stakes involved in making their claim—had a great deal to do with how that claim was received. (They won the Nobel Prize!)

As the example of Watson and Crick illustrates, rhetorical thinking involves certain habits of mind that can and should lead to something—often to an action, to making something happen. And when it comes to taking action, those who think rhetorically are in a very strong position. They have listened attentively, engaged with the words and ideas of others, viewed their topic from many alternate perspectives, and done their homework. This kind of rhetorical thinking will set you up to contribute to conversations—and will increase the likelihood that your ideas will be heard and will inspire real action.

Indeed, the ability to think rhetorically is of great importance in today's global world, as professors Gerald Graff and Cathy Birkenstein explain:

> The ability to enter complex, many-sided conversations has taken on a
> special urgency in today's diverse, post-9/11 world, where the future for

all of us may depend on our ability to put ourselves in the shoes of those who think very differently from us. Listening carefully to others, including those who disagree with us, and then engaging with them thoughtfully and respectfully . . . can help us see beyond our own pet beliefs, which may not be shared by everyone. The mere act of acknowledging that some-one might disagree with us may not seem like a way to change the world; but it does have the potential to jog us out of our comfort zones, to get us thinking critically about our own beliefs, and perhaps even to change our minds.   —GERALD GRAFF AND CATHY BIRKENSTEIN, *"They Say/I Say"*

In the long run, if enough of us learn to think rhetorically, we just might achieve Booth's goal—to use words (and images) in thoughtful and con-structive ways as an alternative to violence and war.

REFLECT. Read Margaret Mead's words below, and then think of at least one historical example in which a "small group of thoughtful citizens" has changed the world for the better. Then think about your own life and the ways in which you have worked with others to bring about some kind of change. In what ways were you called upon to think and act rhetorically in order to do so?

Never doubt that a small group of thoughtful committed citizens can change the world; indeed, it's the only thing that ever has.

—MARGARET MEAD

TWO

Rhetorical Situations

S PART OF A COLLEGE APPLICATION, a high school student writes a personal statement about what she plans to study, and why. A baseball fan posts a piece on a New York Yankees blog analyzing data to show why a beloved pitcher probably won't be elected to the Hall of Fame. Eighty-seven readers respond, some praising his analysis, others questioning his conclusions and offering their own analyses. The officers of a small company address the annual shareholders' meeting to report on how the firm is doing, using *PowerPoint* slides to call attention to their most important points. They take questions afterward, and two people raise their hands. Our baseball fan sees on *Twitter* that the Yankees have signed a star pitcher he thinks they don't really need and fires off a tweet saying so. The student in our first example takes a deep breath and logs on to the website of the college she wants to attend to see if she's been accepted. Good news: she's in. Come September she's at the library, working on an essay for her first-year composition course—and texting her friends as she works.

In each of these scenarios, an author is writing (or speaking) in a different set of specific circumstances—addressing certain audiences for a particular purpose, using certain technologies, and so on. So it is whenever we write. Whether we're texting a friend, outlining an oral presentation, or writing an essay, we do so within a specific rhetorical situation.

Three different rhetorical situations: a lone writer texting (*top left*); a student giving an oral presentation in class (*right*); and members of a community group collaborating on a project (*bottom left*).

We have a purpose, an audience, a stance, a genre, a medium, a design—all of which exist in some larger context. This chapter covers each of these elements and provides prompts to help you think about some of the choices you have as you negotiate your own rhetorical situations.

Every rhetorical situation presents its own unique constraints and opportunities, and as authors, we need to think strategically about our own situation. Adding to a class wiki presents a different challenge from writing an in-class essay exam, putting together a résumé and cover letter for a job, or working with fellow members of a campus choir to draft a grant proposal to the student government requesting funding to go on tour. A group of neighbors developing a proposal to present at a community meeting will need to attend to both the written text they will submit and the oral arguments they will make. They may also need to create slides or other visuals to support their proposal.

The workplace creates still other kinds of rhetorical situations with their own distinctive features. Reporters, for instance, must always consider their deadlines as well as their ethical obligations—to the public, to the persons or institutions they write about, and to the story they are reporting. A reporter working for six months to investigate corporate wrongdoing faces different challenges from one who covers local sports day to day. The medium—print, video, radio, podcast, blog, or some combination of these or other media—also influences how reporters write their stories.

Think about Your Own Rhetorical Situation

Jose Antonio Vargas risked everything by revealing his status as an undocumented immigrant. See how he navigated that rhetorical situation on p. 1078.

It is important to start thinking about your rhetorical situation early in your writing process. As a student, you'll often be given assignments with very specific guidelines—to follow the conventions of a particular genre, in a certain medium, by a specific date. Nevertheless, even the most fully developed assignment cannot specify every aspect of any particular rhetorical situation.

Effective writers—whether students, teachers, journalists, or your mom—know how to analyze their rhetorical situations. They may conduct this analysis unconsciously, drawing on the rhetorical common sense they have developed as writers, readers, speakers, and listeners. Particularly when you are writing in a new genre or discipline—a situation that you'll surely face in college—it can help to analyze your rhetorical situation more systematically.

THINK ABOUT YOUR GENRE

- *Have you been assigned a specific genre?* If not, do any words in the assignment imply a certain genre? *Evaluate* may signal a review, for example, and *explain why* could indicate a causal analysis.

- *If you get to choose your genre*, consider your **PURPOSE**. If you want to convince readers to recycle their trash, you would likely write an argument. If, however, you want to explain how to recycle food waste into compost, your purpose would call for a process analysis.

- *Does your genre require a certain organization?* A process analysis, for instance, is often organized **CHRONOLOGICALLY**, whereas a visual analysis may be organized **SPATIALLY**—and an annotated bibliography is almost always organized alphabetically.

- *How does your genre affect your* TONE *?* A lab report, for example, generally calls for a more matter-of-fact tone than a film review.

- *Are certain* DESIGN *features expected in your genre?* You would likely need to include images in a review of an art show, for instance, or be required to use a standard font for a research paper.

THINK ABOUT YOUR AUDIENCE

- *Who is your intended audience?* An instructor? A supervisor? Classmates? Members of a particular organization? Visitors to a website? Who else might see or hear what you say?

- *How are members of your audience like and unlike you?* Consider demographics such as age, gender, religion, income, education, occupation, or political attitudes.

- *What's your relationship with your audience?* An instructor or supervisor, for example, holds considerable authority over you. Other audiences may be friends, coworkers, or even strangers. What expectations about the text might they have because of your relationship? You'd need to be careful not to sound too informal to a committee considering you for a scholarship, or too bossy to a group of friends.

- *If you have a choice of* MEDIUM, which one(s) would best reach your intended audience?

- *What do you want your audience to think or do* as a result of what you say? Take your ideas seriously? Reflect on their beliefs? Respond to you? Take some kind of action? How will you signal to them what you want?

- *Can you assume your audience will be interested* in what you say, or will you need to get them interested? Are they likely to resist any of your ideas?

- *How much does your audience know about your topic?* How much background information do they need? Will they expect—or be put off by—the use of technical jargon? Will you need to define any terms?

- *Will your audience expect a particular* GENRE *?* If you're writing about Mozart for a music class, you might analyze a piece he composed; if, however, you're commenting on a *YouTube* music video, you'd be more likely to write some kind of review.

To quote further from People's Exhibit A, your Twitter feed, "@holdupguy82 I'm in the getaway vehicle with the money and hostages. Where R U?"

- *What about audience members you don't or can't know?* It goes without saying that you won't always know who could potentially read your writing, especially if you're writing on a site that anyone can access. The ability to reach hundreds, even thousands of readers is part of the web's power, but you will want to take special care when your writing might reach unknown audiences. Remember as well that anything posted on the internet may easily be shared and read out of context, as the above cartoon shows!

THINK ABOUT YOUR PURPOSE

- *How would you describe your own motivation for writing?* To fulfill a course assignment? To meet a personal or professional commitment? To express your ideas to someone? For fun?

- *What is your primary goal?* To inform your audience about something? To persuade them to think a certain way? To call them to action? To entertain them? Something else? Do you have other goals as well?

- *How do your goals influence your choice of genre, medium, and design?* For example, if you want to persuade neighbors to recycle, you may choose to make colorful posters for display in public places. If you want to inform a corporation about what recycling programs accomplish, you may want to write a report using charts and data.

THINK ABOUT YOUR STANCE

- *What's your attitude toward your topic?* Objective? Strongly supportive? Mildly skeptical? Amused? Angry?

- *What's your relationship with your AUDIENCE?* Do they know you, and if so, how? Are you a student? a friend? a mentor? an interested community member? How do they see you, and how do you want to be seen?

- *How can you best convey your stance in your writing?* What TONE do you want it to have?

- *How will your stance and tone be received by your audience?* Will they be drawn in by it?

THINK ABOUT THE LARGER CONTEXT

- *What else has been said about your topic,* and how does that affect what you will say? What would be the most effective way for you to add your voice to the conversation?

- *Do you have any constraints?* When is this writing due and how much time and energy can you put into it? How many pages (or minutes) do you have to deliver your message?

- *How much independence do you have as a writer* in this situation? To what extent do you need to meet the expectations of others, such as an instructor or a supervisor? If this writing is an assignment, how can you approach it in a way that makes it matter to you?

THINK ABOUT YOUR **MEDIUM** AND **DESIGN**

- *If you get to choose your medium,* which one will work best for your audience and purpose? Print? Spoken? Digital? Some combination?

- *How will the medium determine what you can and cannot do?* For example, if you're submitting an essay online, you could include video, but if you were writing the same essay in print, you'd only be able to include a still shot from the video.

- *Does your medium favor certain conventions?* Paragraphs work well in print, but *PowerPoint* presentations usually rely on images or bulleted phrases instead. If you are writing online, you can include links to sources and background information.

- *What's the most appropriate look for your* **RHETORICAL SITUATION**? Plain and serious? Warm and inviting? Whimsical? What design elements will help you project that look?

- *Should you include visuals?* Would any part of your text benefit from them? Will your audience expect them? What kind would be appropriate—photographs? videos? maps? Is there any statistical data that would be easier to understand as a table, chart, or graph?

- *If you're writing a spoken or digital text,* should you include sound? still images? moving images?

REFLECT. Make a list of all the writing that you remember doing in the last week. Be sure to include everything from texts and status updates to more formal academic or work-related writing. Choose three examples that strike you as quite different from one another and analyze the rhetorical situation you faced for each one, drawing upon the guidelines in this chapter.

THREE

Reading Rhetorically

CHANCES ARE, YOU READ MORE than you think you do. You read print texts, of course, but you are probably reading even more on a phone, a tablet, a computer, or other devices. Reading is now, as perhaps never before, a basic necessity. In fact, if you think that reading is something you learned once and for all in the first or second grade, think again.

Today, reading calls for strategic effort. As media critic Howard Rheingold sees it, literacy today involves at least five interlocking abilities: attention, participation, collaboration, network awareness, and critical consumption. Of these, attention is first and foremost. In short, you need to work at *paying attention* to what you read. In his book *The Economics of Attention*, rhetorician Richard Lanham explains: "We're drowning in information. What we lack is the human attention needed to make sense of it all."

When so many texts are vying for our attention, which ones do we choose? In order to decide what to read, what to pay attention to, we need to practice what Rheingold calls *infotention*, a word he came up with to describe a "mind-machine combination of brain-powered attention skills and computer-powered information filters." Rheingold is talking primarily about reading online, but we think that infotention is important for reading any kind of text, because it calls for synthesizing and

So many texts vying for our attention!

thinking rhetorically about the enormous amount of information available to us in both print and digital sources. And while some of us can multitask (fighter pilots are one example Rheingold gives of those whose jobs demand it), most of us are not good at it and must learn to focus our attention when we read.

In other words, we need to learn to read rhetorically. Reading rhetorically means attending carefully and intentionally to a text. It means being open-minded to that text. And it means being an active participant in understanding and thinking about and responding to what is in the text. As Nobel laureate Toni Morrison says, "The words on the page are only half the story. The rest is what you bring to the party."

So how do you learn to read rhetorically and to practice infotention? Some steps seem obvious: especially for high-stakes reading, like much of what you do for school, you need to find space and time in which you can really focus—and turn off social media and put down your phone. Beyond such obvious steps, though, you can improve your reading by approaching texts systematically. This chapter will guide you in doing so, beginning with tips for how to understand and engage effectively with what you read.

READING TO UNDERSTAND AND ENGAGE

Start by previewing the text. Efficient readers tell us that they most often begin not by plunging right into the text but by previewing it, finding out what they can about it and getting a sense of what it's about.

- *What do you know (and think) about the topic?* What do you want to learn about it?

- *Who are the authors or sponsors?* Where do you think they're coming from: might they have a particular agenda or purpose?

- *Who published the text,* and what does that tell you about its intended audience and purpose?

- *Skim the text* to get a sense of what it covers. Does the *title* give you any hint about what's to come? If there's a *subtitle,* does it indicate the author's argument or stance? Scan any *headings* or *menus* to see what's covered, and look at any text that's highlighted. Does the text's *design* and use of *fonts* tell you anything about its content or stance?

Annotate as you read. Author Anatole Broyard said that he used to be intimidated by the texts he read, seeing them as great authorities he should absorb but not respond to. But that changed. Later, he said, he learned when he opened a text to occupy it: "I stomp around in it. I underline passages, scribble in the margins, leave my mark." Broyard's point echoes what experts on reading today say: reading is a thoroughly social activity, bringing you into conversation with the writers, asking you to engage them and their ideas actively. And the digital texts you read today often allow for, even demand, your response. So as you begin to read, you should be ready to engage in that conversation, reading with pen or mouse in hand, ready to "stomp."

NOTE KEY POINTS IN THE ARGUMENT

- Highlight the most important points and any **THESIS** statement.
- Identify key terms (and look them up if necessary).
- Underline things that are unclear or confusing, and jot down your questions in the margins.
- Think about how the content meshes with what you already know about the subject. Is there anything surprising?

CONSIDER THE AUTHOR

- Mark any words that indicate the author's **STANCE**.
- Note places in the text where the author has demonstrated **AUTHORITY** to write on the topic.
- How would you describe the author's **STYLE** and **TONE**? Formal? Casual? Serious? Humorous? Mocking? Informative? Something else? Mark words or passages that establish that style and tone.

THINK ABOUT THE AUDIENCE

- Who do you think the author is addressing? Note any words in the text that make you think so. Are you included in that group?
- What do you know about that audience's values? Highlight words that suggest what the author thinks the audience cares about.

TAKE NOTE OF YOUR REACTIONS

- Make a note of your first impression of the text.
- Do you agree with the author? Disagree? Agree and disagree? Why?
- Note any phrases or passages or points you find surprising—and why.
- After you've read the text thoroughly, sum up your assessment of it. How well do you think it achieves its purpose?

PAY ATTENTION TO THE TEXT'S DESIGN

- How does the design affect the way you understand the text?
- Note any headings, sidebars, or other design features that label or highlight parts of the text.
- Pay attention to the font(s). What do they indicate about the text?
- If the text includes visuals, what do they contribute to the message?

TALK BACK TO THE TEXT

- Comment on any strengths and weaknesses.
- Note any points you want to remember or question.
- Jot down other possible views or **COUNTERARGUMENTS**.

A Sample Annotated Text

Here's the opening of "On Buying Local" by Katherine Spriggs (reprinted on pp. 150–58), along with the annotations one reader has added.

AMERICANS TODAY CAN eat pears in the spring in Minnesota, oranges in the summer in Montana, asparagus in the fall in Maine, and cranberries in the winter in Florida. In fact, we can eat pretty much any kind of produce anywhere at any time of the year. But what is the cost of this convenience? In this essay, I will explore some answers to this question and argue that we should give up a little bit of convenience in favor of buying local.

Thesis statement.

"Buying local" means that consumers choose to buy food that has been grown, raised, or produced as close to their homes as possible ("Buy Local"). Buying local is an important part of the response to many environmental issues we face today (fig. 1). It encourages the development of small farms, which are often more environmentally sustainable than large farms, and thus strengthens local markets and supports small rural economies. By demonstrating a commitment to buying local, Americans could set an example for global environmentalism.

I wonder what she means by "buying local."

This paragraph shows her stance: strongly in favor of sustainable farming and buying local.

In 2010, the international community is facing many environmental challenges, including global warming, pollution, and dwindling fossil fuel resources. Global warming is attributed to the release of greenhouse gases such as carbon dioxide and methane, most commonly emitted in the burning of fossil fuels. It is such a pressing problem that scientists estimate that in the year 2030, there will be no glaciers left in Glacier National Park ("Global Warming Statistics"). The United States is especially guilty of contributing to the problem, producing about a quarter of all global greenhouse gas emissions, and playing a large part in pollution and shrinking world oil supplies as well ("Record Increase"). According to a CNN article published in 2000, the United States manufactures more than 1.5 billion pounds of chemical pesticides a year that can pollute our water, soil, and air (Baum). Agriculture is particularly interconnected with all of these issues. Almost three-fourths of the pesticides produced in the United States are used

Here comes some evidence. Looks like she's done her homework. So far, I'm with her.

I want to check out this source: I'm a little suspicious of what she says here.

Fig. 1. Shopping at a farmers' market is one good way to support small farms and strengthen the local economy. Photograph from Alamy.

Farmers' markets are expensive. Most of us can't afford to shop at them.

Overall, I'm impressed with the research she's done. She's serious about this issue and is making a strong case.

in agriculture (Baum). Most produce is shipped many miles before it is sold to consumers, and shipping our food long distances is costly in both the amount of fossil fuel it uses and the greenhouse gases it produces.

SUMMARIZE the main ideas. If you're reading attentively, you should be able to summarize the main ideas and the major support for those ideas.

- Keep your summary short and sweet, capturing the text's main ideas but leaving out less important information.
- Be careful to summarize the text fairly and accurately.
- Use your own words; if you have included any phrases from the original, enclose them in quotation marks.

Here is a summary of Katherine Spriggs' essay:

> In her essay "On Buying Local," college student Katherine Spriggs argues that consumers should purchase food grown locally whenever possible. After demonstrating the environmental and practical reasons for doing so, Spriggs shows that buying local can offer an alternative to destructive mass farming, help small farmers and their families, build sustainable agricultural models, reduce the cost of shipping food from far-away places, and avoid the exploitation of workers, especially in third-world countries. In spite of a few drawbacks (local food may be more expensive and seasonal variation may reduce the number of choices available), she concludes that "Buying local is an easy step that everyone can take toward 'greener' living."

ANALYZE the text to figure out what makes it tick. How does it achieve its goals and get its message across?

- What claim is the text making? How is the claim **QUALIFIED**, if at all?
- What **REASONS** and **EVIDENCE** support the claim? Examples? Precedents? Personal experience? How effective do you find this support?
- How does the author establish **AUTHORITY** to write on this topic? What does he or she do to gain the audience's confidence?
- What is the author's **STANCE** toward the topic—passionate? critical? neutral?—and what words reflect that stance?
- What **COUNTERARGUMENTS** or other perspectives does the author address—and how does he or she respond to them?
- What overall impression does the text make on you, and what passages create that impression?
- Are you persuaded by the argument? Why or why not?

Consider the larger CONTEXT. Close analysis may leave you looking at a text you're reading as a bunch of parts rather than as a whole. So it's important to put those parts back together again and look at the text within its larger context.

- What seems to have motivated the author to write? Is he or she responding to some other argument—and if so, what is it?
- How does the text fit into the larger conversation on the topic? Is the author's point corroborated by what others have said, or is he or she out on a limb, making a claim that hardly anyone else agrees with?
- Does the author incorporate or fairly acknowledge other perspectives?
- What might the context tell you about the author's stance toward the topic? Is he or she writing as an advocate? a reporter? a critic?
- How do you think others who have thought about the topic would respond to this text?

Say "yes," "no," or "maybe." Before you come to final conclusions about any text—whether it's a newspaper article, an advertisement, a website, a tweet, whatever—take time to read carefully in order to understand the author's point of view as clearly and fully as possible.

- Try "walking a mile" in the author's shoes to understand the way he or she sees the topic.
- Say "yes" first, reading as fairly and open-mindedly as you can.
- Once you have fully understood the author's viewpoint, say "maybe" to any passages that seem problematic, confusing, or poorly supported. Think about why you see these passages as meriting only a "maybe."
- Finally, look for passages, evidence, and anything else to which you feel obligated to say "no." You may find few or none of these, but as a critical reader, you need to look for them. For those you identify, think hard about why they seem unacceptable or just plain wrong.

Take time to reflect. Research shows that there's a strong connection between taking time to think carefully about what you are reading and what researchers call "deep learning," the kind that sticks with you. So when you read an especially important text, it's a good idea to take the time to reflect on what you have learned from it.

- What important information have you gleaned from the text? What are the big takeaways for you?
- What lessons has the text taught you? How might you apply those lessons in your own writing or thinking?
- What impact has the reading had on you—as a person, student, scholar, and researcher?
- What doubts or questions do you still have about the text? What additional information would you have liked to have?

Put your reflections in writing. The act of recording these thoughts will help you remember them.

Respond to what you read. Reading rhetorically calls on you to respond to what you read—to take your reactions to the next level and share your thoughts with others. In other words, it means adding your voice to the larger conversation. Your instructor may assign you to write a response of some kind, but you could also consider sending an email or a letter to the author. If you want to respond to something you read online, see if there's a space for comments.

READING ACROSS MEDIA

Once upon a time "reading" meant attending to words on paper. But today we often encounter texts that convey information in images and in sound as well—and they may be on- or off-screen. So when you approach such texts, be sure to think carefully about how the medium of delivery may affect your understanding, analysis, and response.

Reading Visual Texts

Visual texts present their own opportunities and challenges. As new technologies bring images into our phones and lives on a minute-by-minute basis, visual texts have become so familiar and pervasive that it may seem that "reading" them is just natural. But reading visual texts with a critical eye takes time and patience—and attention.

Take a look at the advertisement for a Shinola watch on the next page. You may know that Shinola is a Detroit-based watchmaker proud that its watches are "made in America"; if not, a quick look at *Shinola.com* will fill in this part of the ad's CONTEXT. But there's a lot more going on in terms of its particular rhetorical situation. The ad first ran in 2015, when it was clearly "talking back" to smart watches in general and to the launch of the Apple watch in particular, with its full panoply of futuristic bells and whistles. "Hey," the ad writers seem to be saying to the smart watch crowd, "our watch is just smart enough."

Thinking through the rhetorical situation tells you something about the ad's purpose and audience. Of course its major PURPOSE is to sell watches, but one other goal seems to be to poke a little fun at all the high-tech, super-smart watches on the market. And what about its AUDIENCE: who do you think the ad addresses most directly? Perhaps Americans who think of themselves as solid "no frills" folks?

Reading a visual begins, then, with studying the purpose, audience, message, and context. But there's a lot more you can do to understand a visual. You can look closely, for instance, at its DESIGN. In the Shinola ad, the stark, high-contrast, black-and-white image takes center stage, drawing our eyes to it and its accompanying captions. There are no other distracting elements, no other colors, no glitz. The simplicity gives the watch a retro look, which is emphasized by its sturdy straps, open face, and clear numerals, its old-fashioned wind-up button and second hand.

You'll also want to take a close look at any words. In this case, the Shinola ad includes a large headline centered above the image, three lines of all caps, sans serif type that match the simplicity and straightforwardness of the image itself. And it's hard to miss the mocking TONE: "A WATCH SO SMART THAT IT CAN TELL YOU THE TIME JUST BY LOOKING AT IT." The small caption below the image underscores this message: "THE RUNWELL. IT'S JUST SMART ENOUGH." Take that, Apple!

Reading Print Texts

Print texts may consist mostly of sentences and paragraphs that (should) follow logically from one to the next, with a clear beginning, middle, and end. For these texts, the familiar practice of reading left to right, top to bottom (at least in English) will carry you through the text, though you may

A WATCH SO SMART
THAT IT CAN TELL YOU THE TIME
JUST BY LOOKING AT IT.

THE RUNWELL. IT'S JUST SMART ENOUGH.™

SMART ENOUGH THAT YOU DON'T NEED TO CHARGE IT AT NIGHT. SMART ENOUGH THAT IT WILL NEVER NEED
A SOFTWARE UPGRADE. SMART ENOUGH THAT VERSION 1.0 WON'T NEED TO BE REPLACED NEXT YEAR,
OR IN THE MANY DECADES THAT FOLLOW. BUILT BY THE WATCHMAKERS OF DETROIT TO LAST
A LIFETIME OR LONGER UNDER THE TERMS AND CONDITIONS OF THE SHINOLA GUARANTEE.

SHINOLA
DETROIT

Where American is made.™

occasionally need to pause to look up the meaning of a word, to take notes, or just to reflect on what you're reading.

"Reading" Spoken Texts

Spoken texts need to be "read" in a different way, by listening to what the speaker is saying while viewing images he or she projects on a screen or has put in a handout. If the presentation is a really good one, these elements will complement each other, joining together to get their message across. Still, you may need to learn to split your attention, making sure you are not focusing so much on any slides or handouts that you're missing what the speaker is saying—or vice versa. Remember, too, that you'll be a better audience member if you look at the speaker and any visuals, rather than staring at your laptop or looking down at the desk.

Reading Digital Texts

Digital texts stretch readers even further, since they blend written words with audio, video, links, charts and graphs, and other elements that you can attend to in any order you choose. In reading such texts, you'll need to make decisions carefully. When exactly should you click on a link, for example? The first moment it comes up? Or should you make a note to check it out later since doing so now may break your concentration—and you might not be able to get back easily to what you were reading. Links are a good thing in that they lead to more information, but following them can interrupt your train of thought. In addition, scrolling seems to encourage skimming and to make us read more rapidly. In short, it can be harder to stay on task. So you may well need to make a special effort with digital texts—to read them attentively, and to pay close attention to what you're reading.

Reading On- and Off-Screen

It's clear by now that our ways of reading are changing in the digital age. If reading was once something we did alone, silently, not so today. Reading now is likely to take place on the run, on digital devices of all kinds. It has also become deeply social, as when we send messages via text or share what we're reading and what we think of it on social media. Between texts, email, *Twitter,* and forums like *Reddit,* you are probably doing a lot of reading, and a lot of it on-screen.

Researchers have found that we often take shortcuts when we read on-line, searching and scanning and jumping around in a text or leaping from link to link. This kind of reading is very helpful for finding answers and information quickly, but it can blur our focus and make it difficult to attend to the text carefully and purposefully. So it's important to learn to make online reading effective for your academic work. Here are a few tips to help you when you're reading on-screen.

- Be clear about your purpose in reading. If you need to understand and remember the text, remind yourself to read carefully and avoid skimming or skipping around.
- Close *Facebook* and other pages that may distract you from reading.
- Learn how to take notes on PDF files and Word documents. Then you can make notes as you read on-screen, just as you would when reading a print text. Or take notes on paper.
- Reading PDFs and websites in full-screen mode will clear away clutter and make it easier to focus on the text.
- Look up terms on the internet as you read, making a note of definitions you may need later.
- For really high-stakes readings, consider printing out the text to read.

The pervasiveness of reading on-screen may suggest that many readers prefer to read that way. But current research suggests that most students still prefer to read print, especially if the reading is important and needs to be internalized and remembered. Print texts, it's worth remembering, are easy to navigate—you can tell at a glance how much you've read and how much you still have to go, and you can move back and forth in the text to find something important.

In addition, researchers have found that students reading on-screen are less likely to reflect on what they read or to make connections and synthesize in ways that bind learning to memory. It's important to note, however, that studies like these almost always end with a caveat: reading practices are changing and technology is making it easier to read on-screen.

We are clearly in a time of flux where reading is concerned, so the best advice is for you to think very carefully about why you are reading. If you need to find some information quickly, to follow a conversation on *Twitter*, or to look for online sources on a topic you're researching, reading on-screen is the way to go. But if you need to fully comprehend and retain the information in a text, you may want to stick with tried-and-true print.

READING ACROSS GENRES

Genres affect how we read—and can help guide our reading. Knowing the characteristic features of a genre, therefore, can help you read more attentively—and more purposefully. When you read a **REPORT**, for example, you expect information you can trust—and you look for signs that the author knows what he or she is writing about and has cited authoritative sources. When you read a **REVIEW**, you expect to find some judgment, along with reasons and evidence to support that judgment. And you know to question any **ARGUMENT** that fails to acknowledge likely counterarguments. This is all to say that what you know about common genres can help you as a reader. Knowing what features to expect will help you read with a critical eye, and just recognizing a genre can help you adjust your reading as need be (reading directions more slowly, for example).

READING ACROSS ACADEMIC DISCIPLINES

An analysis doesn't have to be dry and detached. Read Andy Hinds' analysis of how to pick a favorite sports team on p. 963.

It's especially important to read rhetorically when it comes to encountering texts in different academic fields. Take the word *analysis*, for instance. That little word has a wide range of definitions as it moves from one field to another. In *philosophy*, analysis has traditionally meant breaking down a topic into its constituent parts in order to understand them—and the whole—more completely. In the *sciences*, analysis often involves the scientific method of observing a phenomenon, formulating a hypothesis about it, and experimenting to see whether the hypothesis holds up. And in *business*, analysis usually refers to assessing needs and finding ways to meet them. In *literary studies*, on the other hand, analysis usually calls for close reading in order to interpret a passage of text. When you're assigned to carry out an analysis, then, it's important to know what the particular field of study expects you to do and to ask your instructors if you aren't sure.

Beyond attending to what particular words mean from field to field, you should note that what counts as effective **EVIDENCE** can differ across academic disciplines. In literature and other fields in the *humanities*, textual evidence is often the most important: your job as a reader is to focus on the text itself. For the *sciences*, you'll most often focus on evidence gathered through experimentation, on facts and figures. Some of the *social sciences* also favor the use of "hard" evidence or data, while others are more likely to use evidence drawn from interviews, oral histories, or even anecdotes. As a strong reader, you'll need to be aware of what counts as credible evidence in the fields you study.

Finally, pay attention to the way various disciplines present their information. You'll probably find that articles and books in *literature* and *history* present their information in paragraphs, sometimes with illustrations. *Physics* texts present much important information in equations, while those in *psychology* and *political science* rely more on charts and graphs and other visual representations of quantitative data. In *art history*, you can expect to see extensive use of images, while much of the work in *music* will rely on notation and sound.

So reading calls for some real effort. Whether you're reading words or images or bar graphs, literary analysis or musical notation, in a print book or on a screen, you need to read *rhetorically*—attentively and intentionally and with an open mind. And on top of all that, you need to be an active participant with what you read, just as Toni Morrison says: "The words on the page are only half the story. The rest is what you bring to the party."

＿＿＿ *REFLECT. The next time you're assigned to read a text online, pay attention to your process. Take some notes on just how you read: Do you go straight through, or do you stop often? Do you take notes? Do you take breaks while reading to attend to something else? What do you do if you don't understand a passage? How long can you read at a stretch and maintain full concentration? Then answer the same questions the next time you're assigned to read a print text. What differences do you notice in the way you read each text? What conclusions can you draw about how to be a more effective reader, both on- and off-screen?*

FOUR

Meeting the Demands of Academic Writing

"It's Like Learning a New Language"

LLEN MacNamara arrived at college excited but also anxious. She had grown up in a small town far from the college, had not taken calculus, and had never written more than a five-paragraph essay. So when she got her first college writing assignment—in a political science class, to write a ten-page essay on how the relationship among the three branches of the U.S. government has evolved—she felt a little panic. She had read all her assignments and done some research, and she had even met with her instructor during office hours. She had quite a bit of material. But when she started to write, it just didn't sound right. She wasn't sure what college writing sounded like, but this wasn't it.

Following her instructor's advice, MacNamara studied several of the political science articles on her course reading list. Compared to her usual writing, they were much more formal, full of complicated sentences. What she eventually came up with wasn't a particularly good paper (and she knew it), but it served its purpose: it had gotten her thinking about college-level writing. Looking back at the work she had done to get this far, she thought, "Wow, this is almost like learning a new language."

MacNamara had a point. Many students have experiences similar to hers, especially multilingual students who've grown up in other cultures. One Romanian student we know put it this way:

In my country we care very much about the beauty of what we write. Even with academic and business writing, we try to make our texts poetic in some way. When I got to the U.S.A., I discovered that writing that I thought was beautiful struck my teachers as wordy and off-task. I was surprised about this.

This student, like Ellen MacNamara, needed to set about learning a new language—in this case, the language of U.S. academic writing.

So Just What Is Academic Writing?

Academic writing is the writing you do for school. It follows a fairly strict set of conventions, such as using standard edited English, following logical patterns of organization, and providing support for the points you make. But academic writing reaches beyond the classroom: it's used in many journals, newspapers, and books as well as on the web, especially on blogs that address serious topics like politics, research, or cultural analysis. So "academic writing" is a broad category, one flexible enough to accommodate differences across disciplines, for example, while still remaining recognizably "academic." This chapter considers some of the assumptions that lie behind academic writing in the United States and describes some of the most common characteristics of that writing.

We're giving so much attention to academic writing for a couple of important reasons. First, becoming fluent in it will be of great help to you both in college and well beyond; and second, it poses challenges to both native and nonnative speakers of English. We want to acknowledge these challenges without making them seem too difficult to overcome. Instead, we want to try to demystify some of the assumptions and conventions of academic writing and get you started thinking about how to use them to your advantage.

Joining U.S. Academic Conversations

If you are new to college, you need to learn to "talk the talk" of academic writing as soon as possible so that you can join the conversations in progress all around you. Doing so calls for understanding some common expectations that most if not all of your instructors hold.

You're expected to respond. One important assumption underlying the kind of writing expected in American colleges is that reading and writing are active processes in which students not only absorb information but also respond to and even question it. Not all educational systems view reading and writing in this way. In some cultures, students are penalized if they attempt to read established texts critically or to disagree with authorities or insert their own views. If you are from such a background, you may find it difficult to engage in this kind of active reading and writing. It may feel rude, disrespectful, or risky, particularly if you would be reprimanded for such engagement in your home culture.

Remember, however, that the kind of engagement your instructors want is not hostile or combative; it's not about showing off by beating down the ideas of others. Rather, they expect you to demonstrate your active engagement with the texts you read—and an awareness that in doing so you are joining an academic conversation, one that has been going on for a long time and that will continue. It's fine to express strong opinions, but it's also important to remember—and acknowledge—that there is almost surely some value in perspectives other than your own.

You're expected to ask questions. Because U.S. culture emphasizes individual achievement so much, students are expected to develop authority and independence, often by asking questions. In contrast to cultures where the best students never ask questions because they have already studied the material and worked hard to learn it, in American academic contexts, students are expected and encouraged to voice their questions. In other words, don't assume you have to figure everything out by yourself. Do take responsibility for your own learning whenever possible, but it's fine to ask questions about what you don't understand, especially specific assignments.

You're expected to say what *you* think. American instructors expect that students will progress from relying on the thoughts of others to formulating ideas and arguments of their own. One important way to make that move is to engage in dialogue with other students and teachers. In these dialogues, teachers are not looking for you to express the "right" position; instead, they're looking for you to say what *you* think and provide adequate and appropriate support for that point of view.

You're expected to focus from the start. In contrast to many cultures, where writers start with fairly general background information for read-

Academic writers at work in (*clockwise from top left*) India, Chile, Burkina Faso, the United States, Thailand, and Italy.

ers, American academic writing immediately focuses in on the topic at hand. Thus, even in the introduction of an essay, you begin at a relatively focused level, providing even greater detail in the paragraphs that follow. The point is not to show how much you know but instead to provide as much information as your audience needs to understand the point easily.

Because American academic writers generally open their discussions at a fairly specific level, you wouldn't want to begin with a sentence like "All over the world and in many places, there are families," a thesis statement in an essay one of us once received from a native speaker of Arabic. (Translated into Arabic, this would make a beautiful sentence and an appropriate opening statement for a student essay.) Students educated in Spanish or Portuguese and, to an even greater extent, those educated in Arabic are accustomed to providing a great deal more background information than those educated in English. If you are from one of these cultural backgrounds, do not be surprised if your instructor encourages you to delete most of the first few pages of a draft, for example, and to begin instead by addressing your topic more directly and specifically.

You're expected to state your point explicitly. In U.S. academic English, writers are expected to provide direct and explicit statements that lead readers, step by step, through the text—in contrast to cultures that value indirectness, circling around the topic rather than addressing it head-on. A Brazilian student we knew found it especially hard to state the point of an essay up front and explicitly. From his cultural perspective, it made more sense to develop an argument by building suspense and stating his position only at the end of the essay. As he said, "It took a lot of practice for me to learn how to write the very direct way that professors in the U.S.A. want."

All these expectations suggest that American academic discourse puts much of the burden for successful communication on the author rather than on members of the audience. So with these expectations in mind, let's take a close look at seven common characteristics of U.S. academic writing.

CHARACTERISTIC FEATURES

No list of characteristics can describe all the kinds of texts you'll be expected to write in college, particularly given the differences among disciplines. But there are certain things you're expected to do in college writing:

- Use standard edited English.
- Use clear and recognizable patterns of organization.
- Mark logical relationships between ideas.
- State claims explicitly and provide appropriate support.
- Present your ideas as a response to others.
- Express your ideas clearly and directly.
- Be aware of how genres and conventions vary across disciplines.
- Document sources using the appropriate citation style.

Use Standard Edited English

Academic writing almost always follows the conventions of standard edited English in terms of spelling, grammar, and punctuation. In addition, it is more rather than less formal. Thus, the kinds of abbreviations and other shortcuts you use all the time in text messaging or posting to social media sites usually aren't appropriate in academic writing: you'll have to write out "with respect to" rather than "wrt," and you'll also want to avoid ☺ and other emoticons. Likewise, slang isn't usually appropriate. In some contexts, you'll discover that even contractions aren't appropriate—although we use them in this book because we're aiming for a conversational tone, one that is formal to some degree but not stuffy. As you can probably tell, defining standard edited English is in many ways a matter of cataloging things you *shouldn't* do.

Additionally, however, thinking about the label itself—standard edited English—will give you some insights into the goal you are trying to accomplish. In general, the "standard" variety of any language is the one used in formal contexts, including academic ones, by people who are well educated; thus, the ability to use the standard variety of a language marks its user as educated.

The logic behind a standard language is simple and useful: if everyone can agree on and follow the same basic conventions, whether for spelling or subject-verb agreement, we'll be able to communicate successfully with a broad range of people. It's a good principle in theory, but as you know if you have been to Canada or the United Kingdom, "standard" English varies from country to country. Moreover, standards change over time. So while having a "standard" set of conventions is valuable in many ways, it can't guarantee perfect communication.

"Edited," the second term of the label "standard edited English," reminds you that this variety of English is one that has been looked at very carefully. Many writers, especially those who grew up speaking a variety of English other than the standard and those whose first language is not English, reread their writing several times with great care before submitting it to ensure, for example, that every verb agrees with its subject. This is, of course, the role that good editors play: they read someone else's work and make suggestions about how to improve the quality, whether at the level of the sentence, the paragraph, or the text as a whole. Few of us pay such careful attention to our writing when we tweet, text, or email—but we *all* need to do so with our academic writing.

Use Clear and Recognizable Patterns of Organization

Academic writing is organized in a way that's clear and easy for readers to recognize. In fact, writers generally describe the pattern explicitly early in a text by including a **THESIS** sentence that states the main point and says how the text is structured.

At the level of the paragraph, the opening sentence generally serves as a **TOPIC SENTENCE**, which announces what the paragraph is about. Readers of academic writing expect such signals for the text as a whole and for each paragraph, even within shorter texts like essay exams. Sometimes you'll want to include headings to make it easy for readers to locate sections of text.

Readers of academic writing expect the organization not only to be clear but also to follow some kind of logical progression. For example:

- Beginning with the simplest ideas and then moving step by step to the most complex ideas
- Starting with the weakest claims or evidence and progressing to the strongest ones
- Treating some topics early in the text because readers must have them as background to understand ideas introduced later
- Arranging the text chronologically, starting with the earliest events and ending with the latest ones

Some academic documents in the sciences and social sciences require a specific organization known as **IMRAD** for its specific headings: introduction, methods, results, and discussion. Although there are many possible logical patterns to use, readers will expect to be able to see that pattern with little or no difficulty. Likewise, they generally expect the **TRANSITIONS** between sections and ideas to be indicated in some way, whether with words like *first, next,* or *finally,* or even with full sentences like "Having considered three reasons to support this position, here are some alternative positions."

Finally, remember that you need to conclude your text by somehow reminding your readers of the main point(s) you want them to take away. Often, these reminders explicitly link the conclusion back to the thesis statement or introduction.

Mark Logical Relationships between Ideas

Academic writers are expected to make clear how the ideas they present relate to one another. Thus, in addition to marking the structure of the text, you need to mark the links between ideas and to do so explicitly. If you say in casual conversation, "It was raining, and we didn't go on the picnic," listeners will interpret *and* to mean *so* or *therefore.* In academic writing, however, you have to help readers understand how your ideas are related to one another. For this reason, you'll want to use **TRANSITIONS** like *therefore, however,* or *in addition.* Marking the relationships among your ideas clearly and explicitly helps readers recognize and appreciate the logic of your arguments.

State Claims Explicitly and Provide Appropriate Support

One of the most important conventions of academic writing is to present **CLAIMS** explicitly and support them with **EVIDENCE**, such as examples or statistics, or by citing authorities of various kinds. Notice the two distinct parts: presenting claims clearly and supporting them appropriately. In academic writing, authors don't generally give hints; instead, they state what is on their minds, often in a **THESIS** statement. If you are from a culture that values indirection and communicates by hinting or by repeating proverbs or telling stories to make a point, you'll need to check to be sure that you have stated your claims explicitly. Don't assume that readers will be able to understand what you're saying, especially if they do not have the same cultural background knowledge that you do.

Qualify your statements. It's important to note that being clear and explicit doesn't mean being dogmatic or stubborn. You'll generally want to moderate your claims by using qualifying words like *frequently, often, generally, sometimes,* or *rarely* to indicate how strong a claim you are making. Note as well that it is much easier to provide adequate support for a qualified claim than it is to provide support for a broad unqualified claim.

Choose evidence your audience will trust. Whatever your claim, you'll need to look for **EVIDENCE** that will be considered trustworthy and persuasive by your audience. And keep in mind that what counts as acceptable and appropriate evidence in academic writing often differs from what works in other contexts. Generally, for example, you wouldn't cite sacred religious texts as a primary source for academic arguments.

Consider multiple perspectives. Similarly, you should be aware that your readers may have a range of opinions on any topic, and you should write accordingly. Thus, citing only sources that reflect one perspective won't be sufficient in most academic contexts. Be sure to consider and acknowledge **COUNTERARGUMENTS** and viewpoints other than your own.

Organize information strategically. One common way of supporting a claim is by moving from a general statement to more specific information. When you see words like *for example* or *for instance,* the author is moving from a more general statement to a more specific example.

In considering what kind of evidence to use in supporting your claims, remember that the goal is not to amass and present large quantities of evidence but instead to sift through all the available evidence, choose the evidence that will be most persuasive to your audience, and arrange and present it all strategically. Resist the temptation to include information or **ANECDOTES** that are not directly relevant to your topic or that do not contribute to your argument. Your instructor will likely refer to these as digressions or as "getting off topic" and encourage you to delete them.

Present Your Ideas as a Response to Others

The best academic writers do more than just make well-supported claims. They present their ideas as a response to what else has been said (or might be said) about their topic. One common pattern, introduced by professors Gerald Graff and Cathy Birkenstein, is to start with what others are saying and then to present your ideas as a response. If, as noted earlier in this chapter, academic writing is a way of entering a conversation—of engaging with the ideas of others—you need to include their ideas with your own.

In fact, providing support for your claims will often involve **SYNTHESIS**: weaving the ideas and even the words of others into the argument you are making. And since academic arguments are part of a larger conversation, all of us in some important ways are always responding to and borrowing from others, even as we are developing our own individual ideas.

> Gerald Graff himself provides a good example, on p. 957, of beginning with another's idea and then responding with his own.

Express Your Ideas Clearly and Directly

Another characteristic of academic writing is clarity. You want to be sure that readers can understand exactly what you are writing about. Have you ever begun a sentence by writing "This shows . . ." only to have your teacher ask, "What does *this* refer to?" Such a comment is evidence that the teacher, as reader, isn't sure what the author—you—are referring to: this argument? this evidence? this analysis? this figure? this claim? Be careful and specific in your language. You'll also want to **DEFINE** terms you use, both to be sure readers will not be confused and to clarify your own positions—much as we defined "standard edited English" earlier in this chapter.

Clarity of expression in academic writing also means being direct and concise. Academic writers in the United States, for example, avoid highly elaborate sentence structures or flowery language, and they don't let the metaphors and similes they use get the best of them either, as this author did:

> Cheryl's mind turned like the vanes of a wind-powered turbine, chopping her sparrowlike thoughts into bloody pieces that fell onto a growing pile of forgotten memories.

In fact, this sentence was the winner of an annual "bad writing" contest in which writers try to write the worst sentence they can. It's easy to see why this one was a winner: it has way too much figurative language—chopping wind turbines, bleeding sparrows, thoughts in a pile, forgotten memories—and the metaphors get in the way of one another. Use metaphors carefully in academic writing, making sure they add to what you're trying to say.

Here's one way the prize-winning sentence might be revised to be clearer and more direct: "Cheryl's mind worked incessantly, thought after thought piling up until she couldn't keep track of them all."

Be Aware of How Genres and Conventions Vary across Disciplines

While we can identify common characteristics of all academic writing, it is important to note that some genres and conventions vary across disciplines. Thus, an analytic essay in psychology is similar to one in a literature class, but it is also different in crucial ways. The same will be true for lab reports or position papers in various fields. In this regard, different disciplines are like different cultures, sharing many things but unique in specific ways. Therefore, part of becoming a biologist or an engineer—or even an electrical engineer instead of a civil engineer—is learning the discipline's particular rules and rituals as well as its preferred ways of presenting, organizing, and documenting information.

You'll also find that some rhetorical moves vary across genres. In the humanities, for example, writers often use a quotation to open an essay, as a way of launching an argument—or to close one, as a way of inspiring the audience. Such a move occurs far less often, if at all, in the sciences or social sciences.

Despite these differences in genres across academic disciplines, you'll also find there are some common rhetorical moves you'll make in much of the academic writing you do. You'll find that short essays and research articles generally open with three such moves:

- First, you give the **CONTEXT** or general topic of whatever you are writing; frequently, you will do this by discussing the existing research or commentary on the topic you are writing about.

- Second, you point out some aspect of this topic that merits additional attention, often because it is poorly understood or because there is a problem that needs to be solved—that is, you'll show there is a problem or gap of some kind in our understanding.

- Finally, you'll explain how your text addresses that problem or fills that gap. Notice that this often happens within the first paragraph or two of the text.

By contrast, in writing a response to a question on a timed exam, you might restate the question in some way, using it as the opening line of your response and a thesis statement or topic sentence. For example, if you get an essay exam question asking "How are West African influences evident in coastal southeastern areas of the United States today?" you might begin your response by turning the question into a statement like this: "West African influences on language, music, and food are still very visible in coastal areas of the southeastern United States." You should not spend several sentences introducing your topic while the clock ticks; to do so would be to waste valuable time.

With experience, you will learn the genres and conventions you need to know, especially within your major.

Document Sources Using the Appropriate Citation Style

Finally, academic writers credit and **DOCUMENT** all sources carefully. If becoming fluent in academic discourse is a challenge for all of us, understanding how Western academic culture defines intellectual property and **PLAGIARISM** is even more complicated. Although you will never need to provide a source for historical events that no one disputes (for example, that the U.S. Declaration of Independence was signed on July 4, 1776, in Philadelphia), you will need to provide documentation for words, information, or ideas that you get from others, including any content (words or images) you find on the internet.

What else do you need to learn about academic writing? While we hope this brief list gives you a good idea of the major features of academic writing in the United States, you'll likely still find yourself asking questions. Just what does a direct and concise style look like? How much and what kinds of evidence are necessary to support a claim sufficiently? How much documentation is needed? Should a review of literature primarily describe and summarize existing research, or should it go one step further and critique this research? You will begin to learn the answers to these questions in time, as you advance through college, and especially when you choose your major. But don't be surprised that the immediate answer to all these questions will very often be "It depends." And "it" will always depend on what your purpose is in writing and on the audience you wish to reach.

In the meantime, even as you work to become fluent in U.S. academic writing, it's worth returning to a note we have sounded frequently in this chapter: the U.S. way of writing academically is not the only way. Nor is it a better way. Rather, it is a different way. As you learn about and experience other cultures and languages, you may have an opportunity to learn and practice the conventions those cultures use to guide their own forms of academic writing. When you do so, you'll be learning yet another "new" language, just as you have learned the "academic writing" language of the United States.

FIVE

Writing and Rhetoric as a Field of Study

RHETORICIAN SUSAN MILLER neatly sums up why we study rhetoric: "If you want to know how power works, you must understand how language works—and that's what the study of rhetoric is all about." As Miller's statement underscores, mastery of the tools of rhetoric—writing, reading, speaking, and listening—is crucial, so much so that employers rank the ability to communicate well at the top of their list of the qualities they look for in those they hire. A survey of 120 American corporations, for instance, concludes that in today's workplace writing is a "threshold skill" for hiring and promotion.

So it's no surprise that colleges and universities are responding by establishing departments, programs, and courses that allow students to choose writing and rhetoric as a field of study. Visit the website for the University of Texas's Department of Rhetoric and Writing, for example, and you'll find this statement: "Analytical, communicative, and persuasive skills are in demand in almost every profession. . . . The Rhetoric and Writing major . . . produces sophisticated communicators." Michigan State's Department of Rhetoric, Writing, and American Cultures defines its goal as "preparing excellent communicators in the culturally, technologically, and economically dynamic environments of the . . . twenty-first century."

Educational leaders also speak to the need for careful study of writing and rhetoric. In an interview, Stanford University president John

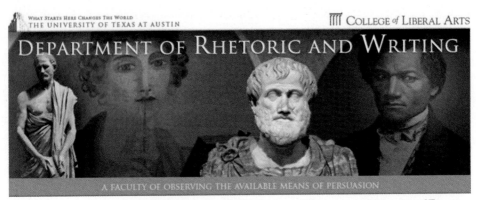

The website of the Department of Rhetoric and Writing at the University of Texas focuses on rhetoricians. From the left: Demosthenes, a Roman woman of Pompeii, Aristotle, and Frederick Douglass.

Hennessy (who was a professor of engineering before he became president) reflected on his own experience to make the point: "[In college] we had a notion that engineers had to know how to use slide rules or calculators or computers, but not how to write. And that is the biggest falsehood you could possibly perpetrate on young people. I think writing and rhetoric . . . are the two most valuable skills across any discipline in any field." You have strong reasons, then, to consider writing and rhetoric as a field of study, whether you choose it as a major or a minor or simply take advantage of opportunities to take classes in writing and rhetoric.

What Will You Learn by Studying Writing and Rhetoric?

What will it mean—what will you learn—if you choose writing and rhetoric as a field of study? As the quotations above suggest, this field focuses on effective, ethical communication, whether written, visual, or spoken—that is, it concentrates on how words and images can change our minds, earn our agreement, and shape our identities and lives. Members of this field recognize that in complex societies such as ours, those who can produce powerful written, spoken, visual, or digital messages have some distinct advantages.

That's the "big picture" of writing and rhetoric as a field of study. But this field will also introduce you to powerful practitioners of rhetoric, from the ancient Sumerian priestess Enheduanna (whose impassioned writing argued for the supremacy of the goddess Inanna over male gods), to the ancient Roman orator Cicero (whose words in support of the Roman Republic were so dangerous that they cost him his life), to twentieth-century rhetorical theorists such as Kenneth Burke (who argues that "wherever there is persuasion, there is rhetoric"), to contemporary leaders like Barack Obama and Aung San Suu Kyi.

Most important, as a student of rhetoric and writing, you will learn to think about how a text gets its message across, rather than just focusing on what the message is. In other words, you will learn to think rhetorically. And in doing so, you'll read, analyze, and respond to important works of rhetoric throughout history, from Plato's attack on rhetoric as deception and trickery in his *Phaedrus* to Sei Shonogan's mischievous and memorable *Pillow Book*, which offers advice and observations about life in eleventh-century Japan, to the powerful speeches of Maria Stewart, Chief Sitting Bull, Sojourner Truth, John F. Kennedy, Cesar Chavez, and Martin Luther King Jr.

> I have something to say to the world, and I have taken English 12 in order to say it well.
> —W. E. B. DU BOIS

You may engage in a variety of research projects. For example, you may study how values and beliefs shape debates over public policy, or you may consider the knowledge, skills, and tools involved in workplace literacy practices. You might study how rhetorical strategies like metaphor and narrative shape communication in the public sphere—or how emerging technologies shape social practices and communication.

Like all fields, this one has a number of subfields:

- The history of rhetoric and writing
- The teaching of rhetoric and writing
- Digital rhetoric
- Visual rhetoric
- Literacy studies
- Gender, identity, and rhetoric
- Technical, professional, and business communication
- Magazine writing and journalism
- Writing program administration
- Teaching English as a second or foreign language

As a student of rhetoric and writing, you will likely find courses on many of these topics. In addition, you may take courses on such topics as rhetoric and performance, the rhetoric of film, the rhetorics of particular cultures, the rhetoric of graphic narratives (comics!), or the rhetoric of science—to name just a few.

Majoring in rhetoric. A sophomore at Whitman College in Washington State, Jesse Moneyhun wasn't sure what he wanted to major in when he first arrived on campus. He describes how he eventually found his way to rhetoric studies, and how he's already starting to see its practical uses:

> There were so many different options: sociology? psychology? English? After a lot of thought, I decided on rhetoric. Studying rhetoric has not only made me a better writer and communicator, but also a better thinker. As a writing tutor, I find that rhetoric helps me analyze and improve any student writing that comes to me, regardless of the discipline. Recently, I helped a foreign exchange student by explaining a difficult prompt in a way I knew she would understand. I was proud when she told me how much it helped her. I know part of that help came from my background in rhetoric. I now have a toolbox of analytical moves and skills that I'll use for the rest of my life, regardless of the career path I choose.

What Jobs Will Studying Rhetoric Prepare You For?

> Don't tell me words don't matter. "I have a dream"—just words? "We hold these truths to be self-evident, that all men are created equal"—just words?
>
> —BARACK OBAMA

A major or minor in rhetoric and writing will prepare you well for any number of pursuits. It offers excellent preparation for law, for example, and it can lead toward any career that calls for effective communication: public relations, advertising, nonprofit work, political and community organizing, publishing, international relations, media, and entertainment.

The study of writing and rhetoric can be a springboard for a number of good jobs. Many of our students, for example, have gone on to become teachers of language arts, history, or social studies; some have gone overseas to teach English as a foreign language. We know one student who, after majoring in writing and rhetoric, became a speechwriter and researcher for a U.S. senator. Still another landed a job as an editorial assistant with a publishing firm in New York City. One former student is now a junior associate in an advertising firm in Chicago, and another is working as an assistant writer for BET. Not long ago, one of us was on an airplane when a fellow passenger noticed the business card on her luggage and said, "You must be a rhetorician; we just hired a rhetorician this week." The fellow passenger was the CEO of an insurance company, and his firm, he said, had hired someone with an extensive background in writing and rhetoric as a group leader in the public relations department. As these examples show, studying writing and rhetoric can lead to many opportunities.

If your school does not offer a major or minor in rhetoric and writing, check out the possibility of developing an independent major or minor. Chances are you'll find courses in a variety of departments that could help you achieve expertise in writing and rhetoric; communications, new media, anthropology, linguistics, English, design, and international relations are just some of the departments that might have courses you could take. But whatever your major, you'll be wise to take courses that focus on rhetoric, writing, or speaking. These are skills that have always been important for success, and in today's world they have become in many ways the new basics.

> When there is more than one language, more than one culture, and more than one rhetorical tradition, the basic question of communication never goes away in terms of who has the floor, who understands what's being said, and who gets listened to.
>
> —LU MING MAO

〰️◎ REFLECT. *Think about what role writing, speaking, and rhetoric are likely to play in your future. Do you expect that you will be giving or attending presentations? reading or writing reports? creating websites? something else?*

SIX

Writing and Rhetoric in the Workplace

LASH FORWARD FIVE OR TEN YEARS. You've graduated from college, maybe from graduate or professional school as well; you're on the job. And whatever that job is, one thing is certain: your ability to communicate—through writing, speaking, and other means—will be crucial to your success. If you're an engineer, you'll likely be writing **PRO-POSALS**, specifications, and directions and maybe giving presentations to prospective clients. If you're a teacher, you'll be writing lesson plans and student **EVALUATIONS**. If you're a health-care practitioner, you'll be writing medical **NARRATIVES** and patient charts and speaking with patients and their families. If you're an accountant, you'll be **ANALYZING** data. If you're a sales representative, you'll be writing **REPORTS** as well as presenting pitches to customers. So strong is the demand for good communicators that virtually every survey of employers reports that the ability to write and speak well is the skill they value most.

Becoming a strong writer, speaker, and presenter isn't rocket science or a gift from the gods: it's a product of careful choices, hard work, and lots of practice. This chapter offers advice on some of the writing and speaking you'll need to do for work, first to get hired and then to succeed once you're on the job.

Strong writing and speaking skills are essential in the workplace—from finding a job to performing the tasks that job will require.

Consider Your Rhetorical Situation

Whether you have a job or are searching for one, you'll be communicating with many different audiences for many different purposes—and so you should get in the habit of thinking systematically about your rhetorical situation. Here are some questions that can guide you:

- *Who's your* AUDIENCE*?* Someone you know or have been referred to? A human resources director? A colleague? A person you would report to? Someone you know nothing about? What can you assume about someone you don't know—and what can you find out by looking on a company website? If you don't know whose desk your message will land on, or if it's likely to be read by multiple people, err on the side of caution: it's better to come across as too formal than too casual.

- *What's your* PURPOSE*?* Are you seeking information? an interview? a specific job? Are you asking someone to do something for you? Are you discussing a possible job, plan, or project? Are you presenting a proposal? negotiating a salary?

- *What* GENRES *should you use?* Are you writing a letter? composing a résumé? reporting information? arguing a position or proposing some kind of action? reviewing someone's work (or being reviewed)? Thinking about genre can help you know what is expected in any of these instances.

- *What's your* STANCE*?* How do you want to present yourself—as eager? curious? confident? knowledgeable? professional? friendly? earnest? If you're looking for a job, what experience do you bring—and how can you demonstrate what you could contribute?

- *What's the* CONTEXT*?* Are you responding to an ad? writing a cover letter to go with an application or a proposal? presenting to a large group? If you're applying for a job, how many steps are involved? What can you find out about the organization online?

- *What* MEDIA *will you use?* If you're sending a letter or résumé, should you use email or snail mail? Or are you required to upload your application to a website? If you're participating in a discussion or interview, will it be face-to-face? on the phone? over *Skype*? in a webinar? If you're giving a presentation, should you include slides or handouts?

Be Professional

The words you choose, the sentences you write, the way you design a letter or résumé, even your email address create an impression for prospective employers—and you want it to be a good one. It's even more important once you're on the job, for then you'll be representing both yourself and the organization you work for. Careless errors that might result in a few points off a grade at school can have greater consequences in the working world, from not getting an interview to not winning a contract to actually losing a job or a promotion. Whether you're on the job or applying for one, every word is crucial for making your goals clear and establishing credibility with employers, colleagues, or clients. This advice is underscored by business schools everywhere:

> Business people who never expected to be doing much writing find that the Internet forces everyone to exchange written messages. . . . Poor writing reflects badly on us, and it limits the influence we can have on others. Excellent writing correlates with the ability to think well, analyze, make decisions and persuade.
> —UNIVERSITY OF CONNECTICUT SCHOOL OF BUSINESS

Job Letters

In email or print, letters are an important part of a job search. You will almost certainly write letters to gather information or ask about possible positions, to apply for specific jobs, and to thank those with whom you have interviewed. For all the job-related letters you'll write, here are some tried-and-true tips:

- Be direct and brief. Say what you want, and why. Assume that your readers will be scanning for just the information they need; make it easy for them to find it.

- Focus more on how you can help the company or organization than on why working there would be good for you. Be careful not to start too many sentences with *I*.

- State your interest and qualifications in a way that makes your readers want to speak with you—or hire you.

- Design letters carefully, making sure they look neat and professional. Use a single typeface—Times New Roman or **Arial** are always appropriate. Remember that the look of your letters says a lot about who you are.

- Use capitalization and punctuation the way you would in an academic essay. Don't include emoticons or too many exclamation points.

- Address readers by name and title (Dear Ms. Willett) or by first name and last if you're not sure about the correct title (Dear Mary Helen Willett). If an advertisement lists only an office, use that in your salutation (Dear Office of Human Resources). If you can't find a person or an office to use, check the company's website—or make a call to the company headquarters to find out more about whom you should address.

- Proofread, proofread, proofread! Make sure that nothing is misspelled.

Inquiry letters. Sometimes you may want to send a letter looking for information about a position, an industry, an organization, or something else. If you admire someone's work, or are interested in a particular company, do some research. You can probably find contact information on the web and some specific names on *LinkedIn*. Write to ask if they would speak with you.

Inquiry letters should be brief but at the same time say what you're looking for, and why. Introduce yourself, and explain your interest in the organization or the person's work. Be enthusiastic but direct about what you're asking for—information about an organization? an opportunity to meet with someone? Remember to include your contact information. If you're looking for a job, you might also attach your résumé.

Shuqiao Song read a book on designing presentations that she liked very much and that helped improve her own presentation skills. When she noticed in the book that the author had a business near her college, Song sent the following email:

From: Shuqiao Song <ssong@gmail.com>

Date: Sunday, May 29, 2009 8:28 PM

To: Nancy Duarte <nduarte@presentations.com>

Subject: Interested in communications design

Dear Ms. Duarte:

I'm a sophomore at Stanford, where I recently took a rhetoric course in which we studied your book *slide:ology* for examples of successful presentations. I loved your book and was inspired to incorporate your suggestions and model my own presentation and slides on the advice you give.

The words and images in the graphic novel that I analyzed in my presentation interact in unusual and fascinating ways, and my research on this topic led me to some insights about the way that speech, written text, and images could interact in my presentation. I've attached a video file of the presentation, which I hope you'll find interesting. My performance is far from perfect, but reading your book really changed the way I thought about presenting and helped me analyze the elements of good (and bad) presentations.

Your book also made me aware of the field of communications design, and I'm interested to learn more about it. Would you be willing to meet with me and to tell me about your work and how I can learn more about the field?

Thank you so much for considering this request. I hope to have the opportunity to speak with you.

Sincerely yours,
Shuqiao Song
650-799-8484

Application letters. When you're writing to apply for a job—or a grant, or something else—you'll usually need to write an application letter. This kind of letter is ordinarily sent along with a résumé, so it should be relatively short and to the point, saying what you are applying for and why you are interested in it. If you're applying for a specific position, say how you heard about it. Most important of all, try to show readers why they should consider your application—and here you need to think in terms of why hiring you would be good for them, not for you. Finally, identify anything you are including with your letter: your résumé, a writing sample, and so on.

Ade Adegboyega saw an advertisement for a summer internship at a ticket sales and service company. He was majoring in exercise science and sport management and had some experience in ticket sales and related services, so he was quick to apply. See the letter he sent on the next page.

An Application Letter

Sender's address.

Frank Miller, Sales Manager
The ASR Group
3120 Industrial Blvd.
Suite A200
Atlanta, GA 30318

Recipient's name and address.

Dear Mr. Miller:

Direct, to-the-point opening that mentions how he heard about the position.

I am writing in response to your Teamworkonline.com posting for a summer intern in ticket sales and services. I believe that I have skills and experience that would enable me to contribute to your organization, and I am interested in this position.

Refers to enclosed résumé and relevant experience and skills.

I am a sophomore at Rutgers University, majoring in exercise science and sport management, graduating in May 2018. The enclosed résumé provides details of my skills, education, and work experience. One item that may be of particular interest to you is my work in the ticket sales department at the Prudential Center. This experience taught me how to analyze sales patterns and meet sales quotas and promotional objectives. I've also worked as an office assistant and would also be able to contribute to the production of reports. All my jobs have helped me learn to communicate effectively with both colleagues and vendors.

I would welcome the opportunity to put my experience and abilities to work for the ASR Group sport management department and to discuss the position further with you. I can be reached at 862-773-4074 or ade.adegbo@scarletmail.rutgers.edu. Thank you for considering my application.

Contact information.

Sincerely,

Ade Adegboyega

Ade Adegboyega

Thank-you letters. Send a thank-you letter to anyone you speak with or who helps you when you're looking for a job. Whether you talk to someone in person, on the phone, or over email, you should thank him or her in writing. Doing so is a sign of respect and demonstrates your seriousness and your ability to follow through. When you're writing to someone who's interviewed you, try to reference something discussed in the interview, to raise a new question that might extend the conversation, and to provide additional thoughts about why the position would be an excellent match for your abilities and interests. And be sure to send a thank-you promptly, within a day or two of your interview. A handwritten note is a nice touch, but it's perfectly appropriate to send the thank-you via email, especially if the employer will be making a decision soon. When Scott Williams was looking for a job, he was careful to write thank-you emails like this one after every interview.

From: Scott Williams <sjwilliams@optonline.net>
Date: Friday, March 25, 2015 4:35 PM
To: Yuri Davison <davisony@graceco.com>
Subject: Thank You

Dear Mr. Davison,

Thank you for meeting with me yesterday and for taking so much time to explain the work your firm does. My studies as an economics major were mostly theoretical so I was especially interested to hear about the day-to-day work at a private equity firm.

It's exciting to know that Grace & Company might be looking for a junior analyst in the near future, and I'm pleased to attach a sample of my writing, as you requested. It's an analytical paper I wrote about the music of Franz Liszt.

Thank you again for your time and consideration. I hope you'll keep me in mind if you do decide you need a junior analyst. In the meantime, would it be a good idea for me to take a class to prepare for the Series 7 exam? There's no telling what the future holds, but I know that I want to work in finance, and that is something I could get working on now.

Sincerely,
Scott Williams
203-875-9634

Note that Williams wrote this letter the day after his interview and that he references some specific things discussed and poses a question that gives reason for the conversation to continue. Now take a look at another letter, which demonstrates what *not* to do:

From: Libby White <lib.white@me.com>

Date: Sunday, October 25, 2015 4:13 PM

To: Alexander Elliott <aelliott@sales.maxco.com>

Subject: Thanks!

Mr. Elliott,

Thank you so much for giving me the opportunity to speak with you about your Sales Representative position. I am extremely excited about the possibility of working for you. Having now received the answers to my many questions about the sales position, I am even more thrilled to have the opportunity to interview for the position.

I greatly appreciate your taking the time to answer my questions so patiently and thoroughly. I hope we speak again in the future.

Thanks again,
Libby White
646-432-2533

While the interview was held on October 19, this email wasn't sent until October 25, suggesting to the employer that the writer was not very efficient or perhaps not genuinely interested in the job—or both. The writer focuses her message more on herself than on the position and the company, and both the subject line (thanks!) and the ending salutation (thanks again) are too informal. You probably won't be surprised to find that this applicant did not get the job.

Résumés

Your résumé provides an overview of your education and work experience—and thus is usually your most important chance to create a strong and favorable impression. While busy employers may not take time to read all the materials you send them, they will certainly take a close look at your résumé. For that reason, you'll need to write and design it carefully. As a piece of writing that represents you, your résumé should look good and be easy to read. Keep it to one page—just enough to showcase your experience and to present yourself thoughtfully. The sample résumés on pages 68 and 69 list experience in chronological order, but you might consider using reverse-chronological order if your recent experiences relate directly to the kind of job you'd like to attain.

Format. Be prepared to submit your document in a variety of ways: Word, rich text format (RTF) or plain text, PDF, HTML, or keyword-optimized. Because browsers or company systems can translate files in different ways, having a clean, simple setup will prevent your résumé from being relegated to the "toss pile" because it has defaulted to something that's difficult to read. If you're submitting your résumé online, check how it looks in the major browsers—*Firefox, Chrome, Safari.* If a company you're applying to wants résumés in a particular format, be sure you deliver yours that way.

Design. Use headings to organize your information and highlight key information with bullets. If you're able to save your résumé as a PDF, you can use some of the design features available in word-processing programs. But because you'll likely have to adapt to various file formats, make your design as simple as possible: fonts and indents won't always carry over, and simpler can often be more readable.

You may also need to create a plain-text *scannable résumé,* designed to be read by a computer. Scannable résumés use a single font, with no italics, boldface, or indents, and they need to use keywords such as *sales* or *analysis* to match terms in job descriptions the computer is likely to be reading for. Scannable résumés use nouns instead of verbs to describe responsibilities and experiences ("*response* to sales calls" rather than "*responded* to sales calls").

If you have a specific job objective, you might list that objective at the top, just under your name and contact information. Be sure to mention any courses and experience that are relevant to that objective. If you're applying to be a teaching assistant at an elementary school, for example, you'll want to list any substitute teaching or babysitting experience and your CPR certification. And you might want to put experience that is most relevant to your goals first, as Ade Adegboyega did on the résumé he sent in for an internship at a ticket sales and service company.

A Print Résumé

Ade Adegboyega
89 Laurel Ave.
Irvington, NJ 07111
862-773-4074
ade.adegbo@scarletmail.rutgers.edu

OBJECTIVE
To obtain an internship related to the field of sport management.

EDUCATION
Rutgers University, New Brunswick, NJ (2014–present)
- School of Arts and Science
- Major: Exercise Science and Sport Management
- Minor: Economics
- Bachelor of Science expected May 2018

EXPERIENCE
Prudential Center, Newark, NJ (Oct. 2012–Sept. 2014)
Ticket Sales Associate
- Responded to inbound sales calls and inquiries, and provided information and/or follow-up materials as requested
- Maintained knowledge of ticket plan programs and ticket holder preferences

Answer, Rutgers University Center for Applied Psychology, Piscataway, NJ (Sept. 2014–present)
Office Assistant at national organization for sex education
- Oversee database management for quality assurance
- Assist staff with administrative duties as requested
- Compile statistical information for program coordinators
- Distribute incoming mail and prepare outgoing mail

Rutgers Recreation, New Brunswick, NJ (Jan. 2015–present)
Intramural Referee
- Look for violations of rules during play
- Impose penalties on players as necessary
- Explain the rules governing a specific sport

COMPUTER SKILLS
Microsoft Word, Excel, PowerPoint, Access, programming

ACTIVITIES
Intramural soccer
Rutgers Brazilian Jiu Jitsu Club

A Scannable Résumé

Ade Adegboyega

Key words: ticket sales; oversight; sport; referee; economics; compilation of statistics; administrative duties

Address
89 Laurel Ave.
Irvington, NJ 07111
Phone: 862-773-4074
Email: ade.adegbo@scarletmail.rutgers.edu

Education
B.S. in Exercise Science and Sport Management, minor in Economics, Rutgers, New Brunswick, NJ, expected May 2018

Experience
Ticket Sales Associate, Oct. 2012–Sept. 2014
Prudential Center, Newark, NJ
Response to inbound sales calls and inquiries; provision of information and/or follow-up materials as requested; knowledge of ticket plan programs and ticket holder preferences

Office Assistant, Sept. 2014–present
Answer, Rutgers University Center for Applied Psychology, Piscataway, NJ
Oversight of database management for quality assurance; assistance of staff with administrative duties as requested; compilation of statistics for program coordinators as requested; distribution of incoming mail and preparation of outgoing mail

Intramural Referee, Jan. 2015–present
Rutgers Recreation, New Brunswick, NJ
Determination of rule violations during play; imposition of penalties on players; explanation of rules governing a specific sport

Computer Skills
Microsoft Word, Excel, PowerPoint, Access, programming

Activities
Intramural soccer
Rutgers Brazilian Jiu Jitsu Club

> Key words for computer searches.

> All information in a single font, flush left, with no bold, italics, or underlining.

> Nouns rather than verbs used to list responsibilities and experiences.

References

Often prospective employers will ask for references—professors or supervisors who can speak about your work and your work ethic. Your first step is to develop relationships with teachers and others who might serve as references. Start early in your college career; visit your teachers during office hours, discuss your goals with them—and keep in touch. When you feel comfortable enough, ask if they would be willing to be a reference for you.

When it comes time to ask for a specific reference, be sure to provide them with helpful information: a description of the position, your résumé and cover letter, and samples of your work. Give ample notice—never less than a week or two to write a letter. If the letter will be mailed, be sure to provide stamped, addressed envelopes. Remember to thank your references at every step: when they agree to be a reference, after they recommend you, and when you get the position!

Writing Samples

You may be asked to submit a writing sample or even a **PORTFOLIO** of your work. For some positions, you may want to choose work that demonstrates writing that relates in some way to the position you're seeking, but often you'll just need to show something that demonstrates your writing ability. Include a brief cover note with your sample explaining what it is, why you are proud of it, and why you've chosen to submit it. Label the sample with your name and contact information, and take care with its presentation: place it in a folder if you're delivering it in person or make sure it's a neatly designed document if you're sending it via email.

When Elizabeth Sanders interviewed for a position as a student events coordinator for a campus research institute that specified "experience organizing and publicizing campus events" as a qualification, she was asked to bring a portfolio of her work along. She chose work that showcased writing that would matter for that job—two brochures she wrote, designed, and produced; an interview she'd conducted with a visiting speaker; and a press release—and then wrote a cover statement listing what was in her portfolio and describing how each item addressed the job she was applying for.

Scott Williams also was asked to submit a writing sample after his interview at a private equity firm. Having just graduated from college, he chose an analytical paper he'd written as a junior and attached it to his thank-you email.

Both Sanders and Williams were careful to choose examples that demonstrated their best work and to present them in a professional manner. In these cases, their hard work paid off: both got the jobs they were seeking. But even if they hadn't, they would have gained important experience to use when starting the next job search.

Job Interviews

When it comes time to interview, you'll need to prepare. Review the job description and plan how you will talk about your experiences. Research the department and organization that you'd be working for. Make a list of questions you can imagine being asked and come up with answers to each. Prepare your own list of questions that you'd like to ask. You may even want to ask a friend to do a mock interview with you for practice.

The day of the interview, be on time, dress appropriately, and bring extra copies of your résumé, cover letter, references, and any other materials that were requested. Of course you'll be nervous, but be sure to *listen*—and to think before responding. And remember to smile! Here are a few questions that interviewers might ask that you can use to practice and build your own list of potential questions:

- Why are you interested in this industry or field?
- What interests you about this specific position?
- What do you know and like about our organization?
- What is your greatest strength? weakness?
- Can you describe a time that you successfully collaborated on a project?

Participating in a video interview. Many employers today use *Skype* or other videoconferencing technologies to conduct interviews. If you're asked to do an interview of this kind, here's some advice:

- Practice speaking over *Skype* with a friend.
- Dress appropriately and in clothing that is easy to move around in: you may be asked to stand, or sit, or both.
- Avoid using overhead lighting, which can appear harsh on camera; try for natural light if at all possible.
- Make sure that you have a reliable internet connection.

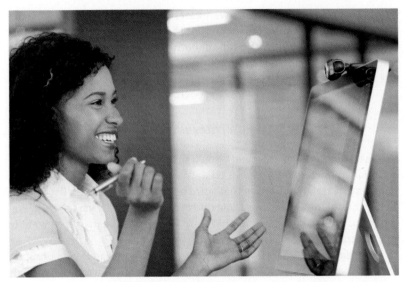

Remember to focus on the camera, rather than the screen, during a videoconference.

- Remember to look and speak directly into the camera in order to come as close as possible to establishing eye contact with your interviewers.
- Be sure to speak carefully, enunciating each word in case the connection is less than ideal.
- Make sure that the area around you is neat—and that your dog isn't barking!

Writing on the Job

The fact is that almost any job you take will call for writing—and for speaking and presenting as well. Regardless of what job you do, you will surely be writing email. You will also likely be composing **EVALUATIONS** as well as letters of recommendation for others and carrying out **ANALYSES** of all kinds. Many jobs will call on you to write a whole range of **REPORTS** and to give presentations incorporating handouts or slides.

As rhetorician Deborah Brandt points out, most of those working in the United States today spend part of their day writing:

A large majority of Americans . . . now make their living in the so-called information economy, people who produce, distribute, process, manipulate or vend mostly written work during a significant percentage of the workday. At the turn of the 20th century, information workers represented 10 percent of all employees. By 1959, they had grown to more than 30 percent; by 1970, they were at 50 percent and now are 75 percent of the employed population. . . . As the nature of work in the United States has changed—toward making and managing information and knowledge—intense pressure has come to bear on the productive side of literacy, the writing side, made all the more intense . . . with the wide distribution of communication technologies that enable writing, that put keyboards and audiences readily at hand.

— DEBORAH BRANDT, "Writing at Work"

So writing will likely be a key part of your day-to-day work, as well as a key to your future success. And the greatest success comes to those who present themselves effectively, develop a strong work ethic, and seek mentorship and constructive criticism—literally writing and speaking their way to success. Remember that getting—and keeping—a job depends on some basic rhetorical principles that will never go out of style:

- Become a strong and proactive team player who **COLLABORATES** well with others.

- Know your **AUDIENCE**, and make the effort to meet them more than halfway, with respect and a willingness to listen and learn from them.

- Clarify your goals and **PURPOSES**, and stick to them—but also know when and how to compromise.

- Consider the **RHETORICAL SITUATION** of any task you face, and make sure that what you are doing is appropriate in that context.

- Know your own strengths and weaknesses, and strive to build on the former and minimize the latter.

- Learn from your mistakes.

Some years ago, when we surveyed members of professional associations about the writing they did as part of their job, we received a letter from an engineer who said the following: "It has come to my attention that those who are skilled in communication—and especially in writing and speaking—are the ones who get ahead in my firm. Would you be willing to correspond with me about how I might improve these skills?" Our guess is that there are thousands of new employees who would echo this sentiment, and this chapter is an attempt to respond to those requests.

REFLECT. Think back to the jobs you've held in high school or college. Whether you were a volunteer at your local hospital or animal shelter, a cashier, a barista, a tutor, or a summer intern, chances are that rhetoric, writing, and collaboration played a role in the work you did. Make some notes about how a particular job required you to use writing or rhetorical strategies. How do you think you might use these skills in future jobs or workplaces?

PART II

Writing Processes

IMAGINE THAT YOU are living in the Middle Ages and that you know how to write (a rare skill at that time). Now imagine the processes you have to engage in to do that writing. You might well begin by making the surface you need to write on, probably parchment or vellum made from animal skins—a process that takes several days.

Once you have something to write on, you make lines across the page to "rule" it and guide your writing. When at last you're ready to begin to write, you do so with a quill pen crafted out of a feather that had its end sharpened into a "nib" with a slit in the middle through

The medieval equivalent to a blank *Word* document: writers began by making their own writing surfaces, first soaking animal skins to remove the fur, then stretching and scraping them until they were the right thickness.

which the ink flows onto the parchment. Woe to you if you make a mistake, for correction is exceedingly difficult—or impossible. And once the writing is done, you still might not be finished if you need to illustrate the manuscript, as in the "illuminated" page from *The Canterbury Tales* on the facing page.

Because the process was so complicated, writing often demanded a team approach. In fact, *book* is defined in an early German encyclopedia as a "work of many hands."

With the advent of the printing press and subsequent technological developments, such material aspects of the writing process became easier, so much so that they became somewhat invisible: writers simply *wrote*. The focus, especially in schools, shifted to the final product, one composed by individual students; any concern with the process, as well as with writing's collaborative aspects, disappeared entirely. And so for many years, the emphasis on the final or "published" piece kept us from seeing the many other processes of writing, from generating ideas to hypothesizing, drafting, revising, and more. Writing involves far more than putting words down on

The Knight. An illuminated page from *The Canterbury Tales*, circa 1410.

a page and checking punctuation. For any important piece of writing, the author must think the message through in many ways to understand and communicate it to an audience. As researcher Janet Emig has concluded, writing is a unique form of learning and understanding it calls for understanding the complex processes involved.

In studying just how those processes work, researchers have lately returned to the medieval notion that a piece of writing is "the work of many hands," recognizing that almost all writing is highly social, created by one or more writers in conversation with many others, from those who have influenced us in the past to those who read and respond to our work. By the end of the twentieth century, the popular image of a writer as a solitary figure (almost always a man) holed up in a tiny room struggling to create an individual work of great genius began to give way to that of a writer as part of an elaborate network, what author Steven Johnson called "connected minds."

The kind of networking now available through the internet and especially through social media surely does involve "connected minds." John Donne's insight that no one "is an island, apart from the main" has never been more true than it is today, as writers around the globe collaborate on everything from a *Google Doc* to a flash mob to a protest movement like Black Lives Matter.

The chapters that follow invite you to think hard about the processes you engage in when you write, about how those processes involve other writers (those you write with and those you write to), and about how writing centers can help. We hope that such thinking will not only make you more aware of how, when, and where you write, but also help to make your writing processes more efficient—and more fun!

SEVEN

Managing the Writing Process

THINK OF SOMETHING YOU LIKE TO DO: ride a bike, play a certain video game, do Sudoku. If you think about it, you'll see that each of these activities involves learning a process that took some effort to get right when you first started doing it. But eventually, the process became familiar, and now you do it almost automatically.

Writing is much the same. It, too, is a process: a series of activities that take some effort to do well. At some level, everyone who writes knows this—from a child who draws a picture and then erases part of it, thinking, "That tree just doesn't look right," to the college student working over an extended period of time on a research paper.

And as with any process, you can manage the writing process by approaching it in parts. This chapter introduces the various stages of the writing process—from generating ideas and coming up with a topic to drafting and revising—and provides strategies that will help you make the most of the many writing demands you'll encounter at school, at work, and elsewhere.

One important aspect of becoming comfortable with the writing process is figuring out what works best for you. No single process works for every author or every writing task, so work instead to develop a repertoire of strategies that will enable you to become an efficient, productive, and effective writer.

Writing involves complex processes and often the "work of many hands."

Develop writing habits that work for you. Think about how you usually approach a writing task. Do you draw up extensive outlines? Do you organize visually or using notecards? Do you write best at a particular time of the day? Do you write best with solitude and quiet—or do you like to have music playing? Think carefully about what habits seem to help you produce your best work. But be careful: if you think you do your best work while multitasking, think again. Research increasingly challenges that assumption!

WRITING PROCESSES / A Roadmap

Whatever processes you find most productive, following are some tips that provide general guidance. If and when you decide on a particular genre, you'll find genre-specific guidance in the Roadmaps in Chapters 11–16.

Understand your assignment. If you're writing in response to an assignment, make sure you understand what it asks you to do. Does it specify a topic? a theme? a genre? Look for words like *argue*, *evaluate*, and *analyze*—words that specify a GENRE and thus point you to approach your topic in a certain way. An assignment that asks you to analyze, for example, lets you know that you should break down your topic into parts that can then be examined closely. If your assignment doesn't name a genre, think about which genre will best suit your rhetorical situation.

Come up with a topic. If you get to choose your topic, think of things you are particularly interested in and want to know more about—or something that puzzles you or poses a problem you'd like to solve or that gets you fired up. A topic you're passionate about is more likely to interest your audience and to keep you engaged as you research and write. If your topic is assigned, try to find an aspect or angle that interests you. Looking for a particular angle on a topic can help you to narrow your focus, but don't worry if the topic you come up with right now isn't very specific: as you do research, you'll be able to narrow and refine it. Coming up with a broad topic that interests you is just the starting point.

Consider your RHETORICAL SITUATION. Whether you're writing an argument or a narrative, working alone or with a group, you'll have an audience, a purpose, a stance, a genre, a medium and design, and a context—all things that you should be thinking about as you write.

- *Audience.* Who are you addressing in your writing, and what are they likely to know or believe about your topic? What do you want them to think or do in response to your writing?

- *Purpose.* What is your goal in writing? What has motivated you to write, and what do you wish to accomplish?

- *Genre.* Have you been assigned a specific genre? If not, which genre(s) will best suit your purpose and audience?

- *Stance.* What is your attitude toward your topic? What perspective do you offer on it? What's your relationship with your audience, and how do you want to be seen by them?

- *Context.* Consider the conversation surrounding your argument. What has been said about your topic, and how does that affect what you say? What about your immediate context—when is your writing due, and are there any other requirements or constraints?

- *Medium and design.* What medium or media will best suit your audience, purpose, and message? What design elements are possible (or required) in these media?

Schedule your time. Remember that you must fit any writing project into your schedule, so think about how to use your time most wisely. However you keep yourself on track, taking a series of small steps is easier than doing it all at once. So schedule periodic goals for yourself: meeting them will build your confidence and reinforce good writing habits.

Generate ideas. Most of us find that writing can help us explore a topic and can even lead us to new ideas. Here are some activities that can help you sort out what you already know about your topic—and come up with new ideas about it:

- *Brainstorming* is a way to generate ideas without worrying about whether they're useful or not. Take a few minutes to focus on your topic or thesis (or a broad idea you want to develop into a specific topic or thesis) and list, using words or phrases, everything that occurs to you about this subject. Then review what you have written, looking for ideas that seem promising and relationships that you can develop. Remember: there are no right answers at this point!

- *Clustering* is a strategy for generating and processing ideas visually. Take a sheet of paper and write a word or phrase that best summarizes or evokes your topic. Draw a circle around this word. Now fill in the page by adding related words and ideas, circling them and connecting them to the original word, forming clusters. Then look at all the clusters to see what patterns you can find or where your ideas seem to be leading.

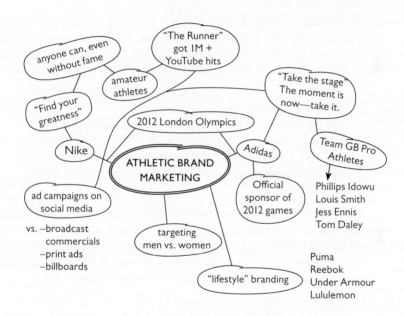

- *Freewriting* is a strategy for writing ideas down quickly, without stopping. To freewrite, simply write about whatever comes into your head in relation to a particular idea or topic for five to ten minutes. Be careful not to censor yourself: let your ideas flow as freely as possible. You may be surprised at the complexity and power of the ideas that you can develop through this process.

- *Looping* is an extended and more focused kind of freewriting. Begin by establishing a subject and then freewrite for five to ten minutes. Look at what you've written. Identify the most important or interesting or promising idea and write a sentence summarizing it. Use this sentence to start another "loop" of freewriting. Repeat this process as many times as necessary.

- *Drawing or sketching a picture of your topic* can help spark and guide your thinking about it. If you're writing about recycling on your campus, what does that topic look like? Drawing it may lead to a creative breakthrough. See if creating a series of sketches can help you figure out the structure of an essay you're writing.

- *Questioning* is an especially good way of exploring a topic. Starting with questions can help you discover what you already know about your topic—and, just as importantly, what you don't know and need to learn. Try starting with the questions *Who? What? Where? When? Why? How?*

  Who was / is involved? What can you say about them?
  What happened / happens?
  Where did / does it occur? What should you describe?
  When did / does it occur? What time?
  Why did / does it happen? What caused / causes it to occur?
  How did / does it happen? Was / is there a process you should describe?

- *Outlining* can help you see connections between ideas and organize information, especially if you're writing about a complex subject. Begin by listing your main ideas in an order that makes sense. Then add supporting evidence or details under each main idea, indenting these subpoints to mark the different levels, as shown below:

  First main idea
      Supporting evidence or detail
      Supporting evidence or detail
  Second main idea
      Supporting evidence or detail
      Supporting evidence or detail

Do some RESEARCH. You may want or need to do some research to better understand your topic, learn more about it, and decide what aspects of it you want to explore further. This could mean reading about your topic, **IN-TERVIEWING** experts about it, conducting **SURVEYS**, **OBSERVING** something firsthand, or some combination of those methods. Learning what others have said about a topic is an important step to figuring out what you want to say—and to joining the conversation.

Come up with a tentative **THESIS**, a statement that identifies your topic and the point you want to make about it. You'll rarely, if ever, have a final thesis when you start writing, but establishing a tentative one will help focus your thinking and any research you may do. Here are some prompts to get you started.

1. *What point do you want to make about your topic?* Try writing it out as a promise to your audience: *In this essay, I will present reasons for becoming a vegetarian.*

2. *Try plotting out a tentative thesis in two parts,* the first stating your topic, the second making some claim about the topic:

   ┌—————— **TOPIC** ——————┓┌——————————— **CLAIM** ———————————
   Adopting a vegetarian diet will improve health, help local farms, and reduce

   ┌———————————————┓
   the carbon footprint.

3. *Ask some questions about what you've written.* Will it engage your intended audience? What's your claim? Is it debatable? There's no point in staking a claim that is a fact, or one that no one would disagree with.

4. *Do you need to narrow or* **QUALIFY** *your thesis?* Can you do what you say you will, given the time and resources available? You don't want to overstate your case—or make a claim that you'll have trouble supporting. Adding words such as *could, might, likely,* or *potentially* can help qualify what you say: *Adopting a vegetarian diet will <u>likely</u> improve health, <u>might</u> help local farms, and <u>could potentially</u> reduce the carbon footprint.*

5. *Is the thesis clear and focused?* Will it tell readers what's coming? And will it help keep you (and your readers) on track?

Keep in mind that at this point in your process, this is a tentative thesis, one that could change as you research, write, and revise. Continue to explore your topic. Don't stop until you feel you've reached a full understanding of your topic. As you learn more about it, you may well find that you want to revise your thesis.

Once you're satisfied that your thesis makes a clear claim that you can support, and one that will interest your readers, gather together the notes from your research. This is the information you'll draw from as support for your thesis.

ORGANIZE your ideas. Whether you like to write out an outline or prefer to do most of your planning on note cards or sticky notes (or in your head!), you'll want to think about how best to organize your text before beginning to write. Writing about events generally works best when told in **CHRONO-LOGICAL ORDER**. And facts, data, and other **EVIDENCE** are usually most effective when stated in order of importance, starting with the information that's most crucial to your argument before stating the less important information. If you're describing something, you might organize your information **SPATIALLY**, beginning at one point and moving from left to right, or top to bottom. As you see, there's no one way to organize your writing; the order in which you present your points will depend on many things, including the topic and what you have to say about it.

Write out a draft. Keep your tentative thesis statement and any other notes and outlines close at hand as you start writing. A complete draft will include an introduction, a body, and a conclusion, though you may not necessarily draft them in that order.

- *The* **INTRODUCTION** is often the most difficult part to write, so much so that some authors decide to write it last. But just as a well-crafted opening can help guide your readers, it can also help you get started writing. A good introduction should grab readers' attention, announce your topic and your claim, and indicate how you plan to proceed. A provocative question, an anecdote, a startling claim: these are some of the ways you might open an essay.

- *The body* of an essay is where you will develop your argument, point by point, paragraph by paragraph. Strategies such as **COMPARISON**, **DE-SCRIPTION**, **NARRATION**, and others can help you develop paragraphs to present **EVIDENCE** in support of your **THESIS**.

- *The* **CONCLUSION** should sum up your argument in a way that readers will remember. You might end by restating your claim, discussing the implications of your argument, calling for some action, or posing further questions—all ways of highlighting the significance of what you've said.

Be flexible, and make changes if you need to. Even the most well-planned writing doesn't show its true shape until you've written a full draft, so don't be surprised if you find that you need to reorganize, do additional research, or otherwise rethink your argument as you go. Be flexible! Rather than sticking stubbornly to a plan that doesn't seem to be working, use each draft and revision as an opportunity to revisit your plan and to think about how you can strengthen your argument or your appeal.

The ancient Greeks had a word for thinking about the opportunities presented by a particular rhetorical situation. They called it *kairos,* and it referred to the ability to seize an opportune and timely moment. Kairos was the ancient Greek god of opportunity and perfect timing, qualities every author needs. He was often depicted as a young man running, and it was said that you must seize the forelock of his hair as he passes by; once he's passed, there's nothing to cling to because the back of his head is completely bald—you've missed your opportunity.

Kairos

This is a concept that can be especially helpful when you're drafting— and that can also help you revise. As you work, think of each paragraph and sentence as an opportunity to add (or eliminate) detail, to reorganize, or to improve your point in some other way. Think about how your sentences and paragraphs might be received by your audience—and about how you can get readers to pay attention to and value what you say.

Get response from others—from your instructor, a classmate, a writing center tutor. Be sure to tell them about any questions or concerns you have about the draft, and ask for their advice. But remember: you don't have to take all the advice you get, just what you consider helpful. You're the author!

Look at your draft with a critical eye and revise. You'll find genre-specific guidelines for reading a draft carefully and revising in the chapters on **ARGUMENTS**, **NARRATIVES**, **ANALYSES**, **REPORTS**, **REVIEWS**, and **PROPOSALS**. For more general advice, following are some prompts to help you read over a draft, either your own or one you're peer reviewing for a fellow writer.

- How does the **INTRODUCTION** capture readers' attention and make them want to read on? Does it indicate that (or why) the topic matters? How else might it begin?

- How does the **AUTHOR** come across—as well-informed? passionate? serious? something else?

- Is it clear what motivated the author to write? Consider the larger **CONTEXT** : what else has been said about the topic, and has the author considered perspectives other than his or her own?

- Is there an explicit **THESIS** ? If not, does there need to be? If so, does it make clear what the author is claiming about the topic?

- Is there sufficient support for the thesis? What **REASONS** and **EVIDENCE** does the author provide? Will they be persuasive for the intended audience?

- Is the draft **ORGANIZED** in a way that is easy to follow? Check to see how each paragraph supports the thesis, and whether it is developed fully enough to make its point. Are there **HEADINGS** —and if not, should there be? Is there any information that would be easier to follow if set off as a list? Are there explicit **TRANSITIONS** to help readers follow the text—and if not, are they needed?

- How does the text **CONCLUDE** ? What does it leave readers thinking? How else might it conclude?

- Is there a title? If so, does it tell readers what your topic is and make them want to read on? If not, think in terms of **KAIROS** : the title is your first opportunity to indicate that this is a text about something that matters and that readers should care about.

Edit and proofread. Now's the time to pay close attention to the details: to check your paragraphs, your **SENTENCES**, your words, and your punctuation. Think about the **STYLE** of your writing: is it appropriate for your purpose and audience? And don't forget to check for **COMMON MISTAKES**. Finally, take the time to proofread. Read with an eye for typos and inconsistencies. Make sure all your sentences are complete. Run a spell checker, but be aware that it is no substitute for careful proofreading.

Approach Your Writing Pragmatically

Even if you have a writing process that works well for you, that doesn't mean you complete all writing tasks the same way—or that you should. It's just common sense that you spend more time and take more care with your writing process for a fifteen-page research paper that counts for 40 percent of your final grade than you do for a much briefer essay that counts for 10 percent of that grade. Take a tip from social scientist Herbert Simon, who coined the word "satisfice," blending *satisfy* and *suffice*. Writers who satisfice approach a writing task pragmatically, considering how important it is, any time constraints, what else they have to do, the nature of the task itself, and how well prepared they feel to complete it. That is, they make *realistic* decisions about their writing processes. So be realistic: what do you *need* to do to complete an assignment effectively—and what *can* you do?

⟋ REFLECT. *Take some time to think about your writing process. What works well? What tends to be a struggle? What do you want to try to do differently? Think about the various ways and places in which you've been able to do good writing. Are you able to make them a regular part of your writing process?*

Gerald Graff's essay on p. 957 might help you appreciate that you already have a lot of everyday skills that you can apply to your own writing process.

EIGHT

The Need for Collaboration

"Here Comes Everybody!"

ERE COMES EVERYBODY is the title of NYU professor Clay Shirky's book about "what happens when people are given the tools to do things together, without needing traditional organizational structures" to do them. Put another way, Shirky's book is about how technology has led to connectivity and how connectivity has led to easy and innovative collaborations. Here's what we mean:

- A group of students creates a *Wikipedia* entry devoted to manga, a genre of Japanese comic books. Within hours, others from around the world have joined in, helping to expand and refine the entry.

- A budding essayist uses the blogging platform *Medium* to publish her writing and interact with readers and other writers. She finds that the online community is full of authors who want to collaborate and discuss their ideas.

- Assigned to write an essay about the dangers faced by independent war journalists, a student starts by researching what has been written on this topic (reading current news magazines, online news sites, and blogs kept by the journalists themselves). When he writes the essay, he weaves the views of others (carefully cited) in with his own, adding his voice to the conversation about that topic.

- Fans of the TV mystery-drama *Veronica Mars* keep the show alive by writing and sharing fanfiction for years after the series ends. The fan base remains so strong that a *Kickstarter* campaign to fund a *Veronica Mars* movie raises over 5 million dollars. The movie hit theaters in 2014, its fans walking down the red carpet alongside the stars.

Even the student mentioned above, researching alone at his computer, depends on others. In short, writers seldom—if ever—write alone. Collaboration has always been inevitable and essential, and now our digital connectivity makes working together easier—and more interesting—than ever. This chapter will help you think about the role that collaboration plays in your life, and especially how it affects the work you do as an author and a reader.

In *Powers of Two*, Joshua Wolf Shenk argues that the real genius of the Beatles and their best work grew out of the collaborative nature of the Lennon-McCartney partnership.

REFLECT. *Think about reading and writing that you do regularly online—status updates, blog posts, wikis—everything. In what ways are you an author, and in what ways are you a member of an audience? To what extent does each activity involve collaboration with others, and how would it be different if there were no collaboration at all?*

What Collaboration Means for Authors—and Audiences

Wikipedia is one of the biggest sites for collaborative authoring today—and might even pop up in your next assignment. Read Larry Gordon's report on *Wikipedia* on p. 952.

The examples above show some of the ways that authors collaborate—and how they sometimes even trade places with their audiences. Readers of the *Wikipedia* entry on manga can take on the role of editors or authors; the student writer using *Medium* becomes an audience for her readers' suggestions and ideas; the student reading and writing about independent war reporters is an audience for those authors whose work he reads and then an author when he responds to their views in his own essay. Welcome to the digital age, where authors and audiences shift roles and collaborate constantly—and indeed, where there's hardly any way to avoid doing so.

Once upon a time, newspapers reported information and events; today, they include blogs that serve as forums for discussing, challenging, even changing that information. Readers who were once passive consumers of the news can now be active participants in responding to and sharing that information with others. As media professor Henry Jenkins puts it, ours is "a world where no one knows everything, but everyone knows something." Putting those somethings together is what happens when we collaborate.

To take another familiar example, players of the first video games were an audience for stories that were written by the games' designers. That's not the case in many of today's role-playing games, however, where the players/audience get to customize their characters and write their own story—very often in collaboration with other players. Consider, for example, the aptly named MMORPGs (massively multiplayer online role-playing games) such as *World of Warcraft,* in which a large number of people play as a group, or the more serious video game *World without Oil,* in which almost 2,000 individuals from twelve countries collaborated over the course of a month to imagine how to deal with a global oil crisis. Not only do such games offer opportunities for collaboration, but it's also actually impossible for any one player to play on his or her own.

Collaboration is an everyday matter. We collaborate for fun, as when a flash mob suddenly appears and starts dancing to "Thriller" or singing the

TAKE A LOOK at some favorite flash mobs at <u>everyonesanauthor.tumblr.com</u>. Some promote a cause, others sell a product, still others celebrate something or someone. The picture above is from a tribute in Berlin to Michael Jackson. We think you'll agree that in addition to fulfilling various purposes, flash mobs can be great fun. What ideas do you have for an effective flash mob? In what ways would a flash mob accomplish your goal better than a piece of writing?

"Hallelujah Chorus" and then just as suddenly disappears. And we collaborate for more serious purposes, as when many people contribute over time to develop a *Wikipedia* entry or when people promoting a particular cause use social media to stay connected and to plan future actions (think Occupy Wall Street). In his book *Net Smart*, digital communications scholar Howard Rheingold argues that collaboration is today's tool for social engagement: "Knowing the importance of participation and how to participate has suddenly become not only an individual survival skill but a key to large-scale social change." For these and other purposes, collaboration is a necessity.

What Collaboration Means for You as a Student

As a student, you'll have many occasions to collaborate, from a simple class discussion to a full-fledged team project to research and write a report, carry out and write up an experiment, or construct a website.

As a writer, you'll be in constant collaboration with others, from teachers and classmates who read and respond to your drafts to the audience you're addressing—and don't forget those whose work you read and cite. Academic writing in particular calls on you to engage with the ideas of others—to listen to and think about what they say, to respond to views you don't agree with, and to weave the ideas of others (those you agree with and those you don't) into your own arguments. Very often you'll want to present your own views as a direct response to what others say—in fact, when you think about it, the main reason we make arguments at all is because someone has said or done something that we want to respond to. And one reason we make academic arguments is to add our voices to conversations about topics that we're studying, things that matter to us.

And consider your nonacademic writing, particularly the writing you do online. Whether you're posting or following others on *Tumblr* or *Instagram*, viewing or contributing to *Wikipedia* or *YouTube* or *Flickr*, it all assumes and makes possible a back-and-forth—a collaboration. You might be an author, an audience, or both. These are all ways that we regularly communicate—and collaborate—with others.

REFLECT. Go to Wikipedia *and work with several classmates to choose an entry that interests you and then revise or add to it. Or, if you don't find what you're looking for, create a new entry yourselves. Revisit in a few days to see what others may have added (or removed). For tips on writing for* Wikipedia, *see p. 771.*

Collaboration at Work

Collaboration almost certainly plays a role in your work life. Indeed, teamwork is central to most businesses and industries. Engineers work in teams to design power plants; editors and designers work together to publish books and magazines; businesses from Best Buy to Google rely on teams to develop and market new products. Given the role that information technologies now play in our lives, whatever work you do—whether it is that of an engineer, health-care worker, bookstore owner, chemist, or teacher—you will find yourself continually communicating with others. The effectiveness of these communications will depend to a large extent on your ability to collaborate effectively.

Today's global culture can raise particular challenges for communication. Increasing numbers of workers are telecommuting—spending time at their home desktops rather than at a desk in an office with other workers.

At ID headquarters in Los Angeles, CEO Kelly Bush leads a videoconference with members of her New York staff.

Even when they are working from a centralized office, workers often need to communicate with colleagues elsewhere in the world and in other time zones. Digital humanities professor Cathy Davidson describes how one company holds global conference calls:

> Everyone chats using Sametime, IBM's internal synchronous chat tool, and has a text window open during the conversation. Anyone can be typing in a comment or a question (backchatting) while any other two people are speaking. Participants are both listening to the main conversation between whichever two people happen to be talking while also reading the comments, questions, and answers that any of the other participants might be texting. The conversation continues in response to both the talk and the text.
>
> —CATHY DAVIDSON, *Now You See It: How the Brain Science of Attention Will Transform the Way We Live, Work, and Learn*

A dizzying scenario to be sure—and an excellent reminder of both the challenges and the opportunities that the future holds for all who wish to make our voices heard in today's global culture. As a student in college, you are well positioned to prepare yourself for this future—which is in fact not the future at all but our present moment. Rather than taking your online writing for granted as "just for fun," learn from it. Take advantage as well of the opportunities that your school provides to learn with and from people with diverse cultural backgrounds. Such collaborative interactions are intrinsically satisfying, and they can also help prepare you to communicate effectively in the twenty-first century.

Some Tips for Collaborating Effectively

As a college student, you will often be asked to work collaboratively with others. Sometimes that collaboration will be fleeting and low risk—for example, to work with a group to respond to questions about a reading and then to share the group's ideas with the class. Other collaborations are more extended and high risk, as when you pick lab partners for the whole term or have a major group project that will count for a significant percentage of everyone's final grade.

Extended collaborative assignments can be a challenge. Members of the group may have differing goals—for instance, two members will accept nothing less than an A and others are just hoping for a C. Other problems can result as well, such as with domineering members of the team or those who don't participate at all. And the logistics of collaborating on a major project can be a challenge. Here are some tips that can help ensure efficient, congenial, and productive team relationships when you are working on an extended collaborative project.

- *Find ways of recognizing everyone.* For example, each group member could talk about a strength that he or she can contribute to the project.

- *Listen carefully*—and respectfully—to every group member.

- *Establish some ground rules.* Whether online or face-to-face, the way your group runs its meetings can make or break your collaborative effort. Spend part of your first meeting exploring your assignment and figuring out how often the group will meet, the responsibilities of each member, and the general expectations you have of each other.

- *Make an effort to develop trust and group identity.* To get started, everyone could share some pertinent information, such as their favorite spots for writing or their typical writing processes. Remember, too, that socializing can play an important role in the development of group identity. Sharing a pizza while brainstorming can pay off down the road. However, remember to stay focused on the project.

- *Get organized.* Use an agenda to organize your meetings, and be sure that someone takes notes. Don't count on anyone's memory, and don't leave all the note-taking to one person! You may want to take turns developing the agenda, reminding everyone of upcoming meetings via email or text message, maintaining written records, and so on.

- *Develop nonthreatening ways to deal with problems.* Rather than telling someone that their ideas are unclear, for instance, you might say, "I'm having trouble making the connection between your suggestion and my understanding of what we're discussing." Just a simple shift from *your* to *my* can defuse difficult situations. And remember that tact, thoughtfulness, and a sense of humor can go a long way toward resolving any interpersonal issues.

- *Build in regular reality checks* to nip any potential problems in the bud—for example, reserve some time to discuss how the group is working and how it could be better. Try not to criticize anyone; instead focus on what's working and what could be improved.

- *Encourage the free play of ideas,* one of the most important benefits of working collaboratively. Think carefully about when your group should strive for consensus and when you should not. You want to avoid interpersonal conflicts that slow you down, yet remain open and consider everyone's ideas.

- *Expect the unexpected.* Someone's computer may crash, interlibrary loan materials may arrive later than expected, someone may be sick on the day when she was supposed to write a key section of the text. Try to build in extra time for the unexpected, and help each other out when some extra teamwork is needed.

- *Be flexible about how you meet.* If getting together in person poses problems, use video chat or *Google Docs* to meet and work. Your school might provide a course management system that includes discussion forums, wikis, and file-sharing folders—all of which will prove helpful for collaborative work.

Remember that when you engage in group work, you need to attend to both the task and the group. And keep in mind that each member of the group should be valued and that the process should be satisfying to all.

NINE

Taking Advantage of the Writing Center

AVE YOU EVER been assigned to write an essay but couldn't quite get started? Perhaps you didn't feel ready to meet with your instructor to discuss your topic (or lack of one), but you wanted to speak with someone about the assignment. Or maybe you had a rough draft, but you weren't sure if your argument made sense. Maybe you're struggling with the conclusion to an essay now, or you don't quite understand how you should be citing sources. Or maybe you just want to know how readers will react to your blog before you post it.

Where can you turn to for help? The writing center! Chances are your school has one, perhaps in the English Department, in an academic skills center, in the library, or online. And if your school does not have a writing center, worry not: you can find help at other online writing centers. In this chapter, you'll learn about the kind of help you can get at a writing center, how to prepare for a tutoring session—and how you can become a writing tutor yourself.

What Writing Centers Offer

All writers need good readers, and the writing center is a place where you can find good readers, generally graduate or undergraduate students who have been trained to respond to student writing. While you may go to the writing center for help on a particular piece of writing, you will usually find that the advice you receive is helpful for almost any kind of writing. In other words, writing centers are places where you can talk with someone else about your writing, and where you can try out ideas with a tutor without worrying about a grade. Keep in mind, though, that tutors will not edit your draft or predict what grade you'll get; they will, however, ask you questions, engage you in discussion about what your goals are, and work to help you meet those goals.

All writers from all disciplines across campus can benefit from feedback: undergraduates in their first year, honors students working on senior theses, graduate students working on dissertations, faculty working on academic articles. Some writers set up regular weekly appointments; others drop by the writing center now and then. Check the website of your campus writing center to determine what options exist for making appointments. You don't even need to have a specific question in mind when you visit the writing center; it often just helps to have another reader look at your work, someone with some distance from your project.

Visiting the writing center can be useful at any stage of the writing process. If you have an assignment and you're having a little trouble getting started, you can brainstorm ideas with a tutor. Or maybe you've written a draft of your essay, but you know the introduction needs work. Perhaps you're struggling to understand a particular grammatical concept or need help with MLA documentation style. Maybe you don't actually have an assignment due, but you're looking for help to strengthen your writing in general. Most writing centers do not require that their clients have specific assignments and will be happy to have you meet with a tutor. In short, writing centers are places where you can go to improve as a writer, not just to ace an important assignment.

Do remember when you visit the writing center, however, that you are the author. Be open to the guidance and advice that your tutor offers, but you should never relinquish control of your draft. You will be the one to implement any changes that you and your tutor discuss.

Remember as well that writing center tutors are not teachers. If you have questions about the specifics of an assignment, or about a grade, you should speak with your instructor. One of the great things about going to the writing center, in fact, is that when you are working with a tutor, you do not have to be concerned about a grade.

Preparing for a Tutoring Session

Before your first visit, check your writing center's website or call to find out its hours, location, and policies. For example, do you need to make an appointment, or is it a walk-in center? How long does a session last? Can you sign up for more than one session with the same tutor if you have a large writing project or want to work over time on improving your writing skills?

Think about what you need to take with you. If you're looking for help with a specific assignment, gather the assignment and any written notes or drafting you've already done. Give some thought to what you most want to work on and prioritize: remember that you have a limited amount of time and that you might not get to everything. It can be helpful to write down questions you have or points you want to cover and to take these notes with you to your tutoring session. If you're looking for help on an assigned piece of writing, be sure to bring the assignment—and if your assignment requires that you respond to something that you've read, bring that, too. If you are looking for help on a particular aspect of your writing, bring some samples of your previous work. Being prepared and having all of your materials will ensure that you have a satisfying, productive conference with your tutor.

Making the Most of a Tutoring Session

Arrive prepared and on time. It's important to be on time so that you can take full advantage of the allotted session.

Tell the tutor what you want to accomplish, and share any concerns. Don't be afraid to share your questions, ideas, and goals.

Set the agenda. If your tutor suggests that you focus on a different aspect of the assignment than you want, ask why. You may want to focus on your organization while the tutor thinks that you should first have a clearer, stronger thesis statement. The tutor may have a good reason for making such a suggestion, so listen and be open to suggestions—but also let him or her know what your concerns are and that you want to spend time on them. The session should be a collaboration between the two of you.

Take notes during the session. Write down changes you want to make to your text. If you do any revising or editing during the session, be sure to write it down then and there. If you see that you need to reorganize your draft, make specific notes about the reorganization—what goes where, what to add or delete, and so on. Tutoring is usually a combination of talking and writing, so it's important to take notes during or immediately after your session. Sometimes the tutor may also take notes and share them with you at the end of the session.

Write down your plan of action. Do not leave your tutoring session without writing down a plan for what you'll do afterward. This plan will be your guide when you next sit down to work on your assignment.

Schedule your next appointment. If you'd like another session, schedule it before you leave the writing center: you're more likely to get your preferred time if you sign up early. The next session can act as a soft deadline for you to work on the issues you and your tutor discussed during the first appointment. At the second session, you can focus on additional writing challenges, get feedback on different aspects of your work, and discuss future writing assignments.

What If English Is Not Your Primary Language?

Writing centers can be especially helpful if English is not your primary language. Perhaps your first language is American Sign Language, or your family communicates primarily in Spanish, or you speak three languages. Or maybe you're an international student studying at an American school, and you don't have previous experience with the kind of explicit argumentation required in U.S. academic contexts. Whatever your situation, you may find it helpful to work with a tutor at the writing center. When you consult with a tutor for the first time, take a moment to talk with him or her about any writing issues that are especially important to you.

Because most tutors are native speakers, they typically recognize when writing is correct or incorrect, idiomatic or nonidiomatic. But this knowledge is often intuitive, and they may not be able to explain just why something is right or wrong. You may need to be patient when a tutor says, "I'm sorry, but I can't explain it. This is just how we say it in English."

Tutors are generally trained not to correct or edit students' writing, but they can help you identify, understand, and correct COMMON ERRORS. They can also teach you about other resources, both print and online, that you can turn to for help. In other words, a good tutor can help you become a proficient editor of your own writing.

Some students find it especially helpful to meet regularly with the same tutor. If your writing center offers this option, you may want to take advantage of the opportunity to work with a tutor who will be familiar with you and the writing issues most important to you.

Visiting an Online Writing Center

At many schools, writing centers have both a physical site and an online site, whereas some schools have only an online site. If your school has an online writing center (often known as an OWL, for online writing lab), it likely conducts virtual tutoring sessions in one of two ways: synchronous or asynchronous.

Like face-to-face sessions, synchronous tutoring sessions are conducted in real time, with tutor and client working together online, usually in a chat program. Synchronous tutorials generally require that you make an appointment and send in a draft sometime before your appointment. Asynchronous online tutoring does not take place in real time, so the tutor and client are not necessarily online at the same time. Usually, the writer sends a series of questions to the tutor along with the draft. The tutor then responds to those questions and may, in return, send the writer questions to think about.

Just as face-to-face writing centers differ from school to school, so do online writing centers. You'll need to check the policies at your school's writing center before signing up for online tutoring.

What if your school does not have either a face-to-face or online writing center? You can still get help from school and commercial sites whose online writing centers offer writing help to the general public. Check out the following links to online writing centers:

Purdue University's OWL: owl.english.purdue.edu

Colorado State's Writing Studio: writing.colostate.edu

The International Writing Center Association also keeps a list of online and face-to-face writing centers at writingcenters.org/links/writing-centers -online.

And most writing centers have resources on their websites to help writers through the writing process—writing thesis statements, writing introductions and conclusions, using various styles of documentation, writing persuasive essays, understanding writing conventions in a variety of disciplines, and so on. Again, check out your writing center's website to see what online resources it offers, and broaden your search to OWLs at other schools too.

What about Becoming a Writing Tutor?

Do you enjoy talking with others about their writing? Do you like working with your peers to help develop their writing and ideas? Do you find that your writing improves when you see how others write and when you provide them with feedback? If you answered yes to any of these questions, you may want to consider becoming a writing tutor.

The first step to becoming a writing tutor is to contact your school's writing center to find out how tutors are selected. Most writing centers require that potential tutors go through an interview process and some kind of training.

Some writing centers, especially those staffed primarily by undergraduates, require that students take a tutor-training course or a one-time orientation or seminar. In such a course, you may be introduced to theories about how people learn to write, how writing centers work, and how writing tutors approach their jobs. You will probably learn a great deal about practical ways to conduct tutoring sessions—nuts-and-bolts advice about how to begin, how to ask questions, what not to do, and so on.

Becoming a writing tutor may help you gain valuable experience working in an educational setting, provide an opportunity to meet new students from diverse backgrounds, and add an impressive accomplishment to your résumé. Best of all, working as a writing tutor nearly guarantees an improvement in your own writing and editing skills—and most tutors say that they really value the collaborative community that writing centers foster.

PART III

Genres of Writing

WHEN YOU WERE A KID, did you have certain kinds of clothes you liked to wear? Six-year-old Lila describes her wardrobe this way: "I have school clothes—they're okay, I guess. And I have dress-up clothes, like for when I go to the *Nutcracker* or a birthday party. But my favorites are my make-believe clothes: Snow White, Alice in Wonderland, and Princess Anna from *Frozen*. She's my favorite!" What Lila displays here is a fairly sophisticated sense of *genres*, ways that we categorize things. You see genres everywhere—in literature (think poetry, fiction, drama), in movies (Westerns, film noir, documentaries), and in music (rap, country, classical). And when we talk about writing, we often talk in terms of genres too: narratives, lab reports, project proposals, movie reviews, argument essays, and so on. Like all genres, those associated with writing are flexible: they expand and change over time as writers find new ways to communicate and express themselves.

In the ancient world, for example, personal communication involved carving symbols into clay tablets or, a bit later, having a scribe record your message on papyrus. For communicating with speed, couriers memorized letters and raced to deliver them orally. Once paper was available and letters were less costly and easier to produce, they evolved into multiple subgenres: the business letter, the personal letter, the condolence letter, the thank you letter, and so on. Today, letters have further evolved into electronic forms—emails, *Facebook* messages, texts. It's hard to predict how these genres of communication will evolve in the future, but when they do, we know they will stretch to accommodate new modes and new media, as genres always do. In short, genres reflect current expectations while also shaping—and sometimes even changing—them.

Instructors will often ask you to use particular genres, most likely including the ones taught in this book: arguments, narratives, analyses, reports, reviews, and proposals. You may need to write a rhetorical analysis of a speech, for instance, or to analyze the causes of the financial crisis in 2008. In either case, knowing the characteristic features of an analysis will be helpful. And you may want or need to combine genres—to introduce an analysis with a short narrative or to conclude it with a proposal of some kind.

Of course, you may not always be assigned to write in a particular genre. Your instructor may give you a topic to write about in whatever way you choose. In this case, you'll need to think carefully about what genre will be most appropriate for addressing that topic—and Chapter 10 will help you choose a genre when the choice is yours.

The chapters that follow introduce most of the genres you'll be assigned to do in college. Each chapter explains the genre's characteristic features; discusses how, when, where, and why you might use the genre most appropriately; provides a roadmap to the process of writing in that genre; and includes several example essays. We hope that you'll use these chapters to explore these common academic genres—and to adapt them as need be to your own purposes and goals.

Communication throughout the ages, from clay tablets to couriers delivering messages to tweets and texts.

TEN

Choosing Genres

COMICS HAVE MANGA, superheroes, and fantasy. Music has hip-hop, country, and folk. Video games? Think shooters, simulation, or role-playing. How about restaurants? Try Italian, Vietnamese, Tex-Mex, vegan, or southern soul food. Or movies: sci-fi, thrillers, drama, anime. These are all genres, and they are one important way we structure our world.

Genres are categorizations, ways of classifying things. The genres this book is concerned with are kinds of writing, but you'll find genres everywhere you look.

In fact, rhetorician and researcher Carolyn Miller has been tracking the use of the word *genre* and has found it everywhere, including on many of the sites you visit every day. *Netflix* lists 19 genres, from action/adventure to sports and thrillers—and many subgenres within each of these. The video game review site *GameSpot* sorts games into 62 genres, and the *iTunes* store lists 346 kinds of music and close to 70 categories of podcasts as this book goes to press. You can even see new genres developing on *YouTube*, including microgenres like "cute babies" or "cats being mean." Indeed, there is now such a proliferation of genres that they've become the subject of parody, with comedians mixing musical genres to make new ones, like honky tonk and techno to make "honky techno" or folk and dubstep to make "folk step." To get a sense of the result, just take a look at the cartoon on the next page.

In this cartoon, Roz Chast comes up with her own new movie genres:
sci-fi/Western, musical/self-help, sports/horror, and documentary/romance.

What You Need to Know about Genres of Writing

Genres are kinds of writing that you can use to accomplish a certain goal and reach a particular audience. As such, they have well-established features that help guide you in your writing. However, they're not fill-in-the-blank templates; you can adapt them to address your own rhetorical situations.

Genres have features that can guide you as a writer and a reader. Argument essays, for instance, take a position supported by reasons and evidence, consider a range of perspectives, and so on. These features help guide you as an author in what you write—and they also set up expectations for you as a reader, affecting the way you interpret what you read. If something's called a report, for instance, you likely assume that it presents information—that it's in some way factual.

This book covers those genres that are most often assigned in school—
ARGUMENTS, **ANALYSES**, **REPORTS**, **NARRATIVES**, **REVIEWS**, **PROPOSALS**, and
ANNOTATED BIBLIOGRAPHIES —and some subgenres: **VISUAL ANALYSES**,
PROFILES, **LITERACY NARRATIVES**, **LITERATURE REVIEWS**, and **PROJECT
PROPOSALS**. These are kinds of writing that have evolved over the years
as a useful means of creating and sharing knowledge. As you advance in a
major, you will become familiar with the most important genres and subgenres in that field. Especially when you are new to a genre, its features can
serve as a kind of blueprint, helping you know how to approach an assignment. Knowing these features helps you organize a text and guides your
choices in terms of content.

Genres are flexible. Keep in mind that genres can be both enabling and con-
straining. Sometimes you'll have reason to adapt genre features to suit your
own goals. One student who was writing an analysis of a sonnet, for example, wanted to bend the analysis genre just a little to include a sonnet of his
own. He checked with his teacher, got approval, and it worked. You probably
wouldn't want to stretch a lab report in this way, however. Lab reports follow a fairly set template, covering purpose, methods, results, summary, and
conclusions to carry out the goals of the scientific fields that use them; they
would not be appropriate (or effective) in a creative writing class.

See how Dana Canedy's narra-tive about a conversation with her son makes an argument on p. 884.

You may also have occasion to combine genres—to tell a story in the
course of arguing a position or to conclude a report with a proposal of some
kind. If ever you decide to adapt or combine genres, think hard about your
rhetorical situation: what genres will help you achieve your purpose? reach
the audience you're addressing? work best in the medium you're using?

Genres evolve. While it is relatively easy to identify some characteristic
genre features, such features are not universal rules. Genres are flexible,
and they evolve across time and in response to shifting cultural contexts.
Letters, for example, followed certain conventions in medieval Europe (they
were handwritten, of course, and they were highly formal); by the twentieth
century, letters had developed dozens of subgenres (thank-you notes, letters
to the editor, application letters). Then, in the 1990s, letters began to morph
into email, adapting in new ways to online situations. Today, text messages
and *Facebook* posts both may be seen as offshoots of the letter genre.

Or think of *Facebook* itself. In the early twentieth century, partygoers
entertained themselves by drawing caricatures of each other and compiling
them in collections they called "face books." Later, some colleges and board-

ing schools extended this practice by creating more formal face books, directories containing the name and photo of every student in a class. And then, in 2004, *Facebook* entered the world of social media.

And as with all genres and subgenres, letters, email, text messages, and *Facebook* pages have developed their own conventions and features, ones that guide you as a writer and a reader.

REFLECT. Think about a favorite song, movie, or game, and then decide what genre it is. How do you know? List the features that help you identify it as belonging to a particular genre. What do you know about that genre? Name a few other examples of that genre, and then think about what features they have in common.

Deciding Which Genres to Use

Sometimes you'll be assigned to write in a particular genre. If that's the case, think about what you know about the genre, about what it expects of you as a writer, and turn to the appropriate chapter in this book for guidance. But other times your assignments won't make the genre perfectly clear. The following advice can help determine which genre(s) to use when the choice is yours. In all cases, remember to consider your **PURPOSE** for writing and the **AUDIENCE** you want to reach in deciding which genres would be most appropriate.

Look for clues in the assignment. Even without a clearly assigned genre, your assignment should be your starting point. Are there any keywords that suggest one? *Discuss*, for example, could indicate a **REPORT** or an **ANALYSIS**. And you might also need to consider how such a keyword is used in the discipline the assignment comes from—*analyze* in a philosophy assignment doesn't likely mean the same thing as in a literature assignment. In either case, you should ask your instructor for clarification.

Consider this assignment from an introductory communications course: "Look carefully at letters to the editor in one newspaper over a period of two weeks, and write an essay describing what you find. Who are the letter writers? What issues are they writing about? How many different perspectives are represented?" Though this assignment doesn't name a genre, it seems to be asking students for a report: to research a topic and then report on what they find.

But what if this were the assignment: "Look carefully at letters to the editor in one newspaper over a period of two weeks, and write an essay describing what you find. Who are the letter writers? What issues are they writing about? How many different perspectives are represented? What rhetorical strategies do the writers use to get their points across? Draw some conclusions based on what you find." This assignment also asks students to research a topic and report on what they find. But in asking them to draw some conclusions based on their findings, it is also prompting them to do some analysis. As you look at your own assignments, look for words or other clues that will help you identify which genres are expected.

If an assignment doesn't give any clues, here are some questions to ask in thinking about which genre may be most appropriate:

- *What discipline is the assignment for?* Say you're assigned to write about obesity and public health. If you're writing for a political science course, you might write an essay **ARGUING** that high-calorie sodas should not be sold in public schools. If, on the other hand, you're writing for a biology class, you might **REPORT** on experiments done on eating behaviors and metabolic rates.

- *What is the topic?* Does it call for a specific genre? If you are asked, for example, to write about the campaign speeches of two presidential candidates, that topic suggests that you're being asked to **ANALYZE** the speeches (and probably **COMPARE** them). On the other hand, if you're writing about an experiment you conducted, you're probably writing a **REPORT** and should follow the conventions of that genre.

- *What is your purpose in writing?* If you want to convince your readers that they should "buy local," for example, your purpose will likely call for an **ARGUMENT**. If, however, you want to explain what buying local means, your purpose will call for a **REPORT**.

- *Who is the audience?* What interests and expectations might they have? Say you're assigned to write about the collective-bargaining rights of unions for a first-year seminar. There your audience would include other first-year students, and you might choose to write a **NARRATIVE** about the father of a friend who lost his job as a high school teacher. Imagine, however, writing on the same topic for a public policy course; there you would be more likely to write an essay **ANALYZING** the costs and benefits of unionized workers in the public sector.

- *What medium will you use?* Are there certain genres that work well— or not—in that medium? If you are assigned to give an oral presentation, for example, you might consider writing a **NARRATIVE** because listeners can remember stories better than they are able to recall other genres. Even if you decide to write an analysis or a report, you might want to include some narrative.

If the assignment is wide open, draw on what you know about genres. Sometimes you may receive an assignment so broad that not only the genre but even the topic and purpose are left up to you. Consider, for example, a prompt one of the authors of this book encountered in college: in an exam for a drama class, the professor came into the room, wrote "Tragedy!" on the blackboard, and said, "You have an hour and a half to respond." We hope you don't run into such a completely open-ended assignment, especially in a timed exam. But if you do, your knowledge of genre can help out. If this assignment came in a Shakespeare course, for example, you might **ARGUE** that *Hamlet* is Shakespeare's most powerful tragedy. Or you could perhaps **ANALYZE** the role of gender in one of his tragedies.

Luckily, such wide-open assignments are fairly rare. It's more likely that you will encounter an assignment like this one: "Choose a topic related to our course theme and carry out sufficient research on that topic to write an essay of eight to ten pages. Refer to at least six sources and follow MLA citation style." In this instance, you know that the assignment calls for some kind of research-based writing and that you need a topic and thesis that can be dealt with in the length specified. You could write an **ARGUMENT**, taking a position and supporting it with the research you have done. Or you could write a **REPORT** that presents findings from your research. At this point, you would be wise to see your instructor to discuss your choices. Once you have decided on a genre, turn to the appropriate chapter in this book (Chapters 11–16) to guide your research and writing.

When an assignment is wide open, try using what you know about genres as a way to explore your topic:

- What are some of the **POSITIONS** on your topic? What's been said or might be said? What controversies or disagreements exist? What's your own perspective?

- What stories— **NARRATIVES** —could you tell about it?

- How might you **ANALYZE** your topic? What are its parts? What caused it—or what effects might it have? Does it follow a certain process?

- What information might be important or interesting to **REPORT** on?
- How can your topic be evaluated, or **REVIEWED**?
- What problems does your topic present for which you can **PROPOSE** a solution?

REFLECT. Look at three writing assignments you have been given for any of your classes. Did the assignments specify a genre? If so, what was it? If not, what genres would you say you were being asked to use—and how can you tell?

ELEVEN

"This Is Where I Stand"

Arguing a Position

O WHAT'S YOUR POSITION ON THAT?" This familiar phrase pops up almost everywhere, from talk radio to blogs, from political press conferences to classroom seminars. In fact, much of the work you do as an author responds, in some way, to this question.

After all, taking a position is something you do many times daily: you visit your advisor's office to explain in person your reasons for dropping a course; you text a friend listing all the reasons she should see a certain film with you; in an economics class discussion, you offer your own position on consumer spending patterns in response to someone else's; you survey research on fracking and then write a letter to the editor of your local newspaper advocating (or protesting) a ban on fracking. In all these cases, you're doing what philosopher Kenneth Burke calls "putting in your oar," taking and supporting positions of your own in conversation with others around you.

Look around, and you'll see other positions being articulated all over the place. Here's one we saw recently on a T-shirt:

Work to eat.

Eat to live.

Live to bike.

Bike to work.

The central argument here is clear: bike to work. One of the reasons it's so effective is the clever way that the last sentence isn't quite parallel to the others. (In the first three, *to* can be replaced by *in order to*; in the last case, it can't.) Another reason it works well is the form of the argument, which is a series of short commands, each beginning with the same word that the previous sentence ends with.

This chapter offers guidelines for writing an academic essay that takes a position. While taking a position in an academic context often differs in crucial ways from doing so in other contexts, many of the principles discussed will serve you well when stating a position generally.

✍ *REFLECT. Stop for a moment and jot down every time you remember having to take a position on something—anything at all—in the last few days. The list will surely soon grow long if you're like most of us. Then take an informal survey, noting and writing down every time in one day someone around you takes a position. This informal research should convince you that the rhetorical genre of taking a position is central to many of your daily activities.*

Across Academic Disciplines

Position papers are written in many fields, and a number of disciplines offer specific guidelines for composing them. In *philosophy*, a position paper is a brief persuasive essay designed to express a precise opinion about some issue or some philosopher's viewpoint. In *computer science*, a position paper considers a number of perspectives on an issue before finally offering the writer's own position. In *political science*, a position paper often critiques a major argument or text, first summarizing and analyzing its main points and then interpreting them in the context of other texts. Many college courses ask students to take a position in response to a course reading, specifying that they state their position clearly, support it with evidence and logical reasons, and cite all sources consulted. So one challenge you'll face when you're asked to write a position paper in various disciplines will be to determine exactly what is expected of you.

Across Media

Different media present different resources and challenges when it comes to presenting your position. Setting up a *website* that encourages people to take action to end animal abuse gives you the ability to link to additional information, whereas writing a traditional *essay* advocating that position for a print magazine requires that you provide all the relevant evidence and reasons on the page. It is very easy to incorporate color images or video clips in the webpage, but the magazine's budget may not allow for color at all. If you make the same argument against animal abuse in an *oral presentation*, you'll mostly be talking, though you may use *PowerPoint* slides to help your listeners follow the structure of your comments, to remind them of your main points, and to show graphs or photos that will appeal to their

**THINK
BEYOND
WORDS**

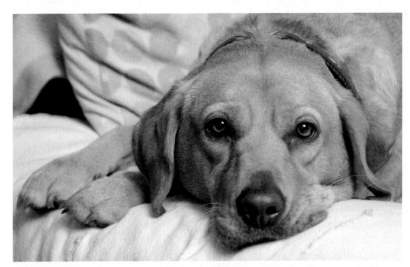

TAKE A LOOK at the website of Mutt Love Rescue, a dog adoption organization in Washington, DC, where you can see photos of available dogs, find out about fostering a dog, and more. Click on "Saving a Life" to see their appeal for donations, along with photos of some of the "lucky pups." How compelling do you find the organization's argument? How does the use of words and images contribute to its appeal—is one more important? How would you revise this site to make it more effective—add video? audio? statistics? testimonials? more written information (or less)? Go to everyonesanauthor.tumblr.com to access the site.

sense of reason or their emotions. Finally, if your marketing class is designing a fundraising *TV commercial* for a nonprofit organization that works to stop animal abuse, you'll likely be able to use images and even music to drive home your point, but you might have only thirty seconds to get the message across.

Remember that persuasion is always about connecting with an audience, meeting them where they are, and helping them see why your position is one they should take seriously or even adopt. To achieve that goal, you have to convey your position in a medium your audience will be receptive to—and can access. Different media serve different purposes, and you will want to consider your own goals as well as your audience's expectations.

Across Cultures and Communities

Taking a position in cultures or communities other than your own poses special challenges. Advertising—a clear case of taking a position—is full of humorous tales of cross-cultural failure. When Pepsi first sought to break into the Chinese market, for example, its slogan, "Pepsi Brings You Back to Life," got mangled in translation, coming out as "Pepsi Brings Your Ancestors Back from the Grave."

Far more problematic than questions of translation are questions of STANCE. When taking a position in American academic contexts, you're almost always expected to state your position explicitly while showing your awareness of other possible positions. In contrast, in some cultures and communities, you would generally avoid stating your opinion directly; rather, you would hint at it. In yet others, you would be expected to state your mind forthrightly, paying little attention to what others think about the issue or to how your words might make them feel.

Equally important, how people are expected to frame positions they take varies within a community, depending on their place in the social hierarchy as supervisor or employee, teacher or student, ruler or governed. To complicate matters, the expectations with respect to outsiders are almost always different from those for the locals. Most people might be quick to criticize their own government among friends, but they don't necessarily grant outsiders the same privilege. A word to the wise: humility is in order, especially when taking a position in communities or cultures of which you're not a member. Don't assume that what works at home will work elsewhere. A safe first step is to listen and observe carefully when in a new context, paying special attention to how people communicate any positions they are taking.

Across Genres

See how Whole Foods states its position on union organizing in its annual report. Go to everyonesanauthor.tumblr.com and scroll to p. 14 of the report.

Arguing a position, as we've pointed out, is something that we do, in small ways or large, almost every day—and even across a range of genres. You might, for instance, write a letter to the editor of your local newspaper lamenting the closure of the local library—and setting forth your **POSITION** that it must be kept open at all costs. Similarly, a company's annual **REPORT** would likely set out its position on how collective bargaining with suppliers will improve the company's bottom line. After taking in a highly anticipated film, you might tweet a 140-character **REVIEW**, arguing that it wasn't as good as you'd expected. In each case, the text states a position.

REFLECT. Look to see where and how positions are expressed around you, considering posters, editorials, songs, Facebook postings, blog entries, and so on. Then choose one that most interests you—or that most irritates you—and spend some time thinking about how it presents its position. How does it appeal to you—or why does it fail to appeal? What kinds of words, images, or sounds does it offer as support for its position? If you were going to revise it for a different audience, what would you do? If you were going to create it in another medium, how would it be different?

CHARACTERISTIC FEATURES

Given the many different forms of writing that take a position, no one-size-fits-all approach to composing them is possible. We can, however, identify the following characteristic features common to writing where the author is arguing a position:

- An explicit position
- A response to what others have said or done
- Appropriate background information
- A clear indication of why the topic matters
- Good reasons and evidence

- Attention to more than one point of view
- An authoritative tone
- An appeal to readers' values

An Explicit Position

Stating a position explicitly is easier said than done, since the complexity of most important issues can make it hard to articulate a position in a crystal-clear way. But it's very important to do so insofar as possible; nothing will lose an audience faster than hemming and hawing or drowning your position in a sea of qualifications. At the same time, in most academic contexts (as well as many others), a position stated baldly with no qualifications or nuances may alienate many readers.

In a syndicated column from 2009, just as the severity of the financial downturn was finally sinking in, *New York Times* columnist Thomas Friedman, writing for an American audience, explained:

> Let's today step out of the normal boundaries of analysis of our economic crisis and ask a radical question: What if the crisis of 2008 represents something much more fundamental than a deep recession? What if it's telling us that the whole growth model we created over the last 50 years is simply unsustainable economically and ecologically and that 2008 was when we hit the wall—when Mother Nature and the market both said: "No more."
>
> We have created a system for growth that depended on our building more and more stores to sell more and more stuff made in more and more factories in China, powered by more and more coal that would cause more and more climate change but earn China more and more dollars to buy more and more U.S. T-bills so Americans would have more and more money to build more and more stores and sell more and more stuff that would employ more and more Chinese. . . .
>
> We can't do this anymore.
>
> —THOMAS FRIEDMAN, "The Inflection Is Near?"

Friedman's position is clear and explicit: Americans' assumptions about their country's economic relationship with China and the behavior growing out of these assumptions must change. Although such a strong position may alienate some readers, all readers have a clear understanding of where Friedman stands.

There are times, however, when you will want to **QUALIFY** your position by using words like *many, some,* or *maybe*—or writing *could* rather than *will*. Not every position you take can be stated with absolute certainty, and a qualified claim is generally easier to support than an unqualified one. When LeBron James decided to return to the Cleveland Cavaliers, many predicted that his return would boost Cleveland's economy. See how one writer for *Time.com* was careful to qualify that position:

> The greatest player on the planet could be an economic catalyst for the Rust Belt city. More fans will flock to Quicken Loans Arena to see James play, more staff will be needed at the arena to handle those larger crowds, more money will be spent during games at local bars and restaurants, and all of that will get pumped back into the region. The result, says LeRoy Brooks, a professor of finance at the Boler School of Business at John Carroll University in suburban Cleveland, could be nearly $500 million added to the local economy. Call it the LeBron Effect.
>
> —SEAN GREGORY, "Economist: LeBron James Worth Almost $500 Million to Cleveland"

Gregory's position is clear—LeBron James' return to the Cleveland Cavaliers will have a major effect on the Cleveland economy—but he is careful to qualify his claim so as not to overstate it. Notice when he uses *will* and when he uses *could*: saying that the difference for Cleveland's economy "could be nearly $500 million" suggests that he cannot provide a definitive dollar amount but can only point to research that offers a reasonable estimate.

Keep in mind that while it may be useful, even necessary, to qualify a statement, you should be careful not to overdo it. You don't want to sound unsure of your position.

A Response to What Others Have Said or Done

Crucially, position papers respond to other positions. That is, they are motivated by something that has been said or done by others—and are part of an ongoing conversation. In the example above, Thomas Friedman explicitly questions a popular position—namely that despite the current economic downturn, Americans and people around the world will eventually be able to continue the patterns of consumption they have created over the past few decades. His response is a rejection of this position, signaled with his emphatic "we can't do this anymore."

In some cases, the position the author is responding to becomes part of the argument. The all-star "Yes, We Can" video that was widely viewed on *YouTube* during the 2008 election uses this strategy. Based on a speech by then-candidate Barack Obama, the video acknowledges the "chorus of cynics" but turns this acknowledgment into part of the argument itself, as you can see in the italicized lines below:

It was a creed written into the founding documents that declared the destiny of a nation. Yes, we can.

It was whispered by slaves and abolitionists as they blazed a trail toward freedom. Yes, we can.

It was sung by immigrants as they struck out from distant shores and pioneers who pushed westward against an unforgiving wilderness. Yes, we can.

It was the call of workers who organized; women who reached for the ballots; a President who chose the moon as our new frontier; and a King who took us to the mountaintop and pointed the way to the Promised Land.

Yes, we can to justice and equality. Yes, we can to opportunity and prosperity. Yes, we can heal this nation. Yes, we can repair this world. Yes, we can.

We know the battle ahead will be long, but always remember that no matter what obstacles stand in our way, nothing can stand in the way of the power of millions of voices calling for change.

We have been told we cannot do this by a chorus of cynics. They will only grow louder and more dissonant.

We've been asked to pause for a reality check. We've been warned against offering the people of this nation false hope.

But in the unlikely story that is America, there has never been anything false about hope.

Now the hopes of the little girl who goes to a crumbling school in Dillon are the same as the dreams of the boy who learns on the streets of LA.

We will remember that there is something happening in America; that we are not as divided as our politics suggests; that we are one people, we are one nation, and together, we will begin the next great chapter in the American story with three words that will ring from coast to coast, from sea to shining sea: Yes, we can.

—BARACK OBAMA, "Yes, We Can"

In fact, the position being taken here extended far beyond what Obama himself said. The video's argument was an explicit response to those who claimed "no, we can't" achieve "justice and equality," "heal this nation," and so on. However, another argument it was making was that U.S. voters could and would elect an African American as their president for the first time, a position that is implicit rather than explicit.

Later in this chapter, you will meet Katherine Spriggs, who staked out a position on "buying local" in an essay written for one of her college courses. In this brief excerpt from her essay, she responds directly to those who say buying local will have negative environmental effects:

> It has also been argued that buying locally will be detrimental to the environment because small farms are not as efficient in their use of resources as large farms. This is a common misconception and actually depends on how economists measure efficiency. Small farms are less efficient than large farms in the total output of one crop per acre, but they are more efficient in total output of all crops per acre (McCauley).
>
> —KATHERINE SPRIGGS, "On Buying Local"

In a short space, Spriggs identifies an argument that others have made about the position she is taking and then responds to it explicitly. In academic position papers, authors are expected to acknowledge and address other positions directly in this way. That is often not the case when you take a position in other contexts and in some cultures. In online writing, for instance, it's not unusual for authors to simply provide a brief mention with a link to refer readers to another position within an ongoing conversation.

REFLECT. *Think about your writing as part of a larger, ongoing conversation. Examine something that you have recently written—an email, a blog post, an essay for a class—that expresses a position about an issue that matters to you. Check to see whether it makes clear your motivation for writing and the position(s) to which you were responding. If these aren't clear, try revising your text to make them more explicit.*

WATCH THE VIDEO of "Yes, We Can." Consider how the medium—video, with the addition of music, voice-overs, written words (like "hope" and "yes, we can"), and images of singers and of Obama delivering the speech—contributes to the power of the argument. Go to the link at everyonesanauthor.tumblr.com *to access the full video.*

Appropriate Background Information

The amount of background information needed—historical background, definitions, contextual information—will vary widely depending on the scope of your topic, your audience, and your medium. If you are preparing a position paper on the effects of global warming for an environmental group, any background information provided will represent extensive, often detailed, and sometimes highly technical knowledge. If, on the other hand, you are preparing a poster to display on campus that summarizes your position on an increase in tuition, you can probably assume your audience will need little background information—for which you will have only limited space anyway.

The "Yes, We Can" video, as an advertisement in a political campaign, provided no background information other than what was contained in segments of the Obama speech on which it is based. Rather, it assumed that viewers would know a great deal about the context of the election and Obama's candidacy. In online writing, links can often do much of the work of filling readers in on background information; they are especially convenient because readers have the option of clicking on them or not, depending on how much information they need or want.

In academic contexts, writers are generally expected to provide a great deal of background information to firmly ground their discussion of a topic. When the president of Rensselaer Polytechnic Institute, Shirley Ann Jackson, spoke at a 2011 symposium celebrating women in science and engineering, she argued that while the number of women graduating with degrees in STEM fields has increased, major obstacles still stand in the way of women academics in the sciences at research universities. To make this argument, she first provided background information about the number of women PhDs leaving the research science track:

> Writing for the *New York Times*, Steven Greenhouse noted that, based on a University of California, Berkeley, study, "Keeping Women in the Science Pipeline," women are far more likely than men to "'leak' out of the research science pipeline before obtaining tenure at a college or university." After receiving a PhD, married women with young children are 35 percent less likely to enter a tenure-track position in science than are married men with young children and PhDs in science. According to the report from the University of California, "women who had children after becoming postdoctoral scholars were twice as likely as their male counterparts to shift their career goals away from being professors with a research emphasis—a 41 percent shift for women versus 20 percent for men." And a 2005 report from Virginia Tech found a disproportionate share of women made up "voluntary departures" from the faculty. Although women represented one-fifth of the faculty, they accounted for two-fifths of departures.
>
> At every step along the way—from entering college as a science or engineering major to graduating with a technical degree, from entering graduate school to exiting successfully, to getting a postdoc, to succeeding as faculty, to attaining tenure—we need to provide women with bridges to the next level. As is clear from the studies I mentioned, the unequal burden of family life turns the gaps in the road into chasms. Help with childcare, which has been provided at MIT, and the establishment of parental childbirth leave, which has been provided at Rensselaer, can help. But there is more to be done.
>
> —SHIRLEY ANN JACKSON, "Leaders in Science
> and Engineering: The Women of MIT"

Many women are earning degrees in STEM fields, and universities need to do more to help young women scientists balance the demands of family life and scientific research.

Hearing about specific research studies helps Jackson's audience see that a disproportionately high number of women scientists are "shift[ing] their career goals away from being professors with a research emphasis"—and supports her argument that universities must do more to ease the "unequal burden of family life" that young women scientists bear.

Background information is not always statistical and impersonal, even in academic contexts. In an essay written for *Academe,* a publication of the American Association of University Professors, Randall Hicks, a professor of chemistry at Wheaton College, argues that it is harder for working-class students to become professors than it is for children of college-educated parents. The background information he provides is startlingly personal:

> "I'll break his goddamned hands," my father said. I wonder if he remembers saying it. Nearly twenty-five years later, his words still linger in my mind. My father had spent the entire day in the auto body shop only to come home and head to the garage for more work on the side. I may have finished my homework, and, tired of roughhousing with my brother,

gone out to help him scrape the paint off his current project, some classic car that he was restoring. "It's okay for a hobby, but if somebody
tells me that he's thinking of doing it for a living, I'll break his goddamned
hands." Although we had no firm plans and little financial means to do
so, he was telling me that he expected me to get an education.

—RANDALL HICKS

Note how this story provides readers with important background information for Hicks's argument. Immediately, we learn relevant information
about him and the environment that shaped him. Thus, we understand part
of his passionate commitment to this topic: he learned, indirectly, from his
father to put a high value on education, since doing so in his father's view
would allow Hicks to get a job that would be better than something that is
just "okay for a hobby."

A Clear Indication of Why the Topic Matters

No matter the topic, one of an author's tasks is to demonstrate that the issue
is real and significant—and thus to motivate readers to read on or listeners
to keep listening. Rarely can you assume your audience sees why your argument matters.

As a student, you'll sometimes be assigned to write a position paper on
a particular topic; in those cases, you may have to find ways to make the topic interesting for you, as the writer, although you can assume the topic matters to the person who assigned it. On other occasions, you may take it upon
yourself to write about something you care deeply about, in which case you
will need to help your audience understand why they should care as well.

See how Mellody Hobson, president of an investment firm and a board
member of DreamWorks, Starbucks, and other prominent companies, begins her 2014 TED Talk with a personal story that is meant to illustrate why
Americans need to talk about race—and why that conversation matters:

So it's 2006. My friend Harold Ford calls me. He's running for U.S. Senate
in Tennessee, and he says, "Mellody, I desperately need some national
press. Do you have any ideas?" So I had an idea. I called a friend who was
in New York at one of the most successful media companies in the world,
and she said, "Why don't we host an editorial board lunch for Harold?
You come with him."

Harold and I arrive in New York. We are in our best suits. We look like shiny new pennies. And we get to the receptionist, and we say, "We're here for the lunch." She motions for us to follow her. We walk through a series of corridors, and all of a sudden we find ourselves in a stark room, at which point she looks at us and she says, "Where are your uniforms?"

Just as this happens, my friend rushes in. The blood drains from her face. There are literally no words, right? And I look at her, and I say, "Now, don't you think we need more than one black person in the U.S. Senate?"   —MELLODY HOBSON, "Color Blind or Color Brave?"

By sharing this story about how she and Ford were assumed to be kitchen staff on the basis of their race, Hobson establishes in a vivid and distressing way why her topic matters—and she uses the fact that this story makes people uncomfortable to show precisely why it is so important that we talk about race. She then goes on to cite statistics about how few people of color hold board seats in corporate America, driving home for her audience the need for this conversation in concrete terms. Like many writers of academic arguments, Hobson uses personal, statistical, and historical data to demonstrate why her argument matters.

Mellody Hobson calls on businesses "not to be color-blind but to be color-brave."

The creators of the "Yes, We Can" video certainly believed the election of 2008 mattered, as demonstrated in the values they appealed to and the range of people they included in the video. (If you watch carefully, you will see that one of the people participating was signing American Sign Language as she sang, explicit evidence that deaf people, too, are part of the "we" who can.) Similarly, Thomas Friedman certainly thinks America's response to the economic downturn that began in 2008 is important. When he writes that the 2008 crisis might be "something much more fundamental than a deep recession" and "the whole growth model . . . is simply unsustainable," his tone in these broad assertions conveys a sense of urgency. In all these cases, the writers share the conviction that what they're writing about matters not just to them but to us all, and they work hard to make that conviction evident.

REFLECT. *Examine something you've written that takes a strong position. Catalog the specific ways you make clear to your readers that the topic matters to you—and that it should matter to them.*

Good Reasons and Evidence

See how Barbara Ehrenreich went about getting firsthand information in order to write about low-wage workers in Florida, p. 917.

Positions are only as good as the reasons and evidence that support them, so part of every author's task in arguing a position is to provide the strongest possible reasons for the position, and evidence for those reasons. Evidence may take many forms, but among the most often used, especially in academic contexts, are facts; firsthand material gathered from observations, interviews, or surveys; data from experiments; historical data; examples; expert testimony (often in the form of what scholars have written); precedents; statistics; and personal experience.

In a 2006 essay from the *New York Times* op-ed page, Jennifer Delahunty, dean of admissions at Kenyon College, seeks to explain to her own daughter why she was rejected by one of the colleges she had applied to. Delahunty's explanation—the position her essay takes—is that the rejection was due at least in part to the fact that young women, even accomplished ones, face particular challenges in getting into prestigious colleges:

> She had not . . . been named a National Merit Finalist, dug a well for a village in Africa or climbed to the top of Mount Rainier. She is a smart,

well-meaning, hard-working teenage girl, but in this day and age of swollen applicant pools that are decidedly female, that wasn't enough. . . .

Had she been a male applicant, there would have been little, if any,
hesitation to admit. The reality is that because young men are rarer,
they're more valued applicants. Today, two-thirds of colleges and universities report that they get more female than male applicants, and more
than 56 percent of undergraduates nationwide are women.

—JENNIFER DELAHUNTY, "To All the Girls I've Rejected"

Delahunty offers two related reasons that her daughter had not been admitted. First, for all her daughter's accomplishments, they were not as impressive as those of other applicants. Here she provides specific evidence (her
daughter was not a National Merit finalist, nor had she "dug a well for a village in Africa or climbed to the top of Mount Rainier") that makes the reason
memorable and convincing.

The second reason focuses on the fact that male applicants in general
have a better chance than female applicants of getting into many schools.
This time her evidence is of a different sort; she uses statistics to show that
"young men are rarer" and "therefore more valued applicants." Note that
Delahunty expects readers to share her knowledge that something seen as
valuable takes on additional value when it is rare.

The scientific community typically takes the long view in terms of
gathering evidence in support of the positions it takes. Certainly that was
true in the case of smoking, when decades of research paved the way for a
statement on the relationship between smoking and cancer. The 1964 Surgeon General's report on the health consequences of smoking notes:

The U.S. Public Health Service first became officially engaged in an ap-
praisal of the available data on smoking and health in June, 1956, when,
under the instigation of the Surgeon General, a scientific Study Group on
the subject was established jointly by the National Cancer Institute, the
National Heart Institute, the American Cancer Society, and the American Heart Association. After appraising sixteen independent studies
carried on in five countries over a period of eighteen years, this group
concluded that there is a causal relationship between excessive smoking
of cigarettes and lung cancer.

—*Smoking and Health: Report of the Advisory Committee*
of the Surgeon General of the Public Health Service

In this case, the Surgeon General's study group analyzed evidence gathered over eighteen years from a range of research conducted by multiple scholars before reaching its conclusion.

Attention to More than One Point of View

Considering multiple, often opposing, points of view is a hallmark of any strong position paper, particularly in an academic context. By showing that you understand and have carefully evaluated other viewpoints, you show respect for the issue's complexity and for your audience, while also showing that you have done your homework on your topic.

In a journal article on human-caused climate change, Naomi Oreskes takes a position based on a careful analysis of 928 scientific articles published in well-known and respected journals. Some people, she says, "suggest that there might be substantive disagreement in the scientific community about the reality of anthropogenic climate change. This is not the case." Yet in spite of the very strong consensus on which Oreskes bases her claim, she still acknowledges other possible viewpoints:

> Admittedly, [some] authors evaluating impacts, developing methods, or studying paleoclimatic change might believe that current climate change is natural. . . . The scientific consensus might, of course, be wrong. If the history of science teaches anything, it is humility, and no one can be faulted for failing to act on what is not known.
>
> —NAOMI ORESKES, "Beyond the Ivory Tower:
> The Scientific Consensus on Climate Change"

Oreskes acknowledges that the consensus she found in the articles she examined might be challenged by other articles she did not consider and that any consensus, no matter how strong, might ultimately prove to be wrong. Thus does she remain respectful of those members of the scientific community who may hold other views.

Sometimes you'll want to both acknowledge and reply to other viewpoints, especially if you can answer any objections persuasively. Here is college admissions officer Jennifer Delahunty, noting—and ruling out—the possible criticism that college admissions officers do not give careful consideration to all applicants:

Rest assured that admissions officers are not cavalier in making their decisions. Last week, the 10 officers at my college sat around a table, 12 hours every day, deliberating the applications of hundreds of talented young men and women. While gulping down coffee and poring over statistics, we heard about a young woman from Kentucky we were not yet ready to admit outright. She was the leader/president/editor/captain/ lead actress in every activity in her school. She had taken six advanced placement courses and had been selected for a prestigious state leadership program. In her free time, this whirlwind of achievement had accumulated more than 300 hours of community service in four different organizations.

Few of us sitting around the table were as talented and as directed at age 17 as this young woman. Unfortunately, her test scores and grade point average placed her in the middle of our pool. We had to have a debate before we decided to swallow the middling scores and write "admit" next to her name.

—JENNIFER DELAHUNTY, "To All the Girls I've Rejected"

Delahunty provides evidence from a specific case, demonstrating persuasively that the admissions officers at her college take their job seriously.

Even bumper stickers can subtly acknowledge more than one position, as does this one from late 2008:

I Support Our Troops / I Question Our Policies

This bumper sticker states two positions that initially might seem contradictory, arguing that supporting the country's troops and questioning our government's foreign policies are not mutually exclusive.

An Authoritative Tone

Particularly in academic contexts, authors make a point of taking an authoritative tone. Even if your goal is to encourage readers to examine a number of alternatives without suggesting which one is best, you should try to do so in a way that shows you know which alternatives are worth examining and why. Likewise, even if you are taking a strong position, you should seek to appear reasonable and rational. The 1964 Surgeon General's report

Nicholas Carr isn't a neuroscientist, but he writes with authority about how using GPS devices changes our brains. See how he does it on p. 889.

on the consequences of smoking does not waver: smoking causes cancer. At the same time, in taking this position, it briefly outlines the history of the issue and the evidence on which the claim is logically based, avoiding emotional language and carefully specifying which forms of smoking ("excessive" cigarettes) and cancer (lung) the claim involves.

Jennifer Delahunty establishes her authority in other ways. Her description of ten admissions officers putting in twelve-hour days going through hundreds of applications and "poring over statistics" backs up her forthright assertion, "Rest assured that admissions officers are not cavalier in making their decisions." Later in the essay, acknowledging her own struggles to weigh issues of fairness to highly qualified young women against the need to maintain gender balance in incoming classes, Delahunty not only demonstrates that she knows what she is writing about but also invites readers to think about the complexity of the situation without offering them any easy answers. In short, she is simultaneously reasonable and authoritative.

An Appeal to Readers' Values

Implicitly or explicitly, authors need to appeal to readers' values, especially when taking a strong position. The creators of the "Yes, We Can" video clearly appealed to a number of cultural values that Americans hold dear, such as justice and equality (with references to the country's founding documents, slaves and abolitionists, the civil rights movement, workers who fought to organize and women who fought to vote) and opportunity, prosperity, and adventure (immigrants, pioneers, the space program). Similarly, we find an appeal to values in President Obama's talk of "hope" and in the use of "from sea to shining sea" from "America the Beautiful," a song known to virtually all Americans. The refrain "yes, we can" is itself a highly charged appeal to the audience's sense of democratic ideals.

Freeman A. Hrabowski III, president of the University of Maryland, Baltimore County, appeals to similar values of opportunity, equality, and democracy in a 2015 essay in *Inside Higher Ed*. His essay responds to the riots in Baltimore that spring, sparked by the death of a black man, Freddie Gray, while in police custody, but which also aired the grievances of a community with a long history of poverty and little opportunity.

As one of my students said to me recently, the Baltimore story—which is the American story—should remind us that issues related to poverty and inequality, crime and opportunity are not about "those people." They are about us—all of us. How we react to events like those in Baltimore speaks volumes about our values. We know we must do much better, especially for people who have not had a chance to thrive in our society. Americans—not just in Baltimore but across the country—have an opportunity now to ask difficult questions and take long-term action. . . . Historically, one of America's greatest strengths has been our ability to look squarely at our problems and to make hard changes. To do so often requires struggle, and we have a responsibility to embrace that struggle. To do so is a fundamental part of the learning and growing process—and it is fundamental to changing issues of systemic injustice and inequality that are neither new nor isolated.

—FREEMAN A. HRABOWSKI III, "After the Cameras Leave"

Hrabowski appeals to readers' patriotic values of unity and democracy, saying that these issues aren't just about certain communities in Baltimore, but "about us—all of us." He goes on to call for universities to engage with underprivileged communities, going by the American ideal of hard work and "struggle" that has led the nation to face difficult problems throughout its history. Writing for *Inside Higher Ed,* Hrabowski was addressing a vast audience of educators—and his text appeals to a wide set of values he can assume his readers to hold: the spirit of the American nation.

Online contexts are particularly interesting for considering appeals to values since you can rarely be sure who your actual readers are, and you certainly can't control who will see a text you create. Yet appealing to values is no less important in online situations and may, in fact, take on a greater role in arguing positions effectively. In this case, writers often seek to create their ideal audience through the words and images they choose. (In the "Yes, We Can" video, every viewer—or at least every American viewer—becomes potentially a part of the "we.") Online environments remind us that as writers, we are always imagining who our audience is and appealing to what we imagine their values to be.

RUSSEL HONORÉ wrote this essay for *This I Believe*, a not-for-profit organiza-tion that sponsors "a public dialogue about belief, one essay at a time." The es-say was later broadcast on *NPR's Weekend Edition* on March 1, 2009. Honoré is a retired lieutenant general in the U.S. Army who has contributed to response efforts to Hurricanes Katrina and Rita in 2005 and other natural disasters.

Work Is a Blessing
RUSSEL HONORÉ

I GREW UP IN Lakeland, Louisiana, one of 12 children. We all lived on my parents' subsistence farm. We grew cotton, sugarcane, corn, hogs, chickens and had a large garden, but it didn't bring in much cash. So when I was 12, I got a part-time job on a dairy farm down the road, helping to milk cows. We milked 65 cows at 5 in the morning and again at 2 in afternoon, seven days a week.

Background information.

In the kitchen one Saturday before daylight, I remember com-plaining to my father and grandfather about having to go milk those cows. My father said, "Ya know, boy, to work is a blessing."

A position taken in response to another position.

I looked at those two men who'd worked harder than I ever had—my father eking out a living on that farm and my grandfather farming and working as a carpenter during the Depression. I had a feeling I had been told something really important, but it took many years before it sunk in.

Admitting his own slowness to understand what his father meant contributes to his authoritative tone.

Going to college was a rare privilege for a kid from Lakeland, Louisiana. My father told me if I picked something to study that I liked doing, I'd always look forward to my work. But he also added, "Even having a job you hate is better than not having a job at all." I wanted to be a farmer, but I joined the ROTC program to help pay for college. And what started out as an obligation to the Army became a way of life that I stayed committed to for 37 years, three months and three days.

Citing his father, Honoré shows his attention to more than one point of view about work.

In the late 1980s, during a visit to Bangladesh, I saw a woman with a baby on her back, breaking bricks with a hammer. I asked a Bangladesh military escort why they weren't using a machine, which would have been a lot easier. He told me a machine would put that lady out of work. Breaking those bricks meant she'd earn enough money to feed herself and her baby that day. And as bad as that woman's job was, it was enough to keep a small family alive. It reminded me of my father's words: To work is a blessing.

Reasons and evidence for how the author came to see work as a blessing.

Serving in the United States Army overseas, I saw a lot of people like that woman in Bangladesh. And I have come to believe that people without jobs are not free. They are victims of crime, the ideology of terrorism, poor health, depression and social unrest. These victims become the illegal immigrants, the slaves of human trafficking, the drug dealers, the street gang members. I've seen it over and over again on the U.S. border, in Somalia, the Congo, Afghanistan and in New Orleans. People who have jobs can have a home, send their kids to school, develop a sense of pride, contribute to the good of the community, and even help others. When we can work, we're free. We're blessed.

Specific examples indicate why the topic matters and show the author's awareness of his audience's values.

I don't think I'll ever quit working. I'm retired from the Army, but I'm still working to help people be prepared for disaster. And I may get to do a little farming someday, too. I'm not going to stop. I believe in my father's words. I believe in the blessing of work.

The author concludes by stating his position explicitly.

Listen to the audio essay at everyonesanauthor.tumblr.com. You'll hear someone who sounds like he grew up on a farm in Louisiana, a fact that contributes to Honoré's authority: this guy knows what he's talking about.

🌀 REFLECT. *Choose a short piece of writing on a website such as* Salon *that takes a position on an issue you care about. Look at the list of characteristic features on pp. 120–21 and annotate your text to point out the ones that are represented in it, using Honoré's essay as a model. Make a list of any features that are not included as well. (While not every effective position paper will include all of the characteristic features, many of them will.) Then consider whether including those features might have improved the text—and if so, how.*

ARGUING A POSITION / A Roadmap

Choose a topic that matters—to you, and to others

If you get to select your topic, begin by examining your own interests and commitments in light of the context you are writing for. Global warming might be an appropriate topic for a course in the life sciences or social sciences, but it's probably not going to serve you well in a course in medieval history unless you can find a direct link between the two topics. You might consider focusing on some issue that's being debated on campus (Are those new rules for dropping classes fair?), a broader political or ethical issue (Is eating meat by definition unethical?), or an issue in which you have a direct stake (Does early admission penalize those who need financial aid?).

Lynda Barry thinks arts education is really important. See how she makes us think the same in "The Sanctuary of School," p. 856.

If you've been assigned a topic, do your best to find an aspect of it that interests you. (If you're bored with your subject, you can be sure your readers will be.) If, for example, you're assigned to write about globalization in a required international studies course, you could tailor that topic to your own interests and write about the influence of American hip-hop on world music.

Be sure that your topic is one that is arguable—and that it matters. Short of astounding new evidence, it's no longer worth arguing that there is no link between smoking and lung cancer. It's a fact. But you can argue about what responsibility tobacco companies now have for tobacco-related deaths, as recent court cases demonstrate.

One sure way to find out whether a topic is arguable is to see if it *is* being debated—and that is a good first step as you explore a topic. You can probably assume that any topic that's being widely discussed matters—and of course you'll want to know what's being said about it in order to write about it. Remember that your essay is part of a larger conversation about your topic: you need to become familiar with that conversation in order to contribute to it.

Consider your rhetorical situation

Looking at your audience, your purpose, and other aspects of your rhetorical situation will help you to think carefully about how to achieve your goals.

Focus on your AUDIENCE. Who are you trying to reach, and what do you hope to persuade them to think or do?

- What are they likely to know about your topic, and what background information will you need to provide?

- How are they like or unlike you—and one another? Consider such things as age, education, gender, abilities and disabilities, cultural and linguistic heritage, and so on. How will such factors influence the way you make your argument?

- What convictions might they hold about the topic you're addressing—and how sympathetic are they likely to be to your position?

If you're trying to convince your fellow business majors of the virtues of free-market capitalism, your task is quite different from if you're trying to convince members of the campus socialist organization. In the first case, you would almost surely be preaching to the choir, whereas in the second, you would likely face a more skeptical audience.

Keep in mind that there's always danger in speaking only to those who already agree with you; if you keep audiences with differing values and viewpoints in mind, you will be more likely to represent all views fairly and hence have others consider your position seriously. Keeping your audience in mind, then, means thinking in terms of who may respond to your position, how they will likely respond, and why.

Think hard about your PURPOSE. Why are you arguing this position? What has motivated you to write on this topic? What do you hope to learn by writing about it? What do you want to convince your audience to think or do? How can you best achieve your purpose or purposes?

Think about your STANCE. Start by asking yourself where you are coming from in regard to this topic. What about the topic captured your interest, and how has that interest led you to the position you expect to take on it? Why do you think the topic matters? How would you describe your attitude toward the topic: are you an advocate, a critic, an observer, an apologist, or something else? How do you want to be seen as an author—as forceful? thoughtful? curious? How can you establish your own authority in writing on this topic?

Consider the larger CONTEXT. What are the various perspectives on the issue? What have others said about it? If you're writing about the use of ethanol as a fuel source, for instance, you'll need to look at what circumstances led to its use, at who's supported and opposed it (and why), and at the economic ramifications both of producing ethanol for fuel and of not doing so.

As you come to understand the larger context, you'll become aware of various positions you'll want to consider, and what factors will be important to consider as you develop your position.

Consider your MEDIUM. Will your writing take the form of a print essay? Will it appear as an editorial in a local paper? on a website? as an audio essay to be broadcast on a local radio station or posted as a podcast? as an oral or multimedia presentation for a class you are taking? The medium you choose should be one that suits both your purpose and your audience.

Consider matters of DESIGN. Think about the "look" you want to achieve and how you can format your text to make it easy to follow. Do you need headings? illustrations? any other graphics? color? Does the discipline you're writing in have any conventions you should follow? Does your medium allow for certain elements such as audio or video links that will help you achieve your purpose?

Research your topic

Begin exploring the topic by looking at it from different points of view. Whatever position you take will ultimately be more credible and persuasive if you can show evidence of having considered other positions.

Begin by assessing what you know—and don't know—about the topic. What interests you about the topic, and why? What more do you want or need to find out about it? What questions do you have about it, and where might you go for answers? To answer these questions, you might try **BRAINSTORMING** or other activities for **GENERATING IDEAS**.

What have others said? What are some of the issues that are being debated now about your topic, and what are the various positions on these issues? What other **POSITIONS** might be taken with respect to the topic? Remember, too, to seek out sources that represent a variety of perspectives.

Where to start your research? Where you start and what sources you consult depend upon your topic and what questions you have about it. If you are focusing on a current issue, turn to news media and to websites, listservs, *Twitter*, or other online groups devoted to the issue. If you are investigating a topic from the distant past, be sure to look for both older sources and more recent scholarship on the topic. For some issues, you might want to interview experts or conduct other sorts of **FIELD RESEARCH**.

Do you need to cut your topic down to size? Few among us know enough to make strong general claims about global warming. While that fact does not and should not keep us from having opinions about the issue, it means that the existence of global warming is likely much too broad a topic to be appropriate for a five-page essay. Instead, you'll need to focus on some aspect of that topic for your essay. What angle you take will depend on the course you're writing for. For a geology class, you might focus on the effects of rising temperatures on melting glaciers; for an international relations course, you could look at climate shift and national security debates. Just remember that your goal is to take an informed position, one that you can support well.

Formulate an explicit position

Once you have sufficient information about your topic and some understanding of the complexity of the issue, you'll need to formulate a position that you can state explicitly and support fully. Let's say you decide to take a position on a current controversy among scientists about climate change. Here's how one author formulated a position:

> Many scientists have argued that climate change has led to bigger and more destructive hurricanes and typhoons. Other researchers, however, have countered by saying that climate change is not linked causally to an increase in hurricane strength. After reviewing both sides of this debate, I see two strong reasons why changes in our climate have not necessarily led to more severe hurricanes.
> —SOFI MINCEY, "On Climate Change and Hurricanes"

These three sentences articulate a clear position—that climate change is not necessarily to blame for bigger hurricanes—and frame that position as a response to an existing debate. Notice also how the writer qualifies her claim: she does not claim definitively that climate change has not led to bigger hurricanes; rather, she promises to present reasons that argue for this view.

By arguing only that the claims of many scientists *may* be wrong, she greatly increases the likelihood that she can succeed in her argument, setting a reasonable goal for what she must achieve. Note that her position still requires support: she needs to present reasonable evidence to challenge the claim that climate change has "necessarily" led to bigger hurricanes.

State your position as a tentative **THESIS**. Once you formulate your position, try stating it several different ways and then decide which one is most compelling. Make sure the position is stated explicitly—no beating around the bush. Your statement should let your audience know where you stand and be interesting enough to attract their attention.

Then think about whether you should **QUALIFY** your position. Should you limit what you claim—is it true only sometimes or under certain circumstances? On the other hand, does it seem too weak or timid and need to be stated more forcefully?

Remember that a good thesis for a position paper should identify your specific topic and make a **CLAIM** about that topic that is debatable. The thesis should also give your audience some idea of your reasons for making this claim. Consider the following thesis statement from two scholars at a public policy institute:

> The case against raising the minimum wage is straightforward: A higher wage makes it more expensive for firms to hire workers.
> —KEVIN A. HASSET AND MICHAEL R. STRAIN,
> "Why We Shouldn't Raise the Minimum Wage"

Hasset and Strain's claim about raising the minimum wage is explicitly stated (they are "against" it), as is a major reason for that position.

Come up with **REASONS** and **EVIDENCE**. List all the reasons supporting your position that you discovered in your research. Which ones will be most persuasive to your audience? Then jot down all the evidence you have to support those reasons—facts, quotations, statistics, examples, testimony, visuals, and so on. Remember that what counts as evidence varies across audiences and disciplines. Some are persuaded by testimonials, while others want statistical data. Finally, look for any **FALLACIES** or weak reasons or evidence, and decide whether you need to do further research.

Identify other positions. Carefully consider **COUNTERARGUMENTS** and other points of view on the topic and how you will account for them. At the very least, you need to acknowledge other positions that are prominent in the larger conversation about the topic and to treat them fairly. If you disagree with a position, you need to offer reasons why and to do so respectfully.

Organize and start writing

Once you have a fair sense of how you will present your position, it's time to write out a draft. If you have trouble getting started, it might help to think about the larger conversation about the topic that's already going on—and to think of your draft as a moment when you get to say what *you* think.

Be guided by your THESIS. As you begin to organize, type it at the top of your page so that you can keep looking back to it to be sure that each part of your text supports the thesis.

Give REASONS for your position, with supporting EVIDENCE. Determine an order for presenting your reasons, perhaps starting with the one you think will speak most directly to your audience.

Don't forget to consider COUNTERARGUMENTS. Acknowledge positions other than your own, and respond to what they say.

Draft an OPENING. Introduce your topic, and provide any background information your audience may need. State your position clearly, perhaps as a response to what others have said about your topic. Say something about why the issue matters, why your audience should care.

Draft a CONCLUSION. You might want to end by summing up your position and by answering the "so what" question: why does your topic matter—and who cares? Make sure you give a strong takeaway message. What are the implications of your argument? What do you want readers to remember or do as a result of reading what you've written?

Look critically at your draft, get response—and revise

Go through your draft carefully, looking critically at the position you stake out, the reasons and evidence you provide in support of it, and the way you present them to your audience. For this review, play the "doubting game" with yourself by asking "Who says?" and "So what?" and "Can this be done better?" at every point.

Being tough on yourself now will pay off by showing you where you need to shore up your arguments. As you work through your draft, make notes on what you plan to do in your revision.

Next, ask some classmates or friends to read and respond to your draft. Here are some questions that can help you or others read over a draft of writing that takes a position.

- *Is the position stated explicitly?* Is there a clear **THESIS** sentence—and if not, is one needed? Does it need to be qualified, or should it be stated more strongly?

- *What positions are you responding to?* What is the larger conversation?

- *Is it clear why the topic matters?* Why do you care about the topic, and why should your audience care?

- *How effective is the* **OPENING** *?* How does it capture your audience's interest? How else might you begin?

- *Is there sufficient background information?* What other information might the audience need?

- *How would you describe the* **STANCE** *and* **TONE** —and are they appropriate to your audience and purpose? Does the tone seem both authoritative and reasonable?

- *What* **REASONS** *do you give for the position, and what* **EVIDENCE** *do you provide for those reasons?* What are the strongest reasons and evidence given? the weakest? What other evidence or reasons are needed to support this position?

- *How trustworthy are the sources you've cited?* Are **QUOTATIONS**, **SUMMARIES**, and **PARAPHRASES** smoothly integrated into the text—and is it clear where you are speaking and where (and why) you are citing others?

- *What other positions do you consider, and do you treat them fairly?* Are there other **COUNTERARGUMENTS** you should address as well? How well do you answer possible objections to your position?

- *How is the draft organized?* Is it easy to follow, with clear **TRANSITIONS** from one point to the next? Are there headings—and if not, would they help? What about the organization could be improved?

- *Is the* **STYLE** *appropriate to the audience and purpose?* Could the style—choice of words, kinds of sentences—be improved in any way?

- *How effective is your text* **DESIGN** *?* Have you used any visuals to support your position—and if so, have you written captions that explain how they contribute to the argument? If not, what visuals might be appropriate? Is there any information that would be easier to follow if it were presented in a chart or table?

- *How does the draft* **CONCLUDE** *?* Is the conclusion forceful and memorable? How else might you conclude?

- *Consider the title.* Does it make clear what the text is about, and does it make a reader want to read on?

- *What is your overall impression of the draft?* Will it persuade your audience to accept the position—and if not, why? Even if they don't accept the position, would they consider it a plausible one?

Revise your draft in light of your own observations and any feedback from others—keeping your audience and purpose firmly in mind, as always.

REFLECT. Once you've completed your essay, let it settle for a while before you look back at it with a critical eye. How well did you argue your point? What additional revisions would you make if you could? Research shows that such reflections help "lock in" what you learn for future use.

In the Minimum Wage Debate, Both Sides Make Valid Points

REX HUPPKE

AFTER TWO WEEKS OF DETAILING THE ARGUMENTS for and against rais-ing the federal minimum wage—interviewing economists and policy experts, poring over a flood of emails from workers and business owners, reading scads of papers pro and con—I've reached an important conclusion: This issue is really complicated.

I realize that doesn't sound important, but in the context of our current national debate over the minimum wage, it's actually quite fundamental.

As I began this series of columns, my gut feeling was: RAISE IT! And if you look at the polling numbers, a sizable majority of Americans share that feeling. That's why Democrats, from President Barack Obama on down, are pushing hard on this issue—it appeals to people, and it sounds like the right thing to do.

But setting emotions aside to look objectively at both sides of the argument takes some of the shine off the idea.

Opponents of boosting the minimum wage focus mainly on the potentially detrimental side effects, like job reduction, and a rise in the cost of consumer goods and services. Some academic studies have confirmed those negative ef-fects; others have shown they don't happen.

5

REX HUPPKE is a columnist for the *Chicago Tribune*. His writing often takes up so-cial and political issues, sometimes humorously. This column appeared in March 2014, in the heat of the debate over raising the federal minimum wage.

You can easily battle to a draw on those issues. I think the truth is that it's wildly difficult to predict exactly how increasing the base wage from $7.25 per hour to $10.10 per hour would play out. Some markets might be able to absorb the change, while others might struggle. Some companies will be able to absorb the increased labor costs, while others with thin profit margins might cut their workforce or raise prices.

But the point that opponents of a minimum wage increase make that strikes me as the most compelling is this: Raising the minimum wage is not a very effective means of addressing poverty. For starters, I had never considered the diversity of minimum wage earners—this swath of the workforce is made up of teenagers working first jobs, older workers supplementing their income and, yes, people who are truly struggling to make ends meet.

It's that latter group that most needs the help, but by raising the minimum wage, you're not targeting those workers alone; you're targeting everyone who happens to get paid minimum wage. And you do so with some level of risk, as detailed in the Congressional Budget Office report that showed a wage increase could lead to the loss of 500,000 jobs. (The report also found that higher wages could push 900,000 people above the poverty line, an unquestionably good outcome.)

Jonathan Guryan, an economist at Northwestern University's Institute for Policy Research, is a neutral observer in this debate, seeing the reasonable arguments on each side.

"The pro argument would be that it's potentially a policy to stem the increases in income inequality that we've seen in the U.S. in the past 30 to 40 years," he said. "The con to that is, if you're trying to reduce income inequality, this is a pretty blunt instrument to do it. It's not helping as many or as large a portion of the labor market as you probably would like. And it has some unintended consequences, potentially." 10

Opponents of the increase say time and money would be better spent improving education and job training programs that will give people a better shot at getting out of minimum wage jobs and into better-paying careers. They also say they would combat poverty using programs like the Earned Income Tax Credit (EITC), a federal wage subsidy for low-income people that directly benefits those who most need help.

I think the EITC and education are two pragmatic tools that are being overshadowed by our focus on the politically attractive minimum wage. (To be fair, a more generous EITC is part of Obama's new budget plan, and it's an issue both sides seem to agree on.)

Guryan said: "If the goal is to reduce inequality or improve the well-being of people currently living in poverty, there are other policies that the evidence suggests would be much more cost-effective in the long run, like investing in education, improving funding for things like food stamps and expanding the EITC."

So, does this mean I think it would be bad to raise the minimum wage? No.

I hear experts opposed to raising the minimum wage talk about education and the EITC. But I don't see Republican lawmakers who oppose raising the minimum wage rallying too hard to promote those ideas—many of them just say "no" to a wage increase and leave it at that.

On the flip side, Democratic lawmakers seem laser-focused on only the increase itself.

The debate we're having right now is: "It's a minimum wage increase or nothing." That's too simplistic an approach for such a complex problem.

If we claim to be concerned about the working poor in this country, then let's demand more of our lawmakers than empty "Raise the Wage!" or "Let the Market Decide!" slogans.

I think our current federal minimum wage, which hasn't been raised since 2009, seems unreasonably low, but I also wonder if a nearly 40 percent increase isn't asking a bit much. If it's going to be raised, it should be tied to inflation so it exists as part of our economic philosophy and can't be used as a political cudgel.

I realize this is impractical in an era of partisan politics, but what I'm in favor of is a comprehensive approach to making life better for American workers. And that will require both sides to compromise.

If the minimum wage is raised, I'll be happy for the working people who benefit and hopeful that the outcomes will be as good as promised. But if all we do is raise the minimum wage, I'll worry we're missing a chance to lift people out of poverty for good, and that a few years from now, we'll be having this same conversation—again.

Thinking about the Text

1. What is Rex Huppke's position on raising the minimum wage? How does his position differ from what we generally expect of authors when they take a stand on an issue?

2. Huppke tells readers about how his thinking on the minimum wage debate changed as he researched the issue. How does this revelation affect his **CREDIBILITY** as an author?

3. Even though Huppke admits that both sides of the minimum wage debate "make valid arguments," he takes a **STANCE**. What parts of his article suggest which side he favors?

4. How does Huppke address the various sides of the debate? How does his treatment of the multiple perspectives affect his own argument?

5. This essay was the last in a two-week series in the *Chicago Tribune*, in which Huppke explored the various sides of the minimum wage debate. Read the series at everyonesanauthor.tumblr.com, briefly **SUMMARIZE** the issues, and then respond by taking a **POSITION** of your own.

On Buying Local

KATHERINE SPRIGGS

AMERICANS TODAY can eat pears in the spring in Minnesota, oranges in the summer in Montana, asparagus in the fall in Maine, and cranberries in the winter in Florida. In fact, we can eat pretty much any kind of produce anywhere at any time of the year. But what is the cost of this convenience? In this essay, I will explore some answers to this question and argue that we should give up a little bit of convenience in favor of buying local.

"Buying local" means that consumers choose to buy food that has been grown, raised, or produced as close to their homes as possible ("Buy Local"). Buying local is an important part of the response to many environmental issues we face today (fig. 1). It encourages the development of small farms, which are often more environmentally sustainable than large farms, and thus strengthens local markets and supports small rural economies. By demonstrating a commitment to buying local, Americans could set an example for global environmentalism.

In 2010, the international community is facing many environmental challenges, including global warming, pollution, and dwindling fossil fuel resources. Global warming is attributed to the release of greenhouse gases such as carbon dioxide and methane, most commonly emitted in the burning of fossil fuels. It is such a pressing problem that scientists estimate that in the year

KATHERINE SPRIGGS wrote this essay for a writing course she took in her first year at Stanford University.

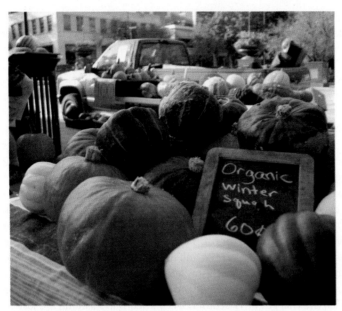

Fig. 1. Shopping at a farmers' market is one good way to support small farms and strengthen the local economy. Photograph from Alamy.

2030, there will be no glaciers left in Glacier National Park ("Global Warming Statistics"). The United States is especially guilty of contributing to the problem, producing about a quarter of all global greenhouse gas emissions, and playing a large part in pollution and shrinking world oil supplies as well ("Record Increase"). According to a CNN article published in 2000, the United States manufactures more than 1.5 billion pounds of chemical pesticides a year that can pollute our water, soil, and air (Baum). Agriculture is particularly interconnected with all of these issues. Almost three-fourths of the pesticides produced in the United States are used in agriculture (Baum). Most produce is shipped many miles before it is sold to consumers, and shipping our food long distances is costly in both the amount of fossil fuel it uses and the greenhouse gases it produces.

A family friend and farmer taught me firsthand about the effects of buying local. Since I was four years old, I have spent every summer on a 150-acre farm in rural Wisconsin, where my family has rented our 75 tillable acres to a farmer who lives nearby. Mr. Lermio comes from a family that has farmed the area for generations. I remember him sitting on our porch at dusk wearing his blue striped overalls and dirty white T-shirt, telling my parents about all of the changes in the area since he was a kid. "Things sure are different around here," he'd say. He told us that all the farms in that region used to milk about 30 head of cattle each. Now he and the other farmers were selling their herds to industrial-scale farms milking 4,000 head each. The shift came when milk started being processed on a large scale rather than at small local cheese factories. Milk is now shipped to just a few large factories where it is either bottled or processed into cheese or other dairy products. The milk and products from these factories are then shipped all across the country. "You see," Mr. Lermio would tell us, "it's just not worth shipping the milk from my 20 cows all the way to Gays Mills. You just can't have a small herd anymore." Farming crops is also different now. Machinery is expensive and hard to pay off with profits from small fields. The Lermio family has been buying and renting fields all around the area, using their tractors to farm hundreds of acres. Because they can no longer sell locally, Mr. Lermio and many other rural farmers have to move towards larger-scale farming to stay afloat.

Buying local could help reverse the trend towards industrial-scale farming,   5 of which the changes in Wisconsin over Mr. Lermio's lifetime are just one ex-

Fig. 2. A small polyculture farm. Photograph from iStockphoto.

ample. Buying local benefits small farmers by not forcing them to compete with larger farms across the country. For example, if consumers bought beef locally, beef cattle would be raised in every region and their meat would be sold locally rather than shipped from a small number of big ranches in Texas and Montana. Small farms are often polycultures—they produce many different kinds of products (fig. 2). The Lermios' original farm, for example, grew corn, hay, oats, and alfalfa. They also had milking cattle, chickens, and a few hogs. Large farms are often monocultures—they raise only one kind of crop or animal (fig. 3). The Lermio family has been moving towards becoming a monoculture; they raise only three field crops and they don't have any animals. Buying local, as was common in the first half of the twentieth century, encourages small polyculture farms that sell a variety of products locally (McCauley).

For environmental purposes, the small polyculture farms that buying local encourages have many advantages over industrial-scale monoculture farms because they are more sustainable. The focus of sustainable farming is on minimizing waste, use of chemicals, soil erosion, and pollution ("Sustainable"). Small farmers tend to value local natural resources more than industrial-scale farmers do and are therefore more conscientious in their farming

Fig. 3. A large monoculture farm. Photograph from iStockphoto.

methods. Small farms are also intrinsically more sustainable. As mentioned, small farms are more likely to be polycultures—to do many different things with the land—and using a field for different purposes does not exhaust the soil the way continually farming one crop does. Rotating crops or using a field alternately for pasture and for crops keeps the land "healthy." On small farms, sometimes a farmer will pasture his cattle in the previous year's cornfield; the cattle eat some of the stubble left from last year's crop and fertilize the field. The land isn't wasted or exhausted from continuous production. I've even seen one organic farmer set up his pigpen so that the pigs plow his blueberry field just by walking up around their pen. This kind of dual usage wouldn't be found on a large monoculture farm. Most big farms use their fields exclusively either for crops or for pasture. Modern fertilizers, herbicides, and pesticides allow farmers to harvest crops from even unhealthy land, but this is a highly unsustainable model. Farming chemicals can pollute groundwater and destroy natural ecosystems.

Not only are small farms a more sustainable, eco-friendly model than big commercial farms, but buying local has other advantages as well. Buying local, for example, would reduce the high cost of fuel and energy used to transport food across the world and would bring long-term benefits as well. It is currently estimated that most produce in the United States is shipped about 1,500 miles before it is sold—it travels about the distance from Nebraska to New York ("Why Buy Local?"). Eighty percent of all strawberries grown in the United States are from California ("Strawberry Fruit Facts Page"). They are shipped from California all around the country even though strawberries can be grown in Wisconsin, New York, Tennessee, and most other parts of the United States. No matter how efficient our shipping systems, shipping food thousands of miles is expensive—in dollars, in oil, and in the carbon dioxide it produces (fig. 4). One of the main reasons that produce is shipped long distances is that fruits and vegetables don't grow everywhere all year around. Even though strawberries grow a lot of places during the early summer, they grow only in Florida in the winter, or in California from spring to fall (Rieger). Americans have become accustomed to being able to buy almost any kind of produce at any time of the year. A true commitment to buying local would accommodate local season and climate. Not everything will grow everywhere, but the goal of buying local should be to eliminate all unnecessary shipping by buying things from as close to home as possible and eating as many things in season as possible.

Some argue that buying local can actually have negative environmental effects; and their arguments add important qualifiers to supporting small local

Fig 4. Interstate trucking is expensive financially and ecologically.
Photograph from iStockphoto.

farms. Alex Avery, the director of research and education at the Center for Global Food Issues, has said that we should "buy food from the world region where it grows best" (qtd. in MacDonald). His implication is that it would be more wasteful to try to grow pineapples in the Northeast than to have them shipped from the Caribbean. He makes a good point: trying to grow all kinds of food all over the world would be a waste of time and energy. Buying local should instead focus on buying *as much as possible* from nearby farmers. It has also been argued that buying locally will be detrimental to the environment because small farms are not as efficient in their use of resources as large farms. This is a common misconception and actually depends on how economists measure efficiency. Small farms are less efficient than large farms in the total output of one crop per acre, but they are more efficient in total output of all crops per acre (McCauley). When buying locally, the consumer should try to buy from these more efficient polyculture farms. Skeptics of buying local also say that focusing food cultivation in the United States will be worse for the environment because farmers here use more industrial equipment than farmers in the third world (MacDonald). According to the Progressive Policy Institute, however, only 13 percent of the American diet is imported ("98.7 Percent"). This is a surprisingly small percentage, especially considering that seafood is one of the top imports. It should also be considered that as countries around the world become wealthier, they will industrialize, so exploiting manual labor in the third world would only be a temporary solution (MacDonald). The environmental benefits now, and in the long run, of buying local outweigh any such immediate disadvantages.

Critics have also pointed to negative global effects of buying local, but buying local could have positive global effects too. In the *Christian Science Monitor*, John Clark, author of *Worlds Apart: Civil Society and the Battle for Ethical Globalization*, argues that buying local hurts poor workers in third world countries. He cites the fact that an estimated fifty thousand children in Bangladesh lost their jobs in the garment industry because of the 1996 Western boycott of clothing made in third world sweatshops (qtd. in MacDonald). It cannot be denied that if everyone buys locally, repercussions on the global market seem unavoidable. Nonetheless, if the people of the United States demonstrated their commitment to buying local, it could open up new conversations about environmentalism. Our government lags far behind the European Union in environmental legislation. Through selective shopping, the people of the United States could demonstrate to the world our commitment to environmentalism.

Arguments that decentralizing food production will be bad for the national   10
economy also ignore the positive effects small farms have on local economies. John Tschirhart, a professor of environmental economics at the University of Wyoming, argues that buying locally would be bad for our national economy because food that we buy locally can often be produced cheaper somewhere else in the United States (qtd. in Arias Terry). This seems debatable since most of the locally grown things we buy in grocery stores today aren't much more expensive, if at all, than their counterparts from far away. In New York City, apples from upstate New York are often cheaper than the industrial, waxed Granny Smiths from Washington State or Chile; buying locally should indeed save shipping costs. Nonetheless, it is true that locally grown food can often be slightly more expensive than "industrially grown" food. Probably one of the biggest factors in the difference in price is labor cost. Labor is cheap in third world countries, and large U.S. farms are notorious for hiring immigrant laborers. It is hard to justify the exploitation of such artificially cheap labor. While the case for the economic disadvantages of buying local is dubious, buying local has clear positive economic effects in local communities. Local farms hire local workers and bring profits to small rural communities. One study of pig farmers in Virginia showed that, compared to corporate-owned farms, small farms created 10 percent more permanent local jobs, a 20 percent higher increase

in local retail sales, and a 37 percent higher increase in local per capita income (McCauley).

Buying locally grown and produced food has clear environmental, social, and economic advantages. On the surface it seems that buying local could constitute a big personal sacrifice. It may be slightly more expensive, and it wouldn't allow us to buy any kind of produce at any time of the year, a change that would no doubt take getting used to. But perhaps these limitations would actually make food more enjoyable. If strawberries were sold only in the summer, they would be more special and we might even enjoy them more. Food that is naturally grown in season is fresher and also tends to taste better. Fresh summer strawberries are sweeter than their woody winter counterparts. Buying local is an easy step that everyone can take towards "greener" living.

Works Cited

Arias Terry, Ana. "Buying Local vs. Buying Cheap." *Conscious Choice: The Journal of Ecology and Natural Living.* Conscious Communications, Jan. 2007. Web. 27 Apr. 2011.

Baum, Michele Dula. "U.S. Government Issues Standards on Organic Food." *CNN.com.* Turner Broadcasting System, 20 Dec. 2000. Web. 25 Apr. 2011.

"Buy Local." *Sustainable Table.* Grace Communications Foundation, Jan. 2007. Web. 27 Apr. 2011.

"Global Warming Statistics." *Effects of Global Warming.* Effects of Global Warming, 2007. Web. 25 Apr. 2011.

MacDonald, G. Jeffrey. "Is Buying Local Always Best?" *Christian Science Monitor.* 24 July 2006: 13+. Print.

McCauley, Marika Alena. "Small Farms: The Optimum Sustainable Agriculture Model." *Oxfam America.* Oxfam America, 2007. Web. 27 Apr. 2011.

"98.7 Percent of Imported Food Never Inspected." *Progressive Policy Institute.* Progressive Policy Institute, 7 Sept. 2007. Web. 25 Apr. 2011.

"Record Increase in U.S. Greenhouse Gas Emissions Reported." *Environment News Service.* Environment News Service, 18 Apr. 2006. Web. 25 Apr. 2011.

Rieger, Mark. "Strawberry—*Fragaria X ananassa*." *Mark's Fruit Crops.* U of Georgia, 2006. Web. 25 Apr. 2011.

"Strawberry Fruit Facts Page." *Grown in California*. Gourmet Shopping Network, LLC. Web. 25 Apr. 2011.

"Sustainable." *Paperback Oxford English Dictionary*. 6th ed. 2001. Print.

"Why Buy Local?" *LocalHarvest*. LocalHarvest, 2007. Web. 23 Apr. 2011.

Thinking about the Text

1. It's clear that this is a topic that matters to Katherine Spriggs. Has she convinced you that it matters—and if so, how? How does Spriggs establish the importance of her topic?

2. What COUNTERARGUMENTS or positions other than her own does Spriggs consider—and how does she respond in each case?

3. Choose a section of Spriggs' essay that you find especially effective or ineffective. Referring to the genre features discussed on pp. 120–21, describe what makes this part of her argument persuasive—or not.

4. Spriggs includes several photos in her essay. How do they contribute to her argument?

5. Consider your own response to Spriggs' position. Write an essay in response to one of the issues she raises. State your POSITION explicitly, and be sure to consider arguments other than your own.

TWELVE

"Here's What Happened"

Writing a Narrative

 O, TELL ME WHAT HAPPENED." Anytime we ask someone about an incident at work or an event at school, we are asking for a narrative: tell us about what happened. Narratives are stories, and they are fundamental parts of our everyday lives. When we tell someone about a movie we've seen or a basketball game we played in, we often use narrative. When we want someone to understand something that we did, we might tell a story that explains our actions. When we post to *Facebook*, we often write about something we've just done or seen.

If you wrote an essay as part of your college applications, chances are that you were required to write a narrative. Here, for instance, are instructions from two colleges' applications:

> Describe a meaningful event or experience and how it has changed or affected the person you are today. —HOFSTRA UNIVERSITY

> Describe a personal moral or ethical dilemma and how it impacted your life. —HAMPTON UNIVERSITY

Each of these prompts asks applicants to write a narrative about some aspect of their lives. In each case they need to do more than just tell a good story; they need to make a clear point about why it matters.

Narrative is a powerful way to get an audience's attention. Telling a good story can even help establish your authority as a writer. Take a look, for example, at the opening paragraphs from an obituary for Michael Jackson from the *Los Angeles Times:*

> Michael Jackson was fascinated by celebrity tragedy. He had a statue of Marilyn Monroe in his home and studied the sad Hollywood exile of Charlie Chaplin. He married the daughter of Elvis Presley.
>
> Jackson met his own untimely death Thursday [June 25, 2009] at age 50, and more than any of those past icons, he left a complicated legacy. As a child star, he was so talented he seemed lit from within; as a middle-aged man, he was viewed as something akin to a visiting alien who, like Tinkerbell, would cease to exist if the applause ever stopped.
>
> —GEOFF BOUCHER AND ELAINE WOO, "Michael Jackson's Life
> Was Infused with Fantasy and Tragedy"

The authors could have opened by saying simply that Michael Jackson had died, but they do more than that, providing details that grab our attention— and that promise a well-told narrative rather than just facts and figures about Jackson's life. The outlines of the story that they offer in these few lines make us want to keep reading.

Images, too, can tell stories, as the cartoon on the following page shows. The writing on the lower left simply records Jackson's name and the years of his life, while the dramatic central image shows a single white-gloved hand, fingers outstretched. Jackson's bejeweled white glove, which he introduced in a 1983 performance of "Billie Jean," became his signature, so ubiquitous that it became an icon of the performer himself. The cartoon thus tells the story of Jackson's life as the story of a man eclipsed by his own enormous star power, a man who became a voice, a figure, and above all a symbol.

Think about some of the powerful personal narratives you've read, perhaps the *Narrative of the Life of Frederick Douglass* or Anne Frank's *Diary of a Young Girl*. We could, of course, read about their lives on *Wikipedia*, but a good narrative provides more than just the facts; it gives us a well-told story that captures not only our attention but also our imagination.

So what exactly is a narrative? For our purposes, narrative is a kind of writing that presents events in some kind of time sequence with a distinct beginning, middle, and ending (but not necessarily in strict chronological order) and that is written for the purpose of making a point. That is, to write a narrative it is not enough to simply report a sequence of events ("this happened, then that happened"), which is often what children do when they tell

One cartoonist's tribute to Michael Jackson.

stories. Narrative essays, especially in college, are meaningful ways of making sense of our experiences, of what goes on around us—and of illustrating a point, making an argument, or writing about the lives of others.

REFLECT. Think about some everyday narratives. Consider stories that are told in your favorite songs or music videos, that you hear in sermons, or that your grandma tells. Make a list of the stories that you hear, read, see, or tell in one day and the subjects of those stories. By doing so, you'll begin to see how narratives are an important way that we communicate with each other.

Across Academic Disciplines

The narrative essay is a common assignment in the humanities and increasingly in other academic fields as well. In a *composition* class, you may be asked to write a literacy narrative about how you learned to read or write or a personal narrative about an important person or experience in your life. In a *history* class, you may be asked to take data from archives and construct a narrative about a particular historical event. (Some think that historians focus on dates and facts about incidents from the past, but actually they are generally piecing together narratives that provide a context

Visit the Digital Archive of Literacy Narratives, a site at Ohio State where you can read literacy narratives as well as post your own. You'll find a link at everyonesanauthor .tumblr.com.

for interpreting what those dates and facts mean.) In *medicine*, patient accounts and medical histories play a key role in diagnosis and treatment and provide important documentation for insurance companies. In the *sciences*, lab reports tell the story of how researchers conducted an experiment and interpreted the data they collected. Since narratives take different forms across disciplines, one challenge you'll face will be to determine which narrative elements are valued or even required in a particular situation.

Across Media

The medium you use makes a huge difference in the way you tell a story. *Videos*, for example, present a wide range of possibilities. TV broadcasts of football games can cut between shots of players, coaches, and fans. Commentators can review key plays in slow motion or from multiple angles, diagram plays on the screen, and pull up player statistics—all of which combine to tell the story of what's happening on the field. These same stories will be told differently in *print*, with written words, still photos, and tables of statistics to show how the players performed.

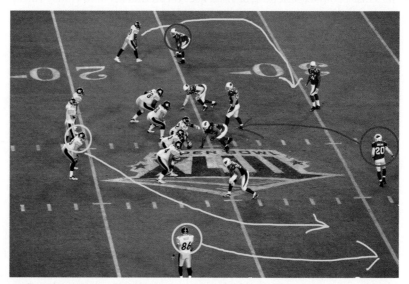

Analysts circle players and draw arrows to show those watching the game on TV what just happened.

When you're writing a narrative, you'll want to think about what media will best suit your audience and purpose. But you won't always have a choice. If you're assigned to work in a specific medium, think about whether a narrative would help get your message across. Well-told stories are a good way to engage your audience's attention in an *oral presentation*, for instance, and to help them remember what you say.

REFLECT. Compare narratives in different media. From the many kinds of narratives you encounter in one day—in books or magazines, on YouTube or in video games, in textbooks or conversations with friends—choose two narratives on the same topic from different media that you find most interesting. Think about the similarities and differences between the ways the two stories are told. How does the medium affect the storytelling in each case? What would change about each narrative if it were presented in a different medium?

Across Cultures and Communities

What makes a good story often depends on who's telling the story and who's listening. Not only is that the case for individuals, but different communities and cultures also tell stories in unique ways and value particular things in them.

Many *Native American tribes* consider narrative an important tradition and art form, so much so that storytellers hold a place of honor. In much of *West Africa*, the griots are the official storytellers, entrusted with telling the history of a village or town through recitation and song. And in many *Appalachian communities*, storytelling functions as a way to pass down family and community history. As in West Africa, good storytellers enjoy high status in Appalachia.

In many cultures and communities, stories are the way that history is passed down from generation to generation. Think about the ways that family histories are passed down in your family or community—through oral stories? photo albums? home videos?

Across Genres

Narrative is often a useful strategy for writers working in other genres. For example, in an essay **ARGUING A POSITION**, you may use a narrative example to prove a point. In a **REVIEW** of a film, in which evaluation is the main

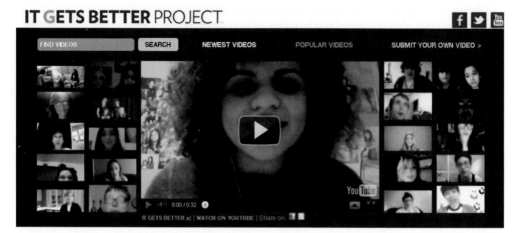

GO TO itgetsbetter.org, the award-winning site of the It Gets Better Project, begun in 2010 to show LGBT youths that life will get better "if they can just get through their teen years." There you'll find thousands of videos, including many personal narratives from gay adults who tell about how their lives got better. There's also a button to add your story, in video or writing. Watch some of the videos and read some of the written stories. Which do you find more powerful, and why?

purpose, you may need to tell a brief story from the plot to demonstrate how the film meets (or does not meet) a specific evaluative criterion. These are only two of the many ways in which narrative can be used as part of a text.

CHARACTERISTIC FEATURES

There is no one way to tell a story. Most written narratives, however, have a number of common features, revolving around the following characteristics and questions:

- A clearly identified event: What happened? Who was involved?
- A clearly described setting: When and where did it happen?
- Vivid, descriptive details: What makes the story come alive?
- A consistent point of view: Who's telling the story?
- A clear point: Why does the story matter?

A Clearly Identified Event:
What Happened? Who Was Involved?

Narratives are based on an event or series of events, presented in a way that makes audiences want to know how the story will turn out. Consider this paragraph by Mike Rose, in which he narrates how he, as a marginal high school student with potential, got into college with the help of his senior-year English teacher, Jack MacFarland:

> My grades stank. I had A's in biology and a handful of B's in a few English and social science classes. All the rest were C's—or worse. MacFarland said I would do well in his class and laid down the law about doing well in others. Still the record for my first three years wouldn't have been acceptable to any four-year school. To nobody's surprise, I was turned down flat by USC and UCLA. But Jack MacFarland was on the case. He had received his bachelor's degree from Loyola, so he made calls to old professors and talked to somebody in admissions and wrote me a strong letter. Loyola finally accepted me as a probationary student. I would be on trial for the first year, and if I did okay, I would be granted regular status. MacFarland also intervened to get me a loan, for I could never have afforded a private college without it. Four more years of religion classes and four more years of boys at one school, girls at another. But at least I was going to college. Amazing.
>
> —MIKE ROSE, *Lives on the Boundary*

This paragraph tells about the series of events that led to Rose's acceptance to Loyola, particularly the assistance he received from MacFarland. As remarkable as it is to think that someone with lots of C's (or worse) could get into college, it's not the actual facts that make this narrative worth reading; rather, it's the way the facts are presented—in other words, the way the story is told.

The narrator grabs our attention with his first sentence ("My grades stank"), then lays out the challenges he faced ("turned down flat by USC and UCLA"), and ends with a flourish ("Amazing"). He could have told us what happened much more briefly—but then it would have been just a sequence of facts; instead, he told us a story. As the author of a narrative, you'll want to be sure to get the facts down, but that won't be enough. Your challenge will be to tell about "what happens" in a way that gets your audience's attention and makes them care enough about what happens to keep on reading.

A Clearly Described Setting:
When and Where Did It Happen?

Narratives need to be situated clearly within time and space in order for readers to understand what's going on. For that reason, you will generally arrange your story in **CHRONOLOGICAL** order starting at the beginning and moving straight ahead to the end. There are times, though, when you may choose to present a narrative in reverse chronological order, starting at the end and looking back at the events that led up to it—or with a flashback or flash-forward that jumps back to the past or ahead to the future. Whether you tell your story in chronological order or not, the sequence of events needs to be clear to your audience.

Also important is that your audience get a clear idea of the place(s) where the events occur. Time and space work together to create a scene that your audience can visualize and follow, as they do in the following example from an *ESPN.com* profile of Myron Rolle, a Rhodes scholar who postponed a career in the NFL to study at Oxford.

> Oxford at first light is an ode to potential. The purple sky throws shadows off churches and their saw-blade spires, bringing definition to the gap-toothed smiles of crenellated walls. The ghosts come out in the dream of early morning. Twelve saints and seven British prime ministers walked these streets. So did Bill Clinton and John Donne, Sir Thomas More and Kris Kristofferson, plus the guy who invented the World Wide Web.
>
> That little list? It always happens. People construct a roster of famous yet diverse alumni when describing Oxford—the quirky sum even more fantastic than the successful parts—implying that greatness comes with the diploma. But a shadow lurks near those collections of names. Oxford University is full of students who will one day change the world, yes, but it is also full of those who have the gifts to change it and will fail. In the hope of morning, though, let your focus fall on Clinton and Donne, More and Kristofferson and now, as the dreamy purple light burns off, as busses chug and belch down the ancient streets and another week of reality begins, Myron Rolle.
>
> Rolle bounds down Banbury Road, long strides chewing up sidewalk, hurrying to his next lecture. Today's topic is "Pain and the Brain." He settles into a seat in the back of the room, the only student whose biceps strain against the fabric of his shirt. Around him, fellow Rhodes scholars open laptops, notebooks or leather-bound Moleskine journals. The

Myron Rolle at the Bodleian Library in Oxford, England, in 2009.

professor, a world-renowned researcher, begins speaking, about Pavlov and the curious case of Phineas Gage. The students take notes furiously.
—WRIGHT THOMPSON, "The Burden of Being Myron Rolle"

Wright Thompson wants his readers to imagine this specific place, Oxford University, at a specific time of day, "first light." He uses vivid details—"the purple sky throws shadows off churches," "busses chug and belch"—to create the scene that helps readers visualize Myron Rolle making his way to a lecture in this famous university town. You should strive, in your narratives, for the same kind of specificity and vividness. You don't want to confuse your audience with a muddled timeline or a vague location.

Vivid, Descriptive Details:
What Makes the Story Come Alive?

You may remember English teachers telling you that good writers "show rather than tell." It's an old adage that applies to narratives in particular.

Vivid, descriptive detail makes the people, places, and events in a narrative come alive for an audience, helping them see, hear, smell, taste, and feel "what happened." See how the following example from *ESPN Magazine* provides colorful detail that shows us Steph Curry's brilliant technique:

> Without ever taking his eyes off the rim, Curry moves to finish his shot. From his toes through his torso to the top of his head, his body is so vertical, he looks as if he's coming down from the ceiling, not jumping toward it. His shooting elbow passes shoulder height, still at a perfect 90-degree angle. And when his arms are straight and extended overhead—elbow over eye, shooters call it—the left hand opens. The path of the ball, like the elbow, stays clean and true, riding the beginning of a Vitruvian arc; it doesn't hitch backward over the crown of his head or veer to the side.
>
> Now the wrist begins its flection. The ball lifts off the tip of his index finger, then off the tip of his middle finger. His palm falls, his fingers now extended to the floor. The left arm stays perfectly still. The head never moves. . . .
>
> Before the game, boyish smile on his face, Curry had laughed, shrugging his shoulders and saying, yeah, he knows the second the ball leaves his hands. As his shot now begins its descent toward the rim, he drops both arms behind his back, palms up, chest out, like a bullfighter. Yeah, he knows. "There's a difference between shooters and shot makers," says [Jerry] West. "This kid is a shot maker."
>
> —DAVID FLEMING, "Sports' Perfect 0.4 Seconds"

Notice how the author slows down the action to show us each step in intricate detail—steps we can't possibly see or understand in the lightning-fast action of real time. With two powerful similes ("his body is so vertical, he looks as if he's coming down from the ceiling," "palms up, chest out, like a bullfighter"), Fleming's text brings Curry to life for readers.

Think about how much detail and what kind of detail your narrative needs to "come to life" for your audience. Remember that you are likely writing for readers (or listeners) unfamiliar with the story you are telling. That means that you need to choose details that help them get a vivid picture of the setting, people, and events in the narrative. When deciding whether to include direct quotations or dialogue, ask yourself if doing so would paint a scene or create a mood more effectively than a summary would.

Steph Curry elevates for a shot during the 2015 NBA finals.

A Consistent Point of View: Who's Telling the Story?

A good narrative is generally told from one consistent point of view. If you are writing about something that happened to you, then your narrative should be written from the first-person point of view (*I, we*). First person puts the focus on the narrator, as Georgina Kleege does in the following example, which recounts the opening moments of one of her classes:

> I tell the class, "I am legally blind." There is a pause, a collective intake of breath. I feel them look away uncertainly and then look back. After all, I just said I couldn't see. Or did I? I had managed to get there on my own—no cane, no dog, none of the usual trappings of blindness. Eyeing me askance now, they might detect that my gaze is not quite focused. My

eyes are aimed in the right direction but the gaze seems to stop short of touching anything. But other people do this, sighted people, normal people, especially in an awkward situation like this one, the first day of class. An actress who delivers an aside to the audience, breaking the "fourth wall" of the proscenium, will aim her gaze somewhere above any particular pair of eyes. If I hadn't said anything, my audience might understand my gaze to be like that, a part of the performance. In these few seconds between sentences, their gaze becomes intent. They watch me glance down, or toward the door where someone's coming in late. I'm just like anyone else. Then what did I actually mean by "legally blind"? They wait. I go on, "Some people would call me 'visually challenged.'" There is a ripple of laughter, an exhalation of relief. I'm making a joke about it. I'm poking fun at something they too find aggravating, the current mania to stick a verbal smiley-face on any human condition which deviates from the status quo. Differently abled. Handicapable. If I ask, I'm sure some of them can tell jokes about it: "Don't say 'bald,' say 'follicularly challenged.'" "He's not dead, he's metabolically stable." Knowing they are at least thinking these things, I conclude, "These are just silly ways of saying I don't see very well."   —GEORGINA KLEEGE, "Call It Blindness"

Notice how the first-person point of view—and the repetition of *I*—keep our attention focused on Kleege. Like the students in her class, we are looking right at her.

If your narrative is about someone else's experience or about events that you have researched but did not witness, then the narrative should probably be written in third person (*he, she, it, they*). Unlike a first-person narrative, a third-person narrative emphasizes someone or something other than the narrator. Historical and medical narratives are usually written in third person, as are newswriting and sportswriting. Look at the following account of the on-field actions leading up to the moment in 1985 when quarterback Joe Theismann was tackled by Lawrence Taylor, suffering a devastating, career-ending broken leg.

From the snap of the ball to the snap of the first bone is closer to four seconds than to five. One Mississippi: The quarterback of the Washington Redskins, Joe Theismann, turns and hands the ball to running back John Riggins. He watches Riggins run two steps forward, turn, and flip the ball back to him. . . . Two Mississippi: Theismann searches for a receiver but instead sees Harry Carson coming straight at him. It's a running down— the start of the second quarter, first and 10 at midfield, with the score

Athletic trainers surround Joe Theismann after a tackle by Lawrence Taylor broke Theismann's leg.

tied 7–7—and the New York Giants' linebacker has been so completely suckered by the fake that he's deep in the Redskins' backfield. Carson thinks he's come to tackle Riggins but Riggins is long gone, so Carson just keeps running, toward Theismann. Three Mississippi: Carson now sees that Theismann has the ball. Theismann notices Carson coming straight at him, and so he has time to avoid him. He steps up and to the side and Carson flies right on by and out of the play. The play is now 3.5 seconds old. Until this moment it has been defined by what the quarterback can see. Now it—and he—is at the mercy of what he can't see.

—MICHAEL LEWIS, *The Blind Side*

The opening sentence takes us right into the game, with "the snap of the ball." The repetition of "one Mississippi . . . two Mississippi . . ." marches us one excruciating second (and sentence) at a time through the actions that led to an injury that became the lead story on every sports broadcast that evening and for days to come. The photograph and caption tell the story of how that play ended for Theismann.

Compare the points of view of Georgina Kleege's first-person narrative and Michael Lewis's third-person one. Notice that there is one consistent point of view in each example. As an author, you will have to determine whether your narrative is most effective told from the first-person or third-person point of view. No matter what you may have been taught in high school, the first person is acceptable in many (though not all) academic contexts. Whatever point of view you use, however, do so consistently. That is, if you refer to yourself in the narrative, do not switch between first (*I, we*) and third (*he, she, they*) person. (Rarely is a narrative told from a second-person—*you*—point of view.)

Part of maintaining a consistent point of view is establishing a clear time frame. Notice Michael Lewis's use of present-tense verbs in the example from *The Blind Side*. By consistently narrating the actions in the game in the present tense, the narrator, much like a play-by-play announcer, places the reader in the moment of the story being told. Using a consistent verb tense situates the actions of the event within a clear time frame.

A clear time frame does not mean that every verb in the narrative has to be in the same tense, only that the writer establishes one primary tense—usually present or past—for the main action of the story. In the example by Mike Rose on page 165, most of the verbs are in the past tense: *said, made, talked*. But other tenses are used to indicate events that, in relation to the main action of the narrative, occurred earlier (*He had received his bachelor's degree from Loyola*) or might occur later (*I would be granted regular status*).

A Clear Point: Why Does the Story Matter?

See how historical events can produce deep personal consequences in Michelle Cacho-Negrete's narrative on p. 876.

Good narratives tell stories that matter. In academic writing in particular, narratives are told to make a point. Whether they begin by stating the point explicitly in a thesis or build toward a point that is expressed at the end, the purpose of the narrative needs to be clear to the audience. Nothing irritates an audience more than reading or listening to a story that has no point. Even if a story is interesting or entertaining, in an academic context, that story will most likely be deemed a failure if it does not make clear why the events matter. Consider how author and English professor bell hooks makes a point about learning to value work:

> "Work makes life sweet!" I often heard this phrase growing up, mainly from old black folks who did not have jobs in the traditional sense of the word. They were usually self-employed, living off the land, selling fishing worms, picking up an odd job here and there. They were people who had a passion for work. They took pride in a job done well. My Aunt

Margaret took in ironing. Folks brought her clothes from miles around because she was such an expert. That was in the days when using starch was common and she knew how to do an excellent job. Watching her iron with skill and grace was like watching a ballerina dance. Like all the other black girls raised in the fifties that I knew, it was clear to me that I would be a working woman. Even though our mother stayed home, raising her seven children, we saw her constantly at work, washing, ironing, cleaning, and cooking (she was an incredible cook). And she never allowed her six girls to imagine we would not be working women. No, she let us know that we would work and be proud to work.

> —BELL HOOKS, "Work Makes Life Sweet"

Hooks opens with her main point, that "work makes life sweet!" In the sentences that follow, she explains how she learned this lesson from "old black folks who did not have jobs in the traditional sense." Through specific examples, she illustrates how they "took pride in a job well done" and passed on this pride in one's work to hooks and her sisters. The explicit restatement of the point in the final sentence—that hooks and her six sisters learned from their mother that they would "work and be proud to work"—recasts the notion of "working woman" in a unique and engaging way.

Now take a look at how author Alice Walker, in a talk to students at Spelman College, leads up to an important point about the relationship between "oppressed hair" and spiritual growth. Walker starts by saying what she is not going to talk about:

> It may surprise you that I do not intend (until the question-and-answer period perhaps) to speak of war and peace, the economy, racism or sexism, or the triumphs and tribulations of black people or of women. Or even about movies. Though the discerning ear may hear my concern for some of these things in what I am about to say, I am going to talk about an issue even closer to home. I am going to talk about hair. Don't give a thought to the state of yours at the moment. Don't be at all alarmed. This is not an appraisal. I simply want to share with you some of my own experiences with our friend hair.

Alice Walker speaking at Spelman College.

Walker purposefully withholds her main point even after announcing her topic—hair. She instead describes the process of realizing that point for herself after letting go all attempts to control her hair, to fit it into some notion of "good" hair:

I found [my hair] to be springy, soft, almost sensually responsive to moisture. As the little braids spun off in all directions but the ones I tried to encourage them to go, I discovered my hair's willfulness, so like my own! I saw that my friend hair, given its own life, had a sense of humor. I discovered I liked it.

Again, I stood in front of the mirror and looked at myself and laughed. My hair was one of those odd, amazing, unbelievable, stop-you-in-your-tracks creations—not unlike a zebra's stripes, an armadillo's ears, or the feet of the electric blue-footed boobie—that the Universe makes for no reason other than to expose its own limitless imagination. I realized I had never been given the opportunity to appreciate hair for its true self. That it did, in fact, have one. I remembered years of enduring hairdressers—from my mother onward—doing missionary work on my hair. They dominated, suppressed, controlled. Now, more or less free, it stood this way and that. . . . It sought more and more space, more light, more of itself. It loved to be washed, but that was it.

Eventually, I knew *precisely* what hair wanted: it wanted to grow, to be itself, to attract lint, if that was its destiny, but to be left alone by anyone, including me, who did not love it as it was. What do you think happened? The ceiling at the top of my brain lifted, once again my mind (and spirit) could get outside itself. I would not be stuck in restless stillness, but would continue to grow.

—ALICE WALKER, "Oppressed Hair Puts a Ceiling on the Brain"

Read Alice Walker's full speech on p. 1088.

In contrast to bell hooks, Alice Walker moves slowly toward her main point, describing her years of worrying about her hair and of experimenting with it before coming to an important realization: her hair wants to be free. This realization leads into her major point, that liberating her hair liberated her mind and her spirit and allowed her to "continue to grow."

As an author, don't assume that your readers will recognize the point you're trying to make. No matter how interesting you think your story is, they need to know why they should care. Why is the story important? State your main point as bell hooks and Alice Walker do.

REFLECT. Look at a narrative in a newspaper or magazine article or on a blog or other website to see what main point it makes and how it does so. Is the main point explicitly stated in a thesis, or is it only implied? Does the narrative make clear to readers why the story is important or why they should care about it?

JAN BRIDEAU is a pediatric nurse practitioner at Massachusetts General Hospital in Boston. She worked in Louisiana in 2005 as part of Operation Helping Hand, a group from Massachusetts General that provided care and assessed medical needs in the aftermath of Hurricane Katrina. Brideau's essay was originally published in 2006 in *Health Affairs*, an American journal about national and global health policy and research issues.

Lydia's Story

JAN BRIDEAU

JUST BEFORE LEAVING LOUISIANA I met a small, slender black woman. She was in her sixties, with her short gray hair neatly tucked up inside a kerchief. Let's call her Lydia. An internist and I had traveled to a rural town's shelter housed in the VFW hall, the temporary home of seventy-some people.

The author opens her narrative by introducing us to an important person in her story.

Entering the large VFW hall, we were struck by the chemical odor of a cleaning solution so strong that it seemed toxic. The hall had no windows; only fluorescent lighting illuminated the large space. Coming from the hot, humid weather outdoors, we found the inside uncomfortably cold from air conditioning. The cackle of a television set was the only sound. There were several rows of cots and mattresses with a few people lying on them. Most of the shelter residents had left for the day, to work or do errands, but they were expected to return later. A local official told us that two adult residents needed medical care.

Vivid, descriptive details make the setting come to life.

One of these was Lydia, who had an abscessed tooth. Lydia was soft-spoken but eager to have her tooth examined. It turned out that she had been unable to chew on the affected side for several months. She hadn't been able to afford $25 for an x-ray, and she didn't have medical insurance; the pain, she told us, waxed and waned. Her cheek was quite tender, and it appeared that the tooth should be extracted. To address her immediate need, we started her on a course of antibiotics and made a note that a dentist should see her soon. The internist asked where she lived and if she knew how her family was doing.

Lydia told us that she lived alone in her home, located in the Eighth Ward in New Orleans, adjacent to that city's devastated Ninth Ward. As the first storm raged, she knew to avoid windows. (Interestingly, she never used the names "Katrina" or "Rita" when speaking about the hurricanes. She, like many people I met, referred to them as the "first storm" and the "second storm.")

Lydia took a sleeping bag into her windowless hallway. She slept on the floor for two nights. Then, one morning, she woke to find that her feet and the sleeping bag were soaking wet, and there was standing water throughout her house.

When she opened the front door, the whole street looked like a river, and water poured in. She described it as "rushing like the Colorado River." She knew that if she went outside, she would be swept up in the current and drown. There was no one in sight.

She was unable to shut the door against the brown rushing water. Horrified, she tried not to panic. Seeking higher ground, she climbed on top of her dining room table. It, like most of her furniture, had been handed down from her grandparents. The table was bulky and heavy; normally, it took three men to move it. But as the water continued to rise, the table started moving,

Rescue personnel searching for victims in New Orleans' Eighth Ward after Katrina struck in August 2005.

then rocking—and Lydia knew she was in trouble. She managed to climb up on her kitchen counter, but that soon became precarious as well. The water continued to rise quickly, and the water pressure was so strong that water spurted out of the kitchen sink like a fountain. Terrified of drowning, she kept reminding herself to think clearly.

The thing to do, she decided, was to find the highest spot in her one-story house. Lydia climbed off the kitchen counter and waded through the deep water, dragging a small kitchen stool behind her. She positioned the stool in front of her linen closet, propping one foot on the stool and the other on the doorknob; then she climbed to the top shelf of her linen closet. She described the shelf area as about three feet wide and about a foot and a half tall. Crouched there, she watched the water continue to rise. Her ceilings, she knew, were twelve feet tall. The water rose to above her height, then to above six feet, finally to about seven feet. (She could estimate numbers, she said, because she had gone to nursing school long ago. Eventually, she had to leave nursing because she cried over her patients' conditions too much, and they ended up consoling her.)

A detail that tells us something about Lydia's character.

Lydia waited, cramped on the top shelf of the linen closet, until the water finally began to recede. When we asked if she got hungry or thirsty, she said that she didn't remember feeling that way. Her tongue became dry and her lips were cracked, but she only was aware of being terrified of the water. When the water receded to about five feet, it was five days later. She was finally able to come down from her perch. The water was up to her chin.

She tried to open the back door near the linen closet. But the wood had swollen from the water, and it wouldn't budge. She knew that the windows were probably swollen shut, too. Then she remembered that she'd never closed the front door because of the strong current. She moved through the water, out the front door, and onto her front porch. She couldn't recall how long she waited alone in the water, holding onto a porch post and screaming for help. Eventually, a far neighbor with a boat rescued her and took her to a larger rescue boat. Then that boat dropped her off at an overpass where, in the sun and the heat, she and a large group of other people waited without food or water.

A clear progression of events helps us picture what happened.

At some point, a small van drove up and stopped directly in front of her. A female driver, dressed in scrubs, jumped out. The van was loaded with medical supplies, and there was room for only one person; she ordered Lydia to get in. The woman told Lydia that she worked in the emergency room of a local hospital and was soon to become a physician. She drove Lydia to a shelter.

As Lydia was telling us her story, I heard strength and resolve in her voice. She was proud that she had "kept her head," which had saved her life. She knew that she didn't have a home to return to, that everything in it was probably destroyed. There was, however, a reason for her to return home one last time. She needed to get back to that linen closet. There, on the top shelf, was her family photo album. It was the only thing Lydia thought might have survived the water. It would be the only thing from her past that she could take with her on her new journey.

The conclusion tells the significance of Lydia's experience, why her story matters.

For me, the enormity of the double hurricanes became clear only after witnessing so many people left without homes. Everywhere we traveled in Louisiana, there were countless people in shelters that had once been a hotel, convention center, sports arena, school, church, YMCA, and, yes, the VFW hall where I met Lydia. It was my privilege to meet and serve them. But it's Lydia's story that stays with me most, probably because it represents the essence of hope and determination in the face of terrible adversity.

REFLECT. *Analyze a short nonfiction narrative that you find in a magazine or on a website. Look at the list of five characteristic features of narratives on p. 164 and annotate the essay to point out these features, using Brideau's essay as a model. Then look at your annotations and the parts of the text they refer to and evaluate how well your chosen narrative illustrates the characteristic features. For example, is the setting clearly described? How vivid are the details?*

LITERACY NARRATIVES

Literacy narratives focus on meaningful experiences with some kind of reading or writing: stories, music, computer code, learning a foreign language, and so on. The focus on learning and literacy makes this sort of narrative a common assignment in first-year writing classes. Professional writers also use the genre to reflect on their craft. Literacy narratives can serve various purposes, but they generally have the following characteristic features.

A Well-Told Story

Whether you're writing about how you learned to do something (or struggled to do so) or why you've always loved a certain book or song, there are some tried-and-true storytelling techniques that can help your literacy narrative interest readers. If you write about something you struggled to learn, for instance, readers will want to know how it turned out, how the story ends. And whatever your topic, make sure your narrative has a clear arc, from a beginning that engages your audience to a conclusion that leaves them understanding why the experience you wrote about matters to you.

A Firsthand Account, Often (but Not Always) about Yourself

You'll want to write about an experience that you know firsthand, not one that you've only read about. Writing about your own experience is the most common way of achieving this close perspective, but you may also reflect on the experiences of others. Perhaps you've observed or had a hand in helping someone else learn to read or write and are able to speak about it firsthand. This, too, could be a productive topic for a literacy narrative.

An Indication of the Narrative's Significance

Readers quickly lose patience with stories that seem to have no point, so you need to make clear what significance your narrative has for those involved. Sometimes you may have an explicit THESIS that makes the point clear from the start; other times, you may prefer to let the narrative play out before explaining its significance.

MELANIE LUKEN was a senior French and English major at The Ohio State University when she wrote this literacy narrative for an English course in which she was being trained to be a writing tutor.

Literacy: A Lineage

MELANIE LUKEN

The author makes her point clear from the start: her father played a large role in her love of reading and writing.

IT WOULD BE IMPOSSIBLE to discuss my path to literacy without talking about my literary guardian, the person who inspired and encouraged my love for reading and writing: my father. I spent a lot of time with my dad as a child, but one of the most important experiences we shared was our Sunday afternoon bike rides. We nearly always took the same route, down to the bike path by the river, circling around, and breaking at Carillon Park under the bell tower. We would just sit, rest, and think under the bells. Etched at the bottom of the bell tower was part of a poem by Henry Wadsworth Longfellow:

> It was as if an earthquake rent
> The hearth-stones of a continent,
> And made forlorn
> The households born
> Of peace on earth, good-will to men!
> And in despair I bowed my head;
> "There is no peace on earth," I said;
> "For hate is strong,

And mocks the song
Of peace on earth, good-will to men!"
Then pealed the bells more loud and deep:
"God is not dead; nor doth he sleep;
The Wrong shall fail,
The Right prevail,
With peace on earth, good-will to men." (lines 21–35)

My dad would inevitably read it aloud, but we both knew it by heart; it is one of the many poems that have come to mean something to me. As I got older, my dad didn't come riding as often with me. He was older and more tired, but I still went by myself. Each time I arrived under the bells, I would recite the poem to myself, even when the weather was cold and my breath made the air foggy. It had become part of me, this poem, this tradition of riding and reading and thinking. In the same way, my passion for reading and writing developed in me through the influence of my father who has a deep love of literature himself. For this reason, my definition of literacy involves more than the ability to read and write; for me, it is also a tradition, an inheritance I received from my father, and an ability to appreciate language because of him and because of many other writers who came before me.

Engaging details draw readers into the story.

You could define my dad as a jack-of-all-trades artist. He has dabbled in almost every art: novel-writing, poetry-writing, song-writing, painting, sculpture, and acting. He was originally in graduate school for English with hopes of becoming a professor. After a couple of years, however, he tired of academia. His tendencies towards creativity and individuality did not mix well with the intense analysis and structure of university life. Eventually, he ended up as a stay-at-home dad, *my* stay-at-home dad, who continues to this day to work on his art and writing. Although our relationship has not always been simple and easy, I benefited greatly from having such an intelligent and imaginative father as my primary caretaker.

For my whole life, my father has quoted the "greats," the "classics," or at least the authors that he admired, in normal conversation. It has become a joke among me and my brothers because we can all recite from memory his favorite lines of books and his favorite poems. Because of him I can quote, "If you can keep your

Vivid details and classic lines from literature bring the story to life.

head when all about you / Are losing theirs and blaming it on you" (Kipling lines 1–2), "And early though the laurel grows / It withers quicker than the rose" (Housman lines 11–12), "I grow old . . . I grow old . . . / I shall wear the bottoms of my trousers rolled" (Eliot lines 120–21), and of course, "Call Me Ishmael" (Melville 3), among many others. Sometimes he will quote things far out of context, and yet I understand and enjoy it because these quotes evoke intense feelings of tradition and love. My father's love of literature pervaded my young mind the way it must pervade his own, and it has stayed with me.

A firsthand account, told from a first-person point of view.

From the time I could read and write, I wrote and acted out princess stories all on my own. I read vociferously, and I loved being told stories. I attribute all of this to my father, who taught me to read and to write, who put *Little Women* in my hands when I was ten years old, and who continued to introduce me to his favorite authors as I got older. The only reason I picked up books like *The Heart Is a Lonely Hunter* or Capote's *Other Voices, Other Rooms*, is because he suggested them or handed them to me. I realize that I did not have a particularly normal American childhood in terms of my relationship with books and literature (most of my friends preferred playing sports or watching TV to reading), but I am blessed to have a father who sees art in language and stories and who passed this gift to me. I have a greater understanding of the diversity of books, authors, and the ways in which language is used because of my father. He always pushed me to read literature other than what I read in school and particularly encouraged me to read female writers like Carson McCullers, Zora Neale Hurston, and Flannery O'Connor to empower me as a young girl and to expand my perspective. Now, everything I read is within this tradition that he and I have established.

Another thing that I vividly remember as a child is spending quite a bit of time in public libraries. My brothers, my dad, and I would visit the library at least once a week, and more often in the summer when we were out of school. We were never allowed to play video games or watch much TV, so our entertainment consisted of what we could create ourselves or what we could gain from books. Our ability to use and understand language proficiently was very important to my father. Although I am the only child who has displayed a penchant for creative writing, I think my father has always held on to the hope that each of his children will spring into novel-writers. Since we were about twelve or thirteen, he has consistently demanded that we each write a story for him at Christmastime rather than buy him a gift. His favorite is a story I wrote for him in high school; it was my own personal version of *A Christmas Carol.*

I began seriously writing creatively towards the end of high school. I have kept journals since I was eight or nine, but in high school, I discovered my true capacity for poetry. I wrote poetry for English classes and for our high school literary magazine. When I got to college, I naturally began taking creative writing classes. I have taken Beginning Poetry, Intermediate Poetry twice, and the Honors 598 seminar with a creative writing component. I improve constantly and with each class my relationship to language changes and grows. Anyone who has taken a workshop knows that, in these courses, you have to be able to stand criticism and to pick out which suggestions are beneficial and which are not. It was my father, the constant in my literacy narrative, who encouraged me through all of these classes, telling me that no matter what anybody thought, I was a poet, a better poet than he had ever been.

I believe that my choice to major in French is also rooted in this tradition of language and literature. Studying a foreign language can, at times, be just like learning how to read and write as a child. Studying French intensely became for me the perfect, impossible challenge: to read and write French like I read and write English. However, it seems that as long and hard as I study French, I will never be quite so comfortable nor quite so capable of understanding it or placing it within a context. I believe that this is partially because tradition plays no role in my study of French. It has nothing to do with my family or my background, and it cannot move me emotionally to the extent that English language can. Unlike French, I have a tradition of reading, speaking, and writing English, and I have a much vaster appreciation for English literature in general.

Because of my father and our shared love of literature, my definition of literacy is intimately linked to the idea of tradition. In a way, my literacy is part of my lineage, part of the legacy of my father. My love for literature and writing, my poetic tendencies, my passion for language are all gifts from him. I think that I tend to have more of an imagination than my peers, and I also love to write and create using words. The reason for these qualities is that my father once

A clear indication of why this story matters to the author.

inspired in me his own creativity and instructed me on the understanding of human experience through writing. In turn, this literacy experience is something I want to pass on to my children someday.

Literacy is generally known as the ability to read and write. My definition of literacy is: the ability to read, write, and understand within a tradition. For me, this is a familial tradition that has permeated my literacy experience. Parents have an incredible power to influence their children through their own behaviors and attitudes, and it is certainly true that my father has impressed upon me his own attitudes towards literacy and literature. Now, every time we talk he asks me, "What are you reading? What do you think about it?" We talk about what each of us is reading, as well as our thoughts and impressions. In this way, the tradition continues.

Some daughters inherit a certain amount of money from their fathers. Some inherit a car or a house. Others inherit jewelry. My father will never have much money or a nice car or many material goods at all. I have, however, received something from him that will last my whole life and will continue to give me joy as long as I live. He has passed on to me his love of language and literature. It is within this tradition that I understand literacy, a tradition that causes me to sometimes think "God is not dead; nor doth he sleep!" (Longfellow 32) when I hear bells ringing.

> The author concludes with a strong statement about why this story is so meaningful.

Works Cited

Eliot, T. S. "The Love Song of J. Alfred Prufrock." *Poets.org.*
  Academy of American Poets, n.d. Web. 12 Oct. 2009.
Housman, A. E. "To an Athlete Dying Young." *Poets.org.*
  Academy of American Poets, n.d. Web. 12 Oct. 2009.
Kipling, Rudyard. "If." *Poets.org.* Academy of American Poets, n.d.
  Web. 12 Oct. 2009.
Longfellow, Henry Wadsworth. "Christmas Bells." *Poets.org.*
  Academy of American Poets, n.d. Web. 12 Oct. 2009.
Melville, Herman. *Moby-Dick.* New York: Penguin Books, 1988.
  Print.

REFLECT on your own experiences as a writer or reader. Identify one person who played a key role in your developing literacy. What did he or she teach you, and how? Whatever it was, what impact has it had on your life?

WRITING A NARRATIVE / A Roadmap

Choose a topic that matters—to you, and to others

Whether you write a narrative for personal reasons or in response to an assignment, choose your own topic or work with an assigned topic, try to write about something that matters to you—and try to make sure that it will matter to your audience as well.

If you are writing a personal narrative, choosing a topic can be difficult because you are deciding to share something personal about yourself or someone you know. You will need to choose an experience or event that you feel comfortable sharing, in some detail, with an audience. Be sure that the experience is not only important to you but is also of enough general interest to engage your audience.

If your narrative is not a personal one, you still want it to be compelling. Narratives that aren't personal are often part of a larger conversation about an event, or some topic that the event represents, which gives the story significance. For example, if you are writing a narrative about how specific students' academic performances changed when they enrolled in a charter school, you need to recognize that such stories are part of an ongoing educational and political debate about the effectiveness of charter schools as an alternative to traditional public schools. You may need to do some research to understand this debate and how your narrative fits into it.

Consider your rhetorical situation

Whenever you write a narrative (or anything, for that matter) you need to consider the following elements of your rhetorical situation:

Think about your AUDIENCE. Who will be reading what you write, and what's your relationship with them?

- Will your audience have any knowledge about your topic? Will you need to explain anything or provide any background information?
- How are they like or unlike you? Consider age, gender, income, cultural heritage, political beliefs, and so on. How will such factors affect how you tell the story?

- Can you assume they'll be interested in what you write? How can you get them interested?
- How are they likely to react to your narrative? What do you want them to think or do as a result of reading what you say?

Think about your PURPOSE. Why are you writing this narrative? What is the significance of this story, and what do you hope it will demonstrate to your readers? Remember that your narrative needs to do more than just tell an engaging story; it needs to make a point of some kind.

Think about your STANCE. Are you telling a story that is very personal to you, or is it one you have some distance from? How do you want to present yourself as the narrator? Do you want to come across as witty and amusing, if you're telling a humorous family story? As knowledgeable but impersonal, if you're recounting historical events for a political science essay? Whatever your stance, how can you make your writing reflect that stance?

Consider the larger CONTEXT. What broader issues are involved in your narrative? What else has been said and written about this topic? Even if your narrative is personal, how might it speak to some larger topic—perhaps a social or political one? Considering the larger context for your narrative can help you see it from perspectives different from your own, and present it in a way that will interest others.

Consider your MEDIUM. Often you won't have a choice—but if you do, think about which medium best suits your goals and audience. The kinds of details you include, the language you use, the way you present materials from sources, and many other things depend on the medium. The conventions of a print essay, for instance, in which you can use written words and images, differ markedly from those of an audio essay (in which you can use sounds but no written words or images).

Consider matters of DESIGN. Does your narrative need headings? Is there anything in the story that could be conveyed better with a photograph than with words alone? Will embedded audio or video clips help you engage your audience? Often in academic writing, you may be expected to use a font and type size or to structure headings a certain way. If you can determine the look of your text, though, remember that design has a powerful impact on the impression your narrative makes.

Explore your topic and do any necessary research

If you are writing a personal narrative, write down all that you remember about your topic. Using **FREEWRITING** or other activities for **GENERATING IDEAS**, write down as many specific details as you can: sounds, smells, textures, colors, and so on. What details will engage your audience? Not all the details that you jot down in this exploratory stage will make it into your essay. You'll need to choose the ones that will engage your audience and support your main point. In addition to sensory details, try to write down direct quotations or dialogue you can remember that will help bring your story to life.

If your narrative is not a personal one, you'll likely need to conduct **RESEARCH** so that you can provide accurate and sufficient details about the topic. Whether your research takes you to sources in the library or online, or into the community to conduct interviews, it's important to get the what, when, and where of the narrative right, and consulting sources will help you do that. The point is that when you write a narrative that is not personal, you'll need to rely on more than your memory for the content.

Decide on a point of view

The subject that you choose to write about will usually determine the point of view from which you write. If you're telling a story in which you are a central participant, you will usually use the first person (*I, we*). In some academic disciplines, however, or if you're narrating a story that is not personal, the third person (*he, she, they*) may be more appropriate.

Also think about what verb tense would be most effective for establishing the point of view in your narrative. Most personal narratives that are arranged in chronological order are written in the past tense ("When I *was* twelve, I *discovered* what I *wanted* to do for the rest of my life"). However, if you want readers to feel like they are actually experiencing an event, you may choose to use the present tense, as Georgina Kleege and Wright Thompson do in examples earlier in this chapter.

Organize and start writing

Once you've chosen a subject and identified your main point, considered your rhetorical situation, come up with enough details, and decided on a point of view (not necessarily in this order), it's time to think about how to organize your narrative.

Keep your main point in mind. As you begin to draft, type out that point as a tentative **THESIS** and keep your eye on it as you write; you can decide later whether you want to include it in your text.

Organize your information. What happened? Where? When? Who was there? What details can you describe to make the story come alive? Decide whether to present the narrative in **CHRONOLOGICAL** order, in reverse chronological order, or in some other order.

Draft an OPENING. A good introduction draws your audience into the story and makes them want to know more. Sometimes you'll need to provide a context for your narrative—to describe the setting and introduce some of the people before getting on with what happened. Other times you might start in the middle of your story, or at the end—and then circle back to tell what happened.

Draft a CONCLUSION. If you organize your narrative chronologically, you'll likely conclude by telling how the story ends. But make sure your readers see the point of your story; if you haven't made that clear, you might end by saying something about the story's significance. Why does it matter to you? What do you want readers to take away—and remember?

Look critically at your draft, get response—and revise

Read your draft slowly and carefully. Try to see it as if for the first time: Does the story grab your attention, and can you follow it? Can you tell what the point is, and will your audience care? If at all possible, get feedback from others. Following are some questions that can help you or others examine a narrative with a critical eye:

- *How does the **OPENING** capture the audience's interest?* Is it clear why you're telling the story, and have you given readers reason to want to find out what happened? How else might the narrative begin?

- *Who's telling the story?* Have you maintained a consistent **POINT OF VIEW**?

- *Is the setting of your story clear?* Have you situated the events in a well-described time and place?

- *Is the story easy to follow?* If it's at all confusing, would **TRANSITIONS** help your audience follow the sequence of events? If it's a lengthy or complex narrative, would headings help?

- *Are there enough vivid, concrete details?* Is there an appropriate balance of showing and telling? Have you included any dialogue or direct quotations—and if not, would adding some help the story come alive?

- *Are there any visuals?* If not, would adding some help bring the narrative to life?

- *How do you establish* **AUTHORITY** *and credibility?* How would you describe the **STANCE** and **TONE**—and are they appropriate for your audience and purpose?

- *Does the story have a clear point?* Is the point stated explicitly—and if not, should it be? If the main point is implied rather than stated, is the significance of the narrative still clear?

- *How satisfying is the* **CONCLUSION**? What does it leave the audience thinking? How else might the narrative end?

- *Does the title suggest what the narrative is about,* and will it make an audience want to read on?

Revise your draft in light of any feedback you receive and your own critique, keeping your purpose and especially your audience firmly in mind.

REFLECT. Once you've completed your narrative, let it settle for a while and then take time to reflect. How well did you tell the story? What additional revisions would you make if you could? Research shows that such reflections help "lock in" what you learn for future use.

Liar's Poker

MICHAEL LEWIS

I T WAS SOMETIME EARLY IN **1986**, the first year of the decline of my firm, Salomon Brothers. Our chairman, John Gutfreund, left his desk at the head of the trading floor and went for a walk. At any given moment on the trading floor billions of dollars were being risked by bond traders. Gutfreund took the pulse of the place by simply wandering around it and asking questions of the traders. An eerie sixth sense guided him to wherever a crisis was unfolding. Gutfreund seemed able to smell money being lost.

He was the last person a nerve-racked trader wanted to see. Gutfreund (pronounced *Good friend*) liked to sneak up from behind and surprise you. This was fun for him but not for you. Busy on two phones at once trying to stem disaster, you had no time to turn and look. You didn't need to. You felt him. The area around you began to convulse like an epileptic ward. People were pretending to be frantically busy and at the same time staring intently at a spot directly above your head. You felt a chill in your bones that I imagine belongs to the same class of intelligence as the nervous twitch of a small furry animal at the silent approach of a grizzly bear. An alarm shrieked in your head: Gutfreund! Gutfreund! Gutfreund!

MICHAEL LEWIS is the author of many best-selling books, including *Moneyball* (2003), *The Blind Side* (2006), and *Flash Boys* (2014). The selection here is the first chapter in *Liar's Poker: Rising through the Wreckage on Wall Street* (1989), which is based on Lewis's experiences as a bond salesman.

Often as not, our chairman just hovered quietly for a bit, then left. You might never have seen him. The only trace I found of him on two of these occasions was a turdlike ash on the floor beside my chair, left, I suppose, as a calling card. Gutfreund's cigar droppings were longer and better formed than those of the average Salomon boss. I always assumed that he smoked a more expensive blend than the rest, purchased with a few of the $40 million he had cleared on the sale of Salomon Brothers in 1981 (or a few of the $3.1 million he paid himself in 1986, more than any other Wall Street CEO).

This day in 1986, however, Gutfreund did something strange. Instead of terrifying us all, he walked a straight line to the trading desk of John Meriwether, a member of the board of Salomon Inc. and also one of Salomon's finest bond traders. He whispered a few words. The traders in the vicinity eavesdropped. What Gutfreund said has become a legend at Salomon Brothers and a visceral part of its corporate identity. He said: "One hand, one million dollars, no tears."

One hand, one million dollars, no tears. Meriwether grabbed the meaning   5 instantly. The King of Wall Street, as *Business Week* had dubbed Gutfreund, wanted to play a single hand of a game called Liar's Poker for a million dollars. He played the game most afternoons with Meriwether and the six young bond arbitrage traders who worked for Meriwether and was usually skinned alive. Some traders said Gutfreund was heavily outmatched. Others who couldn't imagine John Gutfreund as anything but omnipotent—and there were many—said that losing suited his purpose, though exactly what that might be was a mystery.

The peculiar feature of Gutfreund's challenge this time was the size of the stake. Normally his bets didn't exceed a few hundred dollars. A million was unheard of. The final two words of his challenge, "no tears," meant that the loser was expected to suffer a great deal of pain but wasn't entitled to whine, bitch, or moan about it. He'd just have to hunker down and keep his poverty to himself. But why? You might ask if you were anyone other than the King of Wall Street. Why do it in the first place? Why, in particular, challenge Meriwether instead of some lesser managing director? It seemed an act of sheer lunacy. Meriwether was the King of the Game, the Liar's Poker champion of the Salomon Brothers trading floor.

On the other hand, one thing you learn on a trading floor is that winners like Gutfreund always have some reason for what they do; it might not be the best of reasons, but at least they have a concept in mind. I was not privy to Gutfreund's innermost thoughts, but I do know that all the boys on the trading floor gambled and that he wanted badly to be one of the boys. What I think Gutfreund had in mind in this instance was a desire to show his courage, like the boy who leaps from the high dive. Who better than Meriwether for the purpose? Besides, Meriwether was probably the only trader with both the cash and the nerve to play.

The whole absurd situation needs putting into context. John Meriwether had, in the course of his career, made hundreds of millions of dollars for Salomon Brothers. He had an ability, rare among people and treasured by traders, to hide his state of mind. Most traders divulge whether they are making or losing money by the way they speak or move. They are either overly easy or overly tense. With Meriwether you could never, ever tell. He wore the same blank half-tense expression when he won as he did when he lost. He had, I think, a profound ability to control the two emotions that commonly destroy traders—fear and greed—and it made him as noble as a man who pursues his self-interest so fiercely can be. He was thought by many within Salomon to be the best bond trader on Wall Street. Around Salomon no tone but awe was used when he was discussed. People would say, "He's the best businessman in the place," or "the best risk taker I have ever seen," or "a very dangerous Liar's Poker player."

Meriwether cast a spell over the young traders who worked for him. His boys ranged in age from twenty-five to thirty-two (he was about forty). Most of them had Ph.D.'s in math, economics, and/or physics. Once they got onto Meriwether's trading desk, however, they forgot they were supposed to be detached intellectuals. They became disciples. They became obsessed by the game of Liar's Poker. They regarded it as *their* game. And they took it to a new level of seriousness.

John Gutfreund was always the outsider in their game. That *Business Week* ¹⁰ put his picture on the cover and called him the King of Wall Street held little significance for them. I mean, that was, in a way, the whole point. Gutfreund was the King of Wall Street, but Meriwether was King of the Game. When Gutfreund had been crowned by the gentlemen of the press, you could almost hear traders thinking: *Foolish names and foolish faces often appear in public places.* Fair enough, Gutfreund had once been a trader, but that was as relevant as an old woman's claim that she was once quite a dish.

At times Gutfreund himself seemed to agree. He loved to trade. Compared with managing, trading was admirably direct. You made your bets and either you won or you lost. When you won, people—all the way up to the top of the firm—admired you, envied you, and feared you, and with reason: You controlled the loot. When you managed a firm, well, sure you received your quota of envy, fear, and admiration. But for all the wrong reasons. *You did not make the money for Salomon. You did not take risk.* You were hostage to your producers.

They took risk. They proved their superiority every day by handling risk better than the rest of the risk-taking world. The money came from risk takers such as Meriwether, and whether it came or not was really beyond Gutfreund's control. That's why many people thought that the single rash act of challenging the arbitrage boss to one hand for a million dollars was Gutfreund's way of showing he was a player, too. And if you wanted to show off, Liar's Poker was the only way to go. The game had a powerful meaning for traders. People like John Meriwether believed that Liar's Poker had a lot in common with bond trading. It tested a trader's character. It honed a trader's instincts. A good player made a good trader, and vice versa. We all understood it.

The Game: In Liar's Poker a group of people—as few as two, as many as ten—form a circle. Each player holds a dollar bill close to his chest. The game is similar in spirit to the card game known as I Doubt It. Each player attempts to fool the others about the serial numbers printed on the face of his dollar bill. One trader begins by making "a bid." He says, for example, "Three sixes." He means that all told the serial numbers of the dollar bills held by every player, including himself, contain at least three sixes.

Once the first bid has been made, the game moves clockwise in the circle. Let's say the bid is three sixes. The player to the left of the bidder can do one of two things. He can bid higher (there are two sorts of higher bids: the same quantity of a higher number [three sevens, eights, or nines] and more of any number [four fives, for instance]). Or he can "challenge"—that is like saying, "I doubt it."

The bidding escalates until all the other players agree to challenge a single player's bid. Then, and only then, do the players reveal their serial numbers and determine who is bluffing whom. In the midst of all this, the mind of a good player spins with probabilities. What is the statistical likelihood of there being three sixes within a batch of, say, forty randomly generated serial numbers? For a great player, however, the math is the easy part of the game. The hard part is reading the faces of the other players. The complexity arises when all players know how to bluff and double-bluff.

The game has some of the feel of trading, just as jousting has some of the feel of war. The questions a Liar's Poker player asks himself are, up to a point, the same questions a bond trader asks himself. Is this a smart risk? Do I feel lucky? How cunning is my opponent? Does he have any idea what he's doing, and if not, how do I exploit his ignorance? If he bids high, is he bluffing, or does he actually hold a strong hand? Is he trying to induce me to make a foolish bid, or does he actually have four of a kind himself? Each player seeks weakness, predictability, and pattern in the others and seeks to avoid it in himself. The bond traders of Goldman, Sachs, First Boston, Morgan Stanley, Merrill Lynch, and other Wall Street firms all play some version of Liar's Poker. But the place where the stakes run highest, thanks to John Meriwether, is the New York bond trading floor of Salomon Brothers.

The code of the Liar's Poker player was something like the code of the gunslinger. It required a trader to accept all challenges. Because of the code—which was *his* code—John Meriwether felt obliged to play. But he knew it was stupid. For him, there was no upside. If he won, he upset Gutfreund. No good came of this. But if he lost, he was out of pocket a million bucks. This was worse than upsetting the boss. Although Meriwether was by far the better player of the game, in a single hand anything could happen. Luck could very well determine the outcome. Meriwether spent his entire day avoiding dumb bets, and he wasn't about to accept this one.

"No, John," he said, "if we're going to play for those kind of numbers, I'd rather play for real money. Ten million dollars. No tears."

Ten million dollars. It was a moment for all players to savor. Meriwether was playing Liar's Poker before the game even started. He was bluffing. Gutfreund considered the counterproposal. It would have been just like him to accept. Merely to entertain the thought was a luxury that must have pleased him well. (It was good to be rich.)

On the other hand, ten million dollars was, and is, a lot of money. If Gutfreund lost, he'd have only thirty million or so left. His wife, Susan, was busy spending the better part of fifteen million dollars redecorating their Manhattan apartment (Meriwether knew this). And as Gutfreund was the boss, he clearly wasn't bound by the Meriwether code. Who knows? Maybe he didn't even know the Meriwether code. Maybe the whole point of his challenge was to judge Meriwether's response. (Even Gutfreund had to marvel at the king in action.) So Gutfreund declined. In fact, he smiled his own brand of forced smile and said, "You're crazy."

No, thought Meriwether, just very, very good.   20

Thinking about the Text

1. Michael Lewis says that Liar's Poker "has some of the feel of trading, just as jousting has some of the feel of war." What exactly does this **ANALOGY** say about Wall Street? What point did you take away from Lewis's story?

2. How does Lewis use **DESCRIPTION** to help bring his story to life? Find two examples that you find especially vivid and explain what they add to his argument.

3. The events of the story, from Gutfreund's challenge to Meriwether's reply, probably took less than a minute, yet Lewis takes several pages to describe them. How does he build suspense and keep readers engaged?

4. How would you describe Lewis's **TONE**? What words and phrases help create that tone—and what does it convey about his attitude toward Gutfreund, Meriwether, and the others he describes on the Salomon trading floor?

5. Write a **NARRATIVE** about a game—chess, *Angry Birds*, soccer, whatever—describing in detail how it works and why you enjoy it (or not).

The Look

LARRY LEHNA

IFEAR THAT I CARRY FAR MORE BAGGAGE than the typical college student. Unlike Frank Sinatra, regrets I have more than "a few," and even if I do not mention them they weigh heavily upon me. I sometimes regret my wasted life. Then I stop and wonder if it was really wasted. There are so many things I did not accomplish. However, I helped to raise a fine son and he was almost through college before my downfall. My step-daughters were seven and sixteen when I was sent to prison. Yet they both wrote to me for the full eleven years. At different times they have both told me that I am the only real father they have known. Each of them now has children of her own whom I dote upon. So even among the regrets is a modicum of satisfaction.

Always present are my scars, both physical and mental. Mine was not an easy life. I carry many memories. The burning pain of bullet wounds (they really do burn). The agony of stitches going into a fresh knife wound. The nearly immobilizing ache of broken ribs. But most of all I carry emotions. The anguish of being arrested. The despair over lost loves. The disappointment of unfulfilled dreams. I am an emotional cauldron. There is a reason for this.

For eleven years I could not show any emotion. When you go to prison you put on a mask called a "Marquette," the name of Michigan's toughest prison.

LARRY LEHNA was a student at University of Michigan–Dearborn at the time that he wrote this essay for a narrative journalism class. He is now working on an autobiography, of which this story is an important part.

The look says, "I'm tough, I like to fight, and I would just love to hurt you. So mess with me if you dare." When I was in jail awaiting my sentencing I spent hours glaring into the mirror trying to perfect the look, but what gazed back at me was a look that said instead, "I'm constipated." I concluded I would never achieve that look. Little did I know that it would come naturally.

When I was sentenced to ten to thirty years in prison I was stunned. I wanted to cry. I wanted to be hugged. I wanted my mommy. I wanted to hurt someone, but I knew I should not show any emotion. That is when the look appeared on my face. When I got back to the cell-block I noticed a new-found wariness from the other prisoners. They kept their distance. When I went to the bathroom I glanced in the mirror. There it was: the look I would wear for over eleven years, the look that acted like a stopper in the bottle of my emotions. Nothing could faze me, and nothing did. It was more than a look; it was an attitude that was much more severe than mere stoicism. No emotions in, no emotions out.

Over the course of my first year that attitude became ingrained. Part of it 5 was always expecting the worst. I learned to never anticipate anything good from my fellow prisoners or from the institution. When they denied my first attempt at parole, after ten years, I received the information with the same deadpan expression as if they were handing me a pair of socks.

When I finally received my parole I wore the same look. I assumed they would take my parole away, and they did postpone it six months because I had once assaulted a thieving bunkmate. Another bit of news that had no visible effect. I no longer had to try to hide my feelings; I no longer felt any.

When I was released I was sent to a halfway house in Pontiac, one of the few cities in the country in worse shape than Detroit. There were absolutely no job prospects. Add to this the fact that a minimum of three days a week I had to report to either parole, or one of their programs, such as their Job Shop. What a joke. They acted as if they actually spoke with the people offering the jobs. They never did. They found the ads online and printed them. It did not bother these people to send us miles away to apply only to find out that the employer would not even consider a felon. Meanwhile, the amount they spent on counseling and other programs was enormous. It would have been enough to offer a parolee a fresh start, with a car and an apartment and a little bit of a chance at success. But let's not cloud this issue with logic.

The programs, too, were miles away in different directions. It was winter when I was released. I plodded through the snow wearing my cheap state shoes and the look. Whatever they got, I could take it. I only had 90 days to make something happen, and then I had to leave the halfway house. With less than a week left I told my parole officer that I had nowhere to go. When she suggested the homeless shelter, I took her response with a simple nod of my head and the look. With one day to spare I found a place where I could work for my room and board; I was glad to avoid the shelter, but I don't recall a feeling of happiness.

Once ensconced in my palatial new digs, I found my room was actually smaller than my prison cell, but it was all mine. No bunkie for me, but otherwise I continued on as I had done for the past eleven years. I was existing. I had learned that if I applied for a FAFSA educational grant they would pay for my schooling and give me whatever was left over in a check. I applied, was accepted and I made an appointment to see a counselor at Oakland Community College. I expected resistance, having experienced nothing but rejection for the last eleven years. The Secretary of State made it almost impossible to get a driver's license once they saw my prison ID card. Society did not like me; they too had a look when they learned of my past. That was just fine; I didn't like them in return. The pressure was building up like Mount St. Helens.

I arrived for my appointment at OCC less than two weeks before classes   10 were to begin. They ushered me into the office of a woman named Noreen Ruehs. I was fully prepared for her to adopt the look and I was ready to set the counselor straight about how little I cared about her and her fancy college job.

When I told her about my past she raised her eyebrows, nodded and said, "Well, you have some catching up to do. Let's see what kind of degree would suit you best." She proffered a few small pamphlets and suggested I look over the one for General Studies. She asked if I knew about computers. When I admitted my ignorance she recommended a Computer Literacy class. She asked about my typing skills and suggested a keyboarding class. We soon had my whole schedule full and all of it at very convenient times. Her kindness had a remarkable effect. There were times when I had to look at the floor and blink several times before I could speak. Kindness was unexpected and I got choked up. I was starting to believe that I could do this. She asked how I planned to pay for college. I told her about my PELL grant. When she said it could be too late for the summer semester, I know she saw my disappointment.

The counselor picked up the phone. "Have you got a minute or two right now? It's important," she said into the handset. Together we walked to the financial aid office and went straight to the supervisor. Noreen asked the woman if she could rush my paperwork through to get me into the coming semester, adding, "Please do this as a personal favor to me."

"Okay, I will handle this myself," said the supervisor. As we left the office I couldn't speak. I just nodded dumbly. The same thing happened in the enrollment office—straight to the supervisor. The problem was that my financial aid had not been processed and I did not have my transcripts from the 1960's at Henry Ford Community College.

Noreen also asked this woman for a personal favor. "Please, just get him enrolled and make sure he gets these classes," she said. "I guarantee the financial aid will come through and we will have his transcripts in here tomorrow." My eyes were blinking like a strobe light to keep the tears at bay. This woman had spent two hours helping me pick my classes and asking for personal favors on my behalf.

"Well, you're all set. Now it is up to you," she said. I reached out to shake   15
her hand, but she gave me a hug instead and went in to counsel the next student. I was unprepared for a physical demonstration of warmth. I had not been hugged by a woman in eleven years. I walked to the parking structure in a daze. It was darker inside with very few people. By the time I got to my car tears were streaming down my cheeks. When someone walked by I would duck down in the seat. After twenty minutes I managed to slap my mask back on.

But when I walked into my room the mask slipped again. It didn't just slip, the damn thing fell off. This time it was not just tears. My body convulsed in guttural sobs. I fell on the bed, and all of the anguish of the lost years came pouring out. I gagged and gasped and howled. It lasted a good thirty minutes, until I cried myself to sleep. When I woke up an hour later the pillow was wet with tears and drool, and my mustache was stuck to it with dried snot. I got up and washed my face, and afterward I felt remarkably good. I knew I would excel at school. That counselor had given me a new outlook on life. I knew from then on things would change, and they did. But one lingering symptom has refused to go away.

When something good happens to me I get choked up. When someone gives me a compliment I get choked up. While typing this I have used two paper towels just from remembering the counselor's kindness. I blubber through any movie or TV show. It's the same with books. It does not have to be a heart-wrenching scene. If someone succeeds I get tears. If anything good happens I get tears. I sometimes tear up just thinking about good things in my life. There is no returning to what was once my emotional normal. I have turned into a real wuss. Even so, I believe I am a better person now. My look has vanished, but I still get the opposite looks on occasion from people who know about my past. Those looks are the least of my worries; you can't argue with the ignorant.

Noreen Ruehs called Susan Cushner at the University of Michigan–Dearborn and helped me transfer there. I'll graduate in a few weeks with "high distinction" and one of the five Chancellor's Medallions that are awarded to the best in the class. I have tried to thank Noreen but she says that I am the one who did all the work. She has no idea what she did for me. Of course I am wiping tears now.

Thinking about the Text

1. What is Larry Lehna's point in telling this story? Where does he make that point clear?

2. How would you describe the **ORGANIZATION** of Lehna's narrative? Chronological? Reverse chronological? Some other order? Where does the story start and end, and how effective is this structure?

3. Lehna talks about a look he sometimes receives from "people who know about my past," a look that tells him that "society did not like me" and that people doubted his character. We're willing to bet you feel quite differently after reading his story. How does Lehna connect with his **AUDIENCE** in this piece and establish his **CREDIBILITY**?

4. This essay was written for a course in narrative journalism, a genre that uses individual stories to illuminate public issues. Imagine that Lehna told this story as part of an essay on the need for prison reform for a political science course. How might the essay be different for that **PURPOSE**?

5. Identify an experience from your own life that sheds light on a social, political, cultural, or economic issue. Perhaps you were bullied in middle school, for instance—a deeply personal experience that has broader significance. Write a **NARRATIVE** essay in which you bring your own experience to life while also making the broader significance clear.

THIRTEEN

"Let's Take a Closer Look"
Writing Analytically

NALYSIS IS A NECESSARY STEP in much of the thinking that we do, and something that we do every day. What should you wear today? T-shirt and flip-flops? A sweatshirt? Your new red sweater? You consider the weather forecast, what you will be doing, the people you will be with (and might want to impress, or not), and then decide based on those factors. You may not consciously think of it as analysis, but that's what you've done.

When you analyze something, you break it down into its component parts and think about those parts methodically in order to understand it in some way. Since our world is awash in information, the ability to read it closely, examine it critically, and decide how—or whether—to accept or act on it becomes a survival skill. To navigate this sea of information, we rely on our ability to analyze.

Case in point: you want a new set of headphones, but do you want earbuds? over-the-ear? lightweight or full-size? noise canceling? Bluetooth? As you consider your options, your analysis will be driven by a number of questions: What's most important to you—sound quality? comfort? price? brand or look? When will you most often be wearing your headphones—at the gym? on your daily bus commute? while playing video games? You could ask your music-loving friends for their opinions, or you might check websites like *TestFreaks*, which provide expert analysis as well as user reviews and price comparisons. You might test out different styles and designs at your local Best Buy store. These are some of the ways you might analyze the various options, first to understand what they offer and then to decide which one you want to buy.

You have probably analyzed literary texts in English classes. In many college classes, you'll be expected to conduct different kinds of analyses—of texts, and also of events, issues, arguments, and more. Analysis is critical to every academic discipline, useful in every professional field, and essential to everyday decision making. This chapter provides guidelines for conducting an analysis and writing analytically, with specific advice for rhetorical, causal, process, data, and visual analysis.

REFLECT. Think about your own use of analysis. How many decisions— large and small—have you made in the last week? in the last month? in the last year? From small (what to have for breakfast) to major (which college to attend), make a chart listing a representative sample of these decisions and what areas of your life they affected. Then note the information you gathered in each case before you came to a final decision. What does this chart tell you about your interests, activities, and priorities? You've just completed an analysis.

Across Academic Disciplines

Some form of analysis can be found in every academic discipline. In a *history* class, you may be asked to analyze how Russia defeated Napoleon's army in 1812. In *biology*, you might analyze how the body responds to exercise. In *economics*, you might analyze the trade-off between unemployment and inflation rates. In a *technical communication* course, you might analyze a corporate website to understand how it appeals to various audiences. In your *composition* course, you'll analyze your own writing for many purposes, from thinking about how you've appealed to your audience to deciding how you need to revise a draft. So many courses require analysis because looking closely and methodically at something—a text, a process, a philosophy— helps you discover connections between ideas and think about how things work, what they mean, and why.

Across Media

Your medium affects the way you present your analysis. In *print*, you'll be writing mostly in paragraphs, and you might include photos, tables, graphs, diagrams, or other images to make your analysis clear. If you're making an *oral presentation*, you might show some information on slides or handouts. A *digital text* allows you to blend words, images, and audio—and you can embed these elements directly in your text or link to more information elsewhere. See how the following analysis from *Examiner.com* links to a *YouTube* video of Serena Williams practicing her serve to let readers see for themselves the process the author is analyzing. Had he been writing for a print publication, he might have included a still image like the one below.

> Most casual tennis fans may think Williams simply hits the ball harder than any other female on the planet, but the fact of the matter is that Serena Williams' service mechanics are textbook perfect and allow her to maximize every ounce of energy and power she possesses to its fullest extent—all without trying to bash the felt off the ball.
>
> If you watch Williams' entire service motion from beginning to end, you'll see that she has every part of her body working toward one goal, powering up—and through—the tennis ball.

Serena Williams serving at Wimbledon, 2015.

First, Williams gets that familiar "rocking motion" of hers, shifting back and then forward as she begins her swing take-back. Next, the younger tennis-playing Williams sister begins her service toss motion as her body weight begins moving toward the net. Williams then brings her feet together and takes a fantastic knee bend that all players need to copy whether male or female. With her weight shifted and her knees bent significantly and left arm still pointing up, Williams literally explodes upward toward the ball while her racquet head drops as her right elbow stretches up toward the heavens.

Now, with her body launched in the air, Williams reaches up for the ball and just before striking it, she pronates her wrist, arm and racquet as she powers through the ball as only she can.

—ERIC WILLIAMS, "Five Things All Tennis Players
Can Learn from Serena Williams"

**THINK
BEYOND
WORDS**

WATCH THE VIDEO of a TED Talk by statistician Nate Silver on whether race affects voting. Silver includes slides with lists, bar graphs, photos, and maps. How do the visuals contribute to his analysis? A space below the posted video invites viewers to comment. Write a comment about something Silver said in his talk that you find thought-provoking: your challenge will be to frame your comment in response to Silver while adding your own perspective. Go to everyonesanauthor.tumblr.com *to view the video.*

Across Cultures and Communities

Communicating with people from other communities or cultures challenges us to examine our assumptions and think about our usual ways of operating. Analyzing and understanding beliefs, assumptions, and practices that we are not familiar with may take extra effort. We need to be careful not to look at things only through our own frames of reference.

Sheikh Jamal Rahman, Pastor Don Mackenzie, and Rabbi Ted Falcon put in this extra effort in writing their book, *Getting to the Heart of Interfaith: The Eye-Opening, Hope-Filled Friendship of a Pastor, a Rabbi and a Sheikh.* In this book they take on the challenge of working toward interfaith understanding, saying that religion today "seems to be fueling hatred rather than expanding love" and that in order to heal the divisions between us, we must "find ways of entering into conversation with those different from us." And they say that analysis—what they call "inquiring more deeply"—is essential to their ongoing journey toward understanding issues central to each faith.

All three agree that it is critical to discuss the difficult and contentious ideas in faith. For the minister, one "untruth" is that "Christianity is the only way to God." For the rabbi, it is the notion of Jews as "the chosen people." And for the sheikh, it is the "sword verses" in the Koran, like "kill the unbeliever," which when taken out of context cause misunderstanding.

Their book embodies cultural sensitivity and describes the process of creating a text that's respectful of their different faiths. Reading a sentence that the sheikh had written about the security wall in Israel, the rabbi responded, "If that line is in the book, I'm not in the book." Then they analyzed and discussed the sentence, and Sheikh Rahman revised the wording to be "respectful of [both] their principles."

Having respect for the principles, values, and beliefs of others means recognizing and being sensitive to differences among cultures. The best way to demonstrate cultural sensitivity is to use precise language that avoids negative words or stereotypes about gender, religion, race, ethnicity, and such—in short, by carefully selecting the words you use.

Across Genres

Seldom doesny piece of writing consist solely of one genre; in many cases, writers draw on multiple genres as the situation demands. Analysis is a crucial step in writing for many purposes. To **ARGUE A POSITION** on an issue, you'll need to analyze that issue before you can take a stand on it. To compose a **REPORT**, you sometimes have to first analyze the data or the information that the report will be based on. And a **REVIEW** —whether it's of a film, a website, a book, or something else—depends on your analyzing the material before you evaluate it. Likewise, you might use a short **NARRATIVE** as an introductory element in a process or causal analysis.

REFLECT. Look for analysis in everyday use. Find two consumer-oriented websites that analyze something you're interested in—laptops, cell phones, sneakers, places you might like to go, things you might like to do. Study the analyses and decide which one is more useful. Then try to figure out what makes it better. Is it the language? the images? the amount of detail? the format? Keep these observations in mind as you write and design your own analyses.

CHARACTERISTIC FEATURES

While there are nearly as many different kinds of analysis as there are things to be analyzed, we can identify five common elements that analyses share across disciplines, media, cultures, and communities:

- A question that prompts you to take a closer look
- Some description of the subject you are analyzing
- Evidence drawn from close examination of the subject
- Insight gained from your analysis
- Clear, precise language

A Question That Prompts You to Take a Closer Look

Eric Schlosser poses a question that you've probably never considered: why do McDonald's fries taste so good? To find the answer, Schlosser had to analyze. See what he came up with on p. 1051.

If you look at the examples cited earlier in this chapter, you'll note that each is driven by a question that doesn't have a single "right" answer. What should you wear today? Which set of headphones best meets your needs? How can we begin to achieve interfaith understanding? Each question requires some kind of analysis. While an author may not explicitly articulate such a question, it will drive the analysis—and the writing that presents the analysis. In an essay about how partisan politics are driving opinions of President Obama, see how nationally syndicated columnist David Brooks starts by asking a question:

Who is Barack Obama?

If you ask a conservative Republican, you are likely to hear that Obama is a skilled politician who campaigned as a centrist but is governing as a big-government liberal. He plays by ruthless, Chicago politics rules. He is arrogant toward foes, condescending toward allies and runs a partisan political machine.

If you ask a liberal Democrat, you are likely to hear that Obama is an inspiring but overly intellectual leader who has trouble making up his mind and fighting for his positions. He has not defined a clear mission. He has allowed the Republicans to dominate debate. He is too quick to compromise and too cerebral to push things through.

You'll notice first that these two viewpoints are diametrically opposed. You'll observe, second, that they are entirely predictable. Political partisans always imagine the other side is ruthlessly effective and that the public would be with them if only their side had better messaging. And finally, you'll notice that both views distort reality. They tell you more about the information cocoons that partisans live in these days than about Obama himself.   —DAVID BROOKS, "Getting Obama Right"

To begin answering his opening question, Brooks offers brief summaries of both partisan opinions on Obama's leadership; then he takes a closer look, giving us a brief analysis of those opinions. You might not always start an analytical essay as Brooks does, by asking an explicit question, but your analysis will always be prompted by a question of some kind.

Some Description of the Subject You Are Analyzing

To be sure your audience fully understands your analysis, you need to first describe what you are analyzing. How much description you need depends on your subject, your audience, and the medium in which you present your piece. For example, if you are analyzing tropes in George R. R. Martin's *A Song of Fire and Ice* series for your fantasy literature class, you can assume most of your audience will be familiar with your subject. However, if you are analyzing the success of the TV series based on Martin's novels for your marketing class, you will have to describe the elements that make it HBO's most popular series ever. See how Ken Tucker does so in a piece on the British website *BBC Culture* that tackles that question: "Why is *Game of Thrones* so popular?"

Daenerys Targaryen, mother of dragons in HBO's *Game of Thrones*.

The return of *Game of Thrones*, back for a fourth season of sword fighting, bed hopping and mud flinging, reminds us once again what a clever
gamble HBO took in squeezing this massive production through our TV
and laptop screens. Yes, George R.R. Martin's *A Song of Fire and Ice* novels, on which the series is based, were bestsellers. But the size of the
audience for epic fantasy fiction is a fraction of what is needed to make
a profit on television. Martin's forest-dense family trees of characters—
knights in dented armour, damsels in bodice-bursting distress, and a nest
of dragons imported from fairy tales—could not have been an easy sell.
Legend has it that writer-producer Vince Gilligan sold *Breaking Bad* to
TV network AMC with the pithy phrase "Mr. Chips becomes Scarface."
One imagines the folks peddling *Game of Thrones* to HBO calling it "The
Sopranos with swords."

—KEN TUCKER, "Why Is *Game of Thrones* So Popular?"

Writing for this site, Tucker rightly assumes that some in his audience may
know little or nothing about the series and thus he includes descriptions that
help readers understand what the series is about—and what draws so many
viewers to it week after week. Vivid language detailing the show's characters ("knights in dented armour, damsels in bodice-bursting distress, and
a nest of dragons imported from fairy tales") and typical plotlines ("sword
fighting, bed hopping and mud flinging") gives readers a sense of the epic

fantasy fiction genre, and does so in a way that highlights the show's most thrilling and scandalous aspects.

In a similar situation, when you're composing a text that will be read by an audience that may not know your topic well, you'll also need to provide necessary description and details. You might also include an image, embed a video, or include a link to a site offering more information on your subject if the medium you're writing in allows it.

Evidence Drawn from Close Examination of the Subject

Examining the subject of your analysis carefully and in detail and then thinking critically about what you find will help you discover key elements, patterns, and relationships in your subject—all of which provide you with the evidence on which to build your analysis. For example, if you are analyzing a poem, you might examine word choice, rhyme scheme, figurative language, repetition, and imagery. If you are analyzing an ad in a magazine, you might look at the use of color, the choice of fonts, and the placement of figures or logos. Each element contributes something significant to the whole; each carries some part of the message being conveyed. The kinds of elements you examine and the evidence you draw from them will depend on the nature of your subject as well as the kind of analysis you are conducting. Following are discussions and examples of four common kinds of analysis: rhetorical analysis, process analysis, causal analysis, and data analysis.

Rhetorical analysis. This kind of analysis can focus on a written text, a visual text, an audio text, or one that combines words, images, and sound. All of these are rhetorical analyses; that is, they all take a close look at how authors, designers, or artists communicate their messages to an audience. Whether they are using words or images, adjusting font sizes or colors, they all are trying to persuade a particular audience to have a particular reaction to a particular message—theirs.

See how the following example from an article in the online magazine *Macworld* analyzes the core of Apple's "exceptional advertising . . . that indefinable element of cool," something that "Dell, Microsoft, and Hewlett-Packard lack":

> Despite their differences, Apple ads have in common at least one major advantage over many competitors' commercials: regardless of whether

you love or hate the spots, you'll likely *remember* them, and that's the first step to building a successful image. . . .

Apple's current campaign for the Mac, "Get a Mac," conveys just as simple and straightforward a message as the name would suggest. It's a deliberate attempt to appeal to the vast majority of computer users who, as Apple sees it, are using a Windows machine either because they aren't aware they have an alternative or because they're nursing some erroneous preconceptions about Macs.

The ads, which first began airing in May 2006, feature actors Justin Long and John Hodgman as the Mac and PC, respectively—anthropomorphized versions of the long-warring computer platforms.

Aside from a brief shot at the end of the spots, you won't see any actual computers in the "Get a Mac" ads. And there's a good reason for that—computer features are hard to show off in a small space in 30-second segments. Instead, Apple illustrates features by putting the characters into humorous situations. For example, when the PC sports a leg cast due to someone tripping over his power cord, it gives the Mac a chance to bring up the detachable MagSafe adapter.

The result: The ad spells out the Mac's advantages in a way that's both accessible and memorable for the average user. . . .

Because of the "Get a Mac" campaign's reliance on dialogue, Apple has also localized them for other markets. Both the U.K. and Japan now have their own version of the "Get a Mac" ads, with native actors and situations tuned to the nuances of those cultures. It's all part of the attention to detail that Apple knows it needs in order to compete globally.

—DAN MOREN, "Analysis: The Many Faces of Apple Advertising"

To see the "Get a Mac" ads, go to everyonesan author.tumblr.com.

In the rest of his article, Moren takes us methodically through the ad campaigns for other Apple products to provide more evidence for his opening claim that Apple's ads are inherently memorable. And because this article was written for an online publication, he can use multiple media to demonstrate his points. He includes hyperlinks to the online ads, so we can actually listen to the dialogue and see for ourselves that round-faced, balding, pudgy PC is a bit stodgy, dressed in a brown blazer and slacks with white shirt and tie, while lean, shaggy-haired Mac is quintessentially cool, in jeans and a casual shirt, hands tucked into his pockets.

Note how the author moves from a broad statement—"Apple ads have in common at least one major advantage over many competitors' commercials: regardless of whether you love or hate the spots, you'll likely *remember*

John Hodgman and Justin Long as PC and Mac in Apple's "Get a Mac" campaign.

them"—to the supporting evidence, discovered by looking closely at the ads and identifying their essential components and the way each one contributes to make the ads "one of the best campaigns of all time."

In the following example from her study of a literacy tradition in African American churches, rhetorician Beverly Moss uses direct quotations from her field notes to illustrate a key rhetorical pattern she noticed in one preacher's sermons.

> One of the patterns that leapt out at me as I sat in the pew during all the sermons and as I listened to tapes and reviewed fieldnotes was the high level of participation in the sermons by the congregation. . . . It is a pattern that almost any discussion of African American preaching addresses. Just as in the three churches highlighted [earlier], in this church, the congregation and Reverend M. engaged in a call-and-response dialogue. At times during the revival sermons, the feedback from the congregation was so intense that it was impossible to separate speaker from audience. Consider the following exchange. . . .
>
> > When you shout before the battle is over (Preach!)
> > It puts things in a proper perspective (Yeah!)
> > It puts you in a posture of obedience (Yeah!)
> > And it puts things in a proper perspective
> > But finally
> > When you shout before the battle is fought
> > It puts the enemy in confusion (Yeah! That's right!)
>
> The parenthetical expressions, responses from the congregation, do not appear on separate lines because there was little or no pause between the minister's statement and the congregation's response. Often, the congregation's response overlapped with the minister's statement. This type of feedback was typical in the sermons Reverend M. preached to this congregation, as was applause, people standing, cheering, and so on. Practically every sermon Reverend M. preached ended with the majority of the congregation on their feet clapping and talking back to Reverend M.
>
> —BEVERLY MOSS, *A Community Text Arises*

Moss analyzes and presents evidence from a spoken text. Because she was writing a print book, she could not include the actual audio of the sermon, but still she presents evidence in a way that demonstrates a key point of her

Members of a congregation move and shout in response to the preacher's words.

analysis: that the closeness of the preacher's "call" and the congregation's "response" made it almost "impossible to separate speaker from audience." This quoted evidence shows a specific example of how the congregation's response becomes a part of the sermon, filling the church with "applause, people standing, cheering."

Process analysis. Analyzing a process requires you to break down a task into individual steps and examine each one to understand how something works or how something is done. Thus there are two kinds of process analyses: **INFORMATIONAL**, showing how something works; and **INSTRUCTIONAL**, telling how something is done. An analysis of the chemistry that makes a cake rise would be informational, whereas an analysis of how to make a cake would be instructional.

The following example analyzes the process of how skaters make high-speed turns. This is the most critical element in speed skating, for being able to consistently make fast turns without slipping and losing ground can be the difference between winning and losing. This analysis from *Science Buddies*, a website for students and parents, closely examines the key steps of the process. Note how the author provides some information about the basic

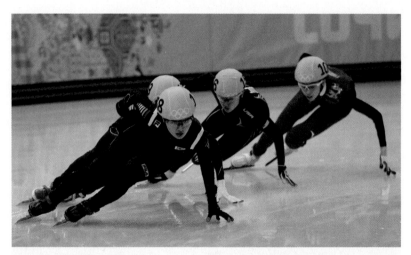

Skating for the finish line in the women's 1,000-meter short-track speed skating finals at the 2014 Winter Olympics in Sochi.

physics of speed and turns and then systematically explains how each element of the action—speed, angle, push-back force from the surface—contributes to the total turn.

Whether it's ice, wood, or a paved surface, the science that governs a skater's ability to turn is essentially the same. It's based on a couple of basic laws of physics that describe speed and the circular motion of turns. The first is Newton's *law of inertia* that says a body in motion will stay in motion unless there is some outside force that changes it. To skaters hoping to make a turn after they speed down the straightaway, that means the force of inertia would tend to keep them going straight ahead if there wasn't a greater force to make them change direction and begin turning.

The force that causes the change in direction comes from the skater's blades or wheels as they cross over at an angle in front of the skater leaning to make a turn. Newton's *law of reaction* explains that the push from the skater's skates generates an equal but opposite push back from the ice or floor. This push back force draws the skater in towards the track and is described as a "center seeking" or *centripetal* type of force. It's the reason why turns are possible in any sport. The wheels of a bicycle, for example, also angle into the road surface when the cyclist leans to begin a turn. As the road pushes back on both bike and rider, it supplies the inward centripetal force to generate the turning motion.

The more a skater leans into a turn, the more powerful the push from the skate, and the greater centripetal force produced to carry the skater through the turn. Leaning in also creates a smaller arc, or tighter turn, making for a shorter distance and a faster path around the turn. However, there's a catch. As the skater leans more and more into the track, the balancing point of the body, or the skater's *center of gravity*, also shifts more and more to the side. If it shifts too far, the skater no longer can maintain balance and ends up splayed out onto the rink rather than happily heading round the turn to the finishing line.

So success in turns, especially fast ones, means skaters must constantly find their center of gravity while teetering on the edge of their skates. To make the turn at all requires that the skater push the skates against the ice with sufficient power to generate enough inward centripetal force to counter the inertia of skating straight ahead. And to keep up speed in a race, a skater must calculate and execute the shortest, or tightest, turns possible around the track.

To read the full analysis, go to everyonesanauthor .tumblr.com.

—DARLENE JENKINS, "Tightening the Turns in Speed Skating: Lessons in Centripetal Force and Balance"

This kind of close examination of the subject is the heart of analysis. Darlene Jenkins explains the key elements in the process of making a high-speed turn—speed, angle, push-back force—and also examines the relationships among these elements as she describes what happens in minute detail, revealing how they all combine to create the pattern of movement that leads to a successful high-speed turn. By including a photograph that shows skaters leaning into a turn, blades and bodies angled precariously, Jenkins shows what the process entails, and readers can actually see what's being described.

Causal analysis. Why did a Malaysia Airlines flight disappear over the Pacific in 2014? What is causing the ongoing drought in California? These and other questions about why something occurs or once occurred call on you to analyze what caused a certain event, but a causal analysis can also investigate the possible effects of an event, or the links in a chain of connected events. Put most simply, causal analyses look at why something happened or will happen as a result of something else.

Go to everyonesan author.tumblr.com to link to the full article, "The Cry Embedded within the Purr."

Behavioral ecologist Karen McComb, who studies communication between animals and humans, wanted to understand why cat owners so often respond to purring cats by feeding them. To answer this question, McComb and a team recorded a number of domestic cats in their homes and discovered what the team termed "solicitation purring"—an urgent high-frequency sound, similar to an infant's cry, that is embedded within the cats' more pleasing and low-pitched purring and that apparently triggered an innate nurturing response in their owners. In an article presenting their findings, the team provided quantitative data about the pitch and frequency of different kinds of purring to support their conclusion about what the data showed: that the similarities in pitch and frequency to the cries of human infants "make them very difficult to ignore."

Using data like these to support an analysis is common in science classes, while in the humanities and social sciences, you're more likely to write about causes that are plausible or probable than ones that can be measured. In a literature class, for example, you might be asked to analyze the influences that shaped F. Scott Fitzgerald's creation of Jay Gatsby in *The Great Gatsby*—that is, to try to explain what caused Fitzgerald to develop Gatsby the way he did. In a sociology class, you might be asked to analyze what factors contributed to a population decline in a certain neighborhood. In both cases, these causes are probabilities—plausible but not provable.

Data analysis. Some subjects will require you to examine data. **QUANTITATIVE** analysis looks at numerical data; **QUALITATIVE** analysis looks at data that's not numerical.

When Beverly Moss analyzed the rhetoric of three ministers, she worked with qualitative data: transcripts of sermons, personal testimonies, her own observations from the church pews. Her data came mostly in the forms of words and text, not statistics.

Now see how blogger Will Moller analyzes the performances of ten major-league baseball pitchers using quantitative data—baseball statistics, in this case—to answer the question of whether New York Yankees pitcher Andy Pettitte is likely to get into baseball's Hall of Fame.

> I prefer to look at Andy versus his peers, because simply put, it would be very odd for 10 pitchers from the same decade to get in (though this number is rather arbitrary). Along that line, who are the best pitchers of Andy's generation, so we can compare them?

	Wins	Win%	WAR	ERA+	IP	K	K/BB	WAR/9IP
Martinez	219	**68.7%**	89.4	**154**	2827	3154	4.15	0.28
Clemens	**354**	65.8%	**145.5**	143	4917	**4672**	2.96	0.27
Johnson	303	64.6%	114.8	136	4135	4875	3.26	0.25
Schilling	216	59.7%	86.1	128	3261	3116	**4.38**	0.24
Maddux	**355**	61.0%	120.6	132	5008	3371	3.37	0.22
Mussina	270	63.8%	85.6	123	3563	2813	3.58	0.22
Smoltz	213	57.9%	82.5	125	3473	3084	3.05	0.21
Brown	211	59.4%	77.2	127	3256	2397	2.66	0.21
Pettitte	240	63.5%	66.9	117	3055	2251	2.34	0.20
Glavine	305	60.0%	67.1	118	4413	2607	1.74	*0.14*

The above table tells the story pretty well. I've bolded the numbers that are particularly absurd, and italicized one in particular which should act as a veto. Though I imagine most of the readers of this blog know full well what these statistics mean at this point, for those of you who don't, a primer:

WAR stands for Wins Above Replacement, and is a somewhat complicated equation which estimates the true value of a pitcher, taking into account league, ERA, park effects, etc. For instance, a pitcher that wins a game but gives up 15 earned runs has probably lost value in their career WAR, even though they get the shiny addition to their win-loss record. We like WAR around these parts.

ERA+ is a normalized version of ERA centered on 100, basically showing how much better or worse a pitcher was compared to their league average (by ERA). 110, for example, would indicate that the pitcher's ERA was 10% better than average. 95, on the other hand, would be roughly 5% worse than average. This is a good statistic for comparing pitchers between different time periods—a 4.00 ERA in 2000 doesn't mean the same thing as a 4.00 ERA in 1920, for example.

To read the full analysis, go to everyonesan author.tumblr.com.

K/BB is how many strikeouts a pitcher had per walk. More is better, less is worse.

As you can see, the above table doesn't do Andy any favors. He's 6th in wins and 5th in winning percentage, but he's 9th in ERA+ and dead last in WAR. His K/BB beats only Tom Glavine, who comes off looking pretty bad on this list. The only thing he has going for him is his playoff record—and frankly, the team he was on won a whole bunch of playoff

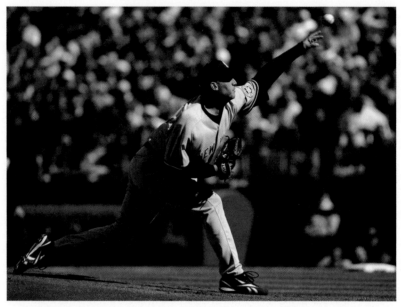

Andy Pettitte pitching against the Kansas City Royals in April 2009.

games while he was on the team, even when he wasn't pitching. Besides, we're pretty much past the point of taking W/L record as a good indication of pitcher skill—why is it that when we slap the word "postseason" onto the statistic, we suddenly devolve 10 years to when such things seemed to matter?   —WILL MOLLER, "A Painful Posting"

Moller's guiding question, "Should Andy Pettitte be in the Hall of Fame?" is unstated in this excerpt, but it is made clear earlier in the piece. He presents the data in a table for readers to see—and then walks us through his analysis of that data. It's critical when using numerical data like these not only to present the information but also to say what it means. That's a key part of your analysis. Using a table to present data is a good way to include numerical evidence, but be careful that you don't just drop the table in; you need to explain to readers what the data mean and to explain any abbreviations that readers may not know, as Moller does. Though he does not state his conclusions explicitly here, his analysis makes clear what he thinks—as does his URL: itsaboutthemoney.net/archives/2011/02/04/sorry-andy/.

Insight Gained from Your Analysis

One key purpose of an analysis is to offer your audience some insight on the subject you are analyzing. As you examine your subject, you discover patterns, data, specific details, and key information drawn from the subject—which will lead you to some insight, a deeper understanding of the subject you're analyzing. The insight that you gain will lead you to your thesis. When the sheikh, pastor, and rabbi mentioned earlier in this chapter analyzed a sentence in their book that offended the rabbi, each gained insight into the others' principles that led them to further understanding. In "Getting Obama Right," these concluding lines make clear the insight David Brooks derived from analyzing the perceptions of Obama expressed by both liberal Democrats and conservative Republicans:

> In a sensible country, people would see Obama as a president trying to define a modern brand of moderate progressivism. In a sensible country, Obama would be able to clearly define this project without fear of offending the people he needs to get legislation passed. But we don't live in that country. We live in a country in which many people live in information cocoons in which they only talk to members of their own party and read blogs of their own sect. They come away with perceptions fundamentally at odds with reality, fundamentally misunderstanding the man in the Oval Office. —DAVID BROOKS, "Getting Obama Right"

From Brooks's insight that both Republicans and Democrats are only reading half the facts and presenting a biased view, we get his message: such misperception is counterproductive to effective government.

Summarizing the study of the way humans react to a cat's purr, Karen McComb and her team note parallels between the isolation cry of domestic cats and the distress cry of human infants as a way of understanding why the "cry embedded within the purr" is so successful in motivating owners to feed their cats. They conclude that the cats have learned to communicate their need for attention in ways that are impossible to ignore, ways that prompt caring responses from people. Thus, their work suggests that much can be learned by studying animal-human communication from both directions, from animals to humans as well as the reverse.

Remember that any analysis you do needs to have a purpose—to discover how cats motivate their owners to provide food on demand, to understand how partisan misperceptions create roadblocks in government,

David Crystal's analysis of our everyday texting conventions leads him to a surprising conclusion. Check it out on p. 899.

to explain why a favorite baseball player's statistics won't get him into the Hall of Fame. In writing up your analysis, your point will be to communicate the insight you gain from the analysis.

Clear, Precise Language

Since the point of an analysis is to help an audience understand something, you need to pay extra attention to the words you use and the way you explain your findings. You want your audience to follow your analysis easily and not get sidetracked. You need to demonstrate that you know what you are talking about. You've studied your subject, looked at it closely, thought about it—*analyzed* it; you know what to say about it and why. Now you have to craft your analysis in such a way that your readers will follow that analysis and understand what it shows. Andy Pettitte doesn't just rank low by his statistics; "he's 9th in ERA+ and dead last in WAR." Democrats and Republicans don't simply have different opinions of Obama; their viewpoints are "diametrically opposed." Like Moller and Brooks, you should be precise in your explanations and in your choice of words.

Analyzing an intricate process or a complicated text requires you to use language that your audience will understand. The analysis of speed skating turns earlier in this chapter was written for an audience of young people and their parents. The language used to describe the physics that govern the process of turning is appropriate for such an audience—precise but not technical. When the author refers to Newton's law of inertia, she defines *inertia* and then explains what it means for skaters. The role of centripetal force is explained as "the more a skater leans into turns, the more powerful the push from the skate." Everything is clear because the writer uses simple, everyday words—"tighter turn," "teetering on the edge of their skates"—to convey complex science.

Look also at the analysis of baseball statistics presented earlier in this chapter; even though it was written for a blog targeting Yankees fans, the author includes a "primer" for those readers who may not understand the kinds of statistics he presents.

You need to consider what your audience knows about your topic and what information you'll need to include to make sure they'll understand what you write. You'll also want to be careful to state your conclusions explicitly—in clear, specific language.

EAMONN FORDE, a British journalist, wrote this article in 2014, analyzing the phenomenal success of "Happy" by Pharrell Williams. It was published in *The Big Issue*, a magazine written by professional journalists and sold by homeless and unemployed people in Great Britain and nine other nations.

"Happy" by Pharrell Williams: Why This Song Has Grabbed the Nation

EAMONN FORDE

YOU KNOW WHEN a song has gone that one step further and connects with people of all ages when it gets the crowd at the World Indoor Bowls Championships in Great Yarmouth clapping and grooving along. "Happy" by Pharrell Williams did exactly that.

In its online version, the article links to a site showing an audience of retirees "clapping and grooving."

"Happy" has sold more than 650,000 copies so far in the UK, was being played more than 5,500 times a week on British radio at its peak, and has become a viral *YouTube* hit (notably a girl dancing down the street to it like it was a Northern Soul classic), but getting an audience reaction like that at the bowls—that's proper success. It now unashamedly sits in the very heart of the mainstream, capturing the hearts and ears of the nation and making everyone who hears it, well, happy.

The author begins by describing the song's success.

Not bad going for a song that was never supposed to be released as a single. Its history is a curious one and drips in serendipity, showing how something in an age of over-marketing can take on a life of its own and pull off the near impossible by appealing to people of all ages.

Here's the insight that the analysis will explain.

[221]

Pharrell Williams at the 2015 Pinkpop Festival in the Netherlands.

Background information provides context for those unfamiliar with how the music industry works.

It was originally released back in June last year, tucked away as track four on the *Despicable Me 2* soundtrack album, released by the Back Lot Music label. Pharrell had signed to Sony Music and the track was considered a "possible" to appear on his new album, which is due out later this year but has no official release date yet. Then dance and urban station Capital Xtra started playing it. Pluggers, as is the norm in radio promotion, had not been knocking on its door. They just decided they liked it and put it on heavy rotation.

This coincided with the DVD release of *Despicable Me 2* and the launch of the 24hoursofhappy.com site that featured, as its name suggests, a 24-hour-long video for the song featuring cameos from Jamie Foxx, Steve Carell and others. RCA hadn't even decided what the lead track from the album would be but quickly swung into action, and it was released as a single by the label.

"Happy" went to number one in the UK at the end of December, selling 107,000 copies in its first week. It dropped to number two the next week but was back at number one the following week, then dipping to number two a week later. RCA is confident it will sell one million copies and has weeks, if not months, in the top 10 to come.

So what is it about the song that has made it so ubiquitous without it becoming irritating?

"It's a very poppy tune and it transcends a few different genres, so maybe people are more open to it," suggests Dr. Lauren Stewart, a reader in psychology at Goldsmiths in London, who has done lengthy research into "earworms"—those songs that burrow into your brain and are difficult to dislodge. "It made me think of that OutKast song 'Hey Ya!,' which had a similar quality to it and seemed to be everywhere."

Key to its success is its musical reiteration and the instructional nature of its lyrics, according to Dr. Elizabeth Margulis, director of the Music Cognition Lab at the University of Arkansas and author of *On Repeat: How Music Plays the Mind*. "That's a pretty repetitive song," she says of "Happy." "There is a catchy bit that expressly invites you to clap along. It is literally inviting you." In that sense, "Happy" is basically an update of "If You're Happy and You Know It (Clap Your Hands)" or "Don't Worry, Be Happy."

She adds, "The thing repetition really does is it captures the motor circuitry of the brain, so you have this sense the music is really pulling you along. It can make people feel really happy. There is something about having a song that is literally about being happy that is using this technique that makes people happy. It just feels good."

But repetition and irritation are often bedfellows, so it is very tricky to pull off just the right amount of recurrence in a song. "If something is really simple and just does all the ordinary things you'd expect it to do . . . repetition can seem really annoying," says Margulis. "If it has enough sparks of new and interesting things going on in there—and not too many to make it overwhelmingly complex—it can get into that sweet spot where you can just listen to it again and again and again and it doesn't seem to get tired."

Margulis says that listening can be tightly defined by age or subculture, so being appealing to one often means being unappealing to another. "So often music is a marker of group identity," she says. "So when a song can do that [cross age boundaries], that's really powerful and unusual."

Pharrell had, of course, been on the two biggest hits of last year in the UK—"Get Lucky" (1.28 million sales) and "Blurred

Lines" (1.47 million sales), both of which relied heavily on repetition—so things were clearly in place for him with whatever song he put out, allowing him to step up as the focal point rather than play a side role as guest vocalist. "Happy" has gone that bit further and has pan-generational appeal.

More evidence to explain the song's great success.

"For an artist to sell a significant amount of music in this day and age you need to be applicable to more than one demographic," says Neil Hughes, the director of promotions at RCA. "The most recent one I can think of that worked in this way was 'Get Lucky,' which was also a Pharrell track. 'Get Lucky' was an event record, but the difference with that was there was an awful lot of clever build-up before they launched the project, whereas this is very much a slow-burner."

"Happy" is going to be everywhere for months to come, lifting spirits and putting springs in steps. Just as he defined the sound of 2013, Pharrell looks set to provide the soundtrack to 2014—but this time with him in the spotlight and, happily, all on the song's own terms.

REFLECT. Find a short analytical article in a newspaper or magazine or online. Look at the list of five characteristic features of analysis on p. 206 and, using Forde's essay as a model, annotate the article to point out these features. Then evaluate how successful the article's analysis is. For example, can you identify the question that drove the analysis? Has the author provided enough description for you to follow the analysis? Is the language clear and precise? Has the author clearly stated the insight the analysis led to? Does he or she provide evidence to support that insight?

VISUAL ANALYSIS

Photos, cartoons, ads, movies, *YouTube* videos—all are visual texts, ones that say something and, just like words alone, make some kind of claim that they hope we will accept. When you analyze a visual, you ask the same questions you would of any text: How does it convey its message? How does it appeal to audiences? To answer such questions for a visual text, you'd begin by considering each of its elements—its use of color, light, and shadow; its perspective; any words or symbols; and its overall composition. Visual analysis takes various forms, but it generally includes the following features:

A Description of the Visual

Include an image of the visual in your analysis, but if that's not possible—in a print essay analyzing a video, for instance—you'll need to describe it. Your description should focus on the most important elements and those you'll point to in your analysis. What draws your eye first, and why? What's most interesting or seems most important? Does any use of contrast affect what you see? Consider the cartoon below. Your eyes were probably first drawn to the white speech balloons, because they stand out against the dark background, and they then bring your attention down to the two phones.

Some Contextual Information

You'll need to provide contextual information about your subject. What's its purpose, and who's the target audience? Is there any historical, political, or cultural context that's important to describe? Such factors are important to think about—and to describe in your analysis. The political cartoon about texting, for instance, was published in the *Atlanta Journal-Constitution* in 2009 and made a point about the need for laws prohibiting the use of hand-held cell phones while driving.

Attention to Any Words

If the visual includes any words, what do they add to its message? Whatever the words—the name of a sculpture, a caption beneath a photo, a slogan in an ad, the words in a speech balloon—you'll want to discuss how they affect the way we understand the visual. The same is true of the typography: words in boldface are likely ones the author wants to emphasize; the fonts affect the tone. If you were analyzing the cartoon about texting, for instance, you might point out that the words themselves are in textese ("Im txtng") and that they say something ridiculous (why would the driver send a text saying he's texting?)—demonstrating that texting while driving is not only dangerous but often stupid.

Close Analysis of the Message

What elements are most important in conveying the message? In the cartoon about texting, for instance, the split screen focuses attention on the contrasts between the two sides—bright colors on one side, dark ones on the other; a busy life, the lone figure of Death. And the words make the point clear: when it comes to texting while driving, Death gets the last laugh. Color, contrast, words, focus, the way it's all framed—these are all details that combine to convey a message, ones that you'll want to consider in analyzing what a visual text "says."

Insight into What the Visual "Says"

Your analysis of the visual will lead you to an understanding of what it's saying. The cartoon about texting argues that doing so while driving could be fatal. Watch ads try to persuade us to buy something—and those Daniel Craig in them suggest that we too can be as cool as James Bo° we need is a watch like his. How does the photo or painting or w' you're analyzing make you feel? What does it suggest that you think o⌐ ⌐ What techniques does it use to make you feel, think, or act in these ways?

Precise Language

It's especially important to use precise words in writing about a visual. Saying that the cartoonist uses "different colors in the driver's panel than in the one about Death" doesn't say much. Better: "the bright colors of the driver's panel—red and yellow against a purple background—present a vivid contrast to the tan and black in Death's panel." When you write about a visual, you need to use language that will help readers see the things that matter.

THINK BEYOND WORDS

TAKE A LOOK at "Paradise, Paved," a photo essay about travelers spending the night in Walmart parking lots. Click through the images and read the surrounding text. Then pick one image to analyze. How are the people in the image portrayed? How is the image itself composed? If this photo essay had a thesis, what would it be? Go to everyonesanauthor.tumblr.com to access the entire piece.

SOMINI SENGUPTA writes about technology and the law for the *New York Times*. She posted this article in 2012 on *Bits*, a *Times* blog about the technology industry.

Why Is Everyone Focused on Zuckerberg's Hoodie?

SOMINI SENGUPTA

Contextual information about the subject of the analysis.

WHO COULD HAVE THOUGHT a hoodie could mean so much? Over the last two days, there has been a great deal of mudslinging and hand-wringing about the significance of what Mark Zuckerberg, 27, the chief executive of Facebook, wore when he went courting would-be investors in New York.

Description of the hoodie that's being analyzed.

On the first stop of the Facebook public offering road show, Mr. Zuckerberg wore a hoodie. The only thing I remember thinking, when I first saw the footage, was that it was not a spring color. It was a dark, drab gray. That made me cringe.

Mr. Zuckerberg, of course, often wears a hoodie. Perhaps he thinks it's fetching. Perhaps, he wears it because it is his trademark, much like the Issey Miyake custom-made black turtlenecks that Steve Jobs, one of Mr. Zuckerberg's executive idols, wore during his public appearances. (Mr. Jobs had hundreds of them made, and he told his biographer, Walter Isaacson, that he had enough of them to wear every day for the rest of his life.)

Analysis of what a hoodie signifies, and of the statement that Zuckerberg was making by wearing one when meeting with investors.

Hoodies, like black turtlenecks, appear casual, like you just threw on the first thing you could find dangling on a hook behind the door. In fact, it carries a lot of meaning. It signifies the opposite of a Hermès tie, the favored accoutrement of Wall Street. It signi-

Mark Zuckerberg in New York during Facebook's road show.

fies that you're busy making things that are really, really important to the world, which is what Silicon Valley believes, and hey—you don't really care what you look like.

Right.

Mr. Zuckerberg is nothing if not a master of optics. Like Mr. Jobs' black turtleneck, the hoodie is his anti-fashion statement.

The hoodie in Manhattan prompted, as Mr. Zuckerberg may have expected, a gush of approval and disdain. Hoodiegate, it came to be called, and it began to show signs of a culture war between the two coasts—Wall Street versus Silicon Valley.

His critics saw it as a sign of immaturity and disrespect for those whom he expected to finance his company. An equities research analyst, Michael Pachter, said it would have been more fitting had he put on a blazer over a T-shirt. Mr. Pachter, incidentally, is so bullish on Facebook he thinks it's worth more than what the company estimates to be its value. But would Mr. Zuckerberg dress like that at church, Mr. Pachter, wearing a pinstripe suit, wondered aloud on a television program.

Naturally, a Twitter hashtag emerged to take up the cause: #zuckerbergshoodie.

His defenders said the hoodie signified Silicon Valley ethos: a brash, youthful self-confidence.

> *Clear and precise language presents the two opposing perceptions of the hoodie: as a sign of "immaturity and disrespect" or of "brash, youthful self-confidence."*

"Mark Zuckerberg really doesn't give a damn about you," Henry Blodget wrote in *Business Insider*. Mr. Blodget continued, in case New York wanted to listen: "I don't mean to be rude, Wall Street, but Mark Zuckerberg is actually wise not to care much about you. First, as discussed, he controls the company. But second, most of you don't do much to deserve much attention from CEOs."

Om Malik, founder of the GigaOm technology blog, opined that Mr. Pachter "is smoking stuff that's outside the realm of legality." The dapper blogger went on to conclude: "Now if you were looking for a problem with Zuckerberg's hoodie, then you should see it for what it really is: a fashion abomination."

On Thursday, Mr. Zuckerberg's sister, Randi, posted on Twitter a link to a pinstripe hoodie that a clothing label had unveiled immediately after hoodiegate began. A post in the *Atlantic Wire* surmised that the hoodie gave Mr. Zuckerberg the magical powers that he—and his investors—would need to keep spinning gold.

The to and fro over hoodiegate of course has been largely about what wealthy and, by and large, white men wear in Silicon Valley and on Wall Street.

But a hoodie is not just a hoodie, except when it's just a hoodie.

A teenage boy named Trayvon Martin was wearing a hoodie the night that he was killed in a gated townhouse community in Sanford, Fla., outside Orlando. His killer, an armed neighborhood watch volunteer, told police he appeared "real suspicious."

The hoodie became a symbol of solidarity in the days after the boy's death. Many people I know took pictures of themselves wearing hoodies. Naturally, they posted their pictures on *Facebook*.

Trayvon's hoodie is a reminder that neither Wall Street nor Silicon Valley is terribly representative of our country.

REFLECT. How surprised were you by the way Somini Sengupta concluded her post? What do you think her main point was in writing this piece? Look again at her title: what do you think it means? Keeping in mind that she posted this piece on a blog read by people in the technology business, what do you think she was saying to them?

WRITING ANALYTICALLY / A Roadmap

Find a topic that matters—to you, and to others

Whether you can choose your topic or have to respond to a specific assignment, find an angle that appeals to you—and to your audience. Write about something that you care about, that engages you. No audience will want to hear about something that you are not interested in writing about.

If you can choose your topic, begin by considering your interests. What do you like to do? What issues do you care about? Do you have a favorite book? If you've read and reread the *Harry Potter* books, you might analyze J. K. Rowling's storytelling style or the causes behind the books' ongoing popularity. An interest in sports could lead you to analyze statistical data on a favorite athlete (as Will Moller does) or to analyze the process of doing something in a particular sport (as Darlene Jenkins does).

If you've been assigned a topic, say to conduct a rhetorical analysis of the Gettysburg Address, find an angle that interests you. If you're a history buff, you might research the particular occasion on which Lincoln spoke and look at how his words were especially appropriate to that audience and event. Or perhaps your interests lie more in current politics, in which case you might compare Lincoln's address to the speeches politicians make today.

Make your topic matter to your audience. Some topics matter to everyone, or nearly everyone; you might be able to identify such topics by checking the media for what's being debated and discussed. But when you're writing about something that may not automatically appeal to a wide audience, it's your responsibility as the writer to tell them why they should care about it. Somini Sengupta does this in her piece about Mark Zuckerberg's hoodie by showing the powerful assumptions we make about people based on their dress—assumptions that, for a different young man wearing a similar hoodie, determined life and death.

Consider your rhetorical situation

Keep in mind the elements of your particular situation—your audience, your specific purpose, your stance, and so on—and how they will or should influence the choices you make in your writing.

Identify your AUDIENCE. Who do you want to reach, and how can you shape your analysis so that you get through to them? Karen McComb's analysis of cat purring was for an audience of scientific peers, whereas Ken Tucker wrote about *Game of Thrones* for BBC's *Culture* site, which is written for the general public. Very different audiences, very different purposes—very different analyses. You, too, should think carefully about who you are trying to reach.

- What do you know about them—their age, gender, cultural and linguistic background?
- What are they likely to know about your subject, and what background information will you need to provide?
- How might they benefit from the analysis and insight you offer?
- Will your subject matter to them—and if not, how can you make them care about it?

If you are writing for the web, you will likely reach a broad audience whose characteristics you can't predict, so you need to assume a range of readers—just as Will Moller does in his blog post about Andy Pettitte. Even though his primary audience is Yankees fans, he knows that some readers won't know much about statistics, so he provides the definitions they need to understand his analysis.

Articulate your PURPOSE. Even if you're writing in response to an assignment, here are some questions that can help you narrow your focus and articulate some more specific purposes:

- What are you analyzing? A text? A process? Causes? Data? A visual?
- What's motivated you to write? Are you responding to some other text or author?
- What do you want to accomplish by analyzing this subject? How can you best achieve your goals?
- What do you want your audience to take away from your analysis?

Think about your STANCE. How do you want to come across as an author? How can your writing reflect that stance? If your subject is surfing and you're writing on a surfers' blog about how to catch a wave for an audience of beginners, your stance might be that of an experienced surfer or a former beginner. Your language would probably be informal, with little or no surfing jargon. If, on the other hand, you're writing an article for *Surfing Magazine* analyzing the process Laird Hamilton developed to ride fifty-foot waves, your stance might be that of an objective reporter, and your language would need to be more technical for that well-informed audience. No matter what your stance or target audience, you need to consider what kind of language is appropriate, what terms need to be defined, and how you can establish your authority as an author.

Consider the larger CONTEXT. If you are analyzing an ad for a composition class, you will want to look at relevant information about its original context. When was the ad created, and who was the target audience? What were the social, economic, and political conditions at the time? All of that is contextual information. If you are preparing a load analysis for an engineering class, you'll need to consider factors such as how, when, and where the structure will be used. Other contextual information comes from what others have said about your subject, and your analysis adds to the conversation.

Consider MEDIA. Will your analysis be delivered in print? on a website? in an oral presentation? Are you writing for an online class? a blog? your campus newspaper? If you get to choose your medium, the choice should depend on how you can best present your subject and reach your intended audience. Do you need to be able to incorporate visuals, or audio or video, or to speak directly to your audience in person? Whether you have a choice or not, the media you use will affect how you design and deliver your analysis.

Consider matters of DESIGN. Think about how to best present your information and whether you need to follow any disciplinary conventions. Does your analysis include data that is easiest to understand in a chart or graph? Would headings help readers follow your analysis? Would illustrations make your point clearer?

Analyze your subject

What kind of analysis is needed for your subject and purpose? You may be assigned to conduct a certain kind of analysis, or you may be inspired by a question, as Will Moller was in analyzing data to determine whether Andy Pettitte is likely to be elected to the Hall of Fame. But sometimes you may be asked simply to "analyze x"—an ad, a game, a historical event, profiles of several companies—in which case you'll need to determine what kind of analysis will work best. The kind of analysis you need to do—*rhetorical analysis, process analysis, causal analysis, data analysis, visual analysis*—will determine the way you study your subject.

If you're analyzing rhetoric, you need to look at what the text you're examining says and how it supports its claims.

- What question are you asking about this text? What specifically are you looking for?
- What **CLAIM** is the text making—and what **REASONS** and **EVIDENCE** does the author provide for the claim? Do they convince you?
- Does the writer acknowledge or respond to **COUNTERARGUMENTS** or other opinions? If so, are they presented fairly?
- Are there any words that indicate what the author thinks—or wants you to think?
- How does the author establish **AUTHORITY** to address the topic?
- Does the text use any **EMOTIONAL APPEALS**? If so, how?

If you're analyzing a process, you'll need to decide whether your analysis will be **INFORMATIONAL** (how something works) or **INSTRUCTIONAL** (how to do something). Writing about how solar panels convert sunshine to energy would be informational, whereas writing about how to install solar panels would be instructional—and would need to explicitly identify all materials needed and then tell readers step-by-step exactly how to carry out the process. Once you've determined the kind of analysis, you might then consider questions like these:

- What question is prompting your analysis?
- If the process is instructional, what materials are needed?
- What are the steps in the process? What does each step accomplish?
- What order do the steps follow? Whether a process follows a set order (throwing a curveball, parallel parking a car) or not (playing sudoku), you'll need to present the steps in some order that makes sense.

If you're analyzing causes, you're looking for answers to why something happened. Why, for instance, have crime rates fallen in a particular city over the past few decades? Is it because police are more actively patrolling neighborhoods? Or because poverty has dropped in some parts of the city? Or because prison programs have expanded?

Questions about causes can rarely be answered definitively, so you'll usually be **ARGUING** that certain causes are the most plausible or the *primary* ones, and that others are less likely or *secondary*. In addition, although an *immediate cause* may be obvious, less obvious *long-term causes* may also have contributed. You'll need to consider all possible causes and provide evidence to support the ones you identify as most plausible.

As you determine which causes are more or less likely, be careful not to confuse coincidence with causation. That two events—such as a new police-patrol policy in a city and a drop in the crime rate—occurred more or less simultaneously, or even that one event preceded the other, does not prove that one *caused* the other.

You'll often need to do some **RESEARCH** to understand all the possible causes and whether they are primary or contributing, immediate or long-term causes. The following questions can guide your research and analysis:

- What question is prompting your analysis?
- List all the causes you can think of. Which seem to be the primary causes and which are contributing or secondary causes? Which are immediate causes and which are long-term causes?
- Might any of the causes on your list be merely coincidences?
- Which causes seem most plausible—and why?
- What research do you need to do to answer these questions?

If you're analyzing data, you're trying to identify patterns in information that you or someone else has gathered in order to answer a question or make an argument. The information collected by the U.S. Census is data. Social scientists looking for patterns to help them make arguments or predictions about population trends might analyze the data on numbers of families with children in urban areas.

In his blog post on Andy Pettitte, Will Moller provides numerical data on ten pitchers' performances, which he then analyzes to determine whether Pettitte is likely to get into the Hall of Fame. His analysis explicitly states his guiding question—"Should Andy Pettitte be in the Hall of Fame?"—and then answers it by considering each element of the data as it relates to Pettitte's performance.

Although the mathematical nature of analyzing **QUANTITATIVE** data can often make it more straightforward than other kinds of analysis, identifying statistical patterns and figuring out their significance can be challenging. Finding and interpreting patterns in **QUALITATIVE** data can also be tricky, especially as the data is more free-form: words, stories, photographs, and so on. Here are some questions to consider when analyzing data:

- What question are you trying to answer?
- Are there any existing data that can help answer your question? If so, will they provide sufficient information, or do you need to conduct any **RESEARCH** of your own to generate the data you need?
- If you're working with existing data, who collected the data, using what methods, and why? How do the data relate to the analysis you're conducting?
- Do the data show the full picture? Are there other data that tell a different story?
- Can you identify patterns in the data? If so, are they patterns you expected, or are any of them surprising?

If you're analyzing a visual, how do specific visual elements convey a message or create an effect?

- What draws your eye first, and why? What seems most interesting or important?
- What's the **PURPOSE** of this visual, and who's its target **AUDIENCE**?
- Is there any larger historical, cultural, or political **CONTEXT** to consider?
- Are there any words, and what do they tell you about the message?
- What's the overall **ARGUMENT** or effect? How do you know?

Determine what your analysis shows

Once you've analyzed your subject, you need to figure out what your analysis shows. What was the question that first prompted your analysis, and how can you now answer that question? What have you discovered about your subject? What have you found that interests you—and how can you make it matter to your audience?

State your insight as a tentative THESIS. Once you've determined what insights your analysis has led to, write it out as a tentative thesis, noting what you've analyzed and why and what conclusions or insights you want to share. Your thesis introduces your point, what you want to say about your subject. Let's say you're writing a rhetorical analysis of the Gettysburg Address. Here's how you might introduce an analysis of that speech:

> Following Edward Everett's two-hour oration, President Lincoln spoke eloquently for a mere two minutes, deploying rhetorical devices like repetition, contrast, and rhythm in a way that connected emotionally with his audience.

This sentence tells us that the writer will describe the event, say something about the length of the speech, and explain how specific words and structures resulted in an eloquently simple but profoundly moving speech.

As you formulate your thesis, begin by thinking about your **AUDIENCE** and how you can make your analysis most compelling to them. What aspects of your analysis will they care most about? How might it apply to them? Does your analysis have important implications beyond the immediate subject, as Somini Sengupta's analysis of a simple hoodie does?

Then list the evidence you found that supports your analysis—examples, quotations, significant data points, and so forth. What of all your evidence will best support your point, and what will your audience find most persuasive?

Organize and start writing

Start with your tentative thesis, being sure that it identifies what you're analyzing, what insights you have to offer, and why it is significant. As you write, be sure you're supporting your thesis—and that it's working. That said, don't hesitate to revise it if you have difficulty supporting it.

Give EVIDENCE that supports your thesis. Depending on the kind of analysis, evidence could include examples, statistics, quotations, definitions, and so on.

Cite other sources, but remember that this is *your* analysis. Your audience wants to hear your voice and learn from your insights. At the same time, don't forget to acknowledge other perspectives.

Draft an **OPENING**. You might begin by describing what you're analyzing and why, explaining what question prompted you to take a closer look at your topic. Provide any background information your audience might need. State your thesis: what are you claiming about your subject?

Draft a **CONCLUSION**. You might reiterate what you've learned from your analysis and what you want your audience to understand about your subject. Make sure they know why your analysis matters, to them and to you.

Look critically at your draft, get response—and revise

Read your draft slowly and carefully to see whether you've made your guiding question clear, described your subject sufficiently, offered enough evidence to support your analysis, and provided your audience with some insight about your subject.

Then ask others to read and respond to your draft. If your school has a writing center, try to meet with a tutor, bringing along any questions you have. Here are some questions that can help you or others read over a draft of analytic writing:

- *Is the question that prompted your analysis clear?* Is it a question worth considering?

- *How does the* **OPENING** *capture the audience's interest?* Does it indicate why this analysis matters? How else might you begin?

- *Is the point of your analysis clear?* Have you stated the point explicitly in a **THESIS** —and if not, do you need to?

- *Is the subject described in enough detail for your audience?* Is there any other information they might need in order to follow your analysis?

- *What* **EVIDENCE** *do you provide to support your point?* Is it sufficient?

- *What insights have you gained from the analysis?* Have you stated them explicitly? How likely is it that readers will accept your conclusions?

- *If you've cited any sources, are they credible and convincing?* Have you integrated them smoothly into your text—is it clear what you are saying and where (and why) you are citing others? And have you **DOCU-MENTED** any sources you've cited?

- *Have you addressed other perspectives?* Do you need to acknowledge possible **COUNTERARGUMENTS**?

- *How would you describe the* **TONE,** and does it accurately convey your **STANCE**? Is the tone appropriate for your audience and purpose?

- *How is the analysis organized?* Is it easy to follow, with clear **TRANSITIONS** from one point to the next? Are there headings—and if not, would adding them help? If you're analyzing a process, are the steps in an order that your audience will be able to follow easily?

- *Consider* **STYLE.** Look at the choice of words and kinds of sentences—are they appropriately formal (or informal) for the audience and purpose? Could the style be improved in any way?

- *How effective is the* **DESIGN**? Have you included any images or other visual elements—and if so, how do they contribute to the analysis? If not, is there any information that might be easier to understand if presented in a table or chart or accompanied by an image?

- *How does the draft* **CONCLUDE**? Is the **CONCLUSION** forceful and memorable? How else might the analysis conclude?

- *Consider the title.* Does it make clear what the analysis is about, and will it make your audience interested in reading on?

Revise your draft in light of your own observations and any feedback you get from others, keeping your audience and purpose firmly in mind. But remember: *you* are the analyst here, so you need to make the decisions.

᙮᙮᙮*REFLECT. Once you've completed your analysis, let it settle for a while and then take time to reflect. How well did you analyze your subject? What insights did your analysis lead to? What additional revisions would you make if you could? Research shows that such reflections help "lock in" what you learn for future use.*

Calvin and Hobbes: The Voice of the Lonely Child
LIBBY HILL

THERE IS A MYTHIC *Calvin and Hobbes* strip that's been bouncing around the internet for years. No one's quite sure where it came from or who's responsible for it. Part of its mystery is likely because it's purported to be the lost final installment of the series, drawn by Bill Watterson himself. In it, a serious-looking Calvin toils away at his schoolwork while Hobbes looks on. The tiger is curious that his friend is being so diligent about his studies, and the boy responds that "the pills" he's taking have started working. Hobbes then asks Calvin to go play, but Calvin is too absorbed in his project to take notice. The final panel is the tiger as "just" a stuffed animal, with Calvin indifferent to the change. It is, in every sense of the word, an abomination.

This is not an actual installment of *Calvin and Hobbes*, and is instead a repurposed strip with a preachy message warning against the dangers of medicating children and ruining their creativity forever. There are any number of ways that this goes against the inherent spirit of the comic, but I will focus my disdain to a single point. *Calvin and Hobbes* was never about hyperactivity and Hobbes himself was never a manifestation of undiagnosed mania: He was a manifestation of pure, unadulterated loneliness.

LIBBY HILL blogs about popular culture for the *New York Times, Salon,* and the *A.V. Club,* a website where this essay appeared in 2015.

Loneliness is a funny thing because generally it has less to do with being alone and more to do with not having other people around. That sounds paradoxical, but being alone and being isolated from your peers are two very different things. The former is a choice, the latter a decree. In truth, it's even more complicated than that, as loneliness can strike at any time, even when surrounded by people. That niggling sense that maybe you don't belong is all it needs to gain a foothold.

For as much as the brain of a child is growing and changing and maturing, for as many distractions as the world provides to developing minds, kids aren't stupid, particularly children as highly sensitive and attuned to the world around them as Calvin. Disappearing into his own world is a coping mechanism for dealing with a world that seems to have little patience or place for him. His isolation breeds fantasy, which breeds isolation, which does him no favors at school or at home. To be a lonely child in the world means creating your own fun, your own friends, your own magic.

There was a linen closet across from my childhood bedroom. It was filled   5
with old sheets and blankets, more than we'd ever need, even with five beds in the house. The old sleeping bags (green nylon, with a red interior, and yellow cotton, with the black interior, which was obviously superior) would be folded and placed on the floor. And there was never enough room in the house, that's important to note. It was three stories, but steam heat, extreme seasons, and a half-finished basement meant that usually we were all grouped into the same two stories. It meant constant bedroom rearrangement, as people graduated or were born or just couldn't stand living with each other anymore. But no matter where I was, I didn't fit. I searched that house high and low, even braved the attic full of cobwebs and crap and maybe bats, looking for the hidden door.

I wanted a wardrobe to take me to another land or a boxcar set up in the backyard. . . . I wanted adventure to find me because I was sure that being misunderstood meant that I was special and destined for something magical. I tried to make the linen closet my secret place, where I could hide away with a flashlight and read, confident that if I fully committed, the magic would find me. But what found me instead were the realizations that the closet of a 100-year-old house is largely unventilated and oxygen becomes a luxury, not a privilege, and that there's never any peace in a five-child household.

I'd pore over *Calvin and Hobbes* time and again, finding renewed joy with every reread, despite being Susie Derkins, stuffed rabbit and all, despite being constantly plagued by a little brother who often seemed like the human incarnation of Calvin himself, despite skipping over most of the Spaceman Spiff fantasies because I just couldn't understand using your imagination that way. What brought me back, even though I didn't understand it at the time, was seeing a child—one who didn't really fit in at school and who had a vague antipathy for almost everyone he met—struggle with the world he inhabited and find a way to make the best of it.

Calvin didn't have trouble focusing on the world around him, he had trouble reconciling himself to the fact that the world around him was such a disappointment. The reason the strip appealed to people both young and old is because Calvin was feeling underwhelmed at a college graduate level. It's not unheard of for children to experience this, particularly those who are more sensitive to their surroundings, and for many it was a relief to know that seeing the world without the luster and facade constantly created for us wasn't so unusual. Calvin made it okay to be disheartened and disappointed by life and normalized the inherent loneliness that childhood can bring. He was there for us as we grew up; and while we learned that things were capable of getting so much better and so much worse as we experienced puberty and beyond, he was still mired in the first grade, raging against the machine.

It's quite the thing to sit down and read 10 years of a comic strip at once. It's a comfort, like going home, the jokes warm and familiar. You grin when you come across the Sunday strips that served as the inspiration for the book collection titles, "Something Under the Bed Is Drooling," "Homicidal Psycho Jungle Cat." And though the strips are the same as they've ever been, you've come to them as a different person. Reading *Calvin and Hobbes* when you're 33 is different from reading it when you're 13. Now you're struck by the struggle Calvin's parents must have had keeping their child in line and loving him even as he drove them out of their minds, and you wonder if their single-income home would still be feasible in the current economic climate. But more than anything, you notice the sorrow buried in the strips, and you wonder how you missed how sad the children in the strips were the whole time.

Loneliness and sadness aren't new fare for comic strips. If anything, Watterson's characters are merely carrying on in the grand tradition of Charles Schultz's *Peanuts*, where preternaturally clever children are nevertheless sty- 10 mied by the world they live in. Like *Peanuts, Calvin and Hobbes* is timeless for the exact same reason: It appealed to adults just as much as it appealed to children. It spoke of things not always acknowledged in polite company, how people are mean, how we wish we had more friends, how being grown up seems weird and being a child even weirder, how the world doesn't make sense, and how it's hard to believe in things even though we desperately want to believe in them.

Calvin was a lot of things, just like every child. He was a budding inventor, a gifted artist, an enterprising entrepreneur, and a self-taught pundit. He was a good friend, an annoying neighbor, clever and conniving, lonely and loyal and, yeah, maybe a little hyperactive. But whatever he was, he taught an entire generation of children that though sadness and disappointment and loneliness may come prepackaged in life, that all could be weathered, so long as you had hope and a really good friend to see you through. For Calvin, that was Hobbes. For us, it was *Calvin and Hobbes*. And when the strip ended its 10-year run in 1995, it left in its wake a generation of children who, though now grown, could move forward in life confident that their magical friend would be with them always.

Thinking about the Text

1. What is Libby Hill's main insight about *Calvin and Hobbes*? Cite specific passages that reveal what she thinks.

2. Hill includes example *Calvin and Hobbes* strips as **EVIDENCE** for her analysis, but she does not discuss any of them in detail. Pick one and write a brief paragraph explaining how it supports Hill's point. Then insert your explanation into Hill's text. Does it improve the overall analysis—why or why not?

3. How does Hill establish her **AUTHORITY** to write on this topic? How does she show that the topic matters to her, and how does she appeal to her **AUDIENCE** to make it matter to them as well? Point to specific passages from the text to support your response.

4. If you were familiar with *Calvin and Hobbes* before you read this essay, do you think Hill describes the comic strip accurately? If you were not familiar with it, do you think you now understand its basic premise—and has Hill made you want to read more of it? Explain.

5. Write an **ANALYSIS** of a favorite cartoon, comic, book series, or other text, following the guidelines in this chapter. Be sure to make clear the question you're exploring, the insight you gain, and the evidence supporting that insight.

Advertisements R Us

MELISSA RUBIN

ADVERTISEMENTS ARE WRITTEN to persuade us—to make us want to support a certain cause, buy a particular car, drink a specific kind of soda. But *how* do they do it? How do they persuade us? Since the beginning of modern consumer culture, companies have cleverly tailored advertisements to target specific groups. To do so, they include text and images that reflect and appeal to the ideals, values, and stereotypes held by the consumers they wish to attract. As a result, advertisements reveal a lot about society. We can learn a great deal about the prevailing culture by looking closely at the deliberate ways a company crafts an ad to appeal to particular audiences.

This ad from the August 1950 *Coca-Cola Bottler* magazine, a trade magazine for Coca-Cola bottlers (fig. 1), features a larger-than-life red Coca-Cola vending machine with the slogan "Drink Coca-Cola—Work *Refreshed*" (Coca-Cola). Set against a bright blue sky with puffy white clouds, an overlarge open bottle of Coke hovers just to the right and slightly above the vending machine, next to the head of "Sprite Boy," a pixie-ish character and onetime Coke symbol, who sports a bottle cap for a hat. Sprite Boy's left hand gestures past the floating Coke bottle and toward a crowd congregating before the vending machine. The group, overwhelmingly male and apparently all white, includes blue-collar workers in casual clothing, servicemen in uniform, and businessmen in suits in the foreground; the few women displayed are in the background, wearing

MELISSA RUBIN wrote this analysis when she was a student at Hofstra University using an early draft of this chapter.

Fig. 1. 1950 ad from *Coca-Cola Bottler* magazine (Coca-Cola).

dresses. The setting is industrialized and urban, as indicated by the factory and smokestacks on the far left side of the scene and by the skyscrapers and apartment building on the right.

Practically since its invention, Coca-Cola has been identified with mainstream America. Born from curiosity and experimentation in an Atlanta pharmacy in 1886, Coke's phenomenal growth paralleled America's in the industrial age. Benefiting from developments in technology and transportation, by 1895 it was "sold and consumed in every state and territory in the United States" (Coca-Cola Company). In 2010, Diet Coke became the second-most-popular carbonated drink in the world . . . behind Coca-Cola (Esterl). In the immediate post-war world, Coke became identified with American optimism and energy, thanks in part to the company's wartime declaration that "every man in uniform gets a bottle of Coca-Cola for 5 cents, wherever he is, and whatever it costs the Company" (Coca-Cola Company). To meet this dictate, bottling plants were built overseas with the result that many people other than Americans first tasted Coke during this war that America won so decisively, and when peace finally came, "the foundations were laid for Coca-Cola to do business overseas" (Coca-Cola Company).

Given the context, just a few years after World War II and at the beginning of the Korean War, the setting clearly reflects the idea that Americans experienced increased industrialization and urbanization as a result of World War II. Factories had sprung up across the country to aid in the war effort, and many rural and small-town Americans had moved to industrial areas and large cities in search of work. In this advertisement, the buildings surround the people, symbolizing a sense of community and the way Americans had come together in a successful effort to win the war.

The ad suggests that Coca-Cola recognized the patriotism inspired by the war and wanted to inspire similar positive feelings about their product. In the center of the ad, the huge red vending machine looks like the biggest skyscraper of all—the dominant feature of the urban industrial landscape. On the upper right, the floating face of Coca-Cola's Sprite Boy towers above the scene. A pale character with wild white hair, hypnotic eyes, and a mysterious smile, Sprite Boy stares straight at readers, his left hand gesturing toward the red machine. Sprite Boy's size and placement in the ad makes him appear godlike, as if he, the embodiment of Coca-Cola, is a powerful force uniting—and refreshing—hardworking Americans. The placement of the vending machine in the center of the ad and the wording on it evoke the idea that drinking Coca-Cola will make a hardworking American feel refreshed while he (and apparently it was rarely she) works and becomes part of a larger community. The text at the bottom of the ad, "A welcome host to workers—*Inviting you to the pause that refreshes with ice-cold Coca-Cola*"—sends the same message to consumers: Coke will refresh and unite working America.

The way that Coca-Cola chooses to place the objects and depict men and women in this ad speaks volumes about American society in the middle of the twentieth century: a white, male-dominated society in which servicemen and veterans were a numerous and prominent presence. The clothing that the men in the foreground wear reflects the assumption that the target demographic for the ad—people who worked in Coca-Cola bottling plants—valued hard workers and servicemen during a time of war. White, uniformed men are placed front and center. One man wears an Army uniform, the one next to him wears a Navy uniform, and the next an Air Force uniform. By placing the servicemen so prominently, Coca-Cola emphasizes their important role in society and underscores the value Americans placed on their veterans at a time when almost all male Americans were subject to the draft and most of them could expect to serve in the military or had already done so. The other men in the foreground—one wearing a blue-collar work uniform and the other formal business attire—are placed on either side of and slightly apart from the soldiers, suggesting that civilian workers played a valuable role in society, but one secondary to that of the military. Placing only a few women dressed in casual day wear in the far background of the image represents the assumption that women played a less important role in society—or at least in the war effort and the workforce, including Coke's.

The conspicuous mixture of stereotypical middle-class and working-class attire is noteworthy because in 1950, the U.S. economy had been marked by years of conflict over labor's unionization efforts and management's opposition to them—often culminating in accommodation between the two sides. The ad seems to suggest that such conflict should be seen as a thing of the past, that men with blue-collar jobs and their bosses are all "workers" whom Coca-Cola, a generous "host," is inviting to share in a break for refreshments. Thus all economic classes, together with a strong military, can unite to build a productive industrial future and a pleasant lifestyle for themselves.

From the perspective of the twenty-first century, this ad is especially interesting because it seems to be looking backward instead of forward in significant ways. By 1950, the highly urban view of American society it presents was starting to be challenged by widespread movement out of central cities to the suburbs, but nothing in the ad hints at this profound change. At the time, offices and factories were still located mostly in urban areas and associated in Americans' minds with cities, and the ad clearly reflects this perspective. In addition, it presents smoke pouring from factory smokestacks in a positive light, with no sign of the environmental damage that such emissions cause, and that would become increasingly clear over the next few decades.

Another important factor to consider: everyone in the ad is white. During the 1950s, there was still a great deal of racial prejudice and segregation in the United States. Coca-Cola was attuned to white society's racial intolerance and chose in this ad to depict what they undoubtedly saw as average Americans, the primary demographic of the audience for this publication: Coca-Cola employees. While Coke did feature African Americans in some ads during the late 1940s and early 1950s, they were celebrity musicians like Louis Armstrong, Duke Ellington, Count Basie, or Graham Jackson (the accordion player who was a huge favorite of Franklin Delano Roosevelt's) or star athletes like Marion Motley and Bill Willis, the first men to break the color barrier in NFL football ("World of Coca-Cola"). The contrast between these extremes underscores the prejudice: "ordinary" people are represented by whites, while only exceptional African Americans appear in the company's ads.

In 1950, then, the kind of diversity that Coke wanted to highlight and appeal   10 to was economic (middle-class and working-class) and war-related (civilian and military). Today, such an ad would probably represent the ethnic diversity missing from the 1950 version, with smiling young people of diverse skin colors and facial features relaxing with Cokes, probably now in cans rather than bottles. But the differences in economic, employment, or military status or in clothing styles that the 1950 ad highlighted would be unlikely to appear, not because they no longer exist, but because advertisers for products popular with a broad spectrum of society no longer consider them a useful way to appeal to consumers.

While initially the ads for Coca-Cola reflected the values of the time, their enormous success eventually meant that Coke ads helped shape the American identity. In them, Americans always appear smiling, relaxed, carefree, united in their quest for well-deserved relaxation and refreshment. They drive convertibles, play sports, dance, and obviously enjoy life. The message: theirs is a life to be envied and emulated, so drink Coca-Cola and live that life yourself.

Works Cited

Coca-Cola. Advertisement. *The Coca-Cola Bottler* 41.6 (1950): n. pag. Web. 5 May 2011.

Coca-Cola Company. "The Coca-Cola Company Heritage Timeline." *Coca-Cola History.* Coca-Cola Company, n.d. Web. 26 June 2011.

Esterl, Mike. "Diet Coke Wins Battle in Cola Wars." *Wall Street Journal.* 17 Mar. 2011: B1. Print.

"The World of Coca-Cola Self-Guided Tour for Teachers. Highlights: African-American History Month." *World of Coca-Cola.* World of Coca-Cola at Pemberton Place, n.d. Web. 26 June 2011.

Thinking about the Text

1. What insight does Melissa Rubin offer about the Coca-Cola ad she analyzes, and what **EVIDENCE** does she provide to support her analysis? Has she persuaded you to accept her conclusions? Why or why not?

2. What historical **CONTEXT** does Rubin provide, and what does that information contribute to her analysis?

3. Rubin's analysis is driven by this question: what can we learn about the culture in which a given ad is created by closely examining how that ad appeals to particular audiences? What other questions might you try to answer by analyzing an ad?

4. Rubin looks closely at the men and women in this ad and makes certain assumptions about them. What sorts of details does she point out to identify who these people are? Do you think she's represented them accurately? If not, how might you identify them differently, and why?

5. Write an **ANALYSIS** of a current ad, looking specifically at how it reflects American values in the twenty-first century. Be sure to include the ad in your essay.

FOURTEEN

"Just the Facts, Ma'am"

Reporting Information

ANY AMERICANS ASSOCIATE THE LINE "Just the facts, ma'am" with *Dragnet*, a 1950s TV crime drama, and more specifically with Sgt. Joe Friday, played by Jack Webb, who used this expression when interviewing women as part of an investigation. Or so people think. In fact, Sgt. Friday never uttered these exact words. He sometimes said, "All we want are the facts, ma'am" or "All we know are the facts," but the expression "Just the facts, ma'am" actually had its origins in a 1953 comedy routine that parodied the show. In the end, however, this line is linked forever with Sgt. Friday and *Dragnet* in the American popular imagination.

This story can be seen as a kind of very short report, and it demonstrates an important aspect of reports: they present information to audiences made up of individuals with varying degrees of knowledge. Perhaps you've heard the phrase "Just the facts, ma'am" but had no idea where it came from. Perhaps you've never heard of *Dragnet*. Now you have, and you know a few things about it. Even if you were familiar with both the program and the expression, you now likely have a new bit of information: the assumption that the expression came directly from the program is not borne out by fact. Thus, this very short report demonstrates how reports are written with a range of readers in mind.

It also reminds us of one of our favorite bumper stickers:

You are entitled to your own
opinions–but not your own facts.

Reports are built of information that is factual in some way. As you no doubt
realize, separating what is factual from what is opinion can be a challenge,
especially when the topic is controversial. Whatever Sgt. Friday may have
said, as a police investigator he was trying to establish factual information
so that he could write an effective police report, one that would help solve a
case and document how he had done so.

The primary goal of a report is to present factual information to educate an audience in some way. The stance of those who write reports is
generally objective rather than argumentative. Thus, newspaper and television reporters—note the word—in the United States have traditionally
tried to present news in a neutral way. Writers of lab reports describe as
carefully and objectively as they can how they conducted their experi-

Sgt. Joe Friday (Jack Webb) in *Dragnet*, a TV series that ran in the 1950s.

ments and what they found. Perhaps even more than authors in other genres, therefore, writers of reports aim to create an **ETHOS** of trustworthiness and reliability.

This chapter offers guidelines for composing reports, including profiles, a kind of report often assigned in college. As you'll see, writing effective reports requires you to pay careful attention to your purpose, audience, and stance as well as to whatever facts you're reporting.

REFLECT. Think about reports you've read, heard, seen, or written recently, and make a list of them. Your list may include everything from a lab report you wrote for a biology class, to a documentary film, to a PowerPoint *presentation you and several classmates created for a course. What similarities do these reports share—and in what ways do they differ?*

Across Academic Disciplines

Reports are found everywhere in academic life. You're certainly familiar with book reports, and you're probably familiar with lab reports from science courses. Students and practitioners in *biology, psychology, engineering*, and most fields in the *physical sciences, social sciences*, and *applied sciences* regularly write reports, generally based on experiments or other kinds of systematic investigation.

Many scientific reports share a common format—often labeled IMRAD (introduction, methods, results, and discussion)—and a common purpose: to convey information. The format mirrors the stages of inquiry: you ask a question, describe the materials and methods you used to try to answer it, report the results you found, and discuss what they mean in light of what you and others already know.

Another kind of report students often write, especially in courses that focus on contemporary society in some way, is the profile, a firsthand report on an individual, a group, an event, or an institution. A profile of a person might be based on an interview, perhaps with an American soldier who served in Iraq, for example, or the first female professor to receive tenure in your college's economics department. Similarly, a profile of an institution might report on the congregation of a specific house of worship, an organization, or a company; such reports often have a specific audience in mind, whether it is donors, investors, members, or clients.

Across Media

When reporting information, you'll find that different media offer you radically different resources. Throughout this chapter, we'll refer to reporting by the *New York Times* on the "double-full-full-full," an especially challenging aerial skiing maneuver involving a triple back flip and four body twists. Just before the 2010 Winter Olympics, the *Times* reported on this jump in three media. It was the subject of a *news article* by Henry Fountain that appeared in the Science section in print and online. It was also the basis of a *video* feature on the *Times* website in which Fountain explains the physics of the flip, as demonstrated by U.S. Olympic skier Ryan St. Onge. Finally, it was the focus of part of a science *podcast* featuring interviews with both St. Onge and Fountain. Two of these reports use images, two use spoken words, and one relies primarily on written words.

In studying these three reports, you'll get a clear idea of how medium influences not only how information is reported but also what kinds of information can be covered. For an example of how much the medium affects the message, consider *Twitter*: imagine what Fountain could have reported about the double-full-full-full in 140 characters.

Across Cultures and Communities

Wherever you find formal organizations, companies, and other institutions, you'll find reports of various kinds. For example, a school board trying to maintain the quality of education in a time of shrinking budgets will surely rely on information in reports written by *parents' organizations, community groups, teachers' unions,* or *outside consultants*. Odds are that the reports from each of these groups would differ in focus and tone. Some of these reports might be based primarily on statistical data while others might feature personal testimonies. Those created by outside consultants would likely be very formal and data-driven and might include a *PowerPoint* presentation to the school board followed by a question-and-answer period. In contrast, a report from a parents' group could include a homemade video consisting primarily of conversations with schoolchildren.

As a student, you'll be working in various academic communities, and you will need to pay attention to the way information is reported across disciplines—and to what is expected of you in any reports that you write.

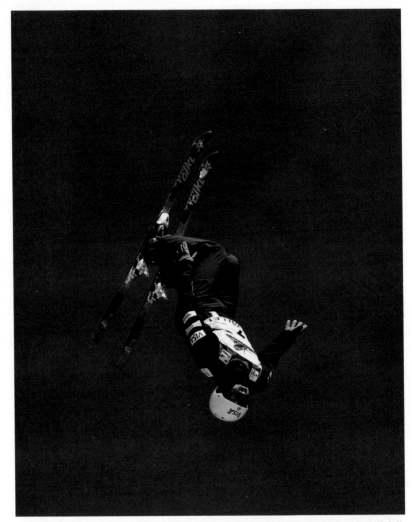

WATCH THE VIDEO of U.S. Olympic skier Ryan St. Onge performing a double-full-full-full, a triple back flip with four body twists. Then listen to the podcast on the physics of aerial skiing. Pay attention to how some of the technical terms are defined (and keep in mind that in the video, definitions may include images as well as words). Describe the double-full-full-full using words alone. Then add an image. Do you need to alter your original description once you add the image? Go to everyonesanauthor.tumblr.com to access the video and podcast.

Across Genres

While reports are a common genre of writing, you'll also have occasion to report information in other genres. **NARRATIVES**, **ANALYSES**, **REVIEWS**, **ARGUMENTS**, and many other kinds of writing contain factual information often presented as neutrally as possible—and you will often report factual evidence to support your claims.

On the other hand, some documents that are called reports present more than "just the facts" and cross the line to **ANALYZE** or interpret the information presented, to make a **PROPOSAL**, and so on. For example, a report on economic development in Austin, Texas, concludes with recommendations for the future. Those recommendations follow many pages of carefully reported information (as well as considerable analysis of that information). When you're assigned to write a report, you will want to determine exactly what the person who assigned it has in mind: a text that only reports information or one that is called a report but that also requires you to analyze the information, make some kind of argument, and so on.

REFLECT. Analyze the purposes of the reports that you listed on p. 254. Who is the intended audience for each? To what degree does each simply report information, and to what degree does it use information to serve some larger goal, for example, to take a position on an issue? Can you distinguish clearly between a report that only presents information and one that presents information and also argues a point?

Sometimes the genre itself becomes part of the story. The humor of the *Onion* article on p. 1025 is that such trivial information could even be reported.

CHARACTERISTIC FEATURES

While you can expect differences across media and disciplines, most of the reports you will write share the following characteristics:

- A topic carefully focused for a specific audience
- Definitions of key terms
- Trustworthy information
- Appropriate organization and design
- A confident, informative tone

A Topic Carefully Focused for a Specific Audience

The most effective reports have a focus, a single topic that is limited in scope by what the audience already knows and what the author's purpose is. For example, in 2008, Liveable City, a nonprofit organization that works to protect the quality of life in Austin, Texas, released a report on economic development in Austin. Liveable City's website offers this summary of the report's content and structure:

> [T]he report [looks at] where Austin's economic development strategy comes from, how it is implemented, and what institutions shape our economic development policies and programs. Focusing on tax incentives and how they fit into broader economic development activities, the study examines why incentives are used, how much the city is giving, and what the taxpayers are getting from the public investment. The study also identifies reforms needed to create a unified, sustainable economic strategy, embraced by the community, to better position Austin for future economic challenges and opportunities.
> —MICHAEL ODEN, "Building a More Sustainable Economy"

Notice how the report's author, Michael Oden, a local professor of urban planning, focuses his report on economic development strategies and tax incentives, and then three related topics: "why incentives are used, how much the city is giving, and what the taxpayers are getting."

Oden assumes that he is writing for people who care about Austin (notice that he refers to "our" policies and programs). His intended readers would have included members of the board of Liveable City as well as indi-

The title page of Michael Oden's report includes three images that capture the essence of his plan for Austin: green industries, transportation, and the arts.

vidual and corporate donors. Because such reports are often cited in news stories and opinion pieces in the local media, we can assume that the intended readers also included Austinites more broadly. But Oden is also writing for audiences beyond Austin, especially those interested in how tax incentives fit into "broader economic development activities." Although the report was distributed as a print document, likely to local members of the intended audience, it is available to anyone with internet access.

In their four-page 2012 annual report for Proud Ground, a nonprofit group that seeks to provide affordable housing for first-time home buyers in Portland, Oregon, the authors have a very different purpose: to show the achievements of the organization over the past year. They do so with minimal text—on page one, a single-paragraph greeting from the executive director and the board chair looks back on the past year and thanks supporters of the program; on page two, a list of all the major accomplishments in 2012 and photographs of new homeowners; on the third page, two pie charts breaking down the year's revenue and expenses; and on the final page, a list

2012

- 42 new home buyers served.
- 484 people attended Homebuying Information Sessions.
- 190 households added to the home buyer wait list.
- 54% of all households served were from communities of color.
- Pipeline of future homebuying opportunities continues to grow: 40+ units, in various stages of development.
- Proud Ground begins administering a Home Repair IDA, providing Proud Ground homeowners with matching grant funds for vital home repair and maintenance projects.
- Proud Ground successfully integrates with Clackamas Community Land Trust and now one organization—Proud Ground—serves the entire region with permanently affordable home buying opportunities.

From Proud Ground's annual report, a list of the year's major accomplishments.

I needed the roots of homeownership. As a Native American I needed to somehow make my place on the land where I raise my children and grow food.

It was meant to be. Proud Ground was the perfect fit for me and my desire for a home of my own that I could really afford.

From Proud Ground's annual report: Natalie and Lisa, two new homeowners.

acknowledging "community investors" (donors and volunteers). The most notable part of the report is the photographs of the families, all visibly happy to have their own homes. These color images and the statements below them about the impact of owning a home appeal to readers' emotions and visually represent the accomplishments of Proud Ground.

In composing this report, the authors were obviously thinking about their primary audience: those who have donated to Proud Ground in the past and those who might do so in the future, and who want to be informed about the work the organization does—what it accomplishes and how economically it does so.

In both the Liveable City and Proud Ground reports, the topic is carefully focused, and the authors approach their task with a keen eye toward the intended audiences and their organization's goals. You'll want to do the same in the reports that you write: to consider carefully whom you're addressing, what they know about your topic, and what information they expect.

Definitions of Key Terms

Effective reports always define key terms explicitly. These definitions serve several functions. Some audience members may not understand some of the technical terms. And even those familiar with the terms pay attention to the definitions for clues about the writer's stance or assumptions. Here's an example of a definition from Michael Oden's report for Liveable City:

> **What Are Economic Incentives?** In addition to . . . general economic strategies, Austin—like most other cities—provides financial incentives designed to encourage specific economic outcomes, such as a desired company locating its headquarters here. Incentives may take many forms including tax abatements or rebates, fee waivers, expedited site approval process, up-zoning, or other types of grants or guarantees. Direct incentives are used to change the economic landscape by attracting new economic activities or new types of physical development that would not be generated by the private sector without specific inducements. In Austin, incentives can be generally categorized in one of two ways: "firm-based" or "project-based."

Notice how Oden explains the purpose of financial incentives ("to encourage specific economic outcomes, such as a desired company locating its headquarters here"), gives examples ("tax abatements or rebates, fee waivers, expedited site approval process, up-zoning, or other types of grants or guarantees"), defines "direct incentives" (those "used to change the economic landscape by attracting new economic activities or new types of physical development that would not be generated by the private sector without specific inducements"), and finally divides incentives into two subcategories ("firm-based" and "project-based"). He then devotes a paragraph to defining and illustrating each of these subcategories of incentives.

It's also worth noting how Oden introduces his definitions. Partly because his report is lengthy, he uses headings to help structure it. Here he introduces his definition by posing a direct question—"What are economic incentives?"—and then answers that question in a paragraph.

In the *New York Times* article on aerial skiing mentioned on page 256, Henry Fountain uses a number of strategies to provide readers with definitions they might need. As a newspaper journalist, Fountain writes for a general audience, and he can safely assume that some readers of the Science section will have a great deal of knowledge about physics. He can likewise assume that some readers will know something about aerial skiing, but he also anticipates that other readers will know little about either. Here's one definition Fountain offers:

> The first time you watch skiers hurtle off a curved ramp at 30 miles per hour, soaring six stories in the air while doing three back flips and up to five body twists, you can't help but think: These people are crazy. . . .
>
> Freestyle aerialists, as these athletes are known, are not actually throwing caution, along with themselves, to the wind.
>
> —HENRY FOUNTAIN, "Up in the Air, and Down, with a Twist"

Here the short phrase "as these athletes are known" refers back to the skiers Fountain has described earlier, and this explains the term "freestyle aerialists."

A few paragraphs later, Fountain explains *torque*, the concept in physics that allows freestyle aerialists to do somersaults, without explicitly defining it:

> "The forces are pretty simple," said Adam Johnston, a physics professor at Weber State University in Ogden, Utah. . . . "There's the force of the ramp on his skis, and the force of gravity on him," Dr. Johnston said, after Ryan St. Onge, the reigning world champion in men's aerials and a mem-

ber of the Olympic team, zipped down a steep inrun, leaned back as he entered the curved ramp until he was nearly horizontal and flew off at a 70-degree angle. "That's all there is."

But it is enough to create torque that sends Mr. St. Onge somersaulting backward as he takes to the air, arcing toward a landing on a steep downslope that the skiers and coaches have chopped and fluffed for safety.

Later in the article, Fountain writes: "In this training jump, Mr. St. Onge adds a full twist in both the second and third flips—a lay-full-full in the language of the sport." Here Fountain provides a technical term used by experts—a "lay-full-full"—immediately after explaining what the term means. In a subsequent paragraph, Fountain uses another strategy, providing a definition of a "double-full-full-full" in a **SUBORDINATE CLAUSE** (italicized here): "And when doing a double-full-full-full, *which requires four full twists, including two in the first flip*, he will use all three methods at takeoff." Note that none of the definitions shown here quote a dictionary, nor do they use the formula "the definition of X is Y"—and that each of the experts offers memorable examples that help readers understand the subject.

Trustworthy Information

Effective reports present information that readers can trust to be accurate. In some cases, writers provide documentation to demonstrate the verifiability of their information, including citations of published research, the dates of interviews they have conducted, or other details about their sources.

In a report for a writing class at Chapman University, Kelley Fox presents information in ways that lead readers to trust the details she presents and, ultimately, the author herself. The report describes how Griffin, Simon, and Andy, three roommates in Room 115 of her dorm, create their identities. Beginning with Muhammad Ali's line "Float like a butterfly, sting like a bee," which is the caption on a large poster of Ali on Griffin's wall, Fox seeks to characterize Griffin as someone who floats at "the top of the pecking order" and who seems "invincible":

> In a sense, Griffin is just that: socially invincible. A varsity basketball athlete, Griffin has no shortage of friends, or of female followers. People seem to simply gravitate toward him, as if being around him makes all

Larry Gordon reports on *Wikipedia*, a site some people associate with the essence of untrustworthiness. See on p. 952 how he inspires trust in both his report and his topic.

their problems trivial. Teammates can often be found in his room, hanging out on his bed, watching ESPN. Girls are certainly not a rarity, and they usually come bearing gifts: pies, CDs, even homework answers. It happens often, and I have a feeling this "social worship" has been going on for a while, although in myriad other forms. Regardless, the constant and excessive positive attention allows Griffin to never have to think about his own happiness; Griffin always seems happy. And it is because of this that, out of the three roommates, it is easiest to be Griffin.

—KELLEY FOX, "Establishing Identities"

Fox's description demonstrates to readers that she has spent considerable time in or around Room 115 and that she knows what she is writing about. Her use of specific details convinces us that Griffin is real and that the things she describes in fact occur—and on a regular basis.

In a report on early language development in children written for a linguistics class at Portland State University, Katryn Sheppard demonstrates the trustworthiness of her information differently, citing both published research and her own primary research on a speech transcript of one-year-old Allison.

One feature of Allison's utterances that did adhere to what is expected for a typical child at this age was related to her use of negatives. Although she used only one negative word—"no"—the word was repeated frequently enough to be the fourth most common category in the transcript. Her use of "no" rather than any other negative conformed to Brown's (1973) finding that other forms of negation like "not" and "don't" appear only in later stages (Santelmann, 2014). In Allison's very early stage of linguistic development, the reliance on "no" alone seems typical.

—KATRYN SHEPPARD, "Early Word Production"

For the full text of Katryn Sheppard's report, go to p. 620. By citing both published research and examples from her own primary research, Sheppard demonstrates that she has spent considerable time researching her topic and can thus make informed observations about Allison's speech. These citations not only let readers know that Sheppard can support her claims, they also indicate where readers can go to verify the information if they so choose; both strategies demonstrate trustworthiness.

Although Fox and Sheppard use different techniques, both of them convince readers that the information being presented and the writers themselves can be trusted.

Appropriate Organization and Design

There is no single best strategy for organizing the information you are reporting. In addition to **DEFINING** (as Henry Fountain does), you'll find yourself **DESCRIBING** (as Kelley Fox does), offering specific **EXAMPLES** and data (as the report from Proud Ground does), **ANALYZING CAUSES AND EFFECTS** (as Michael Oden does), and so on. The specific organizational strategies you'll use will depend on the information you want to report.

In many cases, you'll want to include visuals of some sort, whether photographs, charts, figures, or tables. See, for example, the two pie charts from the Proud Ground annual report. The information they convey would be much harder to understand and thus far less effective if it were presented in a paragraph or even as a table. And as noted on page 261, Proud Ground also uses color photos to make the report more interesting and appealing. Similarly, see on page 256 the way that Henry Fountain uses images in his discussion of aerial skiing.

Sometimes the way in which you organize and present your information will be prescribed. If you're writing a report following the **IMRAD** format, you will have little choice in how you organize and present informa-

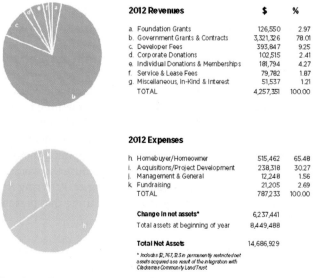

2012 Revenues	$	%
a. Foundation Grants	126,550	2.97
b. Government Grants & Contracts	3,321,326	78.01
c. Developer Fees	393,847	9.25
d. Corporate Donations	102,515	2.41
e. Individual Donations & Memberships	181,794	4.27
f. Service & Lease Fees	79,782	1.87
g. Miscellaneous, In-Kind & Interest	51,537	1.21
TOTAL	4,257,351	100.00

2012 Expenses	$	%
h. Homebuyer/Homeowner	515,462	65.48
i. Acquisitions/Project Development	238,318	30.27
j. Management & General	12,248	1.56
k. Fundraising	21,205	2.69
TOTAL	787,233	100.00

Change in net assets*	6,237,441
Total assets at beginning of year	8,449,488
Total Net Assets	14,686,929

* Includes $2,767,325 in permanently restricted net assets acquired as a result of the integration with Clackamas Community Land Trust

Pie charts from Proud Ground's 2012 annual report.

tion. Everything from the use of headings to the layout of tables to the size of fonts may be dictated.

Some disciplines specify certain format details. Students of *psychology*, for example, are expected to follow **APA STYLE**. On the other hand, a report for a *composition* class may have fewer constraints. For example, you may get to decide whether you will need headings and whether to use personal examples.

A Confident, Informative Tone

James Sanborn's report on Marine Corps body standards is accessible to a general audience, but his tone is thoroughly professional. See how he does it on p. 1043.

Effective reports have a confident tone that assumes the writer is presenting reliable information rather than arguing or preaching. Michael Oden and Henry Fountain both sound like they know what they're writing about. In both these cases, we as readers are by and large getting just "the facts," though it is clear that Oden has strong convictions about what the city of Austin should be doing in the future and that Fountain delights in both the beauty and the science of what freestyle aerialists can achieve.

The line between informing and arguing can become fuzzy, however. If you read reports on any number of hot-button issues—climate change, the economy, gay marriage, abortion—you'll find that they often reflect some kind of position or make recommendations that betray a position. But the authors of such reports usually try to create an informative tone that avoids indicating their own opinions.

You may sometimes find yourself struggling with this line, working to present information while stopping short of telling readers what to think about or how to feel about a topic. Here we can offer two pieces of advice. First, keep in mind that you're aiming to explain something to your audience clearly and objectively rather than to persuade them to think about it a certain way. You'll know you've succeeded here if someone reading a draft of your report can't tell exactly what your own opinion about the topic is. Second, pay special attention to word choice because the words you use give subtle and not-so-subtle clues about your stance. Referring to "someone who eats meat" is taking an objective tone; calling that person a "carnivore" is not.

WIKIPEDIA, the free online encyclopedia that "anyone can edit," has become one of the most-visited sites on the web since it was launched in 2001. Like any encyclopedia, the primary purpose of *Wikipedia* is to report information. Below is the opening section of the entry on same-sex marriage, as it appeared on August 17, 2015. This article offers a good example of how authors negotiate the challenges of reporting information fairly and from a neutral perspective. *Wikipedia* provides many examples of reporting on controversial topics, and the site has explicit policies about the writing of entries and even offers an entry on writing from a "neutral point of view." Readers can also tab over to "Talk," "Edit," and "View History" to read about or report information that is controversial—and *Wikipedia* explicitly acknowledges problematic aspects of an entry, noting when the neutrality of an article has been disputed and pointing out sections that need "additional citations for verification."

Same-Sex Marriage
WIKIPEDIA

SAME-SEX MARRIAGE, also known as **gay marriage**, is marriage between people of the same sex, either as a secular civil ceremony or in a religious setting.

    Same-sex unions are recorded in the history of a number of cultures, but marriage or similarly formalized same-sex unions were rare or nonexistent in other cultures.[specify][when?] In the late 20th century, religious rites of marriage without legal recognition became increasingly common. The first law providing for marriage

A definition of the topic followed by a history of its development.

of people of the same sex in modern times was enacted in 2001 in the Netherlands. As of 26 June 2015, eighteen countries (Argentina, Belgium, Brazil, Canada, Denmark,[nb 1] France, Iceland, Luxembourg, the Netherlands,[nb 2] New Zealand,[nb 3] Norway, Portugal, South Africa, Spain, Sweden, the United Kingdom,[nb 4] the United States[nb 5] and Uruguay) and certain sub-jurisdictions allow same-sex couples to marry. Similar laws in Finland, Ireland and Slovenia are not yet in force. Polls show rising support for legally recognizing same-sex marriage in the Americas, Australia, and most of Europe.[1][2][3] However, with the exception of South Africa and Israel, no country in Africa or Asia recognizes same-sex marriage.

Introduction of same-sex marriage laws has varied by jurisdiction, being variously accomplished through legislative change to marriage laws, a court ruling based on constitutional guarantees of equality, or by direct popular vote (via ballot initiative or referendum). The recognition of same-sex marriage is a political and social issue, and also a religious issue in many countries, and debates continue to arise over whether people in same-sex relationships should be allowed marriage or some similar status (a civil union).[4][5][6] Same-sex marriage can provide those in same-sex relationships who pay their taxes with government services and make financial demands on them comparable to those afforded to and required of those in opposite-sex marriages. Same-sex marriage also gives them legal protections such as inheritance and hospital visitation rights.[7] Various faith communities around the world support allowing those of the same sex to marry, while many major religions oppose same-sex marriage. Opponents of same-sex marriages have argued that recognition of same-sex marriages would erode religious freedoms and undermine a right of children to be raised by their biological mother and father.

Some analysts state that financial, psychological and physical well-being are enhanced by marriage, and that children of same-sex parents or carers benefit from being raised by two parents within a legally recognized union supported by society's institutions.[8][9][10][11][12] Court documents filed by American scientific associations also state that singling out gay men and women as ineligible for marriage both stigmatizes and invites public discrimi-

Underlining signals links to more information.

Notice the organization: definitions first, a brief history, a statement of the issue or controversy, and a review of the major arguments offered by either side.

The tone is confident and avoids taking a stance on this controversial topic.

Footnotes link to evidence that demonstrates the trustworthiness of the information.

nation against them.[13] The <u>American Anthropological Associa-</u><u>tion</u> avers that social science research does not support the view that either civilization or viable social orders depend upon not recognizing same-sex marriage.[14]

Go to everyonesan author.tumblr.com to link to the full *Wikipedia* article.

REFLECT. *Analyze a* Wikipedia *entry on a topic of your choice to see how focused the information is, how key terms are defined, and how the entry is organized. How trustworthy do you find the information—and what makes you trust it (or not)? How would you characterize the tone—informative? informative but somewhat argumentative? something else? Point to words that convey that tone.*

PROFILES

Profiles provide firsthand accounts of people, places, events, institutions, or other things. Newspapers and magazines publish profiles of interesting subjects; college websites often include profiles of the student body; investors may study profiles of companies before deciding whether or not to buy stock. If you're on *Facebook* or *LinkedIn*, you have likely created a personal profile saying something about who you are and what you do. Profiles take many different forms, but they generally have the following features.

A Firsthand Account

In creating a profile, you're always writing about something you know firsthand, not merely something you've read about. You may do some reading for background, but reading alone won't suffice. You'll also need to talk with people or visit a place or observe an event in some way. Keep in mind, however, that while a profile is a firsthand account, it should not be autobiographical. In other words, you can't profile yourself. In his 2002 *New Yorker* profile of soul singer James Brown, Philip Gourevitch describes Brown's performance as he saw it firsthand as a member of the audience.

> There he is: arms out from his sides as if to welcome an embrace, dentistry blazing in a beatific grin, head turning slowly from side to side, eyes goggle-wide—looking down-right blown away to find himself the focus of such a rite of overwhelming acclamation. He lingers thus for several seconds, then, throwing his head back, he lets out a happy scream and rips into the song "Make It Funky." Within seconds, he has sent his microphone stand toppling toward the first row of orchestra seats, only to snatch the cord and yank it back, while spinning on the ball of one foot in a perfect pirouette, so that his mouth returns to the mike and the mike to his mouth in the same instant. He howls. The crowd howls back.
> —PHILIP GOUREVITCH, "Mr. Brown"

Here the author gives readers information about Brown's performance that he could only have gathered from seeing him live, and it's those details of Brown's actions on stage that make the profile come to life.

Detailed Information about the Subject

Profiles are always full of details—background information, descriptive details (sights, sounds, smells), anecdotes, and dialogue. Ideally, these details help bring the subject to life—and persuade your audience that whatever you're writing about is interesting, and worth reading about. What makes the excerpt from the *New Yorker* piece so successful is the kind of details about Brown that the author provides. We can almost see him "spinning on the ball of one foot in a perfect pirouette." Here's another example with different but similarly detailed information about Brown's early musical training (or lack thereof).

> He claims to have mastered the harmonica at the age of five, blowing "Lost John," "Oh, Susannah," and "John Henry," and one afternoon, when he was seven, he taught himself to play the organ by working out the fingering of "Coonshine Baby." Before long, he was picking up guitar licks to such songs as "(Honey) It's Tight Like That" from the great bluesman Tampa Red, who was dating one of Aunt Honey's girls. By the time he was twelve, the young prodigy was fronting his own group.

Much of this information comes from the interviews that Gourevitch conducted while following Brown on tour and visiting his childhood home. The specific details, from the names of songs he sang to the ages when he sang them, go a long way toward establishing his credibility as a writer—and make his profile of Brown even more believable.

Another way that writers of profiles bring their subjects "to life" is by including photos, letting readers see their subjects in action. In the photo on the next page, James Brown seems larger than life, leaping into the air, letting us see what Gourevitch describes.

An Interesting Angle

The best profiles present a new or surprising perspective on whatever is being profiled. In other words, a good profile isn't merely a description; rather, it captures something essential about its subject from an interesting angle, much as a memorable photo does. When you plan a profile, try to come up with an angle that will engage readers. That angle will dictate what infor-

James Brown performing on *Saturday Night Live*, 1980.

mation you include. One thing that makes Gourevitch's profile of James Brown so interesting is the angle that he takes on Brown's life and career, starting with his improbable musical genius.

> He was a middle-school dropout, with no formal musical training (he could not read a chart, much less write one), yet from early childhood he had realized in himself an intuitive capacity not only to remember and reproduce any tune or riff he heard but also to hear the underlying structures of music, and to make them his own.

BILL LAITNER covers local news for the *Detroit Free Press*, specializing in social and political issues and human interest stories like the one below. The following profile, published in the *Free Press* in January 2015, inspired a nationwide response.

Heart and Sole:
Detroiter Walks 21 Miles in Work Commute
BILL LAITNER

Leaving home in Detroit at 8 a.m., James Robertson doesn't look like an endurance athlete.

Pudgy of form, shod in heavy work boots, Robertson trudges almost haltingly as he starts another workday.

But as he steps out into the cold, Robertson, 56, is steeled for an Olympic-sized commute. Getting to and from his factory job 23 miles away in Rochester Hills, he'll take a bus partway there and partway home. And he'll also walk an astounding 21 miles.

Five days a week. Monday through Friday.

It's the life Robertson has led for the last decade, ever since his 1988 Honda Accord quit on him.

Every trip is an ordeal of mental and physical toughness for this soft-spoken man with a perfect attendance record at work. And every day is a tribute to how much he cares about his job,

The profile opens with descriptive details that introduce readers to the subject—and make us want to read on.

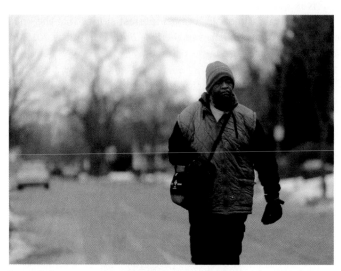

James Robertson commutes 23 miles to and from his job every day—
most of it on foot.

Placing Robertson's challenging commute in the context of the struggles faced by other Detroiters gives it an interesting and meaningful angle.

Another interesting angle: Robertson's extraordinary work ethic in spite of the challenging circumstances.

Interviews with Robertson and his co-workers provide detailed firsthand information.

his boss and his coworkers. Robertson's daunting walks and bus rides, in all kinds of weather, also reflect the challenges some metro Detroiters face in getting to work in a region of limited bus service, and where car ownership is priced beyond the reach of many.

But you won't hear Robertson complain—nor his boss.

"I set our attendance standard by this man," says Todd Wilson, plant manager at Schain Mold & Engineering. "I say, if this man can get here, walking all those miles through snow and rain, well I'll tell you, I have people in Pontiac 10 minutes away and they say they can't get here—bull!"

As he speaks of his loyal employee, Wilson leans over his desk for emphasis, in a sparse office with a view of the factory floor. Before starting his shift, Robertson stops by the office every day to talk sports, usually baseball. And during dinnertime each day, Wilson treats him to fine Southern cooking, compliments of the plant manager's wife.

"Oh, yes, she takes care of James. And he's a personal favorite of the owners because of his attendance record. He's never missed a day. I've seen him come in here wringing wet," says Wilson, 53, of Metamora Township.

With a full-time job and marathon commutes, Robertson is clearly sleep deprived, but powers himself by downing 2-liter bottles of Mountain Dew and cans of Coke.

"I sleep a lot on the weekend, yes I do," he says, sounding a little amazed at his schedule. He also catches zzz's on his bus rides. Whatever it takes to get to his job, Robertson does it.

"I can't imagine not working," he says.

"Lord, Keep Me Safe"

The sheer time and effort of getting to work has ruled Robertson's life for more than a decade, ever since his car broke down. He didn't replace it because, he says, "I haven't had a chance to save for it." His job pays $10.55 an hour, well above Michigan's minimum wage of $8.15 an hour but not enough for him to buy, maintain and insure a car in Detroit.

As hard as Robertson's morning commute is, the trip home is even harder.

At the end of his 2-10 p.m. shift as an injection molder at Schain Mold's squeaky-clean factory just south of M-59, and when his coworkers are climbing into their cars, Robertson sets off, on foot—in the dark—for the 23-mile trip to his home off Woodward near Holbrook. None of his coworkers lives anywhere near him, so catching a ride almost never happens.

Instead, he reverses the 7-mile walk he took earlier that day, a stretch between the factory and a bus stop behind Troy's Somerset Collection shopping mall.

"I keep a rhythm in my head," he says of his seemingly mechanical-like pace to the mall.

At Somerset, he catches the last SMART bus of the day, just before 1 a.m. He rides it into Detroit as far it goes, getting off at the State Fairgrounds on Woodward, just south of 8 Mile. By that time, the last inbound Woodward bus has left. So Robertson foots it the rest of the way—about 5 miles—in the cold or rain or the mild summer nights, to the home he shares with his girlfriend.

"I have to go through Highland Park, and you never know what you're going to run into," Robertson says. "It's pretty dangerous. Really, it is dangerous from 8 Mile on down. They're not the type of people you want to run into.

"But I've never had any trouble," he says. Actually, he did get mugged several years ago—"some punks tuned him up pretty good," says Wilson, the plant manager. Robertson chooses not to talk about that.

So, what gets him past dangerous streets, and through the cold and gloom of night and winter winds?

"One word—faith," Robertson says. "I'm not saying I'm a member of some church. But just before I get home, every night, I say, 'Lord, keep me safe.' "

The next day, Robertson adds, "I should've told you there's another thing: determination."

A Land of No Buses

Detailed information about Robertson's commute, including a graphic with time stamps, helps readers understand it more clearly—and why it's so incredible.

Robertson's 23-mile commute from home takes four hours. It's so time-consuming because he must traverse the no-bus land of rolling Rochester Hills. It's one of scores of tri-county communities (nearly 40 in Oakland County alone) where voters opted not to pay the SMART transit millage. So it has no fixed-route bus service.

Buses provide sparse service on Robertson's long work commute, leaving him to walk most of the way on foot.

Once he gets to Troy and Detroit, Robertson is back in bus country. But even there, the bus schedules are thin in a region that is relentlessly auto-centric.

"The last five years been really tough because the buses cut back," Robertson says. Both SMART and DDOT have curtailed service over the last half decade, "and with SMART, it really affected service into Detroit," said Megan Owens, executive director of Transportation Riders United.

The local angle on this story as an example of the struggles many face in Detroit leads Laitner to include information about the city's transportation services.

Detroit's director of transportation said there is a service Robertson may be able to use that's designed to help low-income workers. Job Access and Reverse Commute, paid for in part with federal dollars, provides door-to-door transportation to low-income workers, but at a cost. Robertson said he was not aware of the program.

Still, metro Detroit's lack of accessible mass transit hasn't stopped Robertson from hoofing it along sidewalks—often snow-covered—to get to a job.

At Home at Work

Robertson is proud of all the miles he covers each day. But it's taking a toll, and he's not getting any younger.

"He comes in here looking real tired—his legs, his knees," says coworker Janet Vallardo, 59, of Auburn Hills.

But there's a lot more than a paycheck luring him to make his weekday treks. Robertson looks forward to being around his co-workers, saying, "We're like a family." He also looks forward to the homemade dinners the plant manager's wife whips up for him each day.

"I look at her food, I always say, 'Excellent. No, not excellent. Phenomenal,' " he says, with Wilson sitting across from him, nodding and smiling with affirmation.

Although Robertson eats in a factory lunchroom, his menus sound like something from a Southern café: Turnip greens with smoked pork neck bones, black-eyed peas and carrots in a brown sugar glaze, baby-back ribs, cornbread made from scratch, pinto beans, fried taters, cheesy biscuits. They're the kind of meal that can fuel his daunting commutes back home.

Though his job is clearly part of his social life, when it's time to work this graduate of Northern High School is methodical. He runs an injection-molding machine the size of a small garage, carefully slicing and drilling away waste after removing each finished part, and noting his production in detail on a clipboard.

Strangers Crossing Paths

Robertson has walked the walk so often that drivers wonder: Who is that guy? UBS banker Blake Pollock, 47, of Rochester, wondered. About a year ago, he found out.

Pollock tools up and down Crooks each day in his shiny black 2014 Chrysler 300.

"I saw him so many times, climbing through snow banks. I saw him at all different places on Crooks," Pollock recalls.

Last year, Pollock had just parked at his office space in Troy as Robertson passed. The banker in a suit couldn't keep from asking the factory guy in sweats, what the heck are you doing, walking out here every day? They talked a bit. Robertson walked off and Pollock ruminated.

From then on, Pollock began watching for the factory guy. At first, he'd pick him up occasionally, when he could swing the time. But the generosity became more frequent as winter swept in. Lately, it's several times a week, especially when metro Detroit sees single-digit temperatures and windchills.

"Knowing what I know, I can't drive past him now. I'm in my car with the heat blasting and even then my feet are cold," Pollock says.

Other times, it's 10:30 or 11 p.m., even after midnight, when Pollock, who is divorced, is sitting at home alone or rolling home from a night out, and wondering how the man he knows only as "James" is doing in the frigid darkness.

On those nights, Pollock runs Robertson all the way to his house in Detroit.

"I asked him, why don't you move closer" to work. "He said his girlfriend inherited their house so it's easy to stay there," Pollock said.

On a recent night run, Pollock got his passenger home at 11

p.m. They sat together in the car for a minute, outside Robert-son's house.

"So, normally you'd be getting here at 4 o'clock (in the morn-ing), right?" the banker asks. "Yeah," Robertson replies. Pollock flashes a wry smile. "So, you're pretty early, aren't you?" he says. Robertson catches the drift.

"Oh, I'm grateful for the time, believe me," Robertson says, then adds in a voice rising with anticipation: "I'm going to take me a bath!"

After the door shuts and Pollock pulls away, he admits that Robertson mystifies him, yet leaves him stunned with admiration for the man's uncanny work ethic and determination.

"I always say to my friends, I'm not a nice guy. But I find myself helping James," Pollock says with a sheepish laugh. He said he's picked up Robertson several dozen times this winter alone.

> *Laitner notes details such as Pollock's "wry smile" and "sheepish laugh" that signal that he is providing details from conversations he heard, adding credibility to his writing.*

Has a Routine

At the plant, coworkers feel odd seeing one of their team num-bers always walking, says Charlie Hollis, 63, of Pontiac. "I keep telling him to get him a nice little car," says Hollis, also a machine operator.

Echoes the plant manager Wilson, "We are very much trying to get James a vehicle." But Robertson has a routine now, and he seems to like it, his coworkers say.

"If I can get away, I'll pick him up. But James won't get in just anybody's car. He likes his independence," Wilson says.

Robertson has simple words for why he is what he is, and does what he does. He speaks with pride of his parents, including his father's military service.

"I just get it from my family. It's a lot of walking, I know."

> *The conclusion brings up another interesting angle to Robertson's story, how he connects his walking to a strong work ethic he inherited from his parents.*

REFLECT. Bill Laitner profiles an ordinary person whose extraordinary commute brought nationwide attention to the challenges of getting to work without a car or public transportation. Think about someone you know whose story might prove significant in this way. If you were to profile this person, what details would bring the person to life and what angle would make his or her story matter to others?

REPORTING INFORMATION / A Roadmap

Choose a topic that matters—to you, and to others

If you get to select your topic, begin by considering topics that you know something about or are interested in learning more about. Whatever your topic, be sure it's one you find intriguing and can be objective about. If you're a devout Catholic and believe that the church is wrong—or right— in its stance on birth control, you're likely to have trouble maintaining the "just the facts" stance necessary for writing a good report.

The more controversial the topic, the more challenging it may be to re- port fairly and accurately on it because the facts themselves likely will be the subject of controversy. So if you're going to write about a controversial topic, you might consider reporting on the controversy itself: the major per- spectives on the issue, the kinds of evidence cited, and so on.

If you've been assigned a topic, find an aspect of it that is both interesting and focused. Unless you've been specifically instructed to address a broad topic (for example, the consequences of World Bank policies for third-world economies), focus on a narrower aspect of the topic (take a single developing country that interests you and report on the consequences of World Bank policies for that economy). Even when you are asked to report on a broad topic, see if it is possible to start out with a specific case and then move to the broader issue.

Consider your rhetorical situation

Analyzing your audience, purpose, and other elements of your rhetorical situation will help you to make the decisions you'll face as you write.

Address your AUDIENCE appropriately. If you're writing a report for an audience you know—your classmates, your instructor—you can some- times assume what they will and won't know about your topic. But if you're writing for a broader audience—all students on campus, readers of a blog—you'll likely be addressing people with different levels of knowl- edge. Your challenge will be to provide enough information without in- cluding irrelevant details. For example, Henry Fountain didn't explain what skiing is or waste his readers' time by including information not directly relevant to his topic. Here are some questions that might guide you in considering your audience:

- What do you know about your audience? To what extent are they like or unlike you—or one another?
- What background information will your audience likely need on your topic? Will their knowledge of it vary?
- What terms need to be defined or illustrated with examples? What sorts of examples will be most effective for your audience?
- What interest does your audience have in your topic? If they're not already interested in it, how can you get them interested—or at least to see that it matters?

Be clear about your PURPOSE. Consider why you are writing a report on this topic for this particular audience. Odds are that you want your report to do more than merely convey information. If you're writing it for a course, you likely want to learn something and to get a good grade. If the report is part of a large project—a campaign to encourage composting on campus, for example—a lot may be riding on the quality of your work. What short-term goals do you have in writing, and do they relate to any longer-term goals?

Consider your STANCE. Think about your own attitudes toward your topic and your audience: What about this topic captured your interest? Why do you think it matters—or should matter—both in general and to your audience? How can you establish your authority on the topic and get your audience to trust you and the information you provide? How do you want them to see you? As a fair, objective reporter? As thoughtful? serious? curious? something else?

Consider the larger CONTEXT. What are the various perspectives on the topic, and what else has been said about it? What larger conversations, if any, is this topic a part of? For a report that's part of a campaign to encourage composting on campus, for example, you'd need to become familiar with how such programs have been conducted at other schools, and what the main challenges and arguments have been.

Think about MEDIA. As the three reports on aerial skiing make clear, the medium you use to say something plays a big role in determining the message you convey. If you have a choice, will your text be presented in print? on the web? as an oral report? Which will be most effective for your subject and audience? If you've got audio of an interview, can you embed it in an online report or incorporate it into an oral report? If your report will be in print, can you summarize or quote from the interview? If your report will be oral, should you prepare slides to help your audience follow your main points?

Think about DESIGN. Consider what design elements are available to you and will help you convey your information in the clearest, most memorable way. For example, much of the effectiveness of Proud Ground's annual report comes from the large color photos and testimonials from new homeowners. Black-and-white images or plain headshots would have been far less effective. Think about whether your report will include any elements that should be highlighted. Do you need headings? Would photos, charts, tables, or other visuals help you convey information more effectively than words alone? Do you have the option of using color in your text—and if so, what colors will set the right tone?

Research your topic

Your goal in researching your topic is first to get a broad overview of what is known about it and second to develop a deeper understanding of the topic. While most high school reports discuss the research of others, those you write in college may call on you to gather data yourself and then write about the data in light of existing research.

LAB REPORTS, for example, describe the results of experiments in engineering and the natural sciences, and reports based on ethnographic observation are common in the social sciences. And whatever your topic or field, reading SECONDARY SOURCES will help you see how your findings relate to what people already know.

Thus, your first task is to read broadly enough to get a feel for the various issues and perspectives on your topic so that you know what you're talking about and can write about it authoritatively.

Begin by assessing what you know—and don't know—about the topic. What aspects of your topic do you need to learn more about? What questions do you have about it? What questions will your audience have? To answer these questions, you might try BRAINSTORMING or other activities for **GENERATING IDEAS**. Such activities may help you focus your topic and also discover areas you need to research further.

Find out what others say. You can research others' **POSITIONS** and perspectives in many different ways. If your topic is a local one, such as alcohol use at your college, you may want to conduct a student survey, interview administrators or counselors who deal with campus drinking problems, or do a search of local newspapers for articles about alcohol-related incidents. But it would also be a good idea to look beyond your own community, in order to gain perspective on how the situation at your school fits into national patterns. You could consult books and periodicals, databases, websites, or online forums devoted to your topic. If your topic doesn't have a local focus, you will likely start out by consulting sources like these. You may also interview people at your school or in the community who are experts on your topic.

Decide whether you need to narrow your topic. What aspect of your topic most interests you, and how much can you cover given the constraints of your assignment? If your political science professor has assigned a five-minute oral report on climate-change legislation, for example, you will need to find a more specific focus than you would for a twenty-page written report on the same general topic. In the first case, you might (with your teacher's permission) focus on one specific bill and its fate in Congress rather than try to cover all of the legislation that falls into this category.

Organize and start writing

Once you've narrowed your topic and have some sense of what you want to say about it, you need to think about how you can frame your topic to appeal to your audience and how you can best organize the information you have collected. As you draft, you may discover that you need to do some additional research as new questions and ideas arise. But for now, just get started.

Come up with a tentative thesis. State your topic and the gist of what you have to say about it in a tentative **THESIS** statement, trying to make it broad enough to cover the range of information you want to share with your audience but limited enough to be manageable—and keeping in mind that your goal is to report information, not to argue a position.

Organize your information. Make a list of the information you want to convey, and think about what details you want to include. You'll find that you need various strategies for presenting information—**DESCRIPTION**, **DEFINITION**, **ANALYSIS**, **EXAMPLES**, and so on.

Then consider how to arrange your material. Some topics call for a **CHRONOLOGICAL** structure, moving from past to present, maybe even projecting into the future, as the report on economic development in Austin does. Or you may find that a **SPATIAL** organization works well—if you're reporting on the design of a new building, for instance—moving from exterior to interior or from top to bottom. There are any number of ways to organize a report in addition to these; you'll just need to work out a structure that will help your audience understand your topic in a systematic way.

Don't be surprised if you find that you do not need to use all of the information that you have collected. Authors often gather far more information than they finally use; your task is to choose the information that is most relevant to your thesis and present it as effectively as possible.

Draft an OPENING. Why do you care about your topic, and how can you get your audience interested in it? You will want to open by announcing your subject in a way that makes your audience want to know more about it. Consider opening with an intriguing example or a provocative question. Perhaps you have a memorable anecdote. It's usually a good idea also to include the thesis somewhere in the introduction so that your audience can follow from the outset where your report is heading and don't have to figure it out for themselves.

Draft a CONCLUSION. What do you want your audience to take away from your report? What do you want them to remember? You could end by noting the implications of your report, reminding them why your topic matters. You could summarize your main points. You could even end with a question, leaving them with something to think about.

Look critically at your draft, get response—and revise

Try rereading your draft several times from different perspectives and imagining how different readers will experience your text. Will readers new to the topic follow what you are saying? Will those who know about the topic think that you have represented it accurately and fairly? If possible, get feedback from a classmate or a tutor at your school's writing center. Following are some questions that can help you and others examine a report with a critical eye:

- *How does the report* OPEN*?* Will it capture your audience's interest? How else might it begin?

- *Is the topic clear and well focused?* Are the scope and structure of the report set out in its opening paragraphs? Is there an explicit THESIS statement—and if not, would it help to add one?

- *Is it clear why the topic matters*—why you care about it and why others should?

- *How does the draft appeal to your* AUDIENCE*?* Will they be able to understand what you say, or do you need to provide more background information or define any terms?

- *How do you establish your* AUTHORITY *on the topic?* Does the information presented seem trustworthy? Are the sources for your information credible, and have you provided any necessary DOCUMENTATION?

- *Is the* TONE *appropriate for your audience and purpose?* If it seems tentative or timid, how could you make it more confident? If it comes across as argumentative, how could you make it focus on "just the facts"?

- *How is the information organized?* Past to present? Simple to complex? Some other way? Does the structure suit your topic and MEDIUM? What strategies have you used to present information— COMPARISON, DESCRIPTION, NARRATION?

- *What* MEDIA *will the report be presented in,* and how does that affect the way it's written? You might consider including photos in a print report, for example, videos and links in an online report, or slides to go along with an oral presentation.

- *Is the report easy to follow?* If not, try adding TRANSITIONS or headings. If it's an oral report, you might put your main points on slides.

- *If you've included illustrations,* are there captions that explain how they relate to the written text? Have you referred to the illustration in your text? Is there information in your text that would be easier to follow in a chart or table?

- *Is the* **STYLE** *appropriate for your audience and purpose?* Consider choice of words, level of formality, and so on.

- *How effective is your* **CONCLUSION** *?* How else might you end?

- *Does the title tell readers what the report is about,* and will it make them want to know more?

Revise your draft in response to any feedback you receive and your own analysis, keeping in mind that your goal is to present "just the facts."

REFLECT. Once you've completed your report, let it settle for a while and then take time to reflect. How well did you report on your topic? How successful do you think you were in making the topic interesting to your audience? What additional revisions would you make if you could? Research shows that such reflections help "lock in" what you learn for future use.

Selling the Farm
BARRY ESTABROOK

LAST FRIDAY, for the first time in 144 years, no one at the Borland family farm got out of bed in the pre-dawn hours—rain, shine, searing heat, or blinding blizzard—to milk the cows. A day earlier, all of Ken Borland's cattle and machinery had been auctioned off. After six generations on the same 400 acres of rolling pastures, lush fields, and forested hillsides tucked up close to the Canadian border in Vermont's remote Northeast Kingdom, the Borlands were no longer a farm family.

It was not a decision they wanted to make. A fit, vigorous 62-year-old, Borland could have kept working. His son, who is 35 and has two sons of his own, was once interested in taking over. But the dismal prices that dairy farmers are receiving for their milk forced the Borlands to sell. "We've gone through hard times and low milk prices before," said Borland's wife, Carol, a retired United Methodist minister. "This time there doesn't seem to be any light at the end of the tunnel. There's no sense working that hard when you're 62 just to go into debt."

For several months I'd been reading headlines and following the statistics behind the current nationwide dairy crisis. The math is stark. Prices paid to farmers per hundredweight (about 12 gallons) have fallen from nearly $20 a

BARRY ESTABROOK, a journalist who concentrates on food politics, writes for the *New York Times*, the *Washington Post*, and a variety of publications. This article appeared in *Gourmet* magazine in August 2009.

year ago to less than $11 in June. Earlier this month, the Federal government raised the support price by $1.25, but that is only a drop in the proverbial bucket. It costs a farmer about $18 to produce a hundredweight of milk. In Vermont, where I live, that translates to a loss of $100 per cow per month. So far this year, 33 farms have ceased operation in this one tiny state.

Meanwhile, the price you and I pay for milk in the grocery store has stayed about the same. Someone is clearly pocketing the difference. Perhaps that explains why profits at Dean Foods—the nation's largest processor and shipper of dairy products, with more than 50 regional brands—have skyrocketed. The company announced earnings of $75.3 million in the first quarter of 2009, more than twice the amount it made during the same quarter last year ($30.8 million). (Dean countered that "current supply and demand is contributing to the low price environment.")

But rote statistics have a way of masking reality. So last week, I drove up to   5
the village of West Glover for a firsthand look at the human side of the dairy crisis by attending the Borland auction. "You will be witnessing what is going to be the fate of all heritage farms," Carol Borland told me.

It was a breathtakingly clear morning in one of the most stunning settings imaginable. The Northeast Kingdom is an undulating patchwork of fields, woodlots, streams, lakes, barns, and white clapboard houses, set against the jagged, blue-gray backdrop of distant mountaintops. I didn't need a sign to direct me to the Borland place: For more than a mile before I crested a hill and saw the barns and silos, the gravel road leading to the farm was lined with dusty, mud-splattered pickup trucks. A crowd of close to 900 had gathered, in part because a country auction is always a major social event, a festive excuse for bone-weary farmers to take a day off, bring the kids, catch up with the gossip, and grumble about the weather, costs, and prices. That made it easy to overlook the sad, serious nature of the business at hand: selling off every last item there (and with any luck, providing the Borlands with a retirement nest egg). Among other things to go on the auction block was a massive amount of equipment, much of which had been shared with neighbors in loose, mutually beneficial arrangements stretching back generations. The demise of one family farm can affect similar small operators for miles in all directions. The auctioneer had to sell a half-dozen tractors, a dump truck, a couple of pickup trucks, manure spreaders, hay balers, wagons, seeders, mowers, milking machines, and assorted antique farm implements. There was feed that Borland had harvested but would no longer have any use for, 50 tons of shelled corn, 800 bales of hay. And, last in the photocopied catalogue, 140 prime Holsteins,

Nearly 900 farmers attended the auction that marked the end of the 144-year-old Borland family farm.

a herd known for its excellence, having earned Borland 16 quality awards over the previous two decades. Unlike the cows that pass their lives in complete confinement on the factory farms that are replacing farms like his, Borland's cows went out on those hilly pastures every day, strengthening their bodies and feeding on grass. Borland worried that with most other farmers as financially strapped as he was, or worse, the cows might not sell. "I didn't spend my whole life breeding up a good herd to see them beefed" (meaning slaughtered for hamburger meat), he said.

Items were sold at a nerve-rattling pace as the auctioneer chanted his frenzied, mesmerizing, "I've got five. Give me ten, ten, ten. Five, gimme ten, ten, ten. A ten dollar bill. Five gimme ten, ten ten." Three "ringmen" worked the crowd, waving their canes to cajole bids, and whooping when the price rose. A John Deere tractor started at $25,000 and was dizzily bid up to $30,000, $40,000, $50,000, and finally $60,000, in a matter of three minutes. Lesser machines sometimes sold in half that time. All morning long, there was no let-up.

Just after the Deere was sold, I asked Borland's son Nathan how he thought things were going. "Online, that tractor would be listed for $75,000, if you can find one half that good, which you can't," he said. "But I guess you can't complain, given how hard it is for everybody."

Making maple syrup a century ago at the sugarhouse built by Ken Borland's great-grandfather in 1898.

After attending college and working out of state for a few years, Nathan came home and joined his father on the farm. But he left to become a paramedic. "I like the work, but it got so bad financially that I felt guilty taking a paycheck," he said. "My sons, they're young. It'd be nice if they wanted to farm one day, but there's not a living to be made in dairy farming."

Carol, who was beside us, added, "The reality of farming is that as a parent, even if you'd like to and they want to, you can't encourage a child to go into something where he won't be able to earn a decent living."

Once the last piece of machinery was gone, the throng moved to folding chairs set up around a fenced ring inside the barn. Borland, who had been taciturn and shy most of the day, stood before the crowd to deliver a short speech. After thanking everybody for coming and expressing his gratitude for the efforts of the auction crew, he said, "I just want to say that these are a good bunch of cows. This auction wasn't their fault. They've always done their part. They have produced well."

Then he told a sad joke. "There was this farmer's son who left the farm and found work as a longshoreman in the city. The first ship that came in carried a cargo of anvils. To impress his new workmates, the boy picked up two anvils, one under each arm. But the gangplank snapped under the weight. He fell

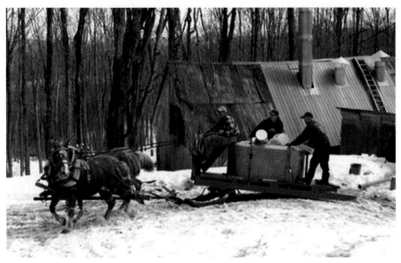

The Borlands still sugar the old-fashioned way, insisting it makes for better-tasting maple syrup.

into the water and sank. He came up one time and shouted for help. No one moved. He went down and came up a second time. Still no help. The third time he came up he hollered, 'If you guys don't help me soon, I'm going to have to let go of one of these anvils.' "

There was nervous laughter. Borland went on, "That's what farming's been these last six months, trying to stay afloat with anvils. This is the day that I let go of mine."

The herd sold well. As an emotional bonus, 20 went to local farmers and would still be grazing on nearby pastures. Borland and Carol were pleased with the overall proceeds of the auction, and doubly pleased because they had been fortunate enough to find a buyer for the property and buildings who would take good care of the land that had supported their family through the generations. The Borlands severed off a piece of land where they will build a house. In the spring, they still plan to tap some maples. The sap will be boiled in the sugarhouse that Borland's great-grandfather built in 1898.

Before the auction, Borland had told his son that he planned to sleep until 15 noon the day afterwards. Fat chance. He was up at 3:30 in the morning, as always. A few cows that had been sold had yet to be picked up, and cows, even ones that now belong to another man, need to be milked. He finished that chore and drove the full milk cans over to a neighbor who was still in the business and had a cooling tank. Borland offered him a lift back to a hayfield he wanted to cut that day. As they rode along in the cab of the truck with the early morning sun streaming over the mountains, the neighbor said, "Ken, do you know how many farmers around here would give anything to be in your shoes? We have to keep struggling. You had a way out."

Thinking about the Text

1. How does Barry Estabrook make this profile of the Borland auction interesting? What details does he provide to show the "human side of the dairy crisis"?

2. "Selling the Farm" is a profile, a firsthand account written for *Gourmet* magazine. How would Estabrook's **AUDIENCE**, readers interested in food and wine, have affected the details he included?

3. How does Estabrook establish his **AUTHORITY** to write on this topic? How does he convince readers that the information he's providing is trustworthy?

4. Imagine Estabrook had written about the Borland auction for a newspaper, as an objective **REPORT** rather than a profile. How would it have been different?

5. Write a **PROFILE** of a person or event, following the guidelines on pp. 280–86. To come up with an interesting angle for your profile, it might help to identify the audience you want to reach: what angle would likely interest them?

The Right to Preach on a College Campus

RYAN JOY

FREE SPEECH ON college campuses has recently become a hotly contested issue in both the popular press and academic circles. The question of whether incendiary speech abides by university guidelines and constitutional protections raises important and fraught questions for both students and the administrators who arbitrate disputes over what qualifies as protected free expression.

Last month, in an area of campus on Park Avenue called the Park Blocks, a street preacher aggressively ministered to the students of Portland State University (PSU) in service to his religious beliefs. On a number of occasions over about a week, he harangued passersby, even instigating verbal altercations with students. The man seems to have been unaffiliated with any student group or organization.

In seeking to understand the significance of such an event, we come to a better comprehension of the larger issue of how college administrators seek to foster a safe and secure environment for students without running afoul of laws protecting the right to freedom of expression.

The question of whether informal public preaching falls within the First

RYAN JOY graduated from Lewis and Clark College with a degree in religious studies and is currently studying economics at Portland State University. He hopes to write professionally in the future and to report on business and economic news. A version of this article was first published in 2015 in the *Portland Spectrum,* a student magazine at Portland State.

Amendment's definition of protected religious speech becomes more complicated when considering a few of the comments this preacher made to specific people. For example, he is purported to have called one woman a "slut" and to have asked others intrusive, personal questions.

When deciding on issues of free speech, administrators must balance the   5 competing interests of a student's right to attend class free of harassment with someone else's right to voice his or her views unimpeded. Indeed, it is often the most objectionable views that require the most steadfast protection. Generally, the Supreme Court disallows speech restrictions that discriminate on the basis of content, and religious speech has been notoriously difficult to proscribe.

Legal precedent has something to say on the subject: in *McGlone v. University of Tennessee*, a 6th U.S. Circuit Court of Appeals decided against the school after the administration sought to bar an itinerant preacher from speaking publicly on campus. Although the preacher, John McGlone, appears to have been moderately respected in the community (the PSU preacher struck many observers as unstable at best), the precedent set by the *McGlone* decision starkly illustrates how our courts balance rival interests in such disputes.

In *McGlone*, the preacher successfully reversed a lower court ruling and affirmed his right to preach on the basis of a rule known as the "vagueness doctrine," a legal test founded in the due process clause of the Fifth and Fourteenth Amendments which requires that laws must be clearly comprehensible and allow for uniform enforcement ("Vagueness Doctrine"). The judge who wrote the opinion in *McGlone* remarked that First Amendment cases must apply the vagueness doctrine stringently. Thus, since John McGlone contends that the university gave him conflicting information about his right to preach on campus, the 6th Circuit Court overturned the lower court's decision to uphold the university's rule barring public speech absent formal permission from a registered student organization or a current student.

Extrapolating from this court's decision, one may wonder whether a clear, unambiguous rule banning unaffiliated speakers would pass constitutional muster if instituted at PSU. As it stands, the university has no restrictions against people wandering onto campus and expounding on their topic of choice. While it is true that PSU has instituted and assiduously promoted its safety guidelines, PSU's codes of conduct stay largely silent on the type of on-campus conflicts that might occur between a student and those unaffiliated with the university— the types of conflicts that are abundant on a downtown college campus.

In response to an emailed list of questions concerning whether PSU might successfully restrict the presence of such visitors, Phillip Zerzan, PSU's Chief of Campus Public Safety, confirmed that "the ability to regulate or control speech in the Park Blocks is guided by the First Amendment" and that while the preacher appears to have harassed students, such "non-physical, generally directed harassment speech is still protected speech."

"There is much case law confirming [that the regulation of speech] must be content neutral," Zerzan added, recognizing that speech restrictions are difficult if not impossible to institute when they restrict speech on a certain topic, especially religion. Even religiously motivated hate-speech enjoys the same protections as more benign forms of expression. "The preachers are a common event on campus, and we encourage students to engage in this conversation in a constructive manner, or otherwise ignore the speech," Zerzan concluded. 10

David Johns, a PSU professor of political science, corroborates this reading of the law as it applies to the preacher, who technically was preaching on public, city-owned property. According to Johns, as long as someone in the Park Blocks is not drawing noise complaints, engaging in disorderly conduct, or specifically threatening students, "they can pretty much say what they want."

To be sure, there are categories of speech that courts have exempted from First Amendment protections. Speech that presents an imminent danger to public health, for instance, and that which intends to do harm enjoy no legal immunity. In the landmark 1942 Supreme Court case *Chaplinsky v. New Hampshire*, the "fighting words" doctrine limited the First Amendment's protection of certain types of speech, including "the lewd and obscene, the profane, the libelous, and the insulting or 'fighting' words—those which by their very utterance inflict injury or tend to incite an immediate breach of the peace" (*Chaplinsky*).

This category may not apply to street preachers, however, regardless of the illicit questions they might pose to students. And while the courts may have once been sympathetic to the notion that large categories of speech deserved little in the way of First Amendment protections, as of the late twentieth century, courts have begun to roll back such exemptions and have granted First Amendment protection to all types of speech. As Johns notes, "although *Chaplinsky* has never been overturned directly . . . its effect has been considerably reduced."

The current Supreme Court seems more inclined than ever to give preference to those claiming immunity under the First Amendment, often invoking the reasoning that more speech equals more freedom. PSU, for one, is in no danger of stifling freedom of expression. Recently, PSU has witnessed a flourishing display of ideas, and while certain visitors may strike some as unworthy of careful consideration, it is the principle that allows them to continue that many consider worthy of protection.

Works Cited

Chaplinsky v. State of New Hampshire. The Oyez Project at IIT Chicago-Kent College of Law, n.d. Web. 24 Aug. 2015.

McGlone v. University of Tennessee at Knoxville. U.S. Court of Appeals for the Sixth Circuit. 2012. Web. 24 Aug. 2015.

"Vagueness Doctrine." Legal Information Inst., Cornell U Law School, n.d. Web. 24 Aug. 2015.

Thinking about the Text

1. A good report generally does not take sides on an issue and instead presents a balanced discussion of the major viewpoints in play. What key positions does Ryan Joy identify in the controversy over the rights of the campus preacher? How fairly does he represent each side?

2. Examine the way that Joy introduces the issue in the first few paragraphs of his report. What kind of background information does he provide? Do you think he should have provided any additional background information or definitions—and if so, why?

3. Joy wrote this report for the *Portland Spectrum*, a student publication about campus issues, yet he addresses a controversy that has wide significance. How does Joy make his report applicable to **AUDIENCES** beyond the Portland State community?

4. What types of **EVIDENCE** does Joy rely on to develop his discussion of the two sides of this issue? How does the range of evidence affect Joy's **CREDIBILITY** as an author?

5. Choose an important campus issue that you want to explore. Research the issue by reading what others have written, speaking to people in your campus community, conducting a survey, or some other method of gathering information. Write a **REPORT** that presents a balanced view of all sides of the issue. Consider submitting the report to a school publication.

FIFTEEN

"Two Thumbs Up"
Writing a Review

ESTAURANTS, CELL PHONES, BOOKS, movies, TV, cars, toaster ovens, employees—just about anything can be reviewed. Nowadays, many people don't buy a new product or try a new restaurant without first checking to see what others have said about it online—and posting their own thoughts on it afterward.

You've probably given casual reviews of this sort yourself. If a friend asks what you think of the TV series *The Walking Dead*, your response would probably constitute a brief review: "It was much better than I'd expected. The special effects were really cool, but sometimes the plot lagged. But I guess I'll keep watching since so many people are talking about it." Even this offhand opinion includes two basic elements of all reviews: a judgment ("cool," "lagged") and the criteria you used to arrive at that judgment, in this case the quality of the special effects, the script, and the show's popularity.

Reviews can vary a good deal, however, as you can see in these examples from other reviews of *The Walking Dead*.

What makes *The Walking Dead* so much more than a horror show is that it plays with theatrical grandeur, on a canvas that feels real, looks cinematic and has an orchestral score to match.

A still from *The Walking Dead*.

For all its set pieces, however, *Walking* is most breathtaking in its small moments, in which the pain and glory of being human are conveyed with only the flick of a filmmaking wrist. We know this series can be something special early on, when Deputy Grimes encounters a crawling zombie too wounded to join the other "walkers." It's just a ravaged head and arms, really, dragging an exposed rib cage and skeletonized legs along the ground as it mewls horribly. In that moment, Grimes can only feel compassion. "I'm sorry this happened to you," he says, before putting a bullet in its head.

—NANCY DEWOLF SMITH, "Everything Old Is New Again"

Check out still another review of *The Walking Dead* on p. 908.

Nancy deWolf Smith's review, written as an essay for the *Wall Street Journal*, makes clear her criteria: the show's cinematic qualities, on the one hand, and its humanity, on the other. Writing for a newspaper, Smith is able to elaborate on these criteria with vivid examples like the scene she describes above.

On the other hand, *Metacritic.com* gives ratings by gathering numerical scores from multiple sources and calculating an average—82 out of 100 in the case of this series, near the lower edge of "Universal Acclaim." The site also provides excerpts and links to full reviews, and lets visitors add their own reviews. On *Metacritic.com*, everyone can be a reviewer.

This chapter provides guidelines for writing reviews—whether an academic book review for a political science class, a product review on *Amazon*, or a review of the literature on a topic you're researching.

REFLECT. Think about reviews you've read. All reviews evaluate something—a product, a performance, a text—and they do so using relevant criteria. Someone reviewing a movie, for instance, would generally consider such factors as the quality of the script, acting, directing, and cinematography. Think about a product you are familiar with or a performance you have recently seen. Develop a list of criteria for evaluating it, and then write an explanation of why these criteria are appropriate for your subject. What does this exercise help you understand about the process of reviewing?

Across Academic Disciplines

Reviews are a common genre in all academic disciplines. As a student, you will often be assigned to write a review of something—a book, a work of art, a musical performance—as a way of engaging critically with the work. While students in the *humanities* and *social sciences* are often asked to write book reviews, students in the *performing arts* may review a performance. In a *business* course, you may be asked to review products or business plans.

In each of these cases, you'll need to develop appropriate criteria for your evaluation and to support that evaluation with substantial evidence. The kind of evidence you show will vary across disciplines. If you're evaluating a literary work, you'll need to show evidence from the text (quotations, for example), whereas if you are evaluating a proposed tax policy for an economics class, you're probably going to be required to show numerical data demonstrating projected outcomes.

Across Media

Reviews can appear in many media—from print to digital, online to television and radio. Each medium offers different resources and challenges. A *television* film critic reviewing a new movie can intersperse clips from the

LOOK AT this illustration of a mola, an art form indigenous to Panama. This image was included in a newspaper review of Testimonios: 100 Years of Popular Expression, *an exhibit at New York's El Museo del Barrio in 2012. The same review on the newspaper's website includes a slideshow of art; see it at* everyonesanauthor.tumblr.com. *The article on the site includes links to further information, but it's otherwise identical to the print version. How else could a review designed specifically for the web take advantage of the medium—with maps? music? video? interviews? What else?*

film to back up her points, but her own comments will likely be brief. A different critic, writing about the same film for a *print magazine*, can develop a fuller, more carefully reasoned review, but will be limited to still images rather than video clips.

The same choices may be available to you when you are assigned to review something. For instance, if you give an *oral presentation* reviewing an art show, you might create slides that show some of the art you discuss. Perhaps your review could be a *video* that includes not only images of the art but also footage of viewers interacting with it. If you get to choose media, you'll need to think about which one(s) will allow you to best cover your subject and reach your audience.

Across Cultures and Communities

Conventions for reviewing vary across communities and cultures. In most U.S. academic contexts, reviews are quite direct, explicitly stating whether something is successful or unsuccessful and why. Especially on the internet, reviews are often very honest, even brutal. In other contexts, reviewers have reason to be more guarded. When the *Detroit News* reviews a new car, for instance, its writers have to keep in mind the sensitivities of the community, many of whom work in the auto industry, and of the company that produces that car, which may be a major advertiser in the newspaper. *Consumer Reports* might review the same car very differently, since it is supported not by advertisers but by subscribers who want impartial data and information that will help them decide whether or not to purchase that car.

A very different sort of review occurs in most workplaces, where employees receive annual performance reviews by their supervisors. There are often explicit criteria for evaluating workers, but these vary across professional communities and institutions: the criteria for someone who works at a hospital (a *medical community*) will be different from those for college instructors (an *academic community*).

In your classes, one challenge will be to figure out what's expected. If you're reviewing a magazine for a journalism class, the expectations will be different from what they would be if you were reviewing a draft by a friend who's writing an article for that magazine. As with any rhetorical situation, you'll need to figure out what's customary and expected.

Across Genres

Evaluation is often used as a strategy in other genres. **PROPOSALS** offer solutions to problems, for example, and in that process they must consider—and review—various other solutions. Evaluation and **ANALYSIS** often go hand in hand as well, as when *Consumer Reports* analyzes a series of smartphones in order to evaluate and rank them for its readers.

REFLECT. Look for several reviews of a favorite movie. You'll likely find many reviews online, but try also to find reviews in print sources or web versions of print publications. How do the reviews differ from one medium to the next? What, if anything, do the online reviews have that the print versions do not? Then check out some fan sites or Twitter *about the same movie. How does the medium affect the decisions that a reviewer makes about content, length, style, and design?*

CHARACTERISTIC FEATURES

Whatever the audience and medium, the most successful reviews share most of the following features:

- Relevant information about the subject
- Criteria for the evaluation
- A well-supported evaluation
- Attention to the audience's needs and expectations
- An authoritative tone
- Awareness of the ethics of reviewing

Relevant Information about the Subject

The background information needed in a review may entail anything from items on a restaurant menu to a description of the graphics of a video game to the plot summary of a novel or movie. What information to include—and how much—depends on your rhetorical situation. In the case of an academic review, your instructor may specify a length, which will affect how much information you can provide. What's needed in nonacademic reviews varies depending on the audience and publication. Someone reviewing a new album by an indie group for *Rolling Stone* may not need to provide much background information since readers are already likely to be familiar with the group. This would not be the case, however, if the same author were writing a review for a more general-interest magazine, such as *Time*.

See how a review of the Nintendo 3DS device opens with background information to help readers appreciate how the new device improves on other 3-D devices:

Nintendo's new 3DS device is quite literally like nothing you have seen before.

Nintendo 3DS

Have you ever watched full-motion 3-D video without wearing those annoying special glasses? Didn't think so. With the 3DS, set to make its debut on Sunday, you will.

In the guise of a hand-held game machine that costs about $250, Nintendo has produced a most astonishing entertainment device. In an age of technical wonders, Nintendo's only competition in innovating personal electronics is Apple.

Though the DS has sold substantially more units than the iPhone (about 145 million DS's worldwide by the end of last year, to about 90 million iPhones), it generally eludes the attention of the technology and media elite because so many of its users are children.

That will change very quickly now. Just about every child in America who likes video games is going to want a 3DS; the clamor will reach a fever pitch this weekend and will continue straight through the summer and into the holiday season. And millions of adults, who previously paid little attention to their kids' game machines, are going to look at it just once and say, "Wow."

—SETH SCHIESEL, "Nintendo's New World of Games"

This example comes from a review written for the *New York Times*; the author assumes that his readers have some familiarity with 3-D images but that they may not have paid much attention to video game machines. Notice the underscored words: in the web version, readers can click on these links to read all about (and purchase) each of the products.

Reviews of films (and other narratives) often provide background information about the story, as does the following example from a newspaper review of *Walk the Line,* the film about the singer Johnny Cash:

Arkansas, 1944. Two brothers walk the long, flat corridor of earth between one corn field and another. Jack Cash, the elder, is memorizing the Bible. His little brother prefers the music of the hymnals and worries that Jack's talent for stories is the nobler enterprise. Jack wants to be a preacher. "You can't help nobody," he explains, "if you don't tell them the right story." Yet we already know it is his little brother, Johnny, who will grow up to tell the memorable stories, the kind you sing, the kind that matter most. In their own generic way, musical biopics are always the right story: the struggle towards self-actualization. With songs. They

Joaquin Phoenix as Johnny Cash in *Walk the Line* (2005).

are as predictable and joyful as Bible stories: the Passion of Tina Turner, the Ascension of Billie Holiday. It is a very hard-hearted atheist indeed who does not believe that Music Saves.   —ZADIE SMITH

This review was written for the *Daily Telegraph*, a British newspaper, by the novelist Zadie Smith. She opens with a summary of the story as the film begins and quotes some dialogue that catches our interest—but she also tells us something about "biopics," the film's genre. In short, this review's opening gives us information we will need, and that makes us want to read on.

Criteria for the Evaluation

Underlying all good reviews are clear criteria—things that matter in deciding whether your subject succeeds or doesn't succeed, is strong or weak, or good in some respects and poor in others. As an author, then, you'll need to establish the criteria for any review you write. Sometimes, the criteria are obvious or can be assumed: criteria for reviewing cars, for example, would almost assuredly include price, style, comfort, performance, safety, gas mileage, and so on. Often, however, you may want to shape the criteria for specific purposes and audiences. In reviewing a concert for your music appreciation class, your professor may expect you to pay attention to certain aspects of the music, yet may not be familiar with the performance you're reviewing, meaning you'll need to state your criteria explicitly: the program, the venue, the soloists, the ensemble, and so on. See how a reviewer of a performance of Handel's vocal music focuses on two criteria as the basis for her evaluation: expressive and technical abilities.

> Forsythe was unquestionably the star of the evening. Her tone was like toasted caramel and her expressiveness and vocal control were astounding. Her embellishments sounded spontaneous and effortless, pinpoint clear and fiendishly twisty but never gratuitous; every display of vocal fireworks had an expressive purpose. I've heard coloratura sopranos with expressive or technical abilities equal to Forsythe's, but almost none so rich in both.   —KATIE TAYLOR, "Handel in Good Hands"

If you were posting a quick review of the same concert on *Twitter*, you might be able to assume that your followers are familiar with these criteria and skip straight to the evaluation. In fact, one tweet about this concert said it simply: "Heart-stopping Handel." No need to name criteria—the author assumed her followers know what it takes for a soprano to stop hearts.

Many reviews combine both **QUANTITATIVE** and **QUALITATIVE** criteria. For example, one well-known source for evaluating colleges and universities is the annual rankings published by *U.S. News & World Report*, whose criteria are mostly quantitative. Here's how Texas A&M University fared in this ranking system in 2014, coming in at number 68:

Tuition	Total Enrollment Fall 2014	Acceptance Rate	6–year Graduation
In-state: $9,180 Out of state: $26,366	44,315	69.21%	81%

In addition, *U.S. News & World Report* often includes brief reviews written by students that rely on qualitative criteria:

> I love Texas A&M for all of its quirks and traditions. There is no other school this large where you will not feel like just another number to the faculty and staff. In fact, I rarely notice that the school is big at all. I love that everything seems to have a tradition to go along with it. While it takes a while to learn them all, and a lot of them seem kind of hokey, the traditions will enrich your college experience, and make you feel a kinship with your fellow schoolmates. Everyone you meet on campus is not a stranger, but merely a friend you've yet to meet! It's so true. Aggies are the friendliest bunch you will encounter. We are always willing to lend a hand, give directions, and answer any question you might have. We would welcome anyone with open arms. And while A&M is in many ways a great school, we do have our quirks, but you learn to live with and love them, to embrace them as your own.   —K'LEE, senior at Texas A&M

K'Lee uses qualitative criteria such as the campus atmosphere ("you will not feel like just another number") and values ("everything seems to have a tradition to go along with it") to give readers a sense of the school that they don't get from just seeing the numbers.

A Well-Supported Evaluation

The foundation of every review is a clear evaluation, a claim that something is good or bad, right or wrong, useful or not. Whatever you're reviewing, you need to give reasons for what you claim and sufficient evidence to support those reasons. And because rarely is anything all good or all bad, you also need to acknowledge any weaknesses in things you praise and any positives in things you criticize. Also, remember to anticipate and acknowledge reasons that others might evaluate your subject differently than you do. In other words, you need to consider other possible perspectives on whatever you're reviewing.

Journalist Amy Goldwasser approached a number of passengers on a New York subway and asked them for impromptu reviews of what they were reading. She then collaborated with the illustrator Peter Arkle to compose graphic reviews for the *New York Times Book Review*. Here's what two readers had to say:

MARIAH ANTHONY, 18, high school senior, on p.133 of <u>THE KITE RUNNER</u>, by Khaled Hosseini (paperback)

DON SHEA, 70, fiction writer, on p. 214 of <u>LIT</u>, by Mary Karr (paperback)

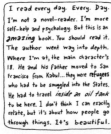

I read every day. Every. Day. I'm not a novel-reader. I'm more self-help and psychology. But this is an amazing book. You should read it. The author went way into depth. Where I'm at, the main character's 18. He and his father moved to San Francisco from Kabul...they were refugees who had to travel inside an oil tank to be here. I don't think I can exactly relate, but it's about how people go through things. It's beautiful.

This is her third book. I've read the first two. She's a poet.... I've been struck by the wonderful metaphors. I'm always surprised when poets really write superb prose. It gets a little draggy in the rehab part. She just keeps slipping and slipping. But it's good—all her stuff is good.

Both readers clearly stated what they thought of the books they were reading ("an amazing book," "it's good"). And then they gave reasons ("the author went way into depth," "all her stuff is good") and evidence to support those reasons ("he had to travel *inside an oil tank* to be here," "wonderful metaphors"). Note as well that one of the readers, Don Shea, acknowledges one weakness in Mary Karr's book ("It gets a little draggy in the rehab part").

When you're writing a review for a college class, you'll need to be more systematic and organized than these off-the-cuff reviews—with an explicitly stated evaluation, for one thing. See how a more formal review opens with a clear evaluation of a documentary film about a cave in southern France that contains paintings thought to have been done more than 30,000 years ago:

> What a gift Werner Herzog offers with *Cave of Forgotten Dreams*, an inside look at the Cave of Chauvet-Pont d'Arc—and in 3-D too.
> —MANOHLA DARGIS, "Herzog Finds His Inner Man"

The reviewer states her evaluation explicitly: the film is so good it is "a gift." As the review continues, she gives her readers background information on the cave and provides good reasons for her evaluation: "It's a blast . . . to see these images, within 3-D grabbing reach"; "Herzog is an agreeable, sometimes . . . funny guide, whether showing you the paintings or talking with the men and women who study them"; and he "also has a talent for tapping into the poetry of the human soul." At the same time, she acknowledges that the film has some shortcomings, though nothing that changes her overall assessment:

> *Cave of Forgotten Dreams* is . . . an imperfect reverie. The 3-D is sometimes less than transporting, and the chanting voices in the composer Ernst Reijseger's new-agey score tended to remind me of my last spa massage. Yet what a small price to pay for such time traveling!

In addition, the reviewer provides an image from the film, visual evidence of the "inside look" *Cave of Forgotten Dreams* offers. This review appeared in the *New York Times*; the print version includes the photo shown here, but the web version also includes four video clips from the film, along with several reviews posted by readers.

A still from *Cave of Forgotten Dreams* (2010).

Attention to the Audience's Needs and Expectations

All authors need to consider what their audience expects from them. But this consideration plays a particularly important role in the case of reviews. In many situations, some audience members will be familiar with what you're reviewing, whereas others will need a detailed summary or description; some will need an explicit statement of the criteria for the evaluation, while others will know what the criteria are without being told.

Audience considerations can also influence the criteria that reviewers identify as most crucial for their evaluation. Consider, for instance, reviews of video games. Gamers might expect one set of criteria, perhaps focusing on the games' playability and entertainment value. Parents and teachers might want entirely different criteria, ones that call attention instead to any violence and strong language.

Here, for instance, is the introduction to a review of *Minecraft: PlayStation 4 Edition* from *GameSpot*, an online forum for news and reviews serving the gaming community. This review was clearly written for an audience concerned with what this game lets them explore and create.

> To say that *Minecraft* is a game about digging and building huts to protect you from zombie attacks is to only scratch the surface of its immense depth. *Minecraft* has evolved considerably since its release to PC more than five years ago. Its boundaries have been tested by its community, which has birthed stunning castles and cities, as well as music machines, calculators, and tender homages to popular television shows and film. While the game eventually made a home on consoles, the aging hardware of the Xbox 360 and PlayStation 3 kept *Minecraft*'s voxel world restrained by an invisible border.
>
> *Minecraft: PlayStation 4 Edition* shatters that barrier, allowing you to fully experience seemingly endless worlds in which to explore and create. The stretching horizon, combined with better performance and sharper aesthetics, do not only make this version of *Minecraft* the best you can find on modern consoles. The boundless delight in creation, coupled by challenging exploration, all shouldered by supreme accessibility, makes *Minecraft: PlayStation 4 Edition* one of the best games to own on PlayStation 4.   —CAMERON WOOLSEY, "Blocky Empires"

Woolsey also assumes his readers are familiar with other gaming systems (Xbox 360, PlayStation 3) and know the language of gamers; later in this review he uses terms like "tooltips" and "four-player cooperative split-screen play" without taking the time to define them. More general audiences would have appreciated it if he had paused to explain, but defining terms his audience already knows would position him as an outsider to the gaming community and thus diminish his credibility with readers of *GameSpot*. Instead, he signals respect for his readers by addressing them as knowledgeable fellow gamers and focusing on issues they will care about.

REFLECT. *Find two reviews of the same subject (a movie, a band, whatever) from two different sources:* Yelp *and* Travel + Leisure, *perhaps, or* Salon *and* Time. *Look over each source, considering both articles and ads, and decide what kind of audience each one addresses. Young? Affluent? Intellectual? A general audience? Then study each review. How much prior knowledge does each one expect of its readers? How much space is devoted to describing the subject and how much to evaluating it? Do the two reviews use the same criteria—and if not, what might account for the difference? What does this analysis suggest about the role that audience plays in the way reviews are written?*

An Authoritative Tone

Authors of reviews have multiple ways of establishing their authority and credibility, and introductions are often crucial to doing so. Here, for instance, is the first paragraph of a lengthy review of several histories of American whaling that appeared in the *New Yorker*:

"Moby Dick swam swiftly round and round the wrecked crew."

If, under the spell of *Moby-Dick*, you decided to run away to the modern equivalent of whaling, where would you go? Because petroleum displaced whale oil as a source of light and lubrication more than a century ago, it might seem logical to join workers in Arabian oil fields or on drilling platforms at sea. On the other hand, firemen, like whalers, are united by their care for one another and for the vehicle that bears them, and the fireman's alacrity with ladders and hoses resembles the whaler's with masts and ropes. Then, there are the armed forces, which, like a nineteenth-century whaleship, can take you around the world in the company of people from ethnic and social backgrounds unfamiliar to you. All these lines of work are dangerous but indispensable, as whaling once was, but none seems perfectly analogous. Ultimately, there is nothing like rowing a little boat up to a sixty-ton mammal that swims, stabbing it, and hoping that it dies a relatively well-mannered death.

—CALEB CRAIN, "There She Blew: The History of American Whaling"

The series of arresting examples not only captures readers' attention but also demonstrates how thoroughly and carefully the reviewer knows his subject, thus making readers trust him and want to hear what he has to say.

Here is the introduction to an essay published in *Harper's Magazine* reviewing a number of works by Egyptian novelists Albert Cossery and Sonallah Ibrahim:

> Egypt is hard on its novelists. Their audience is tiny, their rewards few, their risks considerable. This is true in most if not all Arab countries, but Egypt is notable in having a long and astonishingly varied novelistic tradition, some of which is now becoming available in translation.
>
> —ROBYN CRESWELL, "Undelivered"

The broad generalizations at the start of this review make clear that this reviewer has considerable knowledge about Egyptian novels and Arabic literature more generally.

Finally, here is the introduction to a review of Tim Burton's film version of *Alice in Wonderland*, which appeared on National Public Radio on March 4, 2010:

> To enjoy Tim Burton's *Alice in Wonderland*, you'll need to accept that it's not by any stretch Lewis Carroll's *Alice's Adventures in Wonderland* or its follow-up, *Through the Looking Glass*, but a fancy Hollywood hybrid. Yes, it uses Alice's characters and motifs, but the plot is one part C. S. Lewis [the author of *The Chronicles of Narnia*] to one part *The Wizard of Oz*. You could call it "C. S. Lewis Carroll's *Alice in Narnia* with Johnny Depp as the Mad Scarecrow."
>
> —DAVID EDELSTEIN, "Burton's *Alice*: A Curious Kind of Wonderful"

This introduction shows that the reviewer is knowledgeable about the original novel and also about other children's adventure stories and Hollywood films. Moreover, his use of humor establishes his voice as one you want to listen to. (And note as well that this text was written to be heard on the radio.)

Johnny Depp as the Mad Hatter in *Alice in Wonderland* (2010).

If you get to choose your subject, be sure to select a topic that you know (and care) about, and share some of what you know in your introduction. Telling your audience something interesting about your subject and giving some sense that it matters will help establish your credibility and make them want to know more.

Awareness of the Ethics of Reviewing

Depending on context and purpose, a review can have substantial—or minimal—consequences. When the late, widely syndicated film reviewer Roger Ebert gave a Hollywood movie a thumbs-up or thumbs-down, his judgment influenced whether the movie was shown in theaters across America or went immediately to DVD. Those reviewing Broadway plays for publications like the *New York Times* hold similar powers. And reviews in *Consumers Reports* significantly influence the sale of the products they evaluate.

By comparison, a review of a local high school musical will not determine how long the musical will run or how much money it will make, but an especially negative review, particularly if it is unjustified, will certainly wound the feelings of those involved in the production. And a movie review on the *Internet Movie Database* (*IMDb*) that gives away key elements of a plot without including a "spoiler alert" will ruin the film for some of the audience. So an ethical reviewer will always keep in mind that a review has power—whether economic, emotional, or some other kind—and take care to exercise that power responsibly.

Considering the likely effect of your review on those who created whatever you're reviewing is part of the ethics of reviewing as well. It's one thing to criticize the latest episode of *The Walking Dead* (the creators of that series can afford to laugh all the way to the bank) but quite another when the author, artist, or cook is sitting next to you. It's not that you should hold back criticism (or praise) that you think the subject deserves, but you do need to think about the effect of your judgments before you express them.

How you express them is also important. In academic contexts, remember this responsibility especially when reviewing other students' drafts. Don't avoid mentioning problems just because you might make the writer feel bad, but be sure that any criticisms are constructive. Be sure to mention strengths as well as weaknesses and offer suggestions and encouragement for overcoming those weaknesses if you can.

TIM ALAMENCIAK is a digital media producer at TVOntario. He previously wrote for the *Toronto Star*, Canada's most widely read newspaper, where this book review was published in 2015.

Monopoly: The Scandal Behind the World's Favorite Board Game

TIM ALAMENCIAK

Opening with a mysterious but clever statement that turns out to be about a game many readers will know establishes an authoritative tone; the promise of a good story makes us want to read on.

SOMETIMES THE IRONIES OF THE WORLD are stranger than fiction. That a game based on wheeling and dealing was born of wheeling and dealing writ large is a prime example of this.

Mary Pilon's *The Monopolists* unearths and charts the fascinating history of the popular board game Monopoly and the court battle fought by Ralph Anspach, a quixotic professor trying to save his own game. It's a story rife with controversy and scandal.

The book hitches its narrative on the tale of Anspach, the professor who took umbrage with Monopoly's capitalist focus and created Anti-Monopoly. His move so rankled Parker Brothers, the then-owner of the original game, they started a legal action that unfolded over decades of hearings and appeals.

Once thought to be the brainchild of a man named Charles Darrow, who profited immensely from the game's success, the history is much more complicated than that.

A woman named Elizabeth Magie originally invented "The Landlord's Game" to teach students about Henry George's "single tax" concept—a notion that all land should be owned by the public and simply rented by the occupants. She patented it in 1903—three decades before Darrow attempted to sell the game.

Magie was a prolific advocate for the rights of women but remained hidden for decades—overshadowed by the story Parker Brothers included with every game about Darrow, a down-on-his-luck man during the depression who invented a game for his kids.

Magie made waves in other ways after inventing the game. Finding it difficult to support herself on a stenographer's wage and frustrated with the way things were, she took out an ad in the paper offering herself for sale as a "young woman American slave." The satirical ad spread like wildfire and Magie was eventually hired as a newspaper reporter.

> Alamenciak summarizes the history told in Pilon's book (without giving too much away) and provides relevant background information.

Meanwhile, her game had taken on a life of its own and was being passed around from family to family across the country. While still obscure, its fans were devoted and eager to teach it to others.

The board went through some transformations as others picked up the game and copied it for themselves. The original game was anti-capitalist, with an alternate set of rules to teach the difference. Pilon meticulously charts the path the design took from Magie's hands to Atlantic City, where Quakers penned the famous street names that exist to this day, then to the living room of Darrow.

> Words like "meticulously" and "compelling" (in the following paragraph) establish Alamenciak's criteria for evaluation.

The book is a compelling look at history through the lens of Monopoly. Pilon paints Magie as a heroine long forgotten who contributed more than just a game but also then-rebellious writing that advanced the cause of women.

Pilon's book is full of interesting historical info, but rather than unfolding as a cohesive narrative that follows Anspach's quest to keep Anti-Monopoly alive, it reads more like a book divided into two parts. The reader is provided the true biography of Monopoly and then is asked to accompany Anspach as he uncovers the revelations that were just delivered.

More could have been done to weave the two together and bring the reader with Anspach throughout the text.

> Alamenciak acknowledges the book's limitations, but he also notes its strengths. In considering both and phrasing his criticisms fairly, he shows he is aware of the ethics of reviewing.

That said, Pilon's writing is on-point and the historical information she's uncovered is fascinating. She is not writing about Monopoly; she is writing about American history intertwined with games.

> An explicit statement of another criterion for evaluation.

Quotes and specific examples from the book provide evidence for Alamenciak's claims.

"Games aren't just relics of their makers—their history is also told through their players," writes Pilon. "And like Lizzie's original innovative board, circular and never-ending, the balance between winners and losers is constantly in flux."

This is not just a book for Monopoly fans. It's a great read for anyone who likes to know the quirky, interesting history of board games in twentieth century America. Even discussions on trademarks and brands—which are frequent in the book—are made interesting by Pilon's well-reported examples.

She chronicles the fight by Parker Brothers to keep the sport of ping-pong known as Ping-Pong, their brand name, rather than table tennis. In 1933, the United States Table Tennis Association was formed to oversee the sport.

"It's hard to say just how much money Parker Brothers lost after control of the game slipped out of its grasp, meaning it now produced the game alongside a fleet of competitors," writes Pilon.

Alamenciak concludes by stating his overall evaluation of the book in a way that is useful to his audience.

This is a great book for anyone who likes a good historical read. It moves quickly and provides lots of interesting bits of history, wrapped together in a fascinating package that tells the true story of Monopoly.

REFLECT. Study a review on a subject that interests you and evaluate it, using the list of characteristic features of reviews on p. 302. Annotate the text you have chosen, noting which of the features are included and which are not. For any features you find missing, consider whether including them might have improved the review.

LITERATURE REVIEWS

When instructors refer to "the literature" on a certain topic, they probably aren't talking about poetry or other literary texts. Rather, "literature" in this case means published research on a given topic, and a literature review is a common assignment that asks you to survey, synthesize, and evaluate that research. You may be assigned to write a full essay reviewing a body of research, or to write a literature review as part of a report on research you've conducted. In either case, a literature review contains these features.

A Survey of Relevant Research on a Carefully Focused Topic

The literature you review should be credible, relevant academic sources related to your topic. When the choice is yours, a narrower topic is best: a review of what historians have learned about colonies and postcolonialism could easily run to thirty or more pages, whereas a review of what's been said about just one aspect of one of those topics would be more manageable. If your review is part of a research report, the literature you review will be guided by your **RESEARCH QUESTION** and should cover all the sources your study is based on. In some fields, you may be expected to cite only the most recent research, while in others you would likely begin with foundational studies and then trace the research that's followed. Keep in mind your assignment and the discipline you're working in to determine what kinds of sources are appropriate and how many are required in your review.

An Objective Summary of the Literature

Once you've collected the sources you'll review, you'll need to **SYNTHESIZE** them, looking for significant connections, trends, and themes that have emerged in the scholarship over time. Summarizing the themes and trends shows that you understand how the pieces in your review relate to one another and provides readers with an overview of their significance. In addition, you'll want to look for any ways that sources diverge or disagree. A synthesis of important trends might begin something like this: "Researchers writing about X have generally taken one of three perspectives on it," followed by a section discussing each perspective and what it has contributed to our understanding of the topic.

An Evaluation of the Literature

Like all reviews, literature reviews include an evaluation. The criteria for your evaluation will depend on your purpose for reviewing and the discipline you're writing in. If you're reviewing research as background for a report, its relevance to your project will be a key criterion. In all cases, you will also be looking at whether the research considers important questions and offers new insights—and at the **EVIDENCE** it provides. Your evaluation might point out strengths and weaknesses, as well as any limitations in what the research covers. Are there any important questions that are ignored? Claims for which little evidence exists? Gaps that future research might address?

An Appropriate Organization

It may be easiest to march through your sources one by one, but this sort of organization is hardly the most effective—and may end up reading like an annotated bibliography. When organizing sources for a literature review, think about how the sources relate to one another logically. Do they follow a clear progression that makes a chronological organization the most logical? Do they group by theme? by the authors' perspectives? by research methods? by trends in the results? Looking for ways in which your sources connect with one another will help you both synthesize the information and organize it in a way that helps readers see any significant patterns and trends.

Careful, Accurate Documentation

Be sure to follow carefully any disciplinary conventions for **CITING** and **DOCUMENTING** sources. For guidelines on following MLA and APA style, see Chapters 27 and 28.

CRYSTAL AYMELEK, a psychology and philosophy student at Portland State University, wrote the following literature review as part of a research report for a course in experimental psychology. To frame her research question, she first reviews literature on the nature of memory, then hones in on her topic with research on the effects of stress on memory, on mindfulness meditation and its potential benefits, and on the reported benefits of exercise. Evaluating this literature helps establish how her study attempts to add to our present knowledge of the topic. Her review includes a long list of the sources she reviews, which we've abbreviated here to save space.

The Effects of Mindfulness Meditation and Exercise on Memory

CRYSTAL AYMELEK

ACCORDING TO INFORMATION PROCESSING THEORY (Atkinson & Shiffrin, 1968; Baddeley & Hitch, 1974), human memory comprises three interconnected systems: sensory, working, and long-term memory. Information is initially detected and processed by sensory memory. The quality or quantity of information processed by the senses is determined by one's level of attention. Once information enters the working memory, its ability to be encoded and stored in long-term memory depends on the efficiency by which initial connections are made. Together these systems process information in response to stimuli through encoding, storage, and retrieval.

The opening paragraph establishes the research topic and gives background information about the workings of human memory.

Research has shown that high levels of stress both impede the ability to focus attention and interfere with working memory during the acquisition of information (Al'Absi, Hugdahl, & Lovallo, 2002; Aronen, Vuontela, Steenari, Salmi, & Carlson, 2005; Hadwin, Brogan, & Stevenson, 2005; Owens, Stevenson, Hadwin, & Norgate, 2012). The effects of stress on brain structure have been connected to decreases in gray matter similar to those typically associated with age (Hedden & Gabrieli, 2004). Such changes occur when an excess of cortisol inhibits the production of neurotrophic proteins responsible for the growth of new neurons and synapses. Consequently, this process prevents regions of the brain associated with memory, such as the hippocampus and amygdala, from modulating effectively (Cahill & McGaugh, 1996; Roozendaal, McEwen, & Chattarji, 2009).

Over the last 30 years, mindfulness meditation has acquired popularity in the West thanks to its success in effectively reducing stress (Grossman, Niemann, Schmidt, & Walach, 2004). Moreover, it is increasingly applied in psychotherapeutic programs for the treatment of anxiety and depression (Hofmann, Sawyer, Witt, & Oh, 2010; Salmon, Santorelli, & Kabat-Zinn, 1998). Meditation is the practice of training mental attention to achieve a state of mindfulness. Mindfulness is commonly defined as "paying attention in a particular way: on purpose, in the present moment, and non-judgmentally" (Kabat-Zinn, 1994, p. 4). It is cultivated during meditation and extends beyond the time of formal practice. The major components of mindfulness, awareness and acceptance of both internal (e.g., cognitive-affective-sensory) and external (e.g., social-environmental) experiences in the present moment, are considered effective agents against psychological malaise (Keng, Smoski, & Robins, 2011). The benefits of meditation for anxiety and depression are thought to depend partially on the development of greater attentional control and executive functioning (Baer, 2003). That is, attention and energy previously allocated towards negative stimuli are redirected to more neutral or positive stimuli. The most well known meditation treatment program is Mindfulness-Based Stress Reduction (MBSR; Kabat-Zinn, 1990), which provides comprehensive training in mindfulness meditation.

Recently, meditation has been correlated with improvements

Summarizes a major research finding and cites the relevant sources. Parenthetical citations follow APA style.

Aymelek organizes her literature review by topic; here she surveys literature on mindfulness and meditation.

Such a statement, along with the numerous citations, helps demonstrate Aymelek's awareness of the relevant research literature.

in memory, cognition, and brain composition (Jha, Krompinger, & Baime, 2007; Jha, Stanley, Kiyonaga, Wong, & Gelfand, 2010; Ortner, Kilner, & Zelazo, 2007; Slagter et al., 2007; Zeidan, Johnson, Diamond, David, & Goolkasian, 2010). A study by Hölzel et al. (2011) used the Five Facet Mindfulness Questionnaire (FFMQ; Baer, Smith, Hopkins, Krietemeyer, & Toney, 2006) and magnetic resonance imaging (MRI) to measure subjective mindfulness and neurological changes in participants of the MBSR program. They found that participation in MBSR was associated with increased concentrations of gray matter in the left hippocampus and other regions of the brain connected to learning and memory processes as well as emotion regulation. Regular meditation has also been shown to strengthen one's ability to control impulses and maintain attention with less utilization of the brain's resources (Kozasa et al., 2012). In addition, Pagnoni and Cekic (2007) used voxel-based morphometry (VBM; Ashburner & Friston, 2000) and a computerized neuropsychological test to determine if gray matter in older populations would be more substantial in experienced meditators versus inexperienced meditators. They discovered increases in grey matter volume in the putamen, an area of the brain implicated in attentional processes, in experienced meditators but not in controls.

The benefits of exercise for physical health and stress management have been well documented (Penedo & Dahn, 2005). Current research suggests that frequent exercise may also enhance brain structure and cognition (Griffin et al., 2011; Hillman, Erickson, & Kramer, 2008). A controlled, longitudinal study by Erickson et al. (2011) aimed to determine if aerobic exercise could promote growth in the hippocampus of healthy older adults. They used an MRI to measure volume in the hippocampus at baseline, at 6 months, and at 1 year, and found that the exercise group demonstrated an increase in the left and right hippocampus by 2.12% and 1.97%, respectively, while the control group showed a 1.40% and 1.43% decrease in hippocampal volume. Furthermore, physical activity has been reported potentially to enhance cognitive capacity through the production of brain-derived neurotrophic factors (BDNF), which support the growth of neurons and synapses (Tyler, Alonso, Bramham, & Pozzo-Miller, 2002). Griffin et al. (2011)

Summarizes a recurring research finding, citing the findings of several studies.

measured cognition and blood levels of BDNF in sedentary young males following acute and chronic exercise. To assess cognition, they used a face-name task previously demonstrated by MRI to engage the hippocampus and medial-temporal lobes. Griffin et al. found increases in BDNF concentration in both acute and chronic exercise groups that corresponded with improved scores on the face-name task.

Evaluates earlier research, acknowledging some of its limitations.

Although both meditation and exercise have been associated with enhancements in cognition and memory, it is important to note some of the limitations of past research. For example, many studies on meditation did not randomly assign participants and/ or used small sample sizes (Eberth & Sedlmeier, 2012). In addition, studies frequently used clinical populations, and participants with prior interest in or experience with meditation (Chiesa, Calati, & Serretti, 2011; Hofmann et al., 2010). Likewise, many previous studies on exercise have not controlled and/or randomized designs. Additionally, subjects have often been limited to animals, human adult males, and older populations (Lambourne & Tomporowski, 2010; Smith et al., 2010).

Aymelek concludes by stating her hypotheses, which represent the research questions she will investigate and are clearly based on her review of existing research.

Despite these limitations, the above findings provide evidence that prolonged practice of tasks such as meditation and exercise induce positive changes in anatomical plasticity reflected in both subjective and objective measures of cognition. Based on the success of meditation and exercise in decreasing inhibitory stress levels that interfere with cognition and thus memory function, I hypothesize that: (1) practicing mindfulness meditation over not practicing mindfulness meditation will improve memory function; (2) practicing exercise over not practicing exercise will improve memory function; (3) the effects of mindfulness meditation on memory function will be greater in the exercise group versus the non-exercise group as measured by the Wechsler Memory Scale, fourth edition, adult version (WMS-IV; Wechsler, 2009).

References

Al'Absi, M., Hugdahl, K., & Lovallo, W. R. (2002). Adrenocortical stress responses and altered working memory performance. *Psychophysiology, 39*(1), 95–99.

Aronen, E. T., Vuontela, V., Steenari, M. R., Salmi, J., & Carlson, S. (2005). Working memory, psychiatric symptoms, and academic performance at school. *Neurobiology of Learning and Memory, 83*(1), 33–42.

Ashburner, J., & Friston, K. J. (2000). Voxel-based morphometry: The methods. *Neuroimage, 11*(6), 805–821.

Atkinson, R. C., & Shiffrin, R. M. (1968). Human memory: A proposed system and its control processes. *The Psychology of Learning and Motivation: Advances in Research and Theory, 2*, 89–195.

Baddeley, A. D., & Hitch, G. J. (1974). Working memory. *The Psychology of Learning and Motivation, 8*, 47–89.

Baer, R. A. (2003). Mindfulness training as a clinical intervention: A conceptual and empirical review. *Clinical psychology: Science and Practice, 10*(2), 125–143.

Baer, R. A., Smith, G. T., Hopkins, J., Krietemeyer, J., & Toney, L. (2006). Using self-report assessment methods to explore facets of mindfulness. *Assessment, 13*(1), 27–45.

Cahill, L., & McGaugh, J. L. (1996). Modulation of memory storage. *Current Opinion in Neurobiology, 6*(2), 237–242.

Chiesa, A., Calati, R., & Serretti, A. (2011). Does mindfulness training improve cognitive abilities? A systematic review of neuropsychological findings. *Clinical Psychology Review, 31*(3), 449–464.

. . .

Penedo, F. J., & Dahn, J. R. (2005). Exercise and well-being: A review of mental and physical health benefits associated with physical activity. *Current Opinion in Psychiatry, 18*(2), 189.

Roozendaal, B., McEwen, B. S., & Chattarji, S. (2009). Stress, memory and the amygdala. *Nature Reviews Neuroscience, 10*(6), 423–433.

Salmon, P., Santorelli, S. P., & Kabat-Zinn, J. (1998). Intervention elements promoting high adherence to mindfulness-based stress reduction programs in the clinical behavioral medicine setting. In S. A. Shumaker, E. B. Schron, J. K. Ockene, & W. L. McBee (*Eds*.), *Handbook of health behavior change* (2nd ed., pp. 239–266). New York: Springer.

Slagter, H. A., Lutz, A., Greischar, L. L., Francis, A. D., Nieuwenhuis, S., Davis, J. M., & Davidson, R. J. (2007). Mental training affects distribution of limited brain resources. *PLOS Biology, 5*(6), e138.

Smith, P. J., Blumenthal, J. A., Hoffman, B. M., Cooper, H., Strauman, T. A., Welsh-Bohmer, K., . . . Sherwood, A. (2010). Aerobic exercise and neurocognitive performance: A meta-analytic review of randomized controlled trials. *Psychosomatic Medicine, 72*(3), 239–252.

Tyler, W. J., Alonso, M., Bramham, C. R., & Pozzo-Miller, L. D. (2002). From acquisition to consolidation: On the role of brain-derived neurotrophic factor signaling in hippocampal-dependent learning. *Learning & Memory, 9*(5), 224–237.

Wechsler, D. (2009). *WMS-IV: Wechsler Memory Scale administration and scoring manual* (4th ed). San Antonio, TX: Pearson.

Zeidan, F., Johnson, S. K., Diamond, B. J., David, Z., & Goolkasian, P. (2010). Mindfulness meditation improves cognition: Evidence of brief mental training. *Consciousness and Cognition, 19*(2), 597–605.

REFLECT. Find an article in a scholarly journal in a field you're interested in, perhaps your major. Locate the literature review section of the article (it may or may not be explicitly labeled as such) and analyze it in terms of the genre features on p. 302. What kinds of sources does the author review? What aspects are discussed? How is the review organized? What is the author's evaluation of the literature, and how does that set up the rest of the article?

WRITING A REVIEW / A Roadmap

Choose something to review and find an interesting angle

If you get to choose your topic, pick a subject you're interested in and know something about. Perhaps you're an avid fan of *Harry Potter*. Reviewing the final novel in the series might be a good choice. Or maybe you love mountain biking: you could review three best-selling bikes. Remember that many things can be reviewed—shoes, appliances, restaurants, books, music. Choose a topic you want to learn more about.

If your topic is assigned, try to tailor it to your interests and to find an angle that will engage your audience. For instance, if your assignment is to review a specific art exhibit, see if you can focus on some aspect of the work that intrigues you, such as the use of color or the way the artist represents nature. If you are assigned to review a particular book, try to center your review on themes that you find compelling and that might interest your audience.

Consider your rhetorical situation

Once you have a tentative topic, thinking about your audience and the rest of your rhetorical situation will help you focus on how you ought to address it.

Think about what your AUDIENCE knows and expects. If your review is for an assignment, consider your instructor to be your primary audience (unless he or she specifies otherwise) and know what's expected of a review in your discipline. If, however, you're writing for a specific publication or another audience, you'll have to think about what's appropriate or expected in that situation. Here are some things to consider:

- Who are you trying to reach, and why?
- In what ways are they like or unlike you? Are they likely to agree with you?
- What do they probably know about your subject? What background information will you need to provide?
- Will the subject matter to your audience? If not, how can you persuade them that it matters?
- What will they be expecting to learn from your review? What criteria will they value?

Think about your PURPOSE. Why are you writing this review? If it's for a class, what motivations do you have beyond getting a good grade? To recommend a book or film? evaluate the latest smart gadget? introduce your classmates to a new musical group? What do you expect your audience to do with the information in your review? Do you want them to go see something? buy something (or not)? just appreciate something? How can you best achieve your purpose?

Consider your STANCE. Think about your overall attitude about the subject and how you want to come across as an author. Are you extremely enthusiastic about your subject? firmly opposed to it? skeptical? lukewarm? How can you communicate your feelings? Think also about how you want your audience to see you as author. As well informed? thoughtful? witty? How can your review reflect that stance, and how can you gain your audience's trust and respect?

Think about the larger CONTEXT. What, if any, background information about your subject should you consider—other books on the same subject or by the same author? movies in the same genre? similar products made by different companies? What else has been said about your subject, and how will you respond to it in your review?

Consider MEDIA. Whether or not you have a choice of medium—print, spoken, or electronic—you need to think about how your medium will affect what you can do in your review. If you're presenting it online or to a live audience, you may be able to incorporate video and audio clips—for example, of a film or a concert. If your review will appear in print, can you include still photos? And most important of all: if you get to choose your medium, which one will best reach your audience?

Consider matters of DESIGN. If you are writing for an academic assignment, be sure to follow the format requirements of the discipline you're writing in. If you're writing for a particular publication, you'll need to find out what design options you have. But if you have the option of designing your text yourself, think about what will help readers understand your message. Should you include illustrations? Are you including any information that would be best presented in a list or a graph? Product reviews, for example, often display data in a table so that readers can compare several products.

Evaluate your subject

Think about your own first impressions. What about the subject got your interest? What was your first reaction, and why? What is the first thing you would tell someone who asked your opinion on this subject?

Examine your subject closely. If you're reviewing a performance, take notes as you're watching it; if you're reviewing a book, read it more than once. Look for parts of your subject that are especially powerful, or weak, or unexpected to mention in your review.

Do any necessary RESEARCH. Your subject will be your primary source of information, though you may need to consult other sources to find background information or to become aware of what else has been written about your subject. Would learning more about a book's author or a film's director help you evaluate your subject? If you're writing an academic review, do you need to find out what else has been said about your subject?

Determine the CRITERIA for your evaluation. Sometimes these are obvious: film reviews, for instance, tend to focus on criteria like acting, directing, script, and so forth. At other times, you'll need to establish the criteria that will guide your review. Make a list of criteria that are appropriate for the genre you're reviewing—film, novel, smartphone, whatever—and then decide which criteria matter to you—and will matter to your audience.

Make a judgment about your subject. Based on the criteria you've established, evaluate your subject. Remember that few things are all good or all bad; you will likely find some things to praise, and others to criticize. Whatever you decide, use your criteria to examine your subject carefully, and look for specific **EVIDENCE** you can cite—lines or scenes from a movie, particular features of a product, and so on.

Anticipate other points of view. Not everyone is going to agree with your evaluation, and you need to acknowledge **COUNTERARGUMENTS** to what you think. Even if you don't persuade everyone in your audience to accept your judgment, you can demonstrate that your opinion is worth taking seriously by acknowledging and responding respectfully to those other perspectives.

Think about your mix of DESCRIPTION or SUMMARY and EVALUATION. You need to describe or summarize your subject enough so that readers will understand it, but remember that your primary goal is to evaluate it. The balance will depend on your purpose. Some reviews are expected to give a simple star rating, or a thumbs-up (or down). Others are occasions to write about an issue; one review of a Martin Luther King Jr. memorial, for instance, devoted more space to describing the controversy about the quotes on the monument than to assessing the actual memorial.

Organize and start writing

Once you've determined your overall evaluation of your subject, compiled a list of its strengths and weaknesses, and assembled EVIDENCE you can draw upon to support that evaluation, it's time to organize your materials and start writing. To organize your review, think about what you want to tell readers about your subject, what your evaluation of it is, and why.

Come up with a tentative THESIS. What major point do you want to make about your subject? Try writing this point out as a tentative thesis. Then think about whether the thesis should be stated explicitly or not. Also consider whether to put the thesis toward the end of your introduction or save it for the conclusion.

DESCRIBE or SUMMARIZE the subject you're reviewing, and provide any background information your audience may need.

Evaluate your subject. Using the CRITERIA you identified for your review, present your subject's strengths and weaknesses, generally in order of importance. Provide REASONS and specific EVIDENCE to back them up. Don't forget to acknowledge other points of view.

Draft an OPENING. Introduce your subject in a way that makes clear what you're reviewing and why your audience should care about it—and shows that you know what you're talking about!

Draft a CONCLUSION. Wrap up your review by summarizing your evaluation. If you have any recommendations, here's where to make them known.

Look critically at your draft, get response—and revise

Once you have a complete draft, read it over carefully, focusing on your evaluation, the reasons and evidence you provide as support, and the way you appeal to your audience. If possible, ask others—a writing center tutor, classmate, or friend—for feedback. Be sure to give your readers a clear sense of your assignment or purpose and your intended audience. Here are some questions that can help you or others respond:

- *Is the evaluation stated explicitly?* Is there a clear **THESIS** —and if not, is one needed?

- *How well does the introduction capture the audience's interest?* How well does it establish your **AUTHORITY** as a reviewer? Does it make clear what the review is about? How will it engage your audience's interest? How else might it begin?

- *Is the subject* **DESCRIBED** *or* **SUMMARIZED** *sufficiently* for your audience? Is any additional description or background information needed?

- *How much of the review is* **DESCRIPTION** *and how much is* **EVALUATION** —and does the balance seem right for the subject and purpose?

- *What are the* **CRITERIA** *for the evaluation?* Are they stated explicitly—and if not, should they be? Do the criteria seem appropriate for the subject and audience? Are there other criteria that should be considered?

- *What good* **REASONS** *and* **EVIDENCE** *support the evaluation?* Will your audience be persuaded?

- *What other viewpoints do you consider,* and how well do you respond to these views? Are there other views you should consider?

- *How would you describe the* **STANCE** *and* **TONE** *?* Are they appropriate and authoritative? What words or details create that impression?

- *How is the draft organized?* Is it easy to follow, with clear **TRANSITIONS** from one point to the next?

- *What about* **DESIGN** *?* Should any material be set off as a list or chart or table? Are there any illustrations—and if not, should there be?

- *Is the* **STYLE** —choice of words, kinds of sentences, level of formality— appropriate for the intended audience?

- *How does the draft* CONCLUDE *?* Is the conclusion decisive and satisfy-ing? How else might it conclude?

- *Is this a fair review?* Even if readers do not agree with the evaluation, will they consider it fair?

⟶ *REFLECT. Once you've completed your review, let it settle for a while and then take time to reflect. How well did you argue for your evaluation? How persuasive do you think your readers will find your review? Will those who do not agree with your evaluation consider it fair? What additional revisions would you make if you could? Research shows that such reflections help "lock in" what you learn for future use.*

Ode to Joy (and Sadness, and Anger)

A. O. SCOTT

CAN MOVIES THINK? This is a longstanding critical question, usually answered in the negative. Literature, the thinking goes, is uniquely able to show us the flow of thought and feeling from within, but the camera's eye and the two-dimensional screen can't take us past the external signs of consciousness. We can look at faces in various configurations of pleasure or distress, but minds remain invisible, mysterious, beyond the reach of cinema.

One of the many accomplishments of *Inside Out*—a thrilling return to form for Pixar Animation Studios after a few years of commercially successful sub-masterpieces—is that it demolishes this assumption. The movie, directed by Pete Docter, solves a thorny philosophical problem with the characteristically Pixaresque tools of whimsy, sincerity and ingenious literal-mindedness.

The story takes place mostly in the head of an eleven-year-old girl named Riley (Kaitlyn Dias), who has just moved with her parents (Diane Lane and Kyle MacLachlan) from Minnesota to San Francisco. What happens to Riley on the outside is pretty standard: a dinner-table argument with Mom and Dad; a rough day at school; a disappointing hockey tryout. But anyone who has been or known a child Riley's age will understand that such mundane happenings can be the stuff of major interior drama.

The real action—the art, the comedy, the music and the poetry—unfolds

A. O. SCOTT is chief film critic for the *New York Times* and has written for the paper since 2000. This review appeared in the *Times* in June 2015.

A still from Pixar's *Inside Out* showing eleven-year-old Riley at a moment when she isn't quite the "happy girl" she used to be.

among Riley's personified feelings. There is an old literary tradition of turning what used to be called the Passions into characters, and *Inside Out* updates this tradition with brilliant casting. Riley's brain is controlled by five busy, contentious emotions: Fear, Anger, Disgust, Sadness and Joy. Each one has a necessary role to play, and they all carry out their duties in Riley's neurological command center with the bickering bonhomie of workplace sitcom colleagues.

Their voices, aptly enough, belong to a television-comedy dream team. Anger, a squat, inverted trapezoid of bright red bluster, is the *Daily Show* ranter Lewis Black. Disgust, a green mean girl, is the great Mindy Kaling. Fear, an elastic-limbed goofball, is the former *Saturday Night Live* rubber man Bill Hader. Sadness speaks in the sighing monotone of Phyllis Smith, the most reliable killjoy on *The Office*. She is blue and slow-moving, and the others sometimes wonder what exactly her job is supposed to be.

But Joy reigns supreme. Even without an organizational chart, you can tell she's the boss. She's a sparkling whirlwind of positive energy and friendly micro-management. You might say she's the Leslie Knope* of the cerebral cortex, and not only because her peppy vocalizations belong to Amy Poehler.

---

* *Leslie Knope:* Protagonist of the NBC sitcom *Parks and Recreation*. Knope's character is unfailingly optimistic and hardworking.

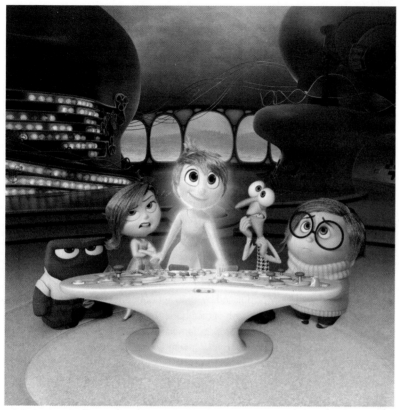

Anger, Disgust, Joy, Fear, and Sadness—the five emotions that control Riley's brain.

In her long run as Leslie on *Parks and Recreation*, Ms. Poehler was frequently and hilariously annoying without ever ceasing to be likable. She performs a similar feat here, to a wonderfully subversive end. We start out rooting for Joy, primed by the Disney logo before the opening titles and the presence of young children in the neighboring seats. We want them—and Riley, and everyone—to be happy.

But the insistence on happiness has its discontents. As a manager, Joy is focused above all on controlling and containing Sadness. She thinks she needs to keep her gloomy co-worker's hands off Riley's core memories. These golden, shiny orbs will be ruined if they turn blue. At one point, Joy draws a small chalk circle on the floor and instructs Sadness to stand inside it, not touching anything lest she wreck the upbeat mood.

That's a pretty powerful metaphor for repression, of course, and *Inside Out* turns a critical eye on the way the duty to be cheerful is imposed on children, by well-intentioned adults and by the psychological mechanisms those grown-up authorities help to install. "Where's my happy girl?" Riley's parents are fond of saying when she seems down, and the forced smile that results is quietly heartbreaking. Not that Riley's mother and father are bad people. We see that their own heads are just as crowded as hers. They also have their own external worries and stresses, including a new house, a fledgling business and a child on the brink of momentous changes.

Those unfold in a mental landscape that ranks among Pixar's grandest visual triumphs, up there with the coral reef in *Finding Nemo*, the post-apocalyptic garbage dump in *Wall-E* and the sinister day care center in *Toy Story 3*. The studio's earlier features have often served as demonstrations of technical breakthroughs. Pixar animators conquered water and piscine movement in *Nemo*, metal in *Cars*, fur in *Monsters, Inc.* and flight in *Up*.

The achievement of *Inside Out* is at once subtler and more impressive. This is a movie almost entirely populated by abstract concepts moving through theoretical space. This world is both radically new—you've never seen anything like it—and instantly recognizable, as familiar aspects of consciousness are given shape and voice. Remember your imaginary childhood friend? Your earliest phobias? Your strangest dreams? You will, and you will also have a newly inspired understanding of how and why you remember those things. You will look at the screen and know yourself.

I would gladly catalog the movie's wittiest inventions and sharpest insights, or try to draw a word map of Riley's brain. Nothing would be spoiled. But I'll leave you the pleasure of discovery, noting only that you should keep an ear out for Michael Giacchino's music and Richard Kind's voice, and your eye peeled for sly philosophical sight gags.

Inside Out is an absolute delight—funny and charming, fast-moving and full of surprises. It is also a defense of sorrow, an argument for the necessity of melancholy dressed in the bright colors of entertainment. The youngest viewers will have a blast, while those older than Riley are likely to find themselves in tears. Not of grief, but of gratitude and recognition. Sadness, it turns out, is not Joy's rival but her partner. Our ability to feel sad is what stirs compassion in others and empathy in ourselves. There is no growth without loss, and no art without longing.

Thinking about the Text

1. Write a one-paragraph SUMMARY of Scott's review, being sure to identify his criteria for evaluation and the extent to which he claims the movie did or did not satisfy them.

2. Do you find Scott's TONE authoritative? Why or why not? How does Scott establish his own AUTHORITY and CREDIBILITY —or fail to do so? Point to specific parts of the text to support your response.

3. What assumptions does Scott make about his AUDIENCE and the things they are familiar with? How do you know? You might start by considering the vocabulary he uses and the topics he mentions as he discusses the film.

4. How does Scott frame his review? In other words, how does the review open, and how does Scott use this OPENING to make a crucial point about the significant achievement of *Inside Out*?

5. As a PG-rated animated film about childhood, *Inside Out* might be considered a "kids' movie," though clearly Scott—and, he suggests, other adults in the audience—found it very relatable. Return to a film or book from your childhood that is especially significant to you, and write a review of it from your current perspective. Be sure to come up with clear CRITERIA for your evaluation and to use EVIDENCE from the text to support your claims.

Serial: A Captivating New Podcast

ANYA SCHULTZ

IN 1999, HAE MIN LEE, a senior at Woodlawn High School in Maryland, went missing. When her body was found a month later, Adnan Syed, her ex-boyfriend, was arrested and convicted of strangling her.

Episode one of *Serial*, the latest podcast series from the creators of *This American Life*, begins with a prepaid call from an inmate at a Maryland correctional facility. It's Adnan, fifteen years after Hae went missing. He is set to spend the rest of his life in prison for a crime he claims he did not commit.

Serial is determined to reveal the truth. Each week the show will release a new episode, and each week public radio enthusiasts nationwide will linger in their driveways minutes after they arrive home to hear the host, veteran radio reporter Sarah Koenig, reinvestigate the case. With a gripping plotline, *Serial* has the potential to secure an enthusiastic audience while delving deep into relevant issues surrounding race and criminal justice.

"For the last year, I've spent every working day trying to figure out where a high school kid was for an hour after school one day in 1999," Koenig says at the start of the first episode. The producers say the show won't stop until they get to the bottom of the case, at which point they will move on to a new story.

ANYA SCHULTZ is a student at the University of California at Berkeley, where she writes for the student newspaper, the *Daily Californian*, and is an editor of the *Weekender*, an online culture magazine where this review was published in 2014. Go to everyonesanauthor.tumblr.com to access the links underlined here.

After the first three episodes, the characters appear rich and intriguing. We 5
learn about Adnan and Hae's forbidden romance—how they kept their relationship a secret from his Islamic family and her Korean family. We learn how
the court based Adnan's conviction largely on the testimony of his friend Jay,
who said he helped Adnan hide Hae's body. But Adnan says he had no reason
to kill Hae—he was at the library after school, he thinks.

It's not surprising how hard it is for one not to remember exactly what they
were doing one Wednesday afternoon fifteen years ago. Unless, of course,
they were killing someone.

Koenig brings us along on her investigation of Hae's murder, admitting to
confusion and sharing exciting leads. According to *Slate*, the producers are
currently researching and producing episodes as they are being released—the
story is still being reported. Koenig's style allows us to stumble through the
story with her, as if we're hearing Sherlock Holmes' diary. What keeps the
story thrilling is that someone, be it Adnan or a perpetrator who we haven't
been introduced to yet, is lying. Someone is a murderer.

After three episodes and a growing stack of questions, what is left is an
intense desire to know the truth of what happened. We learn Adnan was the
prince of his junior prom and an honor roll student. If he was so likeable, how
could he have committed the crime of passion Jay painted to the detectives?
And what was Jay's motivation in cooperating with the police?

As more details emerge, the narrative appears increasingly complex. We
learn how Jay's testimony, the story Adnan's entire conviction rested upon,
kept changing. We learn about relevant cell phone records to scour, potential
witnesses to question, and suddenly podcast listeners around the world have
become detectives bubbling with questions.

Many will listen to *Serial* as pure entertainment, debating theories and de- 10
constructing characters as if it's season three of *Breaking Bad*. But the greater
implications of this investigation have the potential to be life-changing. This
case could take an innocent man out of prison or put a murderer behind bars:
think *Thin Blue Line*.

This is just one case—one boy's story of how the criminal justice system
took over his life. Not every court case gets one of the best radio journalists
to intensely scrutinize and investigate its merits and legitimacy. Most trials go
on without national recognition or interest, but it's no secret that the criminal
justice system needs fixing.

In a recent *New Yorker* piece, reporter Jennifer Gonnerman tells the tragic
story of a man who waited three years in a prison cell for his trial, only to have

his court case thrown out. There are currently more than 2.4 million people incarcerated in the U.S., and in 2008 more than one in 100 adults in the U.S. were in prison, a disproportionate number being African American.

Serial will likely delve further into issues of race and incarceration. But as the season goes on, it gives listeners a unique opportunity to humanize the players. As Adnan becomes more than just an incarceration statistic, hopefully this story can get us talking about who offends and why and whether locking a person behind bars for years repairs the harm their crime caused. At the same time, we could be becoming very sympathetic toward a manipulative murderer.

Eventually, Koenig and listeners will have to step back and face the cruel reality that this story is captivating, because a person's life was lost. Part of the case put up against Adnan was that his relationship with Hae caused him to betray his Islamic family values. When they broke up, he lashed out with anger—or so the jury unanimously agreed.

As Koenig meticulously crafts the story for our ears, we are reminded of the importance of where a story begins and ends—what constitutes truth and how facts can be manipulated. 15

Humans visualize disparate facts in a narrative form—we see our world in stories. In a recent blog post, Koenig wrote about a note Adnan sent her last spring that included two graphs. Each plotted the price of tea at a different store. On first glance, it appeared that the prices fluctuated much more at one store. But in reality, the prices were the same, just plotted with different increments on the y-axis.

His clever analogy goes back to storytelling. How information is framed can drastically determine interpretation. One graph may have been convicted as guilty, the other as innocent.

We have to be weary of Koenig's framing—she starts the story with Adnan, and we learn he was smart and well liked. What facts she decides to deliver and in what order will create the story we walk away with, however close to the truth it may be.

Podcasts give audiences the opportunity to ruminate on and talk about a theme. But instead of a week, we have a whole season to think and theorize. If the first three episodes were this juicy and raw, we can only imagine what is to come ahead. We should keep listening.

Thinking about the Text

1. How does Anya Schultz establish her **AUTHORITY** and credibility as a reviewer? How do the links contribute to her credibility? How would you describe her **TONE**? Point to specific words that create that tone.

2. What is Schultz's **EVALUATION** of this podcast, and what **EVIDENCE** does she offer in support of her views?

3. What **CRITERIA** does Schultz use as a basis for her evaluations? How does she make them clear? Point out specific lines from the text to support your response.

4. Schultz wrote this review for a college newspaper. How does this **RHETORICAL SITUATION** affect the way she wrote the review? Imagine that she reviewed the same podcast for a publication aimed at older readers. What changes, if any, might she have made to reach that **AUDIENCE** and to build their interest in her subject?

5. Imagine that you, like Schultz, wanted to tell your classmates about a book, performance, game, film, or artist that you like—or don't like— in a piece that will be published in your campus newspaper. Write a **REVIEW** to persuade other students to check it out—or not. Take care to introduce your subject, establish criteria for your evaluation, and show evidence from the subject to support what you say.

SIXTEEN

"Here's What I Recommend"
Making a Proposal

 ILL YOU MARRY ME? There is no clearer proposal than the one represented by this question. It proposes something that at least one person thinks ought to be done. Proposals are just that: recommendations that something be done, often to bring about some kind of change or to solve a problem. You'll likely have occasion to write proposals for various purposes; and if you're reading this chapter now, you've probably been assigned to write one for a composition class.

You might propose better financial aid options, a new way of disposing of cafeteria food, a possible solution to the childhood obesity crisis. Like a marriage proposal, each suggests change of some kind; unlike a marriage proposal, however, each of these cases addresses some kind of problem and calls for careful analysis of several possible courses of action. While it may be obvious to your beloved that you are the one, it's less obvious how a more flexible borrowing plan can ease the burden of student debt, how composting can create a more sustainable food system, or how school lunch programs can help end childhood obesity. Proposals of this kind argue for clear solutions to specific problems, and as with any argument, they build a convincing case that what they recommend should be considered—and perhaps acted on.

This chapter provides guidelines for writing proposals that others will take seriously, ones that essentially say, "Here's what I recommend—and why you should take my advice."

REFLECT. Proposals are part of daily life, but some are more compelling than others. Find a proposal that interests you, perhaps an op-ed on a social issue such as homelessness or inequality or a GoFundMe campaign to fund a cause. How does the proposal convince you (or fail to convince you) that it's about something that matters and that the solution it recommends is worth your support?

Across Academic Disciplines

If you've been assigned to write a research paper, chances are that your instructor has asked you to present a proposal before you begin researching and drafting the paper. Such proposals ensure that your topic and your plan of action are appropriate for the assignment. You'll likely have occasion to write these and other kinds of proposals in many courses. For a *biology* course, you may be asked to propose an experiment you want to carry out, explaining why it's important and hypothesizing what you expect to find. And in a *public policy* course, you might work with a group to analyze a particular policy—perhaps your city's policy of providing incentives to encourage the use of solar power—and to propose changes in that policy. In each case, you'll need to think about what's expected, given the topic and the discipline.

Across Media

Authors of proposals often use multiple media to present their recommendations. Crowdfunding sites like *Kickstarter* may use *video* to show their projects in action or to bring audiences face-to-face with their cause. Op-ed columnists writing for *print* newspapers rely on carefully crafted words to make their points, but online versions of the papers may include links to supporting materials. If you're presenting a proposal in an *oral presentation*, slides can help illustrate what you're recommending—and you may be asked to provide a print document to elaborate on what you propose.

Across Cultures and Communities

Proposals of various sorts are common in the United States. At your school, for example, students might band together to propose more effective cam-

CROWDFUNDING SITES are filled with proposals. Take a look at the proposal that three college students posted on **Kickstarter** *seeking funding for Roominate, a build-it-yourself dollhouse that could be wired for electricity, which they hoped would get young girls interested in science and technology. Their proposal stated a problem (not enough women studying in STEM fields) and proposed a solution (the Roominate dollhouse kit). Go to everyonesanauthor.tumblr.com to see their proposal. As you'll see, it includes written words, video, and audio. Imagine these students were presenting this proposal in a meeting with potential investors; what information would they give in speech, on slides, in a video, in a handout?*

pus policies to prevent sexual assault. In business, many companies encourage employees at all levels to share ideas for improving the company's products or services. And in many states voters can propose a ballot initiative to change existing laws.

Proposals are common in cultures and industries that thrive on open discussion and innovation, but not every community is receptive to input from just anyone. Many governments, organizations, and households around the world value the judgment of authorities and community leaders, and proposals from others may be seen as disrespectful. So be aware of the situation you're writing in and the audience you are speaking to, not just to avoid offending someone but to determine how best to present your ideas.

Across Genres

Proposals occur in many kinds of writing. **REVIEWS** sometimes end with proposals for how something could be improved, and many **REPORTS**, especially those on pressing social issues, conclude by proposing a course of action that will address the issue.

    A fully developed proposal is based on an **ANALYSIS** of a problem or situation in great detail. It requires **REPORTING** trustworthy information, and often involves **NARRATING** one or more past events as part of that reporting.

John Maeda weaves elements of several genres into his proposal for improving STEM education on p. 987.

⚰️ *REFLECT. Find two proposals that address the same issue, perhaps one students are currently debating on your campus. How does each proposal define the issue, what solutions does each of them offer, and what evidence does each provide to show that its solutions will work? Which of the two proposals do you find more persuasive, and why?*

CHARACTERISTIC FEATURES

Although there will be variation depending on the topic, you'll find that nearly all proposals share the following characteristics:

- A precise description of the problem
- A clear and compelling solution to the problem
- Evidence that your solution will address the problem
- Acknowledgment of other possible solutions
- A statement of what your proposal will accomplish

A Precise Description of the Problem

The goal of all proposals is to offer a solution for some kind of problem, so most of them begin by explicitly stating the problem and establishing that it is serious enough that it needs a solution. Some problems are obvious—that there's a water shortage in California, for instance, or few women majoring in engineering—and you won't have to say much to convince your audience that they matter. In other cases, though, you'll need to describe the problem in detail and provide data, examples, and other evidence to convince readers that it's serious enough to require a solution.

The title of a controversial article by journalist David Freedman identifies a problem and proposes a possible solution: "How Junk Food Can End Obesity." But in the following passage from that article, Freedman describes a specific problem in the wide debate about obesity that his proposal then responds to.

> If the most-influential voices in our food culture today get their way, we will achieve a genuine food revolution. Too bad it would be one tailored to the dubious health fantasies of a small, elite minority. And too bad it would largely exclude the obese masses, who would continue to sicken and die early. Despite the best efforts of a small army of wholesome-food heroes, there is no reasonable scenario under which these foods could become cheap and plentiful enough to serve as the core diet for most of the obese population—even in the unlikely case that your typical junk-food eater would be willing and able to break lifelong habits to embrace kale and yellow beets. And many of the dishes glorified by the wholesome-food movement are, in any case, as caloric . . . as anything served in a Burger King.
>
> Through its growing sway over health-conscious consumers and policy makers, the wholesome-food movement is impeding the progress of the one segment of the food world that is actually positioned to take effective, near-term steps to reverse the obesity trend: the processed-food industry.   —DAVID FREEDMAN, "How Junk Food Can End Obesity"

Kale and beets are part of the problem? Read David Freedman's full proposal on p. 931 where he explains why.

Not only does Freedman say that the views of many well-known food writers are wrong (that there wouldn't be so much obesity if only we all ate more "wholesome food"); he argues that their "growing sway" over consumers and policy makers is actually "impeding the progress" of one group that might be able to do something to "reverse the obesity trend." In other words, he identifies them as part of the problem.

The authors of the *Kickstarter* proposal illustrated on page 342 to fund a toy meant to interest young girls in scientific and technical fields state the problem directly, noting that they "noticed a BIG problem" in their engineering classes: "Where are all the girls?" They then elaborate on this problem in their proposal:

> We know that girls are great at solving, deducing, and experimenting. Yet . . .
>
> - Only 15% of female first-year college students intend to major in STEM (Science, Technology, Engineering, and Math) fields
> - Less than 11% of engineers are women
>
> And . . .
>
> - Toys for young girls are predominantly dolls and princesses
>
> We think there is a connection.
> We believe that early exposure to STEM through toys will inspire change.
> —"Roominate: Make It Yours!"

The numbers demonstrate that a problem exists (only 15 percent of first-year women students intend to major in a STEM field, less than 11 percent of all engineers are women), and the fact that the toys young girls play with are mostly dolls and princesses shows one possible cause. Together these facts establish the problem that the proposal will then address.

In any proposal, it's important to identify the problem clearly and in a way that sets up the solution you'll be recommending. Defining the problem precisely can also help make your solution realistic: increasing the number of women engineers is a tall order, while creating a toy that might encourage young girls to become interested in engineering seems doable.

A Clear and Compelling Solution to the Problem

Successful proposals offer a compelling solution to the problem at hand. That is, it isn't sufficient merely to have a good idea; in a proposal, you'll have to convince readers that your idea squarely addresses the problem as you've defined it.

You'll want to explain the solution succinctly but in enough detail to make a clear and confident case for it. See how Ras Baraka, the mayor of Newark, New Jersey, and a former teacher in that city's famously struggling school system, calls in a publicly published proposal for the state to return control of the schools to local officials.

> In 1995, the New Jersey State Department of Education took control of Newark's schools, disbanding the local board and appointing its own superintendent. I had just then become a teacher in Newark.
>
> The express intent of the takeover was to intervene temporarily to improve the quality of our schools, increase the achievement of students and better manage the system's finances. . . .
>
> Nearly 20 years later, it is clear that the state has failed on all counts. Local control must be returned to Newark's public schools immediately.
>
> —RAS BARAKA, "A New Start for Newark Schools"

Faced with the problem of the state having "failed on all counts" to improve Newark's schools, Baraka raises a clear solution: to return those schools to local control. And in mentioning the state's long history of failure over the past twenty years, he makes a strong case that change is needed "immediately."

Now consider a proposal for a policy that would provide more affordable housing in Portland, Oregon, from an article by a member of that city's city council written for *Street Roots*, a weekly newspaper often sold by people who've been homeless:

> We can't require developers to build affordable housing; state law prevents it. But we can encourage those who want to build here to be part of the solution. . . . The city currently provides "density bonuses" to developers for including certain public benefits in their projects—meaning they can build taller buildings or get more floor space than would normally be allowed in exchange for including features like eco-roofs or bicycle parking.
>
> Now is the time to restructure our density bonus regulations to prioritize affordable housing development. . . .
>
> Under a proposal that will go before the council on July 9, developers seeking a density bonus must either provide affordable housing within their development or pay a fee into a fund for the creation and preservation of affordable housing. This proposal . . . would require them to contribute to the creation of affordable housing in order to receive the maximum density that our zoning currently allows.
>
> —DAN SALTZMAN, "Incentive for Developers
> Would Spur Affordable Housing"

The proposal Saltzman describes offers a solution that addresses the problem clearly: to build the largest permissible buildings (and hence make more money), developers will have to include affordable units in the development itself *or* contribute to a fund for creating affordable housing. Thus, in return for something a developer would want, the city gets something it wants: more affordable housing.

Evidence That Your Solution Will Address the Problem

A proposal is convincing when the evidence it provides shows that the solution being proposed will, in fact, address the problem. The kind of evidence that will be convincing will vary depending on what it is you're proposing, and to whom. If you're pitching a new business venture to potential investors, your evidence would include numbers showing the projected returns on their investment. If you're proposing a new honor code at your school, your evidence would likely include testimonies and examples of how it would improve the learning environment. In his article on the Portland affordable housing proposal, Dan Saltzman provides data projecting what the proposal could accomplish:

> This "affordable housing incentive zoning proposal" could result in as many as 60 additional units of affordable housing a year on top of those already being developed by the city, or it could mean an additional $120 million to $200 million in funds for affordable housing over the next 20 years.
>
> This proposal alone will not solve our affordable-housing crisis but is a critical step to ensuring more affordable housing in our city.

By acknowledging that this proposal will not totally solve the problem of affordable housing but demonstrating its potential benefits—more affordable housing or funds to create such housing—Saltzman limits his solution to one that Portland will be able to address at the time, thus making a persuasive case that what he is suggesting is in fact feasible.

Another example comes from Appleton, Wisconsin, a city facing the challenge of redesigning its streets and transit systems to accommodate pedestrians and bicyclists. In an eighty-page proposal laying out a twenty-year plan to improve such access, the city's designers offer plenty of evidence to support their ideas: diagrams showing how specific roads will be reconfigured to include bike lanes, charts of costs and funding sources, and a time-table for completing the project over the twenty-year construction period. Some of this evidence illustrates that the proposed changes will achieve the city's goals; others show that they will do so in a feasible manner.

Acknowledgment of Other Possible Solutions

Part of crafting a persuasive proposal is making it clear that your solution is the best course of action—and hence better than other options. To do so, you need to account for other possible solutions and demonstrate the comparative advantages of the solution you're suggesting.

In his article proposing that junk food has the best potential to end obesity, David Freedman describes in great detail what those in the "wholesome food" camp suggest—and then points out why what they advocate is not so good after all. Here he visits his local Whole Foods, where he finds many "wholesome" items:

> One that catches my eye . . . is Vegan Cheesy Salad Booster . . . whose package emphasizes the fact that it is enhanced with spirulina, chlorella, and sea vegetables. The label also proudly lets me know that the contents are raw—no processing!—and that they don't contain any genetically modified ingredients. What it does contain, though, is more than three times the fat content per ounce as the beef patty in a Big Mac . . . and four times the sodium.
>
> —DAVID FREEDMAN, "How Junk Food Can End Obesity"

Later in his article, he does acknowledge that some of the arguments on behalf of "wholesome food" are accurate:

> For the purpose of this article, let's simply stipulate that wholesome foods are environmentally superior. But let's also agree that when it comes to prioritizing among food-related public-policy goals, we are likely to save and improve many more lives by focusing on cutting obesity—through any available means—than by trying to convert all of industrialized agriculture into . . . small organic farms.

Notice that in each case Freedman first describes something others have proposed (or might propose)—and then proceeds to point out their shortcomings.

Other situations call for proposals that consider several possible solutions at the same time, as in the case of the one for creating bicycle and pedestrian access in Appleton, Wisconsin. Because there's no one-size-fits-all solution that will work for every street in the city, the authors of this proposal must suggest several possible configurations, including those shown on the following page in Figures 16.a and 16.b.

Bike lanes, which are meant only for cyclists, and shared lanes, which are shared by bicycles and cars, are two of the possible road configurations the authors of this proposal explore. They provide detailed information about each option, describing its purpose, listing its advantages and disadvantages, and providing a diagram. By presenting multiple design options, the authors address the full range of situations that exist. In situations that call for multiple solutions, considering all possibilities shows that you have fully considered the complexity of the problem.

A Statement of What Your Proposal Will Accomplish

So what if readers decide to follow your proposal? What can they expect it to accomplish? The strongest proposals answer that question explicitly. Given that your goal is to persuade readers to agree with what you suggest and perhaps to take some kind of action, you need to help them understand the likely outcomes. Many proposals end by making clear what's to be gained, what outcomes large and small they might bring about.

Megan Hopkins, a former teacher with Teach For America (TFA), concludes her proposal calling for changes in that program by making clear how her suggestions—a longer commitment period, a full year of training, more incentives to continue teaching—will help TFA realize its mission.

> While these proposals would require substantial redesign of the TFA model, the results are likely to be worth the investment. Teach For America has the potential to effect large-scale change in the field of education. It recruits highly qualified, motivated corps members who appreciate the importance of equal education opportunities, and many go on to devote their lives to this mission. However, these bright individuals are not as effective in the classroom as they could be, and their students do not perform as well as students in classrooms where teachers have more formal training. Corps members who are given a full year to learn effective instructional practices and to fully prepare to work within the

Fig. 16.a BIKE LANE

Description/Purpose: Marked space along length of roadway for exclusive use of cyclists. Bike lanes create separation between cyclists and automobiles.

Advantages
- Provides bicycle access on major through streets
- Clarifies lane use for motorists and cyclists
- Increases cyclists' comfort through visual separation

Disadvantages
- Space requirements may preclude other possible uses like parking or excess travel lane width

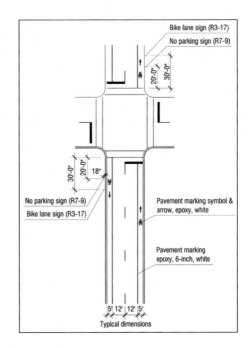

Fig. 16.b SHARED LANE

Description/Purpose: Shared roadway pavement markings, or "sharrows," are markings used to indicate a shared lane environment for bicycles and automobiles. Sharrows identify to all road users where bicycles should operate on a street where a separated facility is not feasible.

Advantages
- Helps cyclists position themselves in lanes too narrow for a motor vehicle and a bicycle to travel side by side
- Provides pavement markings where bike lanes are not possible

Disadvantages
- Maintenance requirements
- Not as effective as a separated bicycle facility

—Wisconsin Department of Transportation, *City of Appleton On-Street Bike Plan*

context of their placement sites will be better prepared to enter their classrooms as skilled teachers. If TFA can prepare its recruits to be more successful in their classrooms from the beginning of their service, it may be able to achieve its vision more effectively, so that, as the TFA mission states, "One day, all children in this nation will have the opportunity to attain an excellent education."

—MEGAN HOPKINS, "Training the Next Teachers for America"

Hopkins states one immediate result of the reforms she's suggesting, namely that corps members will be "better prepared to enter their classrooms." However, to highlight the true impact that her proposal would have, she starts and ends her summary of results by explaining how these adjustments would help TFA realize its "potential to effect large-scale change in the field of education" and thereby "achieve its vision" of providing every child in America with a good education—an inspiring outcome most audiences would happily stand behind, and one that shows persuasively why this proposal matters.

While many proposals are quite concrete, some deal with more abstract topics. Neil deGrasse Tyson's proposal on p. 1069 is as big as the universe itself.

RAS BARAKA is mayor of Newark, New Jersey, and a former teacher and administrator in the Newark school system. In this proposal, published in the *New York Times* in 2014, Baraka offers a first-step measure for solving the struggles of that city's schools. He introduces the problem by laying out the failures of state control—once thought to be a solution itself—before making a strong argument for an alternative.

A New Start for Newark Schools

RAS BARAKA

IN 1995, the New Jersey State Department of Education took control of Newark's schools, disbanding the local board and appointing its own superintendent. I had just then become a teacher in Newark.

The express intent of the takeover was to intervene temporarily to improve the quality of our schools, increase the achievement of students and better manage the system's finances. Since the state was on the receiving end of a 1994 State Supreme Court ruling that the underfunding of public schools in urban districts was unconstitutional, the timing seemed suspicious, to say the least. It felt as if we were being annexed.

A clear description of the problem.

Nearly 20 years later, it is clear that the state has failed on all counts. Local control must be returned to Newark's public schools immediately.

An explicit statement of Baraka's proposed solution.

Over the years, the court-ordered remedies for Newark's schools were eroded or ignored. A $6 billion school construction program never materialized. Instead, thanks to state control, Newark has become a laboratory for experiments in top-down reforms.

Successive state-mandated initiatives came and went. Occasionally, there were useful ideas that yielded results—for example, in lower grades when resources were focused on early childhood learning. But when there was no dramatic breakthrough, programs were withdrawn, and some new plan hatched. Over time, the cycle hurt teachers' morale and bred cynicism among parents.

Evidence that state control—once thought to be a solution—has not succeeded in addressing the issues.

During state control of Newark's schools, a lack of consultation and consent has been a persistent problem. Reports show at least one neighborhood school was shut down and the real estate sold off; others were changed to charter schools* without a vote—a clear violation of state charter laws.

You might think that Mark Zuckerberg's $100 million donation in 2010 to kick-start a foundation for Newark schools would have been a game changer. But little funding went directly to Newark's schools. Instead, the first $1.3 million was wasted on a poorly conducted community outreach campaign. Then another $100 million, including funds from Zuckerberg, went to a program for teacher merit pay.

Consideration of an alternative solution (more funding) and evidence that it has not been effective.

Principals were given the power to re-interview teachers for their jobs and in some cases hire new teachers. But the rejected teachers joined a pool of floating staff members in the "rubber room"** downtown, until reassigned to other schools or bought out. So even as Newark teachers worked without a contract, the state went on a hiring and cash-incentive spree.

There was not enough accountability or transparency about the spending. We only know this much thanks to demands filed by community groups under New Jersey's Open Public Records Act.

The state's maladministration of Newark's public schools con-

---

* *charter schools*: privately run, tuition-free schools that are subject to fewer regulations than public schools but that receive less government funding. Supporters argue that they encourage innovation and competition while detractors say they undermine the mission of public education.

** *rubber room*: a reassignment center where public school teachers accused of misconduct or incompetence are sent, with pay, until their cases are settled, often for a period of years.

tinues to this day. When Superintendent Cami Anderson's "Re-new Schools" reform plan ran into difficulties because of its lack of public consultation, foundation dollars went to a community-engagement program. Yet the latest iteration, the "One Newark" plan, has only plunged the system into more chaos.

Consider the reports I've received of Barringer High School (formerly Newark High School). Three weeks into the school year, students still did not have schedules. Students who had just arrived in this country and did not speak English sat for days in the school library without placement or instruction. Seniors were placed in classes they had already taken, missing the requirements they'd need to graduate. Even the school lunch system broke down, with students served bread and cheese in lieu of hot meals.

Things are no better for parents. Under One Newark's universal enrollment scheme, a secret algorithm determined what school was the "best fit" for each child. Often, this ended up placing each child in a family in a different school, none of which was the neighborhood school the parents chose. The superintendent even had to devise a new busing program service for the unpopular One Newark plan.

To cap it all, last year the school system operated with a deficit of $57 million.

Gov. Chris Christie likes to say that he is "the decider" of what happens in Newark's public schools. What that means is that he and his appointees now own the failure of the state's policies. Advocates of both traditional and charter schools, parent groups, ministers, student organizations and local elected officials have called on New Jersey to relinquish its hold over our schools.

The real issues that reform should address are ensuring that every 3- or 4-year-old child is enrolled in a structured learning environment, and that all our teachers get staff development and training. We must be more effective at sharing best practices and keeping our class sizes manageable. If necessary, we should put more than one teacher in the classroom, especially for students from kindergarten to third grade.

We also need to fix additional problems like a historically seg-regated curriculum, which offers stimulating choices in wealthy suburbs but only the most basic courses to our inner-city chil-

---

Examples provide evidence of the problem.

Links to sources providing evidence of the state's mismanagement.

Baraka declares state control to be the problem that needs a solution.

A discussion of the outcomes readers can expect if control is returned to local officials.

dren. And we must break the cycle of low expectations that some educators have of the children they teach, merely prescribing repeat classes if students don't pass.

The first step in a transition to local control of Newark's schools is a short-term transfer of authority to the mayor. I would quickly appoint a new superintendent. Once basic functions were restored to the district, we would move as soon as possible to return control to an elected school board with full powers.

A statement of what he will do if his proposal is enacted.

It is clear that we cannot rely on the good faith of the state to respond expeditiously. Federal intervention appears our only recourse. I have written to the Justice Department's Office of Civil Rights in support of the lawsuits that parents, students, advocates and educators in our city have brought, requesting that the federal government intercede. The right of Newark's citizens to equitable, high-quality public education demands the return of local, democratic control.

A restatement of why the change he proposes matters to his audience of "Newark's citizens."

REFLECT. *Find a proposal in a campus publication or local newspaper. Read it first to see if you find it persuasive. If not, why not? Then annotate it as we've done with Baraka's proposal to see if it includes all the features listed on p. 343. If not, would it be improved by adding any of the features it's lacking, or by elaborating on any it doesn't demonstrate well?*

PROJECT PROPOSALS

You may be asked to write a project proposal to explain your plans for a large or long-term assignment: what you intend to do, how you'll go about doing it, and why the project is important. Like any proposal, a project proposal makes an argument, demonstrating that the project is worth doing and feasible given the time and resources you have available. Unless the assignment names other requirements, your proposal should cover the following ground:

An Indication of Your Topic and Focus

Explain what your topic is and give any necessary background information. In some cases, you might be required to do some background research and to include a LITERATURE REVIEW summarizing what you find, including any issues or controversies you want to investigate. Say what your research focus will be, with the RESEARCH QUESTION you plan to pursue and a tentative THESIS. Finally, say why the topic matters—so what, and who cares?

An Explanation of Why You're Interested in the Topic

Briefly explain what you already know about your topic and why you've chosen to pursue this line of inquiry. You might describe any coursework, reading, or experience that contributes to your knowledge and interest. Also note what you don't yet know but intend to find out by doing this project.

A Plan

Explain how you will investigate your research question. What types of sources will you need and what will your RESEARCH METHODS be? If you plan to do FIELD RESEARCH, how will you conduct your study? And what GENRE and MEDIUM will you use to present your findings? What steps will be required to bring it all together into the final document?

A Schedule

Break your project into tasks and make a schedule, taking into account all the research, reading, and writing you'll need to do. Include any specific tasks your instructor requires, such as handing in a draft or an ANNOTATED BIBLIOGRAPHY. Be sure also to leave yourself time to get feedback and revise.

DAVID PASINI, an engineering major at The Ohio State University, wrote this project proposal for a first-year writing course on the theme of sports in contemporary American society.

The Economic Impact of Investing Public Funds in Sports Franchises

DAVID PASINI

SINCE THE 1960S, local governments have provided increased funding and subsidies for professional sports franchises. Taxpayer money has gone toward facilities like stadiums and arenas, and many cities have offered tax exemptions and other financial incentives to keep a team in town that has threatened to relocate. Proponents of public funding for privately owned sports franchises argue that cities gain more from the arrangement—namely jobs, status, and tourist dollars—than they lose. Opponents argue that using public funds for these purposes results in long-term financial drains on local governments and point out that many communities have been abandoned by teams even after providing substantial benefits, leaving the city or state holding the proverbial debt-heavy bag.

The introduction announces the topic and summarizes a controversy the project will focus on.

Writing in the *New York Times*, Ken Belson gives an example of one such government-funded project: "The old Giants Stadium, demolished to make way for New Meadowlands Stadium, still carries about $110 million in debt, or nearly $13 for every New Jersey resident, even though it is now a parking lot" (Belson). The image

Figure 1. Left to right: the governor of New Jersey, William T. Cahill; the owner of the Giants, Wellington Mara; and chairman of the New Jersey sports authority, Sonny Werblin, admire a drawing of Giants Stadium. Photo by Neal Boenzi. (Belson A1)

included here shows the governor of New Jersey looking over a drawing of the Giants Stadium, which was completed in 1976 and destroyed in 2010 (fig. 1).

Given the high stakes involved—and particularly the use of taxpayer dollars—it seems important, then, to ask what these sports franchises contribute (or do not contribute) to their cities and wider metropolitan areas. Do these teams "generate positive net economic benefits for their cities," or do they "absorb scarce government funds" that would be better spent on programs that have "higher social or economic payoff" (Noll and Zimbalist 55)? My research project will investigate these questions.

An explicit statement of his research questions.

The question of public funding for sports is important to any resident of a community that has a professional sports franchise or is trying to lure one, as well as to any citizen, sports fan or not, who is interested in the economic and political issues surrounding this topic. I am in the latter group, a nonfan who is simply interested in how public monies are being used to support sports, and whose knowledge about the issues is primarily in the economic domain. At this point in the research process, I am neither a pro-

A statement of why this topic matters, and to whom.

Pasini explains his interest in the topic and his current knowledge of it.

ponent nor an opponent of investing in sports, but I think that it's important to consider just how—and how much—professional sports contribute to the economic well-being of the government that funds them. How much of the money that teams generate supports local businesses, school districts, or other important entities that benefit all citizens? How much of it stays in the owners' pockets? Do the franchises "give back" to their communities in any other tangible or intangible ways? The franchises themselves should consider these questions, since the communities that helped to provide them with the amenities they require to be successful sports teams have a right to expect something in return.

More focused research questions, leading to a tentative thesis statement.

To learn more about investment in sports teams and the teams' economic impact, I will consult business and sports management journals and appropriate news sources, both print and digital. I will also interview stakeholders on both sides of the debate as well as experts on this topic. In my research, I will consider the many factors that must be taken into account, such as the benefits of tourism and the costs of "creating extra demand on local services" (Crompton 33). As a result of my research, I hope to offer insight on whether public funds are in fact put to good use when they are invested in major sports franchises.

A research plan, including kinds of sources he'll consult and field research he plans to conduct.

The conclusion restates why this research matters.

Proposed Schedule

Do library and internet research	April 6–20
Submit annotated bibliography	April 20
Schedule and conduct interviews	April 21–25
Turn in first draft	May 10
Turn in second draft	May 18
Turn in final draft	May 25

A schedule that allows time for research, writing, and revising—and lists assignment deadlines.

Preliminary Works Consulted

Belson, Ken. "As Stadiums Vanish, Their Debt Lives On." *New York Times* 8 Sept. 2010: A1. Print.

Crompton, John L. "Economic Impact Analysis of Sports Facilities and Events: Eleven Sources of Misapplication." *Journal of Sport Management* 9.1 (1995): 14–35. Print.

Pasini uses MLA style for a preliminary list of works consulted.

Noll, Roger G., and Andrew Zimbalist, eds. *Sports, Jobs, and Taxes: The Economic Impact of Sports Teams and Stadiums.* Washington: Brookings Inst., 1997. *Google Books.* Google, 1 Apr. 2011. Web.

Robertson, Robby. "The Economic Impact of Sports Facilities." *Sport Digest* 16.1 (2008): n. pag. Web. 1 Apr. 2011.

REFLECT. *If you're reading about project proposals, you've likely been assigned to write one. Analyze what your assignment is asking for, comparing it with the features described on p. 343. What does this exercise help you appreciate about how such a proposal works? What you can learn from doing one?*

WRITING A PROPOSAL / A Roadmap

Think of a problem you can help solve

If you get to select the topic, begin by identifying an issue you know something about. You'll probably find it easiest—and most rewarding—to tackle an issue on which you can have some real impact. Try choosing a topic you have some knowledge and authority to speak on, and one that is narrowly focused or local enough so that your suggestions may be heard. You can't expect to solve all the problems of America's food system, but you may well be able to propose a more healthy and sustainable dining option on campus.

If you've been assigned a topic, consider ways that you can make it interesting to you and to your readers. This may mean finding an interesting angle on the topic you've been assigned, or, if the assignment is framed in general terms, finding a specific aspect that you can address with a specific solution.

Consider your rhetorical situation

Once you have a topic, thinking about your rhetorical situation will help you focus on how to proceed.

Think about your AUDIENCE. Who do you want your proposal to reach, and why? If you're proposing changes to a campus policy, you would do so differently if you're writing to school administrators in charge of that policy than if you're writing a piece for the student newspaper. Here are some things to consider:

- What do you know about your audience? In what ways are they like or unlike you—and one another?
- What will they likely know about your topic? What background information will you have to provide?
- What interest or stake are they likely to have in the situation you're addressing? Will you need to convince them that the problem matters—and if you do, how can you do so?
- What sorts of evidence will they find most convincing?
- How likely are they to agree with what you propose?

Be clear about your PURPOSE. Odds are that you'll have multiple purposes—everything from getting a good grade to demonstrating your understanding of a situation to making your community a better place for everyone. The more you understand your own motivations, the clearer you can be with your audience about what is at stake.

Be aware of your STANCE. What is your attitude about your topic, and how do you want to come across to your audience? How can your choice of words help convey that stance? When David Freedman refers to those he disagrees with as the "let-them-eat-kale" crowd, his dismissive language tells us as much about him as it does about those he is criticizing.

Examine the larger CONTEXT. What do you know about the problem you're tackling? What might you need to learn? How have others addressed the problem? What solutions have they proposed and how well have those solutions worked?

Think about MEDIA. If the choice is yours, what medium will best reach your audience and suit your purpose? If you're assigned to use a particular medium, how can you use it best? If, for example, you're giving an oral presentation, *PowerPoint* slides can help your audience follow the main points of your proposal, especially if you're presenting quantitative data.

Think about DESIGN. If you have the option of designing your proposal, think about what it needs. If it's lengthy or complex, should you use headings? Is there anything in your proposal that would be hard to follow in a paragraph—and easier to read in a chart or a graph?

Study the situation

Whatever the problem, you have to understand it in all its complexity and think about the many ways different parties will likely understand it.

Begin by thinking about what you know about the situation. What interests you about the issue, and why do you care? What more do you want or need to find out about it? To answer these questions, try BRAINSTORMING or other activities for GENERATING IDEAS.

Be sure you understand the problem. To do so, you'll surely need to do some RESEARCH. What CAUSED this problem, and what are its EFFECTS?

How serious is it? Who cares about it? What's been said about it? What efforts have already been made to address the problem, and how have they succeeded? How have similar problems been handled, and what insights can you gain from studying them?

Consider how you can best present the problem for your **AUDIENCE**. If they're aware of the problem, how likely are they to care about it? Does it affect them? If they're not aware of it, how can you make them aware? What kind of evidence can you provide to show them it exists and make them recognize the potential consequences? Why do you think the issue matters, and how can you persuade others to take it seriously?

For example, if you were writing about the need for a program to raise awareness of the effects of hate speech on campus and needed to persuade readers who have no reason themselves to worry about that, you might open with an anecdote about hateful things that have been said about others to make them aware of the issue. And you could then appeal to their goodwill and concern for fellow students to understand why it's a problem that needs to be solved.

Determine a course of action

Once you've got a thorough understanding of the problem and what others likely think about it, you can start thinking about possible solutions.

Come up with some possible solutions. Start by making a list of options. Which ones seem most feasible and most likely to solve the problem? Is there one that seems like the best approach? Why? Will it solve the problem entirely, or just part of it?

If, for example, you're proposing a program to raise awareness of the effects of hate speech on campus, what are the options? You could suggest an open forum, or a teach-in. Maybe you could get a prominent activist to come speak, or someone from the ACLU.

Decide on the best solution. Determine which of the options would be feasible and which one would work the best. Then think about how far it would go toward actually solving the problem. Hate speech is not a problem easily solved, so this might well be a case when you can realistically only raise awareness of the problem with the ultimate goal of solving it.

These are some of the questions you'll need to ask and answer as you determine the best solution to propose.

Organize and start writing

Once you've clearly defined the problem, figured out a viable solution, and identified evidence to support your proposal, it's time to organize your materials and start drafting.

Come up with a tentative THESIS that identifies the problem and proposes a solution. Use this statement to guide you as you write.

Provide EVIDENCE showing that the problem does in fact exist and is serious enough to demand a solution—and that your proposed solution is feasible and the best among various options.

Acknowledge other possible solutions. Decide how and at what point in your proposal you will address other options. You might start with them and explain their shortcomings one by one, as David Freedman does in "How Junk Food Can End Obesity." Or you could raise them after presenting your own solution, comparing your solution with the others as a way of showing that yours is the most feasible or the most likely to solve the problem.

Draft an OPENING. Identify and describe the problem, making clear why the issue matters—and why the problem needs a solution.

Draft a CONCLUSION. Reiterate the nature of the problem and the solution you're proposing. Summarize the benefits your proposal offers. Most of all: remind readers of why the issue matters, why they should care—and why they should take your proposal seriously (and perhaps take action).

Look critically at your draft, get response—and revise

Once you have a complete draft, read it over carefully, focusing on how you define the problem and support the solution you propose—and the way you appeal to your audience. If possible, ask others—a writing center tutor or classmate—to read it over as well. Here are some questions that can help you or others read over the draft with a critical eye:

- *How does the proposal OPEN?* Will it capture readers' interest? Does it make clear what problem will be addressed and give some sense of why it matters? How else might it begin? Does the title tell readers what the proposal is about, and will it make them want to know more?

- *Is the problem* DESCRIBED *in enough detail?* Will any readers need more information to understand that it's a problem that matters? Have you said anything about its CAUSES and consequences—and if not, do you need to?

- *Is the proposed solution explicit and compelling?* Have you provided enough EVIDENCE to show that it's feasible and will address the problem—and that it's better than other possible solutions? Is there an explicit statement of what it will accomplish?

- *Have other possible solutions been acknowledged fairly*—and how well have you responded to them? Are there any other solutions that need to be considered?

- *Is the proposal easy to follow?* If not, try adding TRANSITIONS or headings.

- *How have you established your* AUTHORITY *to write on this topic?* Does the information seem trustworthy? How do you come across as an author—passionate? serious? sarcastic?—and how does this tone affect the way the proposal comes across to readers?

- *How would you characterize the* STYLE*?* Is it appropriate for your intended audience? Consider the choice of words, the level of formality, and so on.

- *How about* DESIGN*?* Are there any illustrations—and if so, what do they contribute to the proposal? If not, is there any information that would be easier to show with a photo or in a chart? What about the font: is it appropriate for a proposal of this kind? Is the design appropriate for the MEDIUM?

- *How does the proposal* CONCLUDE*?* Will it inspire the change or action you're calling for? How else might it conclude?

Revise your draft in response to any feedback you receive and your own analysis.

REFLECT. Once you've completed your proposal, let it settle for a while and take time to reflect. How well did you define the problem, and how thoroughly did you support your proposed solution? How fairly did you acknowledge and respond to other possible solutions? How persuasively have you demonstrated the feasibility of your solution? Research shows that such reflections help "lock in" what you learn for future use.

Speaking While Female

SHERYL SANDBERG AND ADAM GRANT

YEARS AGO, while producing the hit TV series *The Shield*, Glen Mazzara noticed that two young female writers were quiet during story meetings. He pulled them aside and encouraged them to speak up more.

Watch what happens when we do, they replied.

Almost every time they started to speak, they were interrupted or shot down before finishing their pitch. When one had a good idea, a male writer would jump in and run with it before she could complete her thought.

Sadly, their experience is not unusual.

We've both seen it happen again and again. When a woman speaks in a   5 professional setting, she walks a tightrope. Either she's barely heard or she's judged as too aggressive. When a man says virtually the same thing, heads nod in appreciation for his fine idea. As a result, women often decide that saying less is more.

Some new studies support our observations. A study by a Yale psycholo-

SHERYL SANDBERG serves as the Chief Operating Officer of *Facebook*; she is also founder of *LeanIn.org,* inspired by her bestselling book of the same name. ADAM GRANT teaches at the Wharton School of Business at the University of Pennsylvania; he is the author of *Give and Take: Why Helping Others Drives Our Success* (2013). This essay was the second in a series of four on women in the workplace that Sandberg and Grant wrote for the *New York Times* in 2015. Go to everyones anauthor.tumblr.com to access the links (underscored here) as you read.

gist, Victoria L. Brescoll, found that male senators with more power (as measured by tenure, leadership positions and track record of legislation passed) spoke more on the Senate floor than their junior colleagues. But for female senators, power was not linked to significantly more speaking time.

Suspecting that powerful women stayed quiet because they feared a backlash, Professor Brescoll looked deeper. She asked professional men and women to evaluate the competence of chief executives who voiced their opinions more or less frequently. Male executives who spoke more often than their peers were rewarded with 10 percent higher ratings of competence. When female executives spoke more than their peers, both men and women punished them with 14 percent lower ratings. As this and other research shows, women who worry that talking "too much" will cause them to be disliked are not paranoid; they are often right.

One of us, Adam, was dismayed to find similar patterns when studying a health care company and advising an international bank. When male employees contributed ideas that brought in new revenue, they got significantly higher performance evaluations. But female employees who spoke up with equally valuable ideas did not improve their managers' perception of their performance. Also, the more the men spoke up, the more helpful their managers believed them to be. But when women spoke up more, there was no increase in their perceived helpfulness.

This speaking-up double bind harms organizations by depriving them of valuable ideas. A University of Texas researcher, Ethan Burris, conducted an experiment in which he asked teams to make strategic decisions for a bookstore. He randomly informed one member that the bookstore's inventory system was flawed and gave that person data about a better approach. In subsequent analyses, he found that when women challenged the old system and suggested a new one, team leaders viewed them as less loyal and were less likely to act on their suggestions. Even when all team members were informed that one member possessed unique information that would benefit the group, suggestions from women with inside knowledge were discounted.

Obviously, businesses need to find ways to interrupt this gender bias. Just   10
as orchestras that use blind auditions increase the number of women who are selected, organizations can increase women's contributions by adopting practices that focus less on the speaker and more on the idea. For example, in innovation tournaments, employees submit suggestions and solutions to problems anonymously. Experts evaluate the proposals, give feedback to all participants and then implement the best plans.

Since most work cannot be done anonymously, leaders must also take steps to encourage women to speak and be heard. At *The Shield*, Mr. Mazzara, the show runner, found a clever way to change the dynamics that were holding those two female employees back. He announced to the writers that he was instituting a no-interruption rule while anyone—male or female—was pitching. It worked, and he later observed that it made the entire team more effective.

The long-term solution to the double bind of speaking while female is to increase the number of women in leadership roles. (As we noted in our previous article, research shows that when it comes to leadership skills, although men are more confident, women are more competent.) As more women enter the upper echelons of organizations, people become more accustomed to women's contributing and leading. Professor Burris and his colleagues studied a credit union where women made up 74 percent of supervisors and 84 percent of front-line employees. Sure enough, when women spoke up there, they were more likely to be heard than men. When President Obama held his last news conference of 2014, he called on eight reporters—all women. It made headlines worldwide. Had a politician given only men a chance to ask questions, it would not have been news; it would have been a regular day.

As 2015 starts, we wonder what would happen if we all held Obama-style meetings, offering women the floor whenever possible. Doing this for even a day or two might be a powerful bias interrupter, demonstrating to our teams and colleagues that speaking while female is still quite difficult. We're going to try it to see what we learn. We hope you will, too—and then share your experiences with us all on Facebook or in the comments section.

Thinking about the Text

1. What specific problem do Sheryl Sandberg and Adam Grant seek to solve in this essay? What sorts of **EVIDENCE** do they offer to show that the problem exists?

2. What specific solutions do they suggest? Consider both the short- and long-term solutions that they raise. How practical or compelling do you find these solutions?

3. The problem Sandberg and Grant describe extends beyond women's frustrations in their workplaces. What is the ultimate significance of the problem, and how do these authors make it clear? In other words, what meaningful outcomes do they argue their proposal can ultimately bring about?

4. How did the **AUDIENCE** for this piece, the readers of a major U.S. newspaper, likely affect this essay? How might it have been different had it been written for an audience of male executives? of female employees?

5. Sandberg and Grant tackle a persistent problem of some magnitude, one that is clearly important to them. Choose a problem that matters to you and offer a **PROPOSAL** that addresses some aspect of that problem. You might start by observing issues you see around you, but you'll likely find that you need to do some research to precisely define the problem and propose a solution. Use the genre features on p. 343 as a guide as you construct your proposal.

Let's Start an Education Revolution
MITCHELL OLIVER

HUMAN CAPITAL CONTRACTS (HCCs) could become the new alternative to current public and private debt in America. While revolutionary as a concept, it is one that must be taken into consideration as a unique and efficient way to solve the growing student debt bubble.

A capital contract, in short, is modern indentured servitude. This, of course, is a very distorted parallel but is an effective metaphor. The concept is that you pay nothing upfront with no risk and instead you pay the investor (the government or a private investor) a set percentage of your future income for a set number of years (10 percent for 10 years, 5 percent for 20 years, 2 percent for 5 years, etc.).

This concept isn't new in the world of business. Just look at *Kickstarter*, the hugely popular crowd-funding platform that is taking the world of capital investment by storm. Similar to a human capital contract, the investors pay an inventor or entrepreneur up front in order to land either a pre-order of the future product or a percentage stake in that person's future profits.

These profits might be zero or they could be in the millions. Caveat emptor.*

* *caveat emptor:* Latin for "Let the buyer beware."

MITCHELL OLIVER is a student and staff columnist for Georgia State University's independent student newspaper, *The Signal*. He writes a weekly column, *Dollars and Sense with Mitch*, where this piece was published in 2014.

So let's tackle this concept for college students: You are a company. You ₅ are an entrepreneur and your business is landing a career or job out of college. Right now, you have low capital because you don't have a degree yet (or are going for a masters or PhD). This process of going to college and graduate school serves the purpose of increasing your human capital.

What can you do with more human capital? You can become a more valuable human being, that's what! You become more and more of an asset not only for your future employers but for society as a whole. Increased human capital doesn't always correlate directly to higher income but is commonly believed to grow economies and increase overall societal health.

Increasing overall human capital is essential to our success, and it is why we all go to college today. So why not change the way in which we can obtain this capital? Why not make it available to everyone at no risk or upfront cost?

Here's a revolutionary idea: What if the government were to invest in every young American's future potential earnings (the outcome of increased capital)? What if anyone in America could go to any college they wanted for free? That's the power of human capital contracts.

Let's see how it would work. We'll take a simple example of a college freshman, Jane. Jane goes to Georgia State for four years and lands a job at Geico making $40,000 per year. In her human capital contract, she agreed to pay 10 percent of future income for 10 years after college. This is great for Jane because she is debt free and is making $36,000 out of college (after paying the government $4,000 per year). Over the course of 10 years, Jane will technically have paid $40,000 for her college education, but adjusting for inflation over 14 years, that tuition cost is only about $24,000 in real dollars today.

This percentage system would work for any variation on this example. Say ₁₀ Jane couldn't find work and flipped burgers at McDonalds for 10 years. She would still have to pay only 10 percent of her yearly income. On the other end, she may land a job making $200,000 per year. While unlikely, she would technically pay $200,000 for her education.

I say technically because if you think about it, no one would "pay" anything! You would simply be repaying the investment that the government made in you. Besides, in the above extreme example, Jane would have made $2 million over ten years. A small $20,000 per year for her is not going to break her bank.

A glaring issue with this concept is that it acts as a negative incentive to land a high-paying job. Most opponents of HCCs will say that graduates will begin to aim lower and not push their limits in fear of making too much money, an ironic disincentive.

But to that I pose the question—isn't that already happening in our current system? Aren't students choosing cheaper schools and "safe" degrees because they feel trapped in their student loans? I for one would be hesitant to take out a $50,000 loan and go to Emory in the case that I couldn't find work.

The current loan system is unsympathetic to the student and simply acts as a profit-maker for private loan companies. If you make it after college, you pay off your loan. If the system fails you, you still pay off your loan! Can't we at least *consider* other possibilities?

We as students must demand freedom. Freedom of choice. Freedom of   15
education. I call for a Declaration of Education, creating a real revolution.

We as students must start asking the questions no one wants asked. Are there no alternatives to our current loan system? Is it in our benefit to treat ourselves like companies? Can we do this without losing a sense of self?

Big thinkers and game changers will need to rise up to tackle these questions. The first step is to admit that the system has some flaws and that there are other options to consider. Then the discussion can begin and real change can come about.

Thinking about the Text

1. What problem has Mitchell Oliver defined, and what solution does he **PROPOSE** to solve that problem?

2. How does he demonstrate that his solution will address the problem? What sorts of **EVIDENCE** does he provide, and how well does it support his claim?

3. What **COUNTERARGUMENTS** does Oliver acknowledge? Is his response to these objections satisfactory? What other objections might you raise?

4. How does Oliver establish his **CREDIBILITY** as an author who can speak knowledgeably about the problem he seeks to address?

5. What's your reaction to this proposal? Write an essay to respond—agreeing, disagreeing, or both, and raising any questions that you think need to be considered.

PART IV

The Centrality of Argument

CHANCES ARE THAT your first attempt to communicate was an argument. Your first cry, that is, argued that you were hungry or sleepy or wanted to be held. Later, you could use words to say what you wanted: "More!" "No!" "Candy!" All arguments. So if you think that argument is just about disputes or disagreements, think again. In rhetorical terms, argument refers to any way that human beings express themselves to try to achieve a particular purpose—which, many would say, means any way that people express themselves at all.

If you think about the kinds of writing covered in this book, for example, it is easy to understand that an op-ed taking a position on a political issue or a TV critic's rave review of a new series is "arguing" for or against something. An editorial cartoon about the issue or an ad for the movie is making an obvious argument, too. But even when you post an update on *Facebook* about something you did yesterday, you're implicitly arguing that it will be intriguing or important or perhaps amusing to your audience, those who follow you on *Facebook*. Even when you write a lab report, you'll describe and interpret the results of an experiment, arguing that your findings have certain implications.

In fact, we are immersed in argument. Try counting the number of arguments you either make or encounter in just one day, starting perhaps with the argument you have with yourself over what to wear, moving on to the barrage of posters asking you to support certain causes or attend various concerts, to a biology lecture where the professor explains the conflicting arguments about climate change, and ending only when you and a friend agree to disagree about who's the better quarterback, Tom Brady or Peyton Manning. We bet you'll be surprised by how many arguments you encounter in a day.

The point we want to make is simple: you are the author of many arguments and the target of many more—and you'll be a better reader and writer of your own arguments if you understand how they work.

It's important to mention as well that arguments today often consist of more than just words, from the signs admonishing you to fasten your seat belt, to a big "thumbs up," to an ad for McDonald's. These familiar images demonstrate the way words and pictures and graphics can all make strong visual arguments.

Words and images can make strong visual arguments.

It's also worth noting that arguments today are more seductive than ever. A fifteen-second TV sound bite sways millions of voters; a song you loved as a twelve-year-old now boosts sales of soft drinks; celebrities write op-ed essays in newspapers on issues they care about. Even your school mounts arguments intended to attract prospective students and their parents—and, later, to motivate alumni to give generously. Check out your school's homepage and you'll probably find announcements intended to attract applications and contributions.

Perhaps you think that such arguments are somewhat manipulative, intended to trick you into buying a product or contributing to a cause. But arguments are always trying to achieve some purpose, so it is up to you both as a reader and as a writer to distinguish the good from the bad. And arguments can, of course, be used for good (think of the powerful arguments for human rights) or ill (think of Hitler's hypnotic arguments). They can be deceptive, even silly—does that gorgeous woman holding a can of cleanser really mean to claim that if you buy the cleanser you'll look just like her?

In fact, argument is about many things and has many purposes. Of the many purposes we might name, here are just a few:

to explore

to understand

to find consensus

to make decisions

to convince or persuade

Keep in mind, however, that arguments are always embedded in particular contexts—and that what is persuasive can vary from one context to another, or from one culture to another. The most persuasive evidence in one community might come from religious texts; in another, from personal testimony; in another, from facts or statistics. Especially now that arguments so often take place in cyberspace, reaching people all around the world, it's important to be aware of such differences.

When two brothers attacked the Paris offices of the satiric journal *Charlie Hebdo* in 2015, leaving twelve people dead and eleven others wounded, the entire world was caught up in the story. Why attack a journal that publishes satirical comics? As we later learned, the brothers were acting on their belief that the artists at *Charlie Hebdo* were guilty of (mis)representing Mohammed in cartoons and thus of defiling the prophet and breaking the traditions and laws of Islam as they understood them. Condemnations of the attacks echoed around the world, from Europe to Australia and Japan, arguing that murder is never an appropriate act and that the brothers had struck not only at *Charlie Hebdo* but at a bedrock principle of the Western world: freedom of speech. Yet others disagreed, arguing that the cartoonists had gone too far in their satire, that their work was insulting and destructive of another culture's beliefs; while they did not condone the bloodshed, these critics argued that the cartoonists' work had been deliberately inflammatory. Still others argued that the attack was justified, that the brothers were heroes and martyrs to their faith. Not surprisingly, these opinions varied from culture to culture, religion to religion. In the age of the internet, writers, speakers, cartoonists, and activists need to remember that their intended arguments will be interpreted variably, depending on audience and context.

Posters often make powerful arguments—and those who disagree sometimes argue back on the poster itself.

During his lifetime, Martin Luther King Jr. did not have the benefit of the internet, but the arguments he made eventually reverberated around the world. In his "Letter from Birmingham Jail," King responds to a statement written in 1963 by eight white Alabama clergymen who had urged him to stop his campaign of civil disobedience to protest racial discrimination. This particular context—the U.S. South at the height of the civil rights struggle—informs his argument throughout. And while King's argument remains the same, having been republished countless times, its interpretation varies across time and cultures. Thus when the letter first appeared, it responded point by point to the statement by the eight clergymen, and it

Martin Luther King Jr. in a jail cell in Birmingham, Alabama.

was read in that time and place as an answer to their particular charges. Today, however, it is read as a much more general statement about the importance of civil rights for all people. King's famous conclusion to this letter sums up his argument and consciously addresses an audience that extends far beyond the eight clergymen:

Let us all hope that the dark clouds of racial prejudice will soon pass away and the deep fog of misunderstanding will be lifted from our fear-drenched communities, and in some not too distant tomorrow the radiant stars of love and brotherhood will shine over our great nation with all their scintillating beauty.   —MARTIN LUTHER KING JR., "Letter from Birmingham Jail"

As with all arguments, the effectiveness of King's letter has always varied according to the context in which it is read and, especially, the audience that is reading it. In most of his letter, King addresses eight specific people, and they are clearly part of his primary audience. But his use of "us" and "our" in the passage above works to broaden that audience and reaches beyond that time and place to many other readers and listeners.

Because arguments are so central to our lives, it's important to understand how they work—and to learn how to make effective arguments of your own, remembering that you can do so only by paying very careful attention to your purpose and your intended audience and the rest of your rhetorical situation. The next two chapters focus on how good arguments work and on strategies for supporting the arguments that you make.

SEVENTEEN

Analyzing and Constructing Arguments
Those You Read, Those You Write

HE CLOTHES YOU CHOOSE TO WEAR argue for your own sense of style; the courses your college requires argue for what educators consider important; the kind of transportation you take, the food you eat (or don't eat)—almost everything represents some kind of argument. So it is important to understand all these arguments, those you encounter and those you make yourself. Consider a couple of everyday examples.

What's in an email address? You may not have thought much about the argument that your email address makes, but it certainly does make a statement about who you are. One student we know chose the email address maximman123@yahoo.com, an allusion to the men's magazine. But when it came time to look for meaningful employment, he began to think about what that address said about him. As a result, he chose an address he felt was more appropriate to the image he wanted to convey: whmiller@gmail.com.

If you need to think about what arguments you may be making yourself, it's also important to understand the arguments that come from others. Take a look, for example, at the two images on the next page, both of which appeared after the shootings at Sandy Hook Elementary School in December 2012. The first image shows signs that make the argument that gun control will protect our loved ones; the

Protesters' signs make decidedly different arguments about guns in America.

second takes a very different approach, showing guns rights activists invoking their Constitutional right to bear arms. These two images make radically different arguments about the role guns should play in U.S. society, arguments that call on us to think very carefully before we respond. Crucially, they demonstrate that arguments always exist in a larger context, that they always involve more than just the one person or group making the argument.

You can tell by the brevity and the directness of his language that Brent Staples is jumping right into an ongoing conversation. See what he's done on p. 1065

Arguments, in short, don't appear out of thin air: every argument begins as a response to some other argument—a statement, an event, an image, or something else. From these images we see how important it is to analyze any argument you encounter—and consider the other side—before deciding where you yourself stand. That goes for arguments you read, and for ones you write yourself. Either way, all arguments are part of a larger conversation. Whether you're responding to something you've read, discussing a film you've seen, or writing an essay that argues a position, you enter into a dialogue with the arguments of others.

This chapter will help you analyze the arguments you encounter and compose arguments of your own.

WHERE'S THE ARGUMENT COMING FROM?

As a reader, you need to pay special attention to the source of an argument—literally to where it is coming from. It makes a difference whether an argument appears in the *New York Times* or a school newspaper, in *Physics Review* or on the blog of someone you know nothing about, in an impromptu speech by a candidate seeking your vote or in an analysis of that speech done by the nonpartisan website *FactCheck.org*. And even when you know who's putting forward the argument, you may well need to dig deeper to find out where—what view of the world—that source itself is "coming from."

For example, here's the homepage of the website of Public Citizen, a nonprofit organization founded in 1971 by consumer advocate and social critic Ralph Nader. So what can we tell about where this argument is coming from? We might start with the image in the upper-left corner of Lady Liberty holding up her torch right next to the headline "PUBLIC CITIZEN Protecting Health, Safety and Democracy." Below that is the menu bar and an example of the kind of analysis Public Citizen is known for:

> If President Barack Obama were to issue an executive order requiring government contractors to disclose their political spending, it would reach at least 70 percent of the Fortune 100 companies, a new Public Citizen analysis finds.

The homepage of Public Citizen's website.

Given its stated goals of "defending democracy and resisting corporate power," we can surmise, then, that Public Citizen is coming from a viewpoint that supports the rights of ordinary citizens and liberal democratic values and that opposes the influence of corporations on government. Indeed, if we look a bit further, to the "About" page, we will find the following statement:

> For four decades, we have proudly championed citizen interests before Congress, the executive branch agencies and the courts. We have successfully challenged the abusive practices of the pharmaceutical, nuclear and automobile industries, and many others. We are leading the charge against undemocratic trade agreements that advance the interests of mega-corporations at the expense of citizens worldwide.

Together, these images and statements tell us a lot about Public Citizen's stance, where the organization is coming from. As savvy readers, we then have to assess the claims Public Citizen makes on its website (and elsewhere) in light of this knowledge: knowing where the organization is coming from affects how willing we are to accept what it says.

Or consider a more lighthearted example, this time from a column in the *New York Times* written by political pundit David Brooks:

> We now have to work under the assumption that every American has a tattoo. Whether we are at a formal dinner, at a professional luncheon, at a sales conference or arguing before the Supreme Court, we have to assume that everyone in the room is fully tatted up—that under each suit, dress or blouse, there is at least a set of angel wings, a barbed wire armband, a Chinese character or maybe even a fully inked body suit. We have to assume that any casual anti-tattoo remark will cause offense, even to those we least suspect of self-marking.
> —DAVID BROOKS, "Nonconformity Is Skin Deep"

David Brooks

What can we know about where Brooks is coming from? For starters, it's easy to find out that he is a conservative journalist whose work appears in many publications across the political spectrum and who often appears as a television commentator on the *PBS NewsHour*. We also know that this passage comes from one of his op-ed columns for the *New York Times*. His photo on the *Times* website presents him as a professional, in jacket and tie.

What more can we tell about where he's coming from in the passage itself? Probably first is that Brooks is representing himself here as somewhat old-fashioned, as someone who's clearly an adult and a member of what might be called "the establishment" in the United States (note his offhanded assumption that "we" might be "at a formal dinner" or "arguing before the Supreme Court"). He's someone who almost certainly does not have a tattoo himself. He's also comfortable using a little sarcasm ("everyone in the room is fully tatted up") and exaggeration ("every American has a tattoo") to make a humorous point. Finally, we can tell that he is a self-confident—and persuasive—author and that we'll need to be on our toes to understand the argument that he's actually making.

As an author, you should always think hard about where *you* are coming from in the arguments you make. What's your STANCE, and why? How do you want your audience to perceive you? As reasonable? knowledgeable? opinionated? curious? something else?

How can you convey your stance? Through your choice of words, of course—both *what* you say and *how* you say it—but also through any images you include and the way you design your text. The words you choose not only convey your meaning, they reveal a lot about your attitude—toward your subject and your audience. Introducing a quotation with the words "she insists" indicates a different attitude than the more neutral "she says." And if you highlight certain information by putting it in a box, you're signaling that it's detail that you consider important.

WHAT'S THE CLAIM?

You run into dozens of claims every day. Your brother says the latest Spiderman film is the best one ever; your news feed says that Michigan State will be in the Final Four; a friend's *Facebook* update says it's a waste of time and money to eat at Power Pizza. Each of these statements makes a claim and argues implicitly for you to agree. The arguments you read and write in college often begin with a claim, an arguable statement that must then be supported with good reasons and evidence.

The *New Yorker* cover on the next page titled "Moment of Joy" shows *Sesame Street* character Bert with his arm around Ernie's shoulder as they watch the 2013 Supreme Court ruling overturning the Defense of Marriage Act, which had denied federal benefits to same-sex couples. The cover immediately sparked debate. The creator of the image saw it as portraying a celebratory moment, saying, "It's amazing to witness how attitudes on gay

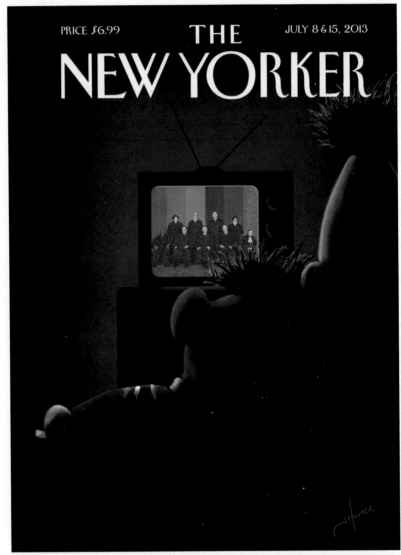

Sesame Street characters Bert and Ernie are featured on this cover from July 2013 marking the Supreme Court's decision to grant federal benefits to same-sex couples.

rights have evolved in my lifetime. This is great for our kids, a moment we can all celebrate." But others read the image differently, saying that using puppets rather than actual people trivialized the issue; still others claimed that the image sexualized the much-loved children's show or even that it promoted child abuse. Images can make powerful arguments, and sometimes ones that spark debate.

The easiest claims to identify are those that are stated directly as an explicit **THESIS**. Look, for instance, at the following paragraph from a journal article by civil rights activist W. E. B. Du Bois in 1922. As you read each sentence, ask yourself what Du Bois's claim is.

> Abraham Lincoln was a Southern poor white, of illegitimate birth, poorly educated and unusually ugly, awkward, ill-dressed. He liked smutty stories and was a politician down to his toes. Aristocrats—Jeff Davis, Seward and their ilk—despised him, and indeed he had little outwardly that compelled respect. But in that curious human way he was big inside. He had reserves and depths and when habit and convention were torn away there was something left to Lincoln—nothing to most of his contemners. There was something left, so that at the crisis he was big enough to be inconsistent—cruel, merciful; peace-loving, a fighter; despising Negroes and letting them fight and vote; protecting slavery and freeing slaves. He was a man—a big, inconsistent, brave man.
>
> —W. E. B. DU BOIS, "Abraham Lincoln"

We think you'll find that the claim is difficult to make out until the last sentence, which lets us know in an explicit thesis that the contradictions Du Bois has been detailing are part of Lincoln's greatness, part of what made him "big" and "brave." Take note as well of where the thesis appears in the text. Du Bois holds his claim for the very end.

Here is a very different example, from a newspaper column about legendary dancer Judith Jamison. Note that it begins with an explicit thesis stating a claim that the rest of the passage expands on—and supports:

> Judith Jamison is my kind of American cultural icon. . . . She has many accolades and awards—among them the National Medal of Arts, the Kennedy Center Honors and an Emmy. . . .
>
> But when I met her . . . she said with a huge smile, "Yes, honey, but you know I still have to do the laundry myself, and no one in New York parts the sidewalk 'cause I am comin' through!"

Judith Jamison dancing with the Alvin Ailey Dance Theater.

I like icons who are authentic and accessible. I think our country benefits from that. It can only serve to inspire others to believe that they can
try to do the same thing.
                                —MARIA HINOJOSA, "Dancing Past the Boundaries"

Notice that although Hinojosa's claim is related to her own personal taste
in American cultural icons, it is not actually about her taste itself. Her argument is not about her preference for cultural icons to be "authentic and
accessible." Instead, she's arguing that given this criterion, Judith Jamison
is a perfect example.

As an author making an argument of your own, remember that a claim shouldn't simply express a personal taste: if you say that you feel lousy or that you hate the New York Yankees, no one could reasonably argue that you don't feel that way. For a claim to be *arguable*—worth arguing—it has to take a **POSITION** that others can logically have different perspectives on. Likewise, an arguable claim can't simply be a statement of fact that no one would disagree with ("Violent video games earn millions of dollars every year"). And remember that in most academic contexts claims based on religious faith alone often cannot be argued since there are no agreed-upon standards of proof or evidence.

In most academic writing, you'll be expected to state your **CLAIM** explicitly as a **THESIS**, announcing your topic and the main point(s) you are going to make about that topic. Your thesis should help readers follow your train of thought, so it's important that it state your point clearly. A good thesis will also engage your audience's interest—and make them want to read on.

Be careful, however, not to overstate your thesis: you may need to **QUALIFY** it with words like *some, might,* or *possible*—saying, for example, that "Recent studies have shown that exercise has a limited effect on a person's weight, so eating less may be a better strategy for losing weight than exercising more." By saying that dieting "may be" more effective than exercise for weight loss, the author of this thesis has limited her claim to one she will be able to support.

In most U.S. academic contexts, authors are expected to make claims directly and get to the point fairly quickly, so you may want to position the thesis near the beginning of your text, often at the end of the introduction or the first paragraph. When your claim is likely to challenge or surprise your audience, though, you may want to build support for it more gradually and hold off stating it explicitly until later in your argument, as Du Bois does. In other situations, you may not need to make a direct statement of your claim at all. But always make sure in such cases that your audience has a clear understanding of what the claim is.

> Bell hooks begins her essay with a simple, direct statement of her thesis. See how much impact her opening has on p. 968.

WHAT'S AT STAKE?

Figuring out the answer to this question takes you to the heart of the argument. Rhetoricians in ancient Rome developed what they called *stasis theory*, a simple system for identifying the crux of an argument—what's at stake in it—by asking four questions in sequence:

1. What are the facts?
2. How can the issue be defined?
3. How much does it matter, and why?
4. What actions should be taken as a result?

Together these questions help determine the basic issues at stake in an argument. A look at the arguments that swirled around Hurricane Katrina and its effects can illustrate how these questions work.

What are the facts? Certainly the hurricane hit the Gulf Coast squarely, resulting in almost unimaginable damage and loss of life, especially in New Orleans, where levees failed along with the city's evacuation plan. Many arguments about the disaster had their crux (or stasis) here, claiming that the most important aspect of "what happened" was not the hurricane itself but the lack of preparation for it and the response to it.

How can the issue be defined? In the case of Katrina, the question of definition turned out to be crucial for many arguments about the event: it was easy enough to define the storm itself as a "category 4 hurricane" but much more difficult to classify the disaster beyond that simple scientific tag. To what extent was it a national disaster and to what extent a local one? To what extent was it a natural disaster and to what extent a man-made one? Was it proof of corruption and incompetence on the part of local and state officials? of FEMA and the Bush administration? Something else?

How much does it matter, and why? In addition to questions of fact and definition, ones about how serious it was also produced many arguments in the wake of Katrina. In the first week or so after the storm hit, the mayor of New Orleans argued that it was the most serious disaster ever to strike that city and that up to 10,000 lives would be lost. Others argued that while the storm represented a huge setback to the people of the region, they could and would overcome their losses and rebuild their cities and towns.

What actions should be taken as a result? Of all the stasis questions, this one was the basis for the greatest number of arguments about Katrina. From those arguing that the federal government should be responsible for fully funding reconstruction, to those arguing that the government should work in concert with insurance agencies and local and state officials, to those arguing that the most damaged neighborhoods should not be rebuilt at all—literally thousands of proposals were offered and debated.

Such questions can help you understand what's at stake in an argument—to help you figure out and assess the arguments put forth by others, to identify which stasis question lies at the heart of an argument—and then to decide whether or not the argument answers the question satisfactorily.

As an author, you can use these questions to identify the main point you want to make in an argument of your own. In the Katrina example, for instance, working through the four stasis questions would help you see the disaster from a number of different perspectives and then to develop a cogent argument related to them. In addition, these questions may help you decide just what **GENRE** of argument you want to make: a question of fact might lead you to write a **NARRATIVE**, explaining what happened, while the question of what action(s) should be taken might lead you to compose a **PROPOSAL**.

MEANS OF PERSUASION: EMOTIONAL, ETHICAL, AND LOGICAL APPEALS

Aristotle wrote that good arguments should make use of "all the available means" of persuading an audience and named three in particular, which he labeled *emotional* appeals (to the heart), *ethical* appeals (about credibility or character), and *logical* appeals (to the mind).

Emotional Appeals

Emotional appeals stir feelings and often invoke values that the audience is assumed to hold. The paragraph on Lincoln on page 385, for example, offers a strong appeal to readers' emotions at the end when it represents Lincoln as "big" and "brave," invoking two qualities Americans traditionally value. Images can make especially powerful appeals to our emotions, such as those on the following page from the Ebola outbreak in West Africa. The first image appeals directly to our hearts, showing a young boy suspected of having Ebola, a table of medications on one side and a healthcare worker in full protective gear on the other. In the second image, from the international relief agency CARE (Cooperative for Assistance and Relief Everywhere), the message is clear and simple: donate now and help halt the Ebola outbreak. As the first example shows, images can appeal very strongly to emotions; in this sense, a picture truly is worth a thousand words. But words too can make a powerful emotional appeal, as in the second example. As a reader, you'll want to consider how any such emotional appeals support an author's claim.

#ENDEBOLA. DONATE TO CARE.

Halt a global outbreak by fighting Ebola in the hardest-hit communities.

These images pull at our heartstrings, leading us both to empathize with the plight of children facing Ebola and to support efforts to end the epidemic.

As an author, you should consider how you can appeal to your audience's emotions and whether such appeals are appropriate to your claim, your purpose, and your audience. And whatever you decide, be careful not to overdo emotional appeals, pulling at the heartstrings so hard that your audience feels manipulated.

Ethical Appeals

Ethical appeals invoke the credibility and good character of whoever is making the argument. See how the blog kept by Lawrence Lessig, an advocate for reform of copyright laws and a critic of institutional corruption, includes information intended to establish his credibility and integrity. Here is part of his "bio" page:

> Lawrence Lessig is the Director of the Edmond J. Safra Foundation Center for Ethics at Harvard University, and a Professor of Law at Harvard Law School. . . .
>
> For much of his academic career, Lessig has focused on law and technology, especially as it affects copyright. He is the author of five books on the subject—*Remix* (2008), *Code v2* (2007), *Free Culture* (2004), *The Future of Ideas* (2001) and *Code and Other Laws of Cyberspace* (1999)—and has served as lead counsel in a number of important cases marking the

boundaries of copyright law in a digital age, including *Eldred v. Ashcroft*, a challenge to the 1998 Sonny Bono Copyright Term Extension Act, and *Golan v. Holder*. . . .

Lessig has won numerous awards, including the Free Software Foundation's Freedom Award, and was named one of *Scientific American*'s Top 50 Visionaries. He is a member of the American Academy of Arts and Sciences, and the American Philosophical Society.   —LESSIG 2.0

All of this information, including his position with a prestigious center at Harvard and his numerous awards, helps establish Lessig's credibility and helps readers decide how much stock they can put in his blog entries.

Citing scholarly positions and awards is only one way of establishing credibility. Here Lessig uses another approach in a keynote address to a 2002 convention devoted to discussion of free and open-source software:

Lawrence Lessig

I have been doing this for about two years—more than 100 of these gigs. This is about the last one. One more and it's over for me. So I figured I wanted to write a song to end it. But then I realized I don't sing and I can't write music. But I came up with the refrain, at least, right? This captures the point. If you understand this refrain, you're gonna understand everything I want to say to you today. It has four parts: Creativity and innovation always build on the past. The past always tries to control the creativity that builds upon it. Free societies enable the future by limiting this power of the past. Ours is less and less a free society.

—LAWRENCE LESSIG, Keynote Address, 2002 Open Source Convention

In this brief opening, Lessig lets listeners know that he has a lot of experience with his topic—in fact, he has spoken on it more than a hundred times. His very informal tone suggests that he is a down-to-earth person who has a simple, direct message to give to his audience. In addition, his self-deprecating humor (he can't sing or write music) underscores his self-confidence: he knows he can create the equivalent of a "good song" on a topic about which he has spoken so frequently.

Building common ground. Lessig's use of simple, everyday language helps establish credibility in another way: by building common ground with his audience. He is not "putting on airs" but speaking directly to them; their concerns, he seems to say, are his concerns.

While building common ground cannot ensure that your audience is "on your side," it does show that you respect your audience and their views and that you've established, with them, a mutual interest in the topic. Each party cares about the issues that you are addressing. Thus, building common ground is a particularly important part of creating an effective argument. Especially if you are addressing an audience unlikely to agree with your position, finding some area of agreement with them, some common ground you can all stand on, can help give the argument a chance of being heard.

No global leader in recent history has been more successful in building common ground than Nelson Mandela, who became the first black president of South Africa in 1994 after the country's harsh apartheid system of racial segregation ended. In *Playing the Enemy: Nelson Mandela and the Game That Made a Nation*, the basis for the 2009 film *Invictus*, author John Carlin recounts hearing Mandela say that "sport has the power to change the world . . . the power to unite people in a way that little else does"—and that "It is more powerful than governments in breaking down racial barriers." Carlin uses this quotation as an example of Mandela's singular ability to "walk in another person's shoes" and to build common ground even where none seems possible. He goes on to detail the ways in which Mandela used white South Africans' love of rugby to build common ground between them and the country's black majority, which had long seen the almost all-white national rugby team, the Springboks, as a symbol of white supremacy:

> He explained how he had . . . used the 1995 Rugby World Cup as an instrument in the grand strategic purpose he set for himself during his five years as South Africa's first democratically elected president: to reconcile blacks and whites and create the conditions for a lasting peace. . . . He told me, with a chuckle or two, about the trouble he had persuading his own people, to back the rugby team. . . . Having won over his own people, he went out and won over the enemy.
>
> —JOHN CARLIN, *Playing the Enemy*

Mandela understood, in short, that when people were as far apart in their thinking as black and white South Africans were when apartheid ended, the only way to move forward, to make arguments for the country's future that both groups would listen to, was to discover something that could bring them together. For Mandela—and for South Africa—rugby provided the common ground. His personal meetings with the Springboks players and his support for the team paid off to such an extent that when they won a stunning upset victory in the 1995 World Cup final in Johannesburg, the

President Nelson Mandela, wearing a Springboks cap and shirt, presents the Rugby World Cup to South African captain Francois Pienaar in June 1995.

multiracial crowd chanted his name and the country united in celebration. And establishing that common ground contributed to Mandela's extraordinary ethical appeal—which he put to good use in the difficult arguments he had to make in the transition to a post-apartheid South Africa.

In all the arguments you encounter, you'll want to consider how much you can trust the author. Does he or she seem knowledgeable? represent opposing positions fairly (or at all)? do anything to build common ground?

As an author, you need to establish your own **AUTHORITY**: to show that you know what you're talking about by citing trustworthy sources; to demonstrate that you're fair by representing other positions even-handedly and accurately; and to establish some kind of common ground with your audience.

Logical Appeals

Appeals to logic have long been regarded as the most important of all the appeals, following Aristotle's definition of humans as rational animals. Recent research has made it increasingly clear, however, that people seldom make decisions based on logic alone and that emotion might actually play a larger role in our decision making than does logic. Nevertheless, in academic contexts, logical appeals still count for a lot. Especially when we make an argument, we need to provide **REASONS** and **EVIDENCE** to support our claims. Such evidence takes many forms, including facts and statistics, data from surveys and questionnaires, direct observations, testimony, experiments, interviews, personal experience, visuals, and more.

Facts and statistics. Facts and statistics are two of the most commonly used kinds of evidence. Facts are ideas that have been proven to be true—and that an audience will accept without further proof. Statistics are numerical data based on research. See how *Men's Health* editor David Zinczenko offers a number of facts and statistics as support for an op-ed argument in the *New York Times* about the effects of fast foods on Americans today:

> Before 1994, diabetes in children was generally caused by a genetic disorder—only about 5 percent of childhood cases were obesity-related, or Type 2 diabetes. Today, according to the National Institutes of Health, Type 2 diabetes accounts for at least 30 percent of all new childhood cases of diabetes in this country.

Not surprisingly, money spent to treat diabetes has skyrocketed, too. The Centers for Disease Control and Prevention estimate that diabetes accounted for $2.6 billion in health care costs in 1969. Today's number is an unbelievable $100 billion a year.

Shouldn't we know better than to eat two meals a day in fast-food restaurants? That's one argument. But where, exactly, are consumers—particularly teenagers—supposed to find alternatives? Drive down any thoroughfare in America, and I guarantee you'll see one of our country's more than 13,000 McDonald's restaurants. Now, drive back up the block and try to find someplace to buy a grapefruit.

—DAVID ZINCZENKO, "Don't Blame the Eater"

The facts about the proliferation of fast-food chains compared to the relative lack of healthier options will be obvious to Zinczenko's readers, and most of his statistics come from respected health organizations whose authority adds to the credibility of his argument. Statistics can provide powerful support for an argument, but be sure they're accurate, up-to-date, from reliable sources—and relevant to the argument. And if you base an argument on facts, be sure to take into account all the relevant information. Realistically, that's hard to do—but be careful not to ignore any important facts available to you.

Surveys and questionnaires. You have probably responded to a number of surveys or questionnaires, and you will often find them used as evidence in support of arguments. When a college student wondered about the kinds of reading for pleasure her dormmates were doing, she decided to gather information through a survey and to present it in a pie chart.

What Genres Students Are Reading

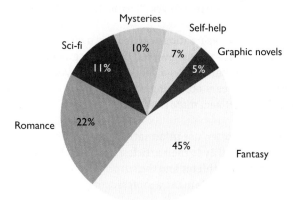

The information displayed in the chart offers evidence that fantasy is the most-read genre, followed by romance, sci-fi, mysteries, self-help, and graphic novels. Before accepting such evidence, however, readers might want to ask some key questions: How many people were surveyed? What methods of analysis did the student use? How were particular works classified? (For example, how did she decide whether a particular book was a "romance" or a "mystery"?) Whether you're reacting to survey data in an essay or a *PowerPoint* presentation, or conducting a survey of your own, you need to scrutinize the methods and findings. Who conducted the survey, and why? (And yes, you need to think about that if you conducted it.) Who are the respondents, how were they chosen, and are they representative? What do the results show?

Observations. A study reported in 2011 in *Science News* demonstrates the way direct observations can form the basis for an argument. In this study, researchers in Uganda observed the way young chimpanzees play, and their findings support arguments about the relative importance of biology and socialization on the way boys and girls play.

> A new study finds that young females in one group of African chimpanzees use sticks as dolls more than their male peers do, often treating pieces of wood like a mother chimp caring for an infant. . . .
>
> Ape observations, collected over 14 years of field work with the Kanyawara chimp community in Kibale National Park, provide the first evidence of a nonhuman animal in the wild that exhibits sex differences in how it plays, two primatologists report in the Dec. 21 *Current Biology*. This finding supports a controversial view that biology as well as society underlies boys' and girls' contrasting toy preferences.
>
> —BRUCE BOWER, "Female Chimps Play with 'Dolls' "

As this study suggests, observations carried out over time are particularly useful as evidence since they show that something is not just a onetime event but a persistent pattern. As a college student, you won't likely have occasion to spend 14 years observing something, but in most cases you'll need to observe your subject more than once.

Interviews. Reporters often use information drawn from interviews to add authenticity and credibility to their articles. In an article on the danger concussions cause to many athletes and the surprising number of such injuries that go unreported, Kristin Sainani, a professor of health policy, interviewed

A young chimp holds a stick in imitation of a mother caring for her child.

Stanford neuroscientists conducting research on concussions as well as one athlete who had suffered several. She included information from these interviews in her article. Here is basketball star Toni Kokenis describing the effects several concussions had on her:

> I felt withdrawn from everything. It was like I was there, but in slow motion. I didn't feel comfortable shooting three-pointers because I couldn't focus on the basket long enough to know that the ball was actually going to go near the hoop. —KRISTIN SAINANI, "Damage Control"

Sainani also cites information she learned from researcher David Camarillo, whose lab is at work on understanding concussions—a science, he says, that is still in its infancy. Preventing concussions won't be possible, he tells us, until we understand them. Camarillo then goes on to describe, in everyday language, what happens during a concussion: "You've got this kind of gelatinous blob in a fluid floating in a sealed pressure vessel. A concussion occurs when the brain is sloshed and bounced around in this fluid."

Unfortunately, he tells Sainani, wearing a helmet does little to prevent concussions, and so the research being conducted in his lab aims to "change the industry standards" for protective equipment.

Throughout this article, Sainani uses evidence and information drawn from interviews to engage readers and convince them that equipment to protect against concussions "needs to be better." As an author, be sure that anyone you interview is an authority on your subject and will be considered trustworthy by your audience.

Good testimony doesn't have to come from experts. See how Barbara Ehrenreich uses the testimony of coworkers in her essay about blue-collar working conditions, on p. 917.

Testimony. Most of us depend on reliable testimony to help us accept or reject arguments: a friend tells us that *Jane the Virgin* is a great TV show, and likely as not we'll watch it at least once. Testimony is especially persuasive evidence when it comes from experts and authorities on the topic. When you cite authorities to support an argument, you help to build your own credibility as an author; readers know that you've done your homework and that you are aware of the different perspectives on your topic. In the example on page 396 about gender-linked behavior among chimpanzees, for example, the *Science News* report notes testimony from the two scientists who conducted the research.

Experiments. Evidence based on experiments is especially important in the sciences and social sciences, where data is often the basis for supporting an argument. In arguing that multitaskers pay a high mental price, Clifford Nass, a professor of communications, based his claims on a series of empirical studies of college students, who were divided into two groups, those identified as "high multitaskers" and those identified as "low multitaskers." In the first studies, which measured attention and memory, Nass and his fellow researchers were surprised to find that the low multitaskers outperformed high multitaskers in statistically significant ways. Still not satisfied that low multitaskers were more productive learners, the researchers designed another test, hypothesizing that if high multitaskers couldn't do well in the earlier studies on attention and memory, maybe they would be better at shifting from task to task more quickly and effectively than low multitaskers.

Wrong again, the study found.

The subjects were shown images of letters and numbers at the same time and instructed what to focus on. When they were told to pay attention to numbers, they had to determine if the digits were even or odd. When told to concentrate on letters, they had to say whether they were vowels or consonants.

Again, the heavy multitaskers underperformed the light multitaskers.

"They couldn't help thinking about the task they weren't doing," the researchers reported. "The high multitaskers are always drawing from all the information in front of them. They can't keep things separate in their minds."   —ADAM GORLICK, "Media Multitaskers Pay Mental Price"

As Gorlick notes, these researchers had evidence to support their hypothesis. Nevertheless, they realized the dangers of generalizing from one set of students to all students. Whenever you use data drawn from experiments, you need to be similarly cautious not to overgeneralize.

Personal experience can provide powerful support for an argument since it brings a kind of "eyewitness" evidence, which can establish a connection between author and audience. In an article for the *Atlantic* about the labor organizer Cesar Chavez, Caitlin Flanagan—who grew up in the San Joaquin Valley, where Chavez's United Farm Workers movement began—recounts her mother's personal experience to support the argument that Chavez had a "singular and almost mystical way of eliciting not just fealty but a kind of awe."

> Of course, it had all started with Mom. Somewhere along the way, she had met Cesar Chavez, or at least attended a rally where he had spoken, and that was it. Like almost everyone else who ever encountered him, she was spellbound. "This wonderful, wonderful man," she would call him, and off we went to collect clothes for the farmworkers' children, and to sell red-and-black UFW buttons and collect signatures.
> —CAITLIN FLANAGAN, "The Madness of Cesar Chavez"

Cesar Chavez

In your own writing, make sure that any personal experience you cite is pertinent to your argument and will be appropriate to your purpose.

Charts, images, and other visuals. Visuals of various kinds often provide valuable evidence to support an argument. Pie charts like the one of the literary genres favored in a college dorm, photographs like the one of the female chimpanzee cradling a stick, and many other kinds of visuals—including drawings, bar and line graphs, cartoons, screenshots, videos, and advertisements—can sometimes make it easier for an audience to see certain kinds of evidence. Imagine how much more difficult it would be to take in the information shown in the pie chart about the genres read by students in the dorm had the data been presented in a paragraph. Remember, though, that visual evidence usually needs to be explained with words—photos may need captions, and any visuals need to be referenced in the accompanying text.

As an author, keep in mind that the MEDIUM you're using affects the kind of EVIDENCE you choose and the way you present it. In a print text, any evidence has to be in the text itself; in a digital medium, you can link directly to statistics, images, and other information. In a spoken text, any evidence needs to be said or shown on a slide or a handout—and anything you say needs to be simple, direct, and memorable (your audience can't rewind or reread what you say). And in every case any evidence drawn from sources needs to be fully DOCUMENTED.

Are There Any Problems with the Reasoning?

Some kinds of appeals use faulty reasoning, or reasoning that some may consider unfair, unsound, or demonstrating lazy or simpleminded thinking. Such appeals are called *fallacies*, and because they can often be very powerful and persuasive, it's important to be alert for them in arguments you encounter—and in your own writing. Here are some of the most common fallacies.

Begging the question tries to support an argument by simply restating it in other language, so that the reasoning just goes around in circles. For example, the statement "We need to reduce the national debt because the government owes too much money" begs the question of whether the debt is actually too large, because the parts of the sentence before and after *because* say essentially the same thing.

Either-or arguments, also called *false dilemmas,* argue that only two alternatives are possible in a situation that actually is more complex. A candidate who declares, "I will not allow the United States to become a defenseless, bankrupt nation—it must remain the military and economic superpower of the world," ignores the many possibilities in between.

Ad hominem (Latin for "to the man") arguments make personal attacks on those who support an opposing position rather than address the position itself: "Of course council member Acevedo doesn't want to build a new high school; she doesn't have any children herself." The council member's childlessness may not be the reason for her opposition to a new high school, and even if it is, such an attack doesn't provide any argument for building the school.

Faulty causality, the mistaken assumption that because one event followed another, the first event caused the second, is also called *post hoc, ergo propter hoc* (Latin for "after this, therefore because of this"). For example, a mayor running for reelection may boast that a year after she began having the police patrol neighborhoods more frequently, the city's crime rate has dropped significantly. But there might be many other possible causes for the drop, so considerable evidence would be needed to establish such a causal connection.

Bandwagon appeals simply urge the audience to go along with the crowd: "Join the millions who've found relief from agonizing pain through Weleda Migraine Remedy." "Everybody knows you shouldn't major in a subject that doesn't lead to a job." "Don't you agree that we all need to support our troops?" Such appeals often flatter the audience by implying that making the popular choice means they are smart, attractive, sophisticated, and so on.

Slippery slope arguments contend that if a certain event occurs, it will (or at least might easily) set in motion a chain of other events that will end in disaster, like a minor misstep at the top of a slick incline that causes you to slip and eventually to slide all the way down to the bottom. For example, opponents of physician-assisted suicide often warn that making it legal for doctors to help people end their lives would eventually lead to an increase in the suicide rate, as people who would not otherwise kill themselves find it easier to do so, and even to an increase in murders disguised as suicide. Slippery slope arguments are not always wrong—an increasingly catastrophic chain reaction does sometimes grow out of a seemingly small beginning. But the greater the difference is between the initial event and the predicted final outcome, the more evidence is needed that the situation will actually play out in this way.

Setting up a straw man misrepresents an opposing argument, characterizing it as more extreme or otherwise different than it actually is, in order to attack it more easily. The misrepresentation is like an artificial figure made of straw that's easier to knock down than a real person would be. For example, critics of the 2010 Affordable Care Act often attacked it as a "government takeover of health care" or a "government-run system." In fact, although the legislation increased the federal government's role in the U.S. health-care system in some ways, it still relied primarily on private systems of insurance and health-care providers.

Hasty generalizations draw sweeping conclusions on the basis of too little evidence: "Both of the political science classes I took were deadly dull, so it must be a completely boring subject." "You shouldn't drink so much coffee—that study that NPR reported on today said it causes cancer." Many hasty generalizations take the form of stereotypes about groups of people, such as men and women, gays and straights, and ethnic and religious groups. It's difficult to make an argument without using some generalizations, but they always need to be based on sufficient evidence and appropriately qualified with words like *most, in many cases, usually, in the United States, in recent years*, and so on.

Faulty analogies are comparisons that do not hold up in some way crucial to the argument they are used to support. Accusing parents who home-school their children of "educational malpractice" by saying that parents who aren't doctors wouldn't be allowed to perform surgery on their children on the kitchen table, so parents who aren't trained to teach shouldn't be allowed to teach their children there either makes a false analogy. Teaching and surgery aren't alike enough to support an argument that what's required for one is needed for the other.

WHAT ABOUT OTHER PERSPECTIVES?

In any argument, it's important to consider perspectives other than those of the author, especially those that would not support the claim or would argue it very differently. As a reader, you should question any arguments that don't acknowledge other positions, and as a writer, you'll want to be sure that you represent—and respond to—perspectives other than your own. Acknowledging other arguments, in fact, is another way of demonstrating that you're fair and establishing your credibility—whereas failing to consider other views can make you seem close-minded or lazy, at best, and unfair or manipulative, at worst. Think of any advertisements you've seen that say, in effect, "Doctors recommend drug X."

The cigarette ad included here is one of the most infamous of these advertising arguments. Of course, this ad doesn't claim that all doctors smoke Camels, but it implies that plenty of them do and that what's good for a doctor

Camels ad, 1946.

is good for other consumers. But what if the ad had been required to consider other viewpoints? The result would have been a more honest and more informative, though perhaps a less successful, argument. Today, cigarette ads are required to carry another point of view: a warning about the adverse effects of smoking. So if an argument does not take other points of view into consideration, you will be right to question it, asking yourself what those other viewpoints might be and why they would not have been taken into account.

Compare the misleading Camels ad to the following discussion of contemporary seismology:

Jian Lin was 14 years old in 1973, when the Chinese government under Mao Zedong recruited him for a student science team called "the earthquake watchers." After a series of earthquakes that had killed thousands in northern China, the country's seismologists thought that if they augmented their own research by having observers keep an eye out for anomalies like snakes bolting early from their winter dens and erratic well-water levels, they might be able to do what no scientific body had managed before: issue an earthquake warning that would save thousands of lives.

In the winter of 1974, the earthquake watchers were picking up some suspicious signals near the city of Haicheng. Panicked chickens were squalling and trying to escape their pens; water levels were falling in wells. Seismologists had also begun noticing a telltale pattern of small quakes. "They were like popcorn kernels," Lin tells me, "popping up all over the general area." Then, suddenly, the popping stopped, just as it had before a catastrophic earthquake some years earlier that killed more than 8,000. "Like 'the calm before the storm,' " Lin says. "We have the exact same phrase in Chinese." On the morning of February 4, 1975, the seismology bureau issued a warning: Haicheng should expect a big earthquake, and people should move outdoors.

At 7:36 p.m., a magnitude 7.0 quake struck. The city was nearly leveled, but only about 2,000 people were killed. Without the warning, easily 150,000 would have died. "And so you finally had an earthquake forecast that did indeed save lives," Lin recalls. . . .

Lin is now a senior scientist of geophysics at Woods Hole Oceanographic Institution, in Massachusetts, where he spends his time studying not the scurrying of small animals and fluctuating electrical current between trees (another fabled warning sign), but seismometer readings, GPS coordinates, and global earthquake-notification reports. He and his longtime collaborator, Ross Stein of the U.S. Geological Survey, are champions of a theory that could enable scientists to forecast earthquakes with more precision and speed.

Some established geophysicists insist that all earthquakes are random, yet everyone agrees that aftershocks are not. Instead, they follow certain empirical laws. Stein, Lin, and their collaborators hypothesized that many earthquakes classified as main shocks are actually aftershocks, and they went looking for the forces that cause faults to fail.

Their work was in some ways heretical: For a long time, earthquakes were thought to release only the stress immediately around them; an earthquake that happened in one place would decrease the possibility of another happening nearby. But that didn't explain earthquake sequences like the one that rumbled through the desert and mountains east of Los Angeles in 1992. . . .

Lin and Stein both admit that [their theory] doesn't explain all earthquakes. Indeed, some geophysicists, like Karen Felzer, of the U.S. Geological Survey, think their hypothesis gives short shrift to the impact that dynamic stress—the actual rattling of a quake in motion—has on neighboring faults.

—JUDITH LEWIS MERNIT, "Seismology: Is San Francisco Next?"

As this excerpt shows, Lin and Stein's research supports the claim that earthquakes can be predicted some of the time, but they—and the author of the article about them—are careful not to overstate their argument or to ignore those who disagree with it. And the author responds to other perspectives in three ways. She *acknowledges* the "all random" theory that is held by "[s]ome established geophysicists"; she provides evidence (including details not shown here) to *refute* the idea that "earthquakes release only the stress immediately around them." And in the last paragraph she *accommodates* other perspectives by qualifying Lin and Stein's claim and mentioning what some critics see as a weakness in it.

As an author, remember to consider what other perspectives exist on your topic—and what COUNTERARGUMENTS someone might have to your position. You may not agree with them, but they might give reason to QUALIFY your thesis—or even to change your position. Whatever you think about other viewpoints, be sure to ACKNOWLEDGE them fairly and respectfully in your writing—and to accommodate or refute them as possible. In any case, they will help you to sharpen your own thinking, and your writing can only improve as a result.

Steven Pinker, writing about cognition and new media, frequently mentions other perspectives. See how he uses them as launching pads for his own arguments on p. 1029.

WAYS OF STRUCTURING ARGUMENTS

You can organize arguments in several ways. You may decide to approach a controversial or surprising argument slowly, *building up to the claim* but withholding it until you have established plenty of evidence to support it, as in this introductory paragraph from an essay about sports injuries:

The flood of media attention highlighting damaged brains, dementia, and suicides in retired NFL players has made concussions synonymous

with football. That attention was greatly needed: the debilitating consequences of brain injuries in football players of all ages has been severely
overlooked. But the focus of this controversy has been far too narrow.
It's true that young players need better equipment and stricter safety
standards on the gridiron. But in many of the most popular sports, boys
aren't the ones most likely to be afflicted by concussions. Girls are.

—MARJORIE A. SNYDER, "Girls Suffer Sports Concussions at a Higher
Rate than Boys. Why Is That Overlooked?"

On the other hand, you may choose to *start right off with the claim* and then
build support for it piece by piece by piece, as in this opening from a 2011
essay in *Wired* on the power of product tie-ins.

Cartoon characters permeate every aspect of our children's existences.
We serve them Transformers Lunchables and have them brush with
SpongeBob-branded toothpaste. We tuck them in on branded sheets,
fix their owies with branded bandages, and change their branded diapers because we know, or at least we think, that the characters will
make them happy. Whether our kids are sleeping, bleeding, or pooping,
Spider-Man is there. Even if you operate one of those rarefied TV-free
households, the brands will penetrate, assuming your children go to pre-
school, have friends, or eat food.

—NEAL POLLACK, "Why Your Kids Are Addicted to *Cars*"

Another common way to begin is to *note what others have said* about your
topic and then to present your own ideas—your claim—as a response.
Whether you agree, disagree, or both, this is a way of adding your voice to
the larger conversation. See how libertarian journalist Radley Balko uses
this framework to begin an essay on government policies on obesity:

This June, *Time* magazine and ABC News will host a three-day summit
on obesity [that] promises to be a pep rally for media, nutrition activists, and policy makers—all agitating for a panoply of government anti-
obesity initiatives. . . . In other words, bringing government between you
and your waistline. . . .

This is the wrong way to fight obesity. Instead of manipulating or in-
tervening in the array of food options available to American consumers,
our government ought to be working to foster a sense of responsibility
in and ownership of our own health and well-being.

—RADLEY BALKO, "What You Eat Is Your Business"

This toy store display argues that if you loved the movie, you should buy
Frozen-themed products.

Whatever the approach, arguments are always inherently social, involving
an author and an audience. They always have certain purpose(s) and make
some kind of debatable claims that the author believes are true or beneficial. In addition, they all provide reasons and evidence as support for their
claims, though what counts as good evidence varies across fields and communities. And finally, arguments almost always rely on assumptions that
may not be explicitly stated but that the audience must agree with in order
to accept the argument. For example:

> *Claim:* Colleges should not rely on standardized tests for admission.
>
> *Reason:* Such tests are socioeconomically biased.
>
> *Evidence:* The disparity in test scores among various groups has been
> linked to cultural biases in the types of questions posed on such tests.
>
> *Assumption:* Questions that favor any group are inherently unfair.

Now let's consider four ways of approaching and structuring an argument:
classical, Toulmin, Rogerian, and invitational.

Classical Arguments

Originating in the ancient Greek law courts and later refined by Roman rhetoricians, the classical system of structuring an argument is still favored by writers in many different fields. Throughout a classically structured argument, you'll rely on **ETHICAL**, **EMOTIONAL**, and **LOGICAL** appeals to your audience. Ethical appeals (those that build your credibility) are especially effective in the introduction, while logical and emotional appeals may be useful anywhere.

The introduction engages the interest and attention of its audience by establishing the importance of the issue, by establishing **COMMON GROUND** with the audience and showing how they are affected by the argument, and by establishing the author's **CREDIBILITY**. To engage the audience, you might begin with a quotation or anecdote, ask a provocative question, or state the issue explicitly. Most writers taking a classical approach state the **CLAIM** in the introduction; students making an academic argument usually do so in an explicit **THESIS** statement.

The body of the argument provides any necessary background information, followed by **REASONS** and **EVIDENCE** in support of the claim. In addition, this section should make clear how the argument you're making is in the best interests of the audience. Finally, it should acknowledge possible **COUNTERARGUMENTS** and alternative points of view, presenting them fairly and respectfully and showing how your own argument is preferable.

The conclusion may summarize your argument, elaborate on its implications, and make clear what you want those in your audience to do in response. Just as it's important to open in a way that will engage their attention, you'll want to close with something that will make them remember your argument—and act on it in some way.

Let's suppose you've been assigned the topic of free speech on campus, and you believe that free speech must always be protected. That's a fairly broad topic, so eventually you decide to focus on the trend at many colleges to withdraw invitations to speakers holding controversial viewpoints. You might begin your introduction with a provocative statement, followed by some facts that will get your readers' attention (both ways of appealing to emotions) and culminating in a statement of your claim:

Our most cherished American freedom is under attack—and not from abroad. On numerous campuses in recent years, an increasing number of invited speakers have been disinvited or driven to decline because various members of the campus community find it offensive to hear from people who hold beliefs or positions that they or others disagree with. However, true freedom of speech requires us to encounter ideas and even language we don't like, don't agree with, or find offensive. To truly protect our freedom, we need to protect everyone else's as well. As students, we need to wrestle with ideas that challenge us, that make us think beyond our personal beliefs and experiences, and that educate us in and out of the classroom.

You might then introduce some background information about this issue, identifying points you'll develop later as support for your claim. Here you might note examples of disinvitation campaigns. Using specific examples will make your argument more credible:

According to the Foundation for Individual Rights in Education (FIRE), 192 college campus speakers have been disinvited since 2000, and most often conservative speakers. As noted by Isaac Chotiner in the *New Republic*, such campaigns indicate "rising levels of liberal intolerance, which is good for neither university campuses nor the truly shun-worthy people in our midst."

And then you might provide support for your claim by noting specific instances when invitations to speak have been withdrawn and giving reasons that free speech applies to everyone:

Former Secretary of State Condoleezza Rice, Director of the International Monetary Fund Christine Lagarde, New York Police Commissioner Ray Kelly, and former U.C. Berkeley Chancellor Robert Birgeneau: each was silenced by hecklers as they attempted to speak or even before they had the opportunity to speak on campus. If we accept only speakers whose political philosophies are ones no one would disagree with, free speech becomes "free only if you agree with me" speech. And then we may as well give up the notion of independent thought.

Acknowledging and responding to counterarguments or other viewpoints strengthens your argument by showing you to be well informed, fair, and open-minded:

> On the other hand, some resistance may well be justified, as when some students and faculty at Brown University protested a speech by Ray Kelly, arguing that it took such a "disruption" to have their voices heard.

And then in your conclusion you might reiterate the major points of your argument and rephrase your claim:

> We should strive to accept diverse voices and viewpoints on campus. Our conversations should challenge us to question our own long-held beliefs and closely examine those of others. We can do so only if we protect and truly embrace the right to freedom of speech—for one and all.

Toulmin Arguments

Philosopher Stephen Toulmin developed a detailed model for analyzing arguments, one that has been widely used for writing arguments as well.

The introduction presents a CLAIM, one that others will find debatable. If need be, you'll want to carefully QUALIFY this claim using words like *something* or *it may be* that limit your argument to one you'll be able to support.

The body of the argument presents good REASONS and EVIDENCE (which Toulmin calls "grounds") in support of the claim and explains any underlying ASSUMPTIONS (Toulmin calls these "warrants") that your audience needs to agree with in order to accept your argument. You may need to provide further evidence (which Toulmin calls "backing") to illustrate the assumptions. Finally, you'd acknowledge and respond to any COUNTERARGUMENTS.

The conclusion restates the argument as strongly and memorably as possible. You might conclude by discussing the implications of your argument, saying why it matters. And you'll want to be clear about what you want readers to think (or do).

For example:

> *Claim:* Our college should ban the smoking of e-cigarettes.
>
> *Qualification:* The ban should be limited to public places on campus.

Good reasons and evidence: E-cigarettes contain some of the same toxins as cigarettes; research shows that they are a hazard to health.

Underlying assumptions: Those who work and study here are entitled to protection from the harmful acts of others; the U.S. Constitution calls for promoting "the general welfare" of all citizens.

Backing for the assumptions: Other colleges and even some cities have banned e-cigarettes; highly respected public health advocates have testified about their ill effects.

Counterarguments: E-cigarettes are less harmful than traditional cigarettes; smokers have rights too. However, this argument limits the ban to public spaces, which means smokers can still use e-cigarettes in their homes and other private places.

Conclusion: Our school should ban the use of e-cigarettes in public places to protect the health of all who work and study here.

Now let's see how an argument about free speech on campus would work using Toulmin's model. You'd begin with your claim, carefully qualified if need be. The italicized words in the following example are qualifiers:

> To be successful as college students, to truly develop into independent thinkers, we need to wrestle with ideas that challenge us and that make us think beyond our personal beliefs and experiences, both in and out of the classroom. Such intellectual challenges are being diminished at *many* colleges as *some* on campus decide that ideas they or others disagree with are more threatening than educational. On numerous campuses in recent years, a number of invited speakers have been disinvited or driven to decline because some on campus find it offensive to hear from those who hold beliefs different from theirs.

You would then follow that claim with the reasons and evidence that support your claim:

> Education requires exposure to multiple points of view, at least according to Aristotle and Martin Luther King Jr. Aristotle notes in his *Metaphysics* that "It is the mark of an educated mind to be able to entertain a thought without accepting it." More than two thousand years later, King defined the purpose of education as enabling a person to "think incisively

and to think for one's self . . . [and not to] let our mental life become invaded by legions of half truths, prejudices, and propaganda."

Then you would make clear the underlying assumptions on which you base your claim:

> Considering a variety of viewpoints is a hallmark of intelligent thinking. Freedom of speech is the right of every American.

And you'd add backing to support your assumptions:

> Freedom of speech requires us to encounter ideas, language, or words we don't like, don't agree with, or find offensive. To truly protect our own right to free speech, we need to protect those rights for everyone.

Next you'd acknowledge and respond to counterarguments and other views, showing yourself to be well-informed, fair, and open-minded:

> Sometimes, supporting free speech on campus calls for just the kind of protests that have led to disinviting speakers. On one such occasion, students and faculty at Brown University protested a speech by New York Police Commissioner Ray Kelly by arguing that it took a disruption to have their voices heard.

Finally, in your conclusion you'd remind your readers of your claim, reiterate why it matters, and let them know what you want them to think or do.

> Free speech is a bedrock value of American life. It's up to all of us to protect it—for ourselves as well as for others.

Rogerian Arguments

Noting that people are more likely to listen to you if you show that you are really listening to them, psychologist Carl Rogers developed a series of non-confrontational strategies to help people involved in a dispute listen carefully and respectfully to one another. Rhetoricians Richard Young, Alton Becker, and Kenneth Pike developed an approach to argument based on Rogers' work as a way to resolve conflict by coming to understand alternative points of view. Rogerian argument aims to persuade by respectfully considering other positions, establishing **COMMON GROUND**, encouraging discussion and an open exchange of ideas, and seeking mutually beneficial compromise. Success depends on a willingness to listen and to try to understand where others are coming from.

The introduction identifies the issue and **DESCRIBES** it as fully and fairly as possible. It then acknowledges the various viewpoints on the issue, using nonjudgmental language to show that you understand and respect the views of others.

The body of the argument discusses the various **POSITIONS** respectfully and in neutral language, presenting **REASONS** and **EVIDENCE** that shows how each position might be valid or acceptable in certain circumstances. Then state your own position, also using neutral language. You'll want to focus on the commonalities among the various positions—and if at all possible, to show how those who hold other positions might benefit from the one you propose.

The conclusion proposes some kind of resolution, including a compromise if possible and demonstrating how it would benefit all parties.

Now let's take a look at how you'd approach the topic of free speech on campus using Rogerian methods. You could begin by identifying the issue, noting that there are a number of different viewpoints, and describing them respectfully:

> On many campuses today, reasonable people are becoming increasingly concerned about the unwillingness of some students and others to listen to people with viewpoints they disagree with—or even to let them speak. As Americans, we can all agree that our right to speak freely is guaranteed by the U.S. Constitution. Yet this principle is being tested at many colleges. Some say that controversial figures should not be invited to speak on campus; others have even argued that certain people who've been invited to speak should be disinivited.

Next you'd discuss each position, showing how it might be reasonable. Then explain your position, being careful to use neutral language and to avoid seeming to claim the moral high ground:

Some speakers may bring messages based on untruths or lies or hate. If such speakers represent a threat to campus life and safety, it seems reasonable that they be disinvited, or simply not invited in the first place. Others feel that speakers who hold extreme or radical positions—on either the right or the left—should not be invited to speak on our campuses. In some cases, this position might be justified, especially if the speaker's position is irrelevant to higher education. Except in such extreme circumstances, however, a very important part of a college education involves exposure to multiple points of view. Such great thinkers as Aristotle and Martin Luther King Jr. have expressed this better than I can: in the *Metaphysics*, Aristotle notes that "It is the mark of an educated mind to be able to entertain a thought without accepting it," and more than two thousand years later, King defined the purpose of education as enabling a person to "think incisively and to think for one's self."

Try to conclude by suggesting a compromise:

Speakers who threaten campus life or safety may be best left uninvited. But while controversial figures may sometimes cause disruption, our community can learn from them even if we disagree with them. Rather than disinviting such speakers, let's invite discussion after they speak— and make it open to all of the interested parties.

Invitational Arguments

Feminist scholars Sonja Foss and Cindy Griffin have developed what they call "invitational" arguments, using an approach that aims to foster conversation as an alternative to confrontation. Rather than trying to convince an audience to accept a position, invitational argument aims to get people to work together toward understanding. This approach begins with listening and demonstrating to your audience that you understand and respect their position, setting the stage for discussion and collaboration in which all parties can benefit.

As you can see, invitational arguments have much in common with the Rogerian approach. One important difference, however, lies in the emphasis on openness and the focus on a shared goal. Rather than presenting the audience with a predetermined position that you then attempt to convince them to accept, an invitational argument starts out by assuming that both author and audience are open to changing their minds.

The introduction presents the topic, acknowledges that there are various **POSITIONS** and perspectives on it, and makes clear that the goal is to understand each viewpoint so that readers can decide what they think.

The body of the argument is where you'd **DESCRIBE** each perspective fairly and respectfully. If you can, **QUOTE** those who favor each viewpoint—a way of letting them speak for themselves.

The conclusion looks for **COMMON GROUND** among the various perspectives and calls on readers to consider each one carefully before making up their minds.

Using an invitational approach to the subject of disinvitations and free speech on campus, you could begin by focusing on the complexity of the issue, noting the ways that well-meaning people can have strong differences of opinion but still aim for a common goal:

> On many campuses today, well-meaning people are increasingly concerned about a tendency to reject others' viewpoints out of hand, without even listening to them. This trend has led to such acts as disinviting speakers to campus or preventing them from speaking, once there. This issue might seem to pit freedom of speech against the right to resist speakers whose views may be harmful in certain ways. Yet looking only at this dichotomy ignores the many other possible perspectives people hold on this issue. The goal of this essay is to bring the major perspectives on free speech on campus together in order to understand each one thoroughly, to identify any common ground that exists among the perspectives, and to provide readers with the information they need to make informed decisions of their own.

Next, you would discuss each perspective fairly and openly, showing its strengths and weaknesses.

> There seem to be at least four perspectives on the issue of free speech on our campus. First, there are those who believe that the principle of free speech is absolute and that anyone should be able to speak on any

issue—period. A second perspective holds that free speech is "free" in context; that is, the right to free speech goes only so far and when it verges on harming others, it is "free" no more. Still a third perspective argues that universities must accept the role of "in loco parentis" and protect students from speech that is offensive, even if it potentially offends only a small group of students. Finally, some hold that universities are indeed responsible for maintaining a safe environment—physically, mentally, and emotionally—and that they can do so while still honoring free speech in most circumstances.

You could then look in detail at the four perspectives, allowing proponents of each to speak for themselves when possible (through quoted and cited passages) and exploring each respectfully and fairly. Following this discussion, you could identify any commonalities among the perspectives:

> Each perspective on this issue has good intentions. Let us use that common ground as the starting point for further exploration, seeing if we can develop guidelines for protecting free speech on campus while also keeping our campus safe. It may well be that considering these perspectives carefully, honestly, and fairly will lead some to change their minds or to come together in certain areas of agreement. I hope that readers of this essay will do just that before taking a position on this issue.

REFLECT. Look for an argument you've read recently that caught your attention and re-read it with an eye for the argumentative strategies it uses. Does it use one particular approach—classical? Toulmin? Rogerian? invitational?—or does it mix strategies from more than one approach? Is the argument persuasive? If not, try revising it using strategies from one of these approaches.

MATTERS OF STYLE

An argument's style usually reinforces its message in as many ways as possible. The ancient Roman orator Cicero identified three basic styles, which he termed "high," "middle," and "low." Today, we can see a wider range of styles, from the highly formal language of U.S. Supreme Court opinions to the informal style of everyday written communication such as memos and email, to the colloquial style of spoken language and the casual shorthand of texts and tweets.

You can learn a lot by looking closely at the stylistic choices in an argument—the use of individual words and figurative language, of personal pronouns (or not), of vivid images (verbal and visual), of design and format. In 2005, the *Los Angeles Times* announced an experiment it called its "Wikitorial," in which the newspaper cautiously invited readers to log on to its website and rewrite editorials:

> Plenty of skeptics are predicting embarrassment; like an arthritic old lady who takes to the dance floor, they say, the *Los Angeles Times* is more likely to break a hip than to be hip. We acknowledge that possibility. Nevertheless, we proceed.

The skeptics turned out to be right, and after three days the paper ended the experiment, saying:

> Unfortunately, we have had to remove this feature, at least temporarily, because a few readers were flooding the site with inappropriate material. Thanks and apologies to the thousands of people who logged on in the right spirit.

Savvy readers will be alert to the power of stylistic choices in these messages. The description of closing down "Wikitorial" as "unfortunate" and the equally careful choice of "a few readers," "flooding," and "inappropriate material" mark this as a formal and judicious message that stands in sharp contrast to the breezy, slightly self-deprecating style of the first announcement, with its casual use of "plenty of " and its play on "hip." How does the sober style of the second announcement influence your response as a reader? How different might your response be if the paper had declared, "We're pulling the plug on this page since a few creeps loaded it with a bunch of crap"?

Now let's look at a visual argument. The spoof ad on the next page was created by Adbusters, whose website identifies it as a "global network of artists, activists, writers, pranksters, students, educators and entrepreneurs" and proclaims that its aim is "to topple existing power structures and forge a major shift in the way we will live in the twenty-first century." The ad satirizes the assumption that drugs can simply "wash your blues away," like laundry detergent. Note especially the retro style, which evokes "the happy housewife" and "the good life" of the 1950s.

Adbusters spoof ad.

As an author, you will need to make such important stylistic choices, beginning—as is almost always the case—with the overall effect you want to create. Try to identify that overall effect in a word or phrase (for instance, concern, outrage, sympathy, or direct action), and then use it to help you choose specific words, images, and design elements that will create that effect and convey it most effectively to your audience.

EIGHTEEN

Strategies for Supporting an Argument

RGUMENTS ARE ONLY AS STRONG as the evidence that supports them. Just as a house built on weak foundations is likely to crumble, so it is with arguments. As an author arguing a point, then, you will need to provide good, strong, reliable evidence to support your position. Ancient Greek rhetoricians developed strategies for finding such support, strategies that continue to serve us well today. This chapter introduces you to those strategies, arranged alphabetically from analogy to reiteration.

Analogy

Analogies are comparisons that point out similarities between things that are otherwise very different. Authors often use them to create vivid pictures in a reader's mind and make abstract ideas more concrete. Analogies can be especially powerful in an **ARGUMENT**, demonstrating that what is true in one case is true in another, usually more complicated, case. Here Annie Dillard draws an analogy between a writer's words and various tools:

> When you write, you lay out a line of words. The line of words is a miner's pick, a wood-carver's gouge, a surgeon's probe. You wield it,

and it digs a path you follow. Soon you find yourself deep in new territory. Is it a dead end, or have you located the real subject? You will know
tomorrow, or this time next year.

—ANNIE DILLARD, *A Writing Life*

Dillard uses this analogy to suggest that writers can use words as tools for
exploring a topic—to "probe" or "dig a path" into whatever subject they're
writing about.

Now see how Malala Yousafzai uses an analogy in a speech to the
United Nations to support her argument that education is the best means of
overcoming poverty and injustice:

> We will continue our journey to our destination of peace and education
> for everyone. No one can stop us. We will speak for our rights and we
> will bring change through our voice. We must believe in the power and
> the strength of our words. Our words can change the world because
> we are all together, united for the cause of education. And if we want
> to achieve our goal, then let us empower ourselves with the weapon of
> knowledge and let us shield ourselves with unity and togetherness.
>
> Dear brothers and sisters, we must not forget that millions of people
> are suffering from poverty, injustice and ignorance. We must not forget
> that millions of children are out of schools. We must not forget that our
> sisters and brothers are waiting for a bright, peaceful future.
>
> So let us wage a global struggle against illiteracy, poverty, and terror-
> ism and let us pick up our books and pens. They are our most powerful
> weapons.
>
> —MALALA YOUSAFZAI, 2013 Speech at the United Nations

Yousafzai, a Pakistani activist for girls' education, builds her argument on
an analogy that compares "the power and strength of our words" to the
power of weapons used by the Taliban and others who would deny women
education. She draws this analogy throughout her speech, calling upon us to
use knowledge to "empower," unity to "shield," and books and pens to "wage
a global struggle" against illiteracy, poverty, and terrorism. If these are our
weapons, she says, then "no one can stop us."

One year later, at age 17, Malala Yousafzai won the Nobel Peace Prize.

Malala Yousafzai addressing the United Nations in 2013.

Cause / Effect

When we analyze causes, we're trying to understand and explain why something happened. Why did the Virgin Galactic spaceship come apart in mid-air seconds after its launch? Why has there been so much extreme weather in recent years? Why did your chocolate chip cookies all run together on the cookie sheet? And when we think about effects, we speculate about what might happen. How will recent weather patterns affect crop yields? What will happen to the cookies if you add more flour?

Authors of **LITERARY NARRATIVES** could focus on teachers or books that caused them to love (or hate) reading, whereas someone writing a **PROPOSAL** may argue that a specific solution will have a particular effect. And in a **NARRATIVE**, you might use cause-and-effect reasoning to explain an event.

Arguing about causes and effects can be tricky, because often it's almost impossible to link a specific cause to one specific effect. That's why it took decades of research to establish a strong enough link between cigarette smoking and cancer to label tobacco products with a warning: researchers had to be able to discount many other possible causes. During the winter of 2015, birds in the San Francisco Bay became soaked in a mysterious goo that kept them from flying. As birds died, researchers frantically looked for

Tressie McMillan Cottom is careful to not claim a direct link between displaying status symbols and receiving certain treatment, but hinting at the effect is all that it takes. Read her essay on p. 1011.

a cause, but that search proved difficult: it took several months, for instance, simply to rule out petrochemicals as part of the mystery substance. As this book goes to press, researchers are still searching for the cause, and even when they identify some possibilities, they will likely present them at first as *probable* or *plausible* causes. Finding definitive causes will probably take much longer, and they may never be identified.

Exact effects are similarly difficult to determine. In 2014, the United Nations released a report on climate change, stating the possible environmental effects if we continue to burn fossil fuels. Notice how the report's authors qualify their statements by noting what effects greenhouse emissions "could" cause to happen:

- The risks of climate change could reverse years of progress against poverty and hunger if greenhouse emissions continue at their present pace.
- The emission of greenhouse gases could cause dangerous warming and long-lasting changes in the climate system, severely impacting people and ecosystems.
- Failure to reduce emissions . . . could cause food shortages, flooding of cities and even nations and a dangerous climate during the hottest times of the year.

— *Climate Change 2014: Synthesis Report*

Often when you write about causes and effects, then, you can only argue that they are likely or probable, not proven. This is just one reason that you'll want to **QUALIFY** what you say: to add words like "might" or "should" that limit your claim.

Causal analysis can sometimes be easier to understand in a chart or graph than in words alone. See one famous example on the facing page, a map created in 1861 that explains the horrific loss of life caused by Napoleon's decision to march on Moscow in 1812. The map shows the dates, the temperatures, the army's movement across Russia, and, most significantly, the dwindling number of soldiers as the temperature dropped farther and farther below zero. The width of the grey and black bands represents the numbers of soldiers: the grey line represents the number of troops marching into Russia (680,000 at the start); the much thinner black line represents the soldiers retreating (27,000 by the end). The graph at the bottom charts the continually dropping temperatures between October and December as the army was retreating, making the causal connection: the colder the temperature, the more soldiers lost.

A map showing Napoleon's invasion of Russia in 1812.

Classification

When you classify, you group items into categories according to their similarities. Tomatoes, for example, can be classified according to their varieties: cherry, plum, grape, heirloom, and so on. Authors often turn to classification in order to organize and elaborate on a topic. Writers of REVIEWS often use classification when focusing on more than one work, as Adam Gopnik does in evaluating a number of books about the internet:

> The Never-Betters believe that we're on the brink of a new utopia, where information will be free and democratic, news will be made from the bottom up, love will reign, and cookies will bake themselves. The Better-Nevers think that we would have been better off if the whole thing had never happened, that the world that is coming to an end is superior to the one that is taking its place, and that, at a minimum, books and magazines create private space for minds in ways that twenty-second bursts of information don't. The Ever-Wasers insist that at any moment in modernity something like this is going on, and that a new way of organizing data and connecting users is always thrilling to some and chilling to others—that something like this is going on is exactly what makes it a modern moment. One's hopes rest with the Never-Betters;

one's head with the Ever-Wasers; and one's heart? Well, twenty or so
books in, one's heart tends to move toward the Better-Nevers, and then
bounce back toward someplace that looks more like home.

—ADAM GOPNIK, "How the Internet Gets Inside Us"

Classification is an essential feature of all websites, one that makes accessible the enormous amount of information available on a site. Take a look
at the homepage on the National Weather Service site at weather.gov and
you'll find various kinds of classification, starting with the horizontal menu
bar at the top that categorizes the information on the site into commonly
consulted topics: forecast, safety, news, and so on. Hovering your mouse
over "Forecast" opens a drop-down menu that classifies forecasts into various categories: Aviation, Marine, Hurricanes, Fire Weather, and so on.

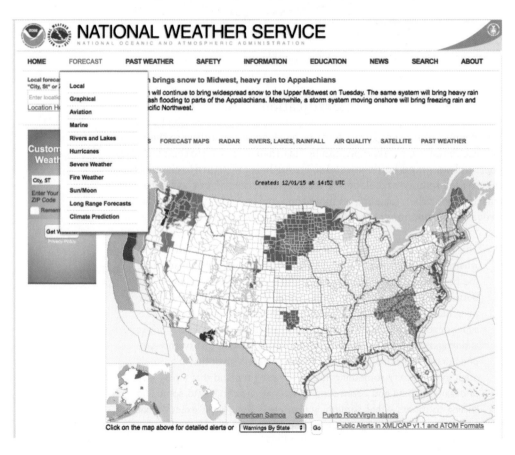

Comparison / Contrast

When you compare things, you focus on their similarities, and when you contrast them, you look at their differences. Both strategies can be very useful in developing an argument, helping to explain something that is unfamiliar by comparing (or contrasting) it with something more familiar. In a book REVIEW, for example, you might compare the *Hunger Games* trilogy to the *Harry Potter* series, or in a REPORT on the decline of the euro, you might compare the situations in Greece and Spain.

There are two ways you can organize a comparison: block and point by point. Using the *block* method, you present the subjects you're comparing one at a time, as in the following paragraphs:

> Most men, I believe, think of themselves as average-looking. Men will think this even if their faces cause heart failure in cattle at a range of 300 yards. Being average does not bother them; average is fine, for men. This is why men never ask anybody how they look. Their primary form of beauty care is to shave themselves, which is essentially the same form of beauty care that they give to their lawns. If, at the end of his four-minute daily beauty regimen, a man has managed to wipe most of the shaving cream out of his hair and is not bleeding too badly, he feels that he has done all he can, so he stops thinking about his appearance and devotes his mind to more critical issues, such as the Super Bowl.
>
> Women do not look at themselves this way. If I had to express, in three words, what I believe most women think about their appearance, those words would be: "not good enough." No matter how attractive a woman may appear to be to others, when she looks at herself in the mirror, she thinks: woof. She thinks that at any moment a municipal animal-control officer is going to throw a net over her and haul her off to the shelter. —DAVE BARRY, "Beauty and the Beast"

Or you can organize your comparison *point by point*, discussing your subjects together, one point at a time, as David Sedaris does in the following paragraph comparing his own childhood in Raleigh, North Carolina, with that of his partner Hugh, a diplomat's son who grew up in Africa:

> Certain events are parallel, but compared with Hugh's, my childhood was unspeakably dull. When I was seven years old, my family moved to North Carolina. When he was seven years old, Hugh's family moved to the Congo. We had a collie and a house cat. They had a monkey and

two horses named Charlie Brown and Satan. I threw stones at stop signs. Hugh threw stones at crocodiles. The verbs are the same, but he definitely wins the prize when it comes to nouns and objects. An eventful day for my mother might have involved a trip to the dry cleaner or a conversation with the potato-chip deliveryman. Asked one ordinary Congo afternoon what she'd done with her day, Hugh's mother answered that she and a fellow member of the Ladies' Club had visited a leper colony on the outskirts of Kinshasa. No reason was given for the expedition, though chances are she was staking it out for a future field trip.

—DAVID SEDARIS, "Remembering My Childhood on the Continent of Africa"

Here's Ashley Highfield, managing director of Microsoft UK, drawing a comparison in a 2005 speech to the Royal Television Society of Britain to illuminate an argument that the "digital revolution is only just beginning":

I was reading an article the other day called "The Dangers of Wired Love," about a teenage girl called Maggie, who helped her dad run a newspaper stand in Brooklyn. Business was booming, so Maggie's dad, George McCutcheon, decided to get wired up, to help him process electronic orders. Being a total technophobe, Mr. McCutcheon got Maggie to operate the thing, but soon found out she was using it to flirt with a number of men, particularly one married man she had met online called Frank. Breaking all the known rules of cyber dating, she invited Frank to visit her in the real world, and of course he accepted. McCutcheon found out, went mad and forbade his daughter to meet up with Frank. But Maggie nevertheless continued to meet him in secret. Her furious father found out and one day followed her to one of the couple's rendezvous. He threatened to blow her brains out. She later had him arrested and charged with threatening behaviour.

An everyday story of modern times maybe? McCutcheon's fathering skills perhaps a bit severe, and Maggie perhaps a little naive? The striking thing about this story is that it was published in a magazine called *Electrical World* in 1886. The Victorian network that McCutcheon got wired to, and Maggie got hooked on, was of course the telegraph.

Those of us in technology like to think we're breaking new ground, that we're creating history through the latest revolution, when we're quite clearly not, as the very modern Maggie McCutcheon illustrates. The telegraph and the internet are perhaps more evolution than revolution: but in a way that means the seismic shifts in society that they cause creep up on us unnoticed. But these cycles of change come round again and again—and people tend to see them as momentous and more often than not scary.   —ASHLEY HIGHFIELD, "Why the Digital Revolution Is Only Just Beginning"

Comparisons of data can often be easier to understand in a chart or graph than in paragraphs. Why spend pages describing changes in demographics over the last fifty years, for example, when a bar graph can make the comparison in a half page? See how the graph below, from an article in the *Atlantic*, compares the number of college graduates in fourteen American cities, helping to support the article's argument that "America's educated elite is clustering in a few cities—and leaving the rest of the country behind."

The Uneven Fortunes of America's Cities

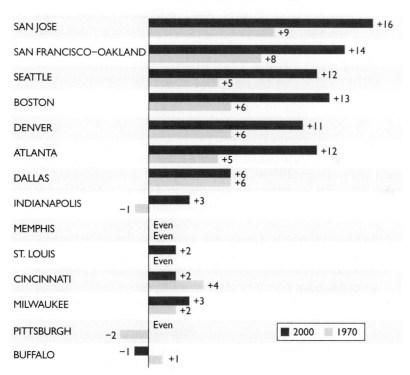

Number of college graduates per 100 people, relative to the national average.
—RICHARD FLORIDA, "Where the Brains Are"

Definition

Mike Rose takes on the way intelligence is defined and demonstrated in our culture. Check out what he says on p. 1033.

Definitions often lie at the heart of an argument: if readers don't agree with your definition of "the good life," for example, they aren't likely to take your advice on how to achieve such a life. As such, definitions themselves are rhetorical choices, especially in the case of controversial topics. Whether you're writing an **ANALYSIS**, a **REPORT**, or using some other genre, you'll often have reason to include definitions in your writing. Good definitions provide a clear explanation of a word, concept, or idea, often by listing their characteristic features, noting any distinguishing details, and perhaps providing an example or illustration as well. A good definition tells readers what something is, and sometimes what it is not.

In a humorous essay about what it means to be a guy, Dave Barry starts out by noting one thing that guys are not:

> And what, exactly, do I mean by "guys"? I don't know. I haven't thought that much about it. One of the major characteristics of guyhood is that we guys don't spend a lot of time pondering our deep innermost feelings. There is a serious question in my mind about whether most guys actually have deep innermost feelings, unless you count, for example, loyalty to the Detroit Tigers, or fear of bridal showers.
>
> —DAVE BARRY, "Guys vs. Men"

One term that is the focus of many arguments is *capitalism*, and such arguments often begin with or include a definition of the word. Here is linguist and social critic Noam Chomsky weighing in with brief but memorable definitions of *democracy* and *capitalism*. As you'll note, his definitions support his argument that capitalism is antidemocratic:

> Personally I'm in favor of democracy, which means that the central institutions of society have to be under popular control. Now, under capitalism, we can't have democracy by definition. Capitalism is a system in which the central institutions of society are in principle under autocratic control.   —NOAM CHOMSKY, *Language and Politics*

Theologian Michael Novak takes a very different view of capitalism, which he defines at much greater length by focusing on what capitalism *does*, in a keynote address to an international conference on economies and nation-states in 2004:

Finally, capitalism instills in tradition-bound populations a new and in some respects a higher personal morality. It demands transparency and honest accounts. It insists upon the rule of law and strict observance of contracts. It teaches hard work, inventiveness, initiative, and a spirit of responsibility. It teaches patience with small gains, incremental but steady and insistent progress. During the 19th century, Great Britain achieved an average of one-and-a-half percent of GDP growth every year, with the happy result that the average income of the ordinary laborer in Britain quadrupled in a single century. The moral habits of invention, discovery, hard work, persistence, saving, investment, and moral seriousness brought about the single greatest transformation in the condition of the poor of all time—the greatest advances in hygiene, medicine, longevity, and physical well-being in all recorded history.

Capitalism brings in its train immense transformation, and the root of this transformation is moral. Those peoples and nations that neglect the moral ecology of their own cultures will not enjoy the fruits of such a transformation—or, having tasted them, will fall into rapid decline.

—MICHAEL NOVAK, "The Spirit of Capitalism"

Visuals can help in making arguments that hinge on definition. Below is a case in which the way the word *capitalism* is designed argues for yet another definition of that word. What argument(s) do you find in this illustration?

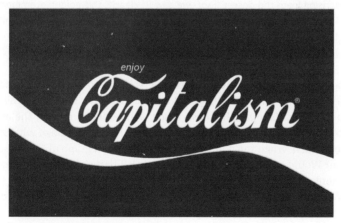

Image from *Daily Wallpapers* blog.

Description

When you describe something, you explain how it looks (or sounds, smells, tastes, or feels). Good descriptions focus on distinctive features and concrete details that add up to some **DOMINANT IMPRESSION** and help readers or listeners imagine what you are describing. You'll have occasion to use description in most of the writing you do—in a **PROFILE** of a neighborhood, you might describe the buildings and people; in a **NARRATIVE**, you'll likely describe people, places, and events.

In writing about atomic testing in Utah in the epilogue to her 1991 book *Refuge: An Unnatural History of Family and Place*, writer and activist Terry Tempest Williams uses description to set the scene for the facts she then presents about the high incidence of breast cancer in that state. She tells her father of a recurring dream she has, of a flash of light in the desert. When her father hears this story, he has a sudden realization:

> "You did see it," he said.
>   "Saw what?"
>   "The bomb. The cloud. We were driving home from Riverside, California. You were sitting on [your mother's] lap. . . . In fact, I remember the day, September 7, 1957. We had just gotten out of the Service. We were driving north, past Las Vegas. It was an hour or so before dawn, when this explosion went off. We not only heard it, but felt it. I thought the oil tanker in front of us had blown up. We pulled over and suddenly, rising from the desert floor, we saw it, clearly, this golden-stemmed cloud, the mushroom. The sky seemed to vibrate with an eerie pink glow. Within a few minutes, a light ash was raining on the car."
>   —TERRY TEMPEST WILLIAMS, "The Clan of One-Breasted Women"

Williams' description lets readers see the "golden-stemmed cloud" and feel the sky "vibrate"—and understand what it must have been like when the bomb exploded. Compare her description with a photograph of the atomic bomb test. Which do you find more powerful—the description of what it was like to be there when the bomb exploded or the photograph of the actual explosion? Would adding the photo have made Williams' description—and her argument—even more forceful?

Williams eventually testified before Congress about the effects of nuclear testing and has also worked as an environmental advocate. In 1995, aghast at a federal wilderness bill that would protect only a tiny fraction of

Utah's wilderness areas, she spoke at a public hearing. In this passage from an interview, see how her description of the hearing helps her make the case that the governmental officials were openly dismissive of her arguments:

> Congressman Jim Hansen and his colleagues sat on a riser above us. I remember how his glasses were perched on the end of his nose, how when I began to speak he was shuffling his papers, yawning, coughing, anything to show his boredom and displeasure. I was half-way through reading the citizens' testimonies—speaking on behalf of those who were at the Indian Walk-In Center the night before. He wasn't even listening—that was clear. Finally, I stopped mid-sentence and said something to the effect, "Congressman Hansen, I have been a resident of Utah all of my life. Is there anything I could say to you that will in some way alter your perspective so that you might consider wilderness in another way?"
>
> What I remember is how he leaned over his elbows and looked down on me over the tops of his glasses and said simply, "I'm sorry, Ms. Williams, there is something about your voice I cannot hear." It was chill-

Fiery mushroom cloud rising above Nevada atomic bomb test site, 1957.

ing—personal. I don't think he was referring to the quality of the micro-phone. And then, it was over.

—TERRY TEMPEST WILLIAMS, interview with David Sumner

Williams could have simply told us who said what and what was decided, but her description helps us picture the congressman "shuffling his pa-pers" and "yawning," hear him "coughing," and sense "his boredom and displeasure."

Examples

Mark Bittman and his colleagues give an example of a food policy exe-cuted by President Nixon in order to show that what they propose is not only possible, but has been done before. See how they argue their point on p. 868.

If a picture is sometimes worth a thousand words, then a good example runs a close second: examples can make abstract ideas more concrete and under-standable and can provide specific instances to back up a claim. See how novelist Gretel Ehrlich uses two examples to support her **ANALYSIS** of what courage means in a cowboy context:

> In a rancher's world, courage has less to do with facing danger than with acting spontaneously—usually on behalf of an animal or another rider. If a cow is stuck in a boghole, he throws a loop around her neck, takes his dally (a half hitch around the saddle horn), and pulls her out with horse-power. If a calf is born sick, he may take her home, warm her in front of the kitchen fire, and massage her legs until dawn.
>
> —GRETEL EHRLICH, "About Men"

You can sometimes draw on personal experience for powerful examples, provided that the experience you cite is pertinent to your point. In a com-mencement address to Stanford University's graduating class of 2005, Apple founder Steve Jobs used the example of his own experience with cancer in **ARGUING** that the graduates should make the most of every moment:

Steve Jobs

> About a year ago I was diagnosed with cancer. . . . The doctors told me this was almost certainly a type of cancer that is incurable, and that I should expect to live no longer than three to six months. My doctor ad-vised me to go home and get my affairs in order, which is doctor's code for prepare to die. . . .
>
> I lived with that diagnosis all day. Later that evening I had a biopsy. . . . I was sedated, but my wife, who was there, told me that when they viewed the cells under a microscope the doctors started crying because

it turned out to be a very rare form of pancreatic cancer that is curable with surgery. . . .

Your time is limited, so don't waste it living someone else's life. Don't be trapped by dogma—which is living with the results of other people's thinking. Don't let the noise of others' opinions drown out your own inner voice. And most important, have the courage to follow your heart and intuition. They somehow already know what you truly want to become. Everything else is secondary.

—STEVE JOBS, Stanford University commencement address

Examples can often be presented visually. See how the following blog posting from *Boing Boing* about the Occupy Wall Street library uses a minimum of words but provides a snapshot that shows a few of the "awesome librarians."

"NYPD & Brookfield have taken the People's Library again, and we love you all," tweet the Occupy Wall Street librarians of Zuccotti Park.

They also raided all the energy bars, waters, and snacks from the re-created library, and threw them away, too. This is not the first time.

Then, shortly after: "A few of our awesome librarians holding up new donations just after NYPD and Brookfield workers took our books tonight."

The librarians are restocking, in case you'd like to donate.

—XENI JARDIN, "NYPD Hates Books: Police and Brookfield
Properties Workers Destroy #OWS Library. Again."

Humor

Humor can sometimes be used to good effect to support an argument—as long as the humor is appropriate to the context and audience. Of course, humor comes in many forms, from a self-deprecating story to a gentle parody or satire, from biting ridicule to a well-worn joke. While few of us are talented enough to write an argument based entirely on humor, it's possible to learn to use it judiciously. Doing so can often help you to connect with your audience, to provide some relief from a serious topic, or just to vary the tone of your argument.

In today's global society, however, you'll want to make sure that most members of your audience will understand the humor. Jokes are notoriously difficult to translate, and what's funny in one language rarely comes through the same way in another.

Sometimes attempts to translate advertisements into various languages or cultures are a source of humor themselves, as when Kentucky Fried Chicken's "finger lickin' good" came out as "eat your fingers off" in Chinese!

And cultural context can also determine if something will be funny at all—or if it will fall flat, or worse, offend. For example, a story beginning "two cows walked into a bar" might seem like a humorous way to introduce an argument about overproduction of beef in the United States, but it probably wouldn't sit too well in India, where cows are sacred.

The late journalist Molly Ivins was famous for the way she used humor in arguing serious positions in her op-ed columns. In the following example from an interview on *Nightline*, Ivins is arguing in favor of gun regulation, but she uses humorous exaggeration—and a bit of real silliness—to help make her point:

> I think that's what we need: more people carrying weapons. I support the [concealed gun] legislation but I'd like to propose one small amendment. Everyone should be able to carry a concealed weapon. But everyone who carries a weapon should be required to wear one of those little beanies on their heads with a little propeller on it so the rest of us can see them coming.
>
> —MOLLY IVINS

See what *The Onion* has to say about how we read on p. 1025.

We're all familiar with the way cartoons use humor to make arguments—as in the one on the facing page, which argues that perhaps airport security has gone just a little overboard.

The 5th Wave — By Rich Tennant

"They won't let me through security until I remove the bullets from my Word document."

The Onion is a satirical news website that regularly uses humor to make its arguments. This article makes an indirect argument that at too many colleges and universities, athletics outweigh academics:

SARASOTA, FL—Bowing to pressure from alumni, students, and a majority of teaching professors of Florida State University, athletic director Dave Hart Jr. announced yesterday that FSU would completely phase out all academic operations by the end of the 2010 school year in order to make athletics the school's No. 1 priority. "It's been clear for a while that Florida State's mission is to provide the young men and women enrolled here with a world-class football program, and this is the best way to cut the fat and really focus on making us No. 1 every year," Hart said. "While it's certainly possible for an academic subsidiary to bring a certain amount of prestige to an athletic program, the national polls have made it clear that our non-athletic operations have become a major distraction." FSU's restructuring program will begin with the elimination of the College of Arts and Sciences, effective October 15.

—*THE ONION*, "Florida State University to Phase Out Academic Operations"

Narration

A good story well-told can engage your audience and help to support an argument. Both writers and speakers use narratives often—in **REPORTS**, **MEMOIRS**, and many other genres. Be sure, however, that any story you tell supports your point, and that it is not the only evidence you offer. In most academic contexts, you shouldn't rely only on stories to support an argument, especially personal stories.

In the following example, author Bich Minh Nguyen writes about her experiences becoming "the good immigrant student." In this essay, she uses narration to capture the tension she felt between wishing to fit in and be obedient, and wanting to rebel:

> More than once, I was given the assignment of writing a report about my family history. I loathed this task, for I was dreadfully aware that my history could not be faked: it already showed on my face. When my turn came to read out loud the teacher had to ask me several times to speak louder. Some kids, a few of them older, in different classes, took to pressing back the corners of their eyes with the heels of their palms while they chanted, "Ching-chong, ching-chong!" during recess. This continued until Anh [Nguyen's sister], who was far tougher than me, threatened to beat them up.
>
> I have no way of telling what tortured me more: the actual snickers and remarks and watchfulness of my classmates, or my own imagination, conjuring disdain. My own sense of shame. At times I felt sickened by my obedience, my accumulation of gold stickers, my every effort to be invisible. —BICH MINH NGUYEN, "The Good Immigrant Student"

Advertisements use narrative to appeal to viewers in many ways, such as in this ad campaign for animal adoption. Using just three frames and eight words, the cartoon below tells a story that argues for adopting an animal.

Narrative is often used to **OPEN** an argument. A good story can get an audience's attention and make them interested in the argument that follows. In arguing for the need to take global warming seriously and rethink our dependence on fossil fuels, Naomi Klein opens with this narrative:

> A voice came over the intercom: would the passengers of Flight 3935, scheduled to depart Washington, D.C., for Charleston, South Carolina, kindly collect their carry-on luggage and get off the plane.
>
> They went down the stairs and gathered on the hot tarmac. There they saw something unusual: the wheels of the US Airways jet had sunk into the black pavement as if it were wet cement. The wheels were lodged so deep, in fact, that the truck that came to tow the plane away couldn't pry it loose. . . . Someone posted a picture: "Why is my flight cancelled? Because DC is so damn hot that our plane sank 4 inches into the pavement."   —NAOMI KLEIN, *Capitalism vs the Climate*

Problem / Solution

Most **PROPOSALS** articulate a problem and then offer a solution that addresses that problem. The following passage from a National Institutes of Health press release sets out a clear problem (drinking among college students) and identifies three elements that must be addressed in any solution:

> The consequences of college drinking are larger and more destructive than commonly realized, according to a new study supported by the National Institute on Alcohol Abuse and Alcoholism (NIAAA). Commissioned by the NIAAA Task Force on College Drinking, the study reveals that drinking by college students age 18–24 contributes to an estimated 1,400 student deaths, 500,000 injuries, and 70,000 cases of sexual assault or date rape each year. It also estimates that more than one-fourth of college students that age have driven in the past year while under the influence of alcohol. . . .
>
> "Prevention strategies must simultaneously target three constituencies: the student population as a whole; the college and its surrounding environment; and the individual at-risk or alcohol-dependent drinker," says [task force co-chair Dr. Mark] Goldman. "Research strongly supports strategies that target each of these factors."
>
>   —"College Drinking Hazardous to Campus Communities: Task Force Calls for Research-Based Prevention Programs"

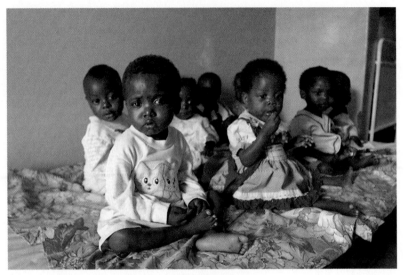

African children who have lost parents to AIDS.

Often writers will open with a statement of the problem, as Rhoi Wangila and Chinua Akukwe do in their article on HIV and AIDS in Africa:

> Simply stated, Africans living with H.I.V./AIDS and the millions of others at high risk of contracting H.I.V. are not benefiting significantly from current domestic, regional, and international high profile remedial efforts.
>
> —RHOI WANGILA AND CHINUA AKUKWE,
> "H.I.V. and AIDS in Africa: Ten Lessons from the Field"

Wangila and Akukwe's article includes a photograph of African children affected by AIDS, which enhances their statement of the problem. The remainder of their essay then tackles the staggering complexities involved in responding to this problem.

Infographics are often used to present problems and solutions. Here's the final panel of an infographic that Chloe Colberg created about saving rhinos from illegal poaching. It identifies three ways of helping solve the problem: "get informed," "spread the word," and "support a campaign." The same information could be communicated in a paragraph or a bulleted list, but the large bold type makes the message much more visible.

What can you do to make a difference?
There are a number of different ways to get involved.

GET INFORMED	**SPREAD THE WORD**	**SUPPORT A CAMPAIGN**
Continue to educate yourself on this issue. Visit the WWF website to learn more specifics and details about the rhino crisis.	The more people that know about this issue, the better! Let your colleagues, friends and families know about this serious problem.	Support the WWF and other organizations' campaigns by learning about their efforts and considering a financial contribution.

SOURCES:
http://www.bbc.co.uk/news/uk-england-11477508
http://www.cites.org/eng/news/pr/2013/20131106_forensics.php
http://www.savetherhino.org/rhino_info/poaching_statistics
http://www.savetherhino.org/rhino_info/thorny_issues/
http://www.worldwildlife.org/species/rhino

DESIGNED FOR:
World Wildlife Fund
Chloe Colberg
December 2013

Reiteration

A form of repetition, reiteration helps support an argument through emphasis: like a drumbeat, the repetition of a key word, phrase, image, or theme can help drive home a point, often in very memorable ways. Reiterating is especially powerful in **PRESENTATIONS** and other spoken texts—think "Yes, we can!" and "Ain't I a Woman?" Martin Luther King Jr. was a master of effective repetition, as is evident in the famous speech he delivered on the steps of the Lincoln Memorial in Washington, D.C., in 1963. Just think for a moment what would be lost in this speech without the power of that repeated phrase, "I have a dream."

> I have a dream that one day this nation will rise up and live out the true meaning of its creed: "We hold these truths to be self-evident, that all men are created equal." I have a dream that one day on the red hills of Georgia, the sons of former slaves and the sons of former slave owners will be able to sit down together at the table of brotherhood. I have

a dream that one day even the state of Mississippi, a state sweltering with the heat of injustice, sweltering with the heat of oppression, will be transformed into an oasis of freedom and justice. I have a dream that my four little children will one day live in a nation where they will not be judged by the color of their skin but by the content of their character.

I have a dream today!

I have a dream that one day, down in Alabama, with its vicious racists, with its governor having his lips dripping with the words of "interposition" and "nullification"—one day right there in Alabama little black boys and black girls will be able to join hands with little white boys and white girls as sisters and brothers.

I have a *dream* today!

I have a dream that one day every valley shall be exalted, and every hill and mountain shall be made low, the rough places will be made plain, and the crooked places will be made straight; "and the glory of the Lord shall be revealed and all flesh shall see it together."

This is our hope, and this is the faith that I go back to the South with.

—MARTIN LUTHER KING JR., "I Have a Dream"

Reiteration also works in visual texts and is a hallmark of graphic novelist Marjane Satrapi's work. Born and raised in Iran before being sent abroad in 1984 to escape what became the country's Islamic revolution, Satrapi tells the story of her childhood in *Persepolis I*, arguing implicitly that repressive regimes squelch individuality. In the frame shown here, Satrapi depicts a class of female students, using reiteration to make her point: all these girls are dressed exactly the same.

Part of a frame from *Persepolis*.

A little reiteration can go a long way. In an article published in *Ebony* magazine about the future of Chicago, see how it drives an argument that Chicago is still a home of black innovation and creativity:

> [Chicago]'s the place where organized Black history was born, where gospel music was born, where jazz and the blues were reborn, where the Beatles and the Rolling Stones went up to the mountaintop to get the new musical commandments from Chuck Berry and the rock 'n' roll apostles.   —LERONE BENNETT JR., "Blacks in Chicago"

Here the reiteration of "where" creates a kind of drumbeat, and the parallel "where" clauses help establish a rhythm of forward movement that drives the argument.

✎ *REFLECT. Choose an example in this chapter that's all words. Think about whether the same argument could be made visually—in a chart, with a photo and caption, and so on. If that doesn't seem possible, how might you illustrate the example?*

PART V

Research

RESEARCH IS AN EVERYDAY MATTER. You gather information from reliable sources all the time to help you make decisions, support arguments, solve problems, become more informed, and for a host of other reasons. Filling out a March Madness basketball bracket? You probably review team records, player profiles, and statistics to help decide which teams you think will win. Going out for dinner and a movie? You probably look up reviews on *Yelp* and the *Internet Movie Database* before deciding where to go. Need directions to the theater? Arguing that this film is better and more critically acclaimed than another? In each case you'd probably do some research—to know what route to take, to locate information, to support an argument. Research helps you do all those things, and you do them all the time.

When you do research, you engage in a process of inquiry: that is, you are guided by questions for which you want answers. You might use a variety of methods—fieldwork, lab experiments, *Google* searches; and you'll find information in a variety of sources—books, articles, news reports, databases, websites, letters, photographs, historical records. However you approach it, research is more than simply a matter of compiling information; the most meaningful research can be a process of discovery and learning.

As a student, you'll engage in research in many of the courses you take and in a variety of disciplines. Research is likely to be part of your work life as well. People working in business, government, and industry all need to follow research in order to make important decisions and keep up with new developments in their fields. Restaurant owners need to do research, for instance, to discover how to maximize profits from menu options and portion sizes. Engineers constantly do research to find equipment and suppliers. When a group of U.S. senators argued for a federal ban on texting while driving, they cited research from a Virginia Tech study as evidence showing the dangers of allowing distracted drivers on the road.

Artists too rely on research for inspiration and also to gather information and materials to use in their artwork. As photographer Laurie Simmons said, "Artists are always doing research on their own behalf and for their work. For some artists, it's reading. For some, it's shopping. For some, it's traveling. And I think that there's always this kind of seeking quality that artists have where they're looking for things that will jog them and move them in one direction or another."

When you do academic research, you'll likely be studying a topic that many scholars before you have examined. You'll want to start by learning what has been written about your topic and then thinking carefully about questions you want to pursue. In this way, you'll be engaging with the ideas of others and participating in discussions about topics that matter—and adding your own insights and discoveries. You'll be joining the larger academic conversation. The following chapters can help you do so.

REFLECT. Think about questions you've had in the past few weeks that have led you to do research to find an answer. List the different kinds of information you've sought and the ways you went about finding it. How did you then use the information or data that you gathered?

NINETEEN

Starting Your Research
Joining the Conversation

 HAT DO YOU FIND MOST DIFFCULT about doing research? Gathering data? Writing it up? Documenting sources? For most students, the hardest part is just getting started. Researchers from Project Information Literacy, an ongoing study at the University of Washington's Information School, have found that U.S. students doing course-related research have the most difficulty with three things: getting started, defining a topic, and narrowing a topic. This chapter will help you tackle these tricky first steps, identify specific questions that will drive your research, and make a schedule to manage the many tasks involved in a research project.

At the same time, we aim to show you that doing research means more than just finding sources. College-level research is a discovery process: it's as much about the search for knowledge and answers as it is about managing sources. When we search, we go down expected and unexpected paths to answer interesting questions, to discover solutions to problems, and to come to new perspectives on old issues. Doing research means learning about something you want to know more about. It means finding out what's been said about that topic, listening to the variety of perspectives (including those that differ from your own)—and then adding your own ideas to that larger conversation when you write about that topic.

While this chapter suggests a sequence of activities for doing research, from finding a topic to coming up with a research question to establishing a schedule, keep in mind that you won't necessarily move through these stages in a fixed order. As you learn more about your topic, you may want to reexamine or change your focus. But first, you have to get started.

Find a Topic That Fascinates You

At its best, research begins as a kind of treasure hunt, an opportunity for you to investigate a subject that you care or wonder about. So finding that topic might be the single most important part of the process.

If you've been assigned a topic, study the instructions carefully so that you understand exactly what you are required to do. Does the assignment give you a list of specific topics to choose from or a general topic or theme to address? Does it specify the **RESEARCH METHODS**? number and kinds of sources? a **GENRE** in which to write up your findings? Even if you've been assigned a particular topic and told how to go about researching it, you'll likely still need to decide what aspect of the topic you'll focus on. Consider the following assignment:

> Identify a current language issue that's being discussed and debated nationally or in your local community. Learn as much as you can about this issue by consulting reliable print and online sources. You may also want to interview experts on the issue. Then write a 5-to-7-page informative essay following MLA documentation style. And remember, your task is to report on the issue, not to pick one side over others.

This assignment identifies a genre (a report), research methods (interviews and published sources), a documentation style (MLA), and a general topic (a current language issue), but it leaves the specific issue up to the author. You might investigate how your local school district handles bilingual education for recent immigrants, for example, or you could research the debate about how texting and social media have affected writing habits.

While this particular assignment is broad enough to allow you to choose a particular issue that interests you, even assignments that are more specific can be approached in a way that will make them interesting. Is there some aspect of the topic related to your major that you'd like to look into? For example, a political science major might research court cases about the issue.

If you get to choose your topic, think of it as an opportunity to learn about something that intrigues you. Consider topics related to your major, or to personal or professional interests. Are you a hunter who is concerned about legislation that impacts land rights in your hometown? Do the restrictions on downloading files from the internet affect you such that you'd like to understand the multiple sides of the issue? Maybe you're an environmentalist interested in your state's policies on fracking.

In addition to finding a topic that interests you, try to pick one that has not been overdone. Chances are, if you're tired of hearing about an issue— and if you've heard the same things said repeatedly—it's not going to be a good topic to research. Instead, pick a topic that is still being debated: the fact that people are talking about it will ensure that it's something others care about as well.

Think about doing research as an invitation to explore a topic that really matters to you. If you're excited about your topic, that excitement will take you somewhere interesting and lead you to ideas that will in turn inform what you know and think.

For ideas and inspiration, visit TED.com, a site devoted to "ideas worth spreading." While there, check out Steven Johnson's talk, "Where Good Ideas Come From."

Consider Your Rhetorical Situation

As you get started, think about your rhetorical situation, starting with the requirements of the assignment. You may not yet know your genre, and you surely won't know your stance, but thinking about those things now will help you when you're narrowing your topic and figuring out a research question.

- **AUDIENCE**. Who will be reading what you write? What expectations might they have, and what will they likely know about your topic? What kinds of sources will they consider credible?

- **PURPOSE**. What do you hope to accomplish by doing this research? Are you trying to report on the topic? argue a position? analyze the causes of something? something else?

- **GENRE**. Have you been assigned to write in a particular genre? Will you **ARGUE A POSITION**? **NARRATE** a historical event? **ANALYZE** some kind of data? **REPORT** information? something else?

- **STANCE**. What is your attitude toward the topic—and toward your audience? How can you establish your authority with them, and how do you want them to see you? As a neutral researcher? an advocate for a cause? something else?

- **CONTEXT**. Do you have any length requirements? When is the due date? What other research has been done on your topic, and how does that affect the direction your research takes?

- **MEDIA**. Are you required to use a certain medium? If not, what media will be most appropriate for your audience, your topic, and what you have to say about it? Will you want or need to include links to other information? audio? video?

- **DESIGN**. Will you include photographs or other illustrations? present any data in charts or graphs? highlight any parts of the text? use headings or lists? Are you working in a discipline with any specific format requirements?

Don't worry if you can't answer all of these questions at this point or if some elements change along the way. Just remember to keep these questions in mind as you work.

Narrow Your Topic

A good academic research topic needs to be substantive enough that you can find adequate information but not so broad that you become overwhelmed by the number of sources you find. The topic "women in sports," for example, is too general; a quick search on *Google* will display hundreds of subtopics, from "Title IX" to "women's sports injuries." One way to find an aspect of a topic that interests you is to scan the subtopics listed in online search results. Additionally, online news sites like *Google News* and *NPR Research News* can give you a sense of current news or research related to your topic. Your goal is to move from a too-general topic to a manageable one, as shown on the facing page:

General topic: women in sports

Narrower topic: injuries among women athletes

Still narrower: injuries among women basketball players

Even narrower: patterns of injuries among collegiate women basketball players compared with their male counterparts

Notice how the movement from a broad topic to one with a much narrower focus makes the number of sources you will consult more manageable. But just as a topic that is too broad will yield an overwhelming number of sources, one that is too narrow will yield too little information. The topic "shin splints among women basketball players at the University of Tennessee," for example, is so narrow that there is probably not enough information available.

Another way of narrowing a topic is to think about what you already know. Have you had any experiences related to your topic? read about it? heard about it? talked with friends about it? Suppose you have been asked to investigate a current health debate for a public health class. You recall a 2015 outbreak of measles in California that prompted a debate about childhood vaccination requirements. Maybe you heard medical experts speaking on the radio about measles and how it spreads. You might also have read about some parents' concern that vaccines cause autism. These are all things that can help you to narrow a topic.

Whatever your topic, write down what you know about it and what you think. Do some **BRAINSTORMING** or some of the other activities for **GENERATING IDEAS**. And if it's an issue that's being debated, you could use a search engine to find out what's being said. Exploring your topic in this way can give you an overview of the issue and help you find a focus that you'd like to pursue.

〰️_REFLECT. *Review your research assignment. Make a list of three topics that you're considering and jot down what you already know about each. Review those notes. What do they suggest to you about your interest in these topics? Finally, narrow each one to a specific, manageable research topic. Which of the three now seems most promising?*

Do Some Background Research

When Andy Hinds wanted to find a sports team to root for, he started by doing some research. Check out what he did on p. 963.

Becoming familiar with some existing research on your topic can provide valuable background information and give you an overview of the topic before you dive into more specialized source. It can also help you discover issues that have not been researched—or perhaps even identified. At this point, your goal should be to see your topic in a larger context and to begin formulating questions to guide the rest of your research.

You may want to take a look at some encyclopedias, almanacs, and other **REFERENCE WORKS**, which can provide an overview of your topic and point you toward specific areas where you might want to follow up. Subject-specific encyclopedias provide more detail, including information about scholarly books to check out.

If you don't have access to a university library, see what information you can find online. Though free online encyclopedias such as *Wikipedia* may not be considered appropriate to cite as authoritative sources, such sites can be helpful in the early stages of research because they link to additional sources and will often summarize any controversies around a topic.

Finally, you might begin your background research by reading articles in popular newsmagazines or newspapers to get a sense of who's talking about the topic and what they're saying.

Articulate a Question Your Research Will Answer

Once you have sufficiently narrowed your topic, you will need to turn it into a question that will guide your research. Start by asking yourself what you'd like to know about your topic. A good research question should be simple and focused, but require more than a "yes" or "no" answer. "Yes" or "no" questions are not likely to lead you anywhere—and often obscure the complexity of an issue. Instead, ask an open-ended question that will lead you to gather more information and explore multiple perspectives on your topic. For example:

Topic: injuries among women soccer players

What you'd like to know: What are the current trends in injuries among women soccer players, and how are athletic trainers responding?

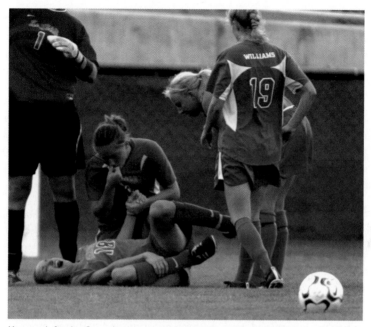

Kansas defender Stacy Leeper is tended to after suffering a game-ending injury.

This is a question that's focused, complex—and meaningful. Before settling on a research question, you should consider why the answer to that question matters. Why is it worth looking into and writing about? And why will others want to read about it? Answering the above question, for instance, can help athletic trainers see if their approach can be improved.

Keep your rhetorical **CONTEXT** in mind as you work to be sure your research question is manageable in the time you have and narrow or open enough to address in the number of pages you plan to write. Consider also any **GENRE** requirements. If you're assigned to argue a position, for example, be sure your research question is one that will lead to an argument. Notice how each question below suggests a different genre:

A question that would lead to a **REPORT**: What are the current trends in injuries among women soccer players?

A question that would lead to an **ANALYSIS** *:* Why do women soccer players suffer specific types of injuries during training?

A question that would lead to an **ARGUMENT** *:* At what age should young girls interested in soccer begin serious athletic training to minimize the chance of injury?

Once you've settled on a research question, your next step is to do some more research. Keeping your question in mind will help you stay focused as you search. Your goal at this point is to look for possible answers to your question—to get a sense of the various perspectives on the issue and to start thinking about where you yourself stand.

REFLECT. Write a research question for your narrowed topic that would lead to a report, one that would lead to an analysis, and one that would lead to an argument. Remember, try to avoid "yes" or "no" questions.

Plot Out a Working Thesis

Once you've determined your research question and gathered more information, you should begin to think about what answers are emerging. When you think you've found the best possible answer, the next step is to turn it into a working thesis. Basically, a working thesis is your hypothesis, your best guess about the claim you will make based on your research thus far.

Your working thesis will not necessarily be your final thesis. As you conduct more research, you may find more support for it, but you may find new information that prompts you to rethink the position you take. Consider one working thesis on the question about why women soccer players experience so many injuries during training:

> Female soccer players sustain more injuries than their male counterparts during training because they use training methods that were developed for men; developing training methods to suit female physiology would reduce the incidence of injuries.

This working thesis makes a clear, arguable claim and provides reasons for that position.

Keeping in mind that your working thesis may well change as you learn more about your topic, stay flexible—and expect to revise it as your ideas develop. The more open your mind, the more you'll learn.

Establish a Schedule

A research project can seem daunting if you think of it as one big undertaking from beginning to end, rather than as a series of gradual tasks. Establishing a schedule will help you break your research into manageable steps, stay organized, and focus on the task at hand—and meet all your deadlines along the way. The following template can help you make a plan:

Working title:

Working thesis:

	Due Date
Choose a topic.	_____
Analyze your rhetorical situation.	_____
Do some preliminary research.	_____
Narrow your topic and decide on a research question.	_____
Plot out a working thesis.	_____
Do library and web research.	_____
Start a working bibliography.	_____
Turn in your research proposal and annotated bibliography.	_____
Plan and schedule any field research.	_____
Do any field research.	_____
Draft a thesis statement.	_____
Write out a draft.	_____
Get response.	_____

Do additional research, if needed.   _____

Revise.   _____

Prepare your list of works cited.   _____

Edit.   _____

Write your final draft.   _____

Proofread.   _____

Turn in the final draft.   _____

TWENTY

Finding Sources

Online, at the Library, in the Field

IF YOU'VE SEEN *The Amazing Race*, a reality show that sends teams of contestants to overcome challenges as they race around the world, then you know what has kept it winning Emmys for more than a decade. Each season, we see the teams learning about cultural traditions in small Italian villages, famous art in German museums, and social practices in little-known regions of the world—all during their wild race to the finish line.

What we don't see is the research on those locations and cultures conducted by the 2,000 crew members who explore potential sites, interview residents and town officials, read histories, pore over maps, and seek information from as many sources as they can before sending the contestants out on their quests.

Like the *Amazing Race* crew, student researchers today have access to a vast number of resources. And with so much information out there, housed in libraries, archives, and museums—not to mention the troves of knowledge and data available online—you too face the challenge of sifting through a lot of information to find the sources you're looking for. A daunting task, perhaps, but much like finding your way to an unfamiliar location, finding sources is a process of exploration that will lead to new discoveries.

Luckily, you have access to a number of resources to ease the journey.

This chapter will teach you how to use these resources, from library catalogs, bibliographies, and reference works to online search engines and even social media as research tools. The following sections introduce you to different types of sources by explaining what's out there, where to find it, how to access it, and how to use it. Finally, this chapter teaches methods of conducting field research firsthand, for examining the many aspects of this world that are still uncharted.

Starting with *Wikipedia*—or *Facebook*

You've probably been told you must use reliable sources, and you may have been steered away from *Wikipedia* or *Google*. But today, these and other casual sources can offer good starting points for your research. Indeed, you might even begin with social media.

One student we know saw a *Facebook* post about a video game developed by Native Alaskans. Curious, she googled the game and found links to information about its origins and artwork, along with a statement about the purpose of the project: "We want to take back our culture out of the museum . . . to share who we are with the world." This statement got our student thinking about how Native Alaskans were representing their own culture in this game compared to how museums were representing it in exhibitions and displays. So she searched the internet for more information about the game, visited her campus library for books and articles on Native Alaskan culture, and perused museum websites to investigate their presentation of it. A casual posting on *Facebook* led this student all the way to the Smithsonian Museum! That's how research often develops: curiosity and the questions that grow out of it lead to valuable and relevant sources.

As this example also demonstrates, the questions that emerge as you examine sources will determine the kinds of information you will seek out. Do you need to learn the history of a group of people or an event? Do you need to research different perspectives on an issue? Do you need statistical data? personal narratives? testimonials? Once you've determined the types of information that will best address your questions, you will need to figure out where to find this information—what sources you will need to locate or what studies you will need to conduct.

WHAT KIND OF SOURCES DO YOU NEED?

The decisions you make about what types of sources you seek, where you look for them, and how authoritative you need them to be will be guided not only by the requirements of your assignment, but also by your **PURPOSE**, **AUDIENCE**, and other elements of the **RHETORICAL SITUATION**. For the research you do in college, an important part of that rhetorical situation may be the discipline you are working in; for example, scientists tend to value research done through observation and experimentation whereas historians tend to value research done in libraries and archives.

You may not always be able to anticipate who will read your writing, especially if you're posting online to a site anyone can access, but you can analyze other aspects of your rhetorical situation to determine what types of sources you'll need. For instance, if your purpose is to convince voters of a political candidate's honesty, what information will be most persuasive and where will you find it? If you're writing about this candidate for a website, what kinds of sources do other writers cite on that site? Who's the site's primary audience? Will you find what you need in the library, online, or will you need to go out and talk to voters? Or will you need to use a variety of sources?

For academic research, you'll also want to keep several other distinctions in mind: the differences between primary and secondary sources, scholarly and popular sources, and older and more current sources.

Primary and secondary sources. Primary sources are original documents or materials, firsthand accounts, or field research like interviews or observations. Secondary sources are texts that analyze and interpret primary sources; they offer background and context that can help you gain perspective on your topic. Secondary sources on a subject might include scholarly books and journal articles about the topic, magazine and newspaper reviews, government research reports, or annotated bibliographies. The student who researched the video game that drew on Native Alaskan culture conducted primary research when she analyzed the game itself and secondary research when she turned to articles about the game's development and books about the politics surrounding the representation of Native Alaskans.

Whether a particular source is considered primary or secondary often depends on what the topic is. If you are analyzing an artistic work, say a film, then the film itself is obviously a primary source, while A. O. Scott's

Research sources vary by topic and discipline: interviews, observations (both in the outdoors and in the lab), library databases and printed resources, and archives can all prove valuable to your research project.

review of the film is a secondary source. But if you are researching Scott's work as a critic, then his review would be a primary source.

Scholarly and popular sources. For most academic assignments, you'll want to consult scholarly sources: articles, books, conference papers, and websites written by authorities in a given field. Such sources have usually been peer-reviewed, evaluated by experts in the field before publication. Because they are written for a knowledgeable audience, scholarly texts go into more depth than popular sources do, citing research and including detailed documentation.

Popular sources, by contrast, are written by journalists and staff writers for a general audience. They may be fact-checked, but they are not likely to be evaluated by experts before publication. Popular magazine articles and websites can play an important role at the start of a research project—for instance, you might consult *Wikipedia* to see if a topic you're interested in but know little about seems viable. Popular magazines can be a good source of information on current issues since they're published so frequently. Like scholarly sources, they often cite research, but rarely do they document those citations. Make sure that any such sources you use serve your subject and purpose. If, for instance, you're writing about fashion, *Vogue* might be a useful source—but its brief reviews of new books would not be appropriate sources in a literary analysis.

DETERMINING IF A SOURCE IS SCHOLARLY

- *What's the title?* Does it sound academic? Scholarly titles often include subtitles indicating a particular focus.

- *What are the author's credentials* to write on the topic?

- *Who's the publisher or sponsor?* Look for academic presses, professional or academic organizations, or government sources.

- *What's the URL,* if it's an online source? Colleges and universities use *edu*, and government agencies use *gov*.

- *Does the source include original research* or interpret research by others that it cites?

- *Does it provide documentation?* Look for a list of works cited or references at the end and parenthetical documentation within the text.

- *Does the text seem authoritative?* Most scholarly texts use FORMAL language and provide evidence that shows the author can be trusted.

- *Does the text* **look** *academic?* Scholarly texts tend to use conservative fonts and often include tables and charts. Popular texts are more likely to include color photos and to highlight certain things in side bars.

- *Are there ads?* Scholarly texts have few, if any, ads; popular articles and sites have many ads.

Considering these questions can help you distinguish between sources such as the two on the facing page, one from the popular magazine *National Geographic*, the other from the scholarly *American Journal of Human Genetics*. While both sources address the legacy of Genghis Khan, note the differences in focus and design. Famous for its photographs, *National Geographic* displays on its cover a striking image of the Khan's face; the article's first pages feature large and colorful photographs, and the typography and layout include some decorative elements. The visuals attract readers' attention. In contrast, the journal's cover includes only its name (which tells us it's a *journal*) and publication information and a picture of a former president of the American Society of Human Genetics. The article looks like serious scholarship; the first page indicates its genre (report), its title ("The Genetic Legacy of the Mongols"), the authors' names and credentials, and includes an abstract.

You may not always be able to judge a source by its cover or homepage, but its design usually offers clues to whether it's appropriate for use in an academic research project.

Older and more current sources. You will need to determine whether older or more current sources are most appropriate for your topic, purpose, and audience. Although you will always want to investigate the latest news and research about your topic, sometimes older works will serve as sources of essential information. Your research question and your discipline may dictate the balance between using older or more current sources. In scientific and technological fields, the most current scholarly sources are usually favored, since change is occurring so rapidly, while in history or literature, older sources that have stood the test of time may offer the best and most appropriate information.

Popular source

Scholarly source

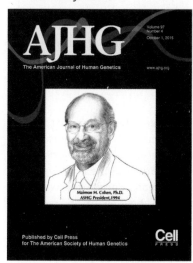

Remember that your professors may expect—or require—certain kinds of sources. They may, for instance, want you to use only scholarly books and articles or require that you look only at primary sources and conduct your own analysis. Most projects, however, call for information drawn from many types of sources. For a report on the impact of recent floods on small farms in your area, for example, you may need to conduct primary research by interviewing local farmers affected by the floods; carry out secondary research online for news reports, photographs, and videos that document the floods; and use library sources to document flood conditions in the past.

TYPES OF SOURCES—AND WHERE TO FIND THEM

Reference Works

General reference sources include general encyclopedias (*Encyclopaedia Britannica, Columbia Encyclopedia*), dictionaries (*Merriam-Webster's, Oxford English Dictionary*), almanacs (*The World Almanac and Book of Facts*), and atlases (*The National Atlas of Canada*), among others. Besides brief overviews of your topic, such sources can be helpful for gathering background information, defining core concepts and terms, and understanding the larger context of your topic—or narrowing it if need be—as well as for getting leads to more specific sources. Your library may have print versions of some of these resources and online subscriptions to others. Still other dictionaries and encyclopedias, such as *Wikipedia*, are online only and give free and open access to all.

Specialized encyclopedias and wikis can give information that is more specifically related to your topic or discipline than general reference works. Through your library or the library website you'll find subject-specific resources ranging from the *Encyclopedia of Ethics* to the *Encyclopedia of Evolution, Encyclopedia Latina*, and many more. Specialized wikis put similar information online in groups of pages about health and medicine, or philosophy, or comic book superheroes of the Marvel universe. Wikis can connect you to information and communities online, but keep in mind that their open, collaborative authoring policy means that anyone can edit the information on a page. So be sure to evaluate the source carefully and, as with reference works generally, use the information only as a starting point.

Bibliographies, also called references or works cited, are lists of books, articles, and other publications that appear at the end of books or scholarly articles and can lead you to further sources on a topic. If you've located a useful source, check its bibliography to find additional sources related to your topic.

Your library may also have compiled longer, standalone bibliographies for popular or widely researched subjects; ask your librarian about availability. Many bibliographies also include descriptive annotations for listed sources that can help you determine if a source will be useful to you.

Directories and indexes. General subject directories such as those provided by *Google* and *Yahoo!* may be helpful in narrowing your topic or directing you to relevant sites. Additionally, many curated directories and indexes collect and evaluate online resources. For example, the *WWW Virtual Library* organizes online texts into subject directories, all maintained by experts on the subject, and includes annotations on many sources as well.

Books

If you're looking for a print book, the first place you think to go is probably the library. But before you venture into the library stacks, you'll want to search a topic or title in the library catalog, accessible through the library website, to see what your library has in its holdings and where a book you're looking for is physically located. The catalog can also tell you if a title is available as an ebook you can access straight from your computer.

In addition to the thousands of print books available through your campus library, you can also access many books online. *Project Gutenberg* makes freely available over 36,000 ebooks and digitized texts that are in the public domain. *Google Books*, like *Project Gutenberg*, provides free digital access to books in the public domain, and it makes these texts searchable.

Rarely will an entire book be relevant to your specific topic, so you'll need to be selective. Reading the table of contents, skimming chapter headings and sections, and examining the list of keywords and topics in the book's catalog or database entry can tell you whether all or part of a book is relevant to your research.

Periodicals

Articles from newspapers, magazines, and scholarly journals are available online through news sites, academic search engines, journal websites, and open-access databases. In addition to these, many more articles may be available to you in your library in print or online or both, depending on the library and the periodical; you can locate such articles through indexes and databases to which the library subscribes. If you can't access an index electronically through your library, ask a reference librarian to help you locate the print version on the library shelves.

Journal articles can be found online through academic search engines such as *Google Scholar* and *JURN*, which yield results from electronic journals and works from academic publishers. *Google Scholar* tends to produce more results in the sciences than in the humanities, while *JURN* focuses on humanities and the arts. But while some of the sources you find online will be free and open-access, you may come across a site that yields an abstract but charges to unlock the full text. In such cases, see whether your library gives you access to the journal. Your campus library may also give you access to subscription-only articles that simply don't turn up on *Google Scholar* and *JURN*, which find a portion of the scholarly texts available online but can miss content held behind paywalls. For this reason, library databases are a good place to go when searching for articles from scholarly journals.

Magazine and news articles are available online through news organizations' websites that provide searchable access to current and archived articles, photos, podcasts, videos, and streaming broadcasts, as well as other resources. Some sites, like that of the *New York Times*, provide only limited access or require subscriptions, but much is available for free—and faster—online. News aggregators like *Google News* and *Bing News* are also useful for searching news on specific subjects, turning up articles from a range of international or local news sources; often you can personalize such aggregators to track news on specific subjects.

    For newspapers that do not archive their articles online, and for older or historical articles that have not been digitized, you can turn to your library's indexes and databases. Because computerized indexing of most magazines and newspapers did not begin until around 1980, to find articles published before then, you'll most likely need to search print indexes such *The Readers' Guide to Periodical Literature, Magazine Index*, and *National Newspaper Index*. Like the index of this book, print indexes list articles by topic and point you to issues and pages where relevant articles can be found. Many databases also include newspaper as well as journal articles and might give you access to articles not openly available online.

Government and Legal Documents

Official reports, legislative records, laws, maps and photos, census data, and other information from federal, state, and local governments are available for free online. Check the websites of government departments and agencies for these resources; you can access such resources for the U.S. government through *USA.gov*. In addition to government reports and documents, the Library of Congress website provides a large archive of photographs, maps, and other U.S. historical and cultural materials.

Primary and Historical Documents

Most university libraries include among their holdings rare and unique materials—books, manuscripts, photographs, fine art, cultural artifacts, maps, and other material—held in the library's archives or special collections. These materials are usually searchable through the library's main catalog, but because the items are often rare and hard, if not impossible, to replace, you'll need to contact your library for access.

Some libraries also house digital images of rare documents in online archives; this is one way of viewing documents held by another institution that you cannot access in person. Many museums, cultural institutions, and historical societies also make their holdings available for viewing through their own online archives—you can explore many rooms of the British Museum, the Smithsonian, and the Museum of Modern Art this way—or through general open-access archives like the *Google Art Project*.

RESEARCH SITES:
ON THE INTERNET, IN THE LIBRARY

Many researchers turn to the internet first for answers to all sorts of questions, and understandably so; you can quickly and easily use it to locate an array of sources from home, from school, or anywhere you have a smartphone and a wireless connection. Convenient and powerful the internet may be, but libraries still provide access to a wealth of resources, from reference works to bibliographies to **PRIMARY SOURCES** (letters, historical documents, rare books, presidential papers, and so on) and **SECONDARY SOURCES** (books based on research, scholarly journals, and magazines). You can visit most college libraries online to access electronic resources such as indexes, databases, and the library catalog remotely. The following sections introduce you to some tools for finding sources on the internet and in the library; knowing how to use these tools effectively will help you take advantage of all that these sites have to offer.

Search sites are a powerful tool for locating materials on the internet. General search sites are a fine starting point, but you can find more specialized sources on your topic if you first identify which sites will be most relevant and useful for your search. For academic searches, try *Google Scholar* or *JURN*. *Google Scholar* locates peer-reviewed articles, books, abstracts, and technical reports by searching the websites of academic publishers, professional societies, and universities. There are also a variety of search sites that can be useful for specific types of searches, including those devoted to maps or image searches (*Google Maps, Bing Images*), news (*Yahoo! News*), and so on. You can also use metasearch sites such as *Dogpile* and *Zoo.com* to collect results from several search engines at once.

As you use search terms to further your research, move from general concepts to more specific ones by configuring short, increasingly narrowed combinations of keywords. Most search sites also allow advanced searches that help you limit results by date, type of source, or other criteria; check the search tips (sometimes you'll need to visit the Help or About pages) for guidelines that are specific to the search engine you're using.

Keep in mind that some search sites allow websites to pay for higher placement or ranking in search results, which means that what comes up first in a search may not be the most useful or relevant to your topic.

Social media may be something you search unconsciously as you scroll through your newsfeed, and indeed the networks you form on social media sites can extend your reach across the web. Sites like *Twitter, Facebook*, and *StumbleUpon* are useful as "sources of sources," where you can connect with people who share your interests to find and share information and sources about those interests. *Twitter* especially has become a popular site for sharing information, following others, and staying on top of the latest news and trends. Many journalists break big stories on *Twitter* before they reach official news sites. With so many prominent people tweeting, the site can also provide you with primary source material. By following experts in the field you're researching, you can find relevant quotes or introductions to a larger discussion.

Online forums, groups, and discussion lists can also connect you with people who share an interest or expertise in specific topics. Many forums and discussion lists archive past posts and threads that you can search to see if your topic has come up in the discussion before; you can also join current discussions and post questions or requests for information. Check *Google Groups* to find forums and lists relevant to your research.

While social media lets you see what others are reading and allows them to recommend sources you might otherwise miss, recent research tells us that people tend to follow like-minded individuals from similar social circles; that is, the view from your newsfeed may not be truly representative of a larger reality. So be sure to evaluate every source: Is the person you are quoting actually an expert? Can you confirm the information in the tweet and follow it to a larger discussion?

Libraries. College libraries are often large and spread across many wings, so it's a good idea to sign up to take a tour of yours. You'll learn the location of key materials and spaces, including the library stacks, special collections, computer rooms, computers designated for searching databases or the catalog, screening and other media rooms, study areas, meeting rooms, and so on. If there are no guided tours available, pick up a library map at the information desk and spend a little time exploring on your own.

Librarians are especially valuable resources. All college libraries are staffed with reference librarians whose major responsibility is to help faculty and students with their research inquiries. While they will not do the research for you, reference librarians can be enormously helpful in showing you where you can find materials specific to your research question or topic and how you can search for them most efficiently. Their advice can save you considerable time and frustration.

In addition to reference librarians, many libraries have specialists in specific academic disciplines. Discipline (or subject) librarians work closely with academic departments to make sure that the relevant journals, databases, and books for that discipline are available to students and faculty.

Schedule a meeting with a reference or discipline librarian, and come to the meeting prepared to discuss your research question or topic. This is also your chance to ask about library resources available on your topic or any specific kinds of sources you're looking for.

Library websites. In addition to information about hours, location, and holdings, library websites often provide useful guides or tutorials to using the library. Many college libraries also provide online research guides that list databases, references, websites, organizations, and other discipline- or subject-specific resources. The image above shows the homepage of the University of Southern Mississippi's library system. Note the links in the horizontal menu bar that allow you to search the library's collections and access its various services, including the help of a research librarian. Farther down you'll see links to information about the multiple libraries on campus, special collections, and other resources.

Clicking on "Research Guides" in the horizontal menu bar takes you to a list you can browse by subject, as shown on the next page. If you're conducting research in a particular discipline, these guides can help you understand its conventions and search for books, journals, and articles in that field.

Library catalogs. Most libraries have electronic catalogs that account for all their holdings. Searching the catalog is the best method for locating books and other materials, such as audio and video recordings, that you can check out from or access through the library. The record for each item includes the author, title, and publication information; a physical description of the item; and sometimes a summary or overview of the contents of the item. The electronic catalog also provides a call number that tells you where the item is physically located in the library stacks (or a networked library), and whether or not it is currently available to be checked out.

You can search a library catalog by author, title, series, subject, or key-word—or some combination of those in an advanced search. On the follow-ing page is an example of the results of a keyword search for *women poets Ireland*. The first image shows the library search page; the second image shows two books from the short list of search results and a link to the full catalog entry for more information.

Databases organize and provide access not only to listings (bibliographic citations) of journal and news articles but also, in many cases, to abstracts and full texts. A variety of open-access databases, such as the *Directory of Open Access Journals*, allow you to search research journals that are freely available on the web. Your library likely also has subscriptions to a number of databases that you can access through its website.

General databases that cover a range of disciplines and topics and include scholarly articles, popular magazines, and news stories may be a good place to start. Here are a few of the ones that are widely used:

- *Academic OneFile* (InfoTrac) provides access to thousands of peer-reviewed journals, including the full text for many of them. This database also offers the full text of the *New York Times* from 1985 on, as well as podcasts and transcripts from CNN, CBC, and NPR.

- *Academic Search Complete* (EBSCO) includes the full text of many periodicals from the humanities, arts, and sciences—the majority of which are peer-reviewed—and provides abstracts for others.

- *ArticleFirst* (OCLC) lists articles, news stories, letters, and other items found in the tables of contents of the journals it indexes. For most items, the database also provides a list of libraries that hold the journal.

- *JSTOR* makes available scanned copies of scholarly journals from many disciplines. It includes issues from further back in time than most other scholarly databases but may not include the most recent issues.

- *LexisNexis Academic* collects full-text documents from news, government, business, and legal sources. Like *Academic OneFile,* this database includes transcripts of broadcast news sources.

- *CQ Researcher* offers issue-focused reports, analyzing topics in the news and from business, the sciences, and social sciences.

Subject-specific databases are useful when you have a focused topic and research question. For example, if you are conducting research on sustainable farming efforts in urban areas, you might begin by searching databases that focus on food and nutrition, such as the *Food Science and Technology Abstracts.* If you are searching for information on trends in sports injuries among soccer players, you might search a sports research database like *SPORTDiscus with Full Text.* Below are some examples of subject-specific databases; ask a subject or reference librarian to direct you to those most relevant to your topic.

- *AGRIS*, from the United Nations Food and Agricultural Organization, provides bibliographic information and full text for a range of agricultural sources, including government and technical reports and conference papers.

- *IEEE Explore* provides access to full-text documents in computer science, electronics, and electrical engineering.

- *PsycINFO* provides indexes and abstracts for peer-reviewed sources in psychology and the behavioral sciences.

- *MLA International Bibliography* indexes scholarly books and articles on literature, languages, linguistics, and folklore from around the world.

- *ERIC* (Educational Resource Information Center) provides bibliographies for journal articles, books, and other materials related to education.

- *SocINDEX*, a sociology-specific research database provided by EBSCO, includes bibliographic records, a sociology-specific thesaurus, author profiles, indexing, and abstracts of journal articles.

RUNNING SEARCHES

Whether you're looking for sources online or in the library, the search typically starts with a website and an open search bar. This is certainly the case if you're using an online search engine like *Google*, and though you may have heard tell of library card catalogs—paper cards that once accounted for all of a library's holdings—that information now lives in a catalog searchable through the library's website. Following are some tips for using search sites, library catalogs, and electronic indexes and databases.

Keyword Searches

Keyword searches allow you to use words and phrases, including author names, titles, and descriptions, to locate sources—but keep in mind that you may need to adjust your keywords or use synonyms if your initial searches don't yield useful results. If searching for *women's sports injuries* doesn't yield much, try *female athlete injuries*. You may also need to try broader keywords (*women sports medicine*). If your search returns too many results, try narrowing your term (*women's sports injuries soccer*).

Following are some advanced search techniques that can help focus your search. *Google* and many search sites provide their own advanced search options—allowing you to limit searches, for example, to items published only during a particular time period.

Quotation marks can be used around terms to search for an exact phrase, such as "International Monetary Fund" or "obesity in American high schools." Using quotation marks may exclude useful results, however—for example, searching for "factory farms" may omit results with "factory farming" in a library search.

Wildcard searches allow you to insert a special symbol (usually ? or *) in the middle or at the end of a word to retrieve multiple forms of that word. For example, typing in *wom?n* would retrieve both *woman* and *women*.

Truncation allows the symbols ? or * to stand in for one or more missing letters at the end of a word; for example, typing in *ethnograph** would retrieve *ethnography, ethnographic, ethnographer,* and so on.

Boolean operators (AND, OR, and NOT) let you refine your search by combining keywords in different ways to include or exclude certain terms. Using AND narrows a search to include all terms joined by AND; using OR broadens a search to include items with any of the terms joined by OR; and using NOT limits a search to exclude items with any term preceded by NOT. For example, if you're researching solar energy, typing in *alternative energy* will bring up many more options than *alternative energy AND solar*, which reduces the number to only those that include the term *solar*. Typing in *alternative energy NOT wind* narrows the search to results that exclude the term *wind*.

Parentheses allow you to combine Boolean searches in a more complex way. For example, a search for *alternative energy AND (solar OR wind)* yields only those items that contain both *alternative energy* and *solar* or both *alternative energy* and *wind*. *Alternative energy NOT (solar OR wind)* yields only items that contain *alternative energy* but do not contain either *solar* or *wind*; this kind of search might be useful, for example, if you are specifically researching forms of alternative energy other than solar or wind energy.

Plus and minus signs are used by some search sites instead of AND and NOT. Using a plus sign (+) in front of words and phrases indicates that those exact words must appear, so +*"alternative energy"* +*solar* will bring up results that include both terms. The minus sign (a hyphen) excludes results, so +*"alternative energy"* -*solar* brings up sources in which *alternative energy* is included but *solar* is not. Searching for +*"alternative energy"* -*solar* -*biofuel* excludes results with both *solar* and *biofuel*.

Author, Title, and Subject Searches

Most library catalogs and many databases are searchable by author, title, and subject as well as by keyword. Using the author and title fields allows you to go directly to a source when you know its title or author. Subject searches allow an overview of your library's holdings on a topic. To do an effective subject search, it helps to know what cataloging system the library uses—most commonly the Library of Congress Subject Headings (LCSH) or the National Library of Medicine's Medical Subject Headings (MeSH). Subject heading searches use what is called "left-hand truncation," which means that you can access a list of headings by entering the first term. These types of searches require terms that are specific to their lists. For example, if you're searching for material on the American Civil War, and you search for the subject *civil war*, you'll get a long list that begins with your term and branches to the right, like this:

Num	Mark	Subjects (1-50 of 870)	Year	Entries 10000 Found
1		Civil War -- See Also the narrower term Insurgency		1
2	☐	Civil War		41
3	☐	Civil War 43 31 B C Rome History		5
4	☐	Civil War 43 31 B C Rome History Drama		7
5	☐	Civil War 49 45 B C Rome History		12
6	☐	Civil War 49 45 B C Rome History Literature And The War		4
7	☐	Civil War 68 69 Rome History		2

These results are not on your topic. If you then go back to the subject search page and type in *American Civil War*, you'll get this suggestion:

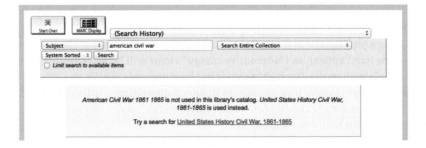

Once you know that the LCSH list uses "United States History Civil War 1861–1865" to begin subject headings on this topic, you'll be on the right track and will get the following search result:

Num	Mark	Subjects (1-50 of 432)	Year	Entries 10000 Found
1		United States History Civil War 1861 1865 -- 2 Related Subjects		2
2	☐	United States History Civil War 1861 1865		1079
3	☐	United States History Civil War 1861 1865 19th Century		3
4	☐	United States History Civil War 1861 1865 Abstracts Periodicals	1984 -	1
5	☐	United States History Civil War 1861 1865 Aerial Operations		2
6	☐	United States History Civil War 1861 1865 Aerial Operations Juvenile Fiction		2
7	☐	United States History Civil War 1861 1865 Aerial Operations Juvenile Literature : Jarrow, Gail.	2010	1

CONDUCTING FIELD RESEARCH

Journalists who interview eyewitnesses, researchers who spend months observing the behavior of a particular population, historians who gather oral histories, and pollsters who conduct surveys on the general public's attitudes about current government policies are all engaging in field research. Depending on your research question, you may need to go "into the field" to conduct research, using data-gathering methods that rely on firsthand accounts. The three most common discovery methods for field research are observation, interviews, and surveys or questionnaires.

Keep in mind that conducting field research on human subjects may require prior approval from your college's Institutional Review Board, a group responsible for making sure that a study will not harm research participants. Observing what kinds of clothing people wear to the mall may not need permission, but observing interactions in a private space like a doctor's office or doing any kind of field research with children probably will. Check with your instructor to find out if your project requires approval. If it does, be sure you understand the approval process and the time required to complete it.

Observations

Observation as a field research method calls for a lot more than casual "people watching." It involves taking careful notice of environments and behaviors, with a clear sense of your purpose and of how your observations will help you answer your research question. Many disciplines use observation to collect data about individuals and communities in order to answer questions about how and why they organize, relate to, or interact with one another and the world around them. In many cases, observation is the best and often the only means of gathering field data.

When reference librarian Linda Bedwell and graduate student Caitlin Banks wanted to find out how the study areas in Canada's Dalhousie University Library were being used, they observed students there, noting behaviors and paying attention to how they themselves used the spaces. Bedwell and Banks were conducting **PARTICIPANT OBSERVATION**, which operates on the principle that researchers can learn by doing as well as by watching. In non-participant observation, on the other hand, researchers focus on the actions of others but do not participate in the situations they're observing.

The process (and resulting information) will differ significantly depending on the type of observation, and you should choose the type most appropriate to the situation and for addressing your research topic and question. If you're studying the winning strategies of video gamers, you might choose to do participant observation if you're an expert gamer yourself and if playing the games would result in more insightful data. If you are researching careers in medicine and want to learn about the typical day of a nurse, participant observation would not be an option—unless you have the credentials, training, and legal standing to provide patient care.

Keep your research question clearly in mind when conducting observations and carefully record what you see. Following are some additional tips for conducting effective observations.

- *Determine your purpose and method for observing.* Is participant observation the appropriate method to pursue your research question? Or do you need to focus only on the actions of others—and not to participate yourself? How do you expect to use the data?

- *Plan ahead.* Decide where you will observe and what materials you'll need—and make sure your equipment is ready and working. Determine whether you'll need permission to observe, photograph, and/or record; if so, secure appropriate permissions ahead of time. Keep in mind that it may not be appropriate to take photographs or record video in some sites—at a church service, for instance.

- *Record your observations.* Take detailed descriptive notes, even if you are also recording audio or video; your notes will add necessary texture. Note who is present, the activities they engage in, where they're situated, and pertinent details about the setting such as the physical design of the space. Be sure to record the date, time, and location. As you observe, focus on recording and describing; save the interpretation and analysis for later, when you review your notes and recordings.

- *Be guided by your purpose for observing,* but don't let that purpose restrain you. Be open to whatever you see. Sometimes in the process of looking for one thing, you may find something else that is equally interesting or important. And don't look only for extraordinary behavior. The goal of observation is generally to look for the routine and for patterns, things that are important because they happen regularly.

- *After your observation,* take a moment to flesh out what you've recorded with notes about any additional thoughts or reflections you have.

- *Review your observation notes* and any audio or videotapes, looking for patterns that emerge. Look for actions that reoccur, for topics that are repeatedly addressed, for individual participants who seem to play important roles. Also note when deviations from patterns occur and what seems to prompt the deviation. You should also consider whether those you observe have changed their behavior because they are being observed and, if so, how these changes may affect your data. You won't be able to correct for these effects, but you can consider and acknowledge them in your analysis. Your goal at this point is to start to analyze and look for an answer to your research question.

Interviews

You may find that the best way to answer your research question is to interview people who have a valuable perspective on your topic, such as experts, witnesses, or key participants in an event. Interviews can provide information that may not be available elsewhere; they can also complement other research and data-gathering methods, such as observations and library research. Just as with observations, you'll need to consider your purpose for conducting an interview and how the information you gain from it will speak to your research question.

You'll also need to decide who to interview. Will one interview provide the needed information, or will you need several? And how qualified are those you're considering to address your research question? As a veteran of the war in Afghanistan, a friend or relative may not be the most credible source for a detailed analysis of the history of U.S. involvement in the region; print sources may be a better starting place for that type of background information. But your friend or relative probably *would* be a valuable, reliable source for a firsthand account of the combat experience and could likely provide details that you would never get from a book or an article.

In any case, remember to ask your interviewees for their written consent to the interview, especially if your work will be published online or elsewhere. Following are additional tips for conducting successful interviews.

- *Plan to conduct your interviews early in your research* in case you have to do follow-up interviews. Contact interviewees well before your research project is due to set up appointments; remember that you will need to schedule interviews at their convenience.

- *Do some background research* on your topic before the interview so that you can ask informed questions.

- *Write out a list of questions* that you will ask in the interview. These questions should be directly related to your research. Avoid questions that are too general that lead to one-word answers like "yes" or "no." For example, don't ask, "Do you like music?" when you want specific details. Try asking "What kind of music do you like?" instead. Also avoid leading questions, ones that prompt answers that you want. The question "Don't you think his campaign tactics were dishonest?" allows the interviewee to disagree, but it still suggests a particular response. A better question would be "What is your opinion on the candidate's campaigning methods?" This question is specific enough to provide a focus yet open enough to let the interviewee answer freely.

- *Decide how you'll record the interview.* Will you rely solely on note taking, or will you combine it with audio or video recording? Remember to ask permission before you tape any part of an interview.

- *If your interview requires any electronic equipment,* test it before the interview to make sure that it is working. And have a back-up plan; there's nothing more frustrating than finding out that you've lost the data from a wonderful interview because batteries died or you pushed the wrong button.

- *Be polite.* Remember that the person you're interviewing is doing you a favor by agreeing to speak with you.

- *Record the date, time, and location* of every interview that you conduct, and write down contact information for the interviewee.

- *Send a thank-you note* to anyone you interview.

- *Check facts, dates, and other information* the interviewee provides, especially about anything controversial. If any of the information seems questionable, try to interview others who can corroborate it or provide another perspective.

Surveys and Questionnaires

You've probably been asked to participate in marketing surveys that review products or services, or maybe you've completed questionnaires for course evaluations. Such surveys and questionnaires can be useful in soliciting information from a large number of people. Most often they aren't meant to poll an entire population; rather, they usually target a *representative sample*, a selected subset of a group that accurately reflects the characteristics of the whole group. The most reliable way to select such a group is by *random sampling*. A true random sample is one in which every member of the target population has the same chance of being selected to participate. Say you want to survey the first-year students in your school. You could try to track down each one—not a problem in a tiny school, but what if there are 5,000? Not feasible. Or you could acquire a list of names from the registrar, assign each name a number (you can use Excel to assign random numbers), and then select a certain percentage of these people.

Unlike interviews, most surveys or questionnaires do not solicit detailed information; generally, researchers use them to gauge trends and opinions on a rather narrow topic. Following are some tips for deciding when to use surveys and how to design and administer them.

Consider your PURPOSE. Will a survey be an effective way to collect the information you need to address your research question? If you are trying to find out how first-year medical residents negotiate the challenges of their demanding schedule, a survey is not likely to provide you with the level of detail you will need; interviews might be more effective. However, if you are researching how the residents account for their time in a typical day, a survey would likely be your best method.

Once you've decided that a survey is the practical way to proceed, think about how you will use the results. Will the results provide essential support for your argument or anecdotal details to make your discussion more interesting and concrete? These considerations will determine the number of people you survey and what sorts of questions you ask them. Imagine, for instance, that you are arguing that your school's library should extend its hours. For survey results to play a meaningful role as major evidence, you will need to survey a representative sample of students on your campus. If, however, you simply hope that your survey will provide some expressions of student opinion on this topic, then a smaller survey will suffice.

Determine your sample. Unless you are only after anecdotal information, you should aim to survey a **REPRESENTATIVE SAMPLE**, a randomly selected subset of a group that reflects the characteristics of the whole group. If you want to discover your college community's level of satisfaction with campus dining services, for example, you'll need to solicit a sample that represents all those who use the services—students, faculty, administrative staff, and visitors—and also reflects the range of ages, genders, ethnicities, and so on. Including only students who eat breakfast in the dining halls on weekends is not likely to give you a viable sample. Most important, decide how many people you will contact; generally, the more of the target population you sample, the more reliably you will be able to claim that your results represent trends in that population.

Choose your distribution method. Will you send a written survey through the mail? through email? Will you use an online service like *SurveyMonkey* or

Google Forms, or administer the survey over the phone or face-to-face? Choose a method that you think will yield the most results—and don't expect a 100 percent response rate. Researchers often distribute surveys multiple times to get as many people in their targeted population to respond as they can.

Write the questions and an introduction, and test the survey. Respondents tend not to complete long or complicated surveys, so the best surveys include only a few questions and are easy to understand. Sequence questions from simple to complex unless there is a good reason not to do so. Also decide what kinds of questions are most likely to yield the information you're after. Here are examples of four common kinds of survey questions: open-ended, multiple-choice, agreement scale, and rating scale.

Open-ended

What genre of books do you like to read?

Where is your favorite place to read?

Multiple-choice

Please select your favorite genre of book (check all that apply):
__ fiction   __ autobiography   __ self-help   __ histories   __ biography

Please indicate your favorite location for reading (check one):
__ coffee shop   __ library   __ home   __ office   __ other

Agreement scale

Indicate your level of agreement with the following statements:

	Strongly Agree	Agree	Strongly Disagree	Disagree
The library should provide both ebooks and print books.	☐	☐	☐	☐
I am more likely to download an ebook than to borrow a print book from the library.	☐	☐	☐	☐

Rating scale

How would you rate your satisfaction with the library?

__ Excellent   __ Good   __ Fair   __ Poor

Your questions should focus on specific topics related to your research question. For example, undergraduate researcher Steven Leone believed that solar energy provided by thin-film solar cells could be an alternative to fossil fuels as an energy source, but he knew many homeowners resist expensive solar installations. His project, "The Likelihood of Homeowners to Implement Thin-Film Solar Cells," was designed to discover the relationship between homeowners' socioeconomic status and their attitudes about alternative energy sources in order to gauge how likely they are to adopt this new technology. These are the questions he asked in a survey of homeowners. Notice that some call for short answers while others ask for detailed responses.

1. What is your combined annual household income?

2. What is the highest level of education you have completed?
   __ high school __ some college __ college __ graduate school

3. How is your home currently heated?

4. How much are you currently spending each year on home energy costs?

5. Which is more important to you—saving money or going green? Why?

6. How knowledgeable are you about solar energy technology?
   __ very knowledgeable   __ somewhat knowledgeable
   __ somewhat unfamiliar   __ very unfamiliar

7. Have you considered using solar energy as your home energy source? Why or why not?

8. Thin-film solar cells cost significantly less than conventional solar installations and offer an energy-cost payback that is twice as fast. Does this information make it more likely you would implement this technology? If so, how much more likely?
   __ very likely   __ somewhat likely
   __ somewhat unlikely   __ very unlikely

9. Thin-film solar cells will increase the resale value of your home. Does this information make it more likely you would implement the technology? If so, how much more likely?
   __ very likely   __ somewhat likely
   __ somewhat unlikely   __ very unlikely

10. If thin-film solar cells were cost-efficient and easy to install, would you consider them to be a good investment for your home? Why or why not?

Leone's questions provided him with data that he then analyzed to determine patterns (education, income, lifestyle) of attitudes on his topic.

Once you're satisfied with your questions, write a brief introductory statement that will let participants know the purpose of the survey and what they can expect, including an estimate of how long it will take to complete.

Manage your results. When you are done collecting data, be sure to carefully record and store your responses. If you are using a print survey, one simple method is to use a blank survey and tally responses next to each question. You can also use a spreadsheet or a similar program to track your findings. When you've tallied or organized your survey responses, then analyze them. If your survey includes open-ended questions, you may want to choose some responses to quote from when you present your results.

ANALYZE your results. After you have tallied up the results, you need to analyze them, looking for patterns that reveal trends and explaining what those trends may mean. Data from survey results do not speak for themselves. You need to analyze the data by looking for similar responses to questions you've asked. Group those that are similar, and label them accordingly. What does that pattern or trend in responses indicate about your research question? When you move from describing the patterns and trends to discussing what they mean, you are interpreting your results. For example, suppose you survey 200 classmates about a recent increase in student fees for using the on-campus fitness center and find that the students, by a significant majority, think the fees are cost-prohibitive. Based on your survey results, your interpretation is that the fee increase is likely to lead to decreased use of the fitness center. You didn't just report the results; you interpreted them as well.

REFLECT on how well the survey worked. When you present your results, be sure to acknowledge any limitations of your survey. What topics were not covered? What populations were not surveyed? Was your sample truly representative?

Information today lives everywhere: in traditional libraries, on the internet, and out "in the field." Your research question and your rhetorical situation—including who will read your research—dictate what kinds of sources you consult and cite. But ultimately, research should be a voyage of discovery, driven by *your* questions based on *your* desire to find out something you didn't know before.

REFLECT. Now that you have thought more about your topic and questions, done some preliminary research, decided on methods, and located some sources, review the types of sources that you've consulted. How did each of those sources help you answer your research question? What other sources do you still need to consult?

TWENTY-ONE

Keeping Track
Managing Information Overload

ESEARCH HAS ALWAYS been a complex, often messy process, but in an age of information overload, it can easily spiral out of control. Where did you save those notes you took? Did that piece of information come from the book you read, or one of the articles you found, or somewhere online? Researchers today have so much information at their fingertips that just managing it has become a primary concern. This chapter aims to help you bring order out of potential chaos by offering tips for keeping track of your sources, taking notes, and maintaining a working bibliography.

Keep Track of Your Sources

The easiest way to keep track of your sources is to save a copy of each one. Especially when your research is spread out over several days or weeks, and when it turns up dozens of potential sources, don't even consider relying on your memory.

Electronic sources. Download and save files, or print them out. Be especially sure to make copies of materials on the web, which can change or even disappear: print out what you might use, or take a screenshot and save the image in your files. Some subscription database services let you

Your research may be spread over a period of weeks or months, with discoveries and epiphanies sprinkled among long hours poring over books or a computer screen. All the more reason, then, not to let your notes sprawl across your desk or your good ideas disappear among the couch cushions.

save, email, or print citations and articles. You might also want to use one of the free online tools that allow you to organize, store, analyze, and share articles, images, snapshots of web pages, even audio and video files; *CiteU-Like* and *Zotero* are two that we've used.

Once you've got copies of your sources, the challenge is to keep them all organized and easy to find. Store all the files for a single project together in one folder, and use a consistent file-naming system so each item is easy to identify. The following example uses the author's last name and keywords from the source's title. All of the sources are saved in a folder under the course title and assignment.

```
ENG1102_ResearchProject
    Ehrenreich_ServingFL
    hooks_TouchingEarth
    Kohls_CleanSweep
    McMillanCottom_LogicOfPoor
    Rose_BlueCollar
    Schlosser_Fries
```

Note the author(s), title, URL, and date of access on each item—and record all the other information needed in a **WORKING BIBLIOGRAPHY**. And be sure to back up your files regularly.

Print sources. Make photocopies, printouts, or scans of everything you think will be useful to your research. Keep a copy of the title and copyright pages of books and of the table of contents or front page of periodicals. Label everything with the author(s), title, and page numbers, and file related materials together in a clearly marked folder.

Take Notes

We cannot stress enough the importance of taking notes systematically *as you go*. But this doesn't mean you should write down everything; carefully select what details you note to be sure they are pertinent to your project.

Take notes in your own words, and be sure to enclose any words taken directly from a source in quotes. Label anything you **QUOTE**, **PARAPHRASE**, or **SUMMARIZE** as such so that you'll remember to acknowledge and document the original source if you use it—and so that you don't accidentally **PLAGIARIZE**. Consider this example:

> Lyon, G. Reid. "Learning Disabilities" *The Future of Children: Special Education for Children with Disabilities* 6.1 (1996): 54-76. Web. 1 June 2014.
>
> Summary: Focuses on problems with reading skills but cautions that early intervention with reading won't address all manifestations of LD.
> - Lyon is chief of Child Development and Behavior in the National Institute of Child Health and Human Development at the NIH.
> - LD is actually several overlapping disorders related to reading, language, and math (paraphrase, p. 54).
> - Lyon: "[L]earning disability is not a single disorder, but is a general category of special education composed of disabilities in any of seven specific areas: (1) receptive language (listening), (2) expressive language (speaking), (3) basic reading skills, (4) reading comprehension, (5) written expression, (6) mathematics calculation, and (7) mathematical reasoning" (direct quotation, p. 55).

Comment: Lyon breaks down LD into more distinctive, precise categories. Defines each category. Will help me define LD.

Notice the specific information included in these notes—all details that will help the researcher later on if she decides to reference this article in her own writing: a full MLA-style citation, a brief summary of the article, and notes about how the source might relate to her research. And notice too that she's indicated when she's paraphrased and quoted from the text, with page numbers in each case. If she does end up citing this source in her own work, she'll already have all the documentation information she'll need.

Label notes with full citation information—the author(s) and title, the page numbers, date of access, and URL.

SUMMARIZE the main point and any other important points you want to remember in a sentence or two, especially if you'll be doing an **ANNOTATED BIBLIOGRAPHY**. Be very careful to write your summary using your own words and sentence patterns.

If you copy any passages by hand, take care to do so accurately, paying attention to both words and punctuation and enclosing the entire passage in quotation marks. If you cut and paste any text from electronic sources, put quotation marks around it.

Record any of your own questions or reactions as you go. Do you see anything that addresses your research question? any interesting ideas? anything you want to know more about? Consider what role this source might play in your own writing. Does it provide evidence? represent perspectives you should consider? show why the topic matters?

Maintain a Working Bibliography

It might seem easiest to keep track only of the sources that you know you will cite. But what if your research takes an interesting twist and you need to include some of the sources that you discarded earlier? Rather than having to stop and search for those earlier sources, you could access the source information right away if you keep a working bibliography—a list of all the sources that you consult.

Unlike a final works cited or reference page, a working bibliography constantly changes as you find more sources to add to it. Therefore, it is probably best to keep it on a computer or individual note cards for easy updating. As you update, note for each source whether you have already used it, rejected it, or are still thinking about it. You may even want to annotate your working bibliography with a sentence or two summarizing each source.

Eventually this information will become your list of works cited or references, so it's a good idea to follow whatever **DOCUMENTATION** style you plan to use. To remind yourself of what information you'll need to note when citing various kinds of sources, see Chapters 27 or 28 on **MLA** and **APA** style.

Consider the working bibliography entries below:

Lyon, G. Reid. "Learning Disabilities" *The Future of Children: Special Education for Children with Disabilities* 6.1 (1996): 54-76. Web. 1 June 2014.

Lyon breaks down LD into more distinct, precise categories. Defines each category. Will help me define LD. (Used)

Brueggemann, Brenda. Personal interview. 10 July 2014.

Professor Brueggemann is one of the world's leading scholars in the field of disability studies. This interview focused on the growth of that field. (Still thinking about it)

WHAT TO PUT IN YOUR WORKING BIBLIOGRAPHY

For books

- Author(s) and any editors or translators
- Title and subtitle
- Edition, volume number
- Publication information: city, publisher, year
- Medium of publication (e.g., Print, Web, Kindle)

For periodicals

- Author(s)
- Title and subtitle
- Name of periodical
- Publisher or sponsor (for online sources)
- Volume and issue numbers, date
- Page numbers
- Medium of publication (i.e., Print or Web)
- Date accessed (for online sources)

Additional items for articles accessed via database

- Name of database and any item number
- Name and URL of subscription service
- DOI, if there is one

For web sources

- Author(s) and any editors of source
- Title and subtitle of source
- Name and URL of site
- Sponsor of site
- Date published, posted, or last updated
- Page or paragraph numbers, if any
- Medium of publication (i.e., Web)
- Date accessed

REFLECT. Review your system for organizing and tracking your sources. Are your sources organized in a way that lets you go back to them easily? Have you recorded the necessary bibliographic information? If you answered "no," take the time now to set up a system that helps you keep track of your sources.

TWENTY-TWO

Evaluating Sources

OUR RESEARCH QUESTION: Is it racist for a school to use American Indian mascots, symbols, or nicknames for its sports teams? To research this topic, rather than merely giving your opinion, you would need to consult reliable sources. Which do you trust more: the official "Statement of the U.S. Commission on Civil Rights on the Use of Native American Images and Nicknames as Sports Symbols," the *Wikipedia* page on the controversy, or a blog entry on the topic posted on ESPN's blog? Is it possible that they could all be useful? How will you know?

Your integrity as an author rests to some degree on the quality of the sources you cite, so your sources need to be appropriate and reliable. You can probably assume that an article or website recommended by a professor or an expert on your topic is a credible source of information.

But in the absence of such advice, and given the overwhelming amount of information available, it can be difficult to know which sources will be useful, appropriate, and relevant. Or, as media expert Howard Rheingold puts it, the unending stream of information on the internet calls for some serious "crap detection": we have to know how to separate the credible sources from the questionable ones. This chapter provides advice for determining which sources are appropriate for your purposes and then for reviewing those sources with a critical eye.

Which would you trust more: the official "Statement of the U.S. Commission on Civil Rights on the Use of Native American Images and Nicknames as Sports Symbols," the *Wikipedia* page on the Native American mascot controversy, or a *YouTube* video?

Is the Source Worth Your Attention?

A database search turns up fifty articles on your topic. The library catalog shows hundreds. *Google?* Thousands. So how do you decide which sources are worth your time and attention? Here are some questions to consider as you scan your search results.

What's the title? Does it sound relevant to your topic? Does it sound serious? humorous? What does the title tell you about the source's purpose?

Who are the authors? Are they experts on your topic? journalists? staff writers? Are they affiliated with any institution that would indicate their expertise—or affect their viewpoints? Check the source for biographical information, or look for this information elsewhere.

If, for example, you were researching brain injuries among NFL players, you might run across the opinions of two medical experts, Dr. Ann McKee and Dr. Elliott Pellman, each offering very different evidence about the long-term effects of concussions. Looking into their credentials and affiliations, you'd learn that McKee is a neurologist who specializes in brain injuries, while Pellman is a rheumatologist who specializes in the body more than the brain—and chairs a medical committee in the NFL—information that tells you something about each one's **STANCE**.

Who's the publisher or sponsor? Is it an academic press? a news organization? a government agency or nonprofit? a business or individual? Knowing the publisher or sponsor can tell you whether the content has been peer reviewed by experts, as is typical for scholarly works and government publications, or fact-checked, as news organizations typically require. Consider also whether the publication or its sponsor has a particular agenda, especially if it presents the opinions of an individual. That said, your topic may call for you to consult the personal blog or even the *Facebook* page of someone with expertise you can trust.

What's the URL, if it's an online source? A site's URL can tell you something about what kind of organization is sponsoring the site: *com* is used by commercial organizations, *edu* by colleges and universities, *org* by nonprofits, *gov* by government agencies.

"On the Internet, nobody knows you're a dog."

When was it published or last updated? Does your topic call for the most current sources or for older historical ones? Even if you're researching a current issue, you may still want to consult older sources to get a sense of the larger context. Likewise, if your topic calls for older sources, you may also want to read the current research on it. And if your source is on a website, check to see that the site itself and any links are still active.

Does it *look* academic? Are there any ads? What impression do you get from the fonts, headings, profile pictures or other images? What does the look of the text suggest about its purpose?

What's the genre? Pay particular attention to whether it's REPORTING information or ARGUING some kind of claim. You'll have reason to look for both, but for those that make an argument, you'll need to find multiple sources expressing a number of different perspectives.

Is it cited in other works? Are there links to it in other online sources? Has it been referenced or reposted? You can determine this by searching for the author and title using *Google Scholar*. For instance, if you enter *Susan Miller "Textual Carnivals,"* the search page returns the information shown below, which lets you know the work has been cited in 541 related articles. If many other writers refer or respond to this author's work, you can probably assume they find it credible.

[BOOK] Textual carnivals: The politics of composition
S **Miller** – 1993 – books.google.com
This is the first book-length study of the status of composition in English studies and the uneasy relationship between composition and literature. Composition studies and institutional histories of English studies have long needed this kind of clarification . . .
Cited by 541 Related articles

Imagine that you are conducting research on the controversy over using Native American mascots for athletic teams. You begin your research by doing an online search and come across a report entitled "Ending the Legacy of Racism in Sports & the Era of Harmful 'Indian' Sports Mascots." Looks promising, but will it be worth your attention? The guidelines above can help you make that decision.

Before you look at the report itself, take a moment to examine its origins and the homepage that hosts it. The report is written by the National Congress of American Indians (NCAI) and published on the organization's site. Note that the site URL ends with *org*, which tells you that the NCAI is a nonprofit organization. The "about NCAI" page tells you that the NCAI is an advocacy group whose mission is to represent the interests of American Indians and Alaskan Natives in a variety of legal, social, and economic issues. The organization also researches and reports on topics concerning Native peoples. Some more searching reveals that the NCAI is supported by government agencies and other organizations that can vouch for its credibility, and that its work is mentioned in such sources as *Slate* and the *Washington Post*. You can also see that the website is clean and professionally designed and (if you scroll to the copyright line at the very bottom of the page) has been recently updated. So far, so good.

Now that you've confirmed the report comes from a credible source, look more closely to see if it is relevant to your research topic. The title tells you that the report is arguing against the use of Native American mascots: one important perspective on your topic. The abstract gives a quick summary of how the report goes about advancing this position. Opening to the table of contents gives still more detail:

    —NATIONAL CONGRESS OF AMERICAN INDIANS, "Ending the Legacy of Racism in Sports & the Era of Harmful 'Indian' Sports Mascots"

From this overview, you learn that the article examines this topic from a historical perspective ("A National Priority for 45 Years"), in both college and professional sports, and focuses on concerns about "racial equality and social justice." The coverage seems both thorough and detailed—and the references and appendices even more so. Finally, note that the report is dated October 10, 2013, so it is recent enough to be useful.

Given all that you know about this source, is it worth your attention? We would say so. Even if you ultimately argue against the NCAI's position on this issue, the report provides valuable information about the history of the debate and one prominent side's argument.

That said, you should be mindful to research other relevant perspectives on your topic. In this case, another internet search turns up a letter from Washington Redskins owner Dan Snyder arguing for a different point of view from the one put forward by the NCAI. Snyder's letter was published in the *Washington Post* under the title "Letter from Washington Redskins owner Dan Snyder to fans." The title announces his stance as the team's owner writing to "Everyone in Our Washington Redskins Nation." In what follows, Snyder explains why he sees the mascot as a way of honoring Native Americans and the team's heritage. He points out that four players and the head coach of the original Redskins team were Native Americans and cites testimony and data from a 2004 survey conducted by the Annenberg Public Policy Center of the University of Pennsylvania, which found that 90 percent of Native Americans interviewed did not find the term "Redskins" offensive. This letter is definitely relevant to your topic and is probably worth your attention. As you go further in your research, you should seek out other credible sources arguing for or against this perspective.

❖ *REFLECT. Read Dan Snyder's letter on* everyonesanauthor.tumblr.com *and the sources he cites as evidence. Evaluate them to determine if they would be credible sources in this research situation. Describe their strengths and weaknesses.*

Reading Sources with a Critical Eye

Once you've determined that a source is credible and appropriate, you'll need to read it closely, thinking carefully about the author's position, how (and how well) it's supported, and how it affects your understanding of the topic as a whole. If the internet has taught us anything, it's to not believe everything that we read. So as you read your sources, approach each one with a critical eye. The following questions can help you do so.

Consider your own RHETORICAL SITUATION. Will the source help you achieve your **PURPOSE**? Look at the preface, abstract, or table of contents to determine how extensively and directly it addresses your topic. Will your **AUDIENCE** consider the source reliable and credible? Are they expecting you to cite certain kinds of materials, such as historical documents or academic journals?

What is the author's STANCE? Does the title indicate a certain attitude or perspective? How would you characterize the **TONE**? Is it objective? argumentative? sarcastic? How does the author's stance affect its usefulness for your project?

Who is the AUDIENCE for this work? Is it aimed at the general public? members of a field? a special interest group? policy makers? Sources written for a general audience may provide useful overviews or explanations. Sources aimed at experts may be more authoritative and provide more detail—but they can be challenging to understand.

What is the main point, and what has motivated the author to write? Is he or she responding to some other argument? What's the larger conversation on this issue? Is it clear why the topic matters?

What REASONS and EVIDENCE does the author provide as support? Are the reasons fair, relevant, and sound? Is the evidence drawn from credible sources? Is the kind of evidence (statistics, facts, examples, expert testimony, and so on) appropriate to the point it's supporting? How persuasive do you find the argument?

Does the author acknowledge and respond to other viewpoints? Look for mention of multiple perspectives, not just the author's own view. And be sure to consider how fairly any **COUNTERARGUMENTS** are represented. The most trustworthy sources represent other views and information fairly and accurately, even (especially) those that challenge their own.

Have you seen ideas given in this source in any other sources? Information found in multiple sources is more reliable than information you can find in only one place. Do other credible sources challenge this information? If so, you should assume that what's said in this source is controversial.

How might you use this source? Source materials can serve a variety of purposes in both your research and your writing. You might consult some sources for background information or to get a sense of the larger context for your topic. Other sources may provide support for your claims—or for your credibility as an author. Still others will provide other viewpoints, ones that challenge yours or that provoke you to respond. Most of all, they'll give you some sense of what's been said about your topic. Then, in writing up your research, you'll get your chance to say what *you* think—and to add your voice to the conversation.

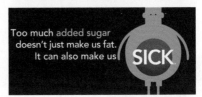

SUPPOSE YOU'RE RESEARCHING current health issues and come across the website SugarScience.org, which claims to be "the authoritative source for evidence-based, scientific information about sugar and its impact on health." A quick look tells you that this site has been developed by a team of health scientists and includes infographics, maps, videos, and "an exhaustive review" of more than 8,000 scientific papers. If you were writing an essay about how sugar consumption has contributed to the obesity crisis, what from this site would you likely cite? How does the way information is presented make it seem more or less credible? For instance, compare the report on sugar "Hidden in Plain Sight" with the infographic shown above. Does one seem more appropriate as a source than the other—and if so, why?

REFLECT. Choose three or four different sources on your chosen topic— possibly one from a government source, one from an academic journal, one from a popular source, and one from a website. Evaluate each of the sources according to the guidelines laid out in this chapter. Explain what makes each source credible (or not).

TWENTY-THREE

Annotating a Bibliography

HEN WE ASSIGN RESEARCH PROJECTS, we often require our students to annotate a bibliography as part of the research process. Instructors do this for a variety of reasons: to ensure that you read sources carefully and critically, summarize useful information about them, and think about how and why you expect to use particular ones. The rhetorical purpose of the annotated bibliography is to inform—and you are part of the audience. Conscientiously done, annotating a bibliography will help you gain a sense of the larger conversation about your topic and think about how your work fits into that conversation.

In a formal annotated bibliography, you **DESCRIBE** each of the sources you expect to consult and state what role each will play in your research. Sometimes you will be asked to **EVALUATE** sources as well—to assess their strengths and weaknesses in one or two sentences.

Characteristic Features

Annotations should be brief, but they can vary in length from a sentence or two to a few paragraphs. They also vary in terms of style: some are written in complete sentences; others consist of short phrases. And like a works cited or reference page, an annotated bibliography is arranged in alphabetical order. You'll want to find out exactly what your instructor expects, but most annotated bibliographies include the following features.

Complete bibliographic information, following whatever documentation style you'll use in your essay— MLA, APA, or another style. This information will enable readers to locate your sources—and can also form the basis for your final works cited or references list.

A brief SUMMARY or DESCRIPTION of each work, noting its topic, scope, and STANCE. If a source reports on research, the research methods may also be important to summarize. Other details you include will depend on your own goals for your project. Whatever you choose to describe, however, be sure that it represents the source accurately and objectively.

Evaluative comments. If you're required to write evaluative annotations, you might consider how AUTHORITATIVE the source is, how up-to-date, whether it addresses multiple perspectives, and so on. Consider both its strengths and its limitations.

Some indication of how each source will inform your research. Explain how you expect to use each source. Does it present a certain perspective you need to consider? report on important new research? include a thorough bibliography that might alert you to other sources? How does each source relate to the others? How does each source contribute to your understanding of the topic and to your research goals? Or if you find that it isn't helpful to your project, explain why you won't use it.

A consistent and concise presentation. Annotations should be presented consistently in all entries: if one is written in complete sentences, they all should be. The amount of information and the way you structure it should also be the same throughout. And that information should be written concisely, summarizing just the main points and key details relevant to your purpose.

Following are two annotated bibliographies, the first descriptive and the second evaluative.

A Descriptive Annotated Bibliography

Renewable and Sustainable Energy in Rural India

SAURABH VAISH

Germany. German Energy Agency. "Renewable Energies."
    Deutsche Energie-Agentur GmbH (dena), n.d. Web.
    12 Apr. 2011.

The German Energy Agency provides information on energy
efficiency, renewable energy sources, and intelligent energy
systems. The website contains some useful databases, including
ones of energy projects in Germany and of recent publications.
It is a useful source of information on the manufacturing and
production of alternative energy systems.

  Though this site does not provide statistical data and
covers only a limited number of projects and publications, it
includes links to much useful information. It's a great source of
publications and projects in both Germany and Russia, and so
it will help me broaden my research beyond the borders of the
United States.

SAURABH VAISH, a management and entrepreneurship major at Hofstra University, wrote this descriptive annotated bibliography for a research project on renewable and sustainable energy in rural India. We then adapted two entries to demonstrate evaluative annotations.

Moner-Girona, Magda, ed. "A New Scheme for the Promotion of Renewable Energies in Developing Countries: The Renewable Energy Regulated Purchase Tariff." *European Commission Joint Research Centre Publications Repository.* European Commission Joint Research Centre, 2008. Web. 12 Apr. 2011.

This report on a study by the PhotoVoltaic Technology Platform discusses how to promote the use of renewable energy in developing countries. The report proposes a new tariff scheme to increase the flow of money where it is most needed, suggests several business models, and estimates the potential success or failure of each. The detailed information it provides about business models, supply-chain setups, and financial calculations will be useful in my analysis, especially in the part of my project that deals with photovoltaic cells.

United States. Energy Information Administration. Renewable & Alternative Fuels Analysis Reports. U.S. Dept. of Energy, 1998–2010. Web. 2 Feb. 2012.

This site reports statistical and graphical data on energy production and consumption, including all major alternative energies. It provides access to numerous databases on energy consumption across the world. This website provides most of the statistical data I will need to formulate conclusions about the efficiency of alternative energies. Its data are reliable, current, and easy to understand.

An Evaluative Annotated Bibliography

Moner-Girona, Magda, ed. "A New Scheme for the Promotion
    of Renewable Energies in Developing Countries: The
    Renewable Energy Regulated Purchase Tariff." *European*
    Commission Joint Research Centre Publications Repository.
    European Commission Joint Research Centre, 2008. Web.
    12 Apr. 2011.

This report on a study by the PhotoVoltaic Technology Platform
discusses how to promote renewable energy in developing
countries. The report proposes a new tariff scheme to increase
the flow of money where it is needed, suggests several business
models, and estimates the potential success or failure of each.

    The detailed information about business models, supply-
chain setups, and financial calculations will be useful, especially in the
part of my project that deals with photovoltaic cells. One potential
drawback is that this report makes premature assumptions: the
proposed business plan is probably not implementable for 20 years.
Even so, this report contains useful data and models, including
graphs and charts, that will support my claims.

Evaluates the source,
acknowledging a potential
weakness—but explains
why it is still useful.

United States. Energy Information Administration. Renewable &
    Alternative Fuels Analysis Reports. U.S. Dept. of Energy,
    1998–2010. Web. 2 Feb. 2012.

This website reports statistical and graphical data on energy
production and consumption, including all major alternative
energies. It provides access to numerous databases on energy
consumption across the world.

    This site provides most of the statistical data I will need
to formulate conclusions about the efficiency of alternative
energies. Its data are reliable, current, and easy to understand.
I see no potential weakness in this source because the data
it presents are non-biased statistics and supporting graphics
pertaining to alternative energies. Using such data will allow me
to shape my own opinions regarding the research I undertake.

TWENTY-FOUR

Synthesizing Ideas

Moving from What Your Sources Say to What You Say

T's Super Bowl Sunday, just before kickoff and just after the teams have been introduced. The broadcast cuts back from a commercial set to DJ Schmolli's "Super Bowl Anthem" and returns to the stadium where Idina Menzel is singing the "Star-Spangled Banner." So you've just heard two anthems. But what else, if anything, do these tunes have in common? Answer: each is a mash-up—a combination of material from a number of different sources. The "Star-Spangled Banner" combines a poem written by Francis Scott Key with the music of an old British drinking song. DJ Schmolli's effort combines clips from more than a dozen popular stadium anthems, from Madonna's "Celebration" to Queen's "We Will Rock You." And each smoothly integrates its sources into one seamless whole. In academic terms, the authors of these mash-ups have effectively engaged in **SYNTHESIS**, bringing together material from various sources to create something new.

Like a good mash-up artist, you don't just patch together ideas from various sources when you do research. Instead, you synthesize what they say to help you think about and understand the topic you're researching—to identify connections among them and blend them into a coherent whole that at the same time articulates *ideas of your own*. This chapter will help you blend ideas from sources with your own ideas smoothly and effectively—just like a really great mash-up.

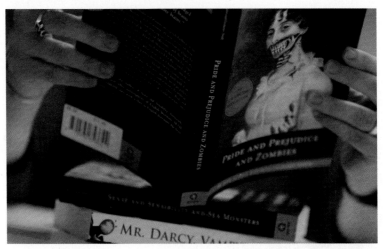

An unlikely mash-up: Jane Austen's *Pride and Prejudice* and . . . zombies! With 85% Austen's original text and 15% zombie blood and gore, *Pride and Prejudice and Zombies* became an instant best-seller, setting off a slew of literary monster mash-ups.

Synthesizing the Ideas in Your Sources

Here are some questions to help you synthesize information as you work with your sources:

- What issues, problems, or controversies do your sources address?
- What else do your sources have in common? Any ideas? facts? examples? statistics? Are any people or works cited in more than one source?
- What significant differences do you find among sources? Different stances? positions? purposes? kinds of evidence? conclusions?
- Do any of your sources cite or refer to one another? Does one source provide details, examples, or explanations that build on something said in another? Does any source respond specifically to something said in another?

Your goal is to get a sense of how the information from your various sources fits together—how the sources speak to one another and what's being said about your topic.

One function of a synthesis is to establish **CONTEXT** and set the scene for what you yourself have to say. See how the following example from an academic article on high-stakes testing brings together information from a number of sources about the history of testing as context for the discussion of trends in school testing today.

> Although the practice of high-stakes testing gained a prominent position in educational reform with the passage of the No Child Left Behind Act (NCLB) of 2002, its use as a lever for school change preceded NCLB. Tests have been used to distribute rewards and sanctions to teachers in urban schools since the mid 1800s (Tyack, 1974) and for most schools throughout the United States since at least the 1970s (Haertel & Herman, 2005). New York state in particular has led the United States in test-based accountability efforts, "implementing state-developed (1965) and mandated minimal competency testing (MCT) before most other states (1978) and disseminating information to the media about local district performance on the state assessments before it became routinely popular (1985)" (Allington & McGill-Franzen, 1992, p. 398).
>
> —SHARON NICHOLS, GENE GLASS, AND DAVID BERLINER,
> "High-stakes Testing and Student Achievement"

Look now at this dramatic opening to a magazine article on actor-comedian Robin Williams' death:

> If you were keeping an eye on Robin Williams' *Twitter* feed these past few months—along with his 875,000 followers—you would have noticed nothing the least bit worrying about the 63-year-old actor-comedian's state of mind. On June 6, he uploaded a photo of himself visiting the San Francisco Zoo, where one of the monkeys had been named after him ("What an honor!"). On July 30, he posted a plug for his December movie, *Night at the Museum: Secret of the Tomb* ("I hope you enjoy it!"). And then, on July 31, in what would turn out to be his last public comment, he tweeted his daughter Zelda a birthday message ("Quarter of a century old today but always my baby girl").
>
> Eleven days later, he was discovered dead at his home in Marin County, California. —BENJAMIN SVETKEY, "Robin Williams Remembered by Critics, Close Friends"

By synthesizing multiple sources—in this case, Williams' *Twitter* posts—and presenting them as one cohesive whole, Svetkey paints a picture of a seemingly happy man.

While these two examples are quite different—one cites academic sources in an academic publication, the other cites social media sources in a popular magazine—they both synthesize information to give readers context for what the authors go on to say. For all writers, including you, that's the next step.

REFLECT. Try your hand at synthesizing the sources you've consulted so far for something you're writing. What patterns do you see? What's being said about your topic?

Moving from What Your Sources Say to What You Say

As a researcher, you'll always be working to synthesize the ideas and information you find in your research, to see the big picture and make sense of it all. At the same time, you'll be striving to connect the data you gather to your own ideas and to your research goals. You'll be learning a lot about what many others have discovered or said about your topic, and that will surely affect what you yourself think—and write—about it. Here are some questions that can help you move from the ideas you find in your sources to the ideas that you'll then write about:

- How do the ideas and information in your sources address your RESEARCH QUESTION? What answers do they give? What information do you find the most relevant, useful, and persuasive?

- How do they support your tentative THESIS? Do they suggest reasons or ways that you should expand, qualify, or otherwise revise it?

- What viewpoints in your sources do you most agree with? disagree with? Why?

- What conclusions can you draw from the ideas and information you've learned from your sources? What discoveries have you made in studying these sources, and what new ideas have they led you to?

- Has your research changed your own views on your topic? Do any of your sources raise questions that you can pursue further?
- Have you encountered any ideas that you would like to build on— or challenge?
- From everything you've read, what is the significance of the topic you're researching? Who cares, and why does it matter?

When you work with your sources in this way, you can count on your ideas to grow—and maybe to change. As we've been saying, research is an act of learning and inquiry, and you never know where it will lead. But as soon as you sit down and write, no matter what you say or how you say it, you will be, as Kenneth Burke says, "putting in your oar," adding your voice *and your ideas* to the very conversation you've been researching.

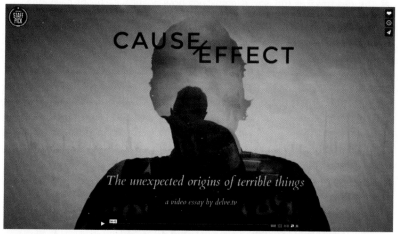

WATCH Cause/Effect: The Unexpected Origins of Terrible Things, *a video essay by Adam Westbrook that makes a fascinating argument about what caused World War I. (You'll find it at* everyonesanauthor.tumblr.com.*) As you'll see, Westbrook synthesizes many kinds of sources and information—history books, maps, cartoons, newspapers, archival photographs and video, data from public records, and more—to build a case for his argument. How does he synthesize all these sources in a video? How does he go about introducing each one and weaving them together with his own ideas?*

THINK
BEYOND
WORDS

Entering the Conversation You've Been Researching

Once you've thought carefully about what others have said about your topic, you can add your own voice to the conversation. Look at the following example from the introduction to an essay tracing the changes in political cartoons in the United States between World War II and the Iraq War. See how the writer synthesized ideas from her research into her writing in a way that set up her own questions and thoughts.

> A cartoon shows carolers at the White House door making a choral argument to then president George W. Bush that "we gotta get out of this place," referring to America's involvement in the war in Iraq (fig. 1). Bush appears completely oblivious to their message.
>
> First published in 2006, this cartoon offered a critique of America's continued presence in Iraq by criticizing the president's actions and attitudes towards the war, exemplifying how political cartoons have long been, and continue to be, a prominent part of wartime propaganda. Combining eye-catching illustrations with textual critique, such cartoons

Fig. 1. A cartoon criticizing war in Iraq (Copley News Service, 2006).

do more than merely convey messages about current events. Rather, political cartoons serve as a tool for shaping public opinion. In fact, since the 1500s, political cartoons have used satirical critiques to persuade the general public about matters large and small (McCloud 16–17).

In the United States, the political (or editorial) cartoon is a form of editorializing that began as "scurrilous caricatures," according to Stephen Becker, author of *Comic Art in America*. His book looks, in part, at the social history of political cartoons and states that it was only after "newspapers and magazines came to be published regularly . . . that caricatures, visual allegories, and the art of design were combined to form . . . modern editorial art" (15). As all-encompassing as that description of "modern editorial art" seems to be, it suggests several questions that remain unanswered: Do cartoonists use common themes to send their critical messages? As society and regulations change from generation to generation, do the style and content of political cartoons change as well? Have political cartoons become "modernized" since World War II? The essay that follows aims to answer as well as draw out the implications of these questions.   —JULIA LANDAUER, "War, Cartoons, and Society: Changes in Political Cartoons between World War II and the Iraq War"

Landauer begins with a cartoon (a primary source) that illustrates a point she is making—that editorial cartoons are known for stinging political critiques. She then refers to a source (McCloud) to provide some background information and then another (Becker) to provide additional commentary on the "modern editorial art" she intends to examine in her essay. At that point, she raises questions "that remain unaddressed"—and says that answering them will be the work of her essay. Thus she uses ideas drawn from her sources to introduce her own ideas—and weave them all together into a strong introduction to her essay.

In your college writing, you will have the opportunity to come up with a research question and to dig in and do some research in order to answer it. That digging in will lead you to identify key sources already in conversation about your topic, to read and analyze those sources, and to begin synthesizing them with your own ideas. Before you know it, you won't be just listening in on the conversation: you'll be an active participant in it.

TWENTY-FIVE

Quoting, Paraphrasing, Summarizing

HEN YOU'RE TEXTING or talking with friends, you don't usually need to be explicit about where you got your information; your friends trust what you say because they know you. In academic writing, however, it's important to establish your credibility, and one way to do so is by consulting authoritative sources. Doing so shows that you've done your homework on your topic, gives credit to those whose ideas you've relied on, and helps demonstrate your own authority as an author.

Your challenge in much academic writing is to integrate other voices with your own. How do you let your audience hear from expert sources while ensuring that their words don't eclipse yours? How do you pick and choose brief segments from long passages of text—or condense those passages into much briefer statements—without misrepresenting someone's ideas? How do you then introduce these segments and integrate them with your own words and ideas? This chapter provides guidelines on the three ways you can incorporate sources into your writing: quoting, paraphrasing, and summarizing.

A **QUOTATION** consists of someone's exact words, enclosed in quotation marks or set off as a block from the rest of your text. A **PARAPHRASE** includes the details of a passage in your own words and syntax. A **SUMMARY** contains the points of a passage that are important to your purpose, leaving out the other details.

Deciding Whether to Quote, Paraphrase, or Summarize

Quote

- Something that is said so well that it's worth repeating
- Complex ideas that are expressed so clearly that paraphrasing or summarizing could distort or oversimplify them
- Experts whose opinions and exact words help to establish your own **CREDIBILITY** and **AUTHORITY** to write on the topic
- Passages that you yourself are analyzing
- Those who disagree or offer **COUNTERARGUMENTS** —quoting their exact words is a way to be sure you represent their opinions fairly

Paraphrase

- Passages where the details matter, but not the exact words
- Passages that are either too technical or too complicated for your readers to understand

Summarize

- Lengthy passages when the main point is important to your argument but the details are not

Nicholas Carr writes for a general audience, but some of his sources are very technical. See how he uses paraphrases in order to not lose his readers on p. 889.

Whatever method you use for incorporating the words and ideas of others into your own writing, be sure that they work to support what *you* want to say. You're the author—and whatever your sources say needs to connect to what you say—so be sure to make that connection clear. Don't assume that sources speak for themselves. Introduce any source that you cite, naming the authors and identifying them in some way if your audience won't know who they are. In addition, be sure to follow quotations with a comment that explains how they relate to your point.

And regardless of whether you decide to quote, paraphrase, or summarize, you'll need to credit each source. Even if what you include is not a direct quotation, the ideas are still someone else's, and failing to credit your source can result in plagiarism. Indicate the source in a **SIGNAL PHRASE** and include in-text documentation.

Quoting

When you include a direct quotation, be sure to use the exact words of the original source. And while you don't want to include too many quotations—you are the author, after all—using the exact words from a source is sometimes the best way to ensure that you accurately represent what was said. Original quotations can also be an effective way of presenting a point, by letting someone speak in his or her own words. But be sure to frame any quotation you include, introducing it and then explaining why it's important to the point that you are making.

Enclose short quotations in quotation marks within your main text. Such quotations should be no longer than four typed lines (in MLA style) or forty words (in APA style).

> Programmer and digital media pioneer Jaron Lanier describes the problems resulting from "lock-in" (in which software becomes difficult to change because it has been engineered to work with existing programs), arguing that lock-in "is an absolute tyrant in the digital world" (8). By that he means, "lock-in" inhibits creativity as new development is constrained by old software.

In MLA style, short quotations of poetry—no more than three lines—should also be enclosed in quotation marks within the main text. Include slashes (with a space on either side) between each line of verse.

> In "When You are Old," poet William Butler Yeats advises Maud Gonne, the radical Irish nationalist, that when she looks back on her youth from old age, she should consider "How many loved your moments of glad grace, / And loved your beauty with love false or true, / But one man loved the pilgrim soul in you." Yeats thus suggests that he is the "one man" who truly loved her so sincerely all these years.

Set off long quotations as a block by indenting them from the left margin. No need to enclose them in quotation marks, but do indent ten spaces (or one inch) if you are using MLA style and five spaces (or one-half inch) if you are using APA. Use this method for quotations that are more than four lines of prose or three lines of poetry (in MLA) or longer than forty words (in APA).

> In her 1976 keynote address to the Democratic National Convention, Texas congresswoman Barbara Jordan reflects on the occasion:

>> Now that I have this grand distinction, what in the world am I supposed to say? I could easily spend this time praising the accomplishments of this party and attacking the Republicans—but I don't choose to do that. I could list the many problems which Americans have. I could list the problems which cause people to feel cynical, angry, frustrated: problems which include lack of integrity in government; the feeling that the individual no longer counts; the reality of material and spiritual poverty; the feeling that the grand American experiment is failing or has failed. I could recite these problems, and then I could sit down and offer no solutions. But I don't choose to do that either. The citizens of America expect more. They deserve and they want more than a recital of problems. (189)

Go to everyones anauthor.tumblr .com to listen to the full text of Barbara Jordan's speech.

> In this passage, Jordan resists the opportunity to attack the opposing party, preferring instead to offer positive solutions rather than simply a list of criticisms and problems.

Notice that with block quotations, the parenthetical citation falls *after* the period at the end of the quotation.

Indicate changes to the text within a quotation by using brackets to enclose text that you add or change and ellipses to indicate text that you omit.

Use brackets to indicate that you have altered the original wording to fit grammatically within your text or have added or changed wording to clarify something that might otherwise be unclear. In this example, the author changed the verb *had* to *should have*:

Read John Maeda's complete essay on p. 987.

> John Maeda, president of the Rhode Island School of Design, reacts to America's current emphasis on STEM education with the proposal that "just like STEM is made up of science, technology, engineering and math, we [should have] IDEA, made up of intuition, design, emotion and art—all the things that make us humans feel, well, human" ("On Meaningful Observation").

Use ellipsis marks in place of words, phrases, or sentences that you leave out because they aren't crucial or relevant for your purpose. Use three dots, with a space before each one and after the last, when you omit only words and phrases within a sentence. If you leave out the end of a sentence or a whole sentence or more, put a period after the last word before the ellipsis mark. Note how a writer does both in the example below.

> Warning of the effects of GPS on our relationship to the world around us, Nicholas Carr concludes that "the automation of wayfinding . . . encourages us to observe and manipulate symbols on screens rather than attend to real things in real places. . . . What we should be asking ourselves is, *How far from the world do we want to retreat?* " (137)

When you use brackets or ellipses, make sure your changes don't end up misrepresenting the author's original point, which would damage your own credibility. Mark Twain once joked that "nearly any invented quotation, played with confidence, stands a good chance to deceive." Twain was probably right—it's quite easy to "invent" quotations or twist their meaning by taking them out of context or changing some key word. You don't want to be guilty of this! And of course, be careful that you don't introduce any grammatical errors by altering the quotation.

Set off a quotation within a quotation with single quotation marks. In the following passage, the author quotes Nicholas Carr, who himself quotes the writing of anthropologist Tim Ingold:

> Nicholas Carr sums up the difference between navigating with and without a GPS device using two terms borrowed from Scottish anthropologist Tim Ingold. As Carr explains, Ingold "draws a distinction between two very different modes of travel: wayfaring and transport. Wayfaring, he explains, is 'our most fundamental way of being in the world,' " (132). It is navigating by our observations and mental maps of the world around us, as opposed to blindly following GPS-generated directions from point A to point B—the mode Ingold and Carr call "transport."

Punctuate quotations carefully. Parenthetical documentation comes after the closing quotation mark, and any punctuation that is part of your sentence comes after the parentheses (except in the case of a block quote, where the parenthetical documentation goes at the very end).

- *Commas and periods* always go inside the closing quotation marks. If there's parenthetical documentation, however, the period goes after the parentheses.

  > "Everybody worships," said David Foster Wallace in a 2005 commencement speech. "There is no such thing as not worshipping" (8).

- *Colons and semicolons* always go outside closing quotation marks.

  > Wallace warned as well that there are "whole parts of adult American life that nobody talks about in commencement speeches": sometimes, he says, we'll be bored (4).

  > He also once noted that when a lobster is put in a kettle of boiling water, it "behaves very much as you or I would behave if we were plunged into boiling water"; in other words, it acts as if it's in terrible pain (10).

See on p. 884 how Dana Canedy quotes dialogue in writing about a difficult conversation with her eight-year-old son.

- **Question marks and exclamation points** go inside closing quotation marks if they are part of the original quotation, but outside the quotation marks if they are part of your sentence.

> Wallace opened his speech with a now famous joke about how natural it is to be unaware of the world: an old fish swims by two young fish and says, "Morning, boys. How's the water?" They swim on, and after a while one young fish turns to the other and asks, "What the hell is water?" (1)

> So what, according to David Foster Wallace, is the "capital-T Truth about life" (9)?

Paraphrasing

When you paraphrase, you restate information or ideas from a source using your words, your sentence structure, your style. A paraphrase should cover the same points that the original source does, so it's usually about the same length—but sticking too closely to the sentence structures in your source could be plagiarizing. And even though you're using your own words, don't forget where the ideas came from: you should always name the author and include parenthetical documentation.

Here is a paragraph about the search for other life-forms similar to our own in the universe, followed by three paraphrases.

Original source

> As the romance of manned space exploration has waned, the drive today is to find our living, thinking counterparts in the universe. For all the excitement, however, the search betrays a profound melancholy—a lonely species in a merciless universe anxiously awaits an answering voice amid utter silence. That silence is maddening. Not just because it compounds our feeling of cosmic isolation, but because it makes no sense. As we inevitably find more and more exo-planets where intelligent life *can* exist, why have we found no evidence—no signals, no radio waves—that intelligent life *does* exist?
> —CHARLES KRAUTHAMMER, "Are We Alone in the Universe?"

As the underlined words show, the following paraphrase uses too many words from the original.

Unacceptable paraphrase: wording too close to the original

Charles Krauthammer argues that finding our intelligent <u>counterparts in the universe</u> has become more important as the <u>romance of manned space exploration</u> has declined. Even so, the hunt for similar beings also suggests our sadness as a species waiting in vain for an acknowledgment that we aren't alone in <u>a merciless universe</u>. The lack of response, he says, just doesn't make sense because if we keep finding planets that *could* support life, then we should find evidence—like <u>radio waves or signals</u>—of intelligent life out there (A19).

While the next version uses original language, the sentence structures are much too similar to the original.

Unacceptable paraphrase: sentence structures too close to original

As the allure of adventuring into the unknown cosmos has diminished, the desire to discover beings like us out there has grown. There is a sadness to the search though—the calling out into empty space that brings no response. Nothing. Only a vast silence that not only emphasizes our solitary existence but increases our frustration. How can we continue to discover potentially hospitable planets that could sustain life like ours, yet find no evidence—no signs, no data—that such life exists (Krauthammer A19)?

When you paraphrase, be careful not to simply substitute words and phrases while replicating the same sentence structure. And while it may be necessary to use some of the key terms from the original in order to convey the same concepts, be sure to put them in quotation marks—and not to use too many (which would result in plagiarism).

Acceptable paraphrase

Syndicated columnist Charles Krauthammer observes that our current quest to discover other "intelligent life" in the universe comes just as the allure of exploring outer space is dimming. It's a search, he says, that reveals a deep sadness (that we may in fact be living in "cosmic isolation") and a growing frustration: if scientists continue to discover more planets where life like ours can be sustainable, why do we find no actual signs of life (A19)?

Summarizing

Like a paraphrase, a summary presents the source information in your words. However, a summary dramatically condenses the information, covering only the most important points and leaving out the details. Summaries are therefore much briefer than the original texts, though they vary in length depending on the size of the original and your purpose for summarizing; you may need only a sentence or two to summarize an essay, or you may need several paragraphs. In any case, you should always name the author and document the source. The following example appropriately summarizes Krauthammer's passage in one sentence:

> Charles Krauthammer questions whether we will ever find other
> "intelligent life" in the universe—or whether we'll instead discover that
> we do in fact live in "cosmic isolation" (A19).

This summary tells readers Krauthammer's main point, and includes in quotation marks two key phrases borrowed from the original source. If we were to work the summary into an essay, it might look like this:

> Many scientists believe that there is a strong probability—given the
> vastness of the universe and how much of it we have yet to explore,
> even with advances like the Hubble telescope—that there is life
> like ours somewhere out there. In a 2011 opinion piece, however,
> syndicated columnist Charles Krauthammer questions whether we
> will ever find other "intelligent life" in the universe—or whether we'll
> instead discover that we do in fact live in "cosmic isolation" (A19).

Three ways a summary can go wrong are if it represents inaccurately the point of the original source, provides so many details that the summary is too long, or is so general that readers are left wondering what the source is about. Consider the following unsuccessful summaries of Krauthammer's passage:

Unacceptable summary: misrepresents the source

Pulitzer Prize–winning columnist Charles Krauthammer extols the virtues of space exploration.

This summary both misses the point of Krauthammer's questioning our troubled search for "intelligent life" beyond earth and claims that the author praises space exploration when at no point in the passage does he do so.

Unacceptable summary: provides too many details

Award-winning columnist Charles Krauthammer suggests that while sending people into space is no longer as exciting to us as it once was, we are interested in finding out if there is life in the universe beyond Earth. He laments the feeling of being alone in the universe given that all signs point to the very real possibility that intelligent life exists elsewhere. Krauthammer wonders "why we have no evidence . . . of intelligent life" on other habitable planets. He finds this lack of proof confounding.

This summary is almost as long as the original passage and includes as many details. As a summary, it doesn't let readers know what points are most important.

Unacceptable summary: too general

Charles Krauthammer is concerned about the search for life on other planets.

While the statement above is not false, it does not adequately reflect Krauthammer's main point in a way that will help the reader get the gist of the original passage. A better summary would tell readers what precisely about the search for life concerns Krauthammer.

REFLECT. Return to the quotation from Barbara Jordan on p. 515. First, write an appropriate paraphrase of the quotation; then write an appropriate summary.

Incorporating Source Material

Whether you quote, paraphrase, or summarize source material, you need to be careful to distinguish what you say from what your sources say, while at the same time weaving the two together smoothly in your writing. That is, you must make clear how the ideas you're quoting, paraphrasing, or summarizing relate to your own—why you're bringing them into your text.

Use signal phrases to introduce source materials, telling readers who said what and providing some context if need be. Don't just drop in a quotation or paraphrase or summary; you need to introduce it. And while you can always use a neutral signal phrase such as "he says" or "she claims," try to choose verbs that reflect the STANCE of those you're citing. In some cases, a simple "she says" does reflect that stance, but usually you can make your writing livelier and more accurate with a more specific SIGNAL VERB.

Use a signal phrase and parenthetical documentation to clearly distinguish your own words and ideas from those of others. The following paraphrase introduces source material with a signal phrase that includes the author's name and closes with documentation giving the page number from which the information is taken.

> As Ernst Mayr explains, Darwin's theory of evolution presented a significant challenge to then-prevalent beliefs about man's centrality in the world (9).

If you do not give the author's name in a signal phrase, include it in the parenthetical documentation.

> Darwin's theory of evolution presented a significant challenge to then-prevalent beliefs about man's centrality in the world (Mayr 9).

Sometimes you'll want or need to state the author's credentials in the signal phrase, explaining his or her authority on the topic—and at the same time lending credibility to your own use of that source.

> According to music historian Ted Gioia, record sales declined sharply during the Great Depression, dropping by almost 90 percent between 1927 and 1932 (127).

Choose verbs that reflect the author's stance toward the material—or your own stance in including it. Saying someone "notes" means something different than saying he or she "insists" or "implies."

> Because almost anyone can create a blog, most people assume that blogs give average citizens a greater voice in public dialogue. Political scientist Matthew Hindman questions this assumption: "Though millions of Americans now maintain a blog, only a few dozen political bloggers get as many readers as a typical college newspaper" (103).

Signal phrases do not have to come first. To add variety to your writing, try positioning them in the middle or at the end of a sentence.

> "Attracting attention," observes Richard Lanham, "is what style is all about" (xi).

> "We've got to stop the debates! Enough with the debates!" pleaded John McCain last Sunday on *Meet the Press* (31).

> Noting the importance of literacy in American lives today, rhetorician Deborah Brandt argues, "Writing is at the heart of the knowledge economy" (117).

SOME USEFUL SIGNAL VERBS

acknowledges	contends	replies
adds	declares	reports
agrees	disagrees	responds
asserts	implies	says
believes	notes	suggests
claims	objects	thinks
concludes	observes	writes

Verb tenses. The verb tense you use when referring to a text or researcher in a signal phrase will depend on your documentation style. MLA style requires the present tense (*argues*) or the present perfect (*has argued*). Using

MLA style, you might write, "In *Rhetoric*, Aristotle argues" or "In commenting on Aristotle's *Rhetoric*, scholars have argued." An exception involves sentences that include specific dates in the past. In this case, the past tense is acceptable: "In his introduction to the 1960 edition of Aristotle's *Rhetoric*, Lane Cooper argued."

The past tense is conventional in APA style, as is the present perfect. As in, "In *Rhetoric*, Aristotle argued" or "In commenting on Aristotle's *Rhetoric*, scholars have argued." However, use the present tense when you refer to the results of a study ("the results of Conrad (2012) demonstrate") or when you make a generalization ("writing researchers agree").

Parenthetical documentation. If you're following MLA, you'll need to include page numbers for all quotations, paraphrases, and summaries from print sources in your parenthetical documentation. If you're using APA, page numbers are required for quotations; for paraphrases and summaries, they're optional—but it's always a good idea to include them whenever you can do so.

Incorporating Visual and Audio Sources

Sometimes you will want to incorporate visual or audio elements from sources that you cannot write into a paragraph. For example, you may include charts, tables, photographs, or drawings—and in online writing, you might include audio or video clips as well. Remember that any such materials that come from sources need to be introduced, explained, and documented just as you would a quotation. If you're following MLA or APA style, refer to chapters 27 and 28 for specific requirements.

Tables. Label anything that contains facts or figures displayed in columns as a table. Number all tables in sequence, and provide a descriptive title for each one. Supply source information immediately below the table; credit your data source even if you've created the table yourself. If any information within the table requires further explanation (abbreviations, for example), include a note below the source citation.

Figures. Number and label everything that is not a table (photos, graphs, drawings, maps, and so on) as a figure and include a caption letting readers know what the image illustrates. Unless the visual is a photograph or drawing you created yourself, provide appropriate source information after the caption; graphs, maps, and other figures you produce based on information from other sources should still include a full credit. If the visual is discussed in detail within your text, like the Coca-Cola ad in Melissa Rubin's analysis on page 246, you can use an abbreviated citation and include full documentation in your **WORKS CITED** or **REFERENCES** list.

Audio and video recordings. If your medium allows it, provide a link to any recorded element or embed a media player into the text. If you're working in a medium that won't allow linking or embedding, discuss the recording in your text and provide a full citation in your **WORKS CITED** or **REFERENCES** list so your readers can track down the recording themselves.

Captions. Create a clear, succinct caption for each visual or recording: "Fig. 1: The Guggenheim Museum, Spain." The caption should identify and explain the visual—and should reflect your purpose. In an essay about contemporary architecture in Spain, your caption might say "Fig. 1: The Guggenheim

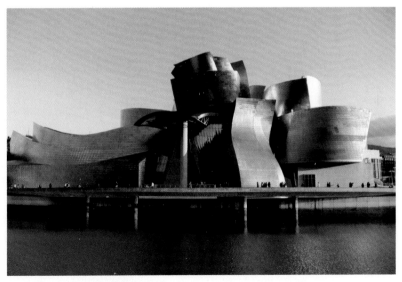

Fig. 1: The Guggenheim Museum, Spain.

Museum, Bilbao. Designed by Frank Gehry." If you're blogging about field research in Bilbao, your caption might say something different, perhaps "A roller coaster building: the Guggenheim!"

Sizing and positioning visuals and recordings. Refer to every visual or embedded recording in your text: "(see fig. 1)," "as shown in Table 3," "in the *YouTube* video below." The element may be on the page where it's discussed, but it should not come before you introduce it to your readers. Think carefully about how you will size and position each visual to be most effective: you want to make sure that your visuals are legible, and that they support rather than disrupt the text. Take a look at the Coca-Cola ad on page 247. Because this ad is the subject of Melissa Rubin's analytical essay, she sized it large enough for readers to be able to see the details she's discussing.

TWENTY-SIX

Giving Credit, Avoiding Plagiarism

HO OWNS WORDS AND IDEAS? Answers to this question differ from culture to culture: In some societies, they are shared resources, not the property of individuals. In others, using another person's words or ideas may be seen as a tribute or compliment that doesn't require specific acknowledgment. In the United States, however (as well as in much of the Western world), elaborate systems of copyright and patent law have grown up to protect the intellectual property (including words, images, voices, and ideas) of individuals and corporations. This system forms the foundation of the documentation conventions currently followed in U.S. schools. And while these conventions are being challenged today by the open-source movement and others who argue that "information wants to be free," the conventions still hold sway in the academy and in the law. As a researcher, you will need to understand these conventions and to practice them in your own writing. Put simply, these conventions allow you to give credit where credit is due and thereby avoid plagiarism (the use of the words and ideas of others as if they were your own work).

But acknowledging your sources is not simply about avoiding charges of plagiarism (although you would be doing that too). Rather, it helps establish your own **CREDIBILITY** as a researcher and an author. It shows that you have consulted other sources of information about your topic and can engage with them in your own work. Additionally, citing and documenting your sources allows readers to locate them for their own purposes if they wish; in effect, it anticipates the needs of your audience.

There are some cases, however, in which you do not need to provide citations for information that you incorporate—for example, if the information is common knowledge. This chapter will help you identify which sources you must acknowledge, explain the basics of documenting your sources, and provide strategies for avoiding plagiarism.

Knowing What You Must Acknowledge

As a general rule, material taken from specific outside sources—whether ideas, texts, images, or sounds—should be **CITED** and **DOCUMENTED**. But there are some exceptions.

You may not know offhand that the next nearest galaxy is 2.5 million light-years away, but it's a fact. See how Neil deGrasse Tyson uses that information (without citing a source) on p. 1069.

INFORMATION THAT DOES NOT NEED TO BE ACKNOWLEDGED

- *Information that is "common knowledge."* Uncontroversial information ("People today get most of their news and information from the internet"), well-known historical events ("Neil Armstrong was the first person to walk on the moon"), facts ("All mammals are warm-blooded"), and quotations (Armstrong's "That's one small step for man, one giant leap for mankind") that are widely available in general reference sources do not need to be cited.

- *Information well known to your audience.* Keep in mind that what is common knowledge varies depending on your audience. While an audience of pulmonary oncologists would be familiar with the names of researchers who established that smoking is linked to lung cancer, for a general audience you might need to cite a source if you give the names.

- *Information from well-known, easily accessible documents.* You do not need to include the specific location where you accessed texts that are available from a variety of public sources and are widely familiar, such as the United States Constitution.

- *Your own work.* If you've gathered data, come up with an idea, or generated a text (including images, multimedia texts, and so on) entirely on your own, you should indicate that to your readers in some way—but it's not necessary to include a formal citation, unless the material has been previously published elsewhere.

INFORMATION THAT MUST BE ACKNOWLEDGED

- *Direct quotations, paraphrases, and summaries.* Exact wording should always be enclosed in quotation marks and cited. And always cite specific ideas taken from another source, even when you present them using your own words.

- *Controversial information.* If there is some debate over the information you're including, cite the source so readers know whose version or interpretation of the facts you're using.

- *Information given in only a few sources.* If only one or two sources make this information available (that is, it isn't common knowledge widely accessible in general sources), include a citation.

- *Any materials that you did not create yourself*—including tables, charts, images, and audio or video segments. Even if you create a table or chart yourself, if it presents information from an outside source, that's someone else's work that needs to be acknowledged.

A word to the wise: it's always better to cite any information that you've taken from another source than to guess wrong and unintentionally plagiarize. If in doubt, err on the safe side and include a citation.

Fair Use and the Internet

In general, principles of fair use apply to the writing you do for your college classes. These principles allow you to use passages and images from the copyrighted work of others without their explicit permission as long as you do so for educational purposes and you fully cite what you use. When you publish your writing online, however, where that material can be seen by all, then you must have permission from the copyright owner in order to post it.

Students across the country have learned about this limitation on fair use the hard way. One student we know won a prize for an essay she wrote, which was then posted on the writing prize website. In the essay, she included a cartoon that was copyrighted by the cartoonist. Soon after the essay was posted, she received a letter from the copyright holder, demanding that she remove the image and threatening her with a lawsuit. Another student, whose essay was published on a class website, was stunned when his instructor got an angry email from a professor at another university, saying that the student writer had used too much of her work in the essay and that, furthermore, it had not been fully and properly cited. The student, who had intended no dishonesty at all, was embarrassed, to say the least.

Many legal scholars and activists believe that fair use policies and laws should be relaxed and that making these laws more restrictive undermines creativity. While these issues get debated in public forums and legal courts, however, you are well advised to be careful not only in citing and documenting all your sources thoroughly but in getting permission in writing to use any copyrighted text or image in anything you plan to post or publish online.

Avoiding Plagiarism

In U.S. academic culture, incorporating the words, ideas, or materials of others into your own work without giving credit through appropriate citations and documentation is viewed as unethical and is considered plagiarism. The consequences of such unacknowledged borrowing are serious: students who plagiarize may receive failing grades for assignments or courses, be subjected to an administrative review for academic misconduct, or even be dismissed from school.

Certainly, the deliberate and obvious effort to pass off someone else's work as your own, such as by handing in a paper purchased online or written by someone else, is plagiarism and can easily be spotted and punished. More troublesome and problematic, however, is the difficulty some students have using the words and ideas of others fairly and acknowledging them fully. Especially when you're new to a field or writing about unfamiliar ideas, incorporating sources without plagiarizing can be challenging.

In fact, researcher Rebecca Moore Howard has found that even expert writers have difficulty incorporating the words and ideas of others acceptably when they are working with material outside their comfort zone or field of expertise. Such difficulty can often lead to what Howard calls **PATCHWRITING**: restating material from sources in ways that stick too closely to the original language or syntax.

But patchwriting can help you work with sources. Some call patchwriting plagiarism, even when it's documented, but we believe that it can be a step in the process of learning how to weave the words and thoughts of others into your own work. Assume, for example, that you want to summarize ideas from the following passage:

> Over the past few decades, scholars from a variety of disciplines have devoted considerable attention toward studying evolving public attitudes toward a whole range of LGBT civil rights issues including support for open service in the military, same-sex parent adoption, employment non-discrimination, civil unions, and marriage equality. In the last 10 years in particular, the emphasis has shifted toward studying the various factors that best explain variation in support for same-sex marriage including demographic considerations, religious and ideological predispositions, attitudes toward marriage and family, and social contact (Baunach 2011, 2012; Becker, 2012a, 2012b; Becker & Scheufele, 2009, 2011; Becker and Todd, 2013; Brewer, 2008; Brewer & Wilcox, Lewis, 2005, 2011; Lewis & Gossett, 2008; Lewis & Oh, 2008).
> —AMY BECKER, "Employment Discrimination, Local School Boards, and LGBT Civil Rights: Reviewing 25 Years of Public Opinion Data"

This passage includes a lot of detailed information in complex sentences that can be hard to process. See how one student first summarized it, and why this summary would be unacceptable in an essay of his own:

A patchwritten summary

For more than 20 years, scholars from many disciplines have committed their energies to examining changing public attitudes toward a variety of LGBT civil rights issues. These encompass things like open military service, same-sex parent adoption, equal employment opportunities, civil unions, and marriage equality. Since 2004, focus has moved toward examining those elements that best account for differences in public support for same-sex marriage like demographic considerations, religious and ideological predispositions, attitudes toward marriage and family, and social contact (Baunach 2011, 2012; Becker, 2012a, 2012b; Becker & Scheufele, 2009, 2011; Becker and Todd, 2013; Brewer, 2008; Brewer & Wilcox, Lewis, 2005, 2011; Lewis & Gossett, 2008; Lewis & Oh, 2008).

This is a classic case of patchwriting that would be considered plagiarism. The sentence structure looks very much like Becker's, and even some of the language is taken straight from the original article. While such a summary would not be acceptable in any writing you turn in, this sort of patchwriting can help you understand what a difficult source is saying.

And once you understand the source, writing an acceptable summary gets a lot easier. In the acceptable summary below, the writer focuses on the ideas in the long second sentence of the original passage, turning those ideas into two simpler sentences and using a direct quotation from the original.

Acceptable summary

Scholars studying changes in public opinion on LGBT issues have increasingly focused on the growing support for same-sex marriage. In looking at the question of why opinions on this issue differ, these scholars have considered factors such as "demographic considerations, religious and ideological predispositions, attitudes toward marriage and family, and social contact" (Becker 342).

An acceptable summary uses the writer's own language and sentence structures, and quotation marks to indicate any borrowed language. To write a summary like this one, you would need to be able to restate the source's main point (that same-sex marriage has gotten greater scholarly attention lately than other LGBT issues) and decide what information is most important for your purposes—what details are worth emphasizing with a quotation or a longer summary. Finally, notice that the citation credits Becker's article, because that is the source this writer consulted, not the research Becker cites. Chapter 25 offers you more guidelines on QUOTING, PARAPHRASING, and SUMMARIZING appropriately.

STEPS YOU CAN TAKE TO AVOID PLAGIARISM

Understand what constitutes plagiarism. Plagiarism includes any unacknowledged use of material from another source that isn't considered common knowledge; this includes phrases, ideas, and materials such as graphs, charts, images, videos, and so on. In a written text, it includes neglecting to put someone else's exact wording in quotation marks; leaving out in-text documentation for sources that you QUOTE, PARAPHRASE, or SUMMARIZE; and borrowing too many of the original sources' words and sentence structures in paraphrases or summaries. Check to see if your school has any explicit guidelines for what constitutes plagiarism.

Take notes carefully and conscientiously. If you can't locate the source of words or ideas that you've copied down, you may neglect to cite them properly. Technology makes it easy to copy and paste text and materials from electronic sources directly into your own work—and then to move on and forget to put such material in quotation marks or record the source. So keep copies of sources, note documentation information, and be sure to put any borrowed language in quotation marks and to clearly distinguish your own ideas from those of others.

Know where your information comes from. Because information passes quickly and often anonymously through the internet grapevine, you may not always be able to determine the origin of a text or image you find online. If you don't know where something came from, don't include it. Not only would you be unable to write a proper citation, chances are you haven't been able to verify the information either.

DOCUMENT sources carefully. Below you'll find an overview of the basics of documenting sources. More detail on using **MLA** and **APA** documentation is given in the next two chapters.

Plan ahead. Work can pile up in a high-pressure academic environment. Stay on top of your projects by scheduling your work and sticking to the deadlines you set. This way, you'll avoid taking shortcuts that could lead to inadvertent plagiarism.

Consult your instructor if necessary. If you're uncertain about how to acknowledge sources properly or are struggling with a project, talk with your instructor about finding a solution. Even taking a penalty for submitting an assignment late is better than being caught cheating or being accused of plagiarism that you didn't intend to commit.

Documenting Sources

When you document sources, you identify the ones you've used and give information about their authors, titles, and publication. Documenting your sources allows you to show evidence of the research you've done and enables your readers to find those sources if they wish to. Most academic documentation systems include two parts: **IN-TEXT DOCUMENTATION**, which you insert in your text after the specific information you have borrowed, and an end-of-text list of **WORKS CITED** or **REFERENCES**, which provides complete bibliographic information for every work you've cited.

This book covers two documentation systems—of the Modern Language Association (**MLA**) and the American Psychological Association (**APA**). MLA style is used primarily in English and other humanities subjects, and APA is used mostly in psychology and other social sciences. Chances are that you will be required to use either MLA or APA style or both in your college courses. Note that some disciplines may require other documentation systems, such as CSE (Council of Science Editors) or Chicago.

MLA and APA both call for the same basic information; you'll need to give the author's name (or sometimes the editor's name or the title) in the in-text citation, and your end-of-text list should provide the author, title, and publication information for each source that you cite. But the two systems differ in some ways. In APA, for example, your in-text documentation always includes the date of publication, but that is not generally done in MLA. You'll find detailed guidance on the specifics of MLA in Chapter 27 and of APA in Chapter 28, with color-coded examples to help you easily distinguish where the author and editor, title, and publication information appear for each type of work you document. Each of these chapters also includes a student paper that uses that style of documentation.

REFLECT. Think about the kinds of information you'll need to give when writing about your research. For your topic and your intended audience, what would be considered common knowledge? What might not be common knowledge for a different audience? What do you know about your audience that can help you make that decision?

TWENTY-SEVEN

MLA Style

MODERN LANGUAGE ASSOCIATION style calls for (1) brief in-text documentation and (2) complete documentation in a list of works cited at the end of your text. The models in this chapter draw on the *MLA Handbook for Writers of Research Papers*, 7th edition (2009). Additional information is available at www.mla.org.

A DIRECTORY TO MLA STYLE

In-Text Documentation 538

Throughout this chapter, you'll find models and examples that are color-coded to help you see how writers include source information in their texts and lists of works cited: brown for author or editor, yellow for title, gray for publication information—place of publication, publisher, date of publication, page number(s), and so on.

IN-TEXT DOCUMENTATION

Brief documentation in your text makes clear to your reader what you took from a source and where in the source you found the information.

In your text, you have three options for citing a source: **QUOTING**, **PARA-PHRASING**, and **SUMMARIZING**. As you cite each source, you will need to decide whether or not to name the author in a signal phrase—"as Toni Morrison writes"—or in parentheses—"(Morrison 24)."

The first examples in this chapter show basic in-text documentation of a work by one author. Variations on those examples follow. The examples illustrate the MLA style of using quotation marks around titles of short works and italicizing titles of long works.

1. Author named in a signal phrase

If you mention the author in a **SIGNAL PHRASE**, put only the page number(s) in parentheses. Do not write *page* or *p*.

> McCullough describes John Adams' hands as those of someone used to manual labor (18).

2. Author named in parentheses

If you do not mention the author in a signal phrase, put his or her last name in parentheses along with the page number(s). Do not use punctuation between the name and the page number(s).

> Adams is said to have had "the hands of a man accustomed to pruning his own trees, cutting his own hay, and splitting his own firewood" (McCullough 18).

Whether you use a signal phrase and parentheses or parentheses only, try to put the parenthetical documentation at the end of the sentence or as close as possible to the material you've cited—without awkwardly interrupting the sentence. Notice that in the example above, the parenthetical reference comes after the closing quotation marks but before the period at the end of the sentence.

3. Two or more works by the same author

If you cite multiple works by one author, include the title of the work you are citing either in the signal phrase or in parentheses. Give the full title if it's brief; otherwise, give a short version.

> Kaplan insists that understanding power in the Near East requires
> "Western leaders who know when to intervene, and do so without
> illusions" (*Eastward* 330).

Include a comma between author and title if you include both in the parentheses.

> Understanding power in the Near East requires "Western leaders
> who know when to intervene, and do so without illusions"
> (Kaplan, *Eastward* 330).

4. Authors with the same last name

Give the author's first name in any signal phrase or the author's first initial in the parenthetical reference.

> *Imaginative* applies not only to modern literature (E. Wilson) but also
> to writing of all periods, whereas *magical* is often used in writing about
> Arthurian romances (A. Wilson).

5. Two or more authors

For a work by two or three authors, name all the authors, either in a signal phrase or in the parentheses.

> Carlson and Ventura's stated goal is to introduce Julio Cortázar,
> Marjorie Agosín, and other Latin American writers to an audience of
> English-speaking adolescents (v).

For a work with four or more authors, either mention all their names or include just the name of the first author followed by *et al.*, Latin for "and others."

> One popular survey of American literature breaks the contents into
> sixteen thematic groupings (Anderson et al. A19-24).

6. Organization or government as author

Acknowledge the organization either in a signal phrase or in parentheses. It's acceptable to shorten long names.

> The U.S. government can be direct when it wants to be. For example,
> it sternly warns, "If you are overpaid, we will recover any payments not
> due you" (Social Security Administration 12).

7. Author unknown

If you don't know the author, use the work's title or a shortened version of the title in the parentheses.

> A powerful editorial in last week's paper asserts that healthy liver
> donor Mike Hurewitz died because of "frightening" faulty postoperative
> care ("Every Patient's Nightmare").

8. Literary works

When referring to literary works that are available in many different editions, give the page numbers from the edition you are using, followed by information that will let readers of any edition locate the text you are citing.

Novels. Give the page and chapter number.

> In *Pride and Prejudice*, Mrs. Bennet shows no warmth toward Jane and
> Elizabeth when they return from Netherfield (105; ch. 12).

Verse plays. Give the act, scene, and line numbers; separate them with periods.

> Macbeth continues the vision theme when he addresses the Ghost
> with "Thou hast no speculation in those eyes / Which thou dost glare
> with" (3.3.96-97).

Poems. Give the part and the line numbers (separated by periods). If a poem has only line numbers, use the word *line(s)* in the first reference.

Whitman sets up not only opposing adjectives but also opposing nouns in "Song of Myself" when he says, "I am of old and young, of the foolish as much as the wise, / . . . a child as well as a man" (16.330-32).

One description of the mere in *Beowulf* is "not a pleasant place!" (line 1372). Later, the label is "the awful place" (1378).

9. Work in an anthology

Name the author(s) of the work, not the editor of the anthology—either in a signal phrase or in parentheses.

"It is the teapots that truly shock," according to Cynthia Ozick in her essay on teapots as metaphor (70).

In *In Short: A Collection of Creative Nonfiction*, readers will find both an essay on Scottish tea (Hiestand) and a piece on teapots as metaphors (Ozick).

10. Encyclopedia or dictionary

Acknowledge an entry in an encyclopedia or dictionary by giving the author's name, if available. For an entry in a reference work without an author, give the entry's title in parentheses. If entries are arranged alphabetically, no page number is needed.

According to *Funk & Wagnall's New World Encyclopedia*, early in his career Kubrick's main source of income came from "hustling chess games in Washington Square Park" ("Kubrick, Stanley").

11. Legal and historical documents

For legal cases and acts of law, name the case or act in a signal phrase or in parentheses. Italicize the name of a legal case.

In 2005, the Supreme Court confirmed in *MGM Studios, Inc. v. Grokster, Ltd.* that peer-to-peer file sharing is illegal copyright infringement.

Do not italicize the titles of laws, acts, or well-known historical documents such as the Declaration of Independence. Give the title and any relevant articles and sections in parentheses. It's okay to use common abbreviations such as *art.* or *sec.* and to abbreviate well-known titles.

> The president is also granted the right to make recess appointments (US Const., art. 2, sec. 2).

12. Sacred text

When citing sacred texts such as the Bible or the Qur'an, give the title of the edition used, and in parentheses give the book, chapter, and verse (or their equivalent), separated by periods. MLA style recommends that you abbreviate the names of the books of the Bible in parenthetical references.

> The wording from *The New English Bible* follows: "In the beginning of creation, when God made heaven and earth, the earth was without form and void, with darkness over the face of the abyss, and a mighty wind that swept over the surface of the waters" (Gen. 1.1-2).

13. Multivolume work

If you cite more than one volume of a multivolume work, each time you cite one of the volumes, give the volume *and* the page number(s) in parentheses, separated by a colon.

> Sandburg concludes with the following sentence about those paying last respects to Lincoln: "All day long and through the night the unbroken line moved, the home town having its farewell" (4: 413).

If your works-cited list includes only a single volume of a multivolume work, give just the page number in parentheses.

14. Two or more works cited together

If you're citing two or more works closely together, you will sometimes need to provide a parenthetical reference for each one.

> Tanner (7) and Smith (viii) have looked at works from a cultural perspective.

If you include both in the same parentheses, separate the references with a semicolon.

> Critics have looked at both *Pride and Prejudice* and *Frankenstein* from a cultural perspective (Tanner 7; Smith viii).

15. Source quoted in another source

When you are quoting text that you found quoted in another source, use the abbreviation *qtd. in* in the parenthetical reference.

> Charlotte Brontë wrote to G. H. Lewes: "Why do you like Miss Austen so very much? I am puzzled on that point" (qtd. in Tanner 7).

16. Work without page numbers

For works without page numbers, including many online sources, identify the source using the author or other information either in a **SIGNAL PHRASE** or in parentheses.

> Studies reported in *Scientific American* and elsewhere show that music training helps children to be better at multitasking later in life ("Hearing the Music").

If the source has paragraph or section numbers, use them with the abbreviation *par.* or *sec.*: ("Hearing the Music," par. 2). If an online work is available as a PDF with page numbers, give the number(s) in parentheses.

17. An entire work or one-page article

If you cite an entire work rather than a part of it, or if you cite a single-page article, identify the author in a signal phrase or in parentheses. There's no need to include page numbers.

> At least one observer considers Turkey and Central Asia explosive (Kaplan).

NOTES

Sometimes you may need to give information that doesn't fit into the text it-self—to thank people who helped you, to provide additional details, to refer readers to other sources, or to add comments about sources. Such informa-tion can be given in a *footnote* (at the bottom of the page) or an *endnote* (on a separate page with the heading *Notes* just before your works-cited list). Put a superscript number at the appropriate point in your text, signaling to read-ers to look for the note with the corresponding number. If you have multiple notes, number them consecutively throughout your paper.

Text

This essay will argue that small liberal arts colleges should not recruit athletes and, more specifically, that giving student athletes preferential treatment undermines the larger educational goals.[1]

Note

1. I want to thank all those who have contributed to my thinking on this topic, especially my classmates and my teachers Marian Johnson and Diane O'Connor.

LIST OF WORKS CITED

A works-cited list provides full bibliographic information for every source cited in your text. See page 573 for guidelines on preparing this list; for a sample works-cited list, see page 590.

Print Books

For most books, you'll need to provide information about the author; the title and any subtitle; and the place of publication, publisher, and date. At the end of the citation, provide the medium—Print.

author   title   publication

Important Details for Documenting Print Books

- **AUTHORS:** Include the author's middle name or initials, if any.
- **TITLES:** Capitalize all principal words in titles and subtitles. Do not capitalize *a, an, the, to,* or any prepositions or coordinating conjunctions unless they are the first or last word of a title or subtitle.
- **PUBLICATION PLACE:** If there's more than one city, use the first.
- **PUBLISHER:** Use a short form of the publisher's name (Norton for W. W. Norton & Company, Yale UP for Yale University Press).
- **DATES:** If more than one year is given, use the most recent one.

1. One author

Author's Last Name, First Name. *Title.* Publication City: Publisher, Year of publication. Medium.

Anderson, Curtis. *The Long Tail: Why the Future of Business Is Selling Less of More.* New York: Hyperion, 2006. Print.

2. Two or more works by the same author(s)

Give the author's name in the first entry, and then use three hyphens in the author slot for each of the subsequent works, listing them alphabetically by the first important word of each title.

Author's Last Name, First Name. *Title That Comes First Alphabetically.* Publication City: Publisher, Year of publication. Medium.

---. *Title That Comes Next Alphabetically.* Publication City: Publisher, Year of publication. Medium.

Kaplan, Robert D. *The Coming Anarchy: Shattering the Dreams of the Post Cold War.* New York: Random, 2000. Print.
---. *Eastward to Tartary: Travels in the Balkans, the Middle East, and the Caucasus.* New York: Random, 2000. Print.

Documentation Map (MLA) / Print Book

Title → PINK SARI REVOLUTION

Subtitle → A TALE OF WOMEN AND POWER IN INDIA

Author → AMANA FONTANELLA-KHAN

Publisher → W. W. NORTON & COMPANY
NEW YORK LONDON

Publication City

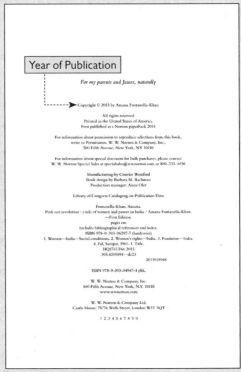

Year of Publication

For my parents and James, naturally

Copyright © 2013 by Amana Fontanella-Khan

All rights reserved
Printed in the United States of America
First published as a Norton paperback 2014

For information about permission to reproduce selections from this book,
write to Permissions, W. W. Norton & Company, Inc.,
500 Fifth Avenue, New York, NY 10110

For information about special discounts for bulk purchases, please contact
W. W. Norton Special Sales at specialsales@wwnorton.com or 800-233-4830

Manufacturing by Courier Westford
Book design by Barbara M. Bachman
Production manager: Anna Oler

Library of Congress Cataloging-in-Publication Data

Fontanella-Khan, Amana.
Pink sari revolution : a tale of women and power in India / Amana Fontanella-Khan.
—First Edition.
pages cm
Includes bibliographical references and index.
ISBN 978-0-393-06297-7 (hardcover)
1. Women—India—Social conditions. 2. Women's rights—India. 3. Feminism—India.
4. Pal, Sampat, 1961– I. Title.
HQ1743.F66 2013
305.4209594—dc23
2013018948

ISBN 978-0-393-34947-4 pbk.

W. W. Norton & Company, Inc.
500 Fifth Avenue, New York, N.Y. 10110
www.wwnorton.com

W. W. Norton & Company Ltd.
Castle House, 75/76 Wells Street, London W1T 3QT

1 2 3 4 5 6 7 8 9 0

Fontanella-Khan, Amana. *Pink Sari Revolution: A Tale of Women and Power in India.* New York: Norton, 2013. Print.

3. Two or three authors

> First Author's Last Name, First Name, Second Author's First and Last Names, and Third Author's First and Last Names. *Title*. Publication City: Publisher, Year of publication. Medium.

Malless, Stanley, and Jeffrey McQuain. *Coined by God: Words and Phrases That First Appear in the English Translations of the Bible.* New York: Norton, 2003. Print.

Sebranek, Patrick, Verne Meyer, and Dave Kemper. *Writers INC: A Guide to Writing, Thinking, and Learning.* Burlington: Write Source, 1990. Print.

4. Four or more authors

You may give each author's name or the name of the first author only, followed by *et al.,* Latin for "and others."

> First Author's Last Name, First Name, Second Author's First and Last Names, Third Author's First and Last Names, and Final Author's First and Last Names. *Title*. Publication City: Publisher, Year of publication. Medium.

Anderson, Robert, John Malcolm Brinnin, John Leggett, Gary Q. Arpin, and Susan Allen Toth. *Elements of Literature: Literature of the United States.* Austin: Holt, 1993. Print.

Anderson, Robert, et al. *Elements of Literature: Literature of the United States.* Austin: Holt, 1993. Print.

5. Organization or government as author

> Organization Name. *Title*. Publication City: Publisher, Year of publication. Medium.

Diagram Group. *The Macmillan Visual Desk Reference.* New York: Macmillan, 1993. Print.

For a government publication, give the name of the government first, followed by the names of any department and agency (see p. 548).

United States. Dept. of Health and Human Services. Natl. Inst. of Mental Health. *Autism Spectrum Disorders*. Washington: GPO, 2004. Print.

6. Anthology

Editor's Last Name, First Name, ed. *Title*. Publication City: Publisher, Year of publication. Medium.

Hall, Donald, ed. *The Oxford Book of Children's Verse in America*. New York: Oxford UP, 1985. Print.

If there is more than one editor, list the first editor last-name-first and the others first-name-first.

Kitchen, Judith, and Mary Paumier Jones, eds. *In Short: A Collection of Brief Creative Nonfiction*. New York: Norton, 1996. Print.

7. Work(s) in an anthology

Author's Last Name, First Name. "*Title of Work*." Title of Anthology. Ed. Editor's First and Last Names. Publication City: Publisher, Year of publication. Pages. Medium.

Achebe, Chinua. "Uncle Ben's Choice." *The Seagull Reader: Literature*. Ed. Joseph Kelly. New York: Norton, 2005. 23-27. Print.

To document two or more selections from one anthology, list each selection by author and title, followed by the anthology editors' names and the pages of the selection. Include an entry for the anthology itself (see no. 6) if you're citing more than one selection.

Author's Last Name, First Name. "Title of Work." Anthology Editor's Last Name Pages.

Hiestand, Emily. "Afternoon Tea." Kitchen and Jones 65-67.

Ozick, Cynthia. "The Shock of Teapots." Kitchen and Jones 68-71.

8. Author and editor

Start with the author if you've cited the text itself.

> Author's Last Name, First Name. *Title*. Ed. Editor's First and Last
> Names. Publication City: Publisher, Year of publication. Medium.

> Austen, Jane. *Emma*. Ed. Stephen M. Parrish. New York: Norton, 2000.
> Print.

Start with the editor to cite his or her contribution rather than the author's.

> Editor's Last Name, First Name, ed. *Title*. By Author's First and Last
> Names. Publication City: Publisher, Year of publication. Medium.

> Parrish, Stephen M., ed. *Emma*. By Jane Austen. New York: Norton,
> 2000. Print.

9. No author or editor

> *Title*. Publication City: Publisher, Year of publication. Medium.

> *2008 New York City Restaurants*. New York: Zagat, 2008. Print.

10. Translation

Start with the author to emphasize the work itself.

> Author's Last Name, First Name. *Title*. Trans. Translator's First and Last
> Names. Publication City: Publisher, Year of publication. Medium.

> Dostoevsky, Fyodor. *Crime and Punishment*. Trans. Richard Pevear and
> Larissa Volokhonsky. New York: Vintage, 1993. Print.

Start with the translator to emphasize the translation.

> Pevear, Richard, and Larissa Volokhonsky, trans. *Crime and Punishment*.
> By Fyodor Dostoevsky. New York: Vintage, 1993. Print.

11. Graphic narrative

Start with the person whose work is most relevant to your research, and include labels to indicate each person's role (more on p. 550).

> Pekar, Harvey, writer. *American Splendor*. Illus. R. Crumb. New York:
> Four Walls, 1996. Print.

> Crumb, R., illus. *American Splendor.* By Harvey Pekar. New York: Four
>   Walls, 1996. Print.

If the work was written and illustrated by the same person, format the entry
like that of a book by one author (see no. 1).

12. Foreword, introduction, preface, or afterword

> Part Author's Last Name, First Name. Name of Part. *Title of Book.*
>   By Author's First and Last Names. Publication City: Publisher, Year
>   of publication. Pages. Medium.

> Tanner, Tony. Introduction. *Pride and Prejudice.* By Jane Austen. London:
>   Penguin, 1972. 7-46. Print.

13. Multivolume work

If you cite more than one volume of a multivolume work, give the total number of volumes after the title.

> Author's Last Name, First Name. *Title of Complete Work.* Number of
>   vols. Publication City: Publisher, Year of publication. Medium.

> Sandburg, Carl. *Abraham Lincoln: The War Years.* 4 vols. New York:
>   Harcourt, 1939. Print.

If you cite only one volume, give the volume number after the title.

> Sandburg, Carl. *Abraham Lincoln: The War Years.* Vol. 2. New York:
>   Harcourt, 1939. Print.

14. Article in a reference book

Provide the author's name if the article is signed. If the reference work is
well known, give only the edition and year of publication.

> Author's Last Name, First Name. "Title of Article." *Title of Reference
>   Book.* Edition number. Year of publication. Medium.

> "Kiwi." *Merriam-Webster's Collegiate Dictionary.* 11th ed. 2003. Print.

If the reference work is less familiar or more specialized, give full publication information. If it has only one volume or is in its first edition, omit that information.

> Author's Last Name, First Name. "Title of Article." *Title of Reference*
> *Book.* Ed. Editor's First and Last Name. Edition number.
> Number of vols. Publication City: Publisher, Year of publication.
> Medium.

> Campbell, James. "The Harlem Renaissance." *The Oxford Companion to*
> *Twentieth-Century Poetry.* Ed. Ian Hamilton. Oxford: Oxford UP,
> 1994. Print.

15. Book in a series

> Editor's Last Name, First Name, ed. *Title of Book.* By Author's First
> and Last Names. Publication City: Publisher, Year of publication.
> Medium. Series Title abbreviated.

> Wall, Cynthia, ed. *The Pilgrim's Progress.* By John Bunyan. New York:
> Norton, 2007. Print. Norton Critical Ed.

16. Sacred text

If you have cited a specific edition of a religious text, you need to include it in your works-cited list.

> *The New English Bible with the Apocrypha.* New York: Oxford UP, 1971. Print.

> *The Torah: A Modern Commentary.* Ed. W. Gunther Plaut. New York:
> Union of Amer. Hebrew Congregations, 1981. Print.

17. Book with a title within the title

When the title of a book contains the title of another long work, do not italicize that title.

> Walker, Roy. *Time Is Free: A Study of* Macbeth. London: Dakers, 1949. Print.

When the book title contains the title of a short work, put the short work in quotation marks, and italicize the entire title (see p. 552).

Thompson, Lawrance Roger. *"Fire and Ice": The Art and Thought of Robert Frost.* New York: Holt, 1942. Print.

18. Edition other than the first

Author's Last Name, First Name. *Title*. Name or number of ed. Publication City: Publisher, Year of publication. Medium.

Hirsch, E. D., Jr., ed. *What Your Second Grader Needs to Know: Fundamentals of a Good Second-Grade Education.* Rev. ed. New York: Doubleday, 1998. Print.

19. Republished work

Give the original publication date after the title, followed by the publication information of the republished edition.

Author's Last Name, First Name. *Title*. Year of original edition. Publication City: Current Publisher, Year of republication. Medium.

Bierce, Ambrose. *Civil War Stories.* 1909. New York: Dover, 1994. Print.

20. Publisher and imprint

Some sources may provide both a publisher's name and an imprint on the title page; if so, include both, with a hyphen between the imprint and the publisher.

Author's Last Name, First Name. *Title*. Publication City: Imprint-Publisher, Year of publication. Medium.

Rowling, J. K. *Harry Potter and the Goblet of Fire.* New York: Levine-Scholastic, 2000. Print.

Print Periodicals

For most articles, you'll need to provide information about the author, the article title and any subtitle, the periodical title, any volume or issue number, the date, inclusive page numbers, and the medium—Print.

author   title   publication

Important Details for Documenting Print Periodicals

- **AUTHORS:** If there is more than one author, list the first author last-name-first and the others first-name-first.
- **TITLES:** Capitalize titles and subtitles as you would for a book. For periodical titles, omit any initial *A, An,* or *The.*
- **DATES:** Abbreviate the names of months except for May, June, or July: Jan., Feb., Mar., Apr., Aug., Sept., Oct., Nov., Dec. Journals paginated by volume or issue need only the year (in parentheses).
- **PAGES:** If an article does not fall on consecutive pages, give the first page with a plus sign (55+).

21. Article in a journal

Author's Last Name, First Name. "Title of Article." *Title of Journal*
       Volume.Issue (Year): Pages. Medium.

Cooney, Brian C. "Considering *Robinson Crusoe*'s 'Liberty of Conscience'
       in an Age of Terror." *College English* 69.3 (2007): 197-215. Print.

22. Article in a journal numbered by issue

Author's Last Name, First Name. "Title of Article." *Title of Journal* Issue
       (Year): Pages. Medium.

Flynn, Kevin. "The Railway in Canadian Poetry." *Canadian Literature*
       174 (2002): 70-95. Print.

23. Article in a magazine

Author's Last Name, First Name. "Title of Article." *Title of Magazine*
       Day Month Year: Pages. Medium.

Walsh, Bryan. "Not a Watt to Be Wasted." *Time* 17 Mar. 2008: 46-47. Print.

For a monthly magazine, include only the month and year.

Fellman, Bruce. "Leading the Libraries." *Yale Alumni Magazine* Feb. 2002:
       26-31. Print.

Documentation Map (MLA) / Article in a Print Journal

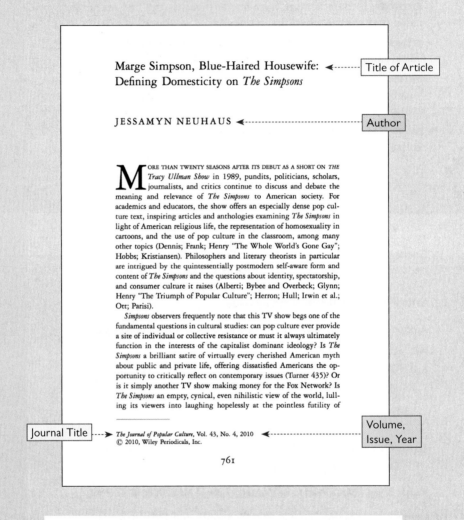

Marge Simpson, Blue-Haired Housewife: **◄-------** Title of Article
Defining Domesticity on *The Simpsons*

JESSAMYN NEUHAUS **◄---------------------------** Author

MORE THAN TWENTY SEASONS AFTER ITS DEBUT AS A SHORT ON *THE Tracy Ullman Show* in 1989, pundits, politicians, scholars, journalists, and critics continue to discuss and debate the meaning and relevance of *The Simpsons* to American society. For academics and educators, the show offers an especially dense pop culture text, inspiring articles and anthologies examining *The Simpsons* in light of American religious life, the representation of homosexuality in cartoons, and the use of pop culture in the classroom, among many other topics (Dennis; Frank; Henry "The Whole World's Gone Gay"; Hobbs; Kristiansen). Philosophers and literary theorists in particular are intrigued by the quintessentially postmodern self-aware form and content of *The Simpsons* and the questions about identity, spectatorship, and consumer culture it raises (Alberti; Bybee and Overbeck; Glynn; Henry "The Triumph of Popular Culture"; Herron; Hull; Irwin et al.; Ott; Parisi).

Simpsons observers frequently note that this TV show begs one of the fundamental questions in cultural studies: can pop culture ever provide a site of individual or collective resistance or must it always ultimately function in the interests of the capitalist dominant ideology? Is *The Simpsons* a brilliant satire of virtually every cherished American myth about public and private life, offering dissatisfied Americans the opportunity to critically reflect on contemporary issues (Turner 435)? Or is it simply another TV show making money for the Fox Network? Is *The Simpsons* an empty, cynical, even nihilistic view of the world, lulling its viewers into laughing hopelessly at the pointless futility of

Journal Title **--->** *The Journal of Popular Culture*, Vol. 43, No. 4, 2010 **◄----------------** Volume, Issue, Year
© 2010, Wiley Periodicals, Inc.

761

Neuhaus, Jessamyn. "Marge Simpson, Blue-Haired Housewife: Defining Domesticity on *The Simpsons*." *Journal of Popular Culture* 43.4 (2010): 761-81. Print.

24. Article in a daily newspaper

> Author's Last Name, First Name. "Title of Article." *Name of Newspaper* Day Month Year: Pages. Medium.

> Springer, Shira. "Celtics Reserves Are Whizzes vs. Wizards." *Boston Globe* 14 Mar. 2005: D41. Print.

To document a particular edition of a newspaper, list the edition (*late ed., natl. ed.,* etc.) after the date. If a section is not identified by a letter or number, put the name of the section after the edition information.

> Burns, John F., and Miguel Helft. "Under Pressure, YouTube Withdraws Muslim Cleric's Videos." *New York Times* 4 Nov. 2010, late ed., sec. 1: 13. Print.

25. Unsigned article

> "Title of Article." *Name of Publication* Day Month Year: Pages. Medium.

> "Being Invisible Closer to Reality." *Atlanta Journal-Constitution* 11 Aug. 2008: A3. Print.

26. Editorial

> "Title." Editorial. *Name of Publication* Day Month Year: Page. Medium.

> "Gas, Cigarettes Are Safe to Tax." Editorial. *Lakeville Journal* 17 Feb. 2005: A10. Print.

27. Letter to the editor

> Author's Last Name, First Name. "Title (if any)." Letter. *Name of Publication* Day Month Year: Page. Medium.

> Festa, Roger. "Social Security: Another Phony Crisis." Letter. *Lakeville Journal* 17 Feb. 2005: A10. Print.

28. Review

Reviewer's Last Name, First Name. "Title (if any) of Review." Rev. of
    Title of Work, by Author's First and Last Names. *Title of Periodical*
    Day Month Year: Pages. Medium.

Frank, Jeffrey. "Body Count." Rev. of *The Exception*, by Christian
    Jungersen. *New Yorker* 30 July 2007: 86-87. Print.

Online Sources

Not every online source gives you all the data that MLA would like to see in
a works-cited entry. Ideally, you will be able to list the author's name, the
title, information about any print publication, information about electronic
publication (title of site, editor, date of first electronic publication and/or
most recent revision, name of the publisher or sponsoring institution), the
publication medium, the date of access, and, if necessary, a URL.

Important Details for Documenting Online Sources

- **AUTHORS OR EDITORS** and **TITLES:** Format authors and titles as you
  would for a print book or periodical.
- **PUBLISHER:** If the name of the publisher or sponsoring institution is unavailable, use *N.p.*
- **DATES:** Abbreviate the months as you would for a print periodical. Although MLA asks for the date when materials were first posted or most
  recently updated, you won't always be able to find that information; if
  it's unavailable, use *n.d.* Be sure to include the date on which you accessed the source.
- **PAGES:** If the documentation calls for page numbers but the source is
  unpaginated, use *n. pag.* in place of page numbers.
- **MEDIUM:** Indicate the medium—web, email, Tweet, and so on.
- **URL:** MLA assumes that readers can locate most sources on the web by
  searching for the author, title, or other identifying information, so they
  don't require a URL for most online sources. When users can't locate the
  source without a URL, give the address of the website in angle brackets.
  When a URL won't fit on one line, break it only after a slash (and do not

author   title   publication

add a hyphen). If a URL is very long, consider giving the URL of the site's home or search page instead.

29. Entire website

For websites with an editor, compiler, director, narrator, or translator, follow the name with the appropriate abbreviation (*ed., comp.*).

> Author's Last Name, First Name. *Title of Site.* Publisher or Sponsoring Institution, Date posted or last updated. Medium. Day Month Year of access.

> Zalta, Edward N., ed. *Stanford Encyclopedia of Philosophy.* Metaphysics Research Lab, Center for the Study of Language and Information, Stanford U, 2007. Web. 14 Nov. 2013.

Personal website

> Author's Last Name, First Name. Home page. Sponsor, Date posted or last updated. Medium. Day Month Year of access.

> Nunberg, Geoffrey. Home page. School of Information, U of California, Berkeley, 2009. Web. 13 Apr. 2013.

30. Work from a website

> Author's Last Name, First Name. "Title of Work." *Title of Site.* Ed. Editor's First and Last Names. Sponsor, Date posted or last updated. Medium. Day Month Year of access.

> Buff, Rachel Ida. "Becoming American." *Immigration History Research Center.* U of Minnesota, 24 Mar. 2008. Web. 4 Apr. 2013.

31. Online book or part of a book

Document a book you access online as you would a print book, adding the name of the site or database, the medium, and the date of access.

> Anderson, Sherwood. *Winesburg, Ohio.* New York: B. W. Huebsch, 1919. *Bartleby.com.* Web. 7 Apr. 2013.

Documentation Map (MLA) / Work from a Website

Title of site; Sponsoring Institution

Title of Work

Date posted

Authors

McIlwain, John, Molly Simpson, and Sara Hammerschmidt. "Housing in
America: Integrating Housing, Health, and Resilience in a Changing
Environment." *Urban Land Institute*. Urban Land Institute, 28 Aug.
2014. Web. 17 Sept. 2016.

To document a part of a book, put the part in quotation marks before the book title. If the online book is paginated, give the pages; if not, use *N. pag.*

> Anderson, Sherwood. "The Strength of God." *Winesburg, Ohio.* New
> York: B. W. Huebsch, 1919. N. pag. *Bartleby.com.* Web. 7 Apr. 2013.

When documenting a book you've downloaded onto a Kindle, iPad, or other digital device, follow the example for a print book, but indicate the ebook format at the end of the reference.

> Larson, Erik. *The Devil in the White City: Murder, Mayhem, and Madness at
> the Fair That Changed America.* New York: Vintage, 2004. Kindle.

32. Article in an online scholarly journal

If a journal does not number pages or if it numbers each article separately, use *n. pag.* in place of page numbers.

> Author's Last Name, First Name. "Title of Article." *Title of Journal*
> Volume.Issue (Year): Pages. Medium. Day Month Year of access.

> Gleckman, Jason. "Shakespeare as Poet or Playwright? The Player's
> Speech in *Hamlet.*" *Early Modern Literary Studies* 11.3 (2006):
> n. pag. Web. 24 June 2013.

33. Article in an online newspaper

> Author's Last Name, First Name. "Title of Article." *Title of Newspaper.*
> Publisher, Day Month Year. Medium. Day Month Year of access.

> Banerjee, Neela. "Proposed Religion-Based Program for Federal
> Inmates Is Canceled." *New York Times.* New York Times, 28 Oct.
> 2006. Web. 24 June 2013.

34. Article in an online magazine

> Author's Last Name, First Name. "Title of Article." *Title of Magazine.*
> Publisher, Date of publication. Medium. Day Month Year of access.

> Lithwick, Dahlia. "Privacy Rights Inc." *Slate.* Washington Post–
> Newsweek Interactive, 14 Oct. 2010. Web. 25 Oct. 2013.

Documentation Map (MLA) /
Article on an Online Magazine

Title of Magazine

Title of Article

Author

Publication Date

Publisher

Segal, Michael. "The Hit Book That Came From Mars." *Nautilus.*
NautilusThink, 8 Jan. 2015. Web. 10 Oct. 2016.

35. Blog entry

> Author's Last Name, First Name. "Title of Entry." *Title of Blog*. Sponsor,
>   Day Month Year posted. Medium. Day Month Year of access.

> Gladwell, Malcolm. "Enron and Newspapers." *Gladwell.com*. N.p., 4 Jan.
>   2007. Web. 26 Aug. 2013.

If the entry has no title, use "Blog entry" without quotation marks. Document a whole blog as you would an entire website (see no. 29). If the publisher or sponsor is unavailable, use *N.p.*

36. Article accessed through a database

For articles accessed through a library's subscription services, such as InfoTrac and EBSCO, give the publication information for the source, followed by the name of the database.

> Author's Last Name, First Name. "Title of Article." *Title of Periodical*
>   Date or Volume.Issue (Year): Pages. *Database Name*. Medium.
>   Day Month Year of access.

> Stalter, Sunny. "Subway Ride and Subway System in Hart Crane's 'The
>   Tunnel.'" *Journal of Modern Literature* 33.2 (2010): 70-91. *Academic
>   Search Complete*. Web. 28 May 2013.

37. Online editorial

> "Title of Editorial." Editorial. *Title of Site*. Publisher, Day Month Year of
>   publication. Medium. Day Month Year of access.

> "Keep Drinking Age at 21." Editorial. *ChicagoTribune.com*. Chicago
>   Tribune, 25 Aug. 2008. Web. 28 Aug. 2013.

38. Online film review

> Reviewer's Last Name, First Name. "Title of Review." Rev. of *Title of
>   Work*, dir. First and Last Names. *Title of Site*. Publisher, Day Month
>   Year posted. Medium. Day Month Year of access.

Documentation Map (MLA) /
Article Accessed through a Database

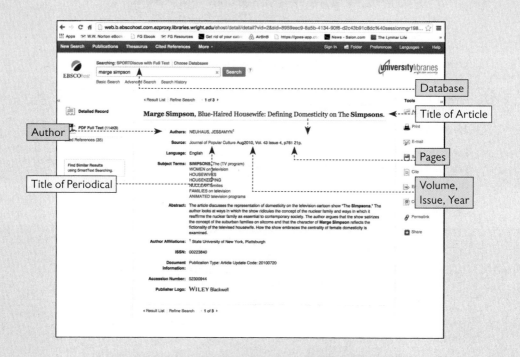

Neuhaus, Jessamyn. "Marge Simpson, Blue-Haired Housewife: Defining
    Domesticity on *The Simpsons*." *Journal of Popular Culture* 43.4 (2010):
    761-81. *SportsDiscus with Full Text*. Web. 24 Mar. 2016.

Edelstein, David. "Best Served Cold." Rev. of *The Social Network,* dir. David Fincher. *New York Magazine.* New York Media, I Oct. 2010. Web. 3 Nov. 2013.

39. Email

Writer's Last Name, First Name. "Subject Line." Message to the author. Day Month Year of message. Medium.

Smith, William. "Teaching Grammar—Some Thoughts." Message to the author. 19 Nov. 2013. Email.

40. Posting on an online forum

Writer's Last Name, First Name. "Title of Posting." *Name of Forum.* Sponsor, Day Month Year of posting. Medium. Day Month Year of access.

Mintz, Stephen H. "Manumission during the Revolution." *H-Net List on Slavery.* Michigan State U, 14 Sept. 2006. Web. 18 Apr. 2013.

41. Article in an online reference work

"Title of Article." *Title of Reference Work.* Sponsor, Date of work. Medium. Day Month Year of access.

"Generation Xerox." *Urban Dictionary.* Urban Dictionary, 13 Sept. 2013. Web. 25 Oct. 2013.

42. Wiki entry

"Title of Entry." *Title of Wiki.* Sponsor, Day Month Year updated. Medium. Day Month Year of access.

"Pi." *Wikipedia.* Wikimedia Foundation, 28 Aug. 2013. Web. 2 Sept. 2013.

43. Podcast

Performer or Host's Last Name, First Name. "Title of Podcast." Host Host's First and Last Name. *Title of Program.* Sponsor, Day Month Year posted. Medium. Day Month Year of access.

Blumberg, Alex, and Adam Davidson. "The Giant Pool of Money." Host Ira Glass. *This American Life*. Chicago Public Radio, 9 May 2008. Web. 18 Sept. 2013.

44. Tweet

Author's Last Name, First Name (User Name). "Full tweet text." Day Month Year, Time. Medium.

Stern, Michael (Roadfood123). "Ice creamorama: Dr. Mike's is now open weekdays." 21 Mar. 2012, 5:21 p.m. Tweet.

Other Kinds of Sources

Many of the sources in this section can be found online, and you'll find examples here for how to document them. If there is no web model here, start with the guidelines most appropriate for the source you need to document, omit the original medium, and end your reference with the title of the website, italicized; the medium (Web); and the day, month, and year of access.

45. Advertisement

Product or Company. Advertisement. *Title of Periodical* Date or Volume.Issue (Year): Page. Medium.

Bebe. Advertisement. *Lucky* Sept. 2011: 112. Print.

Advertisement on the web

Rolex. Advertisement. *Time*. Time, n.d. Web. 1 Apr. 2013.

46. Art

Artist's Last Name, First Name. *Title of Art*. Medium. Year. Institution, City.

Van Gogh, Vincent. *The Potato Eaters*. Oil on canvas. 1885. Van Gogh Museum, Amsterdam.

author   title   publication

Art on the web

Warhol, Andy. *Self-Portrait.* 1979. J. Paul Getty Museum, Los Angeles.
The Getty. Web. 29 Mar. 2007.

Document photographs you find online by giving the photographer, title, and date of the image, if available. If the date is unavailable, use *n.d.* For photographs you take yourself, see no. 65.

Donnell, Ryan. *At a Pre-Civil War Railroad Construction Site Outside of Philadelphia.* 2010. Smithsonian Institution. *Smithsonian.com.*
Web. 3 Nov. 2013.

47. Cartoon

Artist's Last Name, First Name. "Title of Cartoon (if titled)." Cartoon.
Title of Periodical Date or Volume.Issue (Year): Page. Medium.

Chast, Roz. "The Three Wise Men of Thanksgiving." Cartoon. *New Yorker* 1 Dec. 2003: 174. Print.

Cartoon on the web

Horsey, David. Cartoon. *Seattle Post-Intelligencer.* Seattle
Post-Intelligencer, 20 Apr. 2013. Web. 21 Apr. 2013.

48. Dissertation

Treat a published dissertation as you would a book, but after its title, add the abbreviation *Diss.*, the institution, and the date of the dissertation.

Author's Last Name, First Name. *Title.* Diss. Institution, Year.
Publication City: Publisher, Year. Medium.

Goggin, Peter N. *A New Literacy Map of Research and Scholarship in Computers and Writing.* Diss. Indiana U of Pennsylvania, 2000.
Ann Arbor: UMI, 2001. Print.

For unpublished dissertations, put the title in quotation marks and end with the degree-granting institution and the year (see p. 566).

Kim, Loel. "Students Respond to Teacher Comments: A Comparison of Online Written and Voice Modalities." Diss. Carnegie Mellon U, 1998. Print.

49. CD-ROM or DVD-ROM

Title. Any pertinent information about the edition, release, or version. Publication City: Publisher, Year of publication. Medium.

Othello. Princeton: Films for the Humanities and Sciences, 1998. CD-ROM.

To document only part of the CD-ROM or DVD-ROM, name the part as you would a part of a book.

"Snow Leopard." *Encarta Encyclopedia 2007*. Seattle: Microsoft, 2007. CD-ROM.

50. Film, DVD, or video clip

Title. Dir. Director's First and Last Names. Perf. Lead Actors' First and Last Names. Distributor, Year of release. Medium.

Casablanca. Dir. Michael Curtiz. Perf. Humphrey Bogart, Ingrid Bergman, and Claude Rains. Warner, 1942. Film.

To document a particular person's work, such as a screenwriter, start with that name.

Cody, Diablo, scr. *Juno*. Dir. Jason Reitman. Perf. Ellen Page and Michael Cera. Fox Searchlight, 2007. DVD.

Document a video clip as you would a short work from a website.

Director's Last Name, First Name, dir. "Title of Video." *Title of Site*. Sponsor, Day Month Year of release. Medium. Day Month Year of access.

PivotMasterDX, dir. "Bounce!" *YouTube*. YouTube, 14 June 2008. Web. 21 June 2013.

51. Broadcast interview

Subject's Last Name, First Name. Interview. *Title of Program*. Network.
Station, City. Day Month Year. Medium.

Gates, Henry Louis, Jr. Interview. *Fresh Air.* NPR. WNYC, New York.
9 Apr. 2002. Radio.

52. Published interview

Subject's Last Name, First Name. Interview, or "Title of Interview."
Title of Periodical Date or Volume.Issue (Year): Pages. Medium.

Stone, Oliver. Interview. *Esquire* Nov. 2004: 170. Print.

53. Personal interview

Subject's Last Name, First Name. Personal interview. Day Month Year.

Roddick, Andy. Personal interview. 17 Aug. 2013.

54. Unpublished letter

For medium, use MS for a handwritten letter and TS for a typed one.

Author's Last Name, First Name. Letter to the author. Day Month Year.
Medium.

Quindlen, Anna. Letter to the author. 11 Apr. 2013. MS.

55. Published letter

Letter Writer's Last Name, First Name. Letter to First and Last Names.
Day Month Year of letter. *Title of Book*. Ed. Editor's First and Last
Names. City: Publisher, Year of publication. Pages. Medium.

White, E. B. Letter to Carol Angell. 28 May 1970. *Letters of E. B. White.*
Ed. Dorothy Lobarno Guth. New York: Harper, 1976. 600. Print.

56. Map or chart

Title of Map. Map. City: Publisher, Year of publication. Medium.

Toscana. Map. Milan: Touring Club Italiano, 1987. Print.

Map on the web

"Portland, Oregon." Map. Google Maps. Google, 25 Apr. 2013. Web. 25
Apr. 2013.

57. Musical score

Composer's Last Name, First Name. Title of Composition. Year of
composition. Publication City: Publisher, Year of publication.
Medium. Series Information (if any).

Beethoven, Ludwig van. String Quartet No. 13 in B Flat, Op. 130. 1825.
New York: Dover, 1970. Print.

58. Sound recording

Artist's Last Name, First Name. Title of Long Work. Other pertinent
details about the artists. Manufacturer, Year of release. Medium.

Beethoven, Ludwig van. Missa Solemnis. Perf. Westminster Choir and
New York Philharmonic. Cond. Leonard Bernstein. Sony, 1992. CD.

Whether you list the composer, conductor, or performer first depends on
where you want to place the emphasis. If you are discussing a specific song,
put it in quotation marks before the name of the recording.

Brown, Greg. "Canned Goods." The Live One. Red House, 1995. MP3 file.

For a spoken-word recording, you may begin with the writer, speaker, or producer, depending on your emphasis.

Dale, Jim, narr. Harry Potter and the Deathly Hallows. By J. K. Rowling.
Random House Audio, 2007. CD.

59. Oral presentation

Speaker's Last Name, First Name. "Title of Presentation." Sponsoring Institution. Site, City. Day Month Year. Medium.

Cassin, Michael. "Nature in the Raw—The Art of Landscape Painting." Berkshire Institute for Lifetime Learning. Clark Art Institute, Williamstown. 24 Mar. 2005. Lecture.

60. Paper from proceedings of a conference

Author's Last Name, First Name. "Title of Paper." *Title of Conference Proceedings*. Date, City. Ed. Editor's First and Last Names. Publication City: Publisher, Year. Pages. Medium.

Zolotow, Charlotte. "Passion in Publishing." *A Sea of Upturned Faces: Proceedings of the Third Pacific Rim Conference on Children's Literature*. 1986, Los Angeles. Ed. Winifred Ragsdale. Metuchen: Scarecrow P, 1989. 236-49. Print.

61. Performance

Title. By Author's First and Last Names. Other appropriate details about the performance. Site, City. Day Month Year. Medium.

Take Me Out. By Richard Greenberg. Dir. Scott Plate. Perf. Caleb Sekeres. Dobama Theatre, Cleveland. 17 Aug. 2007. Performance.

62. Television or radio program

"Title of Episode." *Title of Program*. Other appropriate information about the writer, director, actors, etc. Network. Station, City, Day Month Year of broadcast. Medium.

"The Silencer." *Criminal Minds*. Writ. Erica Messer. Dir. Glenn Kershaw. NBC. WCNC, Charlotte, 26 Sept. 2012. Television.

Television or radio on the web

"Bush's War." *Frontline*. Writ. and dir. Michael Kirk. PBS, 24 Mar. 2008.
    PBS.org. Web. 10 May 2013.

63. Pamphlet, brochure, or press release

Author's Last Name, First Name. *Title of Publication*. Publication City:
    Publisher, Year. Medium.

Bowers, Catherine. *Can We Find a Home Here? Answering Questions of
    Interfaith Couples*. Boston: UUA Publications, n.d. Print.

To document a press release, include the day and month before the year.

64. Legal source

The name of a court case is not italicized in a works-cited entry.

Names of the First Plaintiff v. First Defendant. Volume Name Page
    numbers of law report. Name of Court. Year of decision. Source
    information for medium consulted.

District of Columbia v. Heller. 540 US 290. Supreme Court of the US.
    2008. *Supreme Court Collection*. Legal Information Inst., Cornell U
    Law School, n.d. Web. 18 Mar. 2013.

For acts of law, include both the Public Law number and the Statutes at Large
volume and page numbers.

Name of Law. Public law number. Statutes at Large Volume Stat. Pages.
    Day Month Year enacted. Medium.

Military Commissions Act. Pub. L. 109-366. 120 Stat. 2083-2521. 17 Oct.
    2006. Print.

65. MP3, JPEG, PDF, or other digital file

For downloaded songs, photographs, PDFs, and other documents stored on
your computer or another digital device, follow the guidelines for the type

author   title   publication

of work you are citing (art, journal article, and so on) and give the file type as the medium.

> Talking Heads. "Burning Down the House." *Speaking in Tongues*. Sire, 1983. Digital file.

> Taylor, Aaron. "Twilight of the Idols: Performance, Melodramatic Villainy, and *Sunset Boulevard*." *Journal of Film and Video* 59 (2007): 13-31. PDF file.

Sources Not Covered by MLA

To document a source for which MLA does not provide guidelines, look for models similar to the source you are citing. Give any information readers will need in order to find your source themselves—author; title, subtitle; publisher and/or sponsor; medium; dates; and any other pertinent information. You might want to try out your reference note yourself, to be sure it will lead others to your source.

FORMATTING A RESEARCH ESSAY

Name, course, title. MLA does not require a separate title page. In the upper left-hand corner of your first page, include your name, your professor's name, the name of the course, and the date. Center the title of your paper on the line after the date; capitalize it as you would a book title.

Page numbers. In the upper right-hand corner of each page, one-half inch below the top of the page, include your last name and the page number. Number pages consecutively throughout your paper.

Font, spacing, margins, and indents. Choose a font that is easy to read (such as Times New Roman) and that provides a clear contrast between regular and italic text. Double-space the entire paper, including your works-cited list. Set one-inch margins at the top, bottom, and sides of your text; do not justify the text. The first line of each paragraph should be indented one-half inch from the left margin.

Long quotations. When quoting more than three lines of poetry, more than four lines of prose, or dialogue between characters in a drama, set off the quotation from the rest of your text, indenting it one inch (or ten to fourteen spaces) from the left margin. Do not use quotation marks, and put any parenthetical documentation *after* the final punctuation.

> In *Eastward to Tartary*, Kaplan captures ancient and contemporary
> Antioch for us:
>> At the height of its glory in the Roman-Byzantine age, when
>> it had an amphitheater, public baths, aqueducts, and sewage
>> pipes, half a million people lived in Antioch. Today the population
>> is only 125,000. With sour relations between Turkey and
>> Syria, and unstable politics throughout the Middle East,
>> Antioch is now a backwater—seedy and tumbledown, with
>> relatively few tourists. I found it altogether charming. (123)

> In the first stanza of Arnold's "Dover Beach," the exclamations make
> clear that the speaker is addressing a companion who is also present in
> the scene:
>> Come to the window, sweet is the night air!
>> Only, from the long line of spray
>> Where the sea meets the moon-blanched land,
>> Listen! You hear the grating roar
>> Of pebbles which the waves draw back, and fling. (6-10)

Be careful to maintain the poet's line breaks. If a line does not fit on one line of your paper, put the extra words on the next line. Indent that line an additional quarter inch (or two spaces).

Illustrations. Insert illustrations in your paper close to the text that discusses them. For tables, provide a number (*Table 1*) and a title on separate lines above the table. Below the table, include a caption and provide information about the source. For figures (graphs, charts, photos, and so on), provide a figure number (*Fig. 1*), caption, and source information below the figure. If you give only brief information about the source (such as a parenthetical note), or if the source is cited elsewhere in your text, include the source in your list of works cited. Be sure to discuss any illustrations, and make it clear how they relate to the rest of your text.

List of works cited. Start your list on a new page, following any notes. Center the title and double-space the entire list. Each entry should begin at the left margin, and subsequent lines should be indented one-half inch (or five to seven spaces). Alphabetize the list by authors' last names (or by editors' or translators' names, if appropriate). Alphabetize works that have no identifiable author or editor by title, disregarding *A*, *An*, and *The*. If you cite more than one work by a single author, list them all alphabetically by title, and use three hyphens in place of the author's name for the second and subsequent titles (see no. 2 on p. 545).

SAMPLE RESEARCH ESSAY

Walter Przybylowski wrote the following analysis, "Holding Up the Hollywood Stagecoach: The European Take on the Western," for a first-year writing course. It is formatted according to the guidelines of the *MLA Handbook for Writers of Research Papers*, 7th edition (2009).

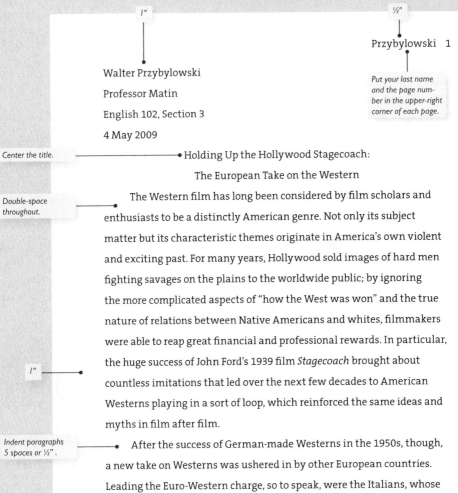

1"   ½"

Przybylowski   1

Put your last name and the page number in the upper-right corner of each page.

Walter Przybylowski

Professor Matin

English 102, Section 3

4 May 2009

Center the title.

Holding Up the Hollywood Stagecoach:

The European Take on the Western

Double-space throughout.

    The Western film has long been considered by film scholars and enthusiasts to be a distinctly American genre. Not only its subject matter but its characteristic themes originate in America's own violent and exciting past. For many years, Hollywood sold images of hard men fighting savages on the plains to the worldwide public; by ignoring the more complicated aspects of "how the West was won" and the true nature of relations between Native Americans and whites, filmmakers were able to reap great financial and professional rewards. In particular, the huge success of John Ford's 1939 film *Stagecoach* brought about countless imitations that led over the next few decades to American Westerns playing in a sort of loop, which reinforced the same ideas and myths in film after film.

1"   1"

Indent paragraphs 5 spaces or ½".

    After the success of German-made Westerns in the 1950s, though, a new take on Westerns was ushered in by other European countries. Leading the Euro-Western charge, so to speak, were the Italians, whose cynical, often politically pointed Westerns left a permanent impact on an American-based genre. Europeans, particularly the Italians, challenged the dominant conventions of the American Western by complicating the morality of the characters, blurring the lines between

1"

Przybylowski 2

good and evil, and also by complicating the traditional narrative, visual, and aural structures of Westerns. In this way, the genre motifs that *Stagecoach* initiated are explored in the European Westerns of the 1950s, 1960s, and early 1970s, yet with a striking difference in style. Specifically, Sergio Leone's 1968 film *Once upon a Time in the West* broke many of the rules set by the Hollywood Western and in the process created a new visual language for the Western. Deconstructing key scenes from this film reveals the demythologization at work in many of the Euro-Westerns, which led to a genre enriched by its presentation of a more complicated American West.

 Stagecoach is a perfect example of almost all the visual, sound, and plot motifs that would populate "classic" Hollywood Westerns for the next few decades. The story concerns a group of people, confined for most of the movie inside a stagecoach, who are attempting to cross a stretch of land made dangerous by Apache Indians on the warpath. Little effort is made to develop the characters of the Indians, who appear mainly as a narrative device, adversaries that the heroes must overcome in order to maintain their peaceful existence. This plot, with minor changes, could be used as a general description for countless Westerns. In his book *Crowded Prairie: American National Identity in the Hollywood Western*, Michael Coyne explains the significance of *Stagecoach* to the Western genre and its influence in solidifying the genre's archetypes:

> [I]t was *Stagecoach* which . . . redefined the contours of the myth. The good outlaw, the whore with a heart of gold, the Madonna/Magdalene dichotomy between opposing female

Quotations of more than 4 lines are set off from the main text and indented 10 to 14 spaces or 1".

Przybylowski   3

leads, the drunken philosopher, the last-minute cavalry rescue, the lonely walk down Main Street--all became stereotypes from *Stagecoach*'s archetypes. *Stagecoach* quickly became the model against which other "A" Westerns would be measured. (18-19)

In a set-off quotation, the parenthetical source citation follows the closing punctuation.

Coyne is not exaggerating when he calls it "the model": in fact, all of these stereotypes became a sort of checklist of things that audiences expected to see. The reliance on a preconceived way to sell Western films to the public--where you could always tell the good characters from the bad and knew before the film ended how each character would end up-- led to certain genre expectations that the directors of the Euro-Westerns would later knowingly reconfigure. As the influential critic Pauline Kael wrote in her 1965 book *Kiss Kiss Bang Bang*, "The original *Stagecoach* had a mixture of reverie and reverence about the American past that made the picture seem almost folk art; we wanted to believe in it even if we didn't" (52).

Verb in signal phrase is past tense because date of source is mentioned.

Parenthetical reference following a quotation within the main text goes before the closing punctuation of the sentence.

There seemed to be a need not just in Americans but in moviegoers around the world to believe that there was (or had been) a great untamed land out there just waiting to be cultivated. More important, as Kael pointed out, Americans wanted to believe that the building of America was a wholly righteous endeavor wherein the land was free for the taking--the very myth that Europeans later debunked through parody and subversive filmmaking techniques. According to Theresa Harlan, author of works on Native American art, the myth was based in the need of early white settlers to make their elimination of American Indians more palatable in light of the settlers' professed Christian beliefs. In her article "Adjusting the Focus for an Indigenous Presence," Harlan writes that

> Eurocentric frontier ideology and the representations of indigenous people it produced were used to convince many American settlers that indigenous people were incapable of discerning the difference between a presumed civilized existence and their own "primitive" state. (6)

Although this myth had its genesis long before the advent of motion pictures, the Hollywood Western drew inspiration from it and continued to legitimize and reinforce its message. *Stagecoach*, with its high level of technical skill and artistry, redefined the contours of the myth, and a close look at the elements that made the film the "classic" model of the Western is imperative in order to truly understand its influence.

The musical themes that underscore the actions of the characters are especially powerful in this regard and can be as powerful as the characters' visual representation on screen. In *Stagecoach*, an Apache does not appear until more than halfway through the movie, but whenever one is mentioned, the soundtrack fills with sinister and foreboding drumbeats. The first appearance of Indians is a scene without dialogue, in which the camera pans between the stagecoach crossing through the land and Apaches watching from afar. The music that accompanies this scene is particularly telling, since as the camera pans between stagecoach and Apaches, the music shifts in tone dramatically from a pleasant melody to a score filled with dread. When the heroes shoot and kill the Apaches, then, the viewer has already been subjected to specific film techniques to give the stagecoach riders moral certitude in their annihilation of the alien menace. To emphasize this point, the music swells victoriously every time an Apache is shown falling from a horse. This kind of score is powerful stuff to accompany an image and does its best to tell the viewers how they should react. When Europeans start to make Westerns, the line of moral certitude will become less distinct.

In her essay "Of Mother Nature and Marlboro Men: An Inquiry into the Cultural Meanings of Landscape Photography," Deborah Bright argues that landscape photography has reinforced certain formulaic myths about landscape, and the same can be said of the Hollywood Western during the 1940s and 1950s. For example, in *Stagecoach*, when the stagecoach finally sets out for its journey through Apache territory, a fence is juxtaposed against the vast wide-open country in the foreground. The meaning is clear--the stagecoach is leaving civilized society to venture into the wilds of the West, and music swells as the coach crosses into that vast landscape (fig. 1). Ford uses landscape in this way to engender in the audience the desired response of longing for a time gone past, where there was land free for the taking and plenty to go around. Yet Bright suggests that "[i]f we are to redeem landscape photography from its narrow self-reflexive project, why not openly question the assumptions about nature and culture that it has traditionally served and use our practice instead to criticize them?" (141).

Figure number calls readers' attention to illustration.

Brackets show that the writer has changed a capital letter to lowercase to make the quotation fit smoothly into his own sentence.

Fig. 1. In *Stagecoach*, swelling music signals the coach's passage through the Western landscape. Photograph from *Internet Movie Database*, www.imdb.com.

This is exactly what Europeans, and Italians in particular, seem to have done with the Western. When Europeans started to make their own Westerns, they took advantage of their outsider status in relation to an American genre by openly questioning the myths that have been established by *Stagecoach* and its cinematic brethren.

Sergio Leone's *Once upon a Time in the West* is a superior example of a European artist's take on the art form of the American Western. The

title alone signals the element of storytelling: in a sublime stroke
of titling, Leone makes the connection between Western films and
fairy tales and announces that the genre myths that *Stagecoach*
presented for audiences to revel in will now be questioned. In his book
Spaghetti Westerns, Christopher Frayling observes that "*Once Upon
a Time* is concerned with the 'language' and 'syntax' of the Western
. . . an unmasking or 'display' of the terminology of the genre" (213).
The "plot" of the film is flimsy, driven by the efforts of a mysterious
character played by Charles Bronson to avenge himself against Henry
Fonda's character, a lowdown gunfighter trying to become a legitimate
businessman. Claudia Cardinale plays a prostitute who is trying to put
her past behind her. All of these classic types from countless American
Westerns are integrated into the "Iron Horse" plotline, wherein
the coming of the railroad signifies great changes in the West. The
similarities to American Westerns, on paper at least, seem to be so great
as to make *Once upon a Time* almost a copy of what had long been done
in Hollywood, but a closer look at European Westerns and at this film in
particular shows that Leone is consciously sending up the stereotypes.
After all, he needs to work within the genre's language if he is to
adequately challenge it.

　　The opening scene of *Once upon a Time* runs roughly ten minutes
and provides an introduction to many of the aesthetic and ideological
changes made by the European Western to the American model. The
viewer quickly notices how little dialogue is spoken during the whole
ten minutes, since the requirements of post-synchronization (the

Przybylowski 8

rerecording of the movie's dialogue after filming in order to produce a clearer soundtrack) and country-specific dubbing into multiple languages resulted in a reliance on strong visual storytelling. Financial reasons made English the default language for most Euro-Westerns since it produced the largest market and, consequently, the greatest monetary rewards. Even cast members who could not speak it would sometimes mouth the words in English. However, the use of post-synchronization has an unsettling effect on any viewer, even an English-speaking one, who is used to the polished soundtracks of a Hollywood film. When viewers experience a post-synchronized film, the result is a distancing from the material; certain characters match the words coming out of their mouths better than others, so the movie takes on a surreal edge. This visual touch perfectly complements Leone's goal--to divorce the reality of the West from the myths encouraged by American Westerns.

During the opening of *Once upon a Time in the West*, the viewer is given a kind of audio and visual tour of Euro-Western aesthetics. Leone introduces three gunmen in typical Italian Western style, with the first presented by a cut to a dusty boot heel from which the camera slowly pans up until it reaches the top of the character's cowboy hat. During this pan, the gunman's gear and its authenticity--a major aspect of the Italian Western--can be taken in by the audience. A broader examination of the genre would show that many Euro-Westerns use this tactic of hyperrealistic attention to costuming and weaponry, which Ignacio Ramonet argues is intended to distract the viewer from the unreality of the landscape:

Przybylowski   9

Extreme realism of bodies (hairy, greasy, foul-smelling), clothes
or objects (including mania for weapons) in Italian films is
above all intended to compensate for the complete fraud of
the space and origins. The green pastures, farms and cattle of
American Westerns are replaced by large, deserted canyons. (32)

In the opening scene, the other two gunfighters are introduced by
a camera panning across the room, allowing characters to materialize
seemingly out of nowhere. Roger Ebert notes that Leone

established a rule that he follows throughout . . . that the
ability to see is limited by the sides of the frame. At important
moments in the film, what the camera cannot see, the
characters cannot see, and that gives Leone the freedom to
surprise us with entrances that cannot be explained by the
practical geography of his shots.

It is these aesthetic touches created to compensate for a fraudulent
landscape that ushered in a new visual language for the Western. The
opening of *Once upon a Time in the West* undercuts any preconceived
notion of how a Western should be filmed, and this is exactly Leone's
intention: "The director had obviously enjoyed dilating the audience's
sense of time, exploiting, in his ostentatious way, the rhetoric of the
Western, and dwelling on the tiniest details to fulfill his intention"
(Frayling 197). By using jarring edits with amplified sounds, Leone
informs the audience not only that he has seen all the popular
Hollywood Westerns, but that he is purposely not going to give them
that kind of movie. The opening ten-minute scene would be considered

No page number
given for online
source.

When no signal
phrase is used to
introduce a quota-
tion, the author's
name is included in
the parenthetical
citation.

needlessly long in a typical Hollywood Western, but Leone is not making a copy of a Hollywood Western, and the length of such scenes allows for more meditation on the styling of the genre. In fact, it is this reliance on the audience's previously established knowledge of Westerns that allows Euro-Westerns to subvert the genre. Barry Langford, writing for *Film History*, claims that

> *Once Upon a Time* strips bare the form's claims on historical verisimilitude and pushes its innately ritualized and stylized aspects to near-parodic extremes that evacuate the film of narrative credibility and psychological realism alike. (31)

Leone and other directors of Euro-Westerns are asking the public to open their eyes, to not believe what is shown; they are attempting to take the camera's power away by parodying its effect. When Leone has characters magically appear in the frame, or amplifies the squeaking of a door hinge on a soundtrack, he is ridiculing the basic laws that govern American Westerns. The opening of *Once upon a Time* can be read as a sort of primer for what is about to come for the rest of the film, and its power leaves viewers more attuned to what they are watching.

Leone's casting also works to heighten the film's subversive effect. Henry Fonda, the quintessential good guy in classic Hollywood Westerns like *My Darling Clementine*, is cast as the ruthless Frank, a gunman shown murdering a small child early in the film. In a 1966 article on Italian Westerns in the *Saturday Evening Post*, Italian director Maurizio Lucidi gave some insight into the European perspective that lay behind such choices:

Przybylowski   11

We're adding the Italian concept of realism to an old American myth, and it's working. Look at Jesse James. In your country he's a saint. Over here we play him as a gangster. That's what he was. Europeans today are too sophisticated to believe in the honest gunman movie anymore. They want the truth and that's what we're giving them. (qtd. in Fox 55)

A citation of a source the writer found quoted in another source.

Leone knew exactly what he was doing, and his casting of Fonda went a long way toward confusing the audience's sympathies and complicating the simple good guy versus bad guy model of Hollywood films. For this reason, Fonda's entrance in the film is worth noting. The scene begins with a close-up of a shotgun barrel, which quickly explodes in a series of (gun)shots that establish a scene of a father and son out hunting near their homestead. Here, Leone starts to move the camera more, with pans from father to son and a crane shot of their house as they return home to a picnic table with an abundance of food: the family is apparently about to celebrate something. Throughout this scene, crickets chirp on the soundtrack--until Leone abruptly cuts them off, the sudden silence quickly followed by close-ups of the uneasy faces of three family members. Leone is teasing the audience: he puts the crickets back on the soundtrack until out of nowhere we hear a gunshot. Instead of then focusing on the source or the target of the gunshot, the camera pans off to the sky, and for a moment the viewer thinks the shot is from a hunter. We next see a close-up of the father's face as he looks off into the distance, then is rattled when he sees his daughter grasping the air, obviously shot. As he runs toward her, tracked by the camera in a startling way, he is quickly shot down himself.

    The family has been attacked seemingly out of nowhere, with only a young boy still alive. During the massacre, there is no musical score, just the abstract brutality of the slayings. Then Leone gives us a long camera shot of men appearing out of dust-blown winds, from nearby brush. It is obvious to the viewer that these men are the killers, but there is no clear sight of their faces: Leone uses long camera shots of their backs and an overhead shot as they converge on the young boy. This is the moment when Leone introduces Henry Fonda; he starts with the camera on the back of Fonda's head and then does a slow track around until his face is visible. At this point, audience members around the world would still have a hard time believing Fonda was a killer of these innocent people. Through crosscutting between the young boy's confused face and Fonda's smiling eyes, Leone builds a doubt in the audience--maybe he will not kill the boy. Then the crosscutting is interrupted with a close-up of Fonda's large Colt coming out of its holster, and Ennio Morricone's score, full of sadness, becomes audible. The audience's fears are realized: Fonda is indeed the killer. This scene is a clear parody of Hollywood casting stereotypes, and Leone toys with audience expectations by turning upside down the myth of the noble outlaw as portrayed by John Wayne in *Stagecoach*.

    During the late 1960s and the early 1970s, Europeans were at odds with many of the foreign policies of the United States, a hostility expressed in Ramonet's characterization of this period as one "when American imperialism in Latin America and Southeast Asia was showing itself to be particularly brutal" (33). Morton, the railroad baron who is Frank's unscrupulous employer in *Once upon a Time in the West*, can easily be read as a critique of the sometimes misguided ways Americans went about bringing their way of life to other countries. Morton represents the bringer of civilization, usually a good thing in the classic Western genre, where civilization meant doctors, schools, homes for everyone. But the Europeans question how this civilization was built. Leone, in a telling quotation, gives his perspective: "I see the history of the West as really the reign of violence by violence" (qtd. in Frayling 134).

Leone's critique of the "civilizing" of the American West becomes apparent in his depiction of Morton's demise at the hands of a bandit gang that Frank has tried to frame for the murder of the family. As Frank returns to Morton's train, wheezing and gasping resonates from the track. In a long, one-take shot, the camera follows Frank as he looks for Morton, and in the process dead and dying bodies in various poses are revealed strewn about the ground. Many people have died for the dream of "civilizing" the West, and there is nothing noble in their deaths. Frank finally finds Morton crawling along outside the train in mud, striving to reach a puddle; as he dies, the lapping waves of the Pacific Ocean--the goal toward which the civilizing of the West always pushes--can be heard.

Instead of the civilizing myth and its representations, the concern of *Once upon a Time*--and the Euro-Western in general--is to give voice to the perspective of the marginal characters: the Native Americans, Mexicans, and Chinese who rarely rated a position of significance in a Hollywood Western. In *Once upon a Time*, Bronson's character Harmonica pushes the plot forward with his need to avenge. Harmonica can be seen as either Mexican or Native American, though it matters little since his character stands in for all the racial stereotypes that populated the American Western genre. When he and Frank meet in the movie's climactic duel, Frank is clearly perplexed about why this man wants to fight him, but his ego makes it impossible for him to refuse (fig. 2).

Fig. 2. The climactic duel in *Once upon a Time in the West* between Frank (Henry Fonda, foreground) and Harmonica (Charles Bronson, background) challenges the casting and costuming stereotypes of the Hollywood Western. Photograph from *Internet Movie Database*, www.imdb.com.

They meet in an abandoned yard, with one character in the extreme foreground and the other in the extreme background. The difference between the two is thus presented from both physical and ideological standpoints: Frank guns down settlers to make way for the railroad (and its owner), whereas Harmonica helps people to fend for themselves. Morricone's score dominates the soundtrack during this final scene, with a harmonica blaring away throughout. The costuming of Frank in black and Harmonica in white is an ironic throwback to classic Hollywood costuming and one that suggests Harmonica is prevailing over the racial stereotypes of American Westerns. Leone milks the scene for all it's worth, with the camera circling Harmonica as Frank looks for a perfect point to start the duel. Harmonica never moves, his face steadily framed in a close-up. Meanwhile, Frank is shown in mostly long shots; his body language shows that he is uncertain about the outcome of the duel, while Harmonica knows the ending.

As the two seem about to draw, the camera pushes into Harmonica's eyes, and there is a flashback to a younger Frank walking toward the camera, putting a harmonica into the mouth of a boy (the young Harmonica), and forcing him to participate in Frank's hanging of the boy's older brother. This brutal scene, in which Frank unknowingly seals his own destiny, is set in actual American locations and is taken directly from John Ford Westerns; Leone is literally bringing home the violence dealt to minorities in America's past. As soon as the brother is hanged, the scene returns to the present, and Frank is shot through the heart. As he lies dying, we see a look of utter disbelief on his face as he asks Harmonica, "Who are you?" At this moment, a harmonica is shoved into his mouth. Only then does recognition play over Frank's face; as he falls to the ground, his face in close-up is a grotesque death-mask not unlike the massacred victims of Morton's train. The idea of past misdeeds coming back to haunt characters in the present is a clear attempt to challenge the idea that the settlers had a moral right to conquer and destroy indigenous people in order to "win" the West.

The tremendous success of *Stagecoach* was both a blessing and curse for the Western genre. Without it, the genre would surely never have gained the success it did, but this success came with ideological and creative limitations. Both the popularity and the limitations of the American Western may have inspired European directors to attempt something new with the genre, and unlike American filmmakers, they could look more objectively at our history and our myths. Leone's demythologization of the American Western has proved a valuable addition to the Western genre. The effect of the Euro-Western can be seen in American cinema as early as *The Wild Bunch* in 1969--and as recently as the attention in *Brokeback Mountain* to types of Western characters usually marginalized. In this way, Italian Westerns forced a new level of viewing of the Western tradition that made it impossible to ever return to the previous Hollywood model.

List of works cited begins on a new page. Heading is centered.

Works Cited

Each entry begins at the left margin, with subsequent lines indented 5 spaces or ½".

Bright, Deborah. "Of Mother Nature and Marlboro Men: An Inquiry into the Cultural Meanings of Landscape Photography." *The Contest of Meaning: Critical Histories of Photography.* Ed. Richard Bolton. Cambridge: MIT P, 1993. 125-43. Print.

List is alphabetized by authors' last names or by title for works with no author.

Coyne, Michael. *The Crowded Prairie: American National Identity in the Hollywood Western.* London: Tauris, 1997. Print.

Ebert, Roger. "The Good, the Bad and the Ugly." *Chicago Sun-Times.* Sun-Times Media, 3 Aug. 2003. Web. 25 Jan. 2012.

Fox, William. "Wild Westerns Italian Style." *Saturday Evening Post* Nov. 1966: 50-55. Print.

Frayling, Christopher. *Spaghetti Westerns: Cowboys and Europeans from Karl May to Sergio Leone.* New York: St. Martin's, 1981. Print.

Harlan, Theresa. "Adjusting the Focus for an Indigenous Presence." *Overexposed: Essays on Contemporary Photography.* Ed. Carol Squiers. New York: New P, 1999. Print.

Kael, Pauline. *Kiss Kiss Bang Bang.* New York: Bantam, 1965. Print.

Langford, Barry. "Revisiting the 'Revisionist' Western." *Film & History* 33.2 (2003): 26-35. *Project Muse.* Web. 2 Feb. 2012.

Once upon a Time in the West. Dir. Sergio Leone. Perf. Henry Fonda, Claudia Cardinale, and Charles Bronson. Paramount, 1968. Film.

Ramonet, Ignacio. "Italian Westerns as Political Parables." *Cineaste* 15.1 (1986): 30-35. Print.

Stagecoach. Dir. John Ford. Perf. John Wayne. United Artists, 1939. Film.

TWENTY-EIGHT

APA Style

AMERICAN **P**SYCHOLOGICAL **A**SSOCIATION (APA) style calls for (1) brief documentation in parentheses near each in-text citation and (2) complete documentation in a list of references at the end of your text. The models in this chapter draw on the *Publication Manual of the American Psychological Association*, 6th edition (2010). Additional information is available at www.apastyle.org.

A DIRECTORY TO APA STYLE

In-Text Documentation   594

Formatting a Research Essay   617

Sample Research Essay   619

Throughout this chapter, you'll find models and examples that are color-coded to help you see how writers include source information in their texts and reference lists: brown for author or editor, yellow for title, gray for publication information—place of publication, publisher, date of publication, page number(s), and so on.

IN-TEXT DOCUMENTATION

Brief documentation in your text makes clear to your reader precisely what you took from a source and, in the case of a quotation, precisely where (usually, on which page) in the source you found the material you are quoting.

PARAPHRASES and **SUMMARIES** are more common than **QUOTATIONS** in APA-style projects. See Chapter 25 for more on all three kinds of citation. As you cite each source, you will need to decide whether to name the author in a signal phrase—"as McCullough (2001) wrote"—or in parentheses—"(McCullough, 2001)." Note that APA requires you to use the past tense or present perfect tense for verbs in **SIGNAL PHRASES:** "Moss (2003) argued," "Moss (2003) has argued."

1. Author named in a signal phrase

If you are quoting, you must give the page number(s). You are not required to give the page number(s) with a paraphrase or a summary, but APA encourages you to do so, especially if you are citing a long or complex work; most of the models in this chapter do include page numbers.

Author quoted

Put the date in parentheses right after the author's name; put the page in parentheses as close to the quotation as possible.

> McCullough (2001) described John Adams as having "the hands of a
> man accustomed to pruning his own trees, cutting his own hay, and
> splitting his own firewood" (p. 18).

Notice that in this example, the parenthetical reference with the page number comes *after* the closing quotation marks but *before* the period at the end of the sentence.

Author paraphrased or summarized

Put the date in parentheses right after the author's name; follow the date with the page.

> John Adams' hands were those of a laborer, according to McCullough
> (2001, p. 18).

2. Author named in parentheses

If you do not mention an author in a signal phrase, put his or her name, a comma, and the year of publication in parentheses as close as possible to the quotation, paraphrase, or summary.

Author quoted

Give the author, date, and page in one set of parentheses, or split the information between two sets of parentheses.

> One biographer (McCullough, 2001) has said John Adams had "the hands of a man accustomed to pruning his own trees, cutting his own hay, and splitting his own firewood" (p. 18).

Author paraphrased or summarized

Give the author, date, and page in parentheses toward the beginning or end of the paraphrase or summary.

> John Adams' hands were those of a laborer (McCullough, 2001, p. 18).

3. Authors with the same last name

If your reference list includes more than one person with the same last name, include initials in all documentation to distinguish the authors from one another.

> Eclecticism is common in modern criticism (J. M. Smith, 1992, p. vii).

4. Two authors

Always mention both authors. Use *and* in a signal phrase, but use an ampersand (&) in parentheses.

> Carlson and Ventura (1990) wanted to introduce Julio Cortázar, Marjorie Agosín, and other Latin American writers to an audience of English-speaking adolescents (p. v).

> According to the Peter Principle, "In a hierarchy, every employee tends to rise to his level of incompetence" (Peter & Hull, 1969, p. 26).

5. Three or more authors

In the first reference to a work by three to five persons, name all contribu-tors. In subsequent references, name the first author followed by *et al.*, Latin for "and others." Whenever you refer to a work by six or more contributors, name only the first author, followed by *et al.* Use *and* in a signal phrase, but use an ampersand (&) in parentheses.

> Faigley, George, Palchik, and Selfe (2004) have argued that where there used to be a concept called *literacy*, today's multitude of new kinds of texts has given us *literacies* (p. xii).

> Peilen et al. (1990) supported their claims about corporate corruption with startling anecdotal evidence (p. 75).

6. Organization or government as author

If an organization name is recognizable by its abbreviation, give the full name and the abbreviation the first time you cite the source. In subsequent references, use only the abbreviation. If the organization does not have a familiar abbreviation, always use its full name.

First reference

> (American Psychological Association [APA], 2008)

Subsequent references

> (APA, 2008)

7. Author unknown

Use the complete title if it is short; if it is long, use the first few words of the title under which the work appears in the reference list.

> *Webster's New Biographical Dictionary* (1988) identifies William James as "American psychologist and philosopher" (p. 520).

> A powerful editorial asserted that healthy liver donor Mike Hurewitz died because of "frightening" faulty postoperative care ("Every Patient's Nightmare," 2007).

8. Two or more works cited together

If you cite multiple works in the same parentheses, place them in the order that they appear in your reference list, separated by semicolons.

> Many researchers have argued that what counts as "literacy" is not necessarily learned at school (Heath, 1983; Moss, 2003).

9. Two or more works by one author in the same year

If your list of references includes more than one work by the same author published in the same year, order them alphabetically by title, adding lowercase letters ("a," "b," and so on) to the year.

> Kaplan (2000a) described orderly shantytowns in Turkey that did not resemble the other slums he visited.

10. Source quoted in another source

When you cite a source that was quoted in another source, let the reader know that you used a secondary source by adding the words *as cited in*.

> During the meeting with the psychologist, the patient stated repeatedly that he "didn't want to be too paranoid" (as cited in Oberfield & Yasik, 2004, p. 294).

11. Work without page numbers

Instead of page numbers, some electronic works have paragraph numbers, which you should include (preceded by the abbreviation *para.)* if you are referring to a specific part of such a source. In sources with neither page nor paragraph numbers, refer readers to a particular part of the source if possible, perhaps indicating a heading and the paragraph under the heading.

> Russell's dismissals from Trinity College at Cambridge and from City College in New York City have been seen as examples of the controversy that marked his life (Irvine, 2006, para. 2).

12. An entire work

You do not need to give a page number if you are directing readers' attention to an entire work.

> Kaplan (2000) considered Turkey and Central Asia explosive.

When you are citing an entire website, give the URL in the text. You do not need to include the website in your reference list. To cite part of a website, see no. 20 on p. 481.

> Beyond providing diagnostic information, the website for the
> Alzheimer's Association includes a variety of resources for family and
> community support of patients suffering from Alzheimer's disease
> (http://www.alz.org).

13. Personal communication

Document email, telephone conversations, interviews, personal letters, messages from nonarchived electronic discussion sources, and other personal texts as *personal communication,* along with the person's initial(s), last name, and the date. You do not need to include such personal communications in your reference list.

> L. Strauss (personal communication, December 6, 2013) told about
> visiting Yogi Berra when they both lived in Montclair, New Jersey.

NOTES

You may need to use *content notes* to give an explanation or information that doesn't fit into your text. To signal a content note, place a superscript numeral at the appropriate point in your text. Include this information as a footnote, and put the notes on a separate page with the heading *Notes,* after your reference list. If you have multiple notes, number them consecutively throughout your text. Here is an example from *In Search of Solutions: A New Direction in Psychotherapy* (2003).

author   title   publication

Text with superscript

An important part of working with teams and one-way mirrors is taking the consultation break, as at Milan, BFTC, and MRI.[1]

Content note

[1]It is crucial to note here that while working within a team is fun, stimulating, and revitalizing, it is not necessary for successful outcomes. Solution-oriented therapy works equally well when working solo.

REFERENCE LIST

A reference list provides full bibliographic information for every source cited in your text with the exception of entire websites and personal communications. See page 618 for guidelines on preparing such a list; for a sample reference list, see page 634.

Print Books

For most books, you'll need to provide the author, the publication date, the title and any subtitle, and the place of publication and publisher.

Important Details for Documenting Print Books

- **AUTHORS:** Use the author's last name, but replace the first and middle names with initials (D. Kinder for Donald Kinder).
- **DATES:** If more than one year is given, use the most recent one.
- **TITLES:** Capitalize only the first word and proper nouns and proper adjectives in titles and subtitles.
- **PUBLICATION PLACE:** Give city followed by state (abbreviated) or country, if outside the United States (for example, Boston, MA; London, England; Toronto, Ontario, Canada). If more than one city is given, use the first. Do not include the state or country if the publisher is a university whose name includes that information.

- **PUBLISHER:** Use a shortened form of the publisher's name (Little, Brown for Little, Brown and Company), but retain *Association, Books,* and *Press* (American Psychological Association, Princeton University Press).

1. One author

Author's Last Name, Initials. (Year of publication). *Title.* Publication City, State or Country: Publisher.

Lewis, M. (2003). *Moneyball: The art of winning an unfair game.* New York, NY: Norton.

2. Two or more works by the same author

If the works were published in different years, list them chronologically.

Lewis, B. (1995). *The Middle East: A brief history of the last 2,000 years.* New York, NY: Scribner.
Lewis, B. (2003). *The crisis of Islam: Holy war and unholy terror.* New York, NY: Modern Library.

If the works were published in the same year, list them alphabetically by title, adding "a," "b," and so on to the year.

Kaplan, R. D. (2000a). *The coming anarchy: Shattering the dreams of the post cold war.* New York, NY: Random House.
Kaplan, R. D. (2000b). *Eastward to Tartary: Travels in the Balkans, the Middle East, and the Caucasus.* New York, NY: Random House.

3. Two or more authors

For two to seven authors, include all names.

First Author's Last Name, Initials, Next Author's Last Name, Initials, & Final Author's Last Name, Initials. (Year of publication). *Title.* Publication City, State or Country: Publisher.

> Levitt, S. D., & Dubner, S. J. (2005). *Freakonomics: A rogue economist explores the hidden side of everything.* New York, NY: Morrow.

For a work by eight or more authors, name just the first six authors, followed by three ellipsis points, and end with the final author (see no. 21 for an example from a magazine article).

4. Organization or government as author

Sometimes an organization or a government agency is both author and publisher. If so, use the word *Author* as the publisher.

> Organization Name or Government Agency. (Year of publication). *Title.* Publication City, State or Country: Publisher.

> Catholic News Service. (2002). *Stylebook on religion 2000: A reference guide and usage manual.* Washington, DC: Author.

5. Author and editor

> Author's Last Name, Initials. (Year of edited edition). *Title.* (Editor's Initials Last Name, Ed.). Publication City, State or Country: Publisher. (Original work[s] published year[s])

> Dick, P. F. (2008). *Five novels of the 1960s and 70s.* (J. Lethem, Ed.). New York, NY: Library of America. (Original works published 1964-1977)

6. Edited collection

> First Editor's Last Name, Initials, Next Editor's Last Name, Initials, & Final Editor's Last Name, Initials. (Eds.). (Year of edited edition). *Title.* Publication City, State or Country: Publisher.

> Raviv, A., Oppenheimer, L., & Bar-Tal, D. (Eds.). (1999). *How children understand war and peace: A call for international peace education.* San Francisco, CA: Jossey-Bass.

Documentation Map (APA) / Print Book

Stiglitz, J. E. (2015). *The great divide: Unequal societies and what we can do about them.* New York, NY: Norton.

7. Work in an edited collection

Author's Last Name, Initials. (Year of publication). Title of article or chapter. In Initials Last Name (Ed.), *Title* (pp. pages). Publication City, State or Country: Publisher.

Harris, I. M. (1999). Types of peace education. In A. Raviv, L. Oppenheimer, & D. Bar-Tal (Eds.), *How children understand war and peace: A call for international peace education* (pp. 46-70). San Francisco, CA: Jossey-Bass.

8. Unknown author

Title. (Year of publication). Publication City, State or Country: Publisher.

Webster's new biographical dictionary. (1988). Springfield, MA: Merriam-Webster.

If the title page of a work lists the author as *Anonymous,* treat the reference list entry as if the author's name were Anonymous, and alphabetize it accordingly.

9. Edition other than the first

Author's Last Name, Initials. (Year). *Title* (name or number ed.). Publication City, State or Country: Publisher.

Burch, D. (2008). *Emergency navigation: Find your position and shape your course at sea even if your instruments fail* (2nd ed.). Camden, ME: International Marine/McGraw-Hill.

10. Translation

Author's Last Name, Initials. (Year of publication). *Title* (Translator's Initials Last Name, Trans.). Publication City, State or Country: Publisher. (Original work published Year)

Hugo, V. (2008). *Les misérables* (J. Rose, Trans.). New York, NY: Modern Library. (Original work published 1862)

11. Multivolume work

Author's Last Name, Initials. (Year). *Title* (Vols. numbers). Publication City, State or Country: Publisher.

Nastali, D. P. & Boardman, P. C. (2004). *The Arthurian annals: The tradition in English from 1250 to 2000* (Vols. 1-2). New York, NY: Oxford University Press USA.

One volume of a multivolume work

Author's Last Name, Initials. (Year). *Title of whole work* (Vol. number). Publication City, State or Country: Publisher.

Spiegelman, A. (1986). *Maus* (Vol. 1). New York, NY: Random House.

12. Article in a reference book

Unsigned

Title of entry. (Year). In *Title of reference book* (Name or number ed., Vol. number, pp. pages). Publication City, State or Country: Publisher.

Macrophage. (2003). In *Merriam-Webster's collegiate dictionary* (11th ed., p. 745). Springfield, MA: Merriam-Webster.

Signed

Author's Last Name, Initials. (Year). Title of entry. In *Title of reference book* (Vol. number, pp. pages). Publication City, State or Country: Publisher.

Wasserman, D. E. (2006). Human exposure to vibration. In *International encyclopedia of ergonomics and human factors* (Vol. 2, pp. 1800-1801). Boca Raton, FL: CRC.

author   title   publication

Print Periodicals

For most articles, you'll need to provide information about the author; the date; the article title and any subtitle; the periodical title; and any volume or issue number and inclusive page numbers.

Important Details for Documenting Print Periodicals

- **AUTHORS:** List authors as you would for a book (see p. 600).
- **DATES:** For journals, give year only. For magazines and newspapers, give year followed by a comma and then month or month and day.
- **TITLES:** Capitalize article titles as you would for a book. Capitalize the first and last words and all principal words of periodical titles. Do not capitalize *a, an, the,* or any prepositions or coordinating conjunctions unless they begin the title of the periodical.
- **VOLUME AND ISSUE:** For journals and magazines, give volume or volume and issue, depending on the journal's pagination method. For newspapers, do not give volume or issue.
- **PAGES:** Use *p.* or *pp.* for a newspaper article but not for a journal or magazine article. If an article does not fall on consecutive pages, give all the page numbers (for example, 45, 75-77 for a journal or magazine; pp. C1, C3, C5-C7 for a newspaper).

13. Article in a journal paginated by volume

Author's Last Name, Initials. (Year). Title of article. *Title of Journal, volume,* pages.

Gremer, J. R., Sala, A., & Crone, E. E. (2010). Disappearing plants: Why they hide and how they return. *Ecology, 91,* 3407-3413.

14. Article in a journal paginated by issue

Author's Last Name, Initials. (Year). Title of article. *Title of Journal, volume*(issue), pages.

Weaver, C., McNally, C., & Moerman, S. (2001). To grammar or not to grammar: That is not the question! *Voices from the Middle, 8*(3), 17-33.

15. Article in a magazine

If a magazine is published weekly, include the day and the month. If there are a volume number and an issue number, include them after the magazine title.

> Author's Last Name, Initials. (Year, Month Day). *Title of article. Title of*
> *Magazine, volume*(issue), page(s).

> Gregory, S. (2008, June 30). Crash course: Why golf carts are more
> hazardous than they look. *Time, 171*(26), 53.

If a magazine is published monthly, include the month(s) only.

16. Article in a newspaper

If page numbers are consecutive, separate them with a hyphen. If not, separate them with a comma.

> Author's Last Name, Initials. (Year, Month Day). Title of article. *Title of*
> *Newspaper,* p(p). page(s).

> Schneider, G. (2005, March 13). Fashion sense on wheels. *The*
> *Washington Post,* pp. F1, F6.

17. Article by an unknown author

> Title of article. (Year, Month Day). *Title of Periodical, volume*(issue), pages
> *or* p(p). page(s).

> Hot property: From carriage house to family compound. (2004,
> December). *Berkshire Living, 1*(1), 99.

> Clues in salmonella outbreak. (2008, June 21). *New York Times,* p. A13.

18. Book review

> Reviewer's Last Name, Initials. (Date of publication). Title of review
> [Review of the book *Title of Work,* by Author's Initials Last Name].
> *Title of Periodical, volume*(issue), page(s).

Brandt, A. (2003, October). Animal planet [Review of the book
    Intelligence of apes and other rational beings, by D. R. Rumb &
    D. A. Washburn]. *National Geographic Adventure, 5*(10), 47.

If the review does not have a title, include the bracketed information about
the work being reviewed immediately after the date of publication.

19. Letter to the editor

Author's Last Name, Initials. (Date of publication). Title of letter [Letter
    to the editor]. *Title of Periodical, volume*(issue), *or* p(p). page(s).

Hitchcock, G. (2008, August 3). Save our species [Letter to the editor].
    San Francisco Chronicle, p. P-3.

Online Sources

Not every online source gives you all the data that APA would like to see in
a reference entry. Ideally, you will be able to list author's or editor's name;
date of first electronic publication or most recent revision; title of document;
information about print publication if any; and retrieval information: DOI
(digital object identifier, a string of letters and numbers that identifies an
online document) or URL. In some cases, additional information about electronic publication may be required (title of site, retrieval date, name of spon
soring institution).

Important Details for Documenting Online Sources

- **AUTHORS:** List authors as you would for a print book or periodical.
- **TITLES:** For websites and electronic documents, articles, or books, capitalize title and subtitles as you would for a book; capitalize periodical
titles as you would for a print periodical.
- **DATES:** After the author, give the year of the document's original publication on the web or of its most recent revision. If neither of those years
is clear, use *n.d.* to mean "no date." For undated content or content that
may change (for example, a wiki entry), include the month, day, and
year that you retrieved the document. You don't need to include the retrieval date for content that's unlikely to change.

- **DOI OR URL:** Include the DOI instead of the URL in the reference whenever one is available. If no DOI is available, provide the URL of the home page or menu page. If you do not identify the sponsoring institution, you do not need a colon before the URL or DOI. When a URL won't fit on the line, break the URL before most punctuation, but do not break *http://*.

20. Work from a nonperiodical website

Author's Last Name, Initials. (Date of publication). Title of work. *Title of site.* DOI or Retrieved Month Day, Year [if necessary], from URL

Cruikshank, D. (2009, June 15). Unlocking the secrets and powers of the brain. *National Science Foundation.* Retrieved from http://www.nsf .gov/discoveries/disc_summ.jsp?cntn_id=114979&org=NSF

When citing an entire website, include the URL in parentheses within the text. Do not include the website in your list of references.

21. Article in an online periodical

When available, include the volume number and issue number as you would for a print source. If no DOI has been assigned, provide the URL of the homepage or menu page of the journal or magazine, even for articles that you access through a database.

Article in an online journal

Author's Last Name, Initials. (Year). Title of article. *Title of Journal, volume*(issue), pages. DOI or Retrieved from URL

Corbett, C. (2007). Vehicle-related crime and the gender gap. *Psychology, Crime & Law, 13,* 245-263. doi:10.1080/10683160600822022

Article in an online magazine

Author's Last Name, Initials. (Year, Month Day). Title of article. *Title of Magazine, volume*(issue). DOI or Retrieved from URL

author   title   publication

Documentation Map (APA) / Work from a Website

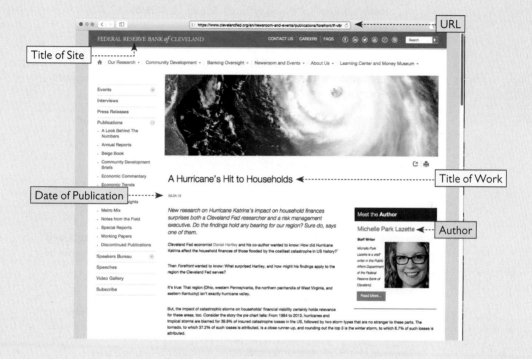

URL

Title of Site

Title of Work

Date of Publication

Author

Lazette, M. P. (2015, February 25). A hurricane's hit to households.
    Federal Reserve Bank of Cleveland. Retrieved from https://www
    .clevelandfed.org/enNewsroom%20and%20Events/Publications/
    Forefront/Katrina.aspx

Barreda, V. D., Palazzesi, L., Tellería, M. C., Katinas, L., Crisci, J. N.,
Bromer, K., . . . Bechis, F. (2010, September 24). Eocene
Patagonia fossils of the daisy family. *Science, 329*(5949).
doi:10.1126=sciences.1193108

Article in an online newspaper

If the article can be found by searching the site, give the URL of the home
page or menu page.

Author's Last Name, Initials. (Year, Month Day). Title of article. *Title of
Newspaper.* Retrieved from URL

Collins, G. (2012, September 12). Game time. *The New York Times.*
Retrieved from http://www.nytimes.com

22. Article available only through a database

Some sources, such as an out-of-print journal or rare book, can be accessed
only through a database. When no DOI is provided, give either the name of
the database or its URL.

Author's Last Name, Initials. (Year). Title of article. *Title of Journal,
volume*(issue), pages. DOI or Retrieved from Name of database or
URL

Simpson, M. (1972). Authoritarianism and education: A comparative
approach. *Sociometry, 35*(2), 223-234. Retrieved from http://
www.jstor.org/stable/2786619

23. Article or chapter in a web document or online reference work

For a chapter in a web document or an article in an online reference work,
give the URL of the chapter or entry if no DOI is provided.

Author's Last Name, Initials. (Year). Title of entry. In Initials Last Name
(Ed.), *Title of reference work.* DOI or Retrieved from URL

Korfmacher, C. (2006). Personal identity. In J. Fieser & B. Dowden
(Eds.), *Internet encyclopedia of philosophy.* Retrieved from http://
www.iep.utm.edu/person-i/

author   title   publication

Documentation Map (APA) / Article in a Journal with DOI

Title of Journal

Volume

Publication Year

Pages

DOI

ETHICS & BEHAVIOR, 23(4), 324–337
Copyright © 2013 Taylor & Francis Group, LLC
ISSN: 1050-8422 print / 1532-7019 online
DOI: 10.1080/10508422.2013.787359

Routledge
Taylor & Francis Group

Smart Technology and the Moral Life

Title of Article

Author

Clifton F. Guthrie
Department of Science and Humanities
Husson University

Smart technology is recording and nudging our intuitive and behavioral reactions in ways that are not fully shaped by our conscious ethical reasoning and so are altering our social and moral worlds. Beyond reasons to worry, there are also reasons to embrace this technology for nudging human behavior toward prosocial activity. This article inquires about four ways that smart technology is shaping the individual moral life: the persuasive effect of promptware, our newly evolving experiences of embodiment, our negotiations with privacy, and our experiences of risk and serendipity.

Keywords: persuasive technology, morality, ethics, virtue

PERSUASIVE TECHNOLOGY

For some time, cars have worked to shape our behaviors, beeping to warn us when a door is unlocked or a seat belt unfastened, or giving us fuel efficiency feedback. These straightforward but persuasive sensor systems nudge us toward a repertoire of safe driving behaviors, and we often cannot override them even if we want to. Newer cars include an increasing number of smart technologies that interact with us more intelligently. Some detect the presence of electronic keys and make it impossible for drivers to lock themselves out. Others use sensors to monitor approaching obstacles or lane boundaries and give warnings or even apply the brakes. We are seeing the emergence of street intersections that communicate directly with cars and cars that can communicate with one another (Dean, Fletcher, Porges, & Ulrich, 2012). These are so-called smart technologies because they draw data from the environment and from us, and often make decisions on our behalf. A leading researcher in automated driving noted, "The driver is still in control. But if the driver is not doing the right thing, the technology takes over" (Markoff & Sengupta, 2013).

As cars become smarter they are helping to lead us into what technologists describe as a pervasive, ambient, or calm computing environment. In 1991, Mark Weiser of the Palo Alto Research Center presciently called it "ubiquitous computing" or "ubicomp" in a much-quoted article from *Scientific American*, in which he outlined what has come to be accepted as a standard interpretation of the history of human interaction with computers. This is the age in which computers are increasingly liberated from manual input devices like laptops and cell phones to become an invisible, interactive, computational sensorium. Early examples include motion sensors, smart

Correspondence should be addressed to Clifton F. Guthrie, Department of Science and Humanities, Husson University, 1 College Circle, Bangor, ME 04401. E-mail: cfguthrie@gmail.com

Guthrie, C. F. (2013). Smart technology and the moral life. *Ethics & Behavior, 23,* 324-337. doi:10.1080/10508422.2013.787359

Documentation Map (APA) / Article Accessed through a Database with DOI

Guthrie, C. F. (2013). Smart technology and the moral life. *Ethics & Behavior*, 23, 324-337. doi:10.1080/10508422.2013.787359

24. Electronic book

Author's Last Name, Initials. (Year). *Title of book.* DOI or Retrieved from
URL

TenDam, H. (n.d.). *Politics, civilization & humanity.* Retrieved from http://
onlineoriginals.com/showitem.asp?itemID=46&page=2

For an ebook based on a print version, include a description of the digital
format in brackets after the book title.

Blain, M. (2009). *The sociology of terror: Studies in power, subjection, and
victimage ritual* [Adobe Digital Editions version]. Retrieved from
http://www.powells.com/sub/AdobeDigitalEditionsPolitics
.html?sec_big_link=1

25. Wiki entry

Give the entry title and the date of posting, or *n.d.* if there is no date. Then
include the retrieval date, the name of the wiki, and the URL for the entry.

Title of entry. (Year, Month Day). Retrieved Month Day, Year, from Title
of wiki: URL

Discourse. (n.d.). Retrieved November 8, 2013, from Psychology Wiki:
http://psychology.wikia.com/wiki/Discourse

26. Online discussion source

If the name of the list to which the message was posted is not part of the
URL, include it after *Retrieved from.* The URL you provide should be for the
archived version of the message or post.

Author's Last Name, Initials. (Year, Month Day). Subject line of message
[Descriptive label]. Retrieved from URL

Baker, J. (2005, February 15). Re: Huffing and puffing [Electronic
mailing list message]. Retrieved from American Dialect Society
electronic mailing list: http://listserv.linguistlist.org/cgi-bin
/wa?A2=ind0502C&L=ADS-L&P=R44

Do not include email or other nonarchived discussions in your list of references. Simply give the sender's name in your text. See no. 13 on page 598 for guidelines on identifying such sources in your text.

27. Blog entry

Author's Last Name, Initials. (Year, Month Day). Title of post [Blog post]. Retrieved from URL

Collins, C. (2009, August 19). Butterfly benefits from warmer springs? [Blog post]. Retrieved from http://www.intute.ac.uk/blog/2009/08/19/butterfly-benefits-from-warmer-springs/

28. Online video

Last Name, Initials (Writer), & Last Name, Initials (Producer). (Year, Month Day posted). *Title* [Descriptive label]. Retrieved from URL

Coulter, J. (Songwriter & Performer), & Booth, M. S. (Producer). (2006, September 23). *Code monkey* [Video file]. Retrieved from http://www.youtube.com/watch?v=v4Wy7gRGgeA

29. Podcast

Writer's Last Name, Initials. (Writer), & Producer's Last Name, Initials. (Producer). (Year, Month Day). Title of podcast. *Title of site or program* [Audio podcast]. Retrieved from URL

Britt, M. A. (Writer & Producer). (2009, June 7). Episode 97: Stanley Milgram study finally replicated. *The Psych Files Podcast* [Audio podcast]. Retrieved from http://www.thepsychfiles.com/

Other Kinds of Sources

30. Film, video, or DVD

Last Name, Initials (Producer), & Last Name, Initials (Director). (Year). *Title* [Motion picture]. Country: Studio.

Wallis, H. B. (Producer), & Curtiz, M. (Director). (1942). *Casablanca* [Motion picture]. United States: Warner.

31. Music recording

Composer's Last Name, Initials. (Year of copyright). Title of song. On *Title of album* [Medium]. City, State or Country: Label.

Veloso, C. (1997). Na baixado sapateiro. On *Livros* [CD]. Los Angeles, CA: Nonesuch.

32. Proceedings of a conference

Author's Last Name, Initials. (Year of publication). Title of paper. In *Proceedings Title* (pp. pages). Publication City, State or Country: Publisher.

Heath, S. B. (1997). Talking work: Language among teens. In *Symposium about Language and Society—Austin* (pp. 27-45). Austin: Department of Linguistics at the University of Texas.

33. Television program

Last Name, Initials (Writer), & Last Name, Initials (Director). (Year). Title of episode [Descriptive label]. In Initials Last Name (Producer), *Series title*. City, State or Country: Network.

Dunkle, R. (Writer), & Lange, M. (Director). (2012). Hit [Television series episode]. In E. A. Bernero (Executive Producer), *Criminal minds*. New York, NY: NBC.

34. Software or computer program

Title and version number [Computer software]. (Year). Publication City, State or Country: Publisher.

Elder Scrolls V: Skyrim [Computer software]. (2012). Rockwood, MD: Bethesda.

35. Government document

> Government Agency. (Year of publication). *Title*. Publication City, State
> 　　or Country: Publisher.

> U.S. Department of Health and Human Services, Centers for Disease Control
> 　　and Prevention. (2009). *Fourth national report on human exposure to*
> 　　*environmental chemicals*. Washington, DC: Government Printing Office.

Online government document

> Government Agency. (Year of publication). *Title* (Publication No. [if
> 　　any]). Retrieved from URL

> U.S. Department of Health and Human Services, National Institutes of
> 　　Health, National Institute of Mental Health. (2006). *Bipolar disorder*
> 　　(NIH Publication No. 06-3679). Retrieved from http://www.nimh.nih
> 　　.gov/health/publications/bipolar-disorder/nimh-bipolar-adults.pdf

36. Dissertation

Include the database name and accession number for dissertations that you
retrieve from a database.

> Author's Last Name, Initials. (Year). *Title of dissertation* (Doctoral
> 　　dissertation). Retrieved from Name of database. (accession
> 　　number)

> Knapik, M. (2008). *Adolescent online trouble-talk: Help-seeking in*
> 　　*cyberspace* (Doctoral dissertation). Retrieved from ProQuest
> 　　Dissertation and Theses database. (AAT NR38024)

For a dissertation that you access on the web, include the name of the institution after *Doctoral dissertation*. For example: (Doctoral dissertation, University of North Carolina). End your documentation with *Retrieved from* and
the URL.

37. Technical or research report

> Author's Last Name, Initials. (Year). *Title of report* (Report number).
> 　　Publication City, State or Country: Publisher.

Elsayed, T., Namata, G., Getoor, L., & Oard., D. W. (2008). *Personal name resolution in email: A heuristic approach* (Report No. LAMP-TR-150). College Park: University of Maryland.

Sources Not Covered by APA

To document a source for which APA does not provide guidelines, look at models similar to the source you have cited. Give any information readers will need in order to find it themselves—author; date of publication; title; publisher; information about electronic retrieval (DOI or URL); and any other pertinent information. You might want to test your reference note to be sure it will lead others to your source.

FORMATTING A RESEARCH ESSAY

Title page. APA generally requires a title page. At the upper left-hand corner of the page, include "Running head:" and a shortened version of your title in capital letters. The page number (1) should go in the upper right-hand corner. Center the full title of the paper, your name, and the name of your school on separate lines about halfway down the page. You may add an "Author Note" at the bottom of the page to provide course information, acknowledgments, or contact information.

Page numbers. Use a shortened title in capital letters in the upper left-hand corner of each page; place the page number in the upper right-hand corner. Number pages consecutively throughout.

Fonts, spacing, margins, and indents. Use a serif font (such as Times New Roman or Bookman) for the text, and a sans serif font (such as Calibri or Verdana) for figure labels. Double-space the entire paper, including any notes and your list of references. Leave one-inch margins at the top, bottom, and sides of your text; do not justify the text. The first line of each paragraph should be indented one-half inch (or five to seven spaces) from the left margin. APA recommends using two spaces after end-of-sentence punctuation.

Headings. Though they are not required in APA style, headings can help readers follow your text. The first level of heading should be bold, centered, and capitalized as you would any other title; the second level of heading should be bold and flush with the left margin; the third level should be bold and indented, with only the first letter and proper nouns capitalized and with a period at the end of the heading, with the text following on the same line.

First Level Heading

Second Level Heading

　　Third level heading. Text follows on the same line.

Abstract. An abstract is a concise summary of your paper that introduces readers to your topic and main points. Most scholarly journals require an abstract; check with your instructor about his or her preference. Put your abstract on the second page, with the word *Abstract* centered at the top. Unless your instructor specifies a length, limit your abstract to 250 words or fewer.

Long quotations. Indent quotations of more than forty words one-half inch (or five to seven spaces) from the left margin. Do not use quotation marks, and place the page number(s) in parentheses *after* the end punctuation.

> Kaplan (2000) captured ancient and contemporary Antioch for us:
>
> > At the height of its glory in the Roman-Byzantine age, when it had an amphitheater, public baths, aqueducts, and sewage pipes, half a million people lived in Antioch. Today the population is only 125,000. With sour relations between Turkey and Syria, and unstable politics throughout the Middle East, Antioch is now a backwater—seedy and tumbledown, with relatively few tourists. (p. 123)
>
> Antioch's decline serves as a reminder that the fortunes of cities can change drastically over time.

Reference list. Start your list on a new page after the text but before any endnotes. Center the title, and double-space the entire list. Each entry should begin at the left margin, and subsequent lines should be indented one-half inch (or five to seven spaces). Alphabetize the list by authors' last names (or by editors' names, if appropriate). Alphabetize works that have no author or editor by title, disregarding *A, An,* and *The.* Be sure every source listed is cited in the text; do not include sources that you consulted but did not cite.

Illustrations. For each table, provide a number (*Table 1*) and a descriptive title on separate lines above the table; below the table, include a note with information about the source. For figures—charts, diagrams, graphs, photos, and so on—include a figure number (*Figure 1*) and information about the source in a note below the figure. Number tables and figures separately, and be sure to discuss any illustrations so that readers know how they relate to the rest of your text.

Table 1
Hours of Instruction Delivered per Week

	American classrooms	Japanese classrooms	Chinese classrooms
First grade			
Language arts	10.5	8.7	10.4
Mathematics	2.7	5.8	4.0
Fifth grade			
Language arts	7.9	8.0	11.1
Mathematics	3.4	7.8	11.7

Note. Adapted from "Peeking Out from Under the Blinders: Some Factors We Shouldn't Forget in Studying Writing," by J. R. Hayes, 1991, National Center for the Study of Writing and Literacy (Occasional Paper No. 25). Retrieved from National Writing Project website: http://www.nwp.org/

SAMPLE RESEARCH ESSAY

Katryn Sheppard wrote the following paper, "Early Word Production: A Study of One Child's Word Productions," for a psychology course. It is formatted according to the guidelines of the *Publication Manual of the American Psychological Association,* 6th edition (2010).

Running head: EARLY WORD PRODUCTION   1

A shortened title in all capital letters is used as a running head in the upper left corner of each page; on the title page, it is preceded by the label "Running head" and a colon. Page numbers appear in the upper right corner.

Early Word Production: A Study of One Child's Word Productions

Katryn Sheppard

Portland State University

The title is centered on the page, with your name and the school name below.

EARLY WORD PRODUCTION 2

Abstract

Early word production, one of the initial stages of language development in children, plays an important role in the development of later language skills. This study identifies the word classes and number of words spoken in a recorded interaction (Bloom, 1973) by one normally developing child of sixteen months and analyzes aspects of the child's speech, with the goal of noting if the characteristics observed were supported by the existing research on early word production or if they deviated from those findings. The words that I analyzed fell into six categories: nouns, spatial terms, adjectives, negatives, social phrases, and verbs. Although the frequency with which the child used words from some of these categories reflected the expectations established by previous research, her use of words in other categories was less predictable. Noting word usage in the six categories led to an analysis of the functions that those categories served in the child's semantic communication at this early stage of language development.

Abstract begins on a new page. Heading is centered.

Abstract text does not need a paragraph indent.

Use two letter spaces after each sentence.

250 words or fewer.

Early Word Production: A Study of One Child's Word Productions

Introduction

Each step in the course of language development and acquisition in children provides a foundation for later skills and eventual mastery of the language. Early word production, a stage of language development in which children have only a few words in their vocabularies, provides the foundation for later vocabulary building and language production and has been shown to be closely linked to later language performance skills (Walker, Greenwood, Hart, & Carta, 1994). The early word production stage is therefore worthy of examination, as it "signals that children have a new tool that will enable them to learn about and participate more fully in their society" (Uccelli & Pan, 2013, p. 95).

Because so few words are produced by children in this early stage, the analysis of their word production focuses on the particular word classes and how frequently each class of words appears in speech. When examining typically developing English-speaking children who have few words in their productive vocabulary, Bates et al. (1994) found that the words produced were most often nouns, while other categories more seldom appeared. These less frequent categories included verbs and closed-class words. *Closed-class* words are function words, which include the categories of articles, conjunctions, numbers, pronouns, and prepositions; they are called closed-class words because new members cannot be added to these categories.

Reporting on the most common kinds of the nouns uttered in early vocabularies, Nelson (1973) found that children "began by naming

---

Title is centered.

First-level headings are centered, bold, and capitalized.

Essay is double-spaced.

Because this source has fewer than six authors, all authors are included in its first citation; subsequent references name only the first author, followed by et al. The year of publication is included in the reference.

Because this source has more than six authors, the signal phrase gives the first author's name followed by et al. The signal phrase uses past tense, and the year of publication is given in parentheses.

Indent each paragraph ½" (5-7 spaces).

EARLY WORD PRODUCTION   4

objects exhibiting salient properties of change whether as the result

of the child's own action . . . or independent of it" (p. 1). In other words,

nouns that point to consistent, concrete objects are most prevalent in

early speech, because "children learn to name and understand categories

that are functionally relevant to them" (Anglin, 1995, p. 165)—they learn

to name the objects they see and interact with day to day.

> The author, year, and page number are given in parentheses right after a quotation.

Although nouns make up the largest percentage of the words

produced by children in the earlier stages of language acquisition, other

word classes like verbs and adjectives also appear. While they do occur

in children's first fifty words, "verbs, adjectives, and function words each

account for less than 10 percent" of total utterances (Uccelli & Pan, 2013,

p. 96). Infrequent use of these categories supports the idea that, while

all word classes are represented, nouns are still expected to occur most

often.

> Because the authors are not named in a signal phrase, their names are given in parentheses, with an ampersand rather than and between them. A page number is provided for a direct quotation.

Other lexical items that can be found in the speech of children

with limited vocabulary are words indicating spatial relationships, how

things relate to one another in physical space. According to Bowerman

(2007), "children's earliest spatial words are topological forms like 'in'

and 'on'" (p. 177). This observation supports the hypothesis that those

prepositions are among the first lexical items children acquire (Brown,

1973; Zukowski, 2013).

> The page number is provided in parentheses for a direct quotation when the author and year of the work are given earlier in the signal phrase.

> Multiple sources cited in the same parentheses are ordered alphabetically and separated by a semicolon.

Overall, the research on early word production in children who are

just beginning to acquire their first language has found that the majority

of words produced will be nouns that refer to concrete objects. According

to Pine (1992), children frequently use their early words to describe or label, or to do both. Pine concluded that "children are making referential statements about the world with the kind of vocabulary items which they happen to have available to them" (p. 53). That is, children try to comment on referents (the things that words stand for) in various ways using just the limited language skills that they possess in their early stage of development.

Taking into account prior research on the early words children produce, I analyzed the classes and categories of words that appear in a transcript of a young child speaking. I wanted to compare this particular child's speech with what is expected during this early stage of language development, knowing that research predicts a higher number of nouns than other word classes in the data. I was interested to know whether nouns would occur as frequently as the literature would have me believe, and whether or not spatial terms would appear in such early speech. Furthermore, I wanted to note whether verbs occur as infrequently as expected and, if so, what words the child used instead of verbs to convey action.

Method

The transcript that I chose to analyze is one sample from a series of six recordings by Bloom (1973) of her daughter, Allison, a normally developing, English-speaking child. Allison's age in the samples ranged from 1 year 4 months and 21 days to 2 years and 10 months. The transcript that I analyzed was the earliest of these. Information about the socioeconomic status of Allison and her family was not available in the transcript or the North American English manual of the CHILDES database (MacWhinney, 2000), from which the transcript came. However, we can assume the family was from the professional class, as Bloom was a professor at Columbia University.

According to information in the CHILDES manual, the recordings took place in the Audio-Visual Studio at Teachers College, Columbia University, in a room that contained some furniture and toys. The sessions were conducted with audio-recording devices alone; as a result, no videos were available through the CHILDES database. Each recording session lasted 40 minutes, for a total of four hours of recording. Bloom (1973) describes her role in the interaction as "more investigator than mother" (p. 11), but the interactions seem to have been more relaxed than one associates with investigators and not structured according to a test or other prearranged activity. Rather, the interactions were led by the child's actions in relation to her mother and objects in the room.

The data are organized in six separate transcripts, arranged chronologically. They contain the actual utterances and morphological notation indicating the parts of speech being used. Bloom initially transcribed the recordings, and later Lois Hood, a fellow researcher, revised the transcript, which was revised again by a larger group of researchers that also included Hood. Each time, the researchers added notes to provide situational context. Each line of the transcript is numbered, and there was an attempt to divide the data in a way that reflected where there was "a shift in topic or focus" (Bloom, 1973, p. 11).

The date is placed right after the author's name; the page number in parentheses is as close to the quotation as possible.

Results

During the 40-minute exchange between Bloom and Allison, Allison produced a total of 362 occurrences of identifiable words. I did not distinguish between single- and multi-word utterances because that distinction was not relevant to the purpose of this study. Not all of Allison's turns in the conversation were intelligible; only intelligible words were included in my analysis. Altogether, I identified 27 different words (types) used by the subject, although there were many repetitions (tokens) of words. I assigned the 27 words to six categories: nouns, spatial terms, adjectives, negatives, social phrases, and verbs.

The category of nouns contained the largest number of distinct words or types as well as the largest number of instances or tokens, as shown in Figure 1. Allison used a total of 12 nouns, and all reflected concrete concepts. These included household objects, nouns that referenced people, and the names of animals referring to toys present at the time of recording. The most frequently used noun was "baby" (n=25); "chair" was second (n= 24). The total number of nouns represented 122 occurrences, or 34% of the total words uttered.

The second most frequent category of words found in Allison's utterances was spatial terms. Five different spatial terms, or types, occurred, with "up" being the most common (n= 48). All of the spatial terms Allison used referred to her immediate surroundings—for example, the chair that she wanted to climb "up" or "down" from. Altogether, 120 of Allison's words were spatial words, accounting for 33% of her speech by word count.

EARLY WORD PRODUCTION   8

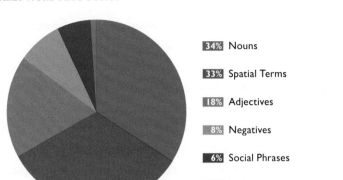

34% Nouns

33% Spatial Terms

18% Adjectives

8% Negatives

6% Social Phrases

1% Verbs

Figure 1. Words uttered by the subject, by word category (n=362). Data recorded in transcripts by L. Bloom (1973), accessed through the CHILDES database (MacWhinney, 2000).

Figure is numbered, and a description and source information are given.

The third most frequently used category of words in the data was adjectives, of which there were three types. Although "more" was the most frequently occurring adjective, "gone" was also often repeated. I will elaborate on the special role that adjectives played in Allison's speech in the discussion and conclusion section.

Negatives also appeared with some frequency in Allison's speech, although the category comprised only one type: "no." The word occurred 28 times (n=28), sometimes referring back to and negating other words that she had previously spoken, at other times negating the word or words that followed. The level of emphasis Allison placed on the word varied: sometimes her utterance was transcribed as "no"; other times, it was transcribed more emphatically, with an exclamation point, as "no!" This negative term accounted for 8% of her total words.

The remaining categories, social phrases and verbs, occurred less frequently. Social phrases—terms or utterances that are appropriately used in specific social contexts—were present in the transcript in two different words: "uhoh" (n= 20), and "oh" (n= 3). Together, these add up to a total of 23 words in the transcript that were social phrases.

The category of verbs was by far the least common in the subject's production. Four different verbs were used, three of which occurred only a single time. "Stop" was used twice, while "turn," "climb," and "sit" were each used once. A total of five words (n=5) were identified as verbs.

Discussion and Conclusion

Allison's single-word utterances fell into six identifiable categories, the frequency of which varied considerably. Some categories contained only a few items that were not repeated often, while other words and categories of words showed up repeatedly. Allison's tendency to use words in certain categories matches the findings of the existing research literature on child language production. In other instances, Allison's use of words differed slightly from what might be expected.

As predicted, nouns made up a large portion of Allison's speech. Since researchers have found the majority of early words to be nouns, it was not surprising that Allison used the greatest number of different words within the noun category and likewise showed the greatest number of repeated tokens in this category. Furthermore, the kinds of nouns Allison used are also in line with the finding that children in

EARLY WORD PRODUCTION   10

the early stages of language acquisition focus on concrete concepts. All of the nouns that Allison used referred to things in the room where the recording took place, mostly common objects that she could draw attention to. For instance, Allison used the noun "baby" when she wanted to communicate something to her mother about a baby doll she wanted to play with.

The category of spatial terms also accounted for a large percentage of the words Allison produced. The most frequent utterance of any word in any category in the transcript was of the word "up." That word, like other spatial terms, was often repeated and sometimes took the place of a more complex construction, as when the subject said "up" as she was struggling to get up onto the chair and "down" when she wished to get back down. Allison's choice of words fits with Bowerman's (2007) descriptions of children's first spatial terms: "early acquired spatial words revolve around relationships of . . . verticality (up, down)" (p. 180). This use of spatial terms contrasts with more complex spatial terms that appear in later development. However, the fact that Allison used five different words within the spatial word category could suggest that those terms play several important roles in her communication at this early stage.

As previously noted, adjectives like "gone" and "more" were words that played important roles in Allison's speech when she wanted to convey something to her mother, as when she finished eating a cookie and repeatedly told her mother "more." This single word seemed to stand in for a more elaborate question or request Allison could not produce at this stage, such as "Give me more." "Gone" was also used repeatedly in the same context to refer to the cookie. The use of "gone" to describe what had happened to the cookie might be seen as evidence of Pine's (1992) observation that children's early words are used to label and describe objects around them.

While the category of adjectives did not form as large a portion of Allison's speech as either nouns or spatial words, it was somewhat surprising that adjectives composed 18% of total words in this transcript. Generally, adjectives and other word classes that are not nouns are expected to account for a much smaller percentage of words spoken in early word production (Bates et al., 1994).

One feature of Allison's utterances that did adhere to what is expected for a typical child at this age was her use of negatives. Although she used only one negative word—"no"—the word was repeated frequently enough to be the fourth most common category in the transcript. Her use of "no" rather than any other negative conformed to Brown's (1973) finding that other forms of negation like "not" and "don't" appear only in later stages of linguistic development. In this very early stage, Allison's reliance on "no" alone seems typical.

There were varied contexts in which Allison used "no." In some cases, the word seemed to convey a lack of something, as when she uttered "cookie," looked around for the cookies, and then said "no." This sequence of events might indicate that Allison was conveying the lack of cookies to her mother. A similar exchange revolved around a picture of a girl, when Allison turned the picture over and, upon finding the

EARLY WORD PRODUCTION   12

other side was blank, said "no," evidently trying to convey that there was nothing on that side of the picture. On other occasions, "no" was produced as an answer to a question. In one example, Bloom asked Allison if the cup was for her (i.e., Bloom), to which the girl replied "no" and took the cup back from her mother. While adhering to the use of the single, simple form of negation that might be expected, Allison's utterances of "no" were varied in purpose and effective in communicating a range of ideas.

The remaining categories, social phrases and verbs, made up only a small percentage of Allison's words. Social words appeared infrequently and sometimes were attached to other words, as when the subject said "uhoh there." The infrequency of social phrases in Allison's early speech reflects typical aspects of early vocabulary development. As Santelmann (2014) explained, at this stage in a child's linguistic development, nearly all lexical items will be nouns and adjectives, with a limited number of social phrases.

True to previous research findings, verbs formed the least frequently used category in Allison's speech. Allison used the four different verbs to describe what something was in the act of doing or what she intended to do. For example, she used "stop" to describe a toy car coming to a stop. The remaining three verbs were produced when Allison was performing an action herself, as when she said "turn" when she was turning the pages of a book, "climb" when she was trying to climb up onto the chair, and "sit" when she was going to sit on the chair. Although four different verbs showed up in Allison's speech, the total number of tokens from the verb category was significantly lower than for any of the other word categories. This follows what researchers generally expect of children's early speech, which includes only a small percentage of verbs (Uccelli & Pan, 2013).

While Allison used these four verbs to communicate action, she often used other words to convey the same meaning. For example, Allison used "up" in two different contexts. The first was in narrating an action she was performing, as when she said "up" while attempting to get up onto the chair. The second was as a request to Bloom to help her up. Allison also used the spatial term "down" to indicate similar intentions.

When not using spatial terms in place of more specific verbs, Allison used nouns to communicate intention and action. For example, one instance of her uttering the word "cookie" was to tell to her mother that she wanted a cookie, indicating this intention without using any verb. This pattern occurred in other contexts, as when she used the concrete noun "chair" but not the verb "sit" to indicate that she wanted to get onto the chair. The use of nouns instead of verbs when communicating certain concepts is perhaps expected, given the established preponderance of nouns in early word production. It also supports the idea that children communicate using the tools at hand (Pine, 1992): since Allison frequently employed nouns and spatial terms, it would seem that those are the tools that she had to rely on to convey whole hosts of meaning.

The results of my analysis of the transcript of Allison interacting

EARLY WORD PRODUCTION   14

with Bloom revealed aspects of the child's speech that were mostly
in line with the established features of early word production. The
frequency of the use of different word classes conformed to previous
findings that concrete nouns are most common, but other categories
varied from the expected patterns. Her choice of the spatial terms "up"
and "down" and the simple negative "no" is typical of children at this
age. However, the uncommon frequency of adjectives in her speech
indicates that they are important to how she communicated certain
meanings; like spatial terms, they often filled in for verbs in cases where
the actual verb was beyond her vocabulary. Her use of verbs, while
predictably limited, showed how she employed the few verbs that she
had and how she conveyed meaning when she did not have the precise
verbs available to her. Overall, Allison used a somewhat varied set of
words to communicate a wide range of meanings even though she had
only a limited vocabulary to work with.

EARLY WORD PRODUCTION   15

References

Anglin, J. M. (1995). Classifying the world through language: Functional relevance, cultural significance, and category name learning. *International Journal of Intercultural Relations, 19*(2), 161-181. Retrieved from http://www.sciencedirect.com/science/journal/01471767

Bates, E., Marchman, V., Thal, D., Fenson, L., Dale, P., Reznick, J. S., & Hartung, J. (1994). Developmental and stylistic variation in the composition of early vocabulary. *Journal of Child Language, 21*(1), 85-123. Retrieved from http://search.proquest.com/docview/58280873?accountid=13265

Bloom, L. (1973). *One word at a time: The use of single-word utterances before syntax.* The Hague, Netherlands: Mouton.

Bowerman, M. (2007). Containment, support, and beyond: Constructing topological spatial categories in first language acquisition. In M. Aurnague, M. Hickmann, & L. Vieu (Eds.), *The categorization of spatial entities in language and cognition* (pp. 177-203). Amsterdam, Netherlands: John Benjamins.

Brown, R. (1973). *A first language: The early stages.* Cambridge, MA: Harvard University Press.

MacWhinney, B. (2000). *The CHILDES Project: Tools for analyzing talk.* (3rd ed.). Mahwah, NJ: Lawrence Erlbaum.

List of references begins on a new page. Heading is centered.

Entries are arranged alphabetically.

All lines except the first are indented ½" (5-7 spaces).

URL given for an article accessed through a database. Do not add a period at the end of a URL.

Entries for a work found in an edited collection includes the editors' names, first initial followed by last name.

EARLY WORD PRODUCTION   16

Nelson, K. (1973). Structure and strategy in learning to talk. *Monographs*
    of the Society for Research in Child Development, 38(1), 1-135.
    Retrieved from http://onlinelibrary.wiley.com/journal/10.1111/%2
    8ISSN%291540-5834

Pine, J. M. (1992). The functional basis of referentiality: Evidence
    from children's spontaneous speech. *First Language, 12*(1), 39-
    55. Retrieved from http://fla.sagepub.com/proxy.lib.pdx.edu/
    content/12/34/39.full.pdf+html

Santelmann, L. (2014). *Development of morphology and syntax*
    [PowerPoint slides]. Retrieved from https://d2l.pdx.edu/d2l/le/
    content/450980/viewContent/1515576/View

Uccelli, P., & Pan, B. A. (2013). Semantic development. In J. Berko Gleason
    & N. Bernstein Ratner (Eds.), *The development of language* (pp. 89-
    112). Boston, MA: Pearson.

Walker, D., Greenwood, C., Hart, B., & Carta, J. (1994). Prediction of school
    outcomes based on early language production and socioeconomic
    factors. *Child Development, 65*(2), 606-621. Retrieved from http://
    onlinelibrary.wiley.com/journal/10.1111/%28ISSN%291467-8624

Zukowski, A. (2013). Putting words together. In J. Berko Gleason &
    N. Bernstein Ratner (Eds.), *The development of language* (pp. 120-
    156). Boston, MA: Pearson.

When the source type is unconventional, unclear, or important to point out, indicate the medium in brackets.

PART VI

Style

ONCE UPON A TIME—and for a long time, too—style in writing meant ornamentation, "dressing up" your writing the way you might dress yourself up for a fancy ball. In fact, ancient images often show rhetoric as a woman in a gaudy flowing gown covered with figures of speech—metaphors, similes, alliteration, hyperbole, and so on—her stylish ornaments.

When we think of style today, however, we think not of ornamentation but of how a message is presented, whether that message is in writing, in speech, in images, or in another form. Think of a movie you like and then list all the things that go into creating its particular style, the *how* of its presentation:

Dame Rhetorica, from Gregor Reisch's *Margarita Philosophica* (1504).

acting, musical score, camera angles, editing—and so on. All these elements interact to give the film a certain style.

What can you use to give your writing your own particular style? To begin with, you have what writers have always had: words, words, words. Choosing just the right word (**DICTION**) and putting it in just the right place (**SYNTAX**) still matter a lot in developing style. And today writers have many other tools to use for creating messages that have style. Think not just word choice and syntax—think also typography, punctuation, color, sound, images, and more. All these elements help you write with style.

Why is style so important to writers? For one thing, we all respond to style, even if unconsciously. When we see something pleasing or arresting, we're much more likely to pay attention to it or agree with it. Simply put, messages that can get and hold our attention are the ones we are most likely to tune in to, remember, and act on. Especially in an age of information overload, it's these messages that will win out in the competition for our attention. Style, then, is not something added on to what you write, like icing on a cake; rather, style is an important ingredient in the substance of what you write.

That's why we take special care in this book to introduce you to issues of style: we want you to be a writer whose texts are distinctive, memorable, and persuasive. Getting and holding an audience's attention, however, is not the only thing that matters when it comes to style. You want to get that attention in ways that are *appropriate* to your topic, your purpose, your audience, and your entire rhetorical situation. If you're dressing for an important job interview, you choose clothes that are pleasing in a businesslike way; if you're dressing for another occasion—a rock concert, a basketball game, a religious service, a funeral—you will dress very differently.

It's difficult, though—even impossible—to set hard-and-fast rules to be sure you're making the right choices for a particular situation. Consider a fascinating analogy from rhetorician Brent Simoneaux about the choices an athlete has to make and the choices we as authors have to make:

> Imagine . . . the relationship between the pitcher and the batter. It's a complicated relationship forged in a complex calculus of the probable, yet unknown. I love those close-up shots on television of the batter studying the pitcher, waiting for the ball. The batter is poised, bat over shoulder, feet planted just so, ready to nimbly meet whatever comes. In that moment, the batter is both *at the mercy of* the pitcher, the rules of game, the equipment, the umpire and also *a participant and creator of* the game.
>
> The ball leaves the pitcher's hand.

In that moment, the coach can't tell the batter exactly what to do at the plate. There's absolutely no way of knowing exactly where that ball is going to go prior to stepping into the situation. There's no way of knowing from which direction the wind will be blowing. There's no way of knowing exactly what the umpire is going to call a strike. The only thing the batter can do is to arrive at the plate poised and remain sensitive to the game unfolding.

Of course, the coach can make a pretty good guess about what will happen and how to react based on what has happened in the past and a myriad of other known factors. The batter can guess as well. And they can both prepare accordingly. But in that utterly kairotic moment when the ball is flying through the air, everything is in flux. . . . And the coach's line has to be: *do the right thing.*

That doesn't mean *do whatever you want.* It doesn't mean *anything goes.* Rather, it's an acknowledgment that . . . the terms of "rightness" are always shifting. . . . Do the *right* thing.

—BRENT SIMONEAUX, "Do the Right Thing"

The same goes for authors. But that's part of the great fun of writing with style. You get to analyze the situation before you, like the batter and the pitcher do, and to think about how to seize the moment in order to get and hold the attention of your audience in the most appropriate ways. You even get something that the batter and pitcher don't have: you can take time to make your rhetorical decisions, to be an author who writes with a powerful and distinctive style.

The chapters that follow all aim to help you achieve that goal.

TWENTY-NINE

What's Your Style?

OES THE TITLE OF THIS CHAPTER sound like a caption in a fashion ad? If so, it's no surprise: we often associate style with clothing, as we see fashions change from season to season or even week to week. What's hot right now will show up in outlet malls in a year or so—and in a decade or two, if you're lucky, those once-trendy clothes at the back of your closet may become retro-chic again. (Do you think there's any hope for these clothes from the 1990s on the left? How about those from the '70s on the right?)

Stars of the TV shows *Beverly Hills, 90210* (1990–2000) and *The Brady Bunch* (1969–74) wear clothing typical of their times.

You might not be caught dead wearing these styles today. Style, after all, is about choices you do *not* make as well as those you do. Wearing a bikini to the beach might seem a perfectly good stylistic choice at twenty—but one you might well question at seventy or in a culture that puts a high value on personal modesty. Of course, there may be some things you would never choose to wear at any time because they just don't suit you at all—bright orange anything, for example, or cowboy boots. Most often, though, you choose your clothing to fit your own sense of yourself and to match the occasion: a business suit for an important interview; shorts and running shoes for the gym. Style, then, is both about creating your own "look" and making sure that look is appropriate to the particular situation.

Style in writing works the same way. As you write, you look for words and ways of using them that match the message you're trying to convey—including the impression of yourself that you want to project. To achieve this goal, you do certain things while not doing others. In this chapter, we aim to give you tools you can use to think about and shape the style of your writing. Specifically, we'll consider the issues of appropriateness, formality, and stance; as you'll see, they're all related.

Appropriateness and Correctness

To understand style in writing, you need to think in terms of a key rhetorical term: appropriateness. Put most simply, an appropriate writing style is one in which your language and the way you arrange it suits your topic, your purpose, your stance, and your audience. But making appropriate stylistic choices in writing can be tricky, especially because we don't have a set of hard-and-fast rules to follow. You may have learned that it's never appropriate to start a sentence with *and* or *but* or to end a sentence with a preposition. But even those "rules" are far from universal—and change over time. In fact, much fine writing today breaks these "rules" to good effect (as we do in the preceding sentence).

So it won't work to think about style simply as a matter of following the rules. In fact, when it comes to being "correct" or being "appropriate," being appropriate wins out in almost all cases. When *Star Trek* announced its mission "to boldly go where no man has gone before," that split infinitive ("boldly" splits the two words of the infinitive "to go") wasn't absolutely "correct," but it created just the emphasis the writers were after. (Say it out loud and see

The crew of the U.S.S. *Enterprise* split infinitives boldly, and with emphasis.

how different "to boldly go" and "to go boldly" sound!) Moreover, it was an appropriate choice for the time (the 1960s) and place (a TV show, not an academic paper). One mark of its stylistic appropriateness: it's still quoted, even in textbooks! Making appropriate stylistic choices, then, will almost always depend on your **RHETORICAL SITUATION** —what you're talking about, where you are, who the audience is, and how you're communicating with them.

Standard edited English: the default choice. In school and in many professional contexts, standard edited English is often seen as the most appropriate choice. Though there's plenty of debate over what standard edited English is, think of it as that variety of English most often used in education, government, and most professional contexts, especially in writing. Like the standard variety of any written language, standard edited English has changed across time—and will continue to change. If you read the stories of Flannery O'Connor, a twentieth-century American fiction writer, you'll notice that she uses the words *man* and *he* to refer to people in general. Choices like this seemed appropriate at the time. But when many criticized the use of *he* to refer to both men and women, conventions changed, and writers looked for more appropriate choices. Were O'Connor, who died in 1964, writing today, it's likely that her use of language would reflect that change.

But the facts that standard languages emerge and change over time and that the appropriate use of a language most often depends on context don't mean that there are no rules at all. There are some rules, and following them—or not—has consequences. After all, the logic behind standard languages is that if users of a language all follow the same rules, then we can focus on content—on *what* is said—rather than being distracted by *how* it is said. When you don't follow these fairly basic rules, readers may end up focusing more on the how than on the what.

"You gotta know the rules to break the rules." This old saying still holds true in many situations. Take a look, for instance, at how linguist Geneva Smitherman breaks the rules of standard edited English brilliantly. In fact, had she stuck with those rules, the following paragraph would have been far less effective than it is.

> Before about 1959 (when the first study was done to change black speech patterns), Black English had been primarily the interest of university academics, particularly the historical linguists and cultural anthropologists. In recent years, though, the issue has become a very hot controversy, and there have been articles on Black Dialect in the national press as well as in the educational research literature. We have had pronouncements on black speech from the NAACP and the Black Panthers, from highly publicized scholars of the Arthur Jensen–William Shockley bent, from executives of national corporations such as Greyhound, and from housewives and community folk. I mean, really, it seem like everybody and they momma done had something to say on the subject!
>
> —GENEVA SMITHERMAN, *Talkin and Testifyin:*
> *The Language of Black America*

Geneva
Smitherman

Smitherman obviously knows the rules of standard edited English but breaks them to support her point and also to create a clear rhetorical stance, as a scholar, a skilled writer, and a proud African American. Writing in the late 1970s, she could assume that her readers would know that the NAACP is the National Association for the Advancement of Colored People, that the Black Panthers were a revolutionary social action group in the 1960s and 1970s, and that Arthur Jensen and William Shockley had made controversial claims about relationships between race and intelligence. She could also assume that readers of her book would expect her to write in standard edited English since the volume was published by a mainstream publisher and treated its subject from an academic perspective.

But Smitherman wasn't interested in writing a book about the vivid, energetic language of African Americans using only standard edited English. After all, one of her claims was that the language practices of African Americans were influencing American culture and language in many ways. Notice how her stylistic choices support that claim. She not only talks the talk of standard edited English but walks the walk of African American English as well. When she switches in her final sentence from standard edited English to African American English, she simultaneously drives home her point—that everyone at that time seemed to have an opinion about the language of African Americans—while demonstrating membership in that community by using the language variety associated with it. In short, she makes sound and appropriate stylistic choices.

Level of Formality

Being appropriate also calls on writers to pay attention to the levels of formality they use. In ancient Rome, Cicero identified three levels of style: low, or plain, style, which was used to teach or explain something; middle style, which was used to please an audience; and high, or grand, style, which was used to move or persuade the audience. Note how these classifications link style with a specific purpose and a likely audience.

Following the January 2011 tragedy in Tucson, Arizona, in which nineteen people, including Congresswoman Gabrielle Giffords, were shot and six died, President Obama delivered an address to the nation. The occasion was solemn and formal, and Obama, speaking as the nation's leader, offered a fine example of grand style, one that sought to move his audience by speaking from his heart to theirs as he sought to console the country.

Early in his speech, Obama quoted a passage from Psalm 46, part of the Hebrew Bible and the Christian Old Testament. He then offered short portraits of the victims of the shooting, those who had died and those who survived, as well as of people who had bravely intervened to limit the scope of the attack. Later in his remarks, he said:

You can find Obama's speech at everyonesanauthor.tumblr.com.

> If this tragedy prompts reflection and debate—as it should—let's make sure it's worthy of those we have lost. . . . The loss of these wonderful people should make every one of us strive to be better. To be better in our private lives, to be better friends and neighbors and coworkers and

parents. And if, as has been discussed in recent days, their death helps usher in more civility in our public discourse, let us remember it is not because a simple lack of civility caused this tragedy—it did not—but rather because only a more civil and honest public discourse can help us face up to the challenges of our nation in a way that would make them proud.

Here Obama used repetition and complex sentence structure appropriate to the gravity of the occasion. If you listen to the speech, you'll also hear how he used pauses to great effect. Note, too, that even in the grand style he used some contractions and that they helped lessen the distance between him and his audience of ordinary Americans; their use humanized him in a moment when his focus was the common humanity of all present. In this case, the level of formality was perfectly appropriate to the occasion. But the president (or anyone else for that matter) doesn't use this level of formality all the time. In a news conference after the Democrats lost the 2010 congressional elections badly, for example, Obama used the slang term "shellacking" to refer to his party's defeat—a good example, we think, of shifting levels of formality to one that was appropriate to that occasion (a press conference) and that audience (Americans who were following the aftermath of the elections).

Stance

Stance refers to the attitude authors take toward their topic and audience. For example, you might write about immigration as an impassioned advocate or critic, someone with strong opinions about the inherent good or evil of immigration; or you might write as a dispassionate analyst, someone trying to weigh carefully the pros and cons of the arguments for and against a particular proposal. Either stance—and any possible stances in between—will affect what style you use, whether in speaking or in writing.

If your audience changes, your language will likely shift, too. Debating immigration issues with close friends whose opinions you're fairly sure of will differ in crucial ways from debating them with people you know less well or not at all because you'll be able to take less for granted. That you will likely shift all aspects of your message—from word choice and sentence structure to amount of background information and choice of examples—

doesn't make you a hypocrite or a flip-flopper; instead, it demonstrates your skill at finding the most effective rhetorical resources to make your point.

In a posting titled "Same Food Planet, Different Food Worlds," blogger Rod Dreher calls attention to the drastically different stances taken by two restaurant reviewers. Here's an excerpt from one, a review of a new Olive Garden restaurant in Grand Forks, North Dakota, by eighty-five-year-old Marilyn Hagerty:

> It had been a few years since I ate at the older Olive Garden in Fargo, so I studied the two manageable menus offering appetizers, soups and salads, grilled sandwiches, pizza, classic dishes, chicken and seafood and filled pastas.
>
> At length, I asked my server what she would recommend. She suggested chicken Alfredo, and I went with that. Instead of the raspberry lemonade she suggested, I drank water.
>
> She first brought me the familiar Olive Garden salad bowl with crisp greens, peppers, onion rings and yes—several black olives. Along with it came a plate with two long, warm breadsticks.
>
> The chicken Alfredo ($10.95) was warm and comforting on a cold day. The portion was generous. My server was ready with Parmesan cheese. . . .
>
> All in all, it is the largest and most beautiful restaurant now operating in Grand Forks. It attracts visitors from out of town as well as people who live here.   —MARILYN HAGERTY, "Long-awaited Olive Garden Receives Warm Welcome"

Hagerty's polite, unpretentious stance is evident in this review—and as it happens, the style of her writing attracted much attention when it went viral, with readers both celebrating and bashing that style.

Dreher contrasts Hagerty's stance with that of Dive Bar Girl (DBG), who writes for a newsletter in Baton Rouge, Louisiana. In fact, DBG starts right out by announcing her stance—she's going to be "mean," not "informative"—and so after saying "a few nice things" about her topic, a restaurant called Twin Peaks, she writes the review that she assumes her readers "want to read":

> Admit it, you like it when DBG is mean. You only send her fan mail when she's mean. She never gets mail for being informative. . . . So she is going to write about the positive things first and then write the review you

Marilyn Hagerty. Read the *Los Angeles Times'* take on the controversy— and Hagerty's son's response in the *Wall Street Journal*—at everyonesan author.tumblr.com.

want to read. The smokehouse burger was above average. The patio was a nice space. The staff, while scantily clad, was professional. The salads even looked good. The place was miles above Hooters.

Here is the review you want: Twin Peaks has to be the brainchild of two 14-year-old boys who recently cracked the parental controls on the home computer. Waitresses are known as "Lumber Jills." In case you are missing the imagery—each Lumber Jill has been endowed with an epic pair of Twin Peaks.   —CHERRYTHEDIVEBARGIRL

These two reviews could hardly be more different in stance: the first is low key and even-handed, well suited to Hagerty's stance as a modest and sincere reviewer. The second is highly opinionated and sarcastic, true to the brash, in-your-face stance of Dive Bar Girl. So both are written in styles that suit (and reflect) their respective stances.

But what happens when that stance doesn't fit well with a particular audience? That's what happened when Hagerty's review went viral: some writers immediately began making fun of her as inept and hopelessly out of it; others jumped in just as quickly to defend Hagerty's review, while still others read her review as an indirect parody of local restaurant reviews. Now imagine that Dive Bar Girl's review appeared in Hagerty's hometown newspaper. Chances are it would attract some hefty criticism as well.

The takeaway lesson here: as a writer, you need to consider whether your **STANCE** is appropriate not only to your topic and audience but also to your **MODE** of distribution. If what you write is going online, then you have to remember that your audience can be very broad indeed.

What do these photos say about Olive Garden (*left*) and Twin Peaks (*right*)?

Thinking about Your Own Style

As you've seen, style is all about making appropriate choices, choices that inevitably depend on your topic and all the elements of your rhetorical situation, especially your STANCE, your PURPOSE, your GENRE, and your AUDIENCE. Have you written a review of something—a restaurant for the campus newspaper? A book on *Amazon*? Your school on *Collegeprowler.com*? If so, take a look at the choices you made in the review, and then compare them to those you made in an essay you wrote for your first-year writing class—or a poster you created for a school project on a subject like alcohol awareness. You'll see right away that you have instinctively used different styles for these different occasions. You may not, however, have paid much attention to the choices you were making to create these styles.

For an example of what we mean about making appropriate stylistic choices, take a look at a paragraph from this book, first as it appears on page 637 and then as it is revised as a tweet, a report, and a flyer (on the following page):

Original text

Once upon a time—and for a long time, too—style in writing meant ornamentation, "dressing up" your writing the way you might dress yourself up for a fancy ball. In fact, ancient images often show rhetoric as a woman in a gaudy flowing gown covered with figures of speech—metaphors, similes, alliteration, hyperbole, and so on—her stylish ornaments.

Revised as a tweet

Writing style used to mean dressing up your words, like Cinderella getting ready for the ball. Not anymore. #rhetorictoday

Revised as a report

For more than 500 years, the definition of "style" held relatively stable. Style was a form of ornamentation that was added to texts in order to make them more pleasing or accessible to an audience. In ancient depictions, Rhetoric is often shown as a woman dressed in elegant attire and "ornamented" with dozens of stylish figures of speech.

Revised as a flyer

O*nce upon a time . . .*

writing style was all about ornamentation.

ℰ *Language* ℛ

in fancy dress

What do you know about writing style?

Join us in the Writing Center to learn how style has changed over time

and how your style can be *in* style.

Sterling C. Evans Library

Room 214

Note how the style changes to match each genre and audience: the tweet is short, of course, and very informal; it uses a sentence fragment and then uses a hashtag to link readers with others talking about rhetoric today. The report is much more formal and is written in standard edited English. The flyer uses a much more conversational style—ellipses to signal a pause, a sentence fragment, a question, and italics for emphasis—and announces an event (the purpose of a flyer).

We hope this chapter has convinced you of the importance of paying attention to the stylistic choices you make—and has shown you that style is the key to getting and holding an audience's attention. As an author, you get to call the shots—and you need to do so with careful attention to your rhetorical situation. And though there may not be any simple do's and don'ts for writing in an appropriate style, here are some questions that can help you think through the stylistic choices you'll need to make in your own writing.

- *What's appropriate?* In short, what word choice, sentence structure, images, punctuation, typography, and other elements of writing will get your message across in a way that is most fitting to your PURPOSE and AUDIENCE as well as the GENRE you are working in?

- *What level of formality should you use?* Think particularly of your topic and audience, and of your audience's expectations, as you decide whether to adopt a colloquial, informal, semiformal, or very formal level of language.

- *What STANCE should you take?* Again, think about matching your stance to your purpose and topic and audience. For a formal college essay, you will probably aim for a serious scholarly stance; for a letter of application, a businesslike stance; and for a letter to the campus newspaper editor poking fun at a recent concert, a satiric, playful stance.

↜ *REFLECT. Have some fun with style by choosing a writer you admire—or one you love to hate!—and then trying your hand at imitating that person's style. Cast a wide net in making your choice: consider songwriters, op-ed writers, cookbook authors (Martha Stewart? Julia Child?), novelists, poets, TV commentators (Stephen Colbert, maybe?). Gather a sample of this person's work, enough to give you a good sense of his or her style and stylistic choices in terms of language, sentence structure, rhythm, imagery, and so on. Then choose a well-known story or song or other text: a children's story like "Little Red Riding Hood," a song like "Uptown Funk" by Mark Ronson and Bruno Mars, or a genre like a tweet or an ad. Now rewrite this text in the style of the author you chose—or ham it up a little by exaggerating the style! Your goal is to exercise your own authorial muscles and have some fun doing so.*

THIRTY

Tweets to Reports

On Social Media
and Academic Writing

 S *GOOGLE* **MAKING US STUPID?** Is *Twitter* destroying our ability to think straight? You're probably aware of these claims, and of the debate about whether the internet is undermining our ability to write well. The cartoon on the following page alludes to this debate, suggesting that online communication is less than "verbal."

It's true enough that online abbreviations such as TMI and OMG sometimes show up in our everyday speech as well as in our online writing. But "undermining our ability to write well"? We don't think so. In fact, our research has shown that most students in first-year writing classes know not to use such abbreviations in their academic writing.

In addition, while you may assume that the informal writing you do on social media sites is totally different from the more formal writing you need to do for school, think again. When you update your status on *Facebook*, you have a pretty good idea who your readers are, and you have a good sense of what's appropriate in terms of topic, language, and style. This is the same kind of rhetorical thinking you need to do for the writing you do in school.

In fact, some of the academic writing you do may well be *in* social media. An instructor may assign you to respond to a video posted on *Tumblr*, you may tweet some information you want to share with classmates, or you may comment online to respond to an article. In addition, you may follow one or more scholars on *Twitter* whose work focuses on a topic you're researching. You may subscribe to their blogs—and later cite something you find there in an academic assignment.

This chapter aims to help you shift easily among the various kinds of writing you do—informal and formal, online and off. Tweets, *Yelp* reviews, MLA-style reports, literary analyses: each has its own conventions, but they all use many of the same rhetorical strategies. And no matter what or where you are writing, it needs to be appropriate to your rhetorical situation, including your audience, your purpose, and your medium.

REFLECT. Take some time to look carefully at a sample of your writing for social media, noting recent Facebook posts, Instagram photos, tweets, and so on. How informal or formal are they? What do they assume your audiences will know about your topic? What are their purposes—to share information? to ask for advice? something else? Then compare these with one or two short pieces of writing you have recently done for a class, asking yourself the same questions. Finally, write a few sentences about what your college writing and your social media writing have in common—and how they differ.

Participating in Conversations

Wonder what other people are thinking about an issue that's important to you? Have something you'd like to shout for the whole world to hear? Today it takes only a couple of clicks to start or join conversations online, conversations that allow you to voice your opinions and to hear what others are thinking.

You're likely familiar with the hashtag #BlackLivesMatter, which took social media by storm in 2014 following the deaths of several unarmed black men at the hands of police officers. But what you may not know is that this hashtag and the conversation it sparked grew from a simple act by three women back in 2012. Grieving over the death of Trayvon Martin and astonished that his killer, George Zimmerman, was not convicted of any crime, Alicia Garza, Opal Tometi, and Patrisse Cullors needed an outlet to talk, to listen, and to share the message that "black lives matter." So they turned to social media, creating pages on *Facebook*, on *Tumblr*, and on *Twitter* where people could post stories, report events, and collaborate. And of course they put a hashtag in front of their message, making it a way to start a conversation—and after the killings of Michael Brown and Eric Garner, a rallying cry for activists across the country.

As this book goes to press, #BlackLivesMatter has been tagged to millions of tweets that together form a conversation about the issue. See how three activists use the hashtag to spin their individual comments into the common thread.

DeRay McKesson @deray 31 Aug 2015
Everyone has a role to play in social justice. #BlackLivesMatter

Connie Collins @khanknee 9 Aug 2015
If all lives mattered, there'd be no need to say #BlackLivesMatter or to film the police, or to fight for fair housing, employment or life.

Jose Antonio Vargas @joseiswriting 8 Aug 2015
If u question #BlackLivesMatter, if u can't see yourself in struggle of undocumented immigrants, u don't know America.

Like many hashtags, #BlackLivesMatter launched a conversation on social media. And once the discussion gathered steam, it became a place where people all over the world could talk, listen, share, and rally.

The point is simple and profound: through social media, individuals can start conversations about issues of great importance and get those messages out to people around the world, who can then join in, adding their voices, their stories, and their points of view. From the Arab Spring to Occupy Wall Street, social media has helped to build those conversations.

As a student, you may already be using social media to tell others about issues you care about or topics that interest you. One student we know, a budding cartoonist, tweets news about where her cartoons are appearing every week, and she's counting on plenty of re-tweets to add to her growing community of followers.

Or you might decide to participate in a conversation already in play on *Twitter, Facebook,* or elsewhere on the web. Here's one Michigan student joining a conversation on *Twitter* following the (very expensive) hiring of San Francisco 49ers coach Jim Harbaugh to lead the Michigan Wolverines. He tags his tweet #UMich to link his comment to others talking about this and other issues related to the University of Michigan.

> Frank Laverne @blueandgold 30 Dec 2014
> Of all places to put $8m, #UMich chooses football? Are we a school or
> a sports team?

Note that Laverne phrases his opinion in the form of a question for others to answer. It is pointed and succinct, designed to encourage others to join in. Now take a look at several tweets in response.

> James Kelcey @Jaymes 30 Dec 2014
> @blueandgold I can think of at least ten causes at #UMich that could better use that kind of money! Better pay for staff and faculty, for instance.

> Alex Jacquette @KitKatJac 30 Dec 2014
> @blueandgold Ridiculous paycheck for a football coach . . . or for anyone.

> Cailin Kassia @CKKass 30 Dec 2014
> @blueandgold Does make you wonder what programs around here are losing out on funding that goes to football instead.

Notice that each writer tweets "@blueandgold" to connect his or her comment to Laverne's original question, joining the conversation and engaging with Laverne directly. Each response is also carefully crafted to make one strong point very succinctly. You'll want to do the same when you join *Twitter* conversations: have something important to add; put it as directly, succinctly, and memorably as possible; and invite response.

These short, informal messages work on *Twitter* and *Facebook*, but making an argument in an academic essay would call for building your case in a different way. You'd need to to weave the ideas of others in with your own: summarizing what's been said about your topic before stating what you want to say, acknowledging and responding to perspectives other than your own, and so on. And more than just adding a **HASHTAG**, you'd need to document any words or ideas that come from others in a works cited or references list. But much like tweeting or posting to social media, writing an essay is one way that you can add your voice to an ongoing conversation.

Sharing Information

Many people post links on social media to disseminate news and other information, or write posts to inform others about things they think worth sharing. Here is Jeffrey Gerson sharing a photo from his travels in Transylvania with his *Instagram* followers, along with a caption with information he hopes will give them some of the flavor of those experiences.

The caption adds descriptive details: the house's location, the "scent of lilacs in the spring." If he were writing about the same subject for a history class, Gerson would probably have to provide much more (and more factual) information.

jeffreydgerson Transylvania smells like lilacs in the springtime. Everywhere we go, in every village and city, courtyard and citadel, there have been fragrant shocks of lilacs drowsily bowing their heads in the breeze. This lone house stands high on the hilltop in Sighisoara, next to a church that has overlooked the city for more than 500 years. This country is more beautiful than I ever could have anticipated, more beautiful even than the scent of lilacs in spring.

But brevity is a common feature of writing on social media, even when the post is for academic rather than personal purposes. Here's one student tweeting an academic link:

Aaron Jackson @Kodacruz 13 Jan 2015
How the Sense of Taste Has Shaped Who We Are
goscientificamerican.com/article/how-th . . . #anthropology #senses

This writer is merely sharing information, linking to an article in *Scientific American* that he tags under two topics: #anthropology and #senses. Like Gerson, he gives just enough information to introduce readers to the information without elaborating on it at length; he simply refers them to an article he thinks they may want to read.

When you cite or link to sources in an academic report, you need to take a couple of important steps that you may skip when you're merely sharing a link. First of all, you need to **EVALUATE** the reliability of the source, and of any research that the source relies on. *Scientific American* is a known and trusted source of scientific and technical information, but before citing an article from a less familiar source in an academic writing assignment, you'd want to identify the credentials of the author and to verify the quality of the evidence he or she provides, including any sources referred to in the text.

And even then, you should look for other credible sources that seem to agree with or support his or her conclusions—as well as ones that offer other viewpoints on the topic that you need to consider and acknowledge. Finally, for any sources you link to, check to be sure that the links are live.

Representing Yourself in Your Writing

Take a look at how some of your friends represent themselves on *Facebook*. What profile pictures do they choose to say "this is who I am"? What personal information do they include? What facts about themselves run under their names? What kind of updates, photos, or links do they post?

Here is Stephanie Parker (on the following page), whose photo shows her with the words "laugh every day" inscribed on her face and hand, suggesting that she doesn't take herself too seriously, that she thinks laughter is a good thing, and that she wants us to think about how this motto might apply to us and our lives. She identifies herself as a student of media studies and lists some of her affiliations: with her college, with *TechSoup*, with Volunteers in Asia. In a recent post, she says:

> WOW!! Words cannot describe how happy I am that I got to meet so many new friends during my trip to Japan! You were all so kind and gracious to me, and made sure I had the best possible time. I will never forget, and look forward to seeing you when you visit the U.S.!

Taken together, Parker's photo and this post depict her as a friendly, happy student who is engaged with friends, travel, and experiencing new things. The language of her posting is informal ("WOW!!") and a bit overstated ("words cannot describe how happy I am," "best possible time"), and even her punctuation (multiple exclamation points) is more casual than she would use in a college essay.

In a more academic context, Parker could also represent herself as friendly and outgoing and enthusiastic, but her **TONE**, sentence structure, and punctuation would be more formal. As part of a statement on the *Facebook* page of the campus organization that funded her trip, she might say something like this:

> Meeting so many new friends on my trip to Japan made me happy and very grateful for the kind and gracious way I was received. I will cherish these memories and look forward to welcoming my hosts when they visit the United States.

Note the more formal word choices ("cherish these memories" rather than "never forget," "United States" rather than "U.S.") and more formal punctuation—no use of all caps for emphasis, for example, and no exclamation points. This version is more restrained and formal, but it still conveys Parker's voice.

Notice that first-person pronouns can be used in both informal and formal writing. You may have been told never to use *I* in academic writing, and especially in the sciences, the first person can sometimes be inappropriate.

Researchers describing an experiment should, after all, put the emphasis on the experiment rather than on themselves—to say "the experiment revealed *x*" rather than "we conducted an experiment that revealed *x*." But in some academic writing, using the first person is perfectly acceptable. Consider the context: if your own experience is pertinent to the topic, saying *I* may be appropriate. But don't overdo it. Even in the most informal writing, too much first person can get a little boring or sound too self-centered, as if everything is about *me*.

Establishing an Appropriate Tone

All of the writing you do—formal, informal, or in between—has a particular **TONE**. You may not think consciously about how to establish that tone, especially when commenting on a friend's *Instagram* photo or tapping out a quick text message, but even in the most informal writing, you are making choices about what attitude you want your text to convey. When you know that your readers are mostly friends and family, your tone can probably be pretty casual, like this *Facebook* update posted by a student in Washington, DC.

> Note to self: avoid union station on weekday mornings. Hordes of angry commuters make getting to the train impossible! #notfun #DCMetro #rushhour #istheworst

Even in this short snippet of writing, this writer's attitude shows. The tone is one of frustration and exasperation, which she expresses in the **HASHTAGS** she adds: #notfun, #istheworst. Such hashtags are a playful and appropriate way for this writer to voice her complaints on social media, but not so in an academic context.

If you were writing a report on commuters in Union Station for your urban studies class instead of a *Facebook* post for friends and family, you'd likely use the more serious tone of a reporter or researcher.

> Walking into Union Station on a weekday morning can be like going against a herd of stampeding cattle. Riders rush from the trains, swinging briefcases and computer bags, knocking over anything or anyone in the way. Rush hour in this station, one of the busiest train stations in the country, is not fun. Looking at some usage statistics and videos will

show just how unpleasant this experience is and how it affects those who regularly ride the Metro.

Here the tone is more serious. The writer opens by describing the scene in the congested station and then moves to introduce an analysis of usage statistics and videos. But even a serious tone doesn't need to be dull. Note the lively description ("stampeding cattle," "swinging briefcases," "knocking over anything or anyone in the way").

Connecting to Audiences

In all your writing—formal and informal, online or off—you need to have a reasonably good sense of your intended audience in order to write effectively. Take a look at the image on the facing page; it's the webpage for a supermarket in a small town in California that appeals directly to its local community. The writers set a friendly, informal tone right away, announcing that "we love good food" and appealing to their audience to "SHOP LOCAL." The emphasis on the local continues as they note that they've been "serving our community" for decades. They also invite readers to visit their *Facebook* page—and learn about "our sustainable fish program." The use of "our" emphasizes the community and establishes COMMON GROUND with readers. The bright colors and simple design add to the warm, inviting tone that underscores the overall message.

A student writing about this same topic for a class project must be more formal and would need to include the background and contextual information that an academic audience expects. Here is Katherine Spriggs arguing for the importance of "buying local":

> "Buying local" means that consumers choose to buy food that has been grown, raised, or produced as close to their home as possible. Buying local is an important part of the response to many environmental issues we face today. It encourages the development of small farms, which are often more environmentally sustainable than large farms, and thus strengthens local markets and supports small rural economies. By demonstrating a commitment to buying local, Americans could set an example for global environmentalism.
>
> —KATHERINE SPRIGGS, "On Buying Local"

The Surf Market in Gualala, California, welcomes customers to its webpage with a friendly, informal tone.

Rather than assuming that her audience already knows what "buying lo-cal" means, Spriggs begins with a careful definition—something the Surf Market webpage doesn't need to do—as a way of laying the groundwork for her argument and demonstrating that she is knowledgeable about her topic. She then starts to build her argument by linking the idea of buying local to environmental issues and community values. Her tone is serious; she gives practical reasons for why buying local is "important," noting that it "encourages the development of small farms" and "supports small rural economies."

Attention to audience is always important in academic writing: you need to think carefully about who will read what you write and how best to connect with them. In classes that invite you to post comments to a course website or conduct peer reviews, a casual tone can serve you well. In other instances, such as communicating with an instructor by email, a more for-mal approach is more appropriate.

Providing Context

When writing informally, you will often leave out a lot of information if you know that your readers are familiar with the context and don't need explicit cues. Especially online, writers sometimes opt for brevity over clarity when writing to friends or peers. Look, for instance, at this short piece of writing about college football posted to *Twitter* by Pat Bostick, a radio analyst and former quarterback for the Pittsburgh Panthers.

> Pat Bostick @pittbostick   24 Sep 2011
> What a great day for college football in the 'Burgh! Mid 60's and overcast for the Panthers vs. the Irish. Go #Pitt!!

The writer of this tweet assumes that his readers will understand a lot about the context for his post—that "the 'Burgh" is short for Pittsburgh, for instance, as is "Pitt"; that the Panthers are the Pitt team and the Irish are Notre Dame; and that the weather will be good. Readers will probably also know that the HASHTAG is used here to link to others tweeting about the University of Pittsburgh. In informal writing, readers are often expected to be able to understand the context or to figure out any context clues—in this case about Pittsburgh football and the *Twitter* format. Informal writing—and especially brief posts like those on *Twitter*—allows you as an author to give readers quick context clues without detailed explanation.

In more formal writing, such as a newspaper article, a statement like this one would need to provide more explicit CONTEXT: to say when and where the game is taking place and why this particular game represents "a great day" for college football. Academic writing follows even more formal conventions. Here's the kind of context you might provide in a proposal arguing that the Pitt football team needs new warm-weather uniforms:

> Close analysis reveals that the University of Pittsburgh football team's record can be correlated with game day weather conditions. Over the last five seasons, the Panthers have recorded 29 percent fewer victories when the temperature exceeds 60 degrees Fahrenheit.

Giving detailed and explicit data—"29 percent fewer victories when the temperature exceeds 60 degrees"—to explain the problem helps establish a context for what you're proposing.

Organizing What You Write

The way you organize what you write plays a big role in making your message clear and persuasive. Even in your most informal writing, you probably intuitively structure what you write in a way that helps make your point. You state a claim, an idea, a thought—and then you offer reasons to support what you've stated. So organization is likely something you already utilize in your informal writing.

Take a look at a very concise review posted on *Yelp* about *Serial,* the 2014 podcast investigating the true story of a murder in Baltimore in 1999. Adnan Syed was found guilty of murdering his ex-girlfriend and sentenced to life in prison, based largely on the testimony of his former friend and classmate Jay. But Syed has always insisted that he is innocent, and *Serial* revisits the evidence. See how Don B. organizes his review in a way that leads us directly to his point:

> **Don B.**
> Portland, OR
> 12/19/2014
>
> Now that it's over, I have to ask what everyone (who has listened to the *Serial* podcast) thinks. Did Adnan do it? Was he framed? Is Jay a mastermind? Even if you think Adnan did it, do you think the jury really had enough to convict him beyond reasonable doubt?
>
> Man, that was a great podcast series.

Don B. uses a simple structure in writing his review, posing the very questions that got millions of people hooked on *Serial* ("Did Adnan do it?") as a way of introducing—and, in a way, of proving—his point: "Man, that was a great podcast series." Quick and to the point, as is appropriate on a site like *Yelp.*

This same point is made in a different way in a review written for the website of the *Guardian*, a British daily newspaper, starting with a title proclaiming *Serial* "the greatest mystery you will ever hear." The author opens by telling readers that they "have to start listening to *Serial,*" next summarizes its basic plot, and then explains in some detail why she thinks it's so good:

> What is really intriguing about *Serial*—what drags you in and keeps you listening—is that it isn't a straightforward case. You assume, when someone protests their innocence, that you will listen to the evidence and say: yes, he did it, or no, he didn't. With *Serial*, nothing is quite so clear-cut. This is partly because, in real life, people don't remember where they

were six weeks ago, let alone 15 years back; partly because, in real life, people have their reasons to be shady about information. Koenig herself flip-flops between thinking that Syed did commit murder and being convinced that he didn't. —MIRANDA SAWYER, "The Greatest Mystery You Will Ever Hear"

This writer follows up her claim that *Serial* is "intriguing" with a reason for why that is: nothing in this story is "quite so clear-cut" as we might expect. Contrary to our usual assumptions that once we hear the evidence in a case we can decide whether someone is innocent or guilty, the evidence in Syed's case is too messy and potentially dubious to lead listeners to a clear conclusion. Even the author of the series "flip-flops" between thinking Syed is guilty and being convinced that he is innocent, keeping the intrigue alive—and keeping audiences listening.

Many college writing assignments will call for you to formulate a claim and then support it, just as the writer of the *Guardian* review does. In most of your college classes, however, you'll have more time and space to make your case than you would on *Yelp*; you'll be able (and expected) to introduce and explain your **CLAIM** and then provide a number of good **REASONS**, and **EVIDENCE** to support those reasons; to consider and respond to alternative points of view; and to say something about the implications of what you say.

Using Images

As the cameras in smartphones get better and better, it's increasingly easy to snap a photo of almost anything. As a result, images are becoming a routine feature of much of the writing we do online. Think about how often you've texted or posted a photo to show a friend something you've just seen. Writers now use images to make our writing more interesting or informative, or to illustrate a point. Take a look on the facing page at an image posted on *Instagram* by photojournalist Benjamin Lowy.

Notice how the image and the caption work together to make a point about "the American ideal." The image shows a ballplayer standing against two big American flags with more players in the distance, a snapshot of patriotism on a cricket field. The caption then explains Lowy's point, a point not evident in the photo alone: that none of the athletes were "born in this country" and yet they play as one team to prove that they "are going some-

Dennis Baron sprinkles his presentation with images that work in concert with the text. Check it out on p. 850.

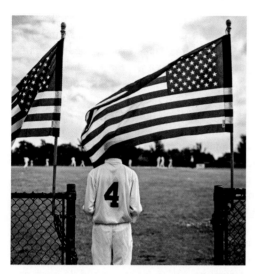

benlowy New York City, NY, July 4, 2014
Two weeks ago I shot the NYC high-school cricket championship for @espn. Athletes, none born in this country, saluted the American flag, hats in hand, the National Anthem playing on a loudspeaker. As a first generation American, this is what the US means to me. It doesn't matter where we came from, only that we are going somewhere together. That is the promise of the American ideal.

where together"—a demonstration of the American ideal that has special meaning to the author as "a first-generation American" himself.

You can use images in your academic writing to powerful effect as well. Adding a map, a diagram or pie chart, a photo, or even something you've drawn by hand is now easy to do and can make a point clear and concrete: sometimes a picture really is worth a thousand words. In Melissa Rubin's essay on Coca-Cola's advertising strategy, for instance, she found that including an image of the Coke ad she was analyzing helped her make the point of her analysis clear. Of course, you need to be more careful about how you use images in your academic writing than you do in social media: insert the image in the appropriate place, label it with a figure number, add an informative caption that credits the artist—and especially make sure readers know how the image supports your argument.

Read Melissa Rubin's essay on p. 246.

Citing Sources

Informal writing—whether it's on the internet or in your daily journal—allows you to skip some of the rules and requirements that formal writing requires. When you send someone a link, for example, you don't need to include formal documentation since readers can simply check out the information for themselves. You may make some reference to your sources; one student we know, a fan of Bollywood films, tweets often about the latest ones he's seen and often includes links to reviews. But when you post to *Facebook* asking if any friends want to go see a new movie you just heard about, you probably don't say where you heard about the movie or who told you about it, much less provide formal documentation.

Nevertheless, letting others know where you are getting your information can be very important. And giving others credit for their work is always important, whether you are writing a blog post or a college essay, even though the standards for documentation are much more relaxed when you are writing for a nonacademic audience. If you re-tweet or share someone else's status update, be sure to mention that fact and to give credit to the original poster.

Take a look at Christina Hernandez Sherwood's post from her blog, *Spaghetti & Meatballs*, which includes links to outside sources. Rather than relying on footnotes or in-text documentation (as she would do in an academic essay), she turned the words referring to the sources ("Gizmodo" and "small portion sizes") into links. She still gives the sources credit for the information she cites, but she does so in an appropriately informal way.

What would Italians think about Starbucks' Trenta?

There's been much hubbub this week over the newest, largest Starbucks drink size: Trenta.

The name means "thirty" in Italian, signifying the 30+ ounces of coffee the cup holds. That's more liquid than the average human stomach can handle, according to Gizmodo.

What would Italians think?

Italian diners, like other Europeans, are known for their small portion sizes. Can you imagine Italians sipping a Big Gulp-sized cappuccino while nibbling on their biscotti?

—CHRISTINA HERNANDEZ SHERWOOD

So this blogger is aware of the need to provide information about sources. If this were an academic essay in print form, the writer would need to provide appropriate **DOCUMENTATION** for the linked references. Note, however, that some online academic journals, especially in the sciences, use links rather than in-text citations.

As we've tried to demonstrate, the internet is not only *not* destroying our ability to write after all, but in fact is providing valuable, everyday practice that is teaching us how to represent ourselves, connect with audiences, and support our arguments—in writing. It's making us *all* writers, and it's one reason that today everyone is an author.

THIRTY-ONE

How to Write Good Sentences

HEN A STUDENT asked author Annie Dillard, "Do you think I could become a writer?" Dillard replied with a question of her own: "Do you like sentences?" French novelist Gustave Flaubert certainly did, once saying that he "itched with sentences." Itching with sentences probably isn't something you've experienced—and liking or not liking sentences might not be something you've ever thought about—but we're willing to bet that you know something about how important sentences are. Anyone who has ever tried to write the perfect tweet or, better yet, the perfect love letter knows about choosing just the right words for each sentence and about the power of the three-word sentence "I love you"—or the even shorter sentence that sometimes follows from such declarations: "I do."

In his book *How to Write a Sentence*, English professor Stanley Fish declares himself to be a "connoisseur of sentences" and offers some particularly noteworthy examples. Here's one, written by a fourth grader in response to an assignment to write something about a mysterious large box that had been delivered to a school:

▶ I was already on the second floor when I heard about the box.

This sentence reminded us of a favorite sentence of our own, this one the beginning of a story written by a third grader:

▶ Today, the monster goes where no monster has gone before: Cincinnati.

Here the student manages to allude to the famous line from *Star Trek*—"to boldly go where no man has gone before"—while suggesting that Cincinnati is the most exotic place on earth and even using a colon effectively. It's quite a sentence.

Finally, here's a sentence that opens a chapter from a PhD dissertation on literacy among young people today:

▶ Hazel Hernandez struck me as an honest thief.

Such sentences are memorable: They startle us a bit and demand attention. They make us want to read more. Who's Hazel Hernandez? What's an honest thief, and what makes her one?

As these examples suggest, you don't have to be a famous author to write a great sentence. In fact, crafting effective and memorable sentences is a skill everyone can master with careful attention and practice. You may not come up with a zinger like the famous sentence John Updike wrote about Ted Williams' fabled home run in his last at bat at Fenway Park—"It was in the books while it was still in the sky"—but you can come close.

Just as certain effects in film—music, close-ups—enhance the story, a well-crafted sentence can bring power to a piece of writing. So think about the kind of effect you want to create in what you're writing—and then look for the type of sentence that will fit the bill. Though much of the power of the examples above comes from being short and simple, remember that some rhetorical situations call for longer, complex sentences—and that the kind of sentence you write also depends on its context, such as whether it's opening an essay, summing up what's already been said, or something else. This chapter looks at some common English sentence patterns and provides some good examples for producing them in your own work.

FOUR COMMON SENTENCE PATTERNS

We make sentences with words—and we arrange those words into patterns. If a sentence is defined as a group of words that expresses a complete thought, then we can identify four basic sentence structures: a **SIMPLE SEN-TENCE** (expressing one idea); a **COMPOUND SENTENCE** (expressing more than one idea, with the ideas being of equal importance); a **COMPLEX SENTENCE** (expressing more than one idea, with one of the ideas more important than the others); and a **COMPOUND-COMPLEX SENTENCE** (with more than one idea of equal importance and at least one idea of less importance).

Simple Sentences: One Main Idea

Let's take a look at some simple sentences:

- ▶ Resist!

- ▶ Consumers revolted.

- ▶ Angry consumers revolted against new debit-card fees.

- ▶ A wave of protest from angry consumers forced banks to rescind the new fees.

- ▶ The growth of the internet and its capacity to mobilize people instantly all over the world have done everything from forcing companies to rescind debit-card fees in the United States to bringing down oppressive governments in the Middle East.

As these examples illustrate, simple sentences can be as short as a single word—or they can be much longer. Each is a simple sentence, however, because it contains a single main idea or thought; in grammatical terms, each contains one and only one **MAIN CLAUSE**. As the name suggests, a simple sentence is often the simplest, most direct way of saying what you want to say—but not always. And often you want a sentence to include more than one idea. In that case, you need to use a compound sentence, a complex sentence, or a compound-complex sentence.

Compound Sentences: Joining Ideas That Are Equally Important

Sometimes you'll want to write a sentence that joins two or more ideas that are equally important, like this one attributed to former president Bill Clinton:

> ▶ You can put wings on a pig, but you don't make it an eagle.

In grammatical terms, this is a compound sentence with two main clauses, each of which expresses one of two independent and equally important ideas. In this case, Clinton joined the ideas with a comma and the coordinating conjunction *but*. But he had several other options for joining these ideas. For example, he could have joined them with only a semicolon:

> ▶ You can put wings on a pig; you don't make it an eagle.

Or he could have joined them with a semicolon, a conjunctive adverb like *however*, and a comma:

> ▶ You can put wings on a pig; however, you don't make it an eagle.

All of these compound sentences are perfectly acceptable—but which seems most effective? In this case, we think Clinton's choice is: it is clear and very direct, and if you read it aloud you'll hear that the words on each side of *but* have the same number of syllables, creating a pleasing, balanced rhythm— and one that balances the two equally important ideas. It also makes the logical relationship between the two ideas explicit: *but* indicates a contrast. The version with only a semicolon, by contrast, indicates that the ideas are somehow related but doesn't show how.

Using *and*, *but*, and other coordinating conjunctions. In writing a compound sentence, remember that different coordinating conjunctions carry meanings that signal different logical relationships between the main ideas in the sentence. There are only seven coordinating conjunctions.

COORDINATING CONJUNCTIONS

and	for	or	yet
but	nor	so	

> ▶ China's one-child policy has slowed population growth, *but* it has helped create a serious gender imbalance in the country's population.

> ▶ Most of us bike to work, *so* many of us stop off at the gym for a shower first.

> ▶ The first two batters struck out, *yet* the Cubs went on to win the game on back-to-back homers.

See how the following sentences express different meanings depending on which coordinating conjunction is used:

▶ You could apply to graduate school, *or* you could start looking for a job.

▶ You could apply to graduate school, *and* you could start looking for a job.

Using a semicolon. Joining clauses with a semicolon only is a way of signaling that they are closely related without saying explicitly how. Often the second clause will expand on an idea expressed in the first clause.

▶ My first year of college was a little bumpy; it took me a few months to get comfortable at a large university far from home.

▶ The Wassaic Project is an arts organization in Dutchess County, New York; artists go there to engage in "art, music, and everything else."

Adding a **CONJUNCTIVE ADVERB** can make the logical relationship between the ideas more explicit:

▶ My first year of college was a little bumpy; *indeed,* it took me a few months to get comfortable at a large university far from home.

Note that the conjunctive adverb in this sentence, *indeed,* cannot join the two main clauses on its own—it requires a semicolon before it. If you use a conjunctive adverb between two clauses with only a comma before it, you've made a mistake called a **COMMA SPLICE**.

SOME CONJUNCTIVE ADVERBS

also	indeed	otherwise
certainly	likewise	similarly
furthermore	nevertheless	therefore
however	next	thus

REFLECT. Read through something you've written recently and identify compound sentences joined with and. *When you find one, ask yourself whether* and *is the best word to use: does it express the logical relationship between the two parts of the sentence that you intend? Would* but, or, so, for, nor, *or* yet *work better?*

Complex Sentences:
When One Idea Is More Important than Another

Many of the sentences you write will contain two or more ideas, with one that you want to emphasize more than the other(s). You can do so by putting the idea you wish to emphasize in the **MAIN CLAUSE**, and then putting those that are less important in **SUBORDINATE CLAUSES**.

▶ Mendocino County is a place in California *where you can dive for abalone.*

▶ *Because the species has become scarce,* abalone diving is strictly regulated.

▶ Fish and Wildlife Department agents *who patrol the coast* use sophisticated methods to catch poachers.

As these examples show, the ideas in the subordinate clauses (italicized here) can't stand alone as sentences: when we read "where you can dive for abalone" or "who patrol the coast," we know that something's missing. Subordinate clauses begin with words such as *if* or *because,* **SUBORDINATING CONJUNCTIONS** that signal the logical relationship between the subordinate clause and the rest of the sentence.

SOME SUBORDINATING CONJUNCTIONS

after	even though	until
although	if	when
as	since	where
because	that	while
before	though	who

Notice that a subordinate clause can come at the beginning of a sentence, in the middle, or at the end. When it comes at the beginning, it is usually followed by a comma, as in the second example. If the opening clause in that sentence were moved to the end, a comma would not be necessary: "Abalone diving is strictly regulated because the species has become scarce."

Grammatically, each of the three examples above is a complex sentence, with one main idea and one other idea of less importance. In writing you will often have to decide whether to combine ideas in a compound sentence, which gives the ideas equal importance, or in a complex sentence, which makes one idea more important than the other(s). Looking once more at our sentence about the pig and the eagle, Bill Clinton could have made it a complex sentence:

▶ Even though you can put wings on a pig, you don't make it an eagle.

Again, though, we think Clinton made a good choice in giving the two ideas equal weight because doing so balances the sentence perfectly—and tells us that both parts are equally important. In fact, neither part of this sentence is very interesting in itself: it's the balancing and the contrast that make it interesting and memorable.

Compound-Complex Sentences: Multiple Ideas—Some More Important, Some Less

When you are expressing three or more ideas in a single sentence, you'll sometimes want to use a compound-complex sentence, which gives some of the ideas more prominence and others less. Grammatically, such sentences have at least two **MAIN CLAUSES** and one **SUBORDINATE CLAUSE**.

▶ 　　　　　　　── MAIN CLAUSE ──　　　　　　── SUBORDINATE CLAUSE ──
We have experienced unparalleled natural disasters that have devastated

　　　　　　　　　　── MAIN CLAUSE ──
entire countries, yet identifying global warming as the cause of these

disasters is difficult.

▶ 　　　── SUBORDINATE CLAUSE ──　　　　　── MAIN CLAUSE ──
Even after distinguished scientists issued a series of reports, critics continued

　　　　　　　　　　── SUBORDINATE CLAUSE ──
to question the findings because they claimed results were falsified;

── MAIN CLAUSE ──
nothing would convince them.

As these examples show, English sentence structure is flexible, allowing you to combine groups of words in different ways in order to get your ideas across to your audience most appropriately and effectively. There's seldom only one way to write a sentence to get an idea across: as the author, you must decide which way works best for your **RHETORICAL SITUATION**.

WAYS OF EMPHASIZING
THE MAIN IDEA IN A SENTENCE

Sometimes, you will want to lead off a sentence with the main point; other times, you might want to hold it in reserve until the end. **CUMULATIVE SENTENCES** start with a main clause and then add on to it, "accumulating" details. **PERIODIC SENTENCES** start with a series of phrases or subordinate clauses, saving the main clause for last.

Cumulative Sentences: Starting with the Main Point

In this kind of sentence, the writer starts off with a **MAIN CLAUSE** and then adds details in phrases and **SUBORDINATE CLAUSES**, extending or explaining the thought. Cumulative sentences can be especially useful for describing a place or an event, operating almost like a camera panning across a room or landscape. The sentences below create such an effect:

▶ The San Bernardino Valley lies only an hour east of Los Angeles by the San Bernardino Freeway but is in certain ways an alien place: not the coastal California of the subtropical twilights and the soft westerlies off the Pacific but a harsher California, haunted by the Mojave just beyond the mountains, devastated by the hot dry Santa Ana wind that comes down through the passes at 100 miles an hour and whines through the eucalyptus windbreaks and works on the nerves.
　　　　　　　　　—JOAN DIDION, "Some Dreamers of the Golden Dream"

▶ Public transportation in Cebu City was provided by jeepneys: refurbished military jeeps with metal roofs for shade, decorated with horns and mirrors and fenders and flaps; painted with names, dedications, quotations, religious icons, logos—and much, much more.

▶ She hit the brakes, swearing fiercely, as the deer leapt over the hood and crashed into the dark woods beyond.

▶ The celebrated Russian pianist gave his hands a shake, a quick shake, fingers pointed down at his sides, before taking his seat and lifting them imperiously above the keys.

These cumulative sentences add details in a way that makes each sentence more emphatic. Keep this principle in mind as you write—and also when you revise. See if there are times when you might revise a sentence or sentences to add emphasis in the same way. Take a look at the following sentences, for instance:

► China has initiated free-market reforms that transformed its economy from a struggling one to an industrial powerhouse. It has become the world's fastest-growing major economy. Growth rates have been averaging 10 percent over the last decade.

These three sentences are clearly related, with each one adding detail about the growth of China's economy. Now look what happens when the writer eliminates a little bit of repetition, adds a memorable metaphor, and combines them as a cumulative—and more emphatic—sentence:

► China's free-market reforms have led to 10 percent average growth over the last decade, transforming it from a paper tiger into an industrial dragon that is now the world's fastest-growing major economy.

Periodic Sentences: Delaying the Main Point until the End

In contrast to sentences that open with the main idea, periodic sentences delay the main idea until the very end. Periodic sentences are sometimes fairly long, and withholding the main point until the end is a way of adding emphasis. It can also help create suspense or build up to a surprise or inspirational ending.

► In spite of everything, in spite of the dark and twisting path he saw stretching ahead for himself, in spite of the final meeting with Voldemort he knew must come, whether in a month, in a year, or in ten, he felt his heart lift at the thought that there was still one last golden day of peace left to enjoy with Ron and Hermione.   —J. K. ROWLING, *Harry Potter and the Half-Blood Prince*

► Unprovided with original learning, uninformed in the habits of thinking, unskilled in the arts of composition, I resolved to write a book.
     —EDWARD GIBBON, *Memoirs of My Life*

► In the week before finals, when my studying and memorizing reached a fever pitch, came a sudden, comforting thought: I have never failed.

Here are three periodic sentences in a row about Whitney Houston, each of which withholds the main point until the end:

> ▶ When her smiling brown face, complete with a close-cropped Afro, appeared on the cover of *Seventeen* in 1981, she was one of the first African-Americans to grace the cover, and the industry took notice. When she belted out a chilling and soulful version of the "Star-Spangled Banner" at the 1991 Super Bowl, the world sat back in awe of her poise and calm. And in an era when African-American actresses are often given film roles portraying them as destitute, unloving, unlovable, or just "the help," Houston played the love interest of Kevin Costner, a white Hollywood superstar.
>
> —ALLISON SAMUELS, "A Hard Climb for the Girl Next Door"

These three periodic sentences create a drumlike effect that builds in intensity as they move through the stages in Houston's career; in all, they suggest that Houston was, even more than Kevin Costner, a "superstar."

Samuels takes a chance when she uses three sentences in a row that withhold the main point until the end: readers may get tired of waiting for that point. And readers may also find the use of too many such sentences to be, well, too much. But as the example above shows, when used carefully a sentence that puts off the main idea just long enough can keep readers' interest, making them want to reach the ending, with its payoff.

You may find in your own work that periodic sentences can make your writing more emphatic. Take a look at the following sentence from an essay on the use of animals in circuses:

> ▶ The big cat took him down with one swat, just as the trainer, dressed in khakis and boots, his whip raised and his other arm extended in welcome to the cheering crowd, stepped into the ring.

This sentence paints a vivid picture, but it gives away all the action in the first six words. By withholding that action until the end, the writer builds anticipation and adds emphasis:

> ▶ Just as the trainer stepped into the ring, dressed in khakis and boots, his whip raised and his other arm extended in welcome to the cheering crowd, the big cat took him down with one swat.

OPENING SENTENCES

The opening sentences in your writing carry big responsibilities, setting the tone and often the scene—and helping draw your readers in by arousing their interest and curiosity. Authors often spend quite a lot of time on opening sentences for this very reason: whether it's a business report or a college essay or a blog posting, the way the piece begins has a lot to do with whether your audience will stay with you and whether you'll get the kind of response you want from them. Here are three famous opening sentences:

> ▶ I am an invisible man.   —RALPH ELLISON, *Invisible Man*

> ▶ The sky above the port was the color of television, tuned to a dead channel.
>   —WILLIAM GIBSON, *Neuromancer*

> ▶ They shoot the white girl first.   —TONI MORRISON, *Paradise*

Each of these sentences is startling, making us read on in order to find out more. Each is brief, leaving us waiting anxiously for what's to come. In addition, each makes a powerful statement and creates some kind of image in readers' minds: an "invisible" person, a sky the color of a "dead" TV channel, someone being shot. These sentences all come from novels, but they use strategies that work in many kinds of writing.

It usually takes more than a single sentence to open an essay. Consider, for example, how Michael Pollan begins a lengthy essay on animal liberation:

> ▶ The first time I opened Peter Singer's *Animal Liberation*, I was dining alone at the Palm, trying to enjoy a rib-eye steak cooked medium-rare. If this sounds like a good recipe for cognitive dissonance (if not indigestion), that was sort of the idea. Preposterous as it might seem to supporters of animal rights, what I was doing was tantamount to reading *Uncle Tom's Cabin* on a plantation in the Deep South in 1852.
>   —MICHAEL POLLAN, "An Animal's Place"

The first sentence presents an incongruous image that holds our attention (he's eating a steak while reading about animal liberation). Then the rest of the paragraph makes this incongruity even more pronounced, even comparing the situation to someone reading the antislavery novel *Uncle Tom's Cabin* while on a slave-owning plantation. It's an opening that makes us read on.

Here is the opening of a blog posting that begins with a provocative question:

> ▶ Have you ever thought about whether to have a child? If so, what factors entered into your decision? Was it whether having children would be good for you, your partner and others close to the possible child, such as children you may already have, or perhaps your parents? For most people contemplating reproduction, those are the dominant questions. Some may also think about the desirability of adding to the strain that the nearly seven billion people already here are putting on our planet's environment. But very few ask whether coming into existence is a good thing for the child itself.
>
> —PETER SINGER, "Should This Be the Last Generation?"

Singer's question is designed to get the reader's attention, and he follows it up with two additional questions that ask readers to probe more deeply into their reasons for considering whether or not to reproduce. In the fifth sentence, he suggests that the answers people give to these questions may not be adequate ones, and in the last sentence he lays down a challenge: perhaps coming into existence is not always good for "the child itself."

Here's another example of an opening that uses several sentences, this one from a student essay about graphic memoirs:

> ▶ In 1974, before the Fall of Saigon, my 14-year-old father, alone, boarded a boat out of Vietnam in search of America. This is a fact. But this one fact can spawn multiple understandings: I could ask a group of students to take a week and write me a story from just this one fact, and I have no doubt that they would bring back a full range of interpretations.
>
> —BRANDON LY, "Leaving Home, Coming Home"

This opening passage begins with a vivid image of a very young man fleeing Vietnam alone, followed by a very short sentence that makes a statement and then a longer one that challenges that statement. This student writer is moving readers toward what will become his thesis: that memoirs can never tell "the whole truth, and nothing but the truth."

Finally, take a look at the opening of the speech Toni Morrison gave when she won the Nobel Prize for Literature:

> ▶ Members of the Swedish Academy, Ladies and Gentlemen:
> Narrative has never been mere entertainment for me. It is, I believe, one of the principal ways in which we absorb knowledge. I hope you will

understand, then, why I begin these remarks with the opening phrase of what must be the oldest sentence in the world, and the earliest one we remember from childhood: "Once upon a time . . ."

—TONI MORRISON, Nobel Prize acceptance speech

Morrison begins with a deceptively simple statement that narrative is for her not just entertainment. In the next sentences, she complicates that statement and broadens her claim that narrative is the way we understand the world, concluding with what she calls "the oldest sentence in the world."

You can use strategies similar to the ones shown here in opening your college essays. Here are just some of the ways you might begin:

- With a strong, dramatic—or deceptively simple—statement
- With a vivid image
- With a provocative question
- With an anecdote
- With a startling claim

Opening sentences online. If the internet lets us send messages to people all over the world, it also challenges us to get and keep their attention. And with limited space and time (small screens, readers in a hurry, scanning for what they need), writers need to make sure the opening sentences of any online text are as attention getting and informative as possible.

In email, for instance, first sentences often show up in auto-preview lines, so it's a good idea to write them carefully. Here's the first line of an email sent recently to everyone at W. W. Norton:

▶ A Ping-Pong table has been set up on the 4th floor in loving memory of Diane O'Connor.

This email was sent by O'Connor's colleagues, honoring her efforts to persuade Norton to have an annual company Ping-Pong tournament. It might have said less ("Ping-Pong on 4," "remembering Diane"), as email usually does—but there was more that they wanted to say.

And then there's *Twitter.* As if it weren't enough of a challenge to say what you want to say in 140 characters, you'd better begin with a sentence that will catch readers' attention. Here are two tweets that got ours:

▶ Steve Jobs was born out of wedlock, put up for adoption at birth, dropped out of college, then changed the world. What's your excuse?   —@JWMOSS

▶ It's so weird because Rush Limbaugh has been such an awesome human being until now.   —@BUCK4ITT

You'll want to think carefully about how you open any text that you post to the web—and to craft opening sentences that will make sense in a *Google* search list. Here are two that we like:

▶ Smith Women Redefine "Pearls and Cashmere."

This is the headline for an article in *Inside Higher Ed,* an online magazine read by educators, but it's also the line that comes up in a *Google* search. The article is about a controversy at Smith College—and we think you'll agree that the headline surely got the attention of those scanning the magazine's list of articles or searching *Google.*

▶ *The Art of Fielding* is a 2011 novel by former *n+1* editor Chad Harbach. It centers on the fortunes of shortstop Henry Skrimshander and his career playing college baseball with the Westish College Harpooners, a Division III (NCAA) team.

This is the start of the *Wikipedia* entry for a novel, which comes up in a *Google* search. As you can see, it identifies the book, says who wrote it, and gives a one-sentence description of the story. Safe to say, the authors of this entry were careful to provide this information in the very first sentences.

CLOSING SENTENCES

Sentences that conclude a piece of writing are where you have a chance to make a lasting impact: to reiterate your point, tell readers why it matters, echo something you say in your opening, make a provocative statement, issue a call for action.

Here's Joe Posnanski, wrapping up an essay on his blog arguing that college athletes should not be paid:

▶ College football is not popular because of the stars. College football is popular because of that first word. Take away the college part, add in money,

and you are left with professional minor league football. . . . See how many
people watch that.   —JOE POSNANSKI, "The College Connection"

These four sentences summarize his argument—and the last one's the zinger, one that leaves readers thinking.

Now take a look at the conclusion to a scholarly book on current neurological studies of human attention, the brain science of attention:

> ▶ Right now, our classrooms and workplaces are structured for success in the
> last century, not this one. We can change that. By maximizing opportunities
> for collaboration, by rethinking everything from our approach to work
> to how we measure progress, we can begin to see the things we've been
> missing and catch hold of what's passing us by.
>
>   If you change the context, if you change the questions you ask, if you
> change the structure, the test, and the task, then you stop gazing one way
> and begin to look in a different way and in a different direction. You know
> what happens next:
>
>   *Now* you see it.   —CATHY DAVIDSON, *Now You See It: How the Brain Science
>   of Attention Will Transform the Way We Live, Work, and Learn*

Cathy Davidson uses two short paragraphs to sum up her argument and
then concludes with a final paragraph that consists of just one very short
four-word sentence. With this last sentence, she uses a tried-and-true strategy of coming full circle to echo the main idea of her book and, in fact, to
reiterate its title. Readers who have worked their way through the book will
take pleasure in that last sentence: *Now* they do see her point.

For another example, note how in the ending to a speech about language and about being able to use "all the Englishes" she grew up with, author Amy Tan closes with a one-sentence paragraph that quotes her mother:

> ▶ Apart from what any critic had to say about my writing, I knew I had
> succeeded where it counted when my mother finished reading my book and
> gave me her verdict: "So easy to read."   —AMY TAN, "Mother Tongue"

Tan's ending sums up one of her main goals as an author: to write so that
readers who speak different kinds of English will find her work accessible,
especially her mother.

Finally, take a look at how Toni Morrison chose to close her Nobel Prize
acceptance speech:

► It is, therefore, mindful of the gifts of my predecessors, the blessing of my sisters, in joyful anticipation of writers to come that I accept the honor the Swedish Academy has done me, and ask you to share what is for me a moment of grace.   —TONI MORRISON, Nobel Prize acceptance speech

In this one-sentence conclusion, Morrison speaks to the past, present, and future when she says she is grateful for those writers who came before her, for those who are writing now (her sisters), and for those yet to come. She ends the sentence by asking her audience to share this "moment of grace" with her and, implicitly, with all other writers so honored.

You may not be accepting a Nobel Prize soon, but in your college writing you can use all the strategies presented here to compose strong closings:

- By reiterating your point
- By discussing the implications of your argument
- By asking a question
- By referring back to your beginning
- By recommending or proposing some kind of action

REFLECT. Identify two memorable openings and closings from a favorite novel, comic book, film, or blog. What makes them so good? Do they follow one of the strategies presented here?

VARYING YOUR SENTENCES

Read a paragraph or two of your writing out loud and listen for its rhythm. Is it quick and abrupt? slow and leisurely? singsong? stately? rolling? Whatever it is, does the rhythm you hear match what you had in mind when you were writing? And does it put the emphasis where you want it? One way to establish the emphasis you intend and a rhythm that will keep readers reading is by varying the length of your sentences and the way those sentences flow from one to the other.

A string of sentences that are too much alike is almost certain to be boring. While you can create effective rhythms in many ways, one of the simplest and most effective is by breaking up a series of long sentences with a shorter one that gives your readers a chance to pause and absorb what you've written.

Take a look at the following passage, from an article in the *Atlantic* about the finale of the *Oprah Winfrey Show*. See how the author uses a mix of long and short sentences to describe one of the tributes to Oprah, this one highlighting her support of black men:

> ▶ Oprah's friend Tyler Perry announced that some of the "Morehouse Men," each a beneficiary of the $12 million endowment she has established at their university, had come to honor her for the scholarships she gave them. The lights were lowered, a Broadway star began singing an inspirational song, and a dozen or so black men began to walk slowly to the front of the stage. Then more came, and soon there were a score, then 100, then the huge stage was filled with men, 300 of them. They stood there, solemnly, in a tableau stage-managed in such a way that it might have robbed them of their dignity—the person serenading them (or, rather, serenading Oprah on their behalf) was Kristin Chenoweth, tiniest and whitest of all tiny white women; the song was from *Wicked,* most feminine of all musicals; and each man carried a white candle, an emblem that lent them the aspect of Norman Rockwell Christmas carolers. But they were not robbed of their dignity. They looked, all together, like a miracle. A video shown before the procession revealed that some of these men had been in gangs before going to Morehouse, some had fathers in prison, many had been living in poverty. Now they were doctors, lawyers, bankers, a Rhodes Scholar—and philanthropists, establishing their own Morehouse endowment.
>
> —CAITLIN FLANAGAN, "The Glory of Oprah"

The passage begins with three medium-length sentences—and then one very long one (seventy-two words!) that points up the strong contrast between the 300 black men filling the stage and the "whitest of white" singer performing a song from the "most feminine" of musicals. Then come two little sentences (the first one eight words long and the second one, seven) that give readers a chance to pause and absorb what has been said while also making an important point: that the men "looked, all together, like a miracle." The remainder of the passage moves back toward longer sentences, each of which explains just what this "miracle" is. Try reading this passage aloud and listen for how the variation in sentences creates both emphasis and a pleasing and effective rhythm.

The Morehouse Men surprise Oprah.

In addition to varying the lengths of your sentences, you can also improve your writing by making sure that they don't all use the same structure or begin in the same way. You can be pretty sure, for example, that a passage in which every sentence is a simple sentence that opens with the subject of a main clause will not read smoothly at all but rather will move along awkwardly. Take a look at this passage, for example:

▶ The sunset was especially beautiful today. I was on top of Table Mountain in Cape Town. I looked down and saw the sun touch the sea and sink into it. The evening shadows crept up the mountain. I got my backpack and walked over to the rest of my group. We started on the long hike down the mountain and back to the city.

There's nothing wrong with these sentences as such. Each one is grammatically correct. But if you read the passage aloud, you'll hear how it moves abruptly from sentence to sentence, lurching along rather than flowing smoothly. The problem is that the sentences are all the same: each one is a simple sentence that begins with the subject of a main clause (*sunset, I, I, evening shadows, I, we*). In addition, the use of personal pronouns at the beginning of the sentences (three *I*'s in only six sentences!) makes for dull reading. Finally, these are all fairly short sentences, and the sameness of the sentence length adds to the abrupt rhythm of the passage—and doesn't keep readers reading. Now look at how this passage can be revised by working on sentence variation:

▶ From the top of Cape Town's Table Mountain, the sunset was especially beautiful. I looked down just as the fiery orb touched and then sank into the sea; shadows began to creep slowly up the mountain. Picking up my backpack, I joined the rest of my group, and we started the long hike down the mountain.

This revision reduces the number of sentences in the passage from six to three (the first simple, the second compound-complex, the third compound) and varies the length of the sentences. Equally important, the revision eliminates all but one of the subject openings. The first sentence now begins with the prepositional phrase ("From the top"); the second with the subject of a main clause ("I"); and the third with a participial phrase ("Picking up my backpack"). Finally the revision varies the diction a bit, replacing the repeated word "sun" with a vivid image ("fiery orb"). Read the revised passage aloud and you'll hear how varying the sentences creates a stronger rhythm that makes it easier to read.

This brief chapter has only scratched the surface of sentence style. But we hope we've said enough to show how good sentences can be your allies, helping you get your ideas out there and connect with audiences as successfully as possible. Remember: authors are only as good as the sentences they write!

REFLECT. Take a look at a writing assignment you've recently completed. Read it aloud, listening for rhythm and emphasis. If you find a passage that doesn't read well or provide the emphasis you want, analyze its sentences for length (count the words) and structure (how does each sentence begin?). Revise the passage using the strategies presented above.

THIRTY-TWO

Checking for Common Mistakes

POET NIKKI GIOVANNI ONCE SAID, "Mistakes are a fact of life. It is the response to the error that counts." Albert Einstein put a little different spin on it when he said, "Anyone who has never made a mistake has never tried anything new." We agree. Anyone who writes is going to make mistakes. That's a given. What matters is to know when something *is* a mistake, to learn from any mistakes we make, and sometimes even to use them, as Einstein might say, to try something new.

Most of all, it means understanding that what may be a mistake in one context may be perfectly appropriate in another, depending—as always—on your purpose, your audience, and the rest of your rhetorical situation. So when you're editing your writing, you need to think about what's appropriate for your particular rhetorical context.

As a college writer, you may sometimes decide to use a sentence fragment or something else that's typically seen as an error for special effect. In most of your academic writing, however, it's wise to play it safe and avoid anything that might be considered a mistake. This chapter offers tips and examples for checking and editing your writing for some common mistakes, arranged alphabetically from articles to verbs.

WHAT'S THE DIFFERENCE between *a dog* and *the dog*? "A" dog could be any dog; it does not matter which one. "The" dog, by comparison, refers to one specific dog. *A, an,* and *the* are articles. Use *a* or *an* with **NOUNS** when their specific identity isn't known or doesn't matter: *I want a golden retriever.* Use *the* with nouns whose specific identity is known or has been mentioned: *I want the golden retriever I told you about last week.*

When to Use *a* or *an*

Use *a* or *an* with singular **COUNT NOUNS** that cannot be identified specifically. Count nouns are those referring to things you can count: *one egg, two chairs, three facts.* Use *a* before words beginning with a consonant sound: *a baby;* use *an* before words beginning with a vowel sound: *an apple.* (And be careful to consider sound rather than spelling: *a uniform, an uncle.*)

Do not use *a* or *an* before a **NONCOUNT NOUN**, one that refers to an abstract concept or something that cannot be counted or made plural such as *loyalty, knowledge,* or *gasoline.*

▶ The vacant apartment looked much better with *furniture* in it.

When to Use *the*

Use *the* with nouns that can be identified specifically—singular and plural, count and noncount.

▶ Many cities have passed laws that require restaurants to provide information about *the ingredients* in their food.

▶ Tyler Cowen criticizes *the eat-local movement* as expensive and snobbish.

When to Use No Article

When you're making a generalization, no article is needed with noncount or count nouns.

▶ Large *corporations* generally offer *health insurance* to *employees.*

▶ *Raccoons* use *sticks* as *tools* to find *food.*

WHEN TO USE *A* OR *AN*

▶ My parents see attending college as *an honor* and *a privilege.*

▶ Studying in another country can give you *a new perspective* on your home country.

▶ The chef added *a little water* to the stew because it was too thick.

▶ When I'm 16, I'm getting ~~the~~ *a* Chrysler because of their Super Bowl ads.

There's more than one kind of Chrysler, and the writer doesn't indicate which one he plans to get.

WHEN TO USE *THE*

▶ *The U.S. Supreme Court* has nine members, who are appointed by *the* president.

▶ After *the attacks* of September 11, 2001, on *the World Trade Center* and *the Pentagon,* Americans recognized *the need* for better security at airports.

▶ Bobby Thomson's home run against *the Brooklyn Dodgers* became known as "*the shot* heard 'round *the world.*" Russ Hodges captured *the excitement* in his radio broadcast, shouting out, "*The Giants* win *the pennant! The Giants* win *the pennant! The Giants* win *the pennant!*"

WHEN TO USE NO ARTICLE

▶ *People* whose bodies are intolerant of *lactose* cannot digest *milk* easily.

▶ Many *people* have found that winning a lottery does not bring them *happiness.*

▶ Airline *passengers* now often have to pay *fees* to check *luggage.*

To SEE HOW IMPORTANT COMMAS ARE, read this sentence: *Let's eat Grandma!* Now see what a difference a comma can make:

▶ Let's eat, Grandma!

We found this sentence on *Facebook*, followed by this excellent advice: "Punctuation saves lives."

    This section focuses on some of the ways that commas help authors and readers, from setting off introductory words to separating items in a series to making sure that Grandma gets to eat rather than be eaten.

To Set Off Introductory Words

Put a comma after any word, PHRASE, or CLAUSE that comes before the SUBJECT of the sentence. Some authors omit a comma after very short introductory elements, but you'll never be wrong to include it.

▶ In 2012, the New York Giants defeated the New England Patriots in the Super Bowl.

▶ Gleefully, New Yorkers celebrated.

▶ Holding up the Vince Lombardi trophy, MVP Eli Manning waved to the fans.

▶ To honor the team, Mayor Bloomberg gave each player a key to the city.

▶ As he accepted his key, Victor Cruz did his signature salsa moves.

Be careful of sentences with inverted word order, where the subject comes after the verb; do not put a comma after a phrase that begins such a sentence.

▶ On the horizon appeared a plane.

▶ In the package were a box of chocolate-chip cookies and various salty snacks.

TO SET OFF INTRODUCTORY WORDS

▶ The marathon completed, the runners greeted their friends and family members.

▶ At the candidate's rally, her supporters waved signs and shouted encouragement.

▶ Because they are dissatisfied with both public and private schools, some parents homeschool their children.

▶ Joyfully, the Heat celebrated after defeating the Thunder in the NBA Finals.

▶ Distracted by a text message, the driver failed to see the stop sign.

▶ Frantically stacking sandbags, the volunteers tried to hold back the rising floodwaters.

▶ To write well, seek out responses to your draft and allow time to revise.

▶ Although many texters enjoy breaking linguistic rules, they also know they need to be understood.

To celebrate World Poetry day in 2007, T-Mobile tried to find the UK's first "Txt laureate" in a competition for the best romantic poem in SMS.

The most important finding is that texting does not erode children's ability to read and write. On the contrary, literacy improves.

In short, it's fun.

—DAVID CRYSTAL, "2b or Not 2b"

To Join Clauses in Compound Sentences

Put a comma before the **COORDINATING CONJUNCTION** (*and, but, for, nor, or, so,* or *yet*) that connects the **MAIN CLAUSES** in a compound sentence.

▶ A balanced budget amendment to the Constitution sounds like a good way to reduce spending, but the government needs more budgetary flexibility for varying economic conditions.

To Set Off Nonessential Elements

Parts of a sentence that are not essential to its meaning should be set off with commas. Parts that are essential to a sentence's meaning should not be set off with commas.

NONESSENTIAL WORDS My sister, Laura, makes the turkey for Thanksgiving.

ESSENTIAL WORDS My sister Susan always brings mashed potatoes for Thanksgiving, while my sister Betty brings pumpkin pie.

In the first sentence, there's only one sister, so her name is not essential to the meaning—and is thus enclosed in commas. In the second, the names of the sisters are essential to the meaning because there is more than one sister.

NONESSENTIAL CLAUSE Opera fans, who are notoriously fickle, loved Luciano Pavarotti throughout his long career.

ESSENTIAL CLAUSE Opera fans who love *The Magic Flute* would especially appreciate Ingmar Bergman's film version.

The first sentence refers to all opera fans, so the information about their fickleness isn't essential to the meaning—and is thus set off by commas. The second sentence refers only to fans of The Magic Flute; *that information is essential to the meaning of the sentence, so there are no commas.*

NONESSENTIAL PHRASE The wood, cut just yesterday, needs to cure before it can be burned in the fireplace.

ESSENTIAL PHRASE Wood cut from hardwood trees burns longer and hotter than wood cut from softwood trees.

TO JOIN CLAUSES IN COMPOUND SENTENCES

▶ The tornado severely damaged the apartment building, but the residents all survived.

▶ Several residents were trapped for hours in the wreckage, and one was not rescued until two days later.

▶ I grew up in Kansas, so I take tornado warning sirens seriously.

TO SET OFF NONESSENTIAL ELEMENTS

▶ Members of the baby boom generation, who were born between World War II and the early 1960s, have started to become eligible for Medicare.

▶ The dramatic increase in childhood obesity in the United States, which public health officials have described as a crisis, has many possible contributing causes.

▶ Fast-food chains, blamed for encouraging fattening food, are starting to offer lower-calorie options.

▶ Daniel Radcliffe, famous for his lead role in the Harry Potter movies, starred on Broadway in *Equus* and *How to Succeed in Business without Really Trying*.

▶ *Glee*, the hit TV show about a high school glee club, made many of its cast members into celebrities.

▶ Congress should increase access to medical and health savings accounts, which give consumers the option of rolling money reserved for health care into a retirement account.
—RADLEY BALKO, "What You Eat Is Your Own Business"

▶ Growing corn, which from a biological perspective had always been a process of capturing sunlight to turn it into food, has in no small measure become a process of converting fossil fuels into food.
—MICHAEL POLLAN, "What's Eating America"

To Separate Items in a Series

Use a comma to separate items in a series of three or more. Some authors omit the comma before the final item in the series, but you'll never be wrong to include it—and sometimes omitting the comma can confuse your readers.

▶ We're planning a special menu for the 4th of July: hamburgers, hot dogs, two kinds of coleslaw, potato salad, roast corn, and watermelon.

The final comma makes it clear that the corn is roasted but the watermelon is not.

To Set Off Interjections, Direct Address, Tag Questions, and Contrasting Elements

INTERJECTIONS	Wow, that was a great film!
DIRECT ADDRESS	"Corporations are people, my friend." ——MITT ROMNEY
TAG QUESTIONS	You're kidding, aren't you?
CONTRASTING ELEMENTS	Tai chi, unlike yoga, is practiced for its martial training as well as for its health benefits.

To Set Off Parenthetical and Transitional Expressions

▶ Umami, by the way, has recently been recognized as a fifth taste, along with sweet, bitter, sour, and salty.

▶ Homemade applesauce, in fact, is both tastier and healthier than store-bought applesauce.

▶ In other words, we're arguing that it makes no sense to build a large waste transfer station in a densely populated residential neighborhood.

TO SEPARATE ITEMS IN A SERIES

▶ My father told me I was going to college even if he had to beg, borrow, or steal the money.

▶ Americans today can eat pears in the spring in Minnesota, oranges in the summer in Montana, asparagus in the fall in Maine, and cranberries in the winter in Florida. —KATHERINE SPRIGGS, "On Buying Local"

▶ Students came to class in cars, on bicycles, on foot, and even on skateboards.

▶ The cat ran out the door, across the road, and into the woods.

TO SET OFF INTERJECTIONS, DIRECT ADDRESS, TAG QUESTIONS, AND CONTRASTING ELEMENTS

▶ "Oh, I think you know what I'm talking about," Samantha said.

▶ Mike laughed and said, "Dude, you need some help."

▶ Members of Congress have to file financial disclosure forms, don't they?

▶ The queen, not the king, is the most powerful piece in chess.

▶ The Notre Dame football program, unlike the programs of many other top-ranked schools, is known for the high graduation rate of its players.

TO SET OFF PARENTHETICAL AND TRANSITIONAL EXPRESSIONS

▶ Investment income, on the other hand, is taxed at a lower rate.

▶ Wind power, however, has environmental disadvantages as well as benefits.

▶ Ultimately, what's at stake is the health of everyone who lives or works in this neighborhood.

With Addresses, Place Names, and Dates

▶ Please send any contributions to The Oregon Cultural Trust, 775 Summer St. NE, Ste. 200, Salem, OR 97301-1280.

▶ Strasbourg, France, is the site of the European Parliament.

▶ No one who experienced the events of September 11, 2001, will ever forget that day.

To Set Off Quotations

▶ "In my view," said Junot Díaz, "a writer is a writer because even when there is no hope, even when nothing you do shows any sign of promise, you keep writing anyway."

▶ "Poetry is not a healing lotion, an emotional massage, a kind of linguistic aromatherapy," said Adrienne Rich in a speech to the National Book Foundation.

▶ "Don't compromise yourself," Janis Joplin advised. "You are all you've got."

Do not use a comma before quotations that are introduced with *that*.

▶ Virginia Woolf wrote that "A woman must have money and a room of her own if she is to write fiction."

Do not use a comma to set off an indirect quotation, one that does not quote someone's exact words.

▶ In a commencement address at Harvard University, J. K. Rowling spoke about failure, saying that failure teaches you who you are and who you can be.

▶ Tallulah Bankhead once said that if she had her life to live over again, she'd make the same mistakes, only sooner.

WITH ADDRESSES, PLACE NAMES, AND DATES

▶ The company's address is 500 Fifth Ave., New York, NY 10110.

▶ The performance venues in Branson, Missouri, have become popular tourist destinations.

▶ The movie director Ang Lee was born in Chaochou, Taiwan, and came to the United States to attend college.

▶ President Franklin Roosevelt said that December 7, 1941, was "a day that will live in infamy."

TO SET OFF QUOTATIONS

▶ The King James Bible warns, "Pride goeth before destruction."

▶ "Life can only be understood backward, but it has to be lived forward," wrote Søren Kierkegaard.

▶ "There have been only two geniuses in the world," insisted Tallulah Bankhead, "Willie Mays and Willie Shakespeare."

▶ When he was asked if Major League Baseball was ready for an openly gay player, Willie Mays was quick to respond, asking, "Can he hit?"

▶ Humphrey Bogart once declared that he'd "rather have a hot dog at the ballpark than a steak at the Ritz."

▶ Lauren Bacall was once quoted as saying that "imagination is the highest kite that one can fly."

Unnecessary Commas

Do not put commas around essential elements

▶ The Galápagos Islands are home to many species of plants and animals,/that are found nowhere else.

The information that many species are unique to those islands is essential and should not be set off by commas.

▶ Shirley Brice Heath's book,/Ways with Words,/is a study of children learning to use language in two communities in the Carolinas.

Since Heath has written more than one book, the title is essential information and should not be set off by commas.

Do not put commas between subjects and verbs

▶ Some basketball players and journalists,/predicted all along that LeBron James would return to the Cleveland team.

▶ The only reason that the committee gave for its decision to end the program,/was lack of funds.

Do not put commas between compound subjects or verbs

▶ People who live in "red" states,/and those who live in "blue" states hold many mistaken beliefs about each other.

▶ The chef whisked the eggs and milk together in a bowl,/and poured the mixture into the omelet pan.

Do not add a comma after a question mark or an exclamation point

▶ "Hi, may I help you?,/" shouted the manager at Gates Bar-B-Q.

▶ "Everybody out of the water!,/" yelled the lifeguard.

UNNECESSARY COMMAS

Around essential elements

▶ The painting/that was found in the abandoned house/sold for ten thousand dollars.

▶ The novelist/Jonathan Franzen/has been invited to speak at a campus writers' seminar next month.

▶ The article argues that children/raised in conditions of poverty/often suffer long-term damage to their cognitive development.

Between subjects and verbs

▶ One of the factors that make the health-care system in the United States so expensive/is the amount spent to extend the last few months of patients' lives.

In compound subjects or verbs

▶ Families looking for more affordable space/and hipsters looking for a cool cultural scene all flocked to Brooklyn.

▶ The earthquake and tsunami devastated the northeastern coast of Honshu/ but mostly spared the densely populated Tokyo and Osaka areas.

After a question mark or an exclamation point

▶ "What can I possibly do about global warming?/" ask many of my friends.

▶ "I want my money back!/" the angry customer yelled.

A **COMMA SPLICE OCCURS** when you join two **MAIN CLAUSES** with only a comma. Leave out the comma, and it's a fused sentence. Writing like this might be perfectly appropriate in a tweet or a comment on a blog, but it's likely to be seen as a mistake in academic writing. This section shows four ways to edit comma splices and fused sentences.

COMMA SPLICE   We don't need a new stadium, the existing one is just fine.

FUSED SENTENCE   She shoots she scores we win!

Make the Clauses into Two Separate Sentences

▶ Tropical Storm Irene caused major flooding in the Northeast *. Hundreds* ~~hundreds~~ of roads and bridges were damaged or destroyed.

Link Clauses with Comma + *and, but, or, nor, for, so,* or *yet*

▶ Tropical Storm Irene caused major flooding in the Northeast *,and* hundreds of roads and bridges were damaged or destroyed.

Link the Clauses with a Semicolon

▶ Tropical Storm Irene caused major flooding in the Northeast *;* hundreds of roads and bridges were damaged or destroyed.

Adding a **TRANSITION** after the semicolon such as *therefore* or *however,* followed by a comma, can help make explicit how the two clauses relate.

▶ Tropical Storm Irene caused major flooding in the Northeast *; as a result,* hundreds of roads and bridges were damaged or destroyed.

Revise One Clause as a Subordinate Clause

▶ *When* Tropical Storm Irene caused major flooding in the Northeast *,* hundreds of roads and bridges were damaged or destroyed.

MAKE THE CLAUSES INTO TWO SEPARATE SENTENCES

▶ The number of landline telephones is decreasing, ~~more~~ **. More** and more people have only a cell phone.

▶ Why build a new stadium, ~~the~~ **? The** existing stadium is just fine.

LINK CLAUSES WITH COMMA + *AND, BUT, OR, NOR, FOR, SO,* OR *YET*

▶ The 2011 Japanese tsunami produced five million tons of trash, **and** most of it stayed near the Japanese coastline.

▶ Some adoptees would like to find their birth parents **, but** they are often thwarted by laws protecting the privacy of the parents.

▶ Many jobs today are not tied to a particular physical location **, so** employees can work anywhere online.

LINK THE CLAUSES WITH A SEMICOLON

▶ Green tea has been gaining in popularity in recent years **;** it has less caffeine than black tea and is seen as a more healthful alternative.

▶ Global warming could have serious consequences **; for example,** many countries and cities might be threatened by rising ocean levels.

REVISE ONE CLAUSE AS A SUBORDINATE CLAUSE

▶ Small Midwestern towns have been losing population **because** young people go elsewhere to find jobs.

▶ **Although** *Moby-Dick* got terrible reviews when it was first published, many people now consider it the greatest American novel ever written.

ABOUT, AT, BY, FOR, FROM, IN, ON, TO—these are all prepositions, words that show relationships between other words. Imagine you've got a book *about* your mom, *by* your mom, *for* your mom, or *from* your mom; each means something different, and the difference is all in the prepositions. Not all languages use prepositions, and if English is not your primary language, they can be a challenge to learn. Following are some tips and examples that can help with three of the most widely used prepositions: *at, in,* and *on.* Remember, though, that there are many exceptions; if in doubt, consult a dictionary.

Prepositions of Place

AT   *a specific address:* the house *at* 54 Main Street

a general kind of place: at home, *at* work, *at* school

a general kind of event: at a concert, *at* a party

IN   *an enclosed space: in* the closet, *in* my pocket, *in* a cup

a geographical area: in Brazil, *in* Chicago, *in* Africa

a printed work: an article *in* a journal, a chapter *in* a book

ON   *a surface:* sitting *on* the bench, a fly *on* the wall, papers *on* a desk

a street: driving *on* Route 17, a restaurant *on* Maple Avenue

an electronic medium: on the web, *on* TV, *on* the radio

Prepositions of Time

AT   *a specific point in time: at* 4:46 a.m., *at* noon, *at* sunrise

IN   *a part of a day: in* the morning, *in* the evening (but *at* night)

a year, month, or season: in 2015, *in* January, *in* the spring

a period of time: graduated *in* three years, return *in* an hour

ON   *a day of the week or month: on* Thursday, *on* March 13

a holiday: travel *on* Thanksgiving, a parade *on* Memorial Day

PREPOSITIONS OF PLACE

▶ Dylan Thomas once lived *in* New York, *at* the Chelsea Hotel *on* Twenty-third Street.

▶ The wifi signal *at* school is usually very good, but it comes and goes *at* home.

▶ Dogs are not allowed *in* most grocery stores *in* the United States.

▶ The story *on* the radio was about the growth of Pentecostal religion *in* South America.

▶ The money *in* the tip jar was divided among the employees.

▶ An accident *on* Interstate 81 injured three people.

▶ Put your papers *in* the envelope *on* my office door.

PREPOSITIONS OF TIME

▶ The Beatles first came to the United States *in* 1964.

▶ Betsye takes classes *in* the evening.

▶ Jamaica Kincaid was the Grinnell College commencement speaker *on* May 21, 2012.

▶ The performance will be *on* July 25 *at* noon.

▶ The earthquake struck *at* three *in* the morning, when most people were sleeping.

▶ Juliet Rose Wright was born *on* April 15, 2012.

▶ The Kenyon Gospel Choir will perform *on* Martin Luther King Jr.'s birthday.

IF YOU'VE EVER BEEN READING SOMETHING and stumbled over a word like *he* or *which* because you couldn't tell what it referred to, you've discovered a problem with pronoun reference. A pronoun needs to have a clear **ANTECEDENT**, a specific word that it refers to in a sentence. And a pronoun needs to agree with that antecedent in gender and number, as the following example demonstrates:

▶ *Coffee shops* are good places to work because *they* offer quiet spaces and comforting beverages.

Clear Pronoun Reference

A pronoun should refer clearly to one and only one antecedent.

AMBIGUOUS   Although Lady Gaga and Madonna are often compared, she is more accomplished as a musician.

Who's more accomplished, Lady Gaga or Madonna? To eliminate the ambiguity, revise the sentence to use pronouns that refer clearly to one woman or the other or to eliminate the need for a pronoun.

EDITED   Although she is often compared to Madonna, Lady Gaga is more accomplished as a musician.

EDITED   Although often compared to Madonna, Lady Gaga is more accomplished as a musician.

This, That, Which

Be sure the pronouns *this*, *that*, and *which* refer to a specific antecedent rather than to an idea or a sentence. Because the context often makes the meaning obvious, this kind of vague reference is common in conversation, but in writing you should eliminate the pronoun or provide a clear antecedent.

▶ Cable television has consistently challenged the domination of the major
         a trend that
networks, ~~which~~ has benefited viewers.
                 ^

▶ Cable provides many more programming options than the networks can,
                              variety
and viewers appreciate this.
                            ^

CLEAR PRONOUN REFERENCE

▶ In the climax of the play, the central character tells his brother that ~~he~~ *the brother* will never measure up to their father.

▶ The management representatives reached a tentative agreement on a new contract with the unions, but ~~their~~ *the management's* tough negotiating stance on the details made a final settlement difficult.

▶ The management representatives reached a tentative agreement on a new contract with the unions, but ~~their~~ *the unions'* tough negotiating stance on the details made a final settlement difficult.

THIS, THAT, WHICH

▶ Most scientists believe that global warming is occurring at least partly because of human activity, but most conservatives reject that *idea*.

▶ Solar energy is becoming cheaper, and this *drop in price* will eventually make it competitive with fossil fuels.

▶ Most Americans have to drive to work~~, which makes them~~ *and therefore are* extremely sensitive to gasoline prices.

▶ Most Americans have to drive to work, ~~which~~ *a fact that* makes them extremely sensitive to gasoline prices.

They, It, You

In informal contexts, we often use *they*, *it*, or *you* without any antecedent. In academic writing, however, *they* and *it* should always have a specific antecedent, and *you* should be used only to refer specifically to the reader.

▶ At some airports, ~~they~~ *TSA agents* do not require passengers to remove belts to go

through the security check.

▶ ~~On the~~ *The* website, ~~it~~ identifies the author as a former writer for

Stephen Colbert.

▶ ~~In many states, you must~~ *Many states require people to* go through a law enforcement background

check before ~~you~~ *they* can work with children.

This use of you *could be appropriate in some rhetorical situations—in a manual for day-care workers, for instance—but is inappropriate in most academic writing.*

Implied antecedents

In informal contexts, we often use pronouns that refer to words clearly implied but not directly stated in a sentence. In academic writing, however, do not use such implied antecedents.

▶ I had planned to *ride my* bike to class yesterday, but it had a flat tire.

Although the pronoun it *implies that* bike *is a noun, it was used as a verb in the original sentence. The revision makes it into a noun.*

▶ In ~~Edward Ball's~~ *Edward Ball* *Slaves in the Family*, ~~he~~ writes about finding and interviewing

the African American descendants of his white slave-owning ancestors.

Although the original sentence is clear, the phrase "Edward Ball's" is possessive, so it cannot serve as the antecedent of he.

THEY, IT, YOU

▶ At some airports, ~~they do not ask~~ passengers^ to remove belts *are not required*

to go through the security check.

▶ ~~On the website, it~~ identifies the author as a former writer for *The "Contributors" link*

Stephen Colbert.

▶ In many states, ~~you~~ must go through a law enforcement background check *job applicants* before ~~you~~ can work with children. *they*

▶ ~~On the~~ voter registration form ~~they ask you for your~~ home address *The* *asks for the voter's*

and phone number.

▶ ~~In the~~ advertisement~~, it~~ claims that the company will pay the shipping *The*

charges for returning items for any reason.

IMPLIED ANTECEDENTS

▶ The children spent the afternoon sledding until a runner broke off of ~~it~~. *the sled*

▶ The contractor repaired several holes in the wall but did not charge for *that part of the work* ~~them~~.

▶ The inscription on Thomas Jefferson's tombstone does not mention that ~~he~~ *Jefferson*

was president of the United States.

Pronoun-Antecedent Agreement

A pronoun has to agree with its antecedent in gender and number.

GENDER   As Speaker of the House of Representatives, *John Boehner* was known for *his* candor and for *his* willingness to let *his* emotions show, sometimes choking up during debates about issues that mattered a lot to *him*.

NUMBER   *Speakers* must often exert *themselves* to persuade *their* party's representatives to side with *them*.

Compound antecedents

Compound antecedents joined with *and* take a plural pronoun unless they are preceded by *each* or *every*.

▶ Because of security concerns, when *the president and vice president* travel to the same event, *they* rarely travel together.

▶ *Every* major-league baseball player has to follow *his* own exercise regimen to stay in shape during the off-season.

When a compound antecedent is joined with *or* or *nor,* the pronoun should agree with the nearest antecedent. If the antecedents are different genders or numbers, you might want to edit the sentence to keep it from being awkward.

AWKWARD   Neither Serena Williams nor Roger Federer was at his best.

EDITED   Serena Williams wasn't at her best, nor was Roger Federer.

AWKWARD   Either the teachers or the principal needs to use her authority.

EDITED   Either the principal needs to use her authority, or the teachers need to use theirs.

Collective nouns as antecedents

COLLECTIVE NOUNS such as *team* or *audience* or the others listed on the facing page take a singular pronoun when the pronoun refers to the unit as a whole but a plural pronoun when the pronoun refers to multiple parts of the unit.

SINGULAR   The *band* changed *its* name to try to attract a different fan base.

PLURAL   The band left *their* instruments in the music room.

PRONOUN-ANTECEDENT AGREEMENT

Compound antecedents

▶ *Every fruit and vegetable* labeled "organic" has to be certified by ~~their~~ *its* grower.

▶ *Each manager and salesperson* is required to set ~~their~~ *his or her* personal goals.

▶ Neither Angela Merkel nor François Hollande felt politically secure enough to risk offending public opinion ~~in his own country~~ *domestic* during the EU crisis.

▶ Under the Articles of Confederation, either the ~~states~~ *national government* or the ~~national government~~ *states* could issue ~~its~~ *their* own currency.

Collective nouns as antecedents

COMMON COLLECTIVE NOUNS

audience	committee	crowd	group	panel
choir	congregation	faculty	herd	platoon
chorus	couple	family	jury	team

▶ Each *committee* is assigned a secretary to assist with *its* clerical duties.

▶ The *committee* took *their* seats, and the meeting began.

▶ The judge told the *jury* to consider only the facts in reaching *its* verdict.

▶ The judge told the *jury* to weigh the evidence in making up *their* minds.

Indefinite pronouns as antecedents

Most **INDEFINITE PRONOUNS** such as *anybody, everyone, nobody,* or *someone* take a singular pronoun.

▶ *Everyone* involved in the negotiations had *his or her* own agenda.

If you find *his or her* awkward, revise the sentence to make both pronouns plural or to eliminate the indefinite pronouns.

▶ *All* of those involved in the negotiations had *their* own agendas.

▶ The *individuals* involved in the negotiations all had *their* own agendas.

In informal conversation, words like *everybody, someone,* and *nobody* are often used with plural pronouns: *Somebody left their coat on the chair.* In academic writing, however, stick to the singular for such references.

Noun antecedents that could be either male or female

If an antecedent could be either male or female, do not use masculine pronouns such as *he* or *him* to refer to it. Use *he or she, her or his,* and so on, or edit the sentence to make the antecedent and pronoun both plural or to eliminate the gendered pronoun.

▶ A *Speaker of the House* has to be good at enforcing party discipline; it is an important part of *his or her* job.

▶ *Speakers of the House* have to be good at enforcing party discipline; it is an important part of *their* job.

▶ A *Speaker of the House* has to be good at enforcing party discipline; it is an important part of *the* job.

Indefinite pronouns as antecedents

SINGULAR INDEFINITE PRONOUNS

another	each	much	one
any	either	neither	other
anybody	everybody	nobody	somebody
anyone	everyone	no one	someone
anything	everything	nothing	something

▶ ~~Anyone who uses~~ *Facebook* ~~has~~ to remember to set up their privacy settings carefully. *[inserted above: Users of ... have]*

▶ Everybody on the women's volleyball team *was* expected to buy ~~their~~ own uniform. *[inserted above: her]*

▶ *Someone* who has served in the military should not have to worry about losing *his or her* health insurance.

▶ *People* in my generation once thought that going to college would guarantee *their* financial security.

Noun antecedents that could be either male or female

▶ A college student often chooses his *[inserted: or her]* major on the basis of expected financial rewards.

▶ A college student often chooses ~~his~~ *[inserted: a]* major on the basis of expected financial rewards.

▶ ~~A college student often chooses his major~~ on the basis of expected financial rewards. *[inserted above: College students often choose their majors]*

A SENTENCE FRAGMENT OCCURS when something less than a sentence is capitalized and punctuated as if it were a complete sentence. Fragments are common in advertising, where they serve to grab the attention of readers and sometimes to create memorable slogans. For example:

▶ A unique mix of clothing and accessories you don't even know you want yet!
—Lizard Lounge ad, *Willamette Week*

As common as they are in many informal contexts, fragments are frowned upon in academic writing. In these contexts, they are considered errors because readers see them as violating the basic rules of sentence structure—and as evidence that the author doesn't know what those rules are.

A sentence fragment occurs when some essential element is missing, usually a **SUBJECT** or a **VERB** —or when it begins with a **SUBORDINATING WORD** like *which* or *because* and is merely a **SUBORDINATE CLAUSE**. To be a sentence, there must be at least one **MAIN CLAUSE**.

NO SUBJECT   Many people could not resist buying homes at very low interest rates. As a result, took on too much debt.

NO VERB   Bank loans available with little or no down payment.

SUBORDINATE CLAUSE   In some regions, many new homes remain empty. Because people are having trouble getting financing.

To edit most fragments, you need to do one of two things: (1) make the fragment into a complete sentence, or (2) attach it to a nearby sentence.

Make the Fragment into a Complete Sentence

ADD A SUBJECT   As a result, ^they^ took on too much debt.

ADD A VERB   Bank loans ^became^ available with little or no down payment.

DELETE THE SUBORDINATING WORD   In some regions, many new homes remain empty. ~~Because people~~ *People* are having trouble getting financing.

MAKE THE FRAGMENT INTO A COMPLETE SENTENCE

▶ *I had*
  ~~Had~~ an accident in my truck and had to spend a lot of money on repairs.

▶ U.S. companies have come under increasing pressure to cut costs. *Many of them have* ~~Have~~ outsourced jobs to China, India, and other Asian countries.

▶ The U.S. housing market *is* still somewhat depressed. *The president and Congress need* ~~Need~~ to figure out a way to help homeowners who cannot pay their mortgages.

▶ The program showed glaciers melting as a result of global warming. Many *are* disappearing faster than predicted a few years ago.

▶ My sister's room *was* always a mess, crammed with posters, athletic equipment, and clothes thrown on the floor.

▶ *It was* ~~Was~~ really exciting and stimulating to live in Tokyo.

▶ He eventually decided to move to New York. *He thought he'd* ~~Because he~~ find more job opportunities there.

▶ *The Best Exotic Marigold Hotel* *starred* ~~starring~~ Judi Dench, Maggie Smith, Bill Nighy, and Tom Wilkinson in an extravagant Indian adventure.

▶ Dad explained how to write checks and balance my checkbook. *He also taught me* ~~Also~~ how to scramble eggs.

▶ Nick worked as an intern at a consulting firm for six months after graduating. *He did so to* ~~To~~ get experience and perhaps to get a permanent position there.

▶ The Semester at Sea students and their instructors sailed around the world on the *MV Explorer.* *They visited* ~~Visiting~~ twelve countries in 106 days.

Attach the Fragment to a Nearby Sentence

▶ A growing number of "medical tourists" travel abroad to have cosmetic
surgery. ~~Or~~ *or* other medical procedures that are much cheaper outside the
United States.

▶ Michael Moore's movie *Sicko* made the American health-care system a topic
of national conversation. ~~Although~~ *, although* even many who share his politics
criticized him for playing fast and loose with the facts.

▶ In 1968, George Romney tried for the Republican presidential ~~nomination.~~ *nomination,*
~~Which~~ *which* his son Mitt won forty-four years later.

▶ Tired of the same old reality shows and reruns on ~~television. Decided~~ *television, we decided*
to go to an a cappella concert on campus.

ATTACH THE FRAGMENT TO A NEARBY SENTENCE

▶ Some older Americans are nostalgic for the 1950s. ~~When~~ *, when* families and

jobs seemed more stable.

▶ The average family size has dropped sharply. ~~Because~~ *because* people are marrying

at later ages and having fewer children than in the baby boom era.

▶ In the 1970s, the United States began losing manufacturing jobs to overseas

competitors. ~~Has~~ *, a trend that has* only recently been reversed.

▶ In recent years, India has begun to develop its own high-tech ~~economy.~~ *economy,*

~~Which~~ *which* is centered in the city of Bangalore.

▶ ABC is broadcasting the NBA finals. ~~With,~~ *with* a panel of experts

breaking down the games afterward.

▶ The farmers market opens Sunday mornings at 9:00. ~~And~~ *and* closes at 1:00.

▶ Much of the country is suffering from a heat wave. ~~Which~~ *, which* makes many

of us especially irritable.

YOU'LL OFTEN HAVE REASON to shift gears when you write, as when you shift from one verb tense to another.

▶ The National Weather Service issued a freeze warning, saying that temperatures will dip into the 20s tomorrow.

This sentence refers to actions occurring at different times, so they require different tenses. But unnecessary shifts in tense—or point of view—can confuse readers.

Shifts in Tense

It's sometimes necessary to shift verb tenses to refer to actions that take place at different times.

▶ The play that *opened* yesterday *will be reviewed* in newspapers tomorrow.

Readers may be confused, however, if you shift from one tense to another in referring to things that happen in the same time frame.

SHIFT   The editorial *noted* the increases in college tuition this year and also *discusses* the causes of skyrocketing tuition costs over the last few decades.

This sentence starts out using the past tense (*noted*) and then switches to the present tense (*discusses*). To eliminate the shift, make both verbs either past tense or present:

▶ The editorial *noted* the increases in college tuition this year and also *discussed* the causes of skyrocketing tuition costs over the last few decades.

▶ The editorial *notes* the increases in college tuition this year and also *discusses* the causes of skyrocketing tuition costs over the last few decades.

Be careful to use the present tense when you're writing about a literary work—and not to accidentally shift to the past tense.

▶ Fitzgerald portrays Gatsby as a boy from a poor family who eventually
becomes rich enough to buy a mansion, where he ~~threw~~ *throws* extravagant
parties in the hope of impressing Daisy.

SHIFTS IN TENSE

▶ After Pearl Harbor, U.S. authorities wrongly suspected that Japanese

Americans living near the Pacific coast ~~are~~ *were* a security risk.

▶ According to several studies, women are more likely than men to develop

the disease, but their symptoms ~~tended~~ *tend* to be less severe.

▶ More than a hundred million people watched the Super Bowl; most were

interested in the game, but many tuned in because the commercials ~~are~~ *were*

so interesting.

▶ In *Moneyball,* Brad Pitt plays Billy Beane, general manager of the Oakland A's,

and ~~showed~~ *shows* how he uses statistics to find undervalued ballplayers.

▶ Only a few countries are major contributors to global warming, but this

phenomenon ~~affected~~ *affects* everyone in the world.

▶ Miguel was paddling his boat swiftly to the pier deep in the Amazon

rainforest; he ~~misses~~ *missed* a stroke and almost ~~falls~~ *fell* overboard.

▶ Chen competed successfully for the women's Olympics semifinal in aerial

acrobatics, but then she ~~fails~~ *failed* to attain the title in the end.

Shifts in Point of View

Sometimes you may have good reason to shift between first person (*I, we*), second person (*you*), or third person (*he, she, they*).

▶ *You* may think that you clearly remember the details of an event, but *scientists* who have studied eyewitness testimony in court cases have found that witnesses' memories are often extremely faulty.

In this sentence, the writer is contrasting readers' beliefs about something with research findings about the same topic, so a shift from second person (*you*) to third (*scientists*) is appropriate. Shifting from one point of view to another when referring to the same subjects, however, would be inconsistent—and could confuse your audience.

SHIFT   *Employees* were stunned by the huge increases in health-insurance premiums. *You* had no choice, though, but to pay or to lose coverage.

Here the point of view shifts from *employees* to *you*, even though both sentences refer to the same group of people. To eliminate this shift, revise one of the sentences to use the same point of view as the other.

▶ *Employees* were stunned by the huge increases in health-insurance premiums. *They* had no choice, though, but to pay or to lose coverage.

Some shifts in number are actually problems in agreement between a **PRONOUN** and its **ANTECEDENT**. Such a shift is often the result of an effort to avoid using *he* to refer to both men and women—or to avoid the awkward *he or she* construction. Here's an example from this book, shown as it was in the first draft, then as it was edited to eliminate the confusing shift.

SHIFT   Today, *anyone* with access to a computer can publish what *they* write.

EDITED   Today, if you have access to a computer, you can publish what you write.

SHIFTS IN POINT OF VIEW

▶ *If you decide* *, you have*
A person who decides to become a vegetarian has to pay careful attention

to your diet to make sure you are getting essential nutrients.

▶ Many Americans want the government to provide services that benefit
they
them, but we do not want to pay for these services through taxes.

▶ The library is so quiet during exams week that one can hear a sheet of paper
one's
fall on the floor or your fingers tapping on a laptop.

▶ When you get to college, you have to grow up and do laundry, balance a
you're on
checkbook, and keep track of all your courses, so for the first time, I'm on
your
my own.

▶ Students working on service-learning projects in Ghana or Kenya or South
they have
Africa are making a difference, even though a student has little power to

change the world.

economists
▶ Even though an economist may understand what's wrong with the economy,

they don't necessarily know how to fix it.

▶ Teachers who speak more than one language are in great demand, and
teachers who speak *have*
a teacher who speaks Spanish in particular probably has many job

opportunities.

Fielders
▶ Our softball team practiced fielding grounders all day. You need to be able

to scoop the ball up quickly and throw it accurately to first or second base.

VERBS NEED TO AGREE (that is, match up) with their subjects in number (singular or plural) and person (first, second, or third): *I smile, you smile, he or she smiles, we smile, they smile*. Sometimes getting subjects and verbs to agree can be tricky, however, especially when other words come between them: *The best paintings in the show were watercolors*. Following are guidelines to help you check for subject-verb agreement in your writing.

When Other Words Come between Subject and Verb

Sometimes the subject is separated from the verb by other words. Be careful that the verb agrees with the subject, not with a word that falls in between.

▶ The *contents* of the old family photo album ~~has~~ *have* provided many clues in our genealogical research.

▶ The *mayor* as well as the taxpayers ~~support~~ *supports* the stadium proposal.

Compound Subjects

If two or more subjects are joined by *and*, they generally take a plural verb.

▶ My math textbook and workbook ~~costs~~ *cost* more than all my other books combined.

However, if two words joined by *and* are considered a single unit, like *fish and chips*, they take a singular verb.

▶ Fish and chips ~~are~~ *is* a dish found on menus everywhere in England.

If two or more subjects are joined by *or* or *nor*, the verb should agree with the closest subject.

▶ Neither the legislators nor the governor ~~were~~ *was* willing to take a stand.

A sentence like this, where the subject includes both singular and plural parts, may read more smoothly if you revise to put the plural part closest to the verb: *Neither the governor nor the legislators were willing to take a stand.*

WHEN OTHER WORDS COME BETWEEN SUBJECT AND VERB

▶ *Institutions* of higher education *continue* to think of ways to increase income.

▶ The *laughter* of the children watching the clowns *was* soothing.

▶ *Produce* grown using organic methods *is* more expensive.

▶ A bowl of ripe yellow pears, which created a delicious smell in the kitchen, ~~were~~ *was* part of the strategy to make the house more inviting to potential buyers.

▶ The case settled shortly after my report, along with other documents, ~~were~~ *was* submitted to the opposing counsel.

COMPOUND SUBJECTS

▶ *Peanut butter and pizza are* my favorite foods.

▶ *Peanut butter and jelly*, however, *is* my favorite sandwich.

▶ I love Justin Bieber, but *neither "What Do You Mean?" nor "Sorry" lives up* to all the hype about his new album.

▶ *The president or the chancellor or the trustees have* the power to overturn decisions of the faculty senate.

▶ *A blanket and a pillow* ~~was~~ *were distributed* to each camper.

▶ Either the workers on the renovation project *or their supervisor* ~~are~~ *is* responsible for the damage.

▶ Neither she nor I know~~s~~ the answer to your question.

Subjects That Follow Verbs

Although verbs usually follow their subjects in English sentences, sometimes this order is reversed. In a sentence that begins with *there is* or *there are,* the subject always follows the verb. In the following example, the subject is *problems.*

▶ There ~~is~~ undoubtedly many unresolved problems with the current proposal.
  ^*are*^

Sentences that begin with a prepositional phrase followed by a verb may also cause problems. In the following sentence, the subject is *rights*, not *importance.*

▶ Of greatest importance ~~is~~ the rights to the performers' videos.
  ^*are*^

Collective Nouns Such as *Audience* or *Team*

In American English, collective nouns like *audience, team,* and *crowd* are usually treated as singular. Sometimes, however, when they refer to individuals in a group rather than to the group as a unit, they take a plural verb.

SINGULAR   The *team wins* convincingly each week.

PLURAL   The *committee disagree* about the report's suggestions.

The members of the committee disagree with each other. If a sentence like this sounds awkward, you can revise to make it clear that you are referring to individuals, not the unit: *The committee members disagree about the report's suggestions.*

COMMON COLLECTIVE NOUNS

audience	class	crowd	jury
board	committee	faculty	panel
choir	congregation	family	team
chorus	couple	herd	troop

SUBJECTS THAT FOLLOW VERBS

▶ There *are a desk and a computer* for each of the temporary employees.

▶ Here ~~is~~ *the plan* for the renovation *and a list* of items to buy.
  `are`

▶ Behind the stage ~~was~~ *a dressing room and storage space* for costumes.
  `were`

COLLECTIVE NOUNS SUCH AS *AUDIENCE* OR *TEAM*

▶ In criminal cases, a *jury needs* to reach a unanimous verdict to convict or acquit; otherwise, a mistrial is declared.

▶ In criminal cases, the *members* of a jury *need* to reach a unanimous verdict to convict or acquit; otherwise, a mistrial is declared.

▶ The *audience were* divided in their opinions of the performance; some people applauded while others jeered.

▶ The *audience was* spellbound; everyone listened with rapt attention.

▶ The *cast* for the San Francisco production of *The Book of Mormon was* different from the one in New York.

▶ The *cast* of a Broadway show sometimes agrees to reduce their salaries to try to keep the show running longer.

Indefinite Pronouns Such as *Everyone* or *Nobody*

Most **INDEFINITE PRONOUNS** —words like *anyone, anything, each, everyone, no-body, no one,* and *something*—take a singular verb, even those that seem to have plural meanings (and are often treated as plural in casual conversation).

▶ *Everyone* at the Academy Awards *likes* to make a fashion statement.

▶ *Each* of the nominees *prepares* an acceptance speech and *hopes* to use it.

A few indefinite pronouns, including *both, few, many, others,* and *several,* are plural and take plural verbs.

▶ *Many* of the athletes in the Ironman Triathlon *have trained* for years.

Some indefinite pronouns, including *all, any, none, some, more, most,* and *enough,* take a singular verb when they refer to a singular or noncount noun or a plural verb when they refer to a plural noun.

SINGULAR *None* of the information given on the site *identifies* the sponsor.

PLURAL *None* of the Greeks interviewed for the article *expect* the country's economic problems to improve in the next few years.

Words Such as *News* That Look Plural but Are Usually Singular

Words such as *news* and *athletics* look plural because they end in –*s*, but they are generally treated as singular. Some such words, notably *physics, mathematics, statistics, politics,* and *economics,* can be singular or plural, depending on the context.

SINGULAR Statistics *is* a required course for political science majors.

PLURAL Statistics *show* that texting while driving is extremely dangerous.

INDEFINITE PRONOUNS SUCH AS *EVERYONE* OR *NOBODY*

▶ *Everyone*, it seems, *wants* to be on a reality show.

▶ *All of the candidates were* nervous about having to take a position on the immigration reform issue.

▶ *All of the media attention was focused* on the female candidates' appearance and the male candidates' sex life.

▶ *Some of the service members* discharged under the "don't ask, don't tell" policy *have reapplied* to the military.

▶ *Some of the debate* over the issues involved *was* similar to the debate over racial integration of the military in the 1940s.

▶ *Each of the traditional neighborhoods* in Chicago *contributes* distinctive qualities to the city.

WORDS SUCH AS *NEWS* THAT LOOK PLURAL BUT ARE USUALLY SINGULAR

▶ *News travels* across the globe in a matter of seconds over the internet.

▶ German *measles* ~~are~~ *is* especially dangerous to pregnant women.

▶ *Economics* ~~have~~ *has* become one of the most popular majors at many colleges.

▶ The *economics* of higher education in the United States *puts* great financial pressure on families with average incomes.

Who, That, Which

The **RELATIVE PRONOUNS** *who, that,* and *which* take singular verbs when they refer to a singular or noncount noun and plural verbs when they refer to a plural noun.

SINGULAR A *cow* that *is* fed only organic feed can be sold for a much higher price on the market.

PLURAL *Cows,* which *produce* methane gas, play a surprisingly important part in global warming.

Problems sometimes occur with the expressions *one of the* and *the only one of the.* Phrases beginning with *the only one of the* always take a singular verb. Those beginning with *one of the* usually take a plural verb.

▶ *The only one of the* candidates who *was* appealing to younger voters was Rand Paul.

▶ A lack of safe drinking water is *one of the* main factors that *reduce* life expectancy in some developing countries.

Subjects That Are Titles

Subjects that are titles of books, movies, and so on use a singular verb even if the title is plural in form.

▶ *The Chronicles of Narnia* ~~have~~ ^has^ been cited as an influence by J. K. Rowling, author of the Harry Potter series.

WHO, THAT, WHICH

▶ Walter Isaacson has written *biographies* of Albert Einstein, Henry Kissinger, Benjamin Franklin, and Steve Jobs that *have* brought him much acclaim.

▶ Makers of flooring are increasingly turning to *bamboo*, which *is* easy to grow and harvest and is environmentally sustainable.

▶ PETA is one of the organizations that oppose*/* using animals in scientific experiments.

▶ Johnson is the only one of the presidential candidates who support*s* legalizing marijuana.

SUBJECTS THAT ARE TITLES

▶ *Friday Night Lights captures* perfectly the atmosphere of a small Texas town and its high school football team.

▶ Released in 1963, Alfred Hitchcock's thriller *The Birds is* still giving moviegoers nightmares half a century later.

▶ *Angry Birds* ~~have~~ *has* become popular through what *Wikipedia* calls "its successful combination of addictive gameplay, comical style, and low price."

WHAT'S THE DIFFERENCE between *lie* and *lay?* When would you say you remembered *to study*, and when would you say you remembered *studying?* Why would you say you'd do something *if you had time* when you know you won't have time? These are all questions about verbs, the subject of this section.

Verb Forms

Every English verb has four forms: base, past tense, past participle, and present participle. For regular verbs, both the past tense and the past participle are formed by adding *-ed* or *-d* to the base (and sometimes dropping a silent *e* or doubling a final consonant): *worked, danced, chatted.* For all verbs, the present participle is formed by adding *–ing* to the base form (again, sometimes dropping an *e* or doubling a consonant): *working, dancing, chatting.*

The problems that some writers have with verb forms are mostly with the past tense and past participle of **IRREGULAR VERBS**, which do not follow the *-ed* or *-d* pattern and thus have to be memorized. A list of the forms of some common irregular verbs appears on the facing page.

Be careful not to confuse the past tense with the past participle. The past tense is used alone, whereas the past participle must be used together with one or more **HELPING VERBS** such as *have* or *be.*

▶ When the maple tree *fell* in the storm, it *broke* the kitchen window.

▶ If other trees *had fallen*, more damage *would have been done.*

Forms of be. The verb *be* is especially irregular, with eight forms that simply must be learned.

BASE FORM	be
PRESENT TENSE	am, is, are
PAST TENSE	was, were
PRESENT PARTICIPLE	being
PAST PARTICIPLE	been

Some Common Irregular Verbs

BASE FORM	PAST TENSE	PAST PARTICIPLE	PRESENT PARTICIPLE
begin	began	begun	beginning
broadcast	broadcast	broadcast	broadcasting
choose	chose	chosen	choosing
do	did	done	doing
eat	ate	eaten	eating
find	found	found	finding
fly	flew	flown	flying
give	gave	given	giving
go	went	gone	going
grow	grew	grown	growing
have	had	had	having
know	knew	known	knowing
lay	laid	laid	laying
lie (recline)	lay	lain	lying
make	made	made	making
prove	proved	proved, proven	proving
read	read	read	reading
rise	rose	risen	rising
set	set	set	setting
sit	sat	sat	sitting
show	showed	showed, shown	showing
think	thought	thought	thinking
win	won	won	winning
take	took	taken	taking
write	wrote	written	writing

Verb Tenses

English verbs have three tenses to indicate time: present, past, and future.

PRESENT	**PAST**	**FUTURE**
I smile	I smiled	I will smile
I speak	I spoke	I will speak

Each tense has progressive forms, which indicate continuing actions.

PRESENT PROGRESSIVE   I *am smiling* in my class photo.

PAST PROGRESSIVE   I *was smiling* when it was taken.

FUTURE PROGRESSIVE   We *will* still *be working* on this book next week.

In addition, each tense has perfect forms. The *present perfect* indicates actions that happened at an indefinite time in the past or that began in the past and continue in the present. The *past perfect* indicates actions that took place before another past action. The *future perfect* indicates actions that will occur in the future before some other action.

PRESENT PERFECT   We *have spoken* about this situation repeatedly.

PAST PERFECT   She *had finished* before I arrived.

FUTURE PERFECT   By this time next year, we *will have been* to Paris.

Verbs can also be both perfect and progressive: I *have been working* late for many months now. This section focuses on several issues with verbs that often cause confusion in academic writing.

Verb Tenses

PRESENT	We *work* hard and *play* hard.
PAST	He *worked* at Northern Trust many years ago.
FUTURE	I *will* never again *work* this hard!
PRESENT PROGRESSIVE	It's midnight, and we *are* just *eating!*
PAST PROGRESSIVE	When I saw her, she *was making* cupcakes.
FUTURE PROGRESSIVE	Our take-out food *will be arriving* soon.
PRESENT PERFECT	That building *has been* empty for many months.
PAST PERFECT	This house *had been* empty for months when we rented it.
FUTURE PERFECT	Tomorrow we *will have been married* a year.
PRESENT PERFECT PROGRESSIVE	She *has been talking* since age two.
PAST PERFECT PROGRESSIVE	I *had been hoping* to see you.
FUTURE PERFECT PROGRESSIVE	We *will be seeing* you soon.

Use the present tense for scientific or general facts, even if the main clause of the sentence is in the past tense.

▶ Magellan's voyage proved conclusively that the world *is* round.

Use the present perfect tense to indicate a past action or state that continues in the present or to specify an action that took place in an indefinite time in the past.

▶ According to the 2010 census, the United States *has become* a predominantly urban nation.

Use the past tense to indicate a specific time in the past.

▶ Once the children moved out, we *decided* to move back to the city.

If you're writing about literature, use the present tense to discuss a text and the past tense to discuss its historical context.

▶ In *Pride and Prejudice and Zombies*, Elizabeth Bennet and Mr. Darcy *defeat* a field of zombies and then *settle* down to live happily ever after.

▶ According to author Seth Grahame-Smith, *Pride and Prejudice was* "just ripe for gore and senseless violence" ("Zombies Literature").

If you're following MLA, use the present tense in SIGNAL PHRASES introducing sources. But if you mention the date of the source, use the past tense.

▶ In his book *Spaghetti Westerns*, Christopher Frayling *observes* that "*Once Upon a Time* is concerned with the 'language' and 'syntax' of the Western" (213).

▶ As Pauline Kael *wrote* in her 1965 book *Kiss Kiss Bang Bang*, "*Stagecoach* had a mixture of reverie and reverence about the American past that made the picture seem almost folk art; we wanted to believe in it even if we didn't" (52).

If you're following APA, use the past tense or the present perfect tense in identifying a source:

▶ Zikmund-Fisher, Smith, Ubel, and Fagerlin (2007) *suggested* that numerical aptitude leads to better risk comprehension.

▶ Research *has shown* that higher mathematical aptitude leads to higher achievement on risk comprehension tasks (Zikmund-Fisher et al., 2007).

Use the present tense for scientific or general facts

▶ Galileo demonstrated that the earth *revolves* around the sun.

Use the present perfect for a past action or state that continues in the present

▶ Since she finished school, Carolina *has had* three different jobs.

▶ She *has received* a big promotion since we last saw her.

▶ Since we arrived in Hong Kong, rents *have* almost *doubled*.

If you're writing about literature

▶ In *Native Son,* Chang-rae Lee *tells* the story of Henry Park, a man of two worlds who fears he belongs to neither one.

▶ Published to great acclaim in 1995, it *was* Lee's first novel.

If you're citing sources MLA style

▶ In his book *Crowded Prairie: American National Identity in the Hollywood Western*, Michael Coyne *explains* the significance of *Stagecoach* to the Western genre and its influence in solidifying the genre's archetypes.

▶ In her 1993 essay on landscape photography, Deborah Bright *argued* that landscape photography has reinforced certain formulaic myths about landscape.

If you're citing sources APA style

▶ Bonari et al. (2005) *found* that pregnant women are more likely to discontinue using antidepressants during pregnancy if their risk assessments are too high.

Gerunds and Infinitives

A **GERUND** is the *-ing* form of a verb that functions as a **NOUN**: *Walking* is a good exercise; I do my best *thinking* after midnight. An **INFINITIVE** is *to* plus the base form of a verb that's also used as a noun: They prefer *to walk* to school. I need *to think* about the proposal. Deciding when to use a gerund or an infinitive can be a challenge, but in general, use gerunds to state facts and use infinitives to state intentions, desires, or expectations.

Use gerunds after verbs that express facts

admit	enjoy	practice	suggest
consider	finish	recall	tolerate
discuss	imagine	resist	understand

▶ Susanna had always *enjoyed making* things, so none of us were at all surprised that she majored in art.

Use infinitives after verbs that express intentions, desires, or expectations

ask	decide	intend	plan
agree	expect	manage	promise
claim	hope	offer	want

▶ She *decided to major* in art.

A few verbs can be followed by either a gerund or an infinitive: *begin, continue, hate, like, love, prefer,* and *start.* In some cases—*forget, remember, stop, try*—the choice of a gerund or infinitive affects the meaning.

▶ He remembered *to call* his mom on her birthday.

  He intended to call, and he did.

▶ He remembered *calling* his mother for her birthday.

  He remembered that he had made the call.

Always use a gerund, not an infinitive, after a preposition

▶ She got college credit *for passing* the Advanced Placement calculus exam.

GERUNDS

▶ Whatever a man's age may be, he can reduce it several years *by putting* a bright-colored flower in his button-hole. —MARK TWAIN

▶ Roger Clemens never *admitted using* steroids, and the jury believed him.

▶ In her most stressful moments, she *imagined being* in Paris.

▶ Who doesn't *enjoy taking* time off every now and then to relax?

▶ *By comparing* the food served in Chinese restaurants in five different countries, Yunshu made progress *in answering* her question about why Chinese food is so universally popular.

▶ In high school, I *avoided taking* courses that *required* a lot of *writing*.

▶ Switzerland has many famous resorts *for skiing*.

INFINITIVES

▶ Television *started to get* big in the US in 1948 with the incredible success of Milton Berle's show, which was so popular that the reservoir levels in Detroit dropped every Tuesday night at 9 p.m. because everyone *waited* until the show was over *to go* to the toilet. —FRANK ROSE, *The Art of Immersion*

▶ The foods *I like to eat* the best, like pizza and hamburgers and ice cream, are not always things that I should eat.

▶ Many college students *plan to study* abroad during their junior year. Some students *hope to learn* a new language, while others simply *want to travel*.

▶ Those with double majors usually can't *manage to take* a semester abroad.

▶ We *decided to get* Dad a shredder for Father's Day when we realized he was burning return-address labels in the barbecue.

▶ Environmentalists *hoped to convince* people that long-life fluorescent bulbs were a good investment.

Mood

English has three moods: indicative, imperative, and subjunctive. Use the indicative to state facts, opinions, or questions. Use the imperative to give commands. Use the **SUBJUNCTIVE** to express wishes, requests, and conditions that are hypothetical, unlikely, or contrary to fact. The subjunctive is also used in clauses introduced by *that* with verbs such as *suggest, demand, insist, recommend,* and *prefer.* Use **MODAL** helping verbs such as *may, might,* or *would* to indicate likelihood or probability.

INDICATIVE   Megastores *have spread* across the country.

IMPERATIVE   *Shop* at Walmart to save money.

SUBJUNCTIVE   I would shop at Target if there *were* a store nearby.
                       They insist that she *send* the documents by registered mail.

Writers are sometimes confused by conditional sentences, especially ones with a clause starting with *if.* Use the indicative if the condition in the *if* clause is possible; use the subjunctive if it's unlikely.

*When the **if** clause expresses a condition that is possible,* use the present tense form in the *if* clause and a modal such as *may, might,* or *will* plus the base form of a verb in the other clause.

▶ If our school *wins* the conference championship, applications *will go* up.

*When the **if** clause expresses a condition that is unlikely, hypothetical, or contrary to fact,* use the past tense form in the *if* clause and *would* or another modal such as *might* plus the base form of a verb in the other clause. Use *were* rather than *was* in the *if* clause.

UNLIKELY   If I *won* the lottery, I *would buy* a house.

CONTRARY TO FACT   If I *were* you, I *would* not *shop* at Target.

In clauses expressing a wish, use the past tense form of the verb—use *were* for *be.*

▶ I *wish* I *were* three inches taller and twenty pounds lighter.

In clauses expressing a request or requirement, use the base form of the verb.

▶ The attorneys ask that the plaintiff *arrive* at the courthouse thirty minutes early.

MOOD

Conditions that are possible

▶ If temperatures *are* warmer than usual, we *will save* on heating bills.

▶ If I *have* time, I *will be* happy to help.

▶ According to the directions on the box, your teeth *will become* white if you *apply* the whitening strips for a half hour a day.

▶ If the company ~~will match~~ matches my other offer, I will stay.

Conditions that are unlikely or hypothetical

▶ If Costco *opened* a store here, my family's store *might not survive*.

▶ If our college *had* a larger endowment, it *could reduce* class sizes.

▶ I *wouldn't do* that if I *were* you!

▶ If a hybrid car ~~wasn't~~ weren't so expensive, we'd buy one.

▶ If Democrats and Republicans ~~would stop~~ stopped bickering, Congress could get something done.

Wishful thinking

▶ I *wish* that I *were* able to attend college full-time.

▶ My mother *wishes* my sisters and I *lived* closer to home.

▶ We *wish* that it *didn't cost* so much to live in Rio.

▶ "If wishes *were* horses, beggars *would ride*" is a saying often used to suggest that it is better to act than to wish.

Request, requirement

▶ The landlord *demands* that my sister *pay* an extra deposit because of her dog.

PART VII

Design and Delivery

ASKED TO NAME the three most important parts of rhetoric, the famous Greek statesman and orator Demosthenes is said to have replied: "Delivery, delivery, delivery." Not too many years ago, that assessment might have seemed overdone: Delivery, more important than content? Delivery, more important than the inventiveness of the message? Delivery, more important than style? But those were the years when print texts still claimed pride of place, when what was most important was "put in writing," and when most messages came to us in black print on white pages. In these instances, the message was carried by words alone, and those words were "delivered" in print texts. Period.

But today, Demosthenes is right on target. With messages of every imaginable sort packaged in ever more alluring garb vying for our attention, just how those messages are delivered matters—a lot. So just what do we mean by "delivery"? For the purposes of this book, we have two senses of the word in mind.

The first refers to how the message is communicated: in what *mode* and through what *medium*. Mode refers to what makes up the message and communicates its meaning: words, sounds, gestures, still and moving images, or some combination of those. Medium is the form in which the audience receives it: these days, that's print, oral, or digital. So a political candidate delivering a campaign speech (the medium) might use words, gestures, and a series of images (the modes) to make a vivid and personal appeal to her audience. Another politician might deliver a proposal for a new ballot measure strictly in a print medium in order to fix the language as precisely as possible.

But there's another important sense of the word "delivery," one that comes down to us through the history of human communication. This sense of the word refers to the *performance* of a text and captures the speaker's tone, pacing, and quality of voice as well as a full range of facial and bodily gestures and movements. In Demosthenes' time, such delivery was of paramount importance in connecting to an audience and gaining its assent, approval, or understanding. And given the ubiquity of television, film, and video (not to mention sites like *YouTube* and *Vine*), these elements of communication are taking on greater and greater significance today.

Savvy authors understand that messages today don't just lie there on the page and wait for readers to discover them. Rather, it's up to us as authors to capture and hold the attention of our audiences. For authors of texts in all media, that means paying careful attention to *design*. A text's design— whether it be the use of color and fonts in a print text, the choice of music and moving images in a video, or the slides and handouts in an oral presentation—often determines your audience's first and lasting impressions. An effective design can draw the notice of your audience, keep their attention on your message, and help you achieve your purpose.

This section of *Everyone's an Author* aims to get *your* attention and to focus it on what delivery can mean for you as an author. The chapters that follow will ask you to consider the choices you'll need to make as an author who is designing texts, and how those choices affect the delivery and reception of your messages. In addition, we will examine the role of delivery in

In the eighteenth century, actors and speakers thought of themselves as occupying 360 degrees of space, which was theirs to use as they wanted in conveying feelings and meanings, as illustrated in this diagram by Gilbert Austin, a writer and orator of that time.

successful oral presentations, multimodal compositions, and portfolios. And last but not least, we'll urge you to deliver some of your ideas to audiences by way of publication, proving once again that, today, everyone's an author.

THIRTY-THREE

Designing
What You Write

ESIGN. IT'S A WORD YOU HEAR ALL THE TIME, one you use without thinking about it. "Kate Middleton walked down the aisle in a wedding dress designed by Sarah Burton for Alexander McQueen." "Have you seen the design for Stephen Colbert's new book?" "Frank Gehry's design of the Disney Concert Hall astonished critics with its waves of gleaming stainless steel." "My essay was designed to get the attention of the college admissions committee."

Fashion, technology, architecture, toys: everything is designed, and that includes everything you write. A slide presentation, a blog post, an essay—you design it, whether you are conscious of doing so or not. You select a medium and tools: a lined notebook and a pencil, a text message and a smartphone, white paper and black printer ink. You choose fonts and colors: big red capital letters for a poster, 12-point black Times New Roman for an essay, your neatest cursive for a thank-you note. You think about including visuals: a bar graph on a slide, a cartoon in a blog, a photo in an essay. You consider whether to use multiple columns, bullet points, numbered lists—and where to leave some white space. You decide what you want readers to notice first and how to make it catch their eye.

This chapter discusses several key design elements: typography, color, visuals, and layout. Whatever fonts or images you choose, though, remember that they are not mere decoration. However you design a text, you need to be guided by your purpose, your audience, and the rest of your rhetorical situation.

THINKING RHETORICALLY ABOUT DESIGN

Researchers point out that being able to design your writing gives you more control over your message than writers had in the past, when they had fewer options and tools at their disposal. That's because your design choices can play a big role in the way your audience receives your message and whether your text achieves its purpose. Look, for example, at the different ways that Coca-Cola was advertised in 1913 and in 2014.

In 1913, Coke was relatively new, and its ads relied on words to introduce it to an audience that was not yet familiar with the drink, telling them it had "character" and was "delicious," "refreshing," and "thirst-quenching." The ad shown here was designed so that these words would pop and be easy to read.

To reach today's audiences, however, advertisers use multiple media—in the case of this 2014 ad aired just before the World Cup in Brazil, print as well as video. Coca-Cola knew the world would be watching the World Cup, and this ad launched a special celebration of the event: mini bottles featuring designs inspired by the flags of World Cup host nations past, present, and future. The message: Coca-Cola is now global, reaching potential customers all over the world.

A print ad for Coca-Cola in Georgia Tech's 1913 yearbook and a video ad presented during the telecast of the 2014 FIFA World Cup.

One thing the two ads have in common, though, is the logo. Whether it's in black ink on white paper or red and white pixels on a screen, the Coca-Cola logo was *designed* to be instantly recognizable.

In designing what you write, you need to think about how you can best reach your audience and achieve your purpose. Given the deluge of words, images, and other data, readers today are less likely than they once were to read anything start to finish. Instead, they may scan for just the information they need. So as an author, you need to design your documents to be user-friendly: easy to access, to navigate, to read—and to remember.

Considering Your Rhetorical Situation

- *Who is your* AUDIENCE, and are there any design elements they expect or need? Large type? Illustrations? Are there any design elements that might not appeal to them—or cause them to question your authority as an author?

- *What is your* PURPOSE, and what design elements can help you achieve that purpose? If you're trying to explain how to do something, would it help to set off the steps in a numbered list? Is there anything that would work against your goals—using a playful typeface in a business letter, for example?

- *What's your* GENRE, and does it have any design requirements?

- *What's your* STANCE *as an author,* and how do you want to come across to your audience? Do you want to seem businesslike? serious? ironic? practical and matter-of-fact? How can your use of fonts, color, images, and other design elements reflect that stance?

- *Consider the larger* CONTEXT. Does your assignment specify any design requirements? What design elements are possible with the technology you have available?

- *What* MEDIA *will you use*—print? digital? spoken?—and what kinds of DESIGN elements are appropriate (or possible)? A print essay, for example, could include photographs but not video.

CHOOSING FONTS

Authors today have hundreds of fonts to choose from, and the choices we make affect the message our readers receive—so it's important to think carefully about what's most appropriate for the particular rhetorical situation.

Serif fonts (fonts with small decorative lines, called serifs, added to the ends of most letters) such as Times New Roman or Bodoni have a traditional look, whereas sans serif fonts (those without serifs) such as Arial or Futura give a more modern look. Your instructors may require you to use a specific font, but if you get to choose, you'll want to think about what look you want for your text—and what will be most readable. Some readers find serif fonts easier to read in longer pieces of writing. Sans serif, on the other hand, tends to be easier to read in slide presentations. Save novelty or decorative fonts such as **Impact** or *Allegro* for your nonacademic writing—and even there, use them sparingly, since they can be difficult (or annoying!) to read.

Most fonts include **bold**, *italics*, and underlining options, which you can use to highlight parts of a text. In academic writing, bold is generally used for headings, whereas italics or underlining is used for titles of books, films, and other long works. If you're following MLA, APA, or another academic style, make sure that your use of fonts conforms to the style's requirements.

Readability matters. For most academic and workplace writing, you'll want to use 10-to-12-point type, and at least 18-point type for most presentation slides. Academic writing is usually double-spaced; letters and résumés are single-spaced.

ADDING HEADINGS

Brief texts may need no headings at all, but for longer texts, headings can help readers follow the text and find specific information. Some kinds of writing have set headings that authors are required to use— **IMRAD** reports, for instance, require introduction, methods, research, and discussion headings. When you include headings, you need to decide on wording, fonts, and placement.

Wording. Make headings succinct and parallel. You could make them all nouns ("Energy Drinks," "Snack Foods"), all gerund phrases ("Analyzing the Contents of Energy Drinks," "Resisting Snack Foods"), or all questions ("What's in Energy Drinks?" and "Why Are Snack Foods So Hard to Resist?").

Fonts. If you've chosen to divide your text further using subheadings under larger headings, distinguish different level headings from one another typographically by using bold, italic, underlining, and capitalization. For example:

FIRST-LEVEL HEADING
Second-Level Heading
Third-Level Heading

When you get to choose, you may want to make headings larger than the main text or to put them in a different font or color (as we do throughout this book). But if you're following MLA or APA styles, be aware that they require headings to be in the same font as the main text.

Placement. You can center headings or set them flush left above the text, or place them to the left of the text; but whatever you do, treat each level of heading consistently throughout the text. If you're following MLA or APA styles, be aware that first-level headings must be centered.

USING COLOR

Sometimes you'll be required to write in black type on a white background, but many times you'll have reason to use colors. In some media, color will be expected or necessary—on websites or presentation slides, for instance. Other times it may be inappropriate—in a thank-you note following a job interview at a law firm or in an application essay to business school. As with any design element, color should be used to help you get a message across and appeal to an audience, never just to decorate your text.

Be aware that certain colors can evoke specific emotional reactions: blue, like the sky and sea, suggests spaciousness and tranquillity; red invokes fire and suggests intense energy and emotions; yellow, the color of our sun, generates warmth and optimism. Also remember that certain colors carry different associations across cultures—to Westerners, white suggests innocence and youth, but in China white is traditionally associated with death (which is why Chinese brides wear red).

Especially if you use more than one color in a text, you'll want to consider how certain colors work together. Look at the color wheel on the next page to see how the colors are related. *Primary colors* (red, blue, and yellow) create

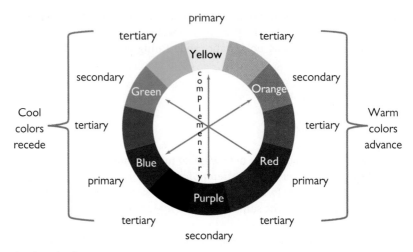

A color wheel.

an effect of simplicity and directness. The more *secondary* and *tertiary colors* you use, the more sophisticated the design. *Complementary colors*, located opposite each other on the color wheel, look brighter when placed next to each other but can sometimes clash and look jarring. (Black and white are also considered complementary colors.) Cool and dark colors appear to recede, whereas warm and bright colors seem to advance. So using both cool and warm colors can create a feeling of movement and energy.

Remember that any color scheme includes the type, the background, and any images or graphics that you use. If colorful photos are an important part of your website, they'll stand out most strongly on a white background and with black type—both of which you may want to use for that reason alone. If you're writing a report that includes multicolored pie charts and want to have color headings, you wouldn't want to use primary colors in the headings and pastels in the charts. In short, if you use colors, make sure they work well with all the other design elements in the text.

Using color to guide readers. Like bold or italic type, color can help guide readers through a text. In fact, that's the way color is used in this book. The headings are all red to make them easy to spot, and key words are color-coded a pale orange to signal that they're defined in the glossary/index. In addition, we've color-coded parts of the book—roadmaps are on yellow pages, readings are light blue, research chapters are green, style chapters are lavender, design and delivery chapters are aqua—to help readers find them easily.

Color is an important navigational element on websites as well, sometimes used to indicate links and to highlight headings. For such uses of color, though, it's important to choose colors that are easy to see.

Considering legibility. Using color can make your writing easier—or harder—to read. Use type and background colors that are compatible. Dark type on a light background works best for lengthy pieces of writing, while less text-heavy projects can use a light text on a dark background for visual effect. In either case, be sure that the contrast is dramatic enough to be legible. Keep in mind that some people can't see or distinguish certain colors (notably, red and green) so be sure to have a good reason if you use these colors together.

USING VISUALS

Authors today write with more than just words. Photos, charts, tables, and videos are just some of the visual elements you can use to present information and to make your writing easier or more interesting to read. Would a photo slideshow help listeners see a scene you're describing in an oral presentation? Would readers of a report be able to compare data better in a table or chart than in a paragraph? Would a map or diagram help readers see how and where an event you're describing unfolded? These are questions you should be asking yourself as you write.

Be sure that any visuals you use are relevant to what you have to say— that you use them to support your point, not just to decorate your text. And remember that even the most spectacular images do not speak for themselves: you need to refer to them in your text and to explain to readers what they are and how they support what you're saying.

Kinds of Visuals

You may be assigned to include certain kinds of visuals in your writing— but if not, a good way to think about what sorts of visuals to use (or not) is by considering your rhetorical situation. What visuals would be useful or necessary for your topic and purpose? What visuals would help you reach

A photo of street art in a Texas parking lot demonstrates the layering effect of graffiti in a way that would be difficult to do with words alone.

your audience? What kinds of visuals are possible in your medium—or expected in your genre?

Photographs can help an audience envision something that's difficult to describe or to explain in words. A good photo can provide powerful visual evidence for an argument and can sometimes move readers in a way that words alone might not. Think of how ads for various charities use photos of hungry children to appeal to readers to donate.

Photos can be useful for many writing purposes, letting readers see something you're **DESCRIBING** or **ANALYZING**, for instance, or even something you're **REPORTING** on. (See how Melissa Rubin needed to include a photo of the ad that she analyzes on p. 246, and how Katherine Spriggs included photos of two different kinds of farms in her argumentative essay on p. 150.) You can take your own photos or use ones that you find in other sources. Remember, however, to provide full documentation for any photos that you don't take yourself and to ask permission before photographing someone and using his or her image in your writing.

Videos are useful for demonstrating physical processes or actions and for showing sequences. Your medium will dictate whether you can include videos in a text. The print version of a newspaper article about aerialist skiers, for instance, includes a still photo of a skier in mid-jump, whereas the same article on the newspaper's website and on a TV news report features videos showing the skier in action. Your topic and genre will affect whether or not you have reason to include video if you can. If you were writing a **PRO-CESS ANALYSIS** to teach a skier how to perform a certain aerial maneuver, a video would be far more useful than the still photo you might include if you were writing a **PROFILE** of a professional skier.

Graphs, charts, and tables. Numerical and statistical data can be easier both to describe and to understand when they are presented visually. See the fantasy sports graphics on this page, for example—and imagine trying to present that data in a paragraph. You'll often have occasion to present data in graphs or charts, in bar graphs, pie charts, and the like, especially in **REPORTS** and **ANALYSES**. In many cases, you'll be able to find tables and graphs in your research and then incorporate them into your own writing. You can also use templates found in *Excel, Word, PowerPoint,* and other programs to create charts and tables yourself. Whether you find or create them, be sure to indicate in your text where the information comes from and how they support your argument.

Line graphs are useful for illustrating trends and changes over time—how unemployment fluctuates over a period of years, for instance. By using more than one line, you can compare changes in different variables, such as unemployment for those with a college education and those with only a high school education. When comparing more

Fantasy sports at a glance

The typical player is a 34-year-old male with a college degree who spends almost nine hours each week consuming fantasy sports.

Fantasy sports players in the U.S.

2004: 13.5 million

2014: 41.5 million

Total for 2013 was unavailable.

2004 2005 2006 2007 2008 2009 2010 2011 2012 2013 2014

Average daily winnings
For daily players

Less than $250: 55%

More than $2,500: 5%

$1,000-$2,500: 9%

$500-$1,000: 15%

$250-$500: 16%

Amount spent on entry fees in a year
For daily players

$1-$50	65%
$51-$100	17%
$101-$300	9%
$301+	9%

Source: Fantasy Sports Trade Association, Eilers Research

Graphic: Chicago Tribune/TNS

A line graph shows the rising number of fantasy sports players over a period of 10 years; a bar chart and a pie chart break down average entry fees and winnings.

than one variable, the lines should be in two different colors so that readers can easily see the comparison.

Bar graphs are useful for comparing quantitative data, such as for different age groups or different years. In the example about fantasy sports, the bars make it easy to see how much most players spend to participate in fantasy sports leagues. It would be easy enough to convey this same information in words alone—but more work to read and harder to remember.

Pie charts give an overview of the relative sizes of parts to a whole, such as what share of a family budget is devoted to food, housing, entertainment, and so on. Pie charts are useful for showing which parts of a whole are more or less significant, but they are less precise (and harder to read) than bar graphs. It's best to limit a pie chart to six or seven slices, since when the slices become too small, it's difficult to see how they compare in size.

Tables are an efficient way of presenting a lot of information concisely by organizing it into horizontal rows and vertical columns. Table 1 below presents data about home internet access in the United States, information that is made easy to scan and compare in a table.

Table I
US Home Internet Access by Age Group, 2009

Age of Householder	No In-Home Internet (%)	In-Home Internet (%)
Under 25 years	33.0	67.0
25-34 years	25.8	74.2
35-44 years	22.2	77.8
45-55 years	24.2	75.8
55 years and older	41.8	58.2

Source: United States Dept. of Commerce, Census Bureau; "Internet Use in the United States: October 2009," Current Population Survey; US Dept. of Commerce, Oct. 2009; Web; 11 June 2012; table 1.

Maps provide geographic context, helping to orient your audience to places mentioned in your text. A report on the 2011 earthquake in New Zealand, for example, includes the maps on the facing page showing where the earthquake was centered and where the most damage was done. Include a map when location is important to your point.

CHRISTCHURCH BUILDINGS DAMAGE

Crust
Upper Mantle
Transition Zone
Lower Mantle
D" Layer
Outer Core
Inner Core

A diagram of the earth's internal structure shows the various layers.

Diagrams are useful for illustrating details that cannot be shown in a photograph. A carefully drawn diagram can deliver a lot of information in a small amount of space.

Infographics bring together several different types of visuals—charts, tables, photos, and so on—to give detailed information and data. They can help simplify a complex subject—or make a potentially dull topic visually interesting. Because infographics can be so densely packed with information, make sure that they are large enough for your audience to be able to read and arranged in a way that they can follow.

Creating Visuals

You can find visuals online, scan them from print sources, or create them yourself using basic software or a digital camera. If you come across an illustration you think would be useful, make or save a copy. Scan or photocopy visuals from print sources, and import a link or take a screen grab from digital sources. Label everything clearly. Be aware that visuals and any data you use to create them need to be **DOCUMENTED** in a **CAPTION** or source note—so keep track of where you found everything as you go.

- *Photographs and videos.* If you plan to print an image, save each file in as high a resolution as possible. If a photo is only available in a very small size or low resolution, try to find a more legible option. Be careful about cropping, adjusting color, and altering images or videos in other ways that could change the meaning; straying too far from the original is considered unethical.

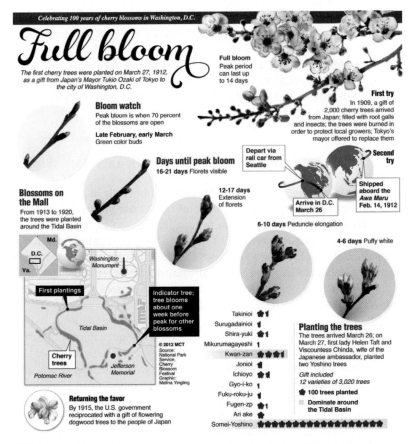

This infographic on the cherry blossom season in Washington, DC, includes photos, diagrams, maps, and a bar chart.

- *Graphs, charts, and tables.* Be consistent in your use of fonts and colors, especially if you include more than one graph, chart, or table. Be sure that the horizontal (*x*) and vertical (*y*) axes are labeled clearly. If you use more than one color, add labels for what each color represents. When you have many rows or columns, alternating colors can make categories easier to distinguish.

- *Maps.* Provide a title and a key explaining any symbols, colors, or other details. If the original is missing these elements, add them. If you create the map yourself, be sure to highlight notable locations or information.

- *Diagrams.* Use a single font for all labels, and be sure to make the diagram large enough to include all of the necessary detail. Make sure these details are clearly and neatly represented, whether they're drawn or created on a computer.

Introducing and Labeling Visuals

Introduce visuals as you would any other source materials, explaining what they show and how they support your point. Don't leave your audience wondering how a photo or chart pertains to your project—spell it out, and be sure to do so *before* the visual appears ("As shown in fig. 3, population growth has been especially rapid in the Southwest"). Number visuals in most academic writing sequentially (Figure 1, Figure 2), counting tables separately (Table 1, Table 2). If you're following MLA, APA, or another academic style, be sure to follow its guidelines for how to label tables and figures.

MLA STYLE. For tables, provide a number ("Table 1") and a descriptive title ("Population Growth by Region, 1990–2010") on separate lines above the table; below the table, add a caption explaining what the table shows and including any source information. For graphs, charts, photos, and diagrams, provide a figure number ("Fig. 1"), caption, and source information below the figure. If you give only brief source information in a parenthetical citation, include the source in your list of works cited.

APA STYLE. For tables, provide a number ("Table 1") and a descriptive title on separate lines above the table; below the table, include a note with information about the source. For charts, diagrams, graphs, and photos, include a figure number ("Figure 1") and source information in a note below the figure.

PUTTING IT ALL TOGETHER

Once you've chosen fonts, colors, and visuals, you need to think about how they all come together as a text. Look, for instance, at the homepage of TED, a nonprofit group dedicated to disseminating "ideas worth spreading." It's easy to read with a sans serif font and minimal text. The logo draws your eye because it's large, red, capitalized, and positioned in the upper left corner of the screen. The soft gray "ideas worth spreading" complements the red and leads your eye to the bold black text below—"Riveting talks by remarkable people, free to the world"—which defines the group's purpose and audience.

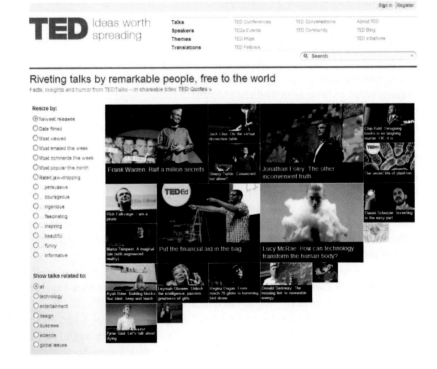

Each of the cascading images is a link to a specific TED talk, and when you mouse over each image, a short summary pops up. Note how white space separates the parts and makes the page easy to read. No surprise that this site won a Webby Award, the online equivalent of an Oscar.

You may not have occasion to design anything as large or complex as the TED site, but the same design principles will apply for all the writing you do. Whether you're designing a report, a photo essay, or a slide presentation, chances are you'll be working with some combination of words, images, graphs, and other graphic elements that you'll need to put on paper or screen in order to reach a certain audience to achieve a certain purpose.

Look beyond the details and think about what you want your design to accomplish. Do you want it to help your audience grasp a message as fast as possible? convey your identity as a hip and creative author? conform to the requirements of a certain academic style? be appealing yet simple enough to implement by an approaching deadline? Thinking about what you want your design to do can help you determine how to put it all together in a way that achieves your end goal.

Keep it simple. Sometimes you'll need to follow a prescribed organization and layout, but if you get to decide how to design your document, here's a piece of advice: don't make your design any more complex than it has to be. Readers want to be able to find the information they need without having to spend time deciphering a complex hierarchy of headings or an intricate navigational system.

Think about how to format your written text. Should it all be in paragraphs, or is there anything that should be set off as a list? If so, should it be a bulleted list to make it stand out, or a numbered list to put items in a sequence? If your text includes numerical data, should any of it be presented in a graph, chart, or table to make it easier for readers to understand? Is there any information that's especially important that you'd like to highlight in some way?

Position visuals carefully. Keep in mind how they will look on a page or screen. Placing them at the top or bottom of a print page will make it easier to lay out pages. If your text will be online, you have more freedom to put visuals wherever you wish. Reproduce visuals at a large enough size so that readers will be able to see all the pertinent detail, but be aware that digital images become fuzzier when they are enlarged. Reduce large image files by saving them in compressed formats such as jpegs or gifs; you don't want readers to have problems loading the image. And once everything is in place, look over your text carefully to be sure that nothing is too small or blurry to read.

Use white space to separate the parts of your text. Add some extra space above headings and around lists, images, graphs, charts, and tables. This will keep your text from looking cluttered and make everything easier to find and read.

Organize the text. Whether your text is a simple five-page report or a full website, readers will need to know how it's organized and how to find the information they're looking for. In a brief essay, you might simply indicate that in a sentence in your introduction, but in lengthier pieces, you may need headings, both to structure your text and to make it easy for readers to navigate.

If you're creating a website, you'll need to figure out how you're dividing materials into pages and to make that clear on the site's homepage. Most homepages have a horizontal navigation bar across the top indicating and linking to the main parts and often another navigation menu going down the left side of the screen, with links to specific materials on the site. These menus should appear in the same position on every page of the site—and every page should include a link to take readers back to the homepage. Take a look at the examples from *National Geographic* on the following page and you'll see the consistent elements that help readers navigate the site: navigation bars at the top, links to popular information in bulleted lists, ads in the bottom right corner, consistent colors and fonts on all the pages.

GETTING RESPONSE TO YOUR DESIGN

Whether you're composing a report, an illustrated essay, or a blog post, try to get response to the design. Enlist the help of friends or classmates, asking them what they think of the "look" of your text, how easy it is to read, and so on. Following are some specific things they (and you) should consider:

- Is the design appropriate to the text's PURPOSE, AUDIENCE, GENRE, and MEDIUM? Consider the fonts and any use of color: do they suit your rhetorical situation?

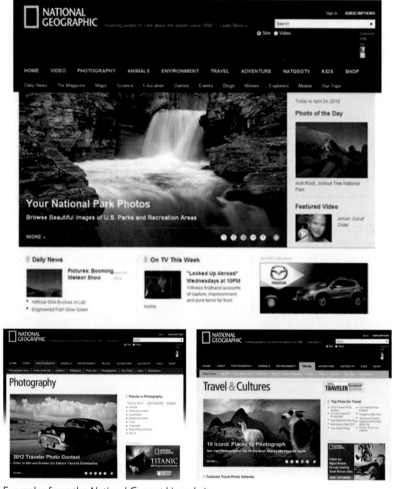

Examples from the *National Geographic* website.

- Does the design make the main parts of your text easy to see? If not, would it help to add headings?

- Is there any information that should be set off as a list?

- Does the text include any data that would be easier to follow in a chart, table, or graph?

- If you've included images, what purpose do they serve? How do they support the point of your text? If some are only decorative, should you delete them?

- Does the overall "look" of your text suit the message that you want to convey?

Remember: your design is often the first impression readers get, and it can make all the difference in getting your message across. There may be a lot at stake in the simple choice of a font or color or image, so make these choices carefully—and make your design work for you.

REFLECT. Find a design that you think is attractive (or not)—a book cover, a magazine spread, a brochure, a poster, a blog, a website, whatever. **ANALYZE** *its use of fonts, colors, and visuals. What works, and what doesn't? How would you revise the design if you could?*

THIRTY-FOUR

Writing in Multiple Modes

Ever since the days of illustrated books and maps, texts have included visual elements for the purpose of imparting information. The contemporary difference is the ease with which we can combine words, images, sound, color, animation, and video . . . so that they are part of our everyday lives.

—NCTE on Multimodal Literacies

HE NATIONAL COUNCIL OF TEACHERS OF ENGLISH made this statement a decade ago, and in the years that have passed, multimodal literacies have indeed become part of the "everyday lives" of students everywhere. Take a look at the cartoon on the next page, for example.

The little boy in this cartoon illustrates the NCTE statement perfectly: he lies in bed, listening to his dad read him a story. But wait a minute! The boy does more than just listen: he compliments his dad on his reading ("darn good job") and offers to record him reading and then "podcast" him on his website. Multimodal, indeed.

Defining Multimodal Writing

So just what are these multimodal texts? Put most simply, they are texts that draw on more than words, bringing in still or moving images, sound, and so on. Researcher Cynthia Selfe identifies five modes writers can use to convey their messages: linguistic (that's words, written or spoken); visual (colors, fonts, images, and so on); audio (tone of voice, music, and

"You know, Dad, you do a darn good job.
You should let me record you sometime, and
I'll podcast you on my website. Just a thought."

other sounds); gestural (body language and facial expression); and spatial (the way elements are arranged on a page or screen).

For hundreds of years, writers have relied primarily on two of these modes, the linguistic and the visual. In this sense, all writing uses multiple modes, so multimodality is nothing new. And just like traditional print texts, more complex multimodal ones call for careful attention to the same conventions of good writing, research, and argument expected of all college writing.

But today writers have easy access to all five modalities and can produce texts that convey meaning not only through words but also through sounds, moving and still images, animations, and more—delivered through print, spoken, and digital media. For you as a writer, that opens up an infinite number of options. This chapter offers some tips for deciding among those options and for making best use of the various technologies available for writing in multiple modes.

REFLECT. Make a list of writing assignments you've done this term and of any writing projects you have worked on out of class. How many of them rely on printed words on a page? How many use multiple modes—and what are they? On the basis of this exercise, write (or draw, or record) a reflection about yourself as a writer of multimodal texts. Then consider the next piece of writing you're preparing to do. How might you use sounds, images, and other modes to get your message across?

Considering Your Rhetorical Situation

Writing in multiple modes calls for the same close attention to rhetorical principles that all writing does. Whatever your topic, the following questions can help you think about your purpose, audience, and the rest of your rhetorical situation:

Consider your PURPOSE. Why are you creating this project? What are your purposes or goals? No doubt one purpose is to fulfill an assignment—and do a good job of it. But you may have other purposes as well: to raise awareness about a problem on campus; to convince someone to support a project you have in mind; to provide information. Consider the message you want to communicate. What do you want to see happen as a result of what you write?

Think about your AUDIENCE. Who are you aiming to reach, and how can you best reach them? If you're writing to all members of your campus community, you'll probably want to post your message online, but if you're writing to neighbors about a lost dog, posters will likely work better. If your intended audience is limited to people you know (such as on a wiki or a blog accessible only to students at your school), you may make some assumptions about them and how they're likely to respond. But remember that most projects you put online may well be accessible to the public—that is, to people you don't and can't know. In this case, it's important not to make assumptions about what they know and to be respectful of the diverse audience that may read what you write.

Think about your STANCE. What is your attitude toward your topic, and how do you want to present yourself as an author—as well-informed? outraged? perplexed? How can you convey that stance? Certain fonts look serious while others look silly; same thing with colors. If you're including music, that too affects the tone. If you're giving an oral presentation, your facial expression and gestures can signal something about your stance.

Choose your GENRE. The kind of writing you're doing can sometimes determine the form that your multimodal project will take. If you're **REPORTING** information, a wiki might be an appropriate choice. But if you're delivering a **PROPOSAL** asking for funding for an event, a print text may be most appropriate. And if afterward you want to write a **NARRATIVE** documenting the event, a video essay might capture the experience most vividly.

Consider the larger CONTEXT. How much time do you have, and is your topic narrow enough that you can do a good job in that amount of time? Do you have access to whatever technology you will need? If you'll need to learn new software, remember to build in time for that. Does your campus offer any services (perhaps at a writing center) where you can get help?

Consider MEDIA. What media will best serve your audience, purpose, and topic? If you're writing about Bollywood films, you might create a blog, which would enable you to embed video clips and to reach a community of fans. If you want to inform fellow students about ways to save water, you might create an infographic to post in restrooms around campus.

KINDS OF MULTIMODAL PROJECTS

A wide range of multimodal projects have made their way into classrooms at colleges and universities across the country. The most prevalent and popular of these kinds of projects include illustrated essays, blogs, wikis, audio essays, video essays, and posters. Following are some tips for composing each of these kinds of writing.

Illustrated Essays

Probably the simplest and most likely multimodal assignment you will encounter is an essay in which you're asked to embed illustrations—photos, drawings, maps, graphs, charts, and so on. Illustrated essays offer you a chance for creativity and for getting your point across in multiple ways; in fact, such writing is a staple in all newspapers and most magazines today. So there's no reason why your college assignments should be words only, not when you have so many other elements to work with.

See how one student used images in an essay about how Japanese video games are no longer being "localized," that is, remade so as to better appeal to foreign audiences.

> Even companies like Nintendo, which had previously relied on the denationalized nature of their characters for international success, have begun capitalizing on uniquely Japanese concepts. For example, the Tanooki Suit is an item introduced with *New Super Mario Bros. 3* that allows Mario to

Figure 1. The box art for *Super Mario Bros. 3* prominently featured Raccoon Mario . . .

Figure 2. . . . while art for later releases focused on Tanooki Mario, who, although present in *Super Mario Bros. 3*, was not nearly as prominent as in *3D Land* or *3D World*.

transform into a tanuki, or Japanese raccoon dog. In the original release of *Super Mario Bros. 3*, Tanooki Mario was de-emphasized in favor of Raccoon Mario, which was prominently featured on the cover art, since Americans were more likely able to identify a raccoon rather than a tanuki (see Figure 1). However, with the release of *Super Mario 3D Land*, which some consider to be a spiritual successor to *Super Mario Bros. 3* (Sterling), Nintendo fully embraced the Tanooki power-up and made it the primary focus both in their advertising and in-game, with many enemies gaining Tanooki tails. This newly realized proliferation of Tanooki extended into its sequel, *Super Mario 3D World* (see Figure 2) and related games, such as *Mario Kart 7*. By embracing their cultural heritage rather than disguising it, Nintendo helps introduce Western gamers to elements of Japanese culture they may otherwise not be aware of, no longer fearful of culture shock.

—RUIZHE (THOMAS) ZHAO, "Word for Word: Culture's Impact on the Localization of Japanese Video Games"

Notice how Zhao has carefully incorporated the two images into his argument, labeling them with figure numbers, referring to them in the text, and providing captions for each one. Though it's not shown here, he also included documentation information in a works cited list. Far from being mere decoration, these images provide essential support for his argument.

Some Tips for Writing Illustrated Essays

- Make sure all illustrations help communicate your message. You never want to use illustrations as mere decoration.

- Refer to each illustration in the text and position each one carefully so that it appears near the text where it's discussed.

- Give each illustration a figure number and a caption that tells readers what it is.

- Provide documentation for any illustrations that you don't create yourself, either in a caption or in a works cited list.

Blogs

Blogs—an abbreviation of "weblogs"—are regularly updated sites on which writers post reflections, ideas, information, and arguments. They often include images, embedded audio or video clips, and links to other sites. Some blogs focus on a single topic (Deb Perelman's *Smitten Kitchen* blog focuses on home cooking; Nate Silver's *FiveThirtyEight* analyzes politics, economics, and sports), but those run by newspapers, advocacy organizations, or other institutions cover a wide range of topics (the *Huffington Post* hosts dozens of blogs by politicians, academics, celebrities, and many ordinary folks who have something to say). Almost all blogs allow readers to comment and thus function as sites where people share and discuss information and ideas. Blogs are now a part of the everyday landscape of the web: as of July 2015, the blogging platform *Tumblr* hosted well over 243 million blogs—including *everyonesanauthor.tumblr.com*, the companion site to this book.

Blogs are frequently assigned in college classes. You may have been assigned to post responses to one, or maybe you have a blog yourself. Check out the following excerpt from a blog posting in the *Huffington Post* by Julia Landauer, who was a college student as well as a NASCAR driver when she wrote this post:

The Lady Up Front

"Boogity boogity boogity, let's just go racing!" screams Darrell Waltrip from the booth. That's when you know the green flag has flown and the Daytona 500 is under way.

Normally Waltrip says, "Boogity boogity boogity, let's go racing,

Julia Landauer,
NASCAR driver.

boys!" But from here on out his trademark phrase will have to be slightly altered to include the sole lady racer, Danica Patrick.

I was thrilled when Danica qualified on pole [won the number one starting position by having the fastest qualifying time] for the 55th running of the Daytona 500. Yes, I wanted to be the first woman to do that, but women in racing is bigger than me. In the effort to draw in more female racers, crewmembers and race/safety officials to the sport, Danica's history-making pole was a huge contribution. Hopefully this contribution will help catapult more women into the sport.

People will critique it, saying that a pole on a super speedway (oval tracks that are over 2 miles long, such as Daytona or Indy) is irrelevant to the rest of the season, so Danica's accomplishment is not a big deal. How wrong! The fact is that success is success and if people consider super speedway poles and wins to be "easy accomplishments," then they should be taken out of the schedule. Or people shouldn't make a big deal about other racers finding success on them. But clearly there is a prestige that goes along with setting pole and winning at Daytona, which can't be taken away from Danica.

The big picture is that Danica showed that women can run up front at the highest levels of racing. There were concerns as to whether she'd

Danica Patrick's race car.

be able to stay up front, and she did; she was in the top five for the majority of the race and even became the first woman to lead laps at the Daytona 500.

Despite finishing 8th, which is still quite respectable, Danica did a great job and set the stage for the future of women in racing. Lyn St. James, retired racer and first female to win the Indianapolis 500 Rookie of the Year award, stated in an interview with CNN, "[Danica] did everything right for the whole race . . . she learned a lot and earned respect from so many people that it was a terrific start of the season and a positive example for women everywhere."

To piggyback off of Lyn's comment, my favorite result from Danica winning the pole comes in something Ella Gordon, Jeff Gordon's daughter, finally realized. As the *Atlantic* pointed out, Danica's pole brought widespread publicity to the fact that women can be racecar drivers too, something that 4-year-old Ella hadn't previously understood to be a possibility. Now think of what all the other little girls who grow up around racing are thinking! We can do it too.

—JULIA LANDAUER, "The Lady Up Front"

Note that the photo of Landauer is one she includes on the blog, in racing gear—a personal touch that helps to build her readership, especially among the women she wants to see join this sport. Her title, "The Lady Up Front," gives a clue about the topic and is meant to intrigue any readers who assume that racing is a man's sport. In providing detailed information about a Daytona 500 race, she quotes from CNN and includes a link to an article in the *Atlantic*. Landauer's writing is informal and friendly, and her point is clear: girls "can do it too."

While you may create a blog of your own, you'll probably also find yourself responding to other people's posts or being assigned to do so for a class. See one response to a post on the *Web of Language* blog run by linguistics professor Dennis Baron. The response is to a posting he wrote in 2010, "Should Everybody Write?"

shon.bacon@ttu.edu Mar 9, 2010 12:08 am

Nice post. This makes me think about a question I've had for a while now with participatory culture and everyone being a producer—producer and user. With the internet and social media, the idea of "audience" has blurred quite a bit considering, as this post notes, that anyone

See Dennis Baron's complete post on p. 840.

can create content. The idea of a participatory culture, of everyone having a voice, sounds great in theory, but I'm not sure how beneficial it is to have all voices create a cacophony instead of a well-blended harmony. I guess this is my longwinded way of answering your question. My short version: "Yes, but . . ."

Note that the author of this response raises a question of his own that relates to Baron's post, about the blurring of the line between author and audience. He builds on what Baron has written and then concludes by answering Baron's original question about whether everyone should write: "Yes, but . . . "

Some Tips for Posting to a Blog

- Blog posts are usually fairly brief and to the point because bloggers assume that their readers are reading for specific information. With this in mind, make sure your posts have a point—and that you make that point clear.
- Blogs tend to be written in fairly informal, conversational language.
- Many readers scan blogs for information, so use lists, headings, italics, and other design elements to make your text easy to scan.
- When appropriate, include images or embed audio or video clips to help make your message clear.
- Include links to guide your readers to additional information.
- Invite feedback: ask questions so that readers will naturally want to comment and respond.
- Give your post a compelling title, one that will make readers want to read on. Try to use keywords that will help your post turn up on a search site.

Wikis

Wikis are collaborative websites that invite readers to add and edit content, allowing them to make changes to an existing page, link to other pertinent pages, or even create new pages. Wikis serve as running records of information that is shared within online communities of various kinds: doctors, gamers, students and staff of a college—or, in the case of *Wikipedia*, the entire internet.

You're no doubt familiar with *Wikipedia,* the "free encyclopedia that anyone can edit." Since it started in 2001, it has grown from a site that many were suspicious of (Can you trust the information is correct? What about all those errors that "anyone" can contribute?) into the first place many people go when looking for information. *Wikipedia* now contains over 4.5 million entries in its English version alone, the majority of which, it turns out, are fairly reliable. And it has set a precedent for just how effective collaboration can be in creating and sharing knowledge. Here is part of *Wikipedia's* entry on "wiki," showing how this particular web format works.

> A wiki is a <u>web application</u> which allows people to add, modify, or delete content in <u>collaboration</u> with others. In a typical wiki, text is written using a simplified <u>markup language</u> (known as "wiki markup") or a <u>rich-text editor</u>.[1][2] While a wiki is a type of <u>content management system</u>, it differs from a <u>blog</u> or most other such systems in that the content is created without any defined owner or leader, and wikis have little implicit structure, allowing structure to emerge according to the needs of the users.[2]   —WIKIPEDIA.ORG, "Wiki"

This entry gives readers options to click for more information. Highlighted terms indicate links to pages about key concepts, and clicking on the numbers takes you to a list of references. The entry also includes—in true multimodal fashion—a video interview with Ward Cunningham, inventor of the wiki.

Some instructors use wikis to collect and add to class notes, creating a collaborative record of what is taught and said in class during the term. Maybe you've been assigned to contribute to an entry on *Wikipedia* or to a wiki for a class.

Whether you build a wiki or add to an existing one, you should think carefully about what community it serves. Wikis are never private sites—they're meant to be collaborative and shared! So in contributing to a wiki, you potentially become part of a huge collaborative project.

Some Tips for Contributing to a Wiki

- Be sure any information you present is authoritative and credible. Information should come from reliable sources, and you should check multiple sources before presenting it as fact.

- Remain fair and be respectful, both in your choice of topic and in what you say about it. Some wikis have rules for what content is allowed, and remember that while you may write whatever you wish, other editors can choose to delete it.

- Anticipate a broad audience. Don't assume others have background knowledge of your subject. Explain terms or events that may be unfamiliar, or link to pages on those topics.

- Offer information that will be useful to others. Write about something others will want to learn about!

- Add links, references, and citations that lead to reliable sources for more information.

- If you are adding links to a wiki entry, be sure that you have correctly coded the links so that they work, and make sure that the pages linked to actually exist.

- Remember that wikis are usually sites for shared revision. You will need to think carefully and respectfully before editing or changing other authors' contributions.

Audio Essays

The University of Wisconsin's Design Lab defines audio essays as ones that "explore topics using spoken text, audio interviews, archival recordings, music, environmental sounds, and/or sound effects" and notes that they "can make unfamiliar materials more accessible to new audiences and/or reveal new perspectives on familiar subjects."

Russel Honoré's essay on p. 136 was written for *This I Believe*. Read it, and then listen to the audio version at everyonesanauthor.tumblr.com. What does he do differently for those listening to his text?

National Public Radio has helped popularize audio essays with its *This I Believe* and *This American Life* series. One of NPR's most popular pieces is humorist David Sedaris reading from his "Santaland Diaries," which chronicles his experiences working as a department store elf one holiday season. Listen to the audio at everyonesanauthor.tumblr.com, paying attention to how the piece is structured in 45-to-50-second segments and how that structure affects the way you follow the story. Here's one segment of Sedaris's tale:

Twenty-two thousand people came to see Santa today, and not all of them were well-behaved. Today I witnessed fistfights and vomiting and magnificent tantrums. The back hallway was jammed with people. There was a line for Santa and a line for the women's bathroom. And one woman, after asking me a thousand questions already, asked, "Which is the line for the women's bathroom?" And I shouted that I thought it was the line with all the women in it. She said, "I'm going to have you fired."

I had two people say that to me today: "I'm going to have you fired." Go ahead. Be my guest. I'm wearing a green velvet costume; it doesn't get any worse than this. Who do these people think they are? "I'm going to have you fired."

And I want to lean over and say, "I'm going to have you killed."

—DAVID SEDARIS, "The Santaland Diaries"

Notice how the music at the beginning and the end of this segment helps bring together the narrative. And listen to Sedaris's voice: how it changes as he imitates the voice of the woman who threatens to have him fired—and then lowers and becomes more menacing at the end, concluding the segment with an unexpected shift in the narrative that keeps listeners engaged (and makes us laugh). That's good radio.

Some Tips for Composing an Audio Essay

- Decide on the software you will use. (*Audacity* and *GarageBand* are widely used.)

- Write out a script, using everyday language, short sentences, strong verbs, and active voice.

- If you are using sources, introduce them at the beginning of the sentence and paraphrase rather than quote.

- Use concrete examples and vivid imagery to help listeners see or imagine what you're describing. Sound effects can help establish setting.

- Organize your audio essay in chronological order, allowing for flashbacks and flashforwards if they are necessary to your story.

- Practice reading your script. Vary your tone of voice to keep listeners engaged. You might change your tone to imitate someone else speaking. (Or better yet, edit in sound clips of others speaking for themselves.)

- Follow *This American Life* host Ira Glass's "45-second rule": listeners expect some kind of break or change of pace every 45 to 50 seconds. Try to pace your essay accordingly.

- Use music to establish a mood, to mark transitions, and to keep your listeners engaged.

Video Essays

Video essays are becoming increasingly popular, and not just on *YouTube*. Some students submit video essays as part of their college applications, and some employers are asking for videos as part of job applications. While anyone with a smartphone can create a video essay, it's not easy.

Just like traditional essays composed with written words alone, video essays need to make some kind of point, to offer good reasons and evidence in support of that point, to acknowledge other points of view, and so on. Unlike print essays, however, video essays can use a combination of images, sounds, and words to make their point.

And you can present these images, sounds, and words in many different ways. Take images: you can use still images, moving images, and stop-motion images. Sounds can include people speaking on camera, voiceover, music, and background sounds. Words can be spoken, or they can be put on-screen as titles, subtitles, credits—even in thought bubbles. All these elements add up to infinite possibilities for authoring.

Multimedia journalist Adam Westbrook combines still photos, moving images, music, maps, charts, and more with spoken commentary in *Cause / Effect: The Unexpected Origins of Terrible Things*, a video essay arguing that World War I was caused not by the assassination of Archduke Franz Ferdinand but by Germany's desire for sea power. The video format allows Westbrook to present audio and visual evidence that makes a persuasive (and engaging) case for his argument—and to use both spoken and written language, from voiceover narration to labels identifying those pictured in historic photos.

Go to everyonesan author.tumblr.com to watch *Cause / Effect: The Unexpected Origins of Terrible Things*.

A map and photograph from the video essay *Cause / Effect*.

Westbrook's example shows how complicated video essays can be to do, with words, images, and sounds all at work in multiple ways. A good way to plan out how all these elements will fit together is by creating a **STORY-BOARD**, a series of sketches that show the sequence of scenes and actions in a film. Take a look at the storyboard on the next page showing five camera shots that follow a man as he walks down a hallway into his office, sits down, and is approached by someone holding a gun. The written words provide directions for the camera operator, noting places where there should be wide-angle shots, close-ups, and so on. A storyboard like this will serve as a blueprint as you shoot and edit a video essay.

Some Tips for Composing a Video Essay

- Decide which program you will use: *iMovie, Final Cut Pro*, and *Windows Live Movie Maker* are popular choices.

- Try to show much of the evidence for your argument visually, with images rather than just words.

- Think about the tone you want to project and how color, lighting, pacing, and music might evoke that tone.

- Draft a script for any text that will be spoken on camera or read as a voiceover—and practice reading it aloud.

- Create a storyboard to map out how the parts of your video essay will fit together. Use your storyboard to plan the shots you need before you begin shooting, and always shoot more than you think you'll need. It's easy to delete footage, much harder to get a single shot you missed.

- Consider a variety of camera angles. Wide-angle shots are useful for setting a scene; medium shots, for framing someone speaking to the camera; close-ups, for showing important details.

- Experiment also with moving the camera—following the subject, zooming in or out, panning left or right—but do so sparingly. You don't want to make your viewers dizzy!

- Display written text on-screen with title cards if need be. You'll probably want to open with your title, and you might add text to give the setting and time, the name and title of someone speaking, captions or subtitles, or to mark transitions.

- Provide a written list of credits on the screen at the end, citing any sources you use and thanking those who helped.

A storyboard lays out the sequence of camera shots and transitions.

Posters

You'll likely have opportunities—and assignments—to create posters for classroom presentations, campus organizations, or academic conferences. And posters aren't what they were back in the day when all that was needed was poster board and some markers; posters today have become sophisticated and multimodal ways of communicating information. Take a look at the poster on the following page that three students created in order to present the results of a research study. The topic is clearly stated in a heading at the top. The text is organized in three columns: one devoted to the motivation for the project, the second to the methods used, and the third to results and future directions. Data is presented in bar graphs, and other images illustrate and underscore key points in the report.

A poster a student research group created to present its study.

Some Tips for Creating a Poster

- People often read posters at a glance, so present the information you want your audience to take away clearly and simply.

- Check to see if there are any guidelines for the size of the poster and whether it should be on a tabletop, an easel—or somewhere else.

- Think hard about how you can get your audience's attention: by asking a provocative question in a large bold font at the top of the poster? with color? an eye-catching image? something else?

- Keep the design simple: too many images, too much text, or distracting fonts make for a cluttered look that can be hard to follow.

- Be sure that any text is large enough to read—and that it is organized in a way that makes it easy to scan and understand quickly.

- Choose colors that will be easy to see. Primary colors are easier to see than pastels, as is dark text on a light background.

MANAGING A MULTIMODAL PROJECT

Managing a multimodal project is a bit like juggling: at any one time, you have multiple balls in the air, each one needing attention, and altogether it takes a lot of skill to keep them all airborne. While we can't provide guidelines for every step of every multimodal project you may encounter, we can offer some general advice about how to approach them.

Whether you're composing an illustrated essay, a blog, a video, or any other multimodal text, you will want to plan carefully for how your project will achieve your purpose with a particular audience and in a particular context. To do so, you'll need to carefully manage your time, your files, your project content, your sources, and more.

Managing your time. Make sure you know exactly how much time you have before your project is due and then be realistic about how to manage that time. Set up a calendar and block out specific times when you know you can work on the project; consider whether you'll have any class time to devote to it. If you're assigned to work with other students, set regular meeting times and draw up a schedule and task list together so that you each know your responsibilities. Breaking a project down into parts and setting deadlines for each part can help keep you on track. And don't forget to build in time to get response to a draft of your project—from your instructor if possible as well as from classmates and friends.

Managing project files. Back in the day, writers used 3 x 5 index cards to keep track of information and sources, which were almost always print. But for many multimodal projects, it's likely you'll be using digital sources: GIF or JPEG image files, M4V or MOV video files, and so on. It can help to make a special folder on your computer and save in one place all the files you may want to use. Organize files according to type (images, charts, video clips, audio clips, and so on) and according to the organization of your project (clips for scene 1 of a video essay, graphs for the results section of a research poster). Be sure to label each file in a way that makes sense to you and to make note of where you found it, the date you downloaded it, and any other relevant source information—so that you can cite your sources properly and go back to them if need be.

Organizing your content. Some writers begin with nothing more than a pack of sticky notes, putting main points and sub-points and supporting reasons and evidence on individual stickies and arranging them on a larger surface. You might even begin with an outline of the main points you want to make and the support for each one. This kind of careful organizing is crucial because it creates a "big picture" of your message and all its parts.

If you're creating a *video essay*, you might create a storyboard to put everything in sequence; another possibility would be a two-column script to line up the video and audio portions. *Audio essays* need some kind of script as well, one that accounts for both words and any music or other sounds. For an *illustrated print essay*, you'll need to decide where to put the images. For *wiki entries*, *blog posts*, and other kinds of web texts that readers navigate by links, you might map out your organization on a large sheet of paper, putting the main page at the center top and then drawing lines out to the various pages you will link to.

Crediting your sources. Be sure to credit your sources. You can do so at the bottom of a poster, as the last slide in an oral presentation, as footnotes in a wiki or links on a blog, or as "credits" at the end of a video or audio essay.

REFLECT. "This is the time for exploration, for experimentation. This is the time when we can create and risk, when we can write graffiti on the walls and color outside the lines. . . . If we are going to fly and find new intellectual spaces . . . we must expand our notion of academic discourse." That's a challenge that Stanford professor Adam Banks issued in 2015 to an audience of college writing instructors. How would you answer his challenge? Find a piece of academic writing you've done and imagine how you would have written it using multiple modes.

THIRTY-FIVE

Making Presentations

HAT GOES INTO a sure-fire great presentation? Author and consultant Nancy Duarte wanted to find out. So she set out to study some great presentations, hundreds of them, beginning with Martin Luther King Jr.'s "I Have a Dream" speech and Steve Jobs' iPhone launch, two speeches that seemed so different to her that she couldn't imagine she would find anything in common. But she did.

She found that these two speeches—and hundreds of other terrific presentations—shared one common structure. Each speech begins by describing "what is"—and then goes on to suggest what it could (or should) be. That's in the introduction. Then in the middle of the speech, the presenter moves back and forth between discussing that status quo and what it could or should be. And in most cases, the conclusion goes full throttle into evoking what could be as vividly as possible and calling for some kind of action.

Duarte's research shows that this basic structure (from what is to what could be) is very widely used, and especially so by activists, politicians, and businesspeople proposing change of some kind. In fact, it's a structure that may work well for many of the presentations you make in your college classes. And there are two common variations on this structure that you may be familiar with. One begins with what *was*, in the past, and then moves on to explain how it changed. The other opens by noting what others have said about a topic and then moves on to what you want to say about it, focusing on the benefits of your position. Start-

Martin Luther King Jr.

Steve Jobs.

ing with what is, what was, or what's been said and then suggesting something "better" uses a classic storytelling technique: setting up a conflict that needs to be resolved. And presenting your main point as a story works well in a spoken presentation because stories are easier to follow and remember than other kinds of evidence and they can often be more persuasive.

In 2014, Michelle Obama used such a story in a high school graduation speech in Topeka, Kansas, where the famous 1954 Supreme Court case *Brown v. Board of Education* originated, in which separate schools for black and white students were ruled unconstitutional. In that speech, she told the story of how that case came into being, what Topeka was like at the time, and then how it had changed in the sixty years since. She brought her main point (and her story) home at the conclusion of the speech by telling the graduates about the grandniece of Lucinda Todd, the very first parent to sign on to the *Brown* lawsuit: that young woman was Obama's "right-hand woman" in the White House. It's this storyline, reaching from the original court case to the present moment, that summed up her point: change is possible, and the students in that audience can help bring about necessary change.

Sounds simple, doesn't it? State your main point, find a story to help get that point across, and inspire the audience to accept what you say. But coming up with these elements in ways that will capture and hold an audience's attention—well, that's not simple. Still, there are some structures and techniques that will help you create presentations that audiences will listen to and remember, and that might even call them to action. This chapter provides guidelines to help you do so.

First, let's take a look at the script one of our students prepared for a presentation on Japanese manga. As you'll see, she used a "what was and how it changed" structure as a foundation for her presentation.

The Rise of Female Heroes in Shoujo Manga

HALLE EDWARDS

HERE'S A QUESTION FOR YOU: [SLIDE] Where are all the strong women heroes in popular comics? In our class we've seen some talented female authors of graphic narratives, but in terms of popular comic book characters (not to mention writers and fans), the girls have been outnumbered.

> # Q: Where are all the strong female heroes?

[SLIDE] So guess what? When I started looking, I found the strong female heroes in comics! The place—Japan. The time period—the 1990s. The genre—Shoujo manga. Literally "girls' comics" in Japanese, Shoujo manga is a

---

HALLE EDWARDS composed this presentation for a second-year writing course that focused on graphic narratives. For this assignment, she first wrote an academic essay and then "translated" it into a ten-minute oral presentation with sixteen slides. As you'll see, we've included only five of these slides.

popular form of comics in Japan typically written by women for women. Prior to the 1990s, Shoujo typically featured weak heroines and plots that revolved around romance. Then, in the 1990s, Shoujo started showing strong female heroes whose first priority wasn't romance. But what did that change look like and, more importantly, why did it happen?

Today I'll explore the answers. First I'll show you an example of this phenomenon, from Naoko Takeuchi's smash hit manga *Sailor Moon*. Then I'll explain what was happening in Japan in the 1990s and why this allowed Shoujo manga to change so drastically.

[SLIDE] Part one. *Sailor Moon* tells the story of Usagi, a clumsy and not particularly smart schoolgirl with a heart of gold. She discovers that she has a secret identity—Sailor Moon—and is destined to fight the forces of evil. [SLIDE] While *Sailor Moon* does have a love story, much of the manga is devoted to expanding on Sailor Moon's relationship with her eventual comrades—Sailors Mars, Mercury, Jupiter, and Venus. [SLIDE] The relationship of these five heroes is usually prioritized over the romance.

Wait a minute. Five female heroes? The romance is just a side plot? Girls described as soldiers who physically fight bad guys? For anyone familiar with traditional Shoujo manga, it's obvious that *Sailor Moon* pushed boundaries.

[SLIDE] This boundary-pushing can be seen in the introduction of the second female hero, Ami, or Sailor Mercury. Introduced as an aloof genius, Ami quickly reveals Takeuchi's friendly, playful side. [SLIDE] From the outset, Sailor Mercury cannot be pinned down to a stereotype—she's neither a cold nerd nor a bubbly teenager. She's very flawed and very real. Takeuchi's female heroes are layered, interesting, and compelling.

Throughout the story, we see Ami develop a close friendship with Usagi, [SLIDE] ultimately ending in a battle where Ami discovers her identity as Sailor Mercury. Meanwhile, Usagi's budding romance is barely a side plot. Throughout *Sailor Moon*'s five-year run, its female heroines were always the heart of the story—not the romance. The funny thing? Despite this drastic departure from typical Shoujo norms, *Sailor Moon* was a smash hit.

[SLIDE] So why was *Sailor Moon* so warmly received, given that it defied so many norms in Shoujo manga? To understand, you need to know a bit about Japan in the early 1990s. [SLIDE] In 1989, the Asset Price Bubble broke—essentially a huge economic bubble that vastly inflated real estate prices. [SLIDE] This sent Japan's economy spiraling into a recession that lasted throughout the entire 1990s, a decade now known as Japan's "lost decade."

[SLIDE] The recession changed many aspects of life in Japan. Before the recession, men could expect to get hired at a company out of college and work there for their whole lives. Meanwhile, women held mainly part-time jobs— think secretaries and office ladies—with few opportunities for advancement. However, once the recession hit, layoffs became rampant. Companies tanked. Men could no longer rely on having lifetime careers, and many in Japan questioned the long hours that were customary in Japan's workplaces.

What made the 1990s in Japan
the "Era of Women"?

- Economic recession lowered job security for men

- More women worked outside the home

- More women voted

- Several female candidates were elected in 1989

[SLIDE] Meanwhile, in the 1989 elections, several female candidates were elected. Also, voter turnout among women was higher than ever. Because of this, the media predicted that the 1990s would be the "era of women." Women were suddenly seen as capable: they could hold real jobs outside the home, run for office, and help save Japan's stumbling economy. These new women were featured in popular soap operas known as "morning dramas" on the government-funded NHK channel.

[SLIDE] Given this media-propelled image of the new, strong woman, several of the major Shoujo magazines began to take note. Thus, when Toshio Irie, the newly minted editor of *Nakayoshi* magazine, learned of *Sailor Moon*, a story with five strong female heroes, he jumped at the opportunity. Not only did he publish Takeuchi's manga; he embraced a mixed-media strategy, including *Sailor Moon*–themed toys with the magazine (to encourage fans to buy their own copies and limit sharing) and selling additional *Sailor Moon* merchandise. [SLIDE] Also, when Toei Animation snapped up the rights to create an animated *Sailor Moon* series, Irie worked with the company to closely match the release of the new *Sailor Moon* chapters and episodes.

Such a media blitz was unheard of for a work of Shoujo manga, and it paid off. By the end of 1995, *Sailor Moon* had made over 300 billion yen in profits and was expanding rapidly worldwide. Circulation figures for the magazine reached an all-time high of 2 million per month. The thirteen volumes that had been released by then had sold over a million copies each and been exported to twenty-three countries.

[SLIDE] The recession, and the media's message that the 1990s would be the "era of women," caused forces in the media to realize that the image of strong women could be popular—and more importantly, profitable. As a result, other manga editors were willing to publish works that featured strong female heroes—knowing that they would make money. This is one way that Shoujo sparked important change.

But why, you might be wondering, does it matter? This was just one time period in one country where comics featured strong women. Was it a phenomenon that spread to other countries? Did more girls start reading comic books and graphic narratives? And did life really change for women in Japan?

The simple answer is no. The "era of women" did not lead to significant change in the lives of women in Japan. They were still mostly relegated to part-time jobs and to most domestic responsibilities. And after the magical girl heroine trends of the 1990s, Shoujo in the 2000s became more focused on "slice of life" stories. This is not to say it went backwards—it just stopped moving forward so daringly.

However, the 1990s in Japan proved that there is a place, and an audience, for strong heroines in graphic narratives. Although there was little or no precedent for introducing strong women characters, a few key people took risks on some new stories, and they paid off. I think this is a lesson we can apply to the graphic novel market today. Just because there are still more male readers and characters in US comics does not mean that the market for strong female characters does not exist. In fact, the success of authors Lynda Barry and Alison Bechdel as well as of the hit TV series Marvel's *Agent* (Peggy) *Carter* suggests that the time may be ripe for many more strong women in graphic narratives. So let's heed the story of Sailor Moon and her crew and read and encourage others to buy works that feature strong women. Then when we're asked "where are all the strong women heroes in popular comics?" we can answer, "They're everywhere!"

[SLIDE] Thank you for listening. I'll be glad to take questions.

Halle Edwards opens her presentation with a statement about "what is"—that is, the status quo, which finds few strong female heroes in popular comic books. She then tells about a similar situation in Japan, and how it changed, exploring some of the issues in Japanese society that allowed women heroes to emerge and using the story of *Sailor Moon*'s success as the major example. Throughout, she poses questions to involve her audience, beginning by asking "Where are all the strong women heroes in popular comics?" Take a moment to count the number of questions in this presentation and where they occur and you'll see that they act as "signpost language," helping the audience follow the presentation and focusing their attention on its most important points. Notice as well that Edwards uses good presentational style: short sentences, simple syntax, clear transitions and other signpost language, active verbs, and vivid description—all things that make the presentation easy to listen to and to follow.

REFLECT. Halle Edwards' presentation grew out of a research paper she had written on the same topic. Look back at an academic essay you have written and then, using this chapter as a guide, make notes on what you would need to do to transform it into a memorable oral presentation.

MAKING A PRESENTATION / A Roadmap

Begin by considering your rhetorical situation

Anticipate who will be in your AUDIENCE. What do they already know about your topic, and what other information might they need? What kinds of evidence will most likely appeal to them? If some will be watching your presentation on video, you can help keep them engaged by looking into the camera some of the time and addressing them directly once or twice.

Be clear about your PURPOSE. Make sure you understand any assignment you've been given for this presentation. Is your goal to provide information? to persuade? to propose some kind of action?

Think about your STANCE. How are you presenting yourself: as an expert? an interested novice? a researcher? an advocate? Be sure that the stance you are taking is an appropriate one for your topic and for your audience. Halle Edwards presents herself as a peer and classmate who has researched her topic and can thus speak with authority about it.

Consider the CONTEXT. Where will the presentation take place? If possible, check it out in advance. What equipment will you need? Whatever it is, be sure to test it in advance—and keep in mind that technology glitches happen, so be sure to have a backup plan. How much time will you have for the presentation? Who will introduce you, or will you introduce yourself?

Think about your GENRE. If you've been assigned a specific genre, say to report on a topic or to present a proposal, consult those chapters in this textbook for guidance. If not, see Chapter 9 for help choosing a genre.

Will you be using any MEDIA elements that need to be DESIGNED? Do you need to show any images or information on a slide or flip chart—or would doing so help your audience follow your presentation? Will they expect some kind of visual aids? Will you be referring to a text or something else that you could put on a handout? Remember that slides and flip charts need to be simple enough and large enough for your audience to read as you speak.

Prepare your presentation

Focus on one main point, and then orchestrate everything else to support it. Halle Edwards begins with a question that signals her main point: where are all the strong women heroes in popular comics? In the rest of the presentation, she provides answers to this question in a story about the appearance of women heroes in Japanese manga, using *Sailor Moon* as her main example.

Gather EVIDENCE to support your point. Once you've decided on your main message, look for examples, statistics, stories, and other evidence that illustrates your point. Halle Edwards uses facts and statistics to support her main point—that, despite some changes, there are still not enough strong female heroes in comic books. Even the huge success of *Sailor Moon*—a franchise that brought in over 300 billion yen—still failed to turn the tide in any permanent way.

Develop a clear structure. You can try using the structure Nancy Duarte recommends, focusing on what is (or was) and moving to what it could or should be (or how it changed). If that doesn't suit your topic, you might start by noting what else has been said about your topic as a way of introducing what you want to say about it. Any of these structures will set up a tension that your presentation then resolves—a storytelling technique that will make your argument easier for your audience to follow.

Use TRANSITIONS and other techniques to help listeners follow your presentation. It's always helpful to provide an overview of your talk, saying something like "In brief, I have four points to make," and then use those points as signposts in the presentation. One other useful technique is repetition. Halle Edwards poses questions repeatedly, and these questions mark turning points in her talk. Still another good technique is to explain what you're saying as you go, using expressions such as "in other words" or "in short."

Use vivid language, images, and metaphors to hammer home your point clearly and memorably. The vivid language ("neither a cold nerd nor a bubbly teenager," "smash hit") and metaphors ("boundary-pushing") that Halle Edwards uses help her audience visualize and follow her argument.

But keep it simple. Remember that your audience doesn't have a script to read, so you need to speak in a way that will be easy to understand. Notice that Halle Edwards uses fairly simple diction throughout—and that her sentences are short and follow a straightforward subject-verb-object structure. Even her paragraphs are short, some only a sentence or two—which helped her keep to her script without having to refer to it often as she spoke.

Develop a dynamic INTRODUCTION, one that will engage your audience's interest and establish some kind of COMMON GROUND with them. You'll also want to establish your CREDIBILITY, to show that you've done your homework and can speak knowledgeably about your topic. Halle Edwards was addressing her classmates, so she didn't need to worry about establishing common ground, but she engaged their interest by asking a provocative question: "Where are all the strong women heroes in popular comics?" The way you open will depend on your topic and rhetorical situation, but whether you start by telling a story, making a startling claim, or summarizing what someone has said about your topic, your goal is to interest your audience in what is to come.

CONCLUDE in a way that leaves your audience thinking. Whether you conclude by reiterating your main point, saying why your argument matters, or some other way, this is a moment when you can make sure your presentation has some kind of impact. Halle Edwards faced a challenge: her research had turned up strong female heroes in Japanese manga, but in the end they did not change the status quo. So she concluded by pointing out that her research showed that there's "a place, and an audience, for strong heroines in graphic narratives." She then turned to her audience and challenged them to seek out such characters and to read the works they appear in.

Think about whether you need any visuals. Images can bring your presentation to life, illustrate important points, and engage your audience. Any slides should support or explain a point you are making and need to be clear and easy to see so that your audience can process the information in a couple of seconds. It's therefore often better to convey one idea per slide than to provide a list of bullet points on a single slide. If you need to communicate complex information, putting it in a chart or graph can make it easier for you to explain—and for your audience to understand. More detailed information or material you want your audience to read is best presented on handouts. Try to distribute the handouts at the point when your audience needs them: if you give them out before then, some in the audience may be focusing on the handouts rather than on you!

If you'll be using slides or other media, you'll need to design them carefully.

- All slides need to be clearly visible to everyone in your audience, so use at least 18-point fonts. Simple bold fonts are easiest to read; italic fonts can be difficult to read, so best to avoid them.

- Don't depend too much on templates for slides: the choices they build in—colors, fonts, layout, and so on—may not be appropriate for your topic or purpose.

- The most effective slides are simple enough for the audience to process the information they contain in a couple of seconds. As a general rule, it's better to convey one idea per slide than to provide a list of bullet points.

- Make sure that any audio or video clips embedded in your slides relate directly to the point you are making and that they are clear and easy to see and hear.

- Decorative backgrounds can be distracting, so avoid them unless they add something very specific to your presentation.

- When possible, present ideas in diagrams or charts that will be easy for the audience to understand.

- Be consistent. Using one font or color for headings and making them parallel in structure will help your audience follow what you are saying.

- Finally, be sure to get responses to your slides just as you would to drafts of your script. Note that Halle Edwards made her slides simple and clearly focused, intended to raise a question or illustrate or underscore a point. She used *PowerPoint* because she was making a linear argument; for less linear structures, you might use *Prezi*, which allows you to zoom in and out, looking at images in detail and from different perspectives.

Give your presentation

Practice, practice, practice. There is no substitute for practice. None. So schedule time to rehearse and make sure you can articulate your main message loud and clear at a moment's notice. Ask friends to serve as an audience for a full rehearsal, and be sure to time your presentation so that you don't go beyond the limit. When you're done, ask your friends to tell you your main point. If they can do so, then you've made an impression! Ask them as well how you came across—as friendly? authoritative? something else? If it's not what you're aiming for, talk through how you *want* to come across and how to get there.

Listen to how you use your voice. Record yourself speaking and then listen to what you sound like. Is your voice clear and loud enough to hear? Do you speak very quickly, or too slowly? Do you vary your tone of voice or tend toward a monotone? What can you do to improve this aspect of your delivery?

Stand up straight! And look at your audience. Try to avoid shifting from foot to foot or jingling change in your pockets. You want the focus to be on you and your message.

THIRTY-SIX

Assembling a Portfolio

OR HIS FIRST-YEAR WRITING CLASS, Julio Martinez was required to create a portfolio of his work to demonstrate how his writing had improved over the term. He included the drafts and final revision of a rhetorical analysis, along with two peer reviews he received; an annotated bibliography; and the drafts and final revision of a research report. Finally, he wrote a cover letter to his instructor in which he described, evaluated, and reflected on his writing—and set out several goals to work on after the term was over. He submitted his portfolio in print.

Not so Susanna Moller, an art major who created a website her sophomore year to host her portfolio of artwork. She included only finished works, organized by subject and style, and updated the site with new pieces as she continued to make art throughout college. When she had her first solo show, she posted the review from the college newspaper. As graduation approached, she put her résumé on the site—and added the URL to résumés she sent to potential employers so they could see her work.

Deborah Burke began her portfolio blog with a first-year essay she was very proud of. The next year, she wrote a radio essay on the same topic; this became another item in her portfolio. Continuing her research, she wrote a play and added the script to her blog, along with a *YouTube* video of a scene from the play. Finally, she added her résumé and a statement reflecting on her work in college. This portfolio helped her to get an internship—and later a job.

Today, portfolios exist on paper and online. You may be required to keep a portfolio of your work for a writing course as a way of thinking about what you've learned, demonstrating and delivering to your instructor what you've written, and reflecting on your strengths and weaknesses as a writer. Or you may assemble a portfolio to showcase your best work to prospective employers. Whatever your purpose, assembling a portfolio offers an excellent opportunity to reflect on your writing and to chart goals for yourself as a writer. This chapter provides guidelines to help you compile a writing portfolio.

What to Include in a Writing Portfolio

A portfolio submitted to your instructor at the end of a course should represent your best work and demonstrate your growth as a writer, so you'll probably include some of the following materials:

- A number of your best essays and other projects
- Writing representing several genres and media
- Freewriting and other notes
- Various drafts, from first to final
- Response from readers
- A statement reflecting on your work

Your instructor may specify what you need to include, but often you'll get to choose. In that case, what you include will depend on what you're trying to show. If you're trying to show your best work, you might include three pieces that you like best; if, on the other hand, you're trying to show a range of what you've written, you would probably choose writing in various **GENRES** and **MEDIA**. If you're trying to show how you've improved, you'll want to include work in several drafts. Just remember that your portfolio is an opportunity for you to evaluate and deliver your own writing: choose work that demonstrates what you want to show.

If you are preparing a portfolio not for class but to highlight your accomplishments for future employers, you will probably make different choices. These choices would be informed by the skills required for the positions you are applying for, and by what you wish to demonstrate to potential employers. If you want to show your abilities as a journalist, you might include in your portfolio a narrative that you wrote for a writing course or a video that you shot and edited. If you are applying for a position in a research lab, you might include a report of a research study and the written proposal that led to that project. Depending on what technology or social media skills employers ask for, you might also include work you've done in multiple modes, such as websites or blogs. You'll certainly want to include a carefully constructed résumé and a cover page introducing yourself and providing an overview of your skills.

Collecting Your Work

Start collecting pieces for your portfolio early in the term. Organization is critical, so create a specific computer folder for the portfolio and give it a name (like "My Portfolio") that you can easily find; inside the folder, create a sub-folder for each piece of writing you include. Identify all drafts with a title and date, as shown in the following example.

If you're required to include a statement reflecting on your writing, take notes on your process and your work *throughout the term*. Also keep copies of any peer responses you receive in your file.

You may also find that you want to add new pieces to your portfolio even after you've submitted it for an assignment, in which case it's all the more important to keep your files neat and organized from the beginning. Adding work is easy, especially to an online portfolio, but anyone visiting your site should see an organized, polished collection of work instead of a site that looks to be under construction.

Reflecting on Your Writing

An essential component of your portfolio is a statement that introduces and reflects on the work that's included in the portfolio. Such a statement should explain what's included and why you included the pieces you did, describe your writing process, assess what you've learned, reflect on your development as a writer, and perhaps establish goals for yourself.

Writing such a statement gives you the opportunity to take a good look at your writing and to evaluate it on your own terms. Maybe the essay on which you received your lowest grade was one where you experienced a breakthrough in your writing process. You may well want to discuss this breakthrough in your statement. Did you discover that freewriting worked better than outlining as a way to generate ideas? These are the kinds of insights you can include in your statement to demonstrate to your instructor that you have thought carefully about your writing and your writing process. Following are some prompts to help you think critically about both:

- **REVIEW** *each piece of writing in your portfolio.* What are the strengths and the weaknesses? Which is your best piece? Explain why it is the best and what it demonstrates about what you've learned. Which would you say is the weakest—and how would you change it if you could?

- **ANALYZE** *your writing process.* Study any drafts, responses, and other materials you're including. How did any responses you received help you revise? Which of them helped the most? Were any not helpful?

- **DESCRIBE** *the strategies you use to write.* Which ones have been most helpful, and which have been less helpful? Which ones do you enjoy?

- **REFLECT** *on your work as an author.* What does the writing in your portfolio show about you? What do you do well—and less well? What kinds of writing do you like the most? Is there any kind of writing that you struggle with or dislike—and if so, why?

- **DEFINE** *goals.* What has your portfolio helped you understand about yourself as a writer? What strengths or weaknesses do you now see? Based on this analysis, what do you now want to work on?

This statement is usually written either as a letter or as an essay. You may or may not have an explicit **THESIS**, but it needs to be clear what your portfolio demonstrates about you as a writer. Remember that the statement itself demonstrates your writing ability: write it thoughtfully and carefully.

A Sample Portfolio Statement

December 7, 2014

Dear Reader,

Writing used to be one of those things I never gave much time to. I'd get it done but without thinking much about how to do it better. It wasn't until coming to Ball State and taking a class with Professor Clark-Upchurch that writing started to be more than just a nuisance. For the first time, I was forced to look at the inner workings of formal writing, to analyze and examine each part, and to learn what each one is supposed to contribute and why it's important. Slowly over the course of this semester, I have moved beyond the simple five-paragraph essay I learned in high school. All in all, I have become a stronger writer.

Writing the first paper, the literacy narrative, came easily to me . . . or so I thought. When my paper came back to me with Professor Clark-Upchurch's questions about my thesis and organization, some irrelevant incidents I included, a lack of illustrations to support my points, and comments about my "repetitive and simplistic sentence structures," I knew I needed to work harder. On the second paper, an analysis of a magazine ad, my thesis was clearer and my paragraphs "flowed, one into the next" with good examples from the ad as support, but I still needed to work on using a variety of sentences to "make the reader want to read on."

It was on my last paper, the research-based essay, that I finally pulled everything together: an engaging introduction, a clear thesis, logical organization, solid development with lots of supporting examples, and (finally!) varied sentences.

Although my writing style has improved and my understanding of all that goes into a paper is at an all-time high, I still struggle with writing a proposal. I'm not sure why, but for some reason writing an essay about writing a future essay leaves me confused. I'd rather just write the essay in the first place instead of wasting time and effort proposing what I'm going to write about. As a result, I never really made a decent effort at the third writing project—the proposal for the research paper. Thus I have decided to exclude that paper from my portfolio as I am sure it is my weakest.

In addition to these three papers, I include drafts with peer responses and Professor Clark-Upchurch's suggestions in order to provide a clear picture of how much I learned this term. One of the most helpful parts of the class was the peer responding sessions, when we analyzed each other's essays. Doing this helped me think about what I do in my own writing, and showed me that other people can learn from what I write—it's not just for the teacher or to get a grade.

The essays you are about to read are just a start, a sturdy base for me to continue developing my writing into something more. Whether willingly or unwillingly, I learned that good writing takes work, but that it also starts to work better when I think about how the parts of my writing fit together. Now whenever I need to write a formal paper, I have some tools I have learned and can use to write for a purpose instead of simply writing to fill the page and finish the assignment.

Sincerely,
Kameron Wiles

Organizing a Portfolio

The way you organize and deliver your portfolio is important; it's part of how you present yourself as a writer. There's no one way to organize a portfolio, but it needs to be carefully arranged so that it's easy to read. Be sure you know if your instructor expects a certain format or system.

Print portfolios can go in a folder (for a small portfolio) or a binder (for a longer one). Begin with a title page that includes your name, the course title and number, the instructor's name, the date, and the portfolio's title. Follow the title page with a table of contents. Next comes your statement, and finally the writing. Unless your instructor asks for papers in a different order, organize the writing by assignments, putting all the materials from each assignment together, with the final draft on top. Label everything. If you're using a binder, add tabbed dividers, one for each assignment. Number the pages consecutively, and be sure each item is labeled.

E-portfolios can be as basic as *Word* documents uploaded to *Blackboard* or some other online course management system. Or you might post texts to an e-portfolio platform like *Google Docs* or use a blogging site like *WordPress*, *Scribd*, or *Tumblr*. You can even create a personal website using a building platform like *Wix*, *Google Sites*, *Squarespace*, or *Weebly*.

And just like a print portfolio, your e-portfolio should be organized by year, course, assignment, or the kind of content on each page. See on the following page how Rae'Johne Smith, an economics major at Spelman College, organizes her e-portfolio. Her homepage features a prominent banner with her name, her photo, and an introductory statement saying who she is and what her portfolio will show—all organized by a menu of links across the top.

As an economics major preparing for a career in finance, Smith presents her writing using the metaphor of a J-curve, one that will make good sense to potential employers. And for those unfamiliar with economics concepts, she clearly explains that a J-curve represents investments and returns over time—and that she's using it here to reflect her growth as a writer

Smith collects her writing—work in which she has obviously invested a lot of time and energy—on the second page, titled "investments," and organizes it into yearly "capital calls," an economics term for money that is put into an investment fund. Then comes a link to "distributions," which is econ-speak for the rewards that have come her way from improving her writing. Next comes an "annual report" that sums up her growth as a student and writer, followed by a page with her contact information.

Some Tips for Compiling an E-portfolio

- Figure out exactly what you're going to put in your portfolio and how you're going to organize it before uploading anything.

- Be sure you know what system your instructor expects you to use, and contact your school's tech desk if you need help.

- If you need to upload files, know what type of file you should use: *Word* documents, PDFs, or something else?

- Double-check that the file you are uploading is the final version.

- If you are working on an e-portfolio website, set up a homepage with your basic information and include links to your statement and to each piece of writing, each on its own page.

- To be sure all of the links work and everything looks the way you expect, check your site in different browsers and on different devices (laptops, desktops, tablets, and phones); you don't want to find out after you've submitted your portfolio that links don't work or some parts aren't visible.

- If you're using a school website or platform to host your work and want to preserve your e-portfolio or continue to add to it, ask your instructor or the tech desk if it will remain online after the term ends. If it will be deleted, you will need to move it to a more permanent platform.

Portfolios are becoming increasingly necessary, both in school and on the job. Your portfolio is more than an archive of your writing—it's a way of looking systematically at your work. Keeping a portfolio of your writing projects enables you to reflect on your development as a writer—on what you've learned and what you need to work on.

REFLECT. Suppose you're putting together a writing portfolio as part of an application for a summer job or a job after graduation. Go through your files to determine which writing samples you would want to include for the kind of job you are applying for. Consider writing in various modes, genres, and media. Read over each piece carefully and then write a brief comment on each one, pointing out its strengths and what it shows about you as a writer.

THIRTY-SEVEN

Publishing Your Writing

NCE UPON A TIME you had to get a newspaper, magazine, or book editor to read and accept your writing in order to be published. Go back further, and even talent (and a cooperative editor) weren't enough to get your work into print—you usually had to be a man as well. Even further back in time, writers who wanted to share their thoughts and ideas with others often had to hire a scribe to handwrite their work since writing was a specialized skill not many people mastered. All this to say, getting published wasn't easy. But today things have changed. Got access to a computer? Then you're only a few clicks away from delivering your writing to audiences far and wide.

The internet not only allows writers to publish their work, but it has also changed how we define "publishing": it no longer only means seeing your work distributed in print by an authoritative source. Today publishing your work means making it available to an audience, whether in print or online.

As a writer today, you have many ways to publish your work. This chapter lists a number of print and online venues where you can do so and includes an award-winning essay, first written for an undergraduate writing course, that went on to be published. We invite you to join the fun—and to publish what you write.

College publications. Most colleges and universities have newspapers and journals that publish the writing of their students. And don't be intimidated: it may be easier to get your work published than you think. Rutgers University's *Daily Targum* is one of the oldest and largest college papers in the country, but it makes it easy for students to submit work for publication:

> Interested in writing, taking photos, editing, reporting or designing for the *Targum*? Drop by our editorial office at 26 Mine Street after 4 p.m., Sunday through Thursday. If you would like to write for the news section, attend our writers meetings: Every Wednesday at 9:30 p.m. in Suite 431 of the Rutgers Student Center. Or, send an email to the head of the respective department. — DAILYTARGUM.COM

Many schools also have literary magazines and journals that publish fiction, poetry, essays, and visual art done by students. *Jabberwock Review*, a student-run journal at Mississippi State University, "welcomes all forms and styles of writing, from traditional to experimental," according to its submission guidelines. And Penn State University lists over twenty campus publications that solicit student work on everything from food culture (*Penn Appétit*) to politics (*Penn Political Review*). If your school does not have a literary magazine, research national undergraduate publications that accept work from students at any institution. DeAnza Community College's literary magazine, *Red Wheelbarrow*, for instance, publishes a national edition open to "everyone around the country and the world."

In addition, some colleges sponsor scholarly journals that publish student work exclusively. The University of Missouri at Kansas City, for example, sponsors a journal called *Young Scholars in Writing*, which publishes articles "written by undergraduates in a wide variety of disciplines associated with rhetoric and writing." These journals offer a way for you to share your academic writing with a wide readership of students as well as researchers in the field.

Essay competitions. Many schools have annual writing contests, often sponsored by the writing program or English department, and publish the winners' work. The University of California at Davis holds such a competition, inviting students to submit essays or scientific or technical writing done for a course at Davis. The winning works are then published in an annual collection called *Prized Writing*. DePaul University holds a similar event and invites all first-year students to submit a piece of writing for The Writers' Showcase, and Morehouse College holds an annual Martin Luther King Jr. Student Essay Contest.

W. W. Norton, the publisher of this book, sponsors an annual prize for an outstanding essay written by an undergraduate student. You'll find an essay written by one recent winner at the end of this chapter and can read all the winning essays at wwnorton.com/books/norton-writers-prize.

Some national organizations and publications sponsor writing competitions as well. The *New York Times* holds annual essay contests for college students. Recent prompts have included the question "What is love like for you as a student in the U.S. today?" and a call to respond to an article asking "What's the Matter with College?" Other publications hold essay contests that offer cash prizes and publication to the winners; the *Nation, Atlantic Monthly*, and *Rolling Stone* are just a few.

And some journals and associations hold annual contests for student work. The Children's Literature Association, for example, gives an award to the best undergraduate essay in its field and publishes the paper online. The Go On Girl Bookclub invites submissions from all historically black colleges and universities to compete for the Unpublished Writers' Award and the Aspiring Author Scholarship.

These are just a few of the places to look into for publishing your work. With a little exploring, you'll surely find other opportunities like these on your own campus and beyond.

Anthologies of student writing. Some publishers issue anthologies of student writing. Norton, for example, invites students to submit essays for publication in *The Norton Pocket Book of Writing by Students* and other Norton textbooks. (You'll find a form for submitting your writing to Norton on pp. 1106–07.)

Publish yourself! What if you pursue some of the options listed above but don't get the recognition or exposure you want? Or what if you want to be published in a book of your own? Print-on-demand and e-publishing technologies enable writers to publish their work, though most such services cost money. Still, there have been some notable works that were self-published. Ever heard of *The Joy of Cooking*? Irma Rombauer self-published that book in 1931, and it has since sold more than 18 million copies. More recently, Amanda Hocking, author of young adult paranormal romance and urban fantasies, self-published nine of her own novels, several of which made the *New York Times* best-seller list.

Kindle Direct Publishing makes it possible to self-publish works and then sell them in the Kindle store. John Locke, who writes crime fiction, sells his books there for $2.99 each—and in 2011 entered the elite "Kindle Million Club" of authors who have sold over 1 million ebooks for the Kindle, joining Stieg Larsson, author of *The Girl with the Dragon Tattoo*, and Suzanne Collins, creator of *The Hunger Games*. Locke was the first independently published author to make the list, but other self-published writers have since joined the ranks.

Blogs. If you're interested in writing about a particular topic, a blog can be a good site for publishing your writing. Many blogs focus on single themes or topics—politics, baseball, coffee, travel, science, whatever—and most of them are interactive, providing space for readers to comment. And comment they do, which often leads to a kind of back-and-forth that brings new insights and ideas to both the author and the reader. Free blogging platforms such as *Blogger, Tumblr, WordPress*, and *Svbtle* make it fairly easy to create and maintain a blog. (For tips on posting to a blog, see Chapter 34.)

Social networks like *Facebook, Tumblr*, and *Instagram* allow you to post your work directly to your friends and followers. Unlike blogs, which may assume a wide audience across the web, social networks give you a degree of control over who you're writing for. Some writers use *Facebook*, for example, to share links to their writing with just their network of friends. *Tumblr* allows you to gather a following and follow others, and on *Instagram* the captions you write may count for as much as the photos you share. Browse the #captionsbywriters hashtag to read the kind of writing being posted on *Instagram*.

Twitter allows you to publish your writing, too, though in very short snippets. But if we understand a publication as work that reaches an audience, then *Twitter* certainly fits the bill: companies tweet about new products, conference goers tweet about presentations they attend, reporters tweet about breaking news. And writers often get around the 140-character limit by posting multiple tweets on a topic in order to get substantial amounts of information out to a worldwide audience.

Collaborative writing and document-sharing tools. You may be familiar with sites like *Google Docs* for managing and storing written documents, but this site and some others can also be used for sharing those documents. You can also try *Draft*, a free web app that lets you share documents with others—who can then comment or edit.

Go to everyonesan
author.tumblr.com
to read a *Wired*
article about one
writer's experience
with *Reddit*.

For bringing your writing to an audience, check out *Medium*, an open reading and writing publication platform built on the mantra that "People create better things together." Its site makes it easy to get feedback and reach an audience.

Another way to share writing is *Reddit*, a link-sharing site that depends on its millions of users for both content and reviews. *Reddit* tracks what's most popular on the web through its users' up-or-down votes and comment threads; the more you participate, the more you gain from the site. And you never know where a *Reddit* thread can lead: one writer was offered a screen-writing deal after a story he posted in response to a question about time travel went viral.

Wikis. If you have ever visited *Wikipedia*, you've used a wiki. **WIKIS** are written collaboratively, which means that anyone can post, update, or add to the information on a page. As a wiki writer, you can choose to be anonymous, and a wiki editor may remove or change what you add. But wikis are a good way to participate in a conversation on a topic you know something about. And wikis are generally visited by a large volume of readers, so you can be certain that if your contribution remains on the site, your writing will reach an audience.

Wikipedia offers the opportunity to write about anything that interests you, from a historical event you're researching to the SXSW festival to your favorite singer or musician. Whatever the topic, there's likely to be an entry on *Wikipedia* that you might contribute to as an author—and if no entry exists already, you can create one yourself! And there are many wikis beyond *Wikipedia*: the *DavisWiki* is devoted to all things about the city of Davis, California; *Foodista* focuses on food and recipes; and *Wookieepedia* is an encyclopedia dedicated to *Star Wars*.

Athlete profile

5:30 A.M. A car horn goes off from Becca Caplin's phone. The blaring continues until Karly Watts, Caplin's teammate and roommate, reaches across the four feet that separate their adjacent bunks and turns off the alarm. Watts rolls out of bed first, as always, and five minutes later Caplin is up too. By 6:00 both women are standing poolside ready to dive back in.

A writer on *Medium* seeks feedback from a friend.

"Is there a section at the bottom for comments?"

Comments. Most newspapers and magazines provide a space in their online versions for readers to post comments on articles and editorials. *YouTube* and other video- and image-sharing sites like *Vine, Vimeo,* and *Imgur* also offer a space for commenting, as do many blogs. In fact, it's rarely the case these days that something on the internet has not been commented on, and reading—and contributing to—those comments can bring you into long and thoughtful discussions with other readers.

Reviews. Maybe you ordered some great (or horrible) take-out food from a new restaurant last night; publish a review on *Yelp* or *Seamless* saying so! Amazon and other online stores also provide space for readers to post reviews of books or other products sold there. These are sites that enable you to reach a large audience—and to offer them some useful advice. Even though some of these venues are anonymous, they allow you to put your perspectives out there, and as often as not to get responses to what you say. (For guidelines on writing a review, see Chapter 15.)

Fan fiction websites. Check out *FanFiction.net*, where you'll find forums to discuss favorite works, writing tips, and a place to write fiction of your own based on works you admire. Write a new ending to *Harry Potter*—or a story about when the heroines in *Pride and Prejudice* go to college. Most fan fiction sites include spaces where writers can discuss their work and also critique

P&P200 – Mr. Collins at Longbourn

Published November 18, 2011 | By Susan Adriani

Mr. Collins was not a sensible man. ~ *from Jane Austen's Pride and Prejudice*

"My dear Mr. Collins," Mrs. Bennet gushed, "I always knew you would be a sensible man!"

Her husband rolled his eyes as the clergyman smiled complacently at Longbourn's mistress, inclining his head in a show of practiced deference while Mrs. Bennet stirred the fire. Mr. Bennet had found the man anything but sensible since his arrival the day before, and was now greatly disappointed that the novelty attached to his ridiculous cousin had lost its luster and rubbed his patience raw so early on in the visit. He shook out his newspaper and reached for his tea, attempting to ignore the other two occupants of the room and their indolent chatter.

A posting from *AustenAuthors*, a Jane Austen fan fiction site.

With the words that you scribble on the back of an envelope or tap out with your thumbs on a little device, you become part of something as big as the world, as near as your heart. Check out how an organization devoted simply to the sharing of words and thoughts has influenced the course of history for nearly a century: pen international.org/.

one another's writing before it is published on the site. Fan fiction websites offer a good way to practice and find an audience and a community—readers who both write and read work like yours.

Almost all writers long to find an audience, and the internet has made it dramatically easier for writers and readers who share an interest to connect. Perhaps you want to start a blog about a favorite basketball team or to share fan fiction with other devotees of the *Harry Potter* series. Perhaps you want to use *Medium* to publish a family history in honor of your grandmother's ninetieth birthday. Or maybe you've written an essay for a college class that you're really proud of and have decided to submit it to the publisher of this book hoping it might be published in another writing textbook. These are just some of the ways that writers today can publish what they write, confirming again that in the twenty-first century everyone can be an author.

We conclude this chapter with a student essay that began as an assignment for an undergraduate writing class and ended up winning the Norton Writer's Prize and later being published in a book—this one! The essay was written by Carrie Barker in response to an assignment asking her to reflect on an important turning point in her life. She chose a crucial moment—an unexpected pregnancy when she already had three children. What should she do? Read on to find out—and then write your own essay to tell us your story and your ideas.

But Two Negatives Equal a Positive

CARRIE BARKER

OH MY GOD. *Oh my God. OH MY GOD! This cannot be happening.* Tears surged down my face, pelting my bare thighs. Two different brands, two different stores, two different bathrooms. Same results. *Are you frickin' kidding me?!* The second one only confirmed the first, and the first only confirmed what I'd recently begun to suspect.

How? I kept demanding. *How could this happen?* Okay, the "how" wasn't the mystery. *This wasn't supposed to happen. Not now.*

I must have sat there for a long time, numb. My head and limbs felt far too heavy to get up, my brain incapable of forming intelligent thought, eyes closed, head tilted backward, positioned awkwardly against the tiled wall behind. At some point, my eyes flickered open to the glare of a recessed floodlight directly above.

Was this the Universe's idea of a sick joke? A test of some kind?

I stared into the white hot light. Mesmerized by the orb, I consented to it cauterizing the tears, scorching my corneas.

What words of wisdom might help here? I needed something. Anything. *When life hands you lemons, make lemonade? What doesn't kill you will only make you stronger?*

CARRIE BARKER wrote this essay as a student at Kirkwood Community College. She then transferred to the University of Iowa, graduating with a BA in English and creative writing. She now works as an administrative assistant in the English department at Kirkwood. The essay here won the Norton Writer's Prize in 2010.

A shoulder angel whispered, "No one ever has to know."

"There *are* options," the other chimed in.

Activity a few feet away briefly interrupted the conversation only I could hear.

"But could she go through with it? Could she live with herself afterward?" the first asked.

"Dunno. She never thought she'd be in this situation," the second answered.

I closed my eyes and gently rubbed the black blobs out of my vision. I dug the other contraption out from a small brown sack at the bottom of my purse and discarded them both in the receptacle mounted in the stall.

"A little different from the typical trash thrown in there," a shoulder angel observed.

"It is ironic," the other agreed.

Go away, I told my shoulder angels. *I don't like you anymore.*

I pulled myself together and made it to the sink. The reflection in the mirror wasn't kind; twin mascara ruts flanked each side of my face, eyelids swollen and naked, the whites bloodshot and raw. The splash of cold water stung my pores. Stalling, I wandered throughout the store and tried to come to terms with this new reality. My loitering terminated in the baby section.

How will Scott react? What will people think? What are we going to do? I tried to put myself in his shoes. *We . . . will there continue to be a "we"?* I just didn't know . . .

I slipped into the house and quickly scanned the rooms. Scott was alone in the kitchen, cleaning out the refrigerator. *Damn, I had bad timing.* I quietly crossed the room and erected myself alongside the sweaty Tupperware and condiment containers sitting on the counter.

I crossed my arms and erupted, "You were right."

He backed out of the fridge and shut the door, giving me his full attention. "About what?" he asked.

Be strong, I told myself, *and do not cry.*

The instant our eyes met, mine started to well up with tears; I looked down and away, focusing on a few stray dust bunnies gathering in the corner. I hesitated. Scott sighed impatiently; he hated to be interrupted in the middle of something. Briefly, my eyes met his arched brows, then darted back to the corner again. *For Christ's sake*, my brain screamed, *he's your husband, not your father!* I took a deep breath and purged, "You were right about me being pregnant." I stole another glance; his expression was impossible to read. I took another breath and elaborated. "When you suggested it earlier, I thought you'd lost your mind. But then I got to thinking . . . the dates, not feeling well. I still thought you were nuts, but I took a test. Two actually, and they were both positive."

Just then, the patter of footsteps getting louder interrupted my confession. "Mom, can I have some crackers?"

"Sure, buddy." I handed him the box, trying to buy us more time alone. "Share with your brother and sister, okay?"

"Okay. Thanks, Mom!" And back to the living room he went.

Scott's silence was unbearable. I forced myself to look directly into his deep blue eyes.

"I haven't cheated on you," I offered.

"I wasn't thinking you did," he countered calmly.

"You weren't?" My brain couldn't comprehend. *How does a man with two surgically cut vas deferens not suspect his knocked-up wife?*

"You remember the numbers the doctor told us," he said.

"Yeah, I remember joking about our odds of having another baby being greater than winning the lottery." *And asking if I could do the honors*, I recalled. (After all, dads were given the option of cutting the umbilical cord after a baby was born; it seemed like a perfectly reasonable request to me.)

"I can't believe I figured out you were pregnant before you did," he said. "What kind of woman are you?" He was teasing, but I failed to see humor in the situation.

"The kind of woman who is done with that part of her life," I belched, sounding defensive. "The kind that gave birth to three babies in thirty-three months and likes eight hours of sleep a night. The kind that is done changing diapers and washing bottles and already got rid of every bit of baby stuff we ever owned." I'm sure he was sorry he asked. "Why would being pregnant even cross my mind?"

If he answered I didn't hear him. My brain was busy cranking out reasons not to have this baby: *Because I was done with that part of my life, because I finally owned clothes that were stain-free, because I was a frazzled, overwhelmed mess when the kids were babies. And because I was tired of feeling like my sole purpose on this earth was to be someone's wife or mother. What about me? When was it my turn?* I stopped, realizing Scott was watching me shake my head back and forth.

"Scott, I can't start over. I don't want to. They're all finally in school." Guilt overwhelmed me. "And you know people are going to assume I had an affair. Everyone knows you got a vasectomy."

"I don't give a shit what they think," he said. "Ultimately, it's your decision and I'll support whatever you decide, but I think we're in a better position now than when we had the first three. Things are better now, right?"

It was true; we weren't exactly living the high life, but we weren't nearly as broke as during those early years. And I couldn't remember the last time we had an argument.

He continued, "I'd say I'm more mature now than at twenty-five. And more patient." I nodded. "Care, it's not like you're going to have three babies again. Just one."

Also good points. Wait a minute—what the hell just happened? Since when was he the voice of reason? That's always been my job!

"Come here," he said, gently pulling me into his protective embrace.

Wow, I thought, dissolving into a blubbering train wreck. *I had prepared for a whole slew of reactions, but that wasn't one of them.*

Exhausted and relieved, I agreed to let the idea of a fourth child marinate awhile.

I knew myself pretty well; I was capable of talking myself into or out of just about anything. I had been known to rationalize, justify, or just procrastinate until someone decided for me. But I wasn't a fan of indecision either, and the gravity of what Oprah called a "defining moment" weighed heavily on my mind and gnawed at my brain stem. During downtimes, my shoulder angels reappeared to duke it out; one would throw out a legitimate objection and the other would counter with an equally valid rebuttal.

In the shower: "She has no baby necessities; it would be absurd to start from scratch."

"She learned the difference between a necessity and a gadget the first time around."

"Has she looked at the prices of the stuff? This is going to cost a bundle."

"It doesn't have to be brand new; there are always garage sales and secondhand stores."

At a stoplight: "Another child is less than ideal in a three-bedroom home; the boys are already sharing a room."

"Maybe it's a girl. Her daughter has always wanted a little sister."

"Yeah, till she actually has one."

"People make do. Years ago, babies slept in dresser drawers."

In line at the grocery store: "A new baby will totally mess up the whole birth-order dynamic."

"It will. There will no longer be a middle child."

"The older kids may resent the baby."

"Maybe they'll be old enough to remember the experience of having a new little brother or sister—being helpers, teaching new things, reveling in all the firsts."

At night in bed: "She lives in a time where women can choose. She doesn't have to blindly accept whatever card life throws her."

"She considered all her options; she feels too often people try to control every aspect of their lives. That's not life, that's a spreadsheet. The bumps in the road are there to teach things—about life, about adversity, about herself."

"But she said she doesn't want this."

"Well, it's not always about getting what you want. She wants chocolate all the time. Wait, that's a bad example."

"But she said she was just starting to get her life back."

"It's true that the timing isn't convenient. But have you noticed that things have a way of working out pretty terrific when given the chance?"

"Wait, does this mean she's having a baby?"

"She's decided; they're having a baby."

"I still can't go to sleep."

"Maybe it's because you consume too much caffeine."

"Maybe. Or maybe it's because I can't turn off my brain. How is it that he can be lying next to her snoring, sixty seconds after his head hits the pillow? She's been lying here for more than an hour."

"She's gonna have to get up to pee soon anyway, so she may as well get used to it."

"Hey, what were all those girls' names we had picked out? Do you remember?"

"Oh, the girls' names were a piece of cake! We found lots of names that we loved. It was the boys' names that were tough. . . . They had to sound masculine, but not too macho."

"Hmm, I wonder where she put that name book."

Shut up! I scolded them. *I'm trying to fall asleep. Maybe I'll look for the book tomorrow.*

REFLECT. If everyone's an author, that includes you too! So get busy. Now's the time to publish something you've written. We hope this book will help you do so.

Readings

IF EVERYONE'S AN AUTHOR, then we are all readers as well. All authors, in fact, learn constantly by engaging with what other authors have written. On the following pages you'll find an anthology of 32 readings, arranged alphabetically by author. And on the inside back cover of the book, we've added a menu that categorizes the readings by both genres and themes. And that's not all. We'll regularly be posting additional essays, articles, cartoons, speeches, videos, and more on everyonesanauthor.tumblr.com for you to read, analyze, reflect on—and respond to. So read on, enjoy, and see what you can learn.

Monsanto's Harvest of Fear

DONALD L. BARLETT & JAMES B. STEELE

ARY RINEHART CLEARLY REMEMBERS the summer day in 2002 when the stranger walked in and issued his threat. Rinehart was behind the counter of the Square Deal, his "old-time country store," as he calls it, on the fading town square of Eagleville, Missouri, a tiny farm community 100 miles north of Kansas City.

The Square Deal is a fixture in Eagleville, a place where farmers and townspeople can go for lightbulbs, greeting cards, hunting gear, ice cream, aspirin, and dozens of other small items without having to drive to a big-box store in Bethany, the county seat, 15 miles down Interstate 35.

Everyone knows Rinehart, who was born and raised in the area and runs one of Eagleville's few surviving businesses. The stranger came up to the counter and asked for him by name.

"Well, that's me," said Rinehart.

As Rinehart would recall, the man began verbally attacking him, saying 5 he had proof that Rinehart had planted Monsanto's genetically modified (G.M.) soybeans in violation of the company's patent. Better come clean and settle with Monsanto, Rinehart says the man told him—or face the consequences.

DONALD L. BARLETT and JAMES B. STEELE have worked together as investigative journalists for more than three decades, winning two Pulitzer Prizes and many other awards. They are contributing editors at *Vanity Fair*, where this article was published in 2008.

Rinehart was incredulous, listening to the words as puzzled customers and employees looked on. Like many others in rural America, Rinehart knew of Monsanto's fierce reputation for enforcing its patents and suing anyone who allegedly violated them. But Rinehart wasn't a farmer. He wasn't a seed dealer. He hadn't planted any seeds or sold any seeds. He owned a small—a *really* small—country store in a town of 350 people. He was angry that somebody could just barge into the store and embarrass him in front of everyone. "It made me and my business look bad," he says. Rinehart says he told the intruder, "You got the wrong guy."

When the stranger persisted, Rinehart showed him the door. On the way out the man kept making threats. Rinehart says he can't remember the exact words, but they were to the effect of: "Monsanto is big. You can't win. We will get you. You will pay."

Scenes like this are playing out in many parts of rural America these days as Monsanto goes after farmers, farmers' co-ops, seed dealers—anyone it suspects may have infringed its patents of genetically modified seeds. As interviews and reams of court documents reveal, Monsanto relies on a shadowy army of private investigators and agents in the American heartland to strike fear into farm country. They fan out into fields and farm towns, where they secretly videotape and photograph farmers, store owners, and co-ops; infiltrate community meetings; and gather information from informants about farming activities. Farmers say that some Monsanto agents pretend to be surveyors. Others confront farmers on their land and try to pressure them to sign papers giving Monsanto access to their private records. Farmers call them the "seed police" and use words such as "Gestapo" and "Mafia" to describe their tactics.

When asked about these practices, Monsanto declined to comment specifically, other than to say that the company is simply protecting its patents. "Monsanto spends more than $2 million a day in research to identify, test, develop and bring to market innovative new seeds and technologies that benefit farmers," Monsanto spokesman Darren Wallis wrote in an e-mailed letter to *Vanity Fair.* "One tool in protecting this investment is patenting our discoveries and, if necessary, legally defending those patents against those who might choose to infringe upon them." Wallis said that, while the vast majority of farmers and seed dealers follow the licensing agreements, "a tiny fraction" do not, and that Monsanto is obligated to those who do abide by its rules to enforce its patent rights on those who "reap the benefits of the technology without paying for its use." He said only a small number of cases ever go to trial.

The report kicks off with an attention-grabbing narrative —a good strategy, and not hard to do. See Ch. 12 and pp. 436–37.

Some compare Monsanto's hard-line approach to Microsoft's zealous ef- 10
forts to protect its software from pirates. At least with Microsoft the buyer
of a program can use it over and over again. But farmers who buy Monsanto's seeds can't even do that.

The Control of Nature

For centuries—millennia—farmers have saved seeds from season to season:
they planted in the spring, harvested in the fall, then reclaimed and cleaned
the seeds over the winter for re-planting the next spring. Monsanto has
turned this ancient practice on its head.

Monsanto developed G.M. seeds that would resist its own herbicide,
Roundup, offering farmers a convenient way to spray fields with weed killer
without affecting crops. Monsanto then patented the seeds. For nearly all
of its history the United States Patent and Trademark Office had refused to
grant patents on seeds, viewing them as life-forms with too many variables
to be patented. "It's not like describing a widget," says Joseph Mendelson III,
the legal director of the Center for Food Safety, which has tracked Monsanto's activities in rural America for years.

Indeed not. But in 1980 the U.S. Supreme Court, in a five-to-four decision,
turned seeds into widgets, laying the groundwork for a handful of corporations to begin taking control of the world's food supply. In its decision, the
court extended patent law to cover "a live human-made microorganism."
In this case, the organism wasn't even a seed. Rather, it was a *Pseudomonas*
bacterium developed by a General Electric scientist to clean up oil spills. But
the precedent was set, and Monsanto took advantage of it. Since the 1980s,
Monsanto has become the world leader in genetic modification of seeds and
has won 674 biotechnology patents, more than any other company, according to U.S. Department of Agriculture data.

Farmers who buy Monsanto's patented Roundup Ready seeds are required to sign an agreement promising not to save the seed produced after
each harvest for re-planting, or to sell the seed to other farmers. This means
that farmers must buy new seed every year. Those increased sales, coupled
with ballooning sales of its Roundup weed killer, have been a bonanza for
Monsanto.

This radical departure from age-old practice has created turmoil in 15
farm country. Some farmers don't fully understand that they aren't sup-

A handful of Monsanto's Roundup Ready soybean seeds saved from a previous season could be grounds for an investigation by the biotech giant.

posed to save Monsanto's seeds for next year's planting. Others do, but ignore the stipulation rather than throw away a perfectly usable product. Still others say that they don't use Monsanto's genetically modified seeds, but seeds have been blown into their fields by wind or deposited by birds. It's certainly easy for G.M. seeds to get mixed in with traditional varieties when seeds are cleaned by commercial dealers for re-planting. The seeds look identical; only a laboratory analysis can show the difference. Even if a farmer doesn't buy G.M. seeds and doesn't want them on his land, it's a safe bet he'll get a visit from Monsanto's seed police if crops grown from G.M. seeds are discovered in his fields.

Most Americans know Monsanto because of what it sells to put on our lawns—the ubiquitous weed killer Roundup. What they may not know is that the company now profoundly influences—and one day may virtually control—what we put on our tables. For most of its history Monsanto was a chemical giant, producing some of the most toxic substances ever created, residues from which have left us with some of the most polluted sites on earth. Yet in a little more than a decade, the company has sought to shed its polluted past and morph into something much different and more far-reaching—an "agricultural company" dedicated to making the world "a better place for future generations." Still, more than one Web log claims to see similarities between Monsanto and the fictional company "U-North" in the movie *Michael Clayton,* an agribusiness giant accused in a multibillion-dollar lawsuit of selling an herbicide that causes cancer.

Monsanto's genetically modified seeds have transformed the company and are radically altering global agriculture. So far, the company has produced G.M. seeds for soybeans, corn, canola, and cotton. Many more products have been developed or are in the pipeline, including seeds for sugar beets and alfalfa. The company is also seeking to extend its reach into milk production by marketing an artificial growth hormone for cows that increases their output, and it is taking aggressive steps to put those who don't want to use growth hormone at a commercial disadvantage.

Even as the company is pushing its G.M. agenda, Monsanto is buying up conventional-seed companies. In 2005, Monsanto paid $1.4 billion for Seminis, which controlled 40 percent of the U.S. market for lettuce, tomatoes, and other vegetable and fruit seeds. Two weeks later it announced the acquisition of the country's third-largest cottonseed company, Emergent Genetics, for $300 million. It's estimated that Monsanto seeds now account for 90 percent of the U.S. production of soybeans, which are used in food products beyond counting. Monsanto's acquisitions have fueled explosive growth, transforming the St. Louis–based corporation into the largest seed company in the world.

In Iraq, the groundwork has been laid to protect the patents of Monsanto and other G.M.-seed companies. One of L. Paul Bremer's last acts as head of the Coalition Provisional Authority was an order stipulating that "farmers shall be prohibited from re-using seeds of protected varieties." Monsanto has said that it has no interest in doing business in Iraq, but should the company change its mind, the American-style law is in place.

To be sure, more and more agricultural corporations and individual farmers are using Monsanto's G.M. seeds. As recently as 1980, no genetically modified crops were grown in the U.S. In 2007, the total was 142 million acres planted. Worldwide, the figure was 282 million acres. Many farmers believe that G.M. seeds increase crop yields and save money. Another reason for their attraction is convenience. By using Roundup Ready soybean seeds, a farmer can spend less time tending to his fields. With Monsanto seeds, a farmer plants his crop, then treats it later with Roundup to kill weeds. That takes the place of labor-intensive weed control and plowing.

Monsanto portrays its move into G.M. seeds as a giant leap for mankind. But out in the American countryside, Monsanto's no-holds-barred tactics have made it feared and loathed. Like it or not, farmers say, they have fewer and fewer choices in buying seeds.

And controlling the seeds is not some abstraction. Whoever provides the world's seeds controls the world's food supply.

Under Surveillance

After Monsanto's investigator confronted Gary Rinehart, Monsanto filed a federal lawsuit alleging that Rinehart "knowingly, intentionally, and willfully" planted seeds "in violation of Monsanto's patent rights." The company's complaint made it sound as if Monsanto had Rinehart dead to rights:

> *During the 2002 growing season, Investigator Jeffery Moore, through surveillance of Mr. Rinehart's farm facility and farming operations, observed Defendant planting brown bag soybean seed. Mr. Moore observed the Defendant take the brown bag soybeans to a field, which was subsequently loaded into a grain drill and planted. Mr. Moore located two empty bags in the ditch in the public road right-of-way beside one of the fields planted by Rinehart, which contained some soybeans. Mr. Moore collected a small amount of soybeans left in the bags which Defendant had tossed into the public right-of-way. These samples tested positive for Monsanto's Roundup Ready technology.*

Faced with a federal lawsuit, Rinehart had to hire a lawyer. Monsanto eventually realized that "Investigator Jeffery Moore" had targeted the wrong man, and dropped the suit. Rinehart later learned that the company had been secretly investigating farmers in his area. Rinehart never heard from Monsanto again: no letter of apology, no public concession that the company had made a terrible mistake, no offer to pay his attorney's fees. "I don't know how they get away with it," he says. "If I tried to do something like that it would be bad news. I felt like I was in another country."

Gary Rinehart is actually one of Monsanto's luckier targets. Ever since commercial introduction of its G.M. seeds, in 1996, Monsanto has launched thousands of investigations and filed lawsuits against hundreds of farmers and seed dealers. In a 2007 report, the Center for Food Safety, in Washington, D.C., documented 112 such lawsuits, in 27 states.

Even more significant, in the Center's opinion, are the numbers of   25 farmers who settle because they don't have the money or the time to fight Monsanto. "The number of cases filed is only the tip of the iceberg," says Bill Freese, the Center's science-policy analyst. Freese says he has been told of many cases in which Monsanto investigators showed up at a farmer's house or confronted him in his fields, claiming he had violated the technology agreement and demanding to see his records. According to Freese, investigators will say, "Monsanto knows that you are saving Roundup Ready seeds, and if you don't sign these information-release forms, Monsanto is going to come after you and take your farm or take you for all you're worth." Investigators will sometimes show a farmer a photo of himself coming out of a store, to let him know he is being followed.

Lawyers who have represented farmers sued by Monsanto say that intimidating actions like these are commonplace. Most give in and pay Monsanto some amount in damages; those who resist face the full force of Monsanto's legal wrath.

Scorched-Earth Tactics

Pilot Grove, Missouri, population 750, sits in rolling farmland 150 miles west of St. Louis. The town has a grocery store, a bank, a bar, a nursing home, a funeral parlor, and a few other small businesses. There are no stoplights, but the town doesn't need any. The little traffic it has comes from trucks on their way to and from the grain elevator on the edge of town. The elevator is owned by a local co-op, the Pilot Grove Cooperative Elevator, which buys soybeans and corn from farmers in the fall, then ships out the grain over the winter. The co-op has seven full-time employees and four computers.

In the fall of 2006, Monsanto trained its legal guns on Pilot Grove; ever since, its farmers have been drawn into a costly, disruptive legal battle against an opponent with limitless resources. Neither Pilot Grove nor Monsanto will discuss the case, but it is possible to piece together much of the story from documents filed as part of the litigation.

Monsanto began investigating soybean farmers in and around Pilot Grove several years ago. There is no indication as to what sparked the probe, but Monsanto periodically investigates farmers in soybean-growing regions such as this one in central Missouri. The company has a staff devoted to enforcing patents and litigating against farmers. To gather leads, the company maintains an 800 number and encourages farmers to inform on other farmers they think may be engaging in "seed piracy."

Once Pilot Grove had been targeted, Monsanto sent private investigators into the area. Over a period of months, Monsanto's investigators surreptitiously followed the co-op's employees and customers and videotaped them in fields and going about other activities. At least 17 such surveillance videos were made, according to court records. The investigative work was outsourced to a St. Louis agency, McDowell & Associates. It was a McDowell investigator who erroneously fingered Gary Rinehart. In Pilot Grove, at least 11 McDowell investigators have worked the case, and Monsanto makes no bones about the extent of this effort: "Surveillance was conducted throughout the year by various investigators in the field," according to court records. McDowell, like Monsanto, will not comment on the case.

Not long after investigators showed up in Pilot Grove, Monsanto subpoenaed the co-op's records concerning seed and herbicide purchases and seed-cleaning operations. The co-op provided more than 800 pages of documents pertaining to dozens of farmers. Monsanto sued two farmers and negotiated settlements with more than 25 others it accused of seed piracy. But Monsanto's legal assault had only begun. Although the co-op had provided voluminous records, Monsanto then sued it in federal court for patent infringement. Monsanto contended that by cleaning seeds—a service which it had provided for decades—the co-op was inducing farmers to violate Monsanto's patents. In effect, Monsanto wanted the co-op to police its own customers.

In the majority of cases where Monsanto sues, or threatens to sue, farmers settle before going to trial. The cost and stress of litigating against a global corporation are just too great. But Pilot Grove wouldn't cave—and ever since, Monsanto has been turning up the heat. The more the co-op has resisted, the more legal firepower Monsanto has aimed at it. Pilot Grove's lawyer, Steven H. Schwartz, described Monsanto in a court filing as pursuing a "scorched earth tactic," intent on "trying to drive the co-op into the ground."

Even after Pilot Grove turned over thousands more pages of sales records going back five years, and covering virtually every one of its farmer customers, Monsanto wanted more—the right to inspect the co-op's hard drives. When the co-op offered to provide an electronic version of any record, Monsanto demanded hands-on access to Pilot Grove's in-house computers.

Monsanto next petitioned to make potential damages punitive—tripling the amount that Pilot Grove might have to pay if found guilty. After a judge denied that request, Monsanto expanded the scope of the pre-trial investigation by seeking to quadruple the number of depositions. "Monsanto is doing its best to make this case so expensive to defend that the Co-op will have no choice but to relent," Pilot Grove's lawyer said in a court filing.

With Pilot Grove still holding out for a trial, Monsanto now subpoenaed 35 the records of more than 100 of the co-op's customers. In a "You are Commanded . . . " notice, the farmers were ordered to gather up five years of invoices, receipts, and all other papers relating to their soybean and herbicide purchases, and to have the documents delivered to a law office in St. Louis. Monsanto gave them two weeks to comply.

Whether Pilot Grove can continue to wage its legal battle remains to be seen. Whatever the outcome, the case shows why Monsanto is so detested in farm country, even by those who buy its products. "I don't know of a company that chooses to sue its own customer base," says Joseph Mendelson, of the Center for Food Safety. "It's a very bizarre business strategy." But it's one that Monsanto manages to get away with, because increasingly it's the dominant vendor in town.

Chemicals? What Chemicals?

The Monsanto Company has never been one of America's friendliest corporate citizens. Given Monsanto's current dominance in the field of bioengineering, it's worth looking at the company's own DNA. The future of the company may lie in seeds, but the seeds of the company lie in chemicals. Communities around the world are still reaping the environmental consequences of Monsanto's origins.

Monsanto was founded in 1901 by John Francis Queeny, a tough, cigar-smoking Irishman with a sixth-grade education. A buyer for a wholesale drug company, Queeny had an idea. But like a lot of employees with ideas, he found that his boss wouldn't listen to him. So he went into business for himself on the side. Queeny was convinced there was money to be made manufacturing a substance called saccharin, an artificial sweetener then imported from Germany. He took $1,500 of his savings, borrowed another $3,500, and set up shop in a dingy warehouse near the St. Louis waterfront. With borrowed equipment and secondhand machines, he began producing saccharin for the U.S. market. He called the company the Monsanto Chemical Works, Monsanto being his wife's maiden name.

The German cartel that controlled the market for saccharin wasn't pleased, and cut the price from $4.50 to $1 a pound to try to force Queeny out of business. The young company faced other challenges. Questions arose about the safety of saccharin, and the U.S. Department of Agriculture even tried to ban it. Fortunately for Queeny, he wasn't up against opponents as aggressive and litigious as the Monsanto of today. His persistence and the loyalty of one steady customer kept the company afloat. That steady customer was a new company in Georgia named Coca-Cola.

Monsanto added more and more products—vanillin, caffeine, and 40
drugs used as sedatives and laxatives. In 1917, Monsanto began making aspirin, and soon became the largest maker worldwide. During World War I, cut off from imported European chemicals, Monsanto was forced to manufacture its own, and its position as a leading force in the chemical industry was assured.

After Queeny was diagnosed with cancer, in the late 1920s, his only son, Edgar, became president. Where the father had been a classic entrepreneur, Edgar Monsanto Queeny was an empire builder with a grand vision. It was Edgar—shrewd, daring, and intuitive ("He can see around the next corner," his secretary once said)—who built Monsanto into a global powerhouse. Under Edgar Queeny and his successors, Monsanto extended its reach into a phenomenal number of products: plastics, resins, rubber goods, fuel additives, artificial caffeine, industrial fluids, vinyl siding, dishwasher detergent, anti-freeze, fertilizers, herbicides, pesticides. Its safety glass protects the U.S. Constitution and the *Mona Lisa*. Its synthetic fibers are the basis of Astroturf.

During the 1970s, the company shifted more and more resources into biotechnology. In 1981 it created a molecular-biology group for research in plant genetics. The next year, Monsanto scientists hit gold: they became the first to genetically modify a plant cell. "It will now be possible to introduce virtually any gene into plant cells with the ultimate goal of improving crop productivity," said Ernest Jaworski, director of Monsanto's Biological Sciences Program.

Over the next few years, scientists working mainly in the company's vast new Life Sciences Research Center, 25 miles west of St. Louis, developed one genetically modified product after another—cotton, soybeans, corn, canola. From the start, G.M. seeds were controversial with the public as well as with some farmers and European consumers. Monsanto has sought to portray G.M. seeds as a panacea, a way to alleviate poverty and feed the hungry. Robert Shapiro, Monsanto's president during the 1990s, once called G.M. seeds "the single most successful introduction of technology in the history of agriculture, including the plow."

By the late 1990s, Monsanto, having rebranded itself into a "life sciences" company, had spun off its chemical and fibers operations into a new company called Solutia. After an additional reorganization, Monsanto reincorporated in 2002 and officially declared itself an "agricultural company."

In its company literature, Monsanto now refers to itself disingenuously as a "relatively new company" whose primary goal is helping "farmers around the world in their mission to feed, clothe, and fuel" a growing planet. In its list of corporate milestones, all but a handful are from the recent era. As for the company's early history, the decades when it grew into an industrial powerhouse now held potentially responsible for more than 50 Environmental Protection Agency Superfund sites—none of that is mentioned. It's as though the original Monsanto, the company that long had the word "chemical" as part of its name, never existed. One of the benefits of doing this, as the company does not point out, was to channel the bulk of the growing backlog of chemical lawsuits and liabilities onto Solutia, keeping the Monsanto brand pure. 45

But Monsanto's past, especially its environmental legacy, is very much with us. For many years Monsanto produced two of the most toxic substances ever known—polychlorinated biphenyls, better known as PCBs, and dioxin. Monsanto no longer produces either, but the places where it did are still struggling with the aftermath, and probably always will be.

"Systemic Intoxication"

Twelve miles downriver from Charleston, West Virginia, is the town of Nitro, where Monsanto operated a chemical plant from 1929 to 1995. In 1948 the plant began to make a powerful herbicide known as 2,4,5-T, called "weed bug" by the workers. A by-product of the process was the creation of a chemical that would later be known as dioxin.

The name dioxin refers to a group of highly toxic chemicals that have been linked to heart disease, liver disease, human reproductive disorders, and developmental problems. Even in small amounts, dioxin persists in the environment and accumulates in the body. In 1997 the International Agency for Research on Cancer, a branch of the World Health Organization, classified the most powerful form of dioxin as a substance that causes cancer in humans. In 2001 the U.S. government listed the chemical as a "known human carcinogen."

On March 8, 1949, a massive explosion rocked Monsanto's Nitro plant when a pressure valve blew on a container cooking up a batch of herbicide. The noise from the release was a scream so loud that it drowned out the emergency steam whistle for five minutes. A plume of vapor and white smoke drifted across the plant and out over town. Residue from the explosion coated the interior of the building and those inside with what workers described as "a fine black powder." Many felt their skin prickle and were told to scrub down.

Within days, workers experienced skin eruptions. Many were soon diagnosed with chloracne, a condition similar to common acne but more severe, longer lasting, and potentially disfiguring. Others felt intense pains in their legs, chest, and trunk. A confidential medical report at the time said the explosion "caused a systemic intoxication in the workers involving most major organ systems." Doctors who examined four of the most seriously injured men detected a strong odor coming from them when they were all together in a closed room. "We believe these men are excreting a foreign chemical through their skins," the confidential report to Monsanto noted. Court records indicate that 226 plant workers became ill.

According to court documents that have surfaced in a West Virginia court case, Monsanto downplayed the impact, stating that the contaminant affecting workers was "fairly slow acting" and caused "only an irritation of the skin."

In the meantime, the Nitro plant continued to produce herbicides, rubber products, and other chemicals. In the 1960s, the factory manufactured Agent Orange, the powerful herbicide which the U.S. military used to defoliate jungles during the Vietnam War, and which later was the focus of lawsuits by veterans contending that they had been harmed by exposure. As with Monsanto's older herbicides, the manufacturing of Agent Orange created dioxin as a by-product.

As for the Nitro plant's waste, some was burned in incinerators, some dumped in landfills or storm drains, some allowed to run into streams. As Stuart Calwell, a lawyer who has represented both workers and residents in Nitro, put it, "Dioxin went wherever the product went, down the sewer, shipped in bags, and when the waste was burned, out in the air."

In 1981 several former Nitro employees filed lawsuits in federal court, charging that Monsanto had knowingly exposed them to chemicals that caused long-term health problems, including cancer and heart disease. They alleged that Monsanto knew that many chemicals used at Nitro were potentially harmful, but had kept that information from them. On the eve of a trial, in 1988, Monsanto agreed to settle most of the cases by making a single lump payment of $1.5 million. Monsanto also agreed to drop its claim to collect $305,000 in court costs from six retired Monsanto workers who had unsuccessfully charged in another lawsuit that Monsanto had recklessly exposed them to dioxin. Monsanto had attached liens to the retirees' homes to guarantee collection of the debt.

Monsanto stopped producing dioxin in Nitro in 1969, but the toxic 55 chemical can still be found well beyond the Nitro plant site. Repeated studies have found elevated levels of dioxin in nearby rivers, streams, and fish. Residents have sued to seek damages from Monsanto and Solutia. Earlier this year, a West Virginia judge merged those lawsuits into a class-action suit. A Monsanto spokesman said, "We believe the allegations are without merit and we'll defend ourselves vigorously." The suit will no doubt take years to play out. Time is one thing that Monsanto always has, and that the plaintiffs usually don't.

Poisoned Lawns

Five hundred miles to the south, the people of Anniston, Alabama, know all about what the people of Nitro are going through. They've been there. In fact, you could say, they're still there.

From 1929 to 1971, Monsanto's Anniston works produced PCBs as industrial coolants and insulating fluids for transformers and other electrical equipment. One of the wonder chemicals of the 20th century, PCBs were exceptionally versatile and fire-resistant, and became central to many American industries as lubricants, hydraulic fluids, and sealants. But PCBs are toxic. A member of a family of chemicals that mimic hormones, PCBs have been linked to damage in the liver and in the neurological, immune, endocrine, and reproductive systems. The Environmental Protection Agency (E.P.A.) and the Agency for Toxic Substances and Disease Registry, part of the Department of Health and Human Services, now classify PCBs as "probable carcinogens."

Today, 37 years after PCB production ceased in Anniston, and after tons of contaminated soil have been removed to try to reclaim the site, the area around the old Monsanto plant remains one of the most polluted spots in the U.S.

People in Anniston find themselves in this fix today largely because of the way Monsanto disposed of PCB waste for decades. Excess PCBs were dumped in a nearby open-pit landfill or allowed to flow off the property with storm water. Some waste was poured directly into Snow Creek, which runs alongside the plant and empties into a larger stream, Choccolocco Creek. PCBs also turned up in private lawns after the company invited Anniston residents to use soil from the plant for their lawns, according to *The Anniston Star.*

So for decades the people of Anniston breathed air, planted gardens, 60 drank from wells, fished in rivers, and swam in creeks contaminated with PCBs—without knowing anything about the danger. It wasn't until the 1990s—20 years after Monsanto stopped making PCBs in Anniston—that widespread public awareness of the problem there took hold.

Studies by health authorities consistently found elevated levels of PCBs in houses, yards, streams, fields, fish, and other wildlife—and in people. In 2003, Monsanto and Solutia entered into a consent decree with the E.P.A. to clean up Anniston. Scores of houses and small businesses were to be razed, tons of contaminated soil dug up and carted off, and streambeds scooped of toxic residue. The cleanup is under way, and it will take years, but some doubt it will ever be completed—the job is massive. To settle residents' claims, Monsanto has also paid $550 million to 21,000 Anniston residents exposed to PCBs, but many of them continue to live with PCBs in their bodies. Once PCB is absorbed into human tissue, there it forever remains.

Monsanto shut down PCB production in Anniston in 1971, and the company ended all its American PCB operations in 1977. Also in 1977, Monsanto closed a PCB plant in Wales. In recent years, residents near the village of Groesfaen, in southern Wales, have noticed vile odors emanating from an old quarry outside the village. As it turns out, Monsanto had dumped thousands of tons of waste from its nearby PCB plant into the quarry. British authorities are struggling to decide what to do with what they have now identified as among the most contaminated places in Britain.

"No Cause for Public Alarm"

What had Monsanto known—or what should it have known—about the potential dangers of the chemicals it was manufacturing? There's considerable documentation lurking in court records from many lawsuits indicating that Monsanto knew quite a lot. Let's look just at the example of PCBs.

The evidence that Monsanto refused to face questions about their toxicity is quite clear. In 1956 the company tried to sell the navy a hydraulic fluid for its submarines called Pydraul 150, which contained PCBs. Monsanto supplied the navy with test results for the product. But the navy decided to run its own tests. Afterward, navy officials informed Monsanto that they wouldn't be buying the product. "Applications of Pydraul 150 caused death in all of the rabbits tested" and indicated "definite liver damage," navy officials told Monsanto, according to an internal Monsanto memo divulged in the course of a court proceeding. "No matter how we discussed the situation," complained Monsanto's medical director, R. Emmet Kelly, "it was impossible to change their thinking that Pydraul 150 is just too toxic for use in submarines."

Ten years later, a biologist conducting studies for Monsanto in streams near 65 the Anniston plant got quick results when he submerged his test fish. As he reported to Monsanto, according to *The Washington Post*, "All 25 fish lost equilibrium and turned on their sides in 10 seconds and all were dead in 3½ minutes."

When the Food and Drug Administration (F.D.A.) turned up high levels of PCBs in fish near the Anniston plant in 1970, the company swung into action to limit the P.R. damage. An internal memo entitled "CONFIDENTIAL—F.Y.I. AND DESTROY" from Monsanto official Paul B. Hodges reviewed steps under way to limit disclosure of the information. One element of the strategy was to get public officials to fight Monsanto's battle: "Joe Crockett, Secretary of the Alabama Water Improvement Commission, will try to handle the problem quietly without release of the information to the public at this time," according to the memo.

Despite Monsanto's efforts, the information did get out, but the company was able to blunt its impact. Monsanto's Anniston plant manager "convinced" a reporter for *The Anniston Star* that there was really nothing to worry about, and an internal memo from Monsanto's headquarters in St. Louis summa-

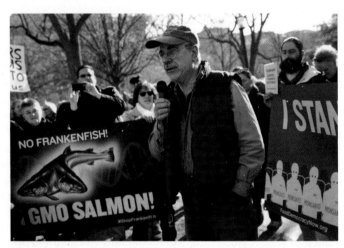

People gather to publicize biologists' findings that chemicals in Monsanto products are having harmful effects on local environments and wildlife.

rized the story that subsequently appeared in the newspaper: "Quoting both plant management and the Alabama Water Improvement Commission, the feature emphasized the PCB problem was relatively new, was being solved by Monsanto and, at this point, was no cause for public alarm."

In truth, there was enormous cause for public alarm. But that harm was done by the "Original Monsanto Company," not "Today's Monsanto Company" (the words and the distinction are Monsanto's). The Monsanto of today says that it can be trusted—that its biotech crops are "as wholesome, nutritious and safe as conventional crops," and that milk from cows injected with its artificial growth hormone is the same as, and as safe as, milk from any other cow.

The Milk Wars

Jeff Kleinpeter takes very good care of his dairy cows. In the winter he turns on heaters to warm their barns. In the summer, fans blow gentle breezes to cool them, and on especially hot days, a fine mist floats down to take the edge off Louisiana's heat. The dairy has gone "to the ultimate end of the earth for cow comfort," says Kleinpeter, a fourth-generation dairy farmer in Baton Rouge. He says visitors marvel at what he does: "I've had many of them say, 'When I die, I want to come back as a Kleinpeter cow.'"

Monsanto would like to change the way Jeff Kleinpeter and his fam- 70 ily do business. Specifically, Monsanto doesn't like the label on Kleinpeter Dairy's milk cartons: "From Cows *Not* Treated with rBGH." To consumers, that means the milk comes from cows that were not given artificial bovine growth hormone, a supplement developed by Monsanto that can be injected into dairy cows to increase their milk output.

No one knows what effect, if any, the hormone has on milk or the people who drink it. Studies have not detected any difference in the quality of milk produced by cows that receive rBGH, or rBST, a term by which it is also known. But Jeff Kleinpeter—like millions of consumers—wants no part of rBGH. Whatever its effect on humans, if any, Kleinpeter feels certain it's harmful to cows because it speeds up their metabolism and increases the chances that they'll contract a painful illness that can shorten their lives. "It's like putting a Volkswagen car in with the Indianapolis 500 racers," he says. "You gotta keep the pedal to the metal the whole way through, and pretty soon that poor little Volkswagen engine's going to burn up."

Kleinpeter Dairy has never used Monsanto's artificial hormone, and the dairy requires other dairy farmers from whom it buys milk to attest that they don't use it, either. At the suggestion of a marketing consultant, the dairy began advertising its milk as coming from rBGH-free cows in 2005, and the label began appearing on Kleinpeter milk cartons and in company literature, including a new Web site of Kleinpeter products that proclaims, "We treat our cows with love . . . not rBGH."

The dairy's sales soared. For Kleinpeter, it was simply a matter of giving consumers more information about their product.

But giving consumers that information has stirred the ire of Monsanto. The company contends that advertising by Kleinpeter and other dairies touting their "no rBGH" milk reflects adversely on Monsanto's product. In a letter to the Federal Trade Commission in February 2007, Monsanto said that, notwithstanding the overwhelming evidence that there is no difference in the milk from cows treated with its product, "milk processors persist in claiming on their labels and in advertisements that the use of rBST is somehow harmful, either to cows or to the people who consume milk from rBST-supplemented cows."

Monsanto called on the commission to investigate what it called the 75 "deceptive advertising and labeling practices" of milk processors such as

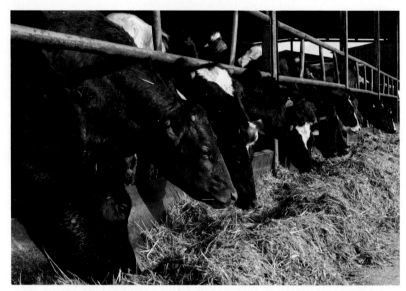

In 1993 the Food and Drug Administration approved the commercial use of rBST, an artificial growth hormone that increases milk production in cows.

Kleinpeter, accusing them of misleading consumers "by falsely claiming that there are health and safety risks associated with milk from rBST-supplemented cows." As noted, Kleinpeter does not make any such claims—he simply states that his milk comes from cows not injected with rBGH.

Monsanto's attempt to get the F.T.C. to force dairies to change their advertising was just one more step in the corporation's efforts to extend its reach into agriculture. After years of scientific debate and public controversy, the F.D.A. in 1993 approved commercial use of rBST, basing its decision in part on studies submitted by Monsanto. That decision allowed the company to market the artificial hormone. The effect of the hormone is to increase milk production, not exactly something the nation needed then—or needs now. The U.S. was actually awash in milk, with the government buying up the surplus to prevent a collapse in prices.

    Monsanto began selling the supplement in 1994 under the name Posilac. Monsanto acknowledges that the possible side effects of rBST for cows include lameness, disorders of the uterus, increased body temperature, di-

Monsanto protested advertisements for milk "From Cows *Not* Treated with rBGH," asserting that the ads implied the possible negative effects of artificial growth hormones and that no studies had shown the hormones to be harmful to cows or people.

gestive problems, and birthing difficulties. Veterinary drug reports note that "cows injected with Posilac are at an increased risk for mastitis," an udder infection in which bacteria and pus may be pumped out with the milk. What's the effect on humans? The F.D.A. has consistently said that the milk produced by cows that receive rBGH is the same as milk from cows that aren't injected: "The public can be confident that milk and meat from BST-treated cows is safe to consume." Nevertheless, some scientists are concerned by the lack of long-term studies to test the additive's impact, especially on children. A Wisconsin geneticist, William von Meyer, observed that when rBGH was approved the longest study on which the F.D.A.'s approval was based covered only a 90-day laboratory test with small animals. "But people drink milk for a lifetime," he noted. Canada and the European Union have never approved the commercial sale of the artificial hormone. Today, nearly 15 years after the F.D.A. approved rBGH, there have still been no long-term studies "to determine the safety of milk from cows that receive artificial growth hormone," says Michael Hansen, senior staff scientist for Consumers Union. Not only have there been no studies, he adds, but the data that does exist all comes from Monsanto. "There is no scientific consensus about the safety," he says.

However F.D.A. approval came about, Monsanto has long been wired into Washington. Michael R. Taylor was a staff attorney and executive assistant to the F.D.A. commissioner before joining a law firm in Washington in 1981, where he worked to secure F.D.A. approval of Monsanto's artificial growth hormone before returning to the F.D.A. as deputy commissioner in 1991. Dr. Michael A. Friedman, formerly the F.D.A.'s deputy commissioner for operations, joined Monsanto in 1999 as a senior vice president. Linda J. Fisher was an assistant administrator at the E.P.A. when she left the agency in 1993. She became a vice president of Monsanto, from 1995 to 2000, only to return to the E.P.A. as deputy administrator the next year. William D. Ruckelshaus, former E.P.A. administrator, and Mickey Kantor, former U.S. trade representative, each served on Monsanto's board after leaving government. Supreme Court justice Clarence Thomas was an attorney in Monsanto's corporate-law department in the 1970s. He wrote the Supreme Court opinion in a crucial G.M.-seed patent-rights case in 2001 that benefited Monsanto and all G.M.-seed companies. Donald Rumsfeld never served on the board or held any office at Monsanto, but Monsanto must occupy a soft spot in the heart of the former defense secretary. Rumsfeld was chairman and C.E.O. of the pharmaceutical maker G. D. Searle & Co. when Monsanto acquired Searle in 1985, after Searle had experienced difficulty in finding a buyer. Rumsfeld's stock and options in Searle were valued at $12 million at the time of the sale.

From the beginning some consumers have consistently been hesitant to drink milk from cows treated with artificial hormones. This is one reason Monsanto has waged so many battles with dairies and regulators over the wording of labels on milk cartons. It has sued at least two dairies and one co-op over labeling.

Critics of the artificial hormone have pushed for mandatory labeling on [80] all milk products, but the F.D.A. has resisted and even taken action against some dairies that labeled their milk "BST-free." Since BST is a natural hormone found in all cows, including those not injected with Monsanto's artificial version, the F.D.A. argued that no dairy could claim that its milk is BST-free. The F.D.A. later issued guidelines allowing dairies to use labels saying their milk comes from "non-supplemented cows," as long as the carton has a disclaimer saying that the artificial supplement does not in any way change the milk. So the milk cartons from Kleinpeter Dairy, for example, carry a label on the front stating that the milk is from cows not treated with rBGH, and the rear panel says, "Government studies have shown no significant difference between milk derived from rBGH-treated and non-rBGH-treated cows." That's not good enough for Monsanto.

The Next Battleground

As more and more dairies have chosen to advertise their milk as "No rBGH," Monsanto has gone on the offensive. Its attempt to force the F.T.C. to look into what Monsanto called "deceptive practices" by dairies trying to distance themselves from the company's artificial hormone was the most recent national salvo. But after reviewing Monsanto's claims, the F.T.C.'s Division of Advertising Practices decided in August 2007 that a "formal investigation and enforcement action is not warranted at this time." The agency found some instances where dairies had made "unfounded health and safety claims," but these were mostly on Web sites, not on milk cartons. And the F.T.C. determined that the dairies Monsanto had singled out all carried disclaimers that the F.D.A. had found no significant differences in milk from cows treated with the artificial hormone.

Blocked at the federal level, Monsanto is pushing for action by the states. In the fall of 2007, Pennsylvania's agriculture secretary, Dennis Wolff, issued an edict prohibiting dairies from stamping milk containers with labels stating their products were made without the use of the artificial hormone. Wolff said such a label implies that competitors' milk is not safe, and noted that non-supplemented milk comes at an unjustified higher price, arguments that Monsanto has frequently made. The ban was to take effect February 1, 2008.

Wolff's action created a firestorm in Pennsylvania (and beyond) from angry consumers. So intense was the outpouring of e-mails, letters, and calls that Pennsylvania governor Edward Rendell stepped in and reversed his agriculture secretary, saying, "The public has a right to complete information about how the milk they buy is produced."

On this issue, the tide may be shifting against Monsanto. Organic dairy products, which don't involve rBGH, are soaring in popularity. Supermarket chains such as Kroger, Publix, and Safeway are embracing them. Some other companies have turned away from rBGH products, including Starbucks, which has banned all milk products from cows treated with rBGH. Although

Monsanto once claimed that an estimated 30 percent of the nation's dairy cows were injected with rBST, it's widely believed that today the number is much lower.

But don't count Monsanto out. Efforts similar to the one in Pennsylva- 85 nia have been launched in other states, including New Jersey, Ohio, Indiana, Kansas, Utah, and Missouri. A Monsanto-backed group called AFACT— American Farmers for the Advancement and Conservation of Technology— has been spearheading efforts in many of these states. AFACT describes itself as a "producer organization" that decries "questionable labeling tactics and activism" by marketers who have convinced some consumers to "shy away from foods using new technology." AFACT reportedly uses the same St. Louis public-relations firm, Osborn & Barr, employed by Monsanto. An Osborn & Barr spokesman told *The Kansas City Star* that the company was doing work for AFACT on a pro bono basis.

Even if Monsanto's efforts to secure across-the-board labeling changes should fall short, there's nothing to stop state agriculture departments from restricting labeling on a dairy-by-dairy basis. Beyond that, Monsanto also has allies whose foot soldiers will almost certainly keep up the pressure on dairies that don't use Monsanto's artificial hormone. Jeff Kleinpeter knows about them, too.

He got a call one day from the man who prints the labels for his milk cartons, asking if he had seen the attack on Kleinpeter Dairy that had been posted on the Internet. Kleinpeter went online to a site called StopLabelingLies, which claims to "help consumers by publicizing examples of false and misleading food and other product labels." There, sure enough, Kleinpeter and other dairies that didn't use Monsanto's product were being accused of making misleading claims to sell their milk.

There was no address or phone number on the Web site, only a list of groups that apparently contribute to the site and whose issues range from disparaging organic farming to downplaying the impact of global warming. "They were criticizing people like me for doing what we had a right to do, had gone through a government agency to do," says Kleinpeter. "We never could get to the bottom of that Web site to get that corrected."

As it turns out, the Web site counts among its contributors Steven Milloy, the "junk science" commentator for FoxNews.com and operator of junkscience.com, which claims to debunk "faulty scientific data and analysis." It may come as no surprise that earlier in his career, Milloy, who calls himself the "junkman," was a registered lobbyist for Monsanto.

Thinking about the Text

1. A good **REPORT** should have a confident **TONE** that informs rather than argues (see p. 266). Does Donald L. Barlett and James B. Steele's report satisfy this criterion? Cite examples from the article to support your answer.

2. Do the dairy products that you consume come from rBGH-fed cows? Has reading this article motivated you to read food labeling more carefully? Should more information be available on labeling? Should it be required? Why or why not?

3. An extensive report about biotechnology, agribusiness, and large-scale litigation runs the risk of being dry and uninteresting to a general audience. Barlett and Steele provide many concrete **EXAMPLES** and **NARRATIVES** to illustrate complex situations and stimulate interest in the topic. The case of Gary Rinehart is one such example. What are three other examples? Which was most interesting or surprising to you? Why?

4. Barlett and Steele say that Monsanto is moving ever closer to controlling the world's agricultural seeds, and they present a variety of **EVIDENCE** to support this conclusion. Do you feel that their evidence is convincing? Why or why not? Is any important kind of evidence lacking? If so, what would it be?

5. Research Monsanto's side of the story. Google "why does Monsanto sue farmers who save seeds?" and read all about it. As you'll see, Monsanto presents its **ARGUMENT** clearly. Whose argument do you find more persuasive—Barlett and Steele's or Monsanto's? Why?

6. Are your food purchases influenced by the information available on packaging about the use of genetically modified organisms or growth hormones? Has Barlett and Steele's article prompted you to think differently about your food choices? Why or why not? Write an essay that explains your reasoning.

Should Everybody Write?

DENNIS BARON

SHOULD EVERYODY WRITE? That's the question to ask when looking at the cyberjunk permeating the World Wide Web. The earlier technologies of the pen, the printing press, and the typewriter, all expanded the authors club, whose members create text rather than just copying it. The computer has expanded opportunities for writers too, only faster, and in greater numbers. More writers means more ideas, more to read. What could be more democratic? More energizing and liberating? But some critics find the glut of internet prose obnoxious, scary, even dangerous. They see too many people, with too little talent, writing about too many things.

Throughout the 5,000-year history of writing, the privilege of authorship was limited to the few: the best, the brightest, the luckiest, those with the right connections. But now, thanks to the computer and the internet, anyone can be a writer: all you need is a laptop, a Wi-Fi card, and a place to sit at Starbucks. The internet allows writers to bypass the usual quality

---

DENNIS BARON is a professor of English and linguistics at the University of Illinois at Urbana-Champaign. His essays and commentaries on language issues have appeared in newspapers and scholarly journals as well as on CNN, NPR, the Voice of America, and the BBC. He tweets @DrGrammar. This piece was first delivered as a lecture with an accompanying slide presentation; this version was published on Baron's blog, *Web of Language*, in 2010.

Today anyone can be a writer.

controls set by reviewers, editors and publishers. Today's authors don't even need a diploma from the Famous Writers School.[1] And they don't need to wait for motivation. Instead of staring helplessly at a blank piece of paper the way writers used to, all they need is a keyboard and right away, they've got something to say.

You may not like all that writing, but somebody does. Because the other thing the internet gives writers is readers, whether it's a nanoaudience of friends and family or a virally large set of FBFs,[2] tweeters, and subscribers to the blog feed. Apparently there are people online willing to read anything.

In the past, writing was restricted to a few diehards and adepts, and the question, "Should everybody write?" if it ever came up, was answered with a resounding, "No!"

Writing itself was a communication technology that came in for plenty of 5 criticism in its early days. Socrates warned that writing was just a shadow of speech. Writing isn't interactive, he tells Phaedrus: you can't ask a text a question, because all it can do is repeat the same words back to you, over and over again. At best, writing is nothing but a mnemonic, a device not to teach us

1. *Famous Writers School:* A correspondence course in writing instruction that was advertised in many magazines in the 1960s and '70s. The school required an aptitude test that would be evaluated by celebrity authors; almost every student was accepted, and investigations revealed that the famous writers did not review any of the submitted tests. [Editor's note]
2. *FBFs:* Facebook friends. [Editor's note]

Visuals can contribute a lot to an argument. See Ch. 33 for tips on using them in your writing.

Socrates and Plato.

new things but to remind us of what we already know. But paradoxically, its danger as a mnemonic is that we will come to rely on it, so that according to Socrates, the ultimate effect of writing will be to weaken memory, not strengthen it. We remember this because Plato wrote it down.

Henry David Thoreau made pencils for a living and sought endorsements for his writing instruments from the likes of Emerson. But in *Walden* Thoreau suggests that not everyone should write, because not everyone has something to say: "We are in great haste to construct a magnetic telegraph from Maine to Texas, but Maine and Texas, it may be, have nothing important to communicate."

Every new communication technology has the capacity to expand the set of who gets to write and talk, who gets to publish and be heard. But expanding the authors club tends to be a by-product of the technologies, not their intent.

When writing came on the scene, very few could read, and fewer still could write. If our interpretation of the Susa stones[3] is correct, writing comes on the scene 7,000–8,000 years ago as a device for Mediterranean traders to track their inventory. The first writers used the technology of shaping and marking stones as a memory device to represent jars of olive oil, goats, and sheep. It was the ancient world's equivalent of a bar tab.

Even after someone repurposed writing as a way to transcribe speech,

3. *Susa stones*: Stones bearing distinctive cup and ring markings (also known as cup-marked stones) that date to prehistoric times. It has been suggested that these markings were used to communicate information. The Susa Valley in Italy contains many examples, but similar markings have been found in coastal Europe and Mexico, Brazil, and India. [Editor's note]

A cup-marked stone from the Susa Valley.

and writers as we might think of them today came on the scene, only a few brave souls were tempted to try the technology, which came with a steep learning curve, required expensive or labor-intensive materials, and for most people, didn't seem to do anything that speech couldn't do better. In order for writing to spread, costs had to come down; materials had to be more easily accessible; writing technologies had to become more user-friendly; and writing itself had to offer something better than communicating the old-fashioned way, by word of mouth.

More and more people began to write, and the new technologies of writ-   10 ing enabled writers to create new genres. But even so, the rise of literacy was painfully slow. Harris reports the literacy rate in Greece during the 4th and 5th century BCE as below 10% (and that was the figure for urban males; literacy among women and in rural areas wasn't much better than 1%). And yet *letters* were everywhere in ancient Greece: inscriptions on public buildings, legal documents, commercial texts, and literary and scientific ones. Even with *arma virumque cano, Gallia est omnes divisa in partes tres,* and *et tu Brute,* literacy rates were no better at the height of Roman civilization. In the Hellenistic period,

Greek coin
c. 6th-century BCE.

the great library at Alexandria may have housed half a million scrolls at its peak, but still the average Egyptian didn't have a library card.

By the 12th century, written documents were becoming *the* way to transact business in England, and scriptoria churned out copies of sacred texts. Still, not everybody wrote. The number of text creators remained small, as did the number of text copiers and the number of people who could sign their names. A late 11th-century Anglo-Norman charter transferring some English land to a French abbey is "signed" by Sir Ilbert de Lacy, his wife Hawise, and King William Rufus, the second son of William the Con-

Charter of King John, 1215, with crosses in place of signatures.

queror. It bears the earliest example of an English knight's seal as an authenticator. But none of the principals could write their names, and it's very likely that none of the signatories, who witnessed the document with three crosses, even made those crosses. The charter was probably created some time after the physical land transfer took place, with the scribe, not the author or the witnesses, filling in all the necessary details to commemorate the act.

Even though the age of print opened up publication opportunities for writers, the printing press is a copying technology, not a technology for text creation. Gutenberg copied Bibles, after all, and while the press eventually created a demand for reading materials—William Caxton was just one early English printer who commissioned original works—many early printed books were reprints of sacred or classical works, or translations, rather than original works.

Gutenberg's press.

Readers as well as writers encountered obstacles. Received wisdom praises Protestantism for spreading literacy as a way to encourage the faithful to read vernacular translations of sacred texts for themselves, but even Martin Luther warned

Martin Luther.

in 1520 of the danger of too many books—in his view, you just need one good book, which you can read over and over—the gift that keeps on giving—not a lot of bad books that will fill your head with error or just confuse you.

And later, in 17th-century England, a period known for the flowering of English letters, where even kings and queens composed poetry and the brand-new Royal Society promoted science writing, literacy in London remained a mere 10% for men, a shocking 1% for women. But who *should* write was not the same population as who *could* write. The route to publication wasn't simple or direct, and even William Shakespeare couldn't put on a play without first getting a license from the Stationers' Company.

Not until the 19th century did literacy in England reach about 70%. And in this period of "exploding" literacy we find explicit concerns being voiced over who gets to read and write, together with a sorting of the literate population into two groups: the functional literates and the literati. Functional literates used their literacy to work in offices, shops, factories. The writers in this group were the copiers, not the creators of text, like the Ruler of the Queen's Navy in Gilbert and Sullivan's *Pirates of Penzance,* a clerk who began his climb from office class to officer class by copying all the letters in a big round hand. The literati were a vastly smaller group whose station in life allowed them to appreciate and exploit a higher education, to create texts, and to consume texts with some sort of higher-order understanding that ordinary people lacked.

The Alphabet is the whole Order of the Letters in any Language, from Alpha and Beta, the two first Letters in the Greek Tongue. The English Alphabet contains twenty six Letters, but others differ

Round-hand writing.

Concerns arose that too much literacy would elevate people above their station in life, causing depression, discontent, or even civil unrest. Victorian essayist Thomas Carlyle complained that the explosion of reading matter made possible by the invention of the steam press in 1810 led to a decline in the quality of what there was to read. At the very least, literacy-controllers argued, reading too much exposed good citizens and the faithful to error and heresy.

Yes, writing expanded the authors club, and later, so did the printing press, and eventually, by the end of the 19th century, literacy levels rose over the 80% mark—in Western Europe and the U.S. But the question of who gets to write has always been a vexed one, and every writing technology came with

Steam-powered printing press.

limits on who gets to be in the authors club—who gets to create texts and not just copy them, and who gets to read—limits that were imposed and that continue to be imposed by governments, by religious authorities, and by social norms. The pencil, the printing press, the typewriter, all expanded opportunities for writers, so long as they could clear the hurdles imposed by publishers, government censors, or the church. In terms of raw numbers, however, all of these technologies benefited copyists more than they benefited the creators of texts.

With the typewriter, as with the press and the big round hand before it, everyone's a copyist. An 1875 ad in *The Nation* for the Remington "Type-Writer" reads, in part,

> a machine now superseding the pen. . . . anyone who can spell can begin to write with it. . . . It is worked without effort, and is not liable to get out of order. . . . Young persons acquire its use with wonderful ease and interest. . . . The benevolent can, by the gift of a "Type-Writer" to a poor, deserving young woman, put her at once in the way of earning a good living as a copyist.

Mark Twain wrote about this newest writing technology,

> I will now claim—until dispossessed—that I was the first person in the world to apply the typewriter to literature. . . . The early machine was full of caprices, full of defects—devilish ones. It had as many immoralities as the machine of today has virtues. After a year or two I found that it was degrading my character, so I thought I would give it to [William Dean] Howells. . . . He took it home to Boston, and my morals began to improve, but his have never recovered. ("The First Writing-Machines")

But to make this early celebrity endorsement of typing, Twain dictated to a typist rather than composing directly at the keyboard.

A 1930s experiment put portable typewriters on the desks of schoolchildren around the country and "proved" that typing students outperformed nontypists on standardized tests in all their subjects. According to teacher reports, typing students even had better handwriting than nontypists. But despite such positive results, two factors combined to keep typewriters off desks: it was the Depression, and schools couldn't afford to replace

Typewriters in the classroom, 1935.

pencils with typewriters; plus it proved too difficult to train the teachers to use typewriters. So instead of a widescale adoption of typewriters to create knowledge, the machines were relegated to dedicated typing classrooms, where students were trained "to copy all the letters" in Courier 12 pt. so that they could eventually win jobs as office clerks.

Unlike other communication technologies, which effectively limited who could read and write, the telephone immediately offered the opportunity for anyone to talk to anyone. Preservers of the social status didn't like this. They sniffed that all you had to have was a nickel for the pay phone, and you could cross social lines at will, entering homes over the wires where you had no hope of being admitted should you knock at the door. But telephones were for talking, not for writing. They might have destabilized social class (and despite complaints about this, it's not clear that they really did), but in the long run people didn't worry so much about the democratizing thrust of the phone, since access to speech was nowhere near as guarded as access to writing. Of course, as we see in this still from Alfred Hitchcock's *Dial M for Murder*, there are times when not everyone should make a call.

Dial M for Murder.

Enter the computer. People worked with text on mainframes, to be sure,

Apple IIe, c. 1983.

but the machines' strength lay in number crunching; they weren't writing machines. The personal computer too was initially billed as a "work processor"—*word* processing, a phrase deployed widely by IBM in its advertising and training literature, was still the province of the typewriter. Like earlier communication technologies, the computer had to overcome some obstacles before it was widely adopted as a writing tool: costs had to come down; the machine had to become user-friendly; and it had to allow writers to do what they used to do with older technologies (pen, typewriter) only better (faster, more efficiently, with a superior product). As word processing software was perfected and hardware improved, the PC replaced the typewriter as the text copying machine of choice in American offices. But along the way something unusual happened: once the PC was hooked up to the internet, copyists of text began to create text as well. And as the personal computer claimed its space in the writer's toolbox, it enabled the creation of new internet-enabled genres: email, web page, IM, blog, social network pages, tweets, and videos.

The computer combined with the internet affords writers something they never really had before, the ability to bypass traditional publication controls. To repeat, all you need is a computer, a Wi-Fi card, and a place to sit at Starbucks. Given that kind of access, more and more of us are finding something to write about, whether momentous or trivial, positive or negative. And while throughout history authors have wondered whether anyone would ever read what they had to say, on the internet there seem to be readers for every text. As a result the authors club is expanding in ways it never has before, and with that expansion comes new concerns about how to control this particular literacy explosion. Because in addition to all the good texts out there in cyberspace, there's pornography, fraud, and hate. And Wikipedia.

In a 1999 *New York Times* op-ed, educational reformer Theodore Roszak complained that computers prevented us from writing. To him, "a child with a pencil in hand is ready to write. A child with a crayon in hand is ready to draw." But the pencil didn't turn us all into writers, and despite the promise of the Famous Artists School,[4] turning us loose with crayons didn't make us all artists either. In contrast, the computer facilitated exactly what Roszak warned that it would prevent, making children, and adults, ready to write, and even Roszak admitted in his critique of the computer-processed word that he much preferred WordPerfect for DOS to the steel-tipped dip pen which had been a torture for him when he learned to write in school.

In any case, today the question, "Should everybody write?" is rendered moot by the fact that everybody appears to be using their computers, and their cell phones, for writing. And so the new question seems to have become, "How can we control these writers and their explosion of text?" Although linguist Geoffrey Nunberg has rightly pointed out that from the earliest days of writing there has always been too much to read, critics bemoan the internet's information glut, and they seek to control access to, or censor outright, the more dangerous parts of cyberspace. There are firewalls and filters to block prohibited topics or content; plus the tethering of devices—like smart phones or the soon-to-be-released iPad—to limit or control what writers can do. But there are other ways that we're controlling authorship that may be less traditional, and a bit more subtle.

As we write on our computers, we're giving up our privacy in ways that 25 writers never did before, not just exposing ourselves—or our personas—on Facebook, Twitter, or a blog, but also by leaving digital fingerprints that allow both businesses and the government to log our keystrokes and track our clicks. Back in 1890, lawyers Samuel D. Warren and Louis D. Brandeis, concerned about the intrusiveness of photographers and journalists, warned in an essay for the *Harvard Law Review,*

> Recent inventions and business methods call attention to the next step which must be taken for the protection of the person, and for securing to the individual . . . the right "to be let alone." Instantaneous photographs and newspaper enterprise have invaded the sacred precincts of private and domestic life; and numerous mechanical devices threaten to make good the prediction that "what is whispered in the closet shall be proclaimed from the house-tops." ("The Right to Privacy")

4. *Famous Artists School*: A correspondence course in painting, illustration/design, and cartooning that began in 1948. This course was the precursor to (and inspiration for) the Famous Writers School. [Editor's note]

Mark Zuckerberg.

We used to think that the internet offered a kind of anonymity that would allow us to express ourselves more freely than ever, taking any pose or persona we want. But if everyone from Sun MicroSystems CEO Scott McNealy, who is supposed to have said back in 1999, "You have zero privacy anyway. Get over it," to Facebook founder Mark Zuckerberg, who insisted in an interview this year that his company is only trying to adapt to the needs of Facebook users, then privacy is indeed dead, even if only college students, Google, and the NSA[5] are willing to admit it. But now that everyone is writing, we're going beyond the simple invasions of privacy outlined by Warren and Brandeis to a more complex inversion of public and private. Putting ourselves online allows other users not just to watch our online behavior and send us context-motivated ads or pack us off to Guantanamo for a nice waterboarding session, but also to remix the posts they find or create mashups of our posts with theirs.

Accompanying the "everyone is writing" phenomenon is a growing amateurization of online text, which is democratic in spirit but which also calls into question the nature of intellectual property, the writing, graphics, and music that we post online. Internet-published text means writers are easily ripped off, and plagiarism has become that much easier—as we see in everything from schoolsucks.com and the online term paper mills to the "creative" plagiarism of the award-winning teenage German novelist Helene Hegemann. But every communication technology brings with it opportunities for fraud and cheating, and eventually we manage to get enough

5. *NSA*: National Security Agency. [Editor's note]

safeguards in place so that any counterfeits that get past the controls can simply be chalked up to the cost of doing business.

Jonathan Zittrain, a professor of internet law and computer science at Harvard, warns that even with plagiarism and mashups, too strict an adherence to traditional notions of copyright may limit the generativity and inventiveness of the Web. *Wired* editor Kevin Kelly goes even further, simply announcing that writers will have to hang on to their day jobs, because royalties will simply dry up because law or no law, online text will inevitably be treated as communal property.

The late John Updike pushed back against Kelly, and historian Anthony Grafton suggests that the age of the seamless cybertext is far from a reality. But since most writers don't live off their royalties anyway, there's a bigger danger to the status of authorship than a revised economic model for writing. It's the growing centralization of online services, with Apple, Microsoft, Google, Amazon, and Wikipedia controlling larger and larger blocks of our information and what we can do with that information (and maybe Zappos controlling the shoes we buy). This represents a particular kind of monopolization of our data by for-profit corporations, who unlike most libraries or public utilities are responsible not to the people as a whole, but to shareholders and boards of directors. The mission of libraries is typically openness and accessibility, but Google & Co. are bastions of secrecy and digital rights management, renting you the privilege of reading online, but retaining ownership of text and limiting access by distributing it according to a carefully calculated business model.

Add to this corporatization of the data stream the trend toward cloud computing. With the spread of the next generation of computers—netbooks, smartphones, and tablets, all of them devices with limited storage space— we will be encouraged more and more to turn to software located not on our hard drives but on a remote server. For some users, that server will be at home or at their university or office. But for most, it will be a Google or Microsoft or other proprietary server, accessible by subscription. And we will be encouraged/forced to cede control of our data to these remote servers as well. The advantage of cloud computing is that all our digital files will be available to us, no matter where we are or what computer or computer-like device we're using to access it. The disadvantage is that our texts will slip from our control to the control of the for-profit corporation that manages the cloud.

Is that so bad? Just as we trade convenience for accuracy when we rely 30 on Wikipedia as our first resort for information, we'll trade convenience for

Diagram of cloud computing via remote server.

control, which may be worth the trade until Amazon decides it doesn't like what's on our Kindle and takes it back; until Facebook decides we've committed an illegal act and blocks us; until Google loses our data or turns it over to the government, or to our employer, or some other third party, with or without a subpoena or warrant. Or until I log on and instead of the draft of my next book I get the dreaded Error 404, file not found.

Of course there's always someone who objects to a new technology rollout. Critics of the first wheel probably argued that round technologies sped up the pace of life too much compared to the old way of doing things, preferring animals for locomotion or simply keeping their feet planted firmly on the ground. And of course, as we see from this 1956 ad for a Chrysler with in-dash record changer, not all new technologies catch on. But the computer is now the writer's tool of choice, and even though pencils still sell in the billions annually, more and more people are joining the authors club and uploading text to the internet.

NEW! — A CAR PHONOGRAPH!

Chrysler introduces the first car phonograph — the Highway Hi Fi — a compact unit that is installed below the instrument panel in the center of the car. It operates electrically, using the regular radio loud speaker. The 16 rpm record will play for forty-five minutes. Have your dealer demonstrate this great new pleasure feature.

Within-dashboard record changer.

One Laptop per Child Program.

So, finally, again, I ask, should everybody write? More people are writing now than ever before, if by writing we mean creating text for readers—whether those readers consist of a nanoaudience of friends and family or a virally large set of FBFs, Twitter followers, or other denizens of cyberspace. More people are writing in North America, in Europe, and even in parts of the world where individuals have not typically had a public voice. Yet one critic of the One Laptop per Child Program[6] echoes Victorian concerns of educating people beyond their station when he argues that giving computers to masses of children will create discontent: "Access to eBay and YouTube isn't going to give them clean water and freedom from disease. But it may help breed resentment and discontent where it hasn't been before" (Gene Spafford, cited in Zittrain's *The Future of the Internet and How to Stop It*, 240). Functional literacy remains a goal, but creative literacy—putting the tools of meaning production into everyone's hands—is still seen as too destabilizing, and not just in China or Myanmar, but also in Silicon Valley.

For those who are already writing, the question is becoming: are they producing anything worth reading? We may not think so—to repeat, there's a lot of junk being cranked out. But then again, somebody seems to think so—there seems to be no lack of readers for even the most inane of cyberposts. Previous technologies of writing did not guarantee quality either. There are plenty of clay tablets, manuscripts, printed books, mimeographed screeds and Xeroxed memos, that should never have seen the light of day. To

6. *One Laptop per Child*: A nonprofit organization that aims to distribute inexpensive but durable computers to children throughout the developing world. [Editor's note]

Nunberg's observation that there has always been too much to read, I might add that there has always been a lot of stuff that no one wants to read.

So, should everybody write? Sure, because it increases the chances that there will be something you will want to read, and you can just ignore the rest. Perhaps the more interesting question is, Will everyone *continue* to write? Cell phone users are texting more than they're talking, and computer users everywhere are creating and publishing text at growing rates. Most digital texts are short, and most aren't "keepers," even though it turns out to be difficult to wipe out a text once it's been uploaded. But there are explosions of fan fiction, online essays, blogs, extended chats and commentaries, and explorations of text, audio and video, and that sort of text production doesn't seem to be slowing down much.

Perhaps the predicted shift from PCs and laptops to tethered devices like 35 the iPad, which really promise to be entertainment devices rather than text-production machines, could signal an eventual decline in internet-enabled authorship. These are machines that permit text entry, though they're billed as entertainment machines, not writing tools. I don't really think the iPad will prompt a decline in card-carrying authors. After all, the original PCs were not text-production machines either. What's more likely to happen is that writers will see the usefulness of tablets, as we once saw, a mere 30 years ago, the usefulness of PCs, for what we do. And developers will reengineer tablets so that, while they satisfy the needs of gamers and video watchers and the readers of ebooks and newspapers, they also allow us to key in and upload our textual, musical, and visual creations.

Maybe one day we'll all use *Star Trek*–like communicators pinned to our chests to create our texts—just tap and talk—but I think that speech-to-text software is still a long way off, and for the near term we'll be keyboarding, and doing so in growing numbers. No matter what you or I think of their products, writers gaining access to the internet seem to have no trouble finding a subject to write about, and no trouble finding readers to read their output. However new communication technologies destabilize the conditions of writers and readers, writers will continue to find ways to get the word out, and new genres to clothe the word in.

Thinking about the Text

1. Dennis Baron **ANALYZES** the very ordinary activity of writing from a historical perspective. A thorough history of the subject, of course, could not have been presented in such a brief article, so Baron carefully selects the information he presents and weaves it into a cohesive whole. **SUMMARIZE** the aspects of writing that Baron chose to trace. What is the unifying theme that pulls them all together?

2. We generally take for granted all of the contemporary technologies of writing that Baron describes; many of us, in fact, have never lived in a world without them. How would your life be different if you could write only with a pen or pencil? In what ways would your social circle be different? How about your work and school life? What changes would need to take place in your daily routine?

3. Baron's article includes many illustrations, not all of which are directly referred to in the text. How do these contribute to your comprehension of his argument? How important are they to it? Which of them do you find particularly effective? Do any just seem distracting? Why do you suppose that Baron included so many illustrations?

4. Baron mentions that in the nineteenth century, concerns were raised that "too much literacy" might cause "depression, discontent, or even civil unrest" (16). At first glance, this claim may seem amusing, even ridiculous, but it bears consideration, if only to be able to refute it. **REFLECT** as openly and as deeply as you can about your own life and the world around you. Depression and discontent certainly exist, as well as civil unrest. Has literacy made any contribution to them?

5. Most modern objects and activities don't have as obviously long a history as writing does, but a little research may reveal deeper roots than you'd realized. Choose a favorite object or activity that you consider very new (skateboards or nail art, perhaps), and do some historical research about it. Write an essay **REPORTING** on the social effects your topic has produced, incorporating the history that you discover.

The Sanctuary of School

LYNDA BARRY

I **WAS 7 YEARS OLD** the first time I snuck out of the house in the dark. It was winter and my parents had been fighting all night. They were short on money and long on relatives who kept "temporarily" moving into our house because they had nowhere else to go.

My brother and I were used to giving up our bedroom. We slept on the couch, something we actually liked because it put us that much closer to the light of our lives, our television.

At night when everyone was asleep, we lay on our pillows watching it with the sound off. We watched Steve Allen's mouth moving. We watched Johnny Carson's mouth moving. We watched movies filled with gangsters shooting machine guns into packed rooms, dying soldiers hurling a last grenade and beautiful women crying at windows. Then the sign-off finally came and we tried to sleep.

LYNDA BARRY is an artist, cartoonist, and teacher, known for her comic strip *Ernie Pook's Comeek* and graphic memoir *One! Hundred! Demons!* (2002) as well as for graphic works on the relationship between creativity and drawing like *What It Is* (2008) and *Picture This* (2010). Now a professor of interdisciplinary creativity at the University of Wisconsin's Image Lab, Barry is the author most recently of *Syllabus: Notes from an Accidental Professor* (2014). The essay here was originally published in the *New York Times* in 1992, when public schools were experiencing severe cutbacks.

The morning I snuck out, I woke up filled with a panic about needing to get to school. The sun wasn't quite up yet but my anxiety was so fierce that I just got dressed, walked quietly across the kitchen and let myself out the back door.

It was quiet outside. Stars were still out. Nothing moved and no one was   5
in the street. It was as if someone had turned the sound off on the world.

I walked the alley, breaking thin ice over the puddles with my shoes. I didn't know why I was walking to school in the dark. I didn't think about it. All I knew was a feeling of panic, like the panic that strikes kids when they realize they are lost.

That feeling eased the moment I turned the corner and saw the dark outline of my school at the top of the hill. My school was made up of about 15 nondescript portable classrooms set down on a fenced concrete lot in a rundown Seattle neighborhood, but it had the most beautiful view of the Cascade Mountains. You could see them from anywhere on the playfield and you could see them from the windows of my classroom—Room 2.

I walked over to the monkey bars and hooked my arms around the cold metal. I stood for a long time just looking across Rainier Valley. The sky was beginning to whiten and I could hear a few birds.

In a perfect world my absence at home would not have gone unnoticed. I would have had two parents in a panic to locate me, instead of two parents in a panic to locate an answer to the hard question of survival during a deep financial and emotional crisis.

But in an overcrowded and unhappy home, it's incredibly easy for any   10
child to slip away. The high levels of frustration, depression and anger in my house made my brother and me invisible. We were children with the sound turned off. And for us, as for the steadily increasing number of neglected children in this country, the only place where we could count on being noticed was at school.

"Hey there, young lady. Did you forget to go home last night?" It was Mr. Gunderson, our janitor, whom we all loved. He was nice and he was funny and he was old with white hair, thick glasses and an unbelievable number of keys. I could hear them jingling as he walked across the playfield. I felt incredibly happy to see him.

He let me push his wheeled garbage can between the different portables as he unlocked each room. He let me turn on the lights and raise the

window shades and I saw my school slowly come to life. I saw Mrs. Holman, our school secretary, walk into the office without her orange lipstick on yet. She waved.

I saw the fifth-grade teacher, Mr. Cunningham, walking under the breezeway eating a hard roll. He waved.

And I saw my teacher, Mrs. Claire LeSane, walking toward us in a red coat and calling my name in a very happy and surprised way, and suddenly my throat got tight and my eyes stung and I ran toward her crying. It was something that surprised us both.

It's only thinking about it now, 28 years later, that I realize I was crying 15 from relief. I was with my teacher, and in a while I was going to sit at my desk, with my crayons and pencils and books and classmates all around me, and for the next six hours I was going to enjoy a thoroughly secure, warm and stable world. It was a world I absolutely relied on. Without it, I don't know where I would have gone that morning.

Mrs. LeSane asked me what was wrong and when I said "Nothing," she seemingly left it at that. But she asked me if I would carry her purse for her, an honor above all honors, and she asked if I wanted to come into Room 2 early and paint.

She believed in the natural healing power of painting and drawing for troubled children. In the back of her room there was always a drawing table and an easel with plenty of supplies, and sometimes during the day she would come up to you for what seemed like no good reason and quietly ask if you wanted to go to the back table and "make some pictures for Mrs. LeSane." We all had a chance at it—to sit apart from the class for a while to paint, draw and silently work out impossible problems on 11×17 sheets of newsprint.

Drawing came to mean everything to me. At the back table in Room 2, I learned to build myself a life preserver that I could carry into my home.

We all know that a good education system saves lives, but the people of this country are still told that cutting the budget for public schools is necessary, that poor salaries for teachers are all we can manage and that art, music and all creative activities must be the first to go when times are lean.

Before- and after-school programs are cut and we are told that public schools 20 are not made for baby-sitting children. If parents are neglectful temporarily or permanently, for whatever reason, it's certainly sad, but their unlucky children must fend for themselves. Or slip through the cracks. Or wander in a dark night alone.

We are told in a thousand ways that not only are public schools not important, but that the children who attend them, the children who need them most, are not important either. We leave them to learn from the blind eye of a television, or to the mercy of "a thousand points of light"[1] that can be as far away as stars.

I was lucky. I had Mrs. LeSane. I had Mr. Gunderson. I had an abundance of art supplies. And I had a particular brand of neglect in my home that allowed me to slip away and get to them. But what about the rest of the kids who weren't as lucky? What happened to them?

By the time the bell rang that morning I had finished my drawing and Mrs. LeSane pinned it up on the special bulletin board she reserved for drawings from the back table. It was the same picture I always drew—a sun in the corner of a blue sky over a nice house with flowers all around it.

Mrs. LeSane asked us to please stand, face the flag, place our right hands over our hearts and say the Pledge of Allegiance. Children across the country do it faithfully. I wonder now when the country will face its children and say a pledge right back.

> Describing how one child was saved by art classes helps argue for funding school programs. See Ch. 18 for more argument strategies.

1. *"A thousand points of light"*: A phrase used by President George H. W. Bush to refer to the many private, nonprofit community organizations that he hoped would step in to help people in need when government-sponsored social programs were cut. [Editor's note]

Thinking about the Text

1. Lynda Barry begins her narrative by revealing some painful personal information, which leads to a damning criticism of the state of education in the United States. Does her personal anecdote enhance her political argument? damage it? How well do these two elements of her essay complement one another? Explain your answer, citing evidence from the text.

2. It could be argued that the art opportunities in Barry's school were more beneficial to her than to other students because she was always artistically inclined and even went on to become a professional artist—or even that there is no reason to have art instruction in elementary schools at all because so few children actually become artists. How would you respond to that argument? Agree or disagree, presenting **EVIDENCE** from your own school experiences.

3. Barry uses the expression "the sound off" or "the sound turned off" three times in the essay (3, 5, 10). In which instances is it meant literally and in which figuratively? How does the repetition of this language help make the point of her narrative?

4. Barry concludes her essay with a call for the United States and its education system to make a "pledge" to children (24). Although her proposals are not spelled out, what can you infer about what Barry is asking the schools to do? Provide **EXAMPLES** from the text that indicate what she thinks is important.

5. Did you ever have a teacher who, in the course of simply doing her or his job, helped you get through a hard time or a tremendous struggle? Write a **NAR-RATIVE** about an experience you had with a memorable teacher, and relate your experience in some way to your adult life.

Compulsory Reading

ALISON BECHDEL

ALISON BECHDEL is a cartoonist and writer. Her serialized comic strip, *Dykes to Watch Out For*, ran in dozens of periodicals from 1983 to 2008. In 2006 she published *Fun Home: A Family Tragicomic*, a graphic memoir that centers on her relationship with her father and addresses matters of gender, sexual orientation, and family—and that has been adapted into a Tony Award–winning musical. Her most recent book, *Are You My Mother? A Comic Drama* (2012), centers on her relationship with her mother. She's currently at work on another memoir, *The Secret to Superhuman Strength*, a book that will focus on her obsession with skiing, running, weight lifting, yoga, and other forms of exercise. In a 2012 interview in the *New Yorker*, Bechdel states that "by looking inward deeply, I'm trying to get outside myself and connect with other people." In 2014, she was awarded a MacArthur "genius" fellowship.

You may have heard of the Bechdel Test. To pass, a movie, TV show, or book has to have at least two female characters talking to each other about something other than a man. Interesting then that Alison Bechdel herself says she's the "number one fan" of *Sex and the City*, a show that would never pass her test. "I would never watch any television or movies if I only watched shows that passed the test," she once explained. Go to bechdeltest.com to see how many of your favorite films have passed the Bechdel Test.

The following piece was written originally for *Entertainment Weekly*'s 1,000th issue, in 2008. If you like it, you can find more of Bechdel's work on her blog, dykestowatchoutfor.com, or on *Twitter* @AlisonBechdel.

THIS COERCIVE PARADIGM BEGAN TO IMPINGE ON MY INNOCENT READING PLEASURE IN OTHER, LESS SUBTLE WAYS.

ARE YOU READING THAT *AGAIN?*

HIGH SCHOOL ENGLISH TEACHER!

SO?

MY FATHER GREW UP IN A BOOKLESS HOME, AND LITERATURE HAD BEEN HIS SALVATION. BUT NOW HE'D BECOME AN ANNOYING MISSIONARY.

READ THIS.

WHAT'S IT ABOUT?

A MAGICAL BIRD-GIRL WHO LIVES IN THE JUNGLE.

THAT'S THE MOST BORING THING I EVER HEARD OF.

GREEN MANSIONS

I DEVELOPED A SEVERE AVERSION TO READING ANYTHING ANYONE ELSE TOLD ME TO, EVEN MY FRIENDS.

YOU'LL LOVE THESE! YOU SHOULD START WITH THIS ONE!

FIVE CHIL-DREN AND IT

THE WORKS OF E. NESBIT, LOST TO ME FOREVER.

ONE DAY WHEN I WAS 11 OR 12, DAD TRIED A NEW TACK.

FIVE DOLLARS TO THE FIRST ONE OF YOU WHO READS *HUCKLEBERRY FINN.*

GIMME ONE!

EIGHTH TIME

I DIDN'T WANT TO GIVE HIM THE SATIS-FACTION, BUT FIVE BUCKS WAS A LOT OF MONEY IN THOSE DAYS.

I WAS RATHER ANNOYED TO FIND MYSELF SO CAUGHT UP IN THE STORY. FOR CHAPTERS ON END, I FORGOT ABOUT THE CONTEST.

AND WHEN I DID INDEED BEAT MY YOUNGER BROTHERS TO THE FINISH, I COULDN'T HELP FEELING A TWINGE OF SUSPICION.

"I BEEN THERE BEFORE." DONE!

NO FAIR!

ALTHOUGH I'D NEVER READ *TOM SAWYER,* THE BOOK'S PREQUEL, EVERYONE KNOWS THE STORY ABOUT THE FENCE—HOW TOM TRICKS THE OTHER KIDS INTO WHITEWASHING BY PRETENDING IT'S FUN.

I'LL GIVE YOU FIVE WHEN YOU FINISH IT, TOO.

THIS INCIDENT LEFT ME BITTER.

I WOULD SHOW MY FATHER. I WOULD FORCE **MYSELF** TO READ THINGS. WHEN I WAS 14, I BEGAN A GRIM LIST.

Summer Reading
1. 1984
2. Animal Farm
3. The Diary of Anne Frank
4. Romeo & Juliet
5. The Count of Monte Cristo

THE VARIOUSLY IMPRISONED AND DOOMED PROTAGONISTS REFLECTED MY OWN JOYLESS SELF-INCARCERATION.

ONE IN A SERIES OF SECOND-DEGREE BURNS.

COUNT OF MONTE CRISTO

I ACTUALLY LIKED ANNE FRANK. AND I GOT THROUGH ORWELL, THOUGH I MISSED ALL THE ALLEGORY. BUT THAT WAS AS FAR AS I GOT WITH MY LIST.

I CAN'T HELP BUT THINK OF MR. KNIGHTLEY'S DRY OBSERVATION ON A SIMILAR PROJECT UNDERTAKEN BY EMMA WOODHOUSE.

'Emma has been meaning to read more ever since she was twelve years old. I have seen a great many lists of her drawing up at various times of books that she meant to read regularly through – and very good lists they were – very well chosen, and very neatly arranged – sometimes alphabetically, and sometimes by some other rule. The list she drew up when only fourteen – I remember thinking it did her judgment so much credit, that I preserved it some time; and I dare say she may have made out a very good list now.

THANK GOD JANE AUSTEN WASN'T IN THE AUTHORS DECK OR I WOULD HAVE NO WAY OF KNOWING THIS.

I LEFT THE COUNT OF MONTE CRISTO LANGUISHING IN THE CHATEAU D'IF BECAUSE I HAD DISCOVERED A KIND OF READING THAT WAS INFINITELY MORE COMPELLING.

THE FORBIDDEN KIND.

MY PARENTS KEPT THE GOOD STUFF UP HERE.

"A MAN OUGHT TO READ JUST AS INCLINATION LEADS HIM; FOR WHAT HE READS AS A TASK WILL DO HIM LITTLE GOOD."

I ABSOLUTELY MUST GET TO BOSWELL'S LIFE OF JOHNSON ONE OF THESE DAYS.

THUP!

IF YOU REALLY WANT YOUR CHILDREN TO READ SOMETHING, FOR GOD'S SAKE, KEEP IT TO YOURSELF.

GUARD THAT BOOK LIKE A PRECIOUS SECRET.

SHELVE IT JUDICIOUSLY.

AND UNDER NO CIRCUMSTANCES PUT IT ON A LIST.

NOW, IF YOU'LL EXCUSE ME, I HAVE SOME READING TO DO.

OH... YOU'RE STILL HERE?!

I'M JUST CHECKING OUT THESE CLASSICAL ALLUSIONS.

WHAT!

Thinking about the Text

1. Alison Bechdel's narrative describes her relationship with reading throughout her life. What is the point of her narrative? In other words, what exactly is her **ARGUMENT**?

2. Bechdel suggests that failing to read is sinful, and she writes of feeling guilty for not reading enough literary novels. Do you enjoy reading? Do you enjoy the reading that you have to do for school? Why or why not? Whatever your relationship to reading, what might make it better?

3. Bechdel's drawings aren't the only element of her narrative that creates images; she uses **FIGURATIVE LANGUAGE** and allusions as well. Find two examples and explain what they contribute to the effect of the narrative.

4. Bechdel advocates the use of reverse psychology to get children to read, suggesting that restricting access to certain books will make them more enticing. Do you think this is an effective strategy? Why or why not? Have you ever read something just because you believed that you weren't supposed to?

5. Write a **LITERACY NARRATIVE** of your lifelong experience with reading (it needn't be in graphic form). Make sure that your narrative has a clear point that readers can identify—and that you provide evidence from your own experience to support that point.

How a National Food Policy Could Save Millions of American Lives

MARK BITTMAN, MICHAEL POLLAN, RICARDO SALVADOR & OLIVIER DE SCHUTTER

MARK BITTMAN writes about food and is a co-founder of The Purple Carrot, a vegan meal-kit delivery company. MICHAEL POLLAN writes about food, agriculture, and health and teaches journalism at the University of California at Berkeley. RICARDO SALVADOR serves as director of the food and environment program at the Union of Concerned Scientists. OLIVIER DE SCHUTTER teaches law at the Université Catholique de Louvain in Belgium. Together, they wrote this op-ed proposing a national food policy, first published in the *Washington Post* in 2014. You can follow them all on *Twitter* @Bittman, @michaelpollan, @cadwego, and @DeSchutterUNSR.

HOW WE PRODUCE AND CONSUME FOOD has a bigger impact on Americans' well-being than any other human activity. The food industry is the largest sector of our economy; food touches everything from our health to the environment, climate change, economic inequality and the federal budget. Yet we have no food policy—no plan or agreed-upon principles—for managing American agriculture or the food system as a whole.

That must change.

The food system and the diet it's created have caused incalculable damage to the health of our people and our land, water and air. If a foreign power were to do such harm, we'd regard it as a threat to national security, if not an act of war, and the government would formulate a comprehensive plan and marshal resources to combat it. (The administration even named an Ebola czar to respond to a disease that threatens few Americans.) So when hundreds of thousands of annual deaths are preventable—as the deaths from the chronic diseases linked to the modern American way of eating surely are—preventing those needless deaths is a national priority.

A national food policy would do that, by investing resources to guarantee that:

- All Americans have access to healthful food;
- Farm policies are designed to support our public health and environmental objectives;
- Our food supply is free of toxic bacteria, chemicals and drugs;
- Production and marketing of our food are done transparently;
- The food industry pays a fair wage to those it employs;
- Food marketing sets children up for healthful lives by instilling in them a habit of eating real food;
- Animals are treated with compassion and attention to their well-being;
- The food system's carbon footprint is reduced, and the amount of carbon sequestered on farmland is increased;
- The food system is sufficiently resilient to withstand the effects of climate change.

Only those with a vested interest in the status quo would argue against 5 creating public policies with these goals. Now weigh them against the reality that our current policies and public investments have given us:

A few statistics make this proposal much stronger. Find out how to use statistics in your writing on pp. 394–95.

Because of unhealthy diets, 100 years of progress in improving public health and extending lifespan has been reversed. Today's children are expected to live shorter lives than their parents. In large part, this is because a third of these children will develop Type 2 diabetes, formerly rare in children and a preventable disease that reduces life expectancy by several years. At the same time, our fossil-fuel-dependent food and agriculture system is responsible for more greenhouse gas emissions than any other sector of the economy but energy. And the exploitative labor practices of the farming and fast-food industries are responsible for much of the rise in income inequality in America.

We find ourselves in this situation because government policy in these areas is made piecemeal. Diet-related chronic disease, food safety, marketing to children, labor conditions, wages for farm and food-chain workers, immigration, water and air quality, greenhouse gas emissions, and support for farmers: These issues are all connected to the food system. Yet they are overseen by eight federal agencies. Amid this incoherence, special interests thrive and the public good suffers.

In the early days of the Obama administration, there were encouraging signs that the new president recognized the problems of our food system and wanted to do something about them. He spoke about the importance of safety, transparency and competition in the food industry.

Since then, the first lady has made childhood obesity her signature issue, elevating food on the national agenda. But as Michelle Obama raises awareness of healthy eating and tries to reform school lunch, she is struggling to undo the damage caused by outmoded agricultural policies that her husband has left largely undisturbed. The result is the spectacle of Michelle Obama warning Americans to avoid high-fructose corn syrup at the same time the president is signing farm bills that subsidize its production.

The contradictions of our government's policies around food become 10 clear as soon as you compare the federal recommendations for the American diet, known as MyPlate, with the administration's agricultural policies. While MyPlate recommends a diet of 50 percent vegetables and fruits, the administration devotes less than 1 percent of farm subsidies to support the research, production and marketing of those foods. More than 60 percent of that funding subsidizes the production of corn and other grains—food that is mostly fed to animals, converted to fuel for cars or processed into precisely the sort of junk the first lady is urging us to avoid.

First Lady Michelle Obama joins the lunch line at Parklawn Elementary School in Alexandria, Virginia, where she spoke about the USDA's improved nutrition standards for school lunches.

How could one government be advancing two such diametrically opposed goals? By failing to recognize that an agricultural policy is not the same as a food policy—and that the former does not necessarily contribute to public health.

Our food system is largely a product of agricultural policies that made sense when the most important public health problem concerning food was the lack of it and when the United States saw "feeding the world" as its mission. These policies succeeded in boosting the productivity of American farmers, yet today they are obsolete and counterproductive, providing billions in public support to an industry that churns out a surfeit of unhealthy calories—while at the same time undermining the ability of the world's farmers to make a living from their land.

These farm policies have nourished an agricultural-industrial complex before which the president and the first lady seem powerless. The administration's early efforts to use antitrust laws to protect farmers and consumers from agribusiness oligopolies were quietly dropped. Promises to regulate the use of antibiotics in animal agriculture—widely acknowledged as a threat to public health—resulted in toothless voluntary guidelines from the Food and Drug Administration.

When it came to regulating methane, one of the most potent greenhouse gases, the Environmental Protection Agency proposed stringent rules for the energy industry—and another voluntary program for agriculture, the single biggest emitter of the gas. And in February the president signed yet another business-as-usual farm bill, which continues to encourage the dumping of cheap but unhealthy calories in the supermarket.

These policies and the diet they sponsor threaten to undermine President Obama's Affordable Care Act. The government now finds itself in the absurd position of financing both sides in the war on Type 2 diabetes, a disease that, along with its associated effects, now costs $245 billion, or 23 percent of the national deficit in 2012, to treat each year. The government subsidizes soda with one hand, while the other writes checks to pay for insulin pumps. This is not policy; this is insanity. [15]

The good news is that solutions are within reach—precisely because the problems are largely a result of government policies. We know that the government has the power to reshape the food system because it has already done so at least once—when President Richard Nixon rejiggered farm policy to boost production of corn and soy to drive down food prices.

Of course, reforming the food system will ultimately depend on a Congress that has for decades been beholden to agribusiness, one of the most powerful lobbies on Capitol Hill. As long as food-related issues are treated as discrete rather than systemic problems, congressional committees in thrall to special interests will be able to block change.

But there is something the president can do now, on his own, to break that deadlock, much as he has done with climate change. In the next State of the Union address, he should announce an executive order establishing a national policy for food, health and well-being. By officially acknowledging the problem and by setting forth a few simple principles on which most Americans agree, the introduction of such a policy would create momentum for reform. By elevating food and farming to a matter of public concern rather than a parochial interest, the president can make it much more difficult for the interests of agribusiness to prevail over those of public and environmental health.

The national food policy could be developed and implemented by a new White House council, which would coordinate among, say, the Department of Health and Human Services and the USDA to align agricultural policies with public health objectives, and the EPA and the USDA to make sure food production doesn't undermine environmental goals. A national food policy would lay the foundation for a food system in which healthful choices are accessible to all and in which it becomes possible to nourish ourselves without exploiting other people or nature.

As Obama begins the last two years of his administration facing an 20 obstructionist Republican Congress, this is an area where he can act on his own—and his legacy may depend on him doing so. For the president won't be able to achieve his goals for health care, climate change, immigration and economic inequality—the four pillars of his second term—if he doesn't address the food system and its negative impact on those issues.

There are precedents for such a policy. Already a handful of states are developing food charters, and scores of U.S. cities have established food policy councils to expand access to healthful food. Brazil and Mexico are far ahead of the United States in developing national food policies. Mexico's recognition of food as a key driver of public health led to the passage last year of a national tax on junk food and soda, which in the first year has reduced consumption of sugary beverages by 10 percent and increased consumption of water.

Brazil has had a national food policy since 2004. In the city of Belo Horizonte that policy—coupled with an investment of 2 percent of the local budget in food-access and farmer-support programs—has reduced poverty by 25 percent and child mortality by 60 percent, and provided access to credit for 2 million farmers, all within a decade.

A well-articulated national food policy in the United States would make it much more difficult for Congress to pass bills that fly in its face. The very act of elevating food among the issues the White House addresses would build public support for reforms. And once the government embraces a goal such as "We guarantee the right of every American to eat food that is healthy, green, fair and affordable"—it becomes far more difficult to pass or sign a farm bill that erodes those guarantees.

Think of the food system as something that works for us rather than exploits us, something that encourages health rather than undermines it. That is the food system the people of the United States deserve, and Obama, in his remaining time in office, can begin to build it.

Thinking about the Text

1. These authors argue that if the United States can appoint an "Ebola czar" to protect the populace from a disease that poses a small and remote threat, then it certainly could institute a national policy regarding food, something that touches *everyone*. Do you find this reasoning persuasive? Why or why not?

2. What **EVIDENCE** do the authors use to show that their proposal would "save millions of American lives"? Point to places in the article where they cite facts, examples, anecdotes, or other evidence. Is it enough to convince you?

3. The **PROPOSAL** for a national food policy is a new idea, but these authors are responding to an ongoing debate about food policy, regulation, and eating practices in the United States. How well do the authors anticipate and address other **POINTS OF VIEW**? Point to specific examples in the text. Does their handling of other viewpoints enhance their argument? Why or why not?

4. If a national food policy such as this were in place, how might your eating habits and food options be different? Would you have access to better food in your town or neighborhood? Might food be more affordable? Would you be more interested in working in a food-related industry? How might the proposed policies change your lifestyle and your perspective on food?

5. The benefits of a national food policy seem attractive, and these authors make their plan sound quite feasible despite its ambitious scope. If you could recommend that the government focus its efforts on just one of the areas they suggest, which would you choose? Why? Write an essay in which you argue for one area of government action on the grounds of practicality, urgency, or both. Support your argument with examples, factual data, and other evidence gathered from recent news and reports.

Tell Me Something

MICHELLE CACHO-NEGRETE

O N A SHELF IN MY HOME I have my brother's record albums, their covers worn with handling, sticky residue evidence of his fondness for candy. Johnny Mathis, Frankie Lyman, the Drifters, Martha and the Vandellas: "Oh, Jimmy Mack, when are you coming back?" On the dull black vinyl of Smokey Robinson and the Miracles, a fingerprint offers itself up like a message from the past. As I slide the record back into its jacket, a photograph tumbles into my lap: my brother, perhaps twelve, eyes closed, pretend microphone in hand, body leaning into the music. I can hear his off-key voice trying to be like Smokey's: "I'm on the outside looking in, and I don't want to be." Everything else in the picture is blurred, as though my brother were the only solid thing.

Everything of my brother's fits on a couple of shelves: boxes of records, books, a few photographs. When you're killed at eighteen, you don't leave much behind.

In December 1968 I was recovering from the birth of my first child three months earlier. A hemorrhage during delivery had left me anemic, and the

MICHELLE CACHO-NEGRETE, a nonfiction writer and psychotherapist, teaches writing in Maine and online. This piece was originally published in 2008 in the *Sun*, an "ad-free monthly magazine that for more than thirty years has used words and photographs to invoke the splendor and heartache of being human."

days had turned hallucinogenic, constructed of jagged shards of color. My brother had shipped out to Vietnam in October. My marriage was faltering. My mother was angry at me for not having married a Jew. My Cuban husband worked six twelve-hour days a week at Grumman Aircraft Engineering Corporation, a leading military contractor. The rent on our Queens apartment would be raised in January. He wanted to buy a house in an isolated section of Long Island, but I'd always lived in the city and had never learned to drive.

Vietnam permeated everything that Christmas. Even the carols seemed part of the national deception: "Peace on earth, goodwill to men."

My anger at my husband had deepened over his views on the war; his 5 cavalier attitude about working for Grumman; his support for the president's policies; his lack of support for me. I dragged myself through the gray-lit days in a stupor. We argued over Vietnam, my exhaustion, his late hours, the mutual hate between my mother and him, whether to have a Christmas tree or a menorah, to move or accept the rent increase. He said I was weak; his grandmother had had fourteen kids and after each birth had gone back to the fields to cut sugar cane. I paced, took iron pills, told him he was unfeeling. I snuck out of the apartment to smoke cigarettes. Finally we agreed to a temporary truce. We agreed to postpone the arguments until an easier time. We agreed to pretend.

It was just before dawn: The baby slept. My husband showered. I stared out the window at the Manhattan skyline ablaze with holiday lights, as if the city were on fire. A Christmas tree twinkled in front of our apartment complex. Dirty snow rimmed the streets, and pigeons rested on windowsills, casting ominous shadows against the panes. A chorus of salt-spattered cars backfired and honked below. The apartment air was oppressive, close. That sorrowful, pleading carol "Have Yourself a Merry Little Christmas" played on the radio: "We'll have to muddle through somehow."

The phone rang. A man with a husky voice gave a name I don't remember, confirmed who I was, then cleared his throat and recited by rote, "We regret to inform you . . ."

I remember little things: The coffee left brewing too long; its bitter, weary smell. Half-browned bread popped up in the toaster. How the street-lights flickered, then went out as the sun began to crack open the early-morning sky.

The man on the phone, who was calling from my mother's home after having delivered the news to her in person, advised me to "come now," as my mother screamed, "No! No! No!" in the background.

I hung up.   10

"My brother is dead!" I yelled into the recesses of the apartment. I drifted up from my seat, my body threatening to collapse. I was entering the baby's room to wake him when my husband stepped out of the bathroom, encircled by mist, and said, "What? I couldn't hear you."

My mother came to stay with us as we waited for the body to be brought back to the U.S. She and I fed the baby, played with him, took him on long walks. My husband went to work. ("Staying home isn't going to change anything.") Friends dropped by with deli sandwiches, baskets of fruit, cookies, chocolate. We received official documents from the military: commendations, explanations, letters of sympathy signed by generals: "A barrage of gunshots . . . mourned by his fellow marines . . . bravery . . . Purple Heart." In bed at night, I conjured a memory of my brother at my wedding: He's standing beside my husband's cousin, whom he has a crush on. His eyes are bright, and he's slimmed down from the chubby child he once was. He says something that makes the cousin laugh, sees me watching him, and winks.

My brother and I had lived much of our lives apart. After having battled with my mother over a phone bill as a teen, he'd gone to live with his father, my stepfather, somewhere in Brooklyn. I didn't know much about how he'd spent those years, but I kept reaching for the sparse memories I did have of him.

When my brother was twelve and I was eighteen, the police left a message that they'd arrested him for stealing a car. My mother wasn't home from work yet, and I ran the eight blocks to the station. The squad room was overheated and stank of sweat and some unidentifiable food. I remember cells, doors leading to shadowy rooms, accused men proclaiming their innocence. The police wouldn't let me see my brother. They stood over me menacingly and called me "street cunt." I went outside and sat on the front steps to wait for my mother. The cops walking in and out glanced at me, nightsticks swinging against their legs, their holstered guns passing me at eye level. A couple of men on the other side of the street shoved each other and screamed in Spanish. Gulls wheeled overhead on the winds off the East River.

When my mother arrived, she straightened her shoulders, said, "Wait   15 here," and went inside.

The first-person "I" provides a powerful focus. See pp. 169–72 for tips on using the first-person point of view.

My brother had been an unsuspecting passenger in the stolen car, but he was sent to a group home for a year anyway. I remember taking the train from Grand Central Station to Pleasantville, New York, to visit him, but I don't remember the visits.

My memories of my brother are disconnected, without contiguous flow: he is two, he is six, he is ten, he is twelve, he is fifteen, he is dead.

When his body finally arrived from Vietnam, they told us it was too perforated with bullet holes to be shown to family members. We stood before the closed coffin at the funeral parlor as if before a holy icon, though the coffin itself was nothing special: standard military issue, as common as M16s. Four marines in crisp blue uniforms and shining brass guarded the body. The proper time to have guarded it, I thought, would have been while it still breathed. As we stared at the coffin, a fantasy seized me: my brother was still alive somewhere in Vietnam; the marines had lost track of him and fabricated this cover story. That Christmas it was easy to disbelieve the government.

I wore a leftover black maternity dress, belted at the waist, and felt unwashed and gritty despite the two showers I'd taken that day. My feet were freezing in tights, wool socks, and scuffed boots. My mother sat crumpled on a chair, a loose arrangement of bent limbs and bowed head. My stepfather, whom I hadn't seen in years, greeted me by saying, "I'm still the handsomest man in Brooklyn, aren't I?" We hugged, and any animosity over his divorce from my mother, after he'd gambled away the rent and food money, was forgiven. A death accomplishes that.

My husband, handsome in the suit he'd worn for our wedding, whispered to his aunts and cousins in the back of the room. The cousin my brother had been attracted to sat in the front row, weeping silent tears beside my mother. I felt as if I were in a foreign movie, something Greek or Italian where everyone wore black and spoke too fast for me to understand. I stared at the coffin and thought about how I'd once had no idea where the Mekong Delta was.

I accepted my share of blame. I'd complained about the war but hadn't protested it. I had been too caught up in my marriage and finding temporary work (I'd been fired when my pregnancy had begun to show) and trying to push through the postpartum exhaustion. I hadn't written letters, gone to demonstrations, participated in sit-ins. I'd done nothing to try to end this war.

The snow was falling heavily when we left for the cemetery, wind whipping up white ghosts. The body was loaded into a hearse with pale satin curtains in the windows and a stealthy engine. Our car skidded and slipped all the way to Long Island National Cemetery, where we stepped onto a plain of squat white stones that must have been churned out by the hundreds. There were fewer of us here than at the funeral parlor: my mother; my husband; a handful of friends, aunts, and cousins; the rabbi assigned by the funeral home. We advanced toward a hole in the ground covered by a black tarp. A couple of men in heavy clothing stood at a distance, shivering. One, in a black wool hat and army jacket, nodded in sympathy to me. My stepfather was already standing over the grave, a slight figure in a skullcap.

As the rabbi moved between the rows, he looked carefully at each name as though making a list. He turned to my mother and said, "Out of the question."

Leaning on my husband's cousin's arm, she stepped around the rabbi the way you'd circle a rock or another nonsentient object in your path. The snow coated the rabbi's black coat and hat as if intending to bury him also.

I waved my husband on and stopped to talk to the rabbi alone. "What are you saying?" I asked. The wind blew the words back into my face.

"There are non-Jews buried here," he said. "How can I pray?" He asked this as though it were a reasonable question.

As I battled my desire to strike him, I thought of my husband's accusation that I would always be a hoodlum from the streets, that anybody could see it. At that moment, I hoped he was right.

I put my face close to the rabbi's, and he took an alarmed step backward. "You *will* pray here," I whispered close to his cheek. "You will pray here because God—the real God, not the one you've made up—mourns every dead child. You will pray here, because otherwise I won't let you leave." I put my hand on his wrist and smiled at him. My lashes were coated with snow, and my scarf flapped around me like a black flag.

The yeshiva had not prepared the rabbi for this threatening woman who would bend him to her will. He glanced from side to side. Nobody was watching. We could have been alone in an alley. Finally he nodded and walked to the graveside. His dark beard caught the pristine snow. He leaned over the coffin and prayed in a low voice, his eyes fixed on the hole in the ground.

25

The Vietnam War Memorial in Washington, DC.

News of the war dominated the papers. Rows of coffins covered with American flags flashed across the television screen. Every night I dreamed my brother was alive, being tortured in a prison camp, running between dense green palms, crawling through rivers, panting, screaming, leaving a trail of blood that his enemies would follow. I'd wake covered with perspiration and gasping for breath. Some friends said I was projecting my own anxiety onto his death, others that I had a telepathic connection, a few that I was having a nervous breakdown.

I prayed that my gentle brother had died instantly rather than suffered pain. I remembered his pride when he'd received his very first paycheck and had "adopted" a Korean war orphan, faithfully paying fifteen dollars a month—until he'd lost his job and enlisted in an act of desperation, believing the military's promise to provide an education. I thought of his certainty that someday he'd leave the city's tenements behind and move to a farm and grow vegetables and flowers, a dream he'd picked up from a book we'd read together as children. I had marveled at his decision, during our poverty-stricken childhood, never to steal, whereas I'd had no problem shoplifting. I wept that my brother—sensitive, good-natured, astonished by cruelty—had been sent to Vietnam. I wanted to prevent the same from happening to any other boy.

I began attending antiwar marches every week, bringing the baby with me: bottles, blankets, diapers, toys. I didn't believe that it would make a difference. I knew it wasn't people protesting in the street that would end the war; it would be over only when it was no longer profitable. But I wanted that spirit of protest to seep into my son. I waved signs and chanted, "Hey, hey, LBJ, how many kids did you kill today?" This became my penance for my previous inertia. It would be five more years before the war ended, and several more after that before my nightmares would be gone and I'd accept that my brother was truly dead.

When the Bush administration decided to invade Iraq in 2003, I protested in Washington, D.C., with a friend and later in New York City with my second husband. Millions of us around the world demonstrated, but it didn't stop the invasion. As I watched the bombs drop on Baghdad, I wondered if we are infected with some malevolent virus that will not let us value peace.

It was nearly Christmas that year when my friend Sarah called to tell me, in a hesitant voice, "Jamie is dead."

The news was on in the background this time. No carols.

"They're bringing his body back from Iraq. No announcement yet on the funeral."

We hung up. What else was there to say?

I'd first met Jamie at a party Sarah had thrown for writers. His wife, Marika, was writing a novel about leaving Russia to seek freedom and opportunity in the U.S. They were newlyweds, both twenty-two, and had met in an English class. Kevin, my husband, spoke with Jamie about his decision to enlist in the National Guard for financial help with college tuition. Marika and I discussed her novel. She was concerned that Americans would be unable to relate to characters based on people she knew in Russia. "Americans seem to have little understanding about life in other countries," she told me. She shook her head and took a sip of her wine. "But I've made such good friends here."

A few weeks later I saw Jamie and Marika's picture in the newspaper above a story about National Guard members shipping out to Iraq. There they were, arms around each other, Marika's eyes full of love and dread, Jamie's smile tentative. (I thought of all the times his mother must have told him to "smile for the camera.") His arm was wound around his young wife, his military beret perched on his head.

35

He lasted one month in Iraq. 40

At the funeral Marika, weeping bitterly, said, "I thought this couldn't happen. He was in the National Guard, not the army."

Jamie's flag-draped coffin was not pictured in the paper. It is forbidden now for returning coffins to be shown in the news.

I recently went to a concert by Anaïs Mitchell, who sang a song called "Tell Me Something," about the invasion of Iraq: "Tell me something good about my country, tell me one good thing."

I have no answer for her, but the lyric still haunts me. It makes me think of my brother, dead in Vietnam, and Jamie, who died thirty-five years later in a different war, which is really the same war. To those who die, they are all the same war.

Thinking about the Text

1. Michelle Cacho-Negrete certainly wrote this narrative to express her pain about the death of her younger brother in Vietnam. What other **PURPOSE** might she have had? How can you tell? How successfully did she achieve this purpose? Provide evidence for your conclusions.

2. In the thematic table of contents for this book, we've classified Cacho-Negrete's narrative in the theme of "Home." Why do you think we made that association? How do you relate the painful and compelling story that Cacho-Negrete tells to your ideas about home?

3. Cacho-Negrete narrates small descriptive details ("A Christmas tree twinkled in front of our apartment complex" [6]) and major revelations ("When you're killed at eighteen, you don't leave much behind" [2]) in the same low-key, matter-of-fact **TONE**. Would her story have been more effective if it were told more dramatically? Explain why or why not.

4. There are eight distinct scenes in Cacho-Negrete's narrative. Which one had the most emotional impact for you? Why?

5. The title of this piece is "Tell Me Something," but not until the end do we learn how it relates to the narrative. What request is Cacho-Negrete making in this title? Is she looking to challenge and criticize? Is she looking for meaning? Think about how you would respond to such a request. Write your own **NARRATIVE** in which you answer the call to "[t]ell me something good about my country" (43).

The Talk: After Ferguson,
a Shaded Conversation about Race

DANA CANEDY

LIKE SO MANY **AFRICAN-AMERICAN PARENTS**, I had rehearsed "the talk," that nausea-inducing discussion I needed to have with my son about how to conduct himself in the presence of the police. I was prepared for his questions, except for one.

"Can I just pretend I'm white?"

Jordan was born to African-American parents, but recessive genes being what they are, he has very fair skin and pale blue eyes. I am caramel brown, and since his birth eight years ago people have mistaken me for his nanny.

When I asked why he would want to "pass" for white, I struggled with how to respond to his answer.

"Because it's safer," Jordan replied. "They won't hurt me."   5

That recent gray day, not long after grand juries failed to indict the police officers who killed unarmed black men in Ferguson, Missouri, and

DANA CANEDY is the author of *A Journal for Jordan: A Story of Love and Honor* (2008), a memoir dedicated to her son after the death of his father and her fiancé, First Sergeant Charles Monroe King. She is an editor at the *New York Times*, where this piece was published in 2014. You can follow her on *Twitter* @DanaCanedy.

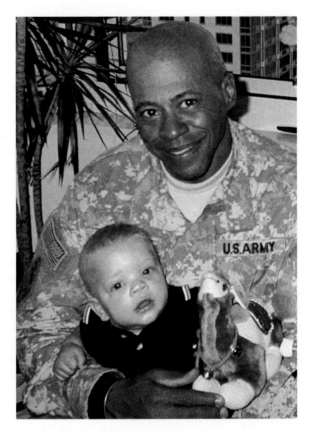

First Sgt. Charles M. King with his son, Jordan. King visited his son on leave before returning to Iraq on a mission that would end his life.

Staten Island, I had steadied myself to lay out the rules: Always address police officers as "sir" or "ma'am." Do not make any sudden moves, even to reach for identification. Do not raise your voice, resist or run.

But now I was taken aback.

Jordan's father and I never had a chance to discuss when we would give him the talk, or what we would say. Our baby was just 6 months old when his dad, a decorated Army soldier, was killed in combat in Iraq. So the timing and the context of the talk were left to me.

I had tried hard to delay it, and make sure he wouldn't know the names Michael Brown or Eric Garner or Tamir Rice.

In the days leading up to the conversation, I asked an African-American 10 male colleague if he thought it was too soon. When did he tell his own boys?

"Before they were no longer seen as cute," he said, making me wince.

I hadn't fully processed that someday my son would be seen as suspect instead of sweet. So I told him, and then Jordan asked if it was rare for the police to hurt black people. I said that, just like his father when he wore his military uniform, most police officers are dedicated to protecting us. But, no, I added, it is unfortunately not uncommon.

"Then I don't want to be black anymore," Jordan declared.

He asked if I was crying. I dabbed at my eyes and searched my mind for what to say.

"Son, your father was an incredible African-American man," I told him. 15 "And you are an amazing boy who is going to grow into just such a man. Please be proud of that."

"Yes," he responded emphatically, "but can't I just pretend to be white?"

The message that Jordan's appearance affords him the option to check "other" on the race card comes at him constantly. After his second-grade class created self-portraits last year, I noticed that his was the only one not hanging on the classroom wall. His teacher explained that his portrait was "a work in progress." The brown crayon he had used to color in his face was several shades too dark, she thought, and so she wanted him to "lighten it up" to more accurately reflect his complexion.

It is not just the overt signals that have convinced Jordan that he can choose to blend in to a white world. It is also that we live a life of relative affluence. I am a journalist and author whose inner circle includes prominent black writers, television anchors and doctors. We live in a high-rise in Manhattan with a doorman and round-the-clock security. Jordan attends an elite private school and an exclusive summer camp.

A white friend calls him "the boy who lives in the sky" because of the vast city view from the nine-foot windows in his bedroom. "He lives in a bubble and is always with responsible adults," she said recently, trying to assure me that our status makes him safer than many black boys.

You may not be a mother. Or black. Or wealthy. In any case, it's important to really listen to what Dana Canedy is saying— pp. 8–10 explain why.

That is true, mostly. And if my parenting pays off, I will be able to mini- 20
mize his contact with the police. He will be law-abiding. He will respect authority. He'll understand the perception of black boys wearing hoodies or
sagging pants. But will it be enough?

Just last month a video went viral that showed a black man in Pontiac,
Michigan, being questioned by a sheriff's deputy because someone reported
feeling nervous after seeing him walking in the cold with his hands in his
pockets. So as much as I want to believe that our upper-middle-class status
will protect my son from many of society's social ills, it could not provide
him the white privilege he seeks.

Nor would "passing" protect Jordan entirely, for the internal damage
from living that lie would surely be as painful as any blow from a police
baton. To deny his blackness would be to deny me. It would be to deny our
enslaved ancestors who were strong enough to endure that voyage. It would
mean rejecting the reflection he sees every time he looks in a mirror.

For at least a little while longer, Jordan is too young to understand any
of this. He does not know the racial indignity of having jobs and promotions denied or delayed, does not know the humiliation of being stopped
and frisked. He has never heard the mantra "I can't breathe."

I know that our talk was just the start of a conversation that will go
deeper as he moves into his teen years in a post-Obama America. My fervent
hope is that, by then, I will have found a way to help him embrace the privilege of being black.

Thinking about the Text

1. What is Dana Canedy's **PURPOSE** in publicly exposing such a painful and private conversation between her and her son? What point is she trying to make?
   And how persuasively does she make it? Explain your response.

2. It's true: numerous studies confirm that white youth are not targeted by police
   nearly as often as black youth. Still, pretending to be white, as Canedy's son
   proposed, is both unsuitable as a solution and hurtful to Canedy personally.
   Why? Explain the dilemma.

3. Canedy's narrative was published in the *New York Times*, a daily newspaper
   with a large nationwide circulation. What background information about "the

talk" does Canedy provide for this **AUDIENCE**? What might she have done differently if she were writing for a magazine with a primary readership of black parents? What information could she have omitted, and what might she have included that she chose not to include here?

4. A good narrative includes **DESCRIPTIVE** details that make the story come alive. What part of Canedy's narrative touched you the deepest? Why? Describe your reaction.

5. At some time in our lives, we've all had a run-in with some form of authority. Think of a frightening or otherwise memorable encounter with an authority figure. In what ways did your skin color, gender, stature, dress, or other factors in how you look or present yourself affect that encounter? Did any characteristics work in your favor or against you—and if so, how? Write a brief **NARRATIVE** of the encounter as you remember it, reflecting in particular on how your physical presence affects your life.

World and Screen

NICHOLAS CARR

THE WORLD is a strange, changeable, and dangerous place. Getting around in it demands of any animal a great deal of effort, mental and physical. For ages, human beings have been creating tools to reduce the strain of travel. History is, among other things, a record of the discovery of ingenious new ways to ease our passage through our environs, to make it possible to cross greater and more daunting distances without getting lost, roughed up, or eaten. Simple maps and trail markers came first, then star maps and nautical charts and terrestrial globes, then instruments like sounding weights, quadrants, astrolabes, compasses, octants and sextants, telescopes, hourglasses, and chronometers. Lighthouses were erected along shorelines, buoys set in coastal waters. Roads were paved, signs posted, highways linked and numbered. It has, for most of us, been a long time since we've had to rely on our wits to get around.

GPS receivers and other automated mapping and direction-plotting devices are the latest additions to our navigational toolkit. They also give the

NICHOLAS CARR is the author of *The Shallows: What the Internet Is Doing to Our Brains* (2011) and *The Big Switch: Rewiring the World from Edison to Google* (2008). His books about technology, economy, and culture have sparked much conversation on those topics, and the catchphrase "Is Google Making Us Stupid?" comes from his 2008 essay in the *Atlantic*. He blogs at roughtype.com and tweets @roughtype. This essay comes from his latest book, *The Glass Cage: Automation and Us* (2014).

Amerigo Vespucci, a fifteenth-century navigator, uses an astrolabe to find the Southern Cross.

old story a new and worrisome twist. Earlier navigational aids, particularly those available and affordable to ordinary folks, were just that: aids. They were designed to give travelers a greater awareness of the world around them—to sharpen their sense of direction, provide them with advance warning of danger, highlight nearby landmarks and other points of orientation, and in general help them situate themselves in both familiar and alien settings. Satellite navigation systems can do all those things, and more, but they're not designed to deepen our involvement with our surroundings. They're designed to relieve us of the need for such involvement. By taking control of the mechanics of navigation and reducing our own role to following routine commands—turn left in five hundred yards, take the next exit, stay right, destination ahead—the systems, whether running through a dashboard, a smartphone, or a dedicated GPS receiver, end up isolating us from the environment. As a team of Cornell University researchers put it in a 2008 paper, "With the GPS you no longer need to know where you are and where your destination is, attend to physical landmarks along the way, or get assistance from other people in the car and outside of it." The automation of wayfinding serves to "inhibit the process of experiencing the physical world by navigation through it."[1]

As is so often the case with gadgets and services that ease our way through life, we've celebrated the arrival of inexpensive GPS units. The *New York Times* writer David Brooks spoke for many when, in a 2007 op-ed titled "The Outsourced Brain," he raved about the navigation system installed in his new car: "I quickly established a romantic attachment to my GPS. I found comfort in her tranquil and slightly Anglophilic voice. I felt warm and safe following her thin blue line." His "GPS goddess" had "liberated" him from the age-old "drudgery" of navigation. And yet, he grudgingly confessed, the emancipation delivered by his in-dash muse came at a cost: "After a few weeks, it occurred to me that I could no longer get anywhere without her. Any trip slightly out of the ordinary had me typing the address into her system and then blissfully following her satellite-fed commands. I found that I was quickly shedding all vestiges of geographic knowledge." The price of convenience was, Brooks wrote, a loss of "autonomy."[2] The goddess was also a siren.

We want to see computer maps as interactive, high-tech versions of paper maps, but that's a mistaken assumption. . . . Traditional maps give us context. They provide us with an overview of an area and require us to figure out our current location and then plan or visualize the best route to our next stop. Yes, they require some work—good tools always do—but the mental effort aids our mind in creating its own cognitive map of an area. Map reading, research has shown, strengthens our sense of place and hones our navigational skills—in ways that can make it easier for us to get around even when we don't have a map at hand. We seem, without knowing it, to call on our subconscious memories of paper maps in orienting ourselves in a city or town and determining which way to head to arrive at our destination. In one revealing experiment, researchers found that people's naviga-

1. Gilly Leshed et al., "In-Car GPS Navigation: Engagement with and Disengagement from the Environment," in *Proceedings of the SIGCHI Conference on Human Factors in Computing Systems* (New York: ACM, 2008), 1675–1684.
2. David Brooks, "The Outsourced Brain," *New York Times*, October 26, 2007.

tional sense is actually sharpest when they're facing north—the same way maps point.[3] Paper maps don't just shepherd us from one place to the next; they teach us how to think about space.

The maps generated by satellite-linked computers are different. They usually provide meager spatial information and few navigational cues. Instead of requiring us to puzzle out where we are in an area, a GPS device simply sets us at the center of the map and then makes the world circulate around us. In this miniature parody of the pre-Copernican universe, we can get around without needing to know where we are, where we've been, or which direction we're heading. We just need an address or an intersection, the name of a building or a shop, to cue the device's calculations. Julia Frankenstein, a German cognitive psychologist who studies the mind's navigational sense, believes it's likely that "the more we rely on technology to find our way, the less we build up our cognitive maps." Because computer navigation systems provide only "bare-bones route information, without the spatial context of the whole area," she explains, our brains don't receive the raw material required to form rich memories of places. "Developing a cognitive map from this reduced information is a bit like trying to get an entire musical piece from a few notes."[4]

Other scientists agree. A British study found that drivers using paper maps developed stronger memories of routes and landmarks than did those relying on turn-by-turn instructions from satellite systems. After completing a trip, the map users were able to sketch more precise and detailed diagrams of their routes. The findings, reported the researchers, "provide strong evidence that the use of a vehicle navigation system will impact negatively on the formation of drivers' cognitive maps."[5] A study of drivers conducted at the University of Utah found evidence of "inattentional blindness" in GPS users, which impaired their "wayfinding performance" and their ability to form visual memories of their surroundings.[6] . . .

Nicholas Carr cites an interesting mix of scholarly and popular sources. For some tips on finding sources, see Ch. 20.

3. Julia Frankenstein et al., "Is the Map in Our Head Oriented North?," *Psychological Science* 23, no. 2 (2012): 120–125.
4. Julia Frankenstein, "Is GPS All in Our Heads?," *New York Times*, February 2, 2012.
5. Gary E. Burnett and Kate Lee, "The Effect of Vehicle Navigation Systems on the Formation of Cognitive Maps," in Geoffrey Underwood, ed., *Traffic and Transport Psychology: Theory and Application* (Amsterdam: Elsevier, 2005), 407–418.
6. Elliot P. Fenech et al., "The Effects of Acoustic Turn-by-Turn Navigation on Wayfinding," *Proceedings of the Human Factors and Ergonomics Society Annual Meeting* 54, no. 23 (2010): 1926–1930.

Which raises the obvious question: *Who cares?* As long as we arrive at our destination, does it really matter whether we maintain our navigational sense or offload it to a machine? An Inuit elder on Igloolik may have good reason to bemoan the adoption of GPS technology as a cultural tragedy, but those of us living in lands crisscrossed by well-marked roads and furnished with gas stations, motels, and 7-Elevens long ago lost both the custom of and the capacity for prodigious feats of wayfinding. Our ability to perceive and interpret topography, especially in its natural state, is already much reduced. Paring it away further, or dispensing with it altogether, doesn't seem like such a big deal, particularly if in exchange we get an easier go of it.

But while we may no longer have much of a cultural stake in the conservation of our navigational prowess, we still have a personal stake in it. We are, after all, creatures of the earth. We're not abstract dots proceeding along thin blue lines on computer screens. We're real beings in real bodies in real places. Getting to know a place takes effort, but it ends in fulfillment and in knowledge. It provides a sense of personal accomplishment and autonomy, and it also provides a sense of belonging, a feeling of being at home in a place rather than passing through it. Whether practiced by a caribou hunter on an ice floe or a bargain hunter on an urban street, wayfinding opens a path from alienation to attachment. We may grimace when we hear people talk of "finding themselves," but the figure of speech, however vain and shopworn, acknowledges our deeply held sense that *who we are* is tangled up in *where we are*. We can't extract the self from its surroundings, at least not without leaving something important behind.

A GPS device, by allowing us to get from point A to point B with the least possible effort and nuisance, can make our lives easier, perhaps imbuing us, as David Brooks suggests, with a numb sort of bliss. But what it steals from us, when we turn to it too often, is the joy and satisfaction of apprehending the world around us—and of making that world a part of us. Tim Ingold, an anthropologist at the University of Aberdeen in Scotland, draws a distinction between two very different modes of travel: *wayfaring* and *transport*. Wayfaring, he explains, is "our most fundamental way of being in the world." Immersed in the landscape, attuned to its textures and features, the wayfarer enjoys "an experience of movement in which action and perception are intimately coupled." Wayfaring becomes "an ongoing process of growth and development, or self-renewal." Transport, on the other hand, is "essentially destination-oriented." It's not so much a process of discovery "*along* a way of life" as a mere "carrying *across*, from location to location, of people and goods in such a way as to leave their basic natures unaffected." In transport, the traveler doesn't actually move in any meaningful way. "Rather, he is moved, becoming a passenger in his own body."[7]

Wayfaring is messier and less efficient than transport, which is why it has become a target for automation. "If you have a mobile phone with Google Maps," says Michael Jones, an executive in Google's mapping division, "you can go anywhere on the planet and have confidence that we can give you directions to get to where you want to go safely and easily." As a result, he declares, "No human ever has to feel lost again."[8] That certainly sounds appealing, as if some basic problem in our existence had been solved forever. And it fits the Silicon Valley obsession with using software to rid people's lives of "friction." But the more you think about it, the more you realize that to never confront the possibility of getting lost is to live in a state of perpetual dislocation. If you never have to worry about not knowing where you are, then you never have to know where you are. It is also to live in a state of dependency, a ward of your phone and its apps.

Problems produce friction in our lives, but friction can act as a catalyst, pushing us to a fuller awareness and deeper understanding of our situation. "When we circumvent, by whatever means, the demand a place makes of us to find our way through it," the writer Ari Schulman observed in his 2011 *New Atlantis* essay "GPS and the End of the Road," we end up foreclosing "the best entry we have into inhabiting that place—and, by extension, to really *being* anywhere at all."[9]

We may foreclose other things as well. Neuroscientists have made a series of breakthroughs in understanding how the brain perceives and remembers space and location, and the discoveries underscore the elemental role that navigation plays in the workings of mind and memory. . . .

In a 2013 article in *Nature Neuroscience*, Edvard Moser and his colleague György Buzsáki provided extensive experimental evidence that "the neuronal mechanisms that evolved to define the spatial relationship among landmarks can also serve to embody associations among objects, events and other types of factual information." Out of such associations we weave the memories of our lives. It may well be that the brain's navigational sense—its

---

7. Tim Ingold, *Being Alive: Essays on Movement, Knowledge and Description* (London: Routledge, 2011), 149–152. The emphasis is Ingold's.
8. Quoted in James Fallows, "The Places You'll Go," *Atlantic*, January/February 2013.
9. Ari N. Schulman, "GPS and the End of the Road," *New Atlantis*, Spring 2011.

ancient, intricate way of plotting and recording movement through space—is the evolutionary font of all memory.[10]

What's more than a little scary is what happens when that font goes dry. Our spatial sense tends to deteriorate as we get older, and in the worst cases we lose it altogether.[11] One of the earliest and most debilitating symptoms of dementia, including Alzheimer's disease, is hippocampal and entorhinal degeneration and the consequent loss of locational memory.[12] Victims begin to forget where they are. Véronique Bohbot, a research psychiatrist and memory expert at McGill University in Montreal, has conducted studies demonstrating that the way people exercise their navigational skills influences the functioning and even the size of the hippocampus—and may provide protection against the deterioration of memory.[13] The harder people work at building cognitive maps of space, the stronger their underlying memory circuits seem to become. They can actually grow gray matter in the hippocampus—a phenomenon documented in London cab drivers—in a way that's analogous to the building of muscle mass through physical exertion. But when they simply follow turn-by-turn instructions in "a robotic fashion," Bohbot warns, they don't "stimulate their hippocampus" and as a result may leave themselves more susceptible to memory loss.[14] Bohbot worries that, should the hippocampus begin to atrophy from a lack of use in navigation, the result could be a general loss of memory and a growing risk of dementia. "Society is geared in many ways toward shrinking the hippocampus," she told an interviewer. "In the next twenty years, I think we're going to see dementia occurring earlier and earlier."[15]

Even if we routinely use GPS devices when driving and walking out- ⒖

10. György Buzsáki and Edvard I. Moser, "Memory, Navigation and Theta Rhythm in the Hippocampal-Entorhinal System," *Nature Neuroscience* 16, no. 2 (2013): 130–138. See also Neil Burgess et al., "Memory for Events and Their Spatial Context: Models and Experiments," in Alan Baddeley et al., eds., *Episodic Memory: New Directions in Research* (New York: Oxford University Press, 2002), 249–268.

11. See, for example, Jan M. Wiener et al., "Maladaptive Bias for Extrahippocampal Navigation Strategies in Aging Humans," *Journal of Neuroscience* 33, no. 14 (2013): 6012–6017.

12. See, for example, A. T. Du et al., "Magnetic Resonance Imaging of the Entorhinal Cortex and Hippocampus in Mild Cognitive Impairment and Alzheimer's Disease," *Journal of Neurology, Neurosurgery and Psychiatry* 71 (2001): 441–447.

13. Kyoko Konishi and Véronique D. Bohbot, "Spatial Navigational Strategies Correlate with Gray Matter in the Hippocampus of Healthy Older Adults Tested in a Virtual Maze," *Frontiers in Aging Neuroscience* 5 (2013): 1–8.

14. Email from Véronique Bohbot to author, June 4, 2010.

15. Quoted in Alex Hutchinson, "Global Impositioning Systems," *Walrus*, November 2009.

A smartphone displays an indoor map of the Florida Mall.

doors, it's been suggested, we'll still have to rely on our own minds to get around when we're walking through buildings and other places that GPS signals can't reach. The mental exercise of indoor navigation, the theory goes, may help protect the functioning of our hippocampus and related neural circuits. While that argument may have been reassuring a few years ago, it is less so today. Hungry for more data on people's whereabouts and eager for more opportunities to distribute advertising and other messages keyed to their location, software and smartphone companies are rushing to extend the scope of their computer-mapping tools to indoor areas like airports, malls, and office buildings....

Indoor mapping promises to ratchet up our dependence on computer navigation and further limit our opportunities for getting around on our own. Should personal head-up displays, such as Google Glass, come into wide use, we would always have easy and immediate access to turn-by-turn instructions. We'd receive, as Google's Michael Jones puts it, "a continuous stream of guidance," directing us everywhere we want to go.[16] Google and Mercedes-Benz are already collaborating on an app that will link a Glass headset to a driver's in-dash GPS unit, enabling what the carmaker calls "door-to-door navigation."[17] With the GPS goddess whispering in our ear, or

16. Quoted in Fallows, "Places You'll Go."
17. Damon Lavrinc, "Mercedes Is Testing Google Glass Integration, and It Actually Works," *Wired*, August 15, 2013, wired.com/autopia/2013/08/google-glass-mercedes-benz/.

beaming her signals onto our retinas, we'll rarely, if ever, have to exercise our mental mapping skills.

Bohbot and other researchers emphasize that more research needs to be done before we'll know for sure whether long-term use of GPS devices weakens memory and raises the risk of senility. But given all we've learned about the close links between navigation, the hippocampus, and memory, it is entirely plausible that avoiding the work of figuring out where we are and where we're going may have unforeseen and less-than-salubrious consequences. Because memory is what enables us not only to recall past events but to respond intelligently to present events and plan for future ones, any degradation in its functioning would tend to diminish the quality of our lives.

Through hundreds of thousands of years, evolution has fit our bodies and minds to the environment. We've been formed by being, to appropriate a couple of lines from the poet Wordsworth,

> Rolled round in earth's diurnal course,
> With rocks, and stones, and trees.

The automation of wayfinding distances us from the environment that shaped us. It encourages us to observe and manipulate symbols on screens rather than attend to real things in real places. The labors our obliging digital deities would have us see as mere drudgery may turn out to be vital to our fitness, happiness, and well-being. So *Who cares?* probably isn't the right question. What we should be asking ourselves is, *How far from the world do we want to retreat?*

Thinking about the Text

1. Nicholas Carr argues that satellite navigation systems "are not designed to deepen our involvement with our surroundings." What does he mean by that? **SUMMARIZE** his argument. Is it persuasive? Why or why not?

2. Although it is still a matter of speculation, how might the long-term use of a GPS device contribute to the development of dementia in later life, according to Carr? What does he say happens in the brain? **EVALUATE** the **EVIDENCE** that Carr presents for what he says. Does it seem reliable? Explain.

3. Carr borrows two terms from the work of anthropologist Tim Ingold: *wayfaring* and *transport*. How does he **DEFINE** each of these terms? What is the key distinction between them, and how is that distinction important to Carr's argument?

4. How do you get around in the world? When navigating a new place, do you use a map? a GPS device? landmarks, or street signs, or something else? **REFLECT** on your preferences. How do they contribute (or not) to your feeling comfortable in your surroundings and grounded in the world?

5. Imagine that someone has asked you for directions from one location in your neighborhood or on your campus to another spot nearby. Try giving them directions by drawing a map, sketching in relevant streets and landmarks; by describing how to get there with words alone; and by listing directions as a GPS device would. Was one set of directions easier (or harder) to articulate than the others? Write a brief essay **COMPARING** these three ways of giving directions.

2b or Not 2b?

DAVID CRYSTAL

LAST YEAR, IN A NEWSPAPER ARTICLE headed "I h8 txt msgs: How texting is wrecking our language," John Humphrys argued that texters are "vandals who are doing to our language what Genghis Khan did to his neighbours 800 years ago. They are destroying it: pillaging our punctuation; savaging our sentences; raping our vocabulary. And they must be stopped."

As a new variety of language, texting has been condemned as "textese," "slanguage," a "digital virus." According to John Sutherland of University College London, writing in this paper in 2002, it is "bleak, bald, sad short-hand. Drab shrinktalk . . . Linguistically it's all pig's ear . . . it masks dyslexia, poor spelling and mental laziness. Texting is penmanship for illiterates."

Ever since the arrival of printing—thought to be the invention of the devil because it would put false opinions into people's minds—people have been arguing that new technology would have disastrous consequences for language. Scares accompanied the introduction of the telegraph, telephone, and broadcasting. But has there ever been a linguistic phenomenon that has aroused such curiosity, suspicion, fear, confusion, antagonism, fascination,

---

DAVID CRYSTAL is a linguist and prolific author on themes as far-flung as Shakespearean English and language use in digital contexts. He is currently professor of linguistics at Bangor University in Wales. This piece was published in the *Guardian*, a London daily, in 2008.

excitement and enthusiasm all at once as texting? And in such a short space of time. Less than a decade ago, hardly anyone had heard of it.

The idea of a point-to-point short message service (or SMS) began to be discussed as part of the development of the Global System for Mobile Communications network in the mid-1980s, but it wasn't until the early 90s that phone companies started to develop its commercial possibilities. Text communicated by pagers were replaced by text messages, at first only 20 characters in length. It took five years or more before numbers of users started to build up. The average number of texts per GSM customer in 1995 was 0.4 per month; by the end of 2000 it was still only 35.

The slow start, it seems, was because the companies had trouble working out reliable ways of charging for the new service. But once procedures were in place, texting rocketed. In the UK, in 2001, 12.2bn text messages were sent. This had doubled by 2004, and was forecast to be 45bn in 2007. On Christmas Day alone in 2006, over 205m texts went out. World figures went from 17bn in 2000 to 250bn in 2001. They passed a trillion in 2005. Text messaging generated around $70bn in 2005. That's more than three times as much as all Hollywood box office returns that year. 5

People think that the written language seen on mobile phone screens is new and alien, but all the popular beliefs about texting are wrong. Its graphic distinctiveness is not a new phenomenon, nor is its use restricted

Teenagers texting on mobile phones.

to the young. There is increasing evidence that it helps rather than hinders literacy. And only a very tiny part of it uses a distinctive orthography. A trillion text messages might seem a lot, but when we set these alongside the multi-trillion instances of standard orthography in everyday life, they appear as no more than a few ripples on the surface of the sea of language. Texting has added a new dimension to language use, but its long-term impact is negligible. It is not a disaster.

Although many texters enjoy breaking linguistic rules, they also know they need to be understood. There is no point in paying to send a message if it breaks so many rules that it ceases to be intelligible. When messages are longer, containing more information, the amount of standard orthography increases. Many texters alter just the grammatical words (such as "you" and "be"). As older and more conservative language users have begun to text, an even more standardised style has appeared. Some texters refuse to depart at all from traditional orthography. And conventional spelling and punctuation is the norm when institutions send out information messages, as in this university text to students: "Weather Alert! No classes today due to snow storm," or in the texts which radio listeners are invited to send in to programmes. These institutional messages now form the majority of texts in cyberspace—and several organisations forbid the use of abbreviations, knowing that many readers will not understand them. Bad textiquette.

Research has made it clear that the early media hysteria about the novelty (and thus the dangers) of text messaging was misplaced. In one American study, less than 20% of the text messages looked at showed abbreviated forms of any kind—about three per message. And in a Norwegian study, the proportion was even lower, with just 6% using abbreviations. In my own text collection, the figure is about 10%.

People seem to have swallowed whole the stories that youngsters use nothing else but abbreviations when they text, such as the reports in 2003 that a teenager had written an essay so full of textspeak that her teacher was unable to understand it. An extract was posted online, and quoted incessantly, but as no one was ever able to track down the entire essay, it was probably a hoax.

There are several distinctive features of the way texts are written 10 that combine to give the impression of novelty, but none of them is, in fact, linguistically novel. Many of them were being used in chatroom interactions that predated the arrival of mobile phones. Some can be found in precomputer informal writing, dating back a hundred years or more.

The most noticeable feature is the use of single letters, numerals, and symbols to represent words or parts of words, as with b "be" and 2 "to." They are called rebuses, and they go back centuries. Adults who condemn a "c u" in a young person's texting have forgotten that they once did the same thing themselves (though not on a mobile phone). In countless Christmas annuals, they solved puzzles like this one:

YY U R YY U B I C U R YY 4 ME
("Too wise you are . . .")

Similarly, the use of initial letters for whole words (n for "no," gf for "girlfriend," cmb "call me back") is not at all new. People have been initialising common phrases for ages. IOU is known from 1618. There is no difference, apart from the medium of communication, between a modern kid's "lol" ("laughing out loud") and an earlier generation's "Swalk" ("sealed with a loving kiss").

In texts we find such forms as msg ("message") and xlnt ("excellent"). Almst any wrd cn be abbrvted in ths wy—though there is no consistency between texters. But this isn't new either. Eric Partridge published his *Dictionary of Abbreviations* in 1942. It contained dozens of SMS-looking examples, such as agn "again," mth "month," and gd "good"—50 years before texting was born.

English has had abbreviated words ever since it began to be written down. Words such as exam, vet, fridge, cox and bus are so familiar that they have effectively become new words. When some of these abbreviated forms first came into use, they also attracted criticism. In 1711, for example, Joseph Addison complained about the way words were being "miserably curtailed"—he mentioned pos(itive) and incog(nito). And Jonathan Swift thought that abbreviating words was a "barbarous custom."

What novelty there is in texting lies chiefly in the way it takes further 15 some of the processes used in the past. Some of its juxtapositions create forms which have little precedent, apart from in puzzles. All conceivable types of feature can be juxtaposed—sequences of shortened and full words (hldmecls "hold me close"), logograms and shortened words (2bctnd "to be continued"), logograms and nonstandard spellings (cu2nite) and so on. There are no less than four processes combined in iowan2bwu "I only want to be with you"—full word + an initialism + a shortened word + two logograms + an initialism + a logogram. And some messages contain unusual processes:

in iohis4u "I only have eyes for you," we see the addition of a plural ending to a logogram. One characteristic runs through all these examples: the letters, symbols and words are run together, without spaces. This is certainly un-usual in the history of special writing systems. But few texts string together long sequences of puzzling graphic units.

There are also individual differences in texting, as in any other linguistic domain. In 2002, Stuart Campbell was found guilty of the murder of his 15-year-old niece after his text message alibi was shown to be a forgery. He had claimed that certain texts sent by the girl showed he was innocent. But a detailed comparison of the vocabulary and other stylistic features of his own text messages and those of his niece showed that he had written the messages himself. The forensic possibilities have been further explored by a team at the University of Leicester. The fact that texting is a relatively un-standardised mode of communication, prone to idiosyncrasy, turns out to be an advantage in such a context, as authorship differences are likely to be more easily detectable than in writing using standard English.

Texters use deviant spellings—and they know they are deviant. But they are by no means the first to use such nonstandard forms as cos "be-cause," wot "what," or gissa "give us a." Several of these are so much part of English literary tradition that they have been given entries in the *Oxford English Dictionary*. "Cos" is there from 1828 and "wot" from 1829. Many can be found in literary dialect representations, such as by Charles Dickens, Mark Twain, Walter Scott, DH Lawrence, or Alan Bleasdale ("Gissa job!").

Sending a message on a mobile phone is not the most natural of ways to communicate. The keypad isn't linguistically sensible. No one took letter-frequency considerations into account when designing it. For example, key 7 on my mobile contains four symbols, pqrs. It takes four key-presses to access the letter s, and yet s is one of the most frequently occurring letters in English. It is twice as easy to input q, which is one of the least frequently occurring let-ters. It should be the other way round. So any strategy that reduces the time and awkwardness of inputting graphic symbols is bound to be attractive.

Abbreviations were used as a natural, intuitive response to a techno-logical problem. And they appeared in next to no time. Texters simply trans-ferred (and then embellished) what they had encountered in other settings. We have all left notes in which we have replaced an *and* by an &, a three by a 3, and so on. Anglo-Saxon scribes used abbreviations of this kind.

But the need to save time and energy is by no means the whole sto-ry of texting. When we look at some texts, they are linguistically quite 20 complex. There are an extraordinary number of ways in which people play with language—creating riddles, solving crosswords, playing Scrabble, inventing new words. Professional writers do the same—providing catchy copy for advertising slogans, thinking up puns in newspaper headlines, and writing poems, novels and plays. Children quickly learn that one of the most enjoyable things you can do with language is to play with its sounds, words, grammar—and spelling.

The drive to be playful is there when we text, and it is hugely powerful. Within two or three years of the arrival of texting, it developed a ludic dimension. In short, it's fun.

To celebrate World Poetry day in 2007, T-Mobile tried to find the UK's first "Txt laureate" in a competition for the best romantic poem in SMS. They had 200 entrants, and as with previous competitions the entries were a mixture of unabbreviated and abbreviated texts.

The winner, Ben Ziman-Bright, wrote conventionally:

> The wet rustle of rain
> can dampen today. Your text
> buoys me above oil-rainbow puddles
> like a paper boat, so that even
> soaked to the skin
> I am grinning.

The runner-up did not:

> O hart tht sorz
> My luv adorz
> He mAks me liv
> He mAks me giv
> Myslf 2 him
> As my luv porz

(The author of the latter was, incidentally, in her late 60s.)

The length constraint in text-poetry fosters economy of expression in much the same way as other tightly constrained forms of poetry do, such as the haiku or the Welsh englyn. To say a poem must be written within 160 characters at first seems just as pointless as to say that a poem must be written in three lines of five, seven, and five syllables. But put such a discipline into the hands of a master, and the result can be poetic magic. Of course,

SMS poetry has some way to go before it can match the haiku tradition; but then, haikus have had a head-start of several hundred years.

There is something about the genre which has no parallel elsewhere. [25] This is nothing to do with the use of texting abbreviations. It is more to do with the way the short lines have an individual force. Reading a text poem, wrote Peter Sansom, who co-judged a *Guardian* competition in 2002, is "an urgent business . . . with a text poem you stay focused as it were in the now of each arriving line." The impact is evident even in one-liners, whose effect relies on the kind of succinctness we find in a maxim or proverb. UA Fanthorpe, Sansom's fellow judge, admired "Basildon: imagine a carpark." And they both liked "They phone you up, your mum and dad."

Several competitions have focussed on reworking famous lines, titles, or quotations:

> txt me ishmael
> zen & T @ f m2 cycl mn10nc

The brevity of the SMS genre disallows complex formal patterning—of, say, the kind we might find in a sonnet. It isn't so easy to include more than a couple of images, such as similes, simply because there isn't the space. Writers have nonetheless tried to extend the potential of the medium. The SMS novel, for example, operates on a screen-by-screen basis. Each screen is a "chapter" describing an event in the story. Here is an interactive example from 2005, from an Indian website called "Cloakroom":

> Chptr 6: While Surching 4 Her Father, Rita Bumps In2 A Chaiwalla & Tea Spills On Her Blouse. She Goes Inside Da Washroom, & Da Train Halts @ A Station.

In Japan, an author known as Yoshi has had a huge success with his text-messaging novel *Deep Love*. Readers sent feedback as the story unfolded, and some of their ideas were incorporated into it. He went on to make a film of the novel.

A mobile literature channel began in China in 2004. The "m-novel," as it is called, started with a love story, "Distance," by writer and broadcaster Xuan Huang. A young couple get to know each other because of a wrongly sent SMS message. The whole story is 1008 Chinese characters, told in 15 chapters, with one chapter sent each day.

Plainly, there are severe limits to the expressive power of the medium, when it is restricted to a screen in this way. So it is not surprising that, very early on, writers dispensed with the 160-character constraint, and engaged in SMS creative writing of any length using hard copy. Immediately there was a problem. By taking the writing away from the mobile phone screen, how could the distinctiveness of the genre be maintained? So the stylistic character of SMS writing changed, and texting abbreviations, previously optional, became obligatory.

Several SMS poets, such as Norman Silver, go well beyond text-messag- 30
ing conventions, introducing variations in line-shape, type-size, font, and colour that are reminiscent of the concrete poetry creations of the 1960s. They illustrate the way the genre is being shaped by the more powerful applications available on computers.

In 2007 Finnish writer Hannu Luntiala published *The Last Messages,* in which the whole 332-page narrative consists of SMS messages. It tells the story of an IT executive who resigns his job and travels the world, using text messages to keep in touch with everyone. And the growing independence of the genre from its mobile-phone origins is well illustrated by the French novelist Phil Marso, who published a book in 2004 written entirely in French SMS shorthand, *Pas Sage a Taba vo SMS*—a piece of word-play intended to discourage young people from smoking. The next year he produced *L,* an SMS retelling of French poetic classics.

An extraordinary number of doom-laden prophecies have been made about the supposed linguistic evils unleashed by texting. Sadly, its creative potential has been virtually ignored. But five years of research has at last begun to dispel the myths. The most important finding is that texting does not erode children's ability to read and write. On the contrary, literacy improves. The latest studies (from a team at Coventry University) have found strong positive links between the use of text language and the skills underlying success in standard English in pre-teenage children. The more abbreviations in their messages, the higher they scored on tests of reading and vocabulary. The children who were better at spelling and writing used the most textisms. And the younger they received their first phone, the higher their scores.

Children could not be good at texting if they had not already developed considerable literacy awareness. Before you can write and play with abbreviated forms, you need to have a sense of how the sounds of your language relate to the letters. You need to know that there are such things as alternative spellings. If you are aware that your texting behaviour is different, you

See Ch. 30 on how to move smoothly between texts and the formal rigors of academic writing.

must have already intuited that there is such a thing as a standard. If you are using such abbreviations as lol and brb ("be right back"), you must have developed a sensitivity to the communicative needs of your textees.

Some people dislike texting. Some are bemused by it. But it is merely the latest manifestation of the human ability to be linguistically creative and to adapt language to suit the demands of diverse settings. There is no disaster pending. We will not see a new generation of adults growing up unable to write proper English. The language as a whole will not decline. In texting what we are seeing, in a small way, is language in evolution.

Thinking about the Text

1. David Crystal's **ANALYSIS** includes the results of a study of students that found a positive correlation between the use of texting abbreviations and scores on reading and vocabulary tests. Think about your own experience texting. Does it match the results of that study? How might you explain any differences?

2. Crystal says it's pointless to send a message "if it breaks so many rules that it ceases to be intelligible" (7). Can you decipher all the text messages that you receive? Do you use any texting shorthand with close friends that others might not understand? Are you always careful to text intelligibly? Why or why not?

3. Crystal could be fairly certain that he and his credentials were known to the *Guardian*'s audience. If you were to write a similar article for your hometown newspaper, what could you include to establish an authoritative **TONE**?

4. Crystal's **EVIDENCE** that texting conventions are no cause for alarm falls into two main categories: historical (that the abbreviation strategies used in texts have been around for a long time, with no ill effect) and cognitive (that the more such strategies students use, the better they do on reading and vocabulary tests). Which do you find more convincing, and why?

5. Crystal presents a strong argument in support of texting conventions as a perfectly normal use of the language. Still, many people prefer to use standard spelling and punctuation in their text messages. Write an essay in which you support or refute Crystal's position, using as evidence your own practices and those of people you text with.

The Walking Dead Opens Its Season
in Lively Fashion

MARK DAWIDZIAK

IF YOU LIKE *THE WALKING DEAD,* you're just going to love the horror show's hit-the-ground-running fifth-season opener.

And if you don't like *The Walking Dead* . . . well, come on, it's the fifth-season opener, for crying out loud, and you long ago decided this isn't your cup of intestines. You're running from the room like an unarmed human being chased by a horde of flesh-craving zombies.

But for those who are addicted to AMC's zombie-apocalypse drama, the action-packed fifth-season premiere serves up a bounty of everything you savor about this supernatural series: nerve-jangling suspense, grand gross-outs, intriguing character study, razor-sharp dialogue, heart-thumping action, psychologically riveting moral dilemmas, state-of-the-art monster makeup and scream-inducing special effects. Eat hearty, me hearties.

It has been said that horror can work on three levels. It can be cerebral, giving your mind profoundly metaphoric material to chew over. It can be emotional, making your heart beat faster. And it can be repulsive, aiming

---

MARK DAWIDZIAK has written nonfiction books about Mark Twain, vampires, and—his favorite—the horror genre and has also edited several anthologies of horror stories. He is the television critic for the *Cleveland Plain Dealer*, where this review was published in October 2014.

Rick Grimes (Andrew Lincoln) and Daryl Dixon (Norman Reedus) in *The Walking Dead*.

for the gut and turning your stomach. At its frightening best, *The Walking Dead* works on all three levels, and don't sell the first one short.

For all of the rotting zombies limping through these eerie episodes, this remains a show about human beings constantly struggling to hold on to their humanity. For all of those bone-snapping, flesh-tearing, vein-squishing, skull-smashing special effects, *The Walking Dead* is a drama about what it means to be human . . . under the most desperate of circumstances.

Those questions hang over the fifth-season opener, which airs at 9 p.m. Sunday, October 12, on AMC. And you get the feeling from this episode that those questions will take on increased resonance as we make our way through the season.

Referencing Joseph Conrad, series star Andrew Lincoln has said that the show is entering "the heart of darkness" this season. That's precisely the feeling you get when the time-shifting season opener is over.

When we last left Rick Grimes (Lincoln), Daryl (Norman Reedus) and Michonne (Danai Guria), they and most of the other scrappy survivors were being held captive in a railroad car in the Terminus compound. The fourth season ended with Rick ominously promising that "they're screwing with the wrong people."

Very quickly, we learn the true motives of the Termians, and it's every bit as twisted as you suspect it is. Rick, Daryl and Glenn (Steven Yeun) are placed in imminent and immediate danger, and it sure doesn't look like there's any way out of this one. Don't you just love those moments? If you love *The Walking Dead*, you sure do.

Unlike the more deliberately paced fourth-season opener, which picked up after the loss of the prison and the death of the Governor (David Morrissey), the fifth-season opener hits the accelerator and races through revelation after revelation, battle after battle.

There's grim talk about the Terminus philosophy and there's chatter about hopes for a cure in Washington, D.C. And why shouldn't we put our trust in Washington, D.C.?

And that's about all you're getting out of me. If you want any more hints about what the new season might hold, stick with the official (and appropriately vague) description released by AMC. It says we'll learn about "the fate of the group's lost comrades, as well as new locales, new conflicts, and new obstacles in keeping the group together and staying alive. Stories will break apart and intersect. The characters will find love and hate. Peace and conflict. Contentment and terror. And, in the quest to find a permanent,

Yuck! No lack of descriptive detail here! See pp. 430–32 on adding rich detail to your writing.

safe place to call home, one question will haunt them . . . After all they've seen, all they've done, all they've sacrificed, lost, and held on to no matter what the cost . . . Who do they become?"

They become a tasty part of TV terror history, of course—a show that's already won a place in any discussion of the best horror, fantasy and science-fiction shows the medium has fielded. Have they taken wrong steps along the way? Show me a horror series that hasn't.

But *The Walking Dead* still has a strong grip on our imagination as it continues to aim at all three levels—brain, heart and stomach—with deadly accuracy.

Thinking about the Text

1. Mark Dawidziak provides numerous **CRITERIA** in his review of *The Walking Dead*. List the criteria he mentions, and note how much emphasis he places on each. Is the emphasis appropriate, or would the review have been stronger with a more balanced discussion of the criteria? Why?

2. Consider Dawidziak's use of ellipses (. . .). He uses them conventionally to mark omitted words, but also for stylistic effect—such as in paragraphs 2 and 5. How does the stylistic use of ellipses affect the way you read and understand these sentences? How would each sentence have read differently without ellipses? Explain.

3. How does Dawidziak anticipate criticisms of *The Walking Dead*? What concessions does he make to opposing views, and how fairly does he present them? Support your response with examples from the text.

4. Dawidziak may be addressing his comments to *Walking Dead* fans, but he knows that his actual **AUDIENCE** is much broader. How does he make the review speak to readers who may not be familiar with the show? Which of his statements specifically help those who are not already *Walking Dead* fans understand and appreciate this review?

5. Dawidziak asserts that *The Walking Dead* is a drama about "what it means to be human," as many other dramas are as well. Write a **REVIEW** of a movie or TV show that you feel examines "what it means to be human." Be sure to establish criteria for your review and to provide background information for readers who may not be familiar with the show or movie.

The Money

JUNOT DÍAZ

ALL THE DOMINICANS I KNEW IN THOSE DAYS sent money home. My
mother certainly did. She didn't have a regular job outside of caring for us five kids so she scrimped the loot together from whatever came
her way. My father was always losing his forklift jobs so it wasn't like she
had a steady flow ever. But my mother would rather have died than not
send money back home to my grandparents in Santo Domingo. They were
alone down there and those remittances, beyond material support, were a
way, I suspect, for Mami to negotiate the absence, the distance caused by
our diaspora. Hard times or not she made it happen. She chipped dollars
off from the cash Papi gave her for our daily expenses, forced our already
broke family to live even broker. In those times when nobody gave a damn
about nutrition we alone among our friends never had juice, soda, snacks
in our apartment. Not ever. And you can forget about eating at McDonald's
or having clothes with real labels. The family lived tight and that was how

JUNOT DÍAZ teaches writing at MIT and is the author of *Drown* (1996), *The Brief
Wondrous Life of Oscar Wao* (2007) (which won the Pulitzer Prize), and *This Is How
You Lose Her* (2012). Born in the Dominican Republic, Díaz moved with his family to
the United States when he was six, and he writes often of his experiences growing
up in a Dominican neighborhood in New Jersey. This narrative originally appeared
in the *New Yorker* in 2011.

she built the nut that she sent home every six months or so to the grand-parents.

We're not talking about a huge amount either. Two, maybe three hundred dollars. But in the Santo Domingo of those years, in the neighborhood in which my abuelos lived, that 300 smackers was the difference between life with meat and life without, between electricity and stone age. All of us kids knew where that money was hidden too—our apartment wasn't huge—but we also knew that to touch it would have meant a violence approaching death. I, who could take the change out of my mother's purse without even thinking, couldn't have brought myself to even look at that forbidden stash.

So what happened? Exactly what you would think. The summer I was twelve my family went away on a "vacation"—one of my father's half-baked get-to-know-our-country-better, sleep-in-the-van extravaganzas—and when we returned to Jersey, exhausted, battered, we found our front door unlocked. Stuff was knocked over, including the empty Presidente can my mother considered a decoration. My parents' room, which was where the thieves had concentrated their search, looked like it had been tornado-tossed. The thieves had kept it simple; they'd snatched a portable radio, some of my Dungeons & Dragons hardcovers, and of course: the remittances my mother had kept hidden back in a drawer.

It's not like the robbery came as some huge surprise. In our neighbor-hood cars and apartments were always getting jacked and the kid stupid enough to leave a bike unattended for more than a tenth of a second was the kid who was never going to see that bike again. There was no respect. Every-body got hit; no matter who you were, eventually it was your turn.

And that summer it was ours.   5

Still we took the burglary pretty hard. When you're a recent immigrant and you've put up with a lot of bullshit because of it, it's easy to feel targeted. Like it wasn't just a couple of assholes that had it in for you but the whole neighborhood—hell, maybe the whole country.

I felt that for certain and felt shame too, wondered if it was something we'd done, but I was also pissed. I was at the stage in my nerdery when I thought Dungeons & Dragons was going to be my life so the loss of those books was akin to having my kidney nicked while I slept.

No one took the robbery as hard as my mom, though. My father for his part shrugged it off, wasn't his money or his parents after all; went right back to running the streets but my mother stayed angry in a Hulkish way none of us had seen before. You would have thought the thieves had run off with 10 million dollars, how she was carrying on. It was bad. She cursed the neighborhood, she cursed the country, she cursed my father and of course she cursed us kids, swore that the only reason that the robbery happened was because we had run our gums to our idiot friends and they had done it. Something we all denied of course. And at least once a day, usually while we were eating, she'd say: I guess your abuelos are going to starve now.

Just in case we kids didn't feel impotent and responsible enough.

Anyway, this is where the tale should end, right? Wasn't as if there was   10 going to be any CSI-style investigation or anything. Should have been bye-bye money, bye-bye Dungeon Masters Guide. Except that a couple of days later I was moaning about the robbery to these guys I was hanging with at that time and they were cursing sympathetically and out of nowhere it struck me. You know when you get one of those moments of mental clarity? When the nictitating membrane obscuring the world suddenly lifts? That's what happened. For no reason whatsoever I realized that these two dopes that I called my friends had done it. They'd broken into the apartment while we were away and taken our shit. I couldn't have been any more sure if you'd shown me a video of them doing it. They were shaking their heads, mouthing all the right words, but I could see the way they looked at each other, those Raskolnikov glances. I *knew*.

Now it wasn't like I could publicly denounce these dolts or go to the police. That would have been about as useless as crying. Here's what I did: I asked the main dope to let me use his bathroom (we were in front of his apartment) and while I pretended to piss I unlatched the window and then we all headed down to the community pool as usual. But while they dove in I pretended to forget something back home. Ran back to the dope's apartment, slid open the bathroom window and in broad daylight wriggled my skinny ass into his apartment; his mom was of course at work.

Where the hell did I get these ideas? I have not a clue. I guess I was reading way too much Encyclopedia Brown and The Three Investigators in those days. What can I tell you—that's just the kind of moron I was.

Because if mine had been the normal neighborhood this is when the cops would have been called and my ass would have been caught *burglarizing*. Oh the irony—imagine me trying to explain that one to my mother. But no matter: mine wasn't a normal neighborhood and so no one called anybody. The dolt's family had been in the U. S. all their lives and they had a ton of stuff in their apartment, a TV in every room, but I didn't have

Junot Díaz sets a tone that's appropriate for his story. See pp. 642–45 for help setting an appropriate tone in your writing.

to do a great amount of searching. I popped up the dolt's mattress and underneath I found my D&D books and most of my mother's money. He had thoughtfully kept it in the same envelope. Walked out the front door and on the run back to my apartment I kept waiting for the SWAT team to zoom up but it never happened.

And that was how I solved the Case of the Stupid Morons. My one and only case.

The next day at the pool the dolt announced that someone had broken into *his* apartment and stolen all of *his* savings. This place is full of thieves, he complained bitterly; and I was like: No kidding. 15

Took me two days to return the money to my mother. Truth was I was seriously considering keeping it. I'd never had that much money in hand and who in those days didn't want a Colecovision? But in the end the guilt got to me and I gave it to her and told her what had happened. I guess I was expecting my mother to run around in joy, to crown me her favorite son, to at least cook me my favorite meal. Nada. She just looked at the money and then at me and went back to her bedroom and put it back in its place. I'd wanted a party or at least to see her happy but there was nothing. Just two hundred and some odd dollars and fifteen hundred or so miles—that's all there was.

Thinking about the Text

1. On the surface, this is a **NARRATIVE** about a sequence of events that happened when Junot Díaz was twelve. On a deeper level, the story touches on broader themes: family, justice, ethics, the immigrant experience. Choose one of these themes and discuss what Díaz is saying about it through his narrative.

2. Díaz uses a lot of slang ("300 smackers," "nicked," "run our gums"). He also uses academic words ("diaspora") and makes some literary references ("Raskolnikov"). And he sprinkles in Spanish words, untranslated ("abuelos," "nada," "Papi"). Why do you think he mixes language this way? What if anything would be lost if he did not?

3. Notice the way Díaz uses the word "you." Sometimes he seems to be addressing his readers directly, as in paragraph 10, when he says, "You know when you get one of those moments of mental clarity?" In other places, it's less clear what he means. Study his use of "you" and "your" throughout the narrative. How does it affect the way Díaz comes across as an author?

4. Díaz was surprised not to be given the hero's treatment when he gave the money to his mother. What might she have been feeling: happiness? relief? sadness? despair? What is the **TONE** of the ending, particularly in the last sentence, and how does Díaz communicate that emotion to his readers?

5. Díaz poignantly describes his experience with something we've all felt—the tension and conflict between our own desires and our sense of loyalty and duty to family. Think of a time that you've experienced that tension and write a **NARRATIVE** about it. Include descriptive details that allow the reader to enter your thoughts and perceptions.

Serving in Florida

BARBARA EHRENREICH

MOSTLY OUT OF LAZINESS, I decide to start my low-wage life in the town nearest to where I actually live, Key West, Florida, which with a population of about 25,000 is elbowing its way up to the status of a genuine city. The downside of familiarity, I soon realize, is that it's not easy to go from being a consumer, thoughtlessly throwing money around in exchange for groceries and movies and gas, to being a worker in the very same place. I am terrified, especially at the beginning, of being recognized by some friendly business owner or erstwhile neighbor and having to stammer out some explanation of my project. Happily, though, my fears turn out to be entirely unwarranted: during a month of poverty and toil, no one recognizes my face or my name, which goes unnoticed and for the most

BARBARA EHRENREICH holds a PhD in cell biology but became a journalist and an activist after working with a nonprofit organization to improve public access to health care. She is the author of *Bait and Switch: The (Futile) Pursuit of the American Dream* (2006), *Living with a Wild God: A Nonbeliever's Search for the Truth about Everything* (2014), and many more books. This piece is a chapter from her 2001 book, *Nickel and Dimed: On (Not) Getting By in America*, a memoir of her experiences working—and living on minimum wages—as a waitress, as a hotel maid, and in other service jobs.

part unuttered. In this parallel universe where my father never got out of the mines and I never got through college, I am "baby," "honey," "blondie," and, most commonly, "girl."

My first task is to find a place to live. I figure that if I can earn $7 an hour—which, from the want ads, seems doable—I can afford to spend $500 on rent or maybe, with severe economies, $600 and still have $400 or $500 left over for food and gas. In the Key West area, this pretty much confines me to flophouses and trailer homes—like the one, a pleasing fifteen-minute drive from town, that has no air-conditioning, no screens, no fans, no television, and, by way of diversion, only the challenge of evading the landlord's Doberman pinscher. The big problem with this place, though, is the rent, which at $675 a month is well beyond my reach. All right, Key West is expensive. But so is New York City, or the Bay Area, or Jackson, Wyoming, or Telluride, or Boston, or any other place where tourists and the wealthy compete for living space with the people who clean their toilets and fry their hash browns. Still, it is a shock to realize that "trailer trash" has become, for me, a demographic category to aspire to.

So I decide to make the common trade-off between affordability and convenience and go for a $500-a-month "efficiency" thirty miles up a two-lane highway from the employment opportunities of Key West, meaning forty-five minutes if there's no road construction and I don't get caught behind some sun-dazed Canadian tourists. I hate the drive, along a roadside studded with white crosses commemorating the more effective head-on collisions, but it's a sweet little place—a cabin, more or less, set in the swampy backyard of the converted mobile home where my landlord, an affable TV repairman, lives with his bartender girlfriend. Anthropologically speaking, the trailer park would be preferable, but here I have a gleaming white floor and a firm mattress, and the few resident bugs are easily vanquished.

The next piece of business is to comb through the want ads and find a job. I rule out various occupations for one reason or another: hotel front-desk clerk, for example, which to my surprise is regarded as unskilled and pays only $6 or $7 an hour, gets eliminated because it involves standing in one spot for eight hours a day. Waitressing is also something I'd like to avoid, because I remember it leaving me bone-tired when I was eighteen, and I'm decades of varicosities and back pain beyond that now. Telemarketing, one of the first refuges of the suddenly indigent, can be dismissed on grounds of personality. This leaves certain supermarket jobs, such as deli clerk, or housekeeping in the hotels and guest houses, which pays about $7 and, I imagine, is not too different from what I've been doing part-time, in my own home, all my life.

So I put on what I take to be a respectable-looking outfit of ironed Bermuda shorts and scooped-neck T-shirt and set out for a tour of the local hotels and supermarkets. Best Western, Econo Lodge, and HoJo's all let me fill out application forms, and these are, to my relief, mostly interested in whether I am a legal resident of the United States and have committed any felonies. My next stop is Winn-Dixie, the supermarket, which turns out to have a particularly onerous application process, featuring a twenty-minute "interview" by computer since, apparently, no human on the premises is deemed capable of representing the corporate point of view. I am conducted to a large room decorated with posters illustrating how to look "professional" (it helps to be white and, if female, permed) and warning of the slick promises that union organizers might try to tempt me with. The interview is multiple-choice: Do I have anything, such as child care problems, that might make it hard for me to get to work on time? Do I think safety on the job is the responsibility of management? Then, popping up cunningly out of the blue: How many dollars' worth of stolen goods have I purchased in the last year? Would I turn in a fellow employee if I caught him stealing? Finally, "Are you an honest person?"

Apparently I ace the interview, because I am told that all I have to do is show up in some doctor's office tomorrow for a urine test. This seems to be a fairly general rule: if you want to stack Cheerios boxes or vacuum hotel rooms in chemically fascist America, you have to be willing to squat down and pee in front of a health worker (who has no doubt had to do the same thing herself).[1] The wages Winn-Dixie is offering—$6 and a couple of dimes to start with—are not enough, I decide, to compensate for this indignity.

I lunch at Wendy's, where $4.99 gets you unlimited refills at the Mexican part of the Super-bar, a comforting surfeit of refried beans and cheese sauce. A teenage employee, seeing me studying the want ads, kindly offers me an application form, which I fill out, though here, too, the pay is just $6 and change an hour. Then it's off for a round of the locally owned inns and guest houses in Key West's Old Town, which is where all the seri-

---

1. Eighty-one percent of large employers now require preemployment drug testing, up from 21 percent in 1987. Among all employers, the rate of testing is highest in the South. The drug most likely to be detected—marijuana, which can be detected weeks after use—is also the most innocuous, while heroin and cocaine are generally undetectable three days after use. Alcohol, which clears the body within hours after ingestion, is not tested for.

ous sightseeing and guzzling goes on, a couple of miles removed from the functional end of the island, where the discount hotels make their homes. At The Palms, let's call it, a bouncy manager actually takes me around to see the rooms and meet the current housekeepers, who, I note with satisfaction, look pretty much like me—faded ex-hippie types in shorts with long hair pulled back in braids. Mostly, though, no one speaks to me or even looks at me except to proffer an application form. At my last stop, a palatial B & B, I wait twenty minutes to meet "Max," only to be told that there are no jobs now but there should be one soon, since "nobody lasts more than a couple weeks."

Three days go by like this and, to my chagrin, no one from the approximately twenty places at which I've applied calls me for an interview. I had been vain enough to worry about coming across as too educated for the jobs I sought, but no one even seems interested in finding out how overqualified I am. Only later will I realize that the want ads are not a reliable measure of the actual jobs available at any particular time. They are, as I should have guessed from Max's comment, the employers' insurance policy against the relentless turnover of the low-wage workforce. Most of the big hotels run ads almost continually, if only to build a supply of applicants to replace the current workers as they drift away or are fired, so finding a job is just a matter of being in the right place at the right time and flexible enough to take whatever is being offered that day. This finally happens to me at one of the big discount chain hotels where I go, as usual, for housekeeping and am sent instead to try out as a waitress at the attached "family restaurant," a dismal spot looking out on a parking garage, which is featuring "Polish sausage and BBQ sauce" on this 95-degree day. Phillip, the dapper young West Indian who introduces himself as the manager, interviews me with about as much enthusiasm as if he were a clerk processing me for Medicare, the principal questions being what shifts I can work and when I can start. I mutter about being woefully out of practice as a waitress, but he's already on to the uniform: I'm to show up tomorrow wearing black slacks and black shoes; he'll provide the rust-colored polo shirt with "Hearthside," as we'll call the place, embroidered on it, though I might want to wear my own shirt to get to work, ha ha. At the word *tomorrow*, something between fear and indignation rises in my chest. I want to say, "Thank you for your time, sir, but this is just an experiment, you know, not my actual life."

So begins my career at The Hearthside, where for two weeks I work from 2:00 till 10:00 P.M. for $2.43 an hour plus tips.[2] Employees are barred from using the front door, so I enter the first day through the kitchen, where a red-faced man with shoulder-length blond hair is throwing frozen steaks against the wall and yelling, "Fuck this shit!" "That's just Billy," explains Gail, the wiry middle-aged waitress who is assigned to train me. "He's on the rag again"—a condition occasioned, in this instance, by the fact that the cook on the morning shift had forgotten to thaw out the steaks. For the next eight hours, I run after the agile Gail, absorbing bits of instruction along with fragments of personal tragedy. All food must be trayed, and the reason she's so tired today is that she woke up in a cold sweat thinking of her boyfriend, who was killed a few months ago in a scuffle in an upstate prison. No refills on lemonade. And the reason he was in prison is that a few DUIs caught up with him, that's all, could have happened to anyone. Carry the creamers to the table in a "monkey bowl," never in your hand. And after he was gone she spent several months living in her truck, peeing in a plastic pee bottle and reading by candlelight at night, but you can't live in a truck in the summer, since you need to have the windows down, which means anything can get in, from mosquitoes on up.

At least Gail puts to rest any fears I had of appearing overqualified.   10 From the first day on, I find that of all the things that I have left behind, such as home and identity, what I miss the most is competence. Not that I have ever felt 100 percent competent in the writing business, where one day's success augurs nothing at all for the next. But in my writing life, I at least have some notion of *procedure:* do the research, make the outline, rough out a draft, etc. As a server, though, I am beset by requests as if by bees: more iced tea here, catsup over there, a to-go box for table 14, and where are the high chairs, anyway? Of the twenty-seven tables, up to six are usually mine at any time, though on slow afternoons or if Gail is off, I sometimes have the whole place to myself. There is the touch-screen computer-ordering system to master, which I suppose is meant to minimize server-cook contacts but in practice requires constant verbal fine-tuning: "That's gravy on the mashed,

2. According to the Fair Labor Standards Act, employers are not required to pay "tipped employees," such as restaurant servers, more than $2.13 an hour in direct wages. However, if the sum of tips plus $2.13 an hour falls below the minimum wage, or $5.15 an hour, the employer is required to make up the difference. This fact was not mentioned by managers or otherwise publicized at either of the restaurants where I worked.

OK? None on the meatloaf," and so forth. Plus, something I had forgotten in the years since I was eighteen: about a third of a server's job is "side work" invisible to customers—sweeping, scrubbing, slicing, refilling, and restocking. If it isn't all done, every little bit of it, you're going to face the 6:00 P.M. dinner rush defenseless and probably go down in flames. I screw up dozens of times at the beginning, sustained in my shame entirely by Gail's support—"It's OK, baby, everyone does that sometime"—because, to my total surprise and despite the scientific detachment I am doing my best to maintain, I *care*.

The whole thing would be a lot easier if I could just skate through it like Lily Tomlin in one of her waitress skits, but I was raised by the absurd Booker T. Washingtonian precept that says: If you're going to do something, do it well. In fact, "well" isn't good enough by half. Do it better than anyone has ever done it before. Or so said my father, who must have known what he was talking about because he managed to pull himself, and us with him, up from the mile-deep copper mines of Butte to the leafy suburbs of the Northeast, ascending from boiler-makers to martinis before booze beat out ambition. As in most endeavors I have encountered in my life, "doing it better than anyone" is not a reasonable goal. Still, when I wake up at 4 A.M. in my own cold sweat, I am not thinking about the writing deadlines I'm neglecting; I'm thinking of the table where I screwed up the order and one of the kids didn't get his kiddie meal until the rest of the family had moved on to their Key lime pies. That's the other powerful motivation—the customers, or "patients," as I can't help thinking of them on account of the mysterious vulnerability that seems to have left them temporarily unable to feed themselves. After a few days at Hearthside, I feel the service ethic kick in like a shot of oxytocin, the nurturance hormone. The plurality of my customers are hardworking locals—truck drivers, construction workers, even housekeepers from the attached hotel—and I want them to have the closest to a "fine dining" experience that the grubby circumstances will allow. No "you guys" for me; everyone over twelve is "sir" or "ma'am." I ply them with iced tea and coffee refills; I return, midmeal, to inquire how everything is; I doll up their salads with chopped raw mushrooms, summer squash slices, or whatever bits of produce I can find that have survived their sojourn in the cold storage room mold-free.

There is Benny, for example, a short, tight-muscled sewer repairman who cannot even think of eating until he has absorbed a half hour of air-conditioning and ice water. We chat about hyperthermia and electrolytes until he is ready to order some finicky combination like soup of the day, garden salad, and a side of grits. There are the German tourists who are so touched by my pidgin *"Wilkommen"* and *"Ist alles gut?"* that they actually tip. (Europeans, no doubt spoiled by their trade union–ridden, high-wage welfare states, generally do not know that they are supposed to tip. Some restaurants, the Hearthside included, allow servers to "grat" their foreign customers, or add a tip to the bill. Since this amount is added before the customers have a chance to tip or not tip, the practice amounts to an automatic penalty for imperfect English.) There are the two dirt-smudged lesbians, just off from their shift, who are impressed enough by my suave handling of the fly in the piña colada that they take the time to praise me to Stu, the assistant manager. There's Sam, the kindly retired cop who has to plug up his tracheotomy hole with one finger in order to force the cigarette smoke into his lungs.

Sometimes I play with the fantasy that I am a princess who, in penance for some tiny transgression, has undertaken to feed each of her subjects by hand. But the nonprincesses working with me are just as indulgent, even when this means flouting management rules—as to, for example, the number of croutons that can go on a salad (six). "Put on all you want," Gail whispers, "as long as Stu isn't looking." She dips into her own tip money to buy biscuits and gravy for an out-of-work mechanic who's used up all his money on dental surgery, inspiring me to pick up the tab for his pie and milk. Maybe the same high levels of agape can be found throughout the "hospitality industry." I remember the poster decorating one of the apartments I looked at, which said, "If you seek happiness for yourself you will never find it. Only when you seek happiness for others will it come to you," or words to that effect—an odd sentiment, it seemed to me at the time, to find in the dank one-room basement apartment of a bellhop at the Best Western. At Hearthside, we utilize whatever bits of autonomy we have to ply our customers with the illicit calories that signal our love. It is our job as servers to assemble the salads and desserts, pour the dressings, and squirt the whipped cream. We also control the number of butter pats our customers get and the amount of sour cream on their baked potatoes. So if you wonder why Americans are so obese, consider the fact that waitresses both express their humanity and earn their tips through the covert distribution of fats.

Ten days into it, this is beginning to look like a livable lifestyle. I like Gail, who is "looking at fifty," agewise, but moves so fast she can alight in one place and then another without apparently being anywhere between. I clown around with Lionel, the teenage Haitian busboy, though we don't have much vocabulary in common, and loiter near the main sink to listen

Barbara Ehrenreich's evidence comes from personal experience. See more examples of this strategy on pp. 399 and 432–33.

to the older Haitian dishwashers' musical Creole, which sounds, in their rich bass voices, like French on testosterone. I bond with Timmy, the fourteen-year-old white kid who buses at night, by telling him I don't like people putting their baby seats right on the tables: it makes the baby look too much like a side dish. He snickers delightedly and in return, on a slow night, starts telling me the plots of all the *Jaws* movies (which are perennial favorites in the shark-ridden Keys): "She looks around, and the water-skier isn't there anymore, then SNAP! The whole boat goes . . ."

I especially like Joan, the svelte fortyish hostess, who turns out to be a   15 militant feminist, pulling me aside one day to explain that "men run every-thing—we don't have a chance unless we stick together." Accordingly, she backs me up when I get overpowered on the floor, and in return I give her a chunk of my tips or stand guard while she sneaks off for an unauthorized cigarette break. We all admire her for standing up to Billy and telling him, after some of his usual nastiness about the female server class, to "shut the fuck up." I even warm up to Billy when, on a slow night and to make up for a particularly unwarranted attack on my abilities, or so I imagine, he tells me about his glory days as a young man at "coronary school" in Brooklyn, where he dated a knockout Puerto Rican chick—or do you say "culinary"?

I finish up every night at 10:00 or 10:30, depending on how much side work I've been able to get done during the shift, and cruise home to the tapes I snatched at random when I left my real home—Marianne Faithfull, Tracy Chapman, Enigma, King Sunny Adé, Violent Femmes—just drained enough for the music to set my cranium resonating, but hardly dead. Midnight snack is Wheat Thins and Monterey Jack, accompanied by cheap white wine on ice and whatever AMC has to offer. To bed by 1:30 or 2:00, up at 9:00 or 10:00, read for an hour while my uniform whirls around in the landlord's washing machine, and then it's another eight hours spent following Mao's central instruction, as laid out in the Little Red Book, which was: Serve the people.

I could drift along like this, in some dreamy proletarian idyll, except for two things. One is management. If I have kept this subject to the margins so far it is because I still flinch to think that I spent all those weeks under the surveil-lance of men (and later women) whose job it was to monitor my behavior for signs of sloth, theft, drug abuse, or worse. Not that managers and especially "assistant managers" in low-wage settings like this are exactly the class en-emy. Mostly, in the restaurant business, they are former cooks still capable of pinch-hitting in the kitchen, just as in hotels they are likely to be former clerks, and paid a salary of only about $400 a week. But everyone knows they have crossed over to the other side, which is, crudely put, corporate as opposed to human. Cooks want to prepare tasty meals, servers want to serve them graciously, but managers are there for only one reason—to make sure that money is made for some theoretical entity, the corporation, which exists far away in Chicago or New York, if a corporation can be said to have a physical existence at all. Reflecting on her career, Gail tells me ruefully that she swore, years ago, never to work for a corporation again. "They don't cut you no slack. You give and you give and they take."

Managers can sit—for hours at a time if they want—but it's their job to see that no one else ever does, even when there's nothing to do, and this is why, for servers, slow times can be as exhausting as rushes. You start dragging out each little chore because if the manager on duty catches you in an idle moment he will give you something far nastier to do. So I wipe, I clean, I consolidate catsup bottles and recheck the cheesecake supply, even tour the tables to make sure the customer evaluation forms are all standing perkily in their places—wondering all the time how many calories I burn in these strictly theatrical exercises. In desperation, I even take the desserts out of their glass display case and freshen them up with whipped cream and bright new maraschino cherries; anything to look busy. When, on a particularly dead afternoon, Stu finds me glancing at a *USA Today* a customer has left behind, he assigns me to vacuum the entire floor with the broken vacuum cleaner, which has a handle only two feet long, and the only way to do that without incurring orthopedic damage is to proceed from spot to spot on your knees.

On my first Friday at Hearthside there is a "mandatory meeting for all restaurant employees," which I attend, eager for insight into our overall marketing strategy and the niche (your basic Ohio cuisine with a tropical twist?) we aim to inhabit. But there is no "we" at this meeting. Phillip, our top manager except for an occasional "consultant" sent out by corporate headquarters, opens it with a sneer: "The break room—it's disgusting. Butts in the ashtrays, newspapers lying around, crumbs." This windowless little room, which also houses the time clock for the entire hotel, is where we stash our bags and civilian clothes and take our half-hour meal breaks. But a break room is not a right, he tells us, it can be taken away. We should also know that the lockers in the break room and whatever is in them can be searched at any time. Then comes gossip; there has been gossip; gossip (which seems to mean employees talking among themselves) must stop. Off-duty employees are henceforth barred from eating at the restaurant, because "other servers gather around them and gossip." When Phillip has exhausted his agenda of rebukes, Joan complains about the condition of the ladies' room and I throw in my two bits about the vacuum cleaner. But I don't see any backup coming from my fellow servers, each of whom has slipped into her own personal funk; Gail, my role model, stares sorrowfully at a point six inches from her nose. The meeting ends when Andy, one of the cooks, gets up, muttering about breaking up his day off for this almighty bullshit.

Just four days later we are suddenly summoned into the kitchen at 3:30 20 P.M., even though there are live tables on the floor. We all—about ten of us— stand around Phillip, who announces grimly that there has been a report of some "drug activity" on the night shift and that, as a result, we are now to be a "drug-free" workplace, meaning that all new hires will be tested and possibly also current employees on a random basis. I am glad that this part of the kitchen is so dark because I find myself blushing as hard as if I had been caught toking up in the ladies' room myself: I haven't been treated this way—lined up in the corridor, threatened with locker searches, peppered with carelessly aimed accusations—since at least junior high school. Back on the floor, Joan cracks, "Next they'll be telling us we can't have *sex* on the job." When I ask Stu what happened to inspire the crackdown, he just mutters about "management decisions" and takes the opportunity to upbraid Gail and me for being too generous with the rolls. From now on there's to be only one per customer and it goes out with the dinner, not with the salad. He's also been riding the cooks, prompting Andy to come out of the kitchen and observe—with the serenity of a man whose customary implement is a butcher knife—that "Stu has a death wish today."

Later in the evening, the gossip crystallizes around the theory that Stu is himself the drug culprit, that he uses the restaurant phone to order up marijuana and sends one of the late servers out to fetch it for him. The server was caught and she may have ratted out Stu, at least enough to cast some suspicion on him, thus accounting for his pissy behavior. Who knows? Personally, I'm ready to believe anything bad about Stu, who serves no evident function and presumes too much on our common ethnicity, sidling up to me one night to engage in a little nativism directed at the Haitian immigrants: "I feel like I'm the foreigner here. They're taking over the country." Still later that evening, the drug in question escalates to crack. Lionel, the busboy, entertains us for the rest of the shift by standing just behind Stu's back and sucking deliriously on an imaginary joint or maybe a pipe.

The other problem, in addition to the less-than-nurturing management style, is that this job shows no sign of being financially viable. You might imagine, from a comfortable distance, that people who live, year in and year out, on $6 to $10 an hour have discovered some survival stratagems unknown to the middle class. But no. It's not hard to get my coworkers talking about their living situations, because housing, in almost every case, is the principal source of disruption in their lives, the first thing they fill you in on when they arrive for their shifts. After a week, I have compiled the following survey:

Gail is sharing a room in a well-known downtown flophouse for $250 a week. Her roommate, a male friend, has begun hitting on her, driving her nuts, but the rent would be impossible alone.

Claude, the Haitian cook, is desperate to get out of the two-room apartment he shares with his girlfriend and two other, unrelated people. As far as I can determine, the other Haitian men live in similarly crowded situations.

Annette, a twenty-year-old server who is six months pregnant and abandoned by her boyfriend, lives with her mother, a postal clerk.

Marianne, who is a breakfast server, and her boyfriend are paying $170 a week for a one-person trailer.

Billy, who at $10 an hour is the wealthiest of us, lives in the trailer he owns, paying only the $400-a-month lot fee.

The other white cook, Andy, lives on his dry-docked boat, which, as far as I can tell from his loving descriptions, can't be more than twenty feet long. He offers to take me out on it once it's repaired, but the offer comes with inquiries as to my marital status, so I do not follow up on it.

Tina, another server, and her husband are paying $60 a night for a room in the Days Inn. This is because they have no car and the Days Inn is in walking distance of the Hearthside. When Marianne is tossed out of her trailer for subletting (which is against trailer park rules), she leaves her boyfriend and moves in with Tina and her husband.

Joan, who had fooled me with her numerous and tasteful outfits (hostesses wear their own clothes), lives in a van parked behind a shopping center at night and showers in Tina's motel room. The clothes are from thrift shops.[3]

It strikes me, in my middle-class solipsism, that there is gross improvidence in some of these arrangements. When Gail and I are wrapping silverware in napkins—the only task for which we are permitted to sit—she tells me she is thinking of escaping from her roommate by moving into the Days Inn herself. I am astounded: how she can even think of paying $40 to $60 a day? But if I was afraid of sounding like a social worker, I have come out just sounding like a fool. She squints at me in disbelief: "And where am I supposed to get a month's rent and a month's deposit for an apartment?" I'd been feeling pretty smug about my $500 efficiency, but of course it was made possible only by the $1,300 I had allotted myself for start-up costs when I began my low-wage life: $1,000 for the first month's rent and deposit, $100 for initial groceries and cash in my pocket, $200 stuffed away for emergencies. In poverty, as in certain propositions in physics, starting conditions are everything.

There are no secret economies that nourish the poor; on the contrary, there are a host of special costs. If you can't put up the two months' rent you need to secure an apartment, you end up paying through the nose for a room by the week. If you have only a room, with a hot plate at best, you can't save by cooking up huge lentil stews that can be frozen for the week ahead. You eat fast food or the hot dogs and Styrofoam cups of soup that can be microwaved in a convenience store. If you have no money for health insurance— and the Hearthside's niggardly plan kicks in only after three months—you go without routine care or prescription drugs and end up paying the price. Gail, for example, was doing fine, healthwise anyway, until she ran out of money for estrogen pills. She is supposed to be on the company health plan by now, but they claim to have lost her application form and to be beginning the paperwork all over again. So she spends $9 a pop for pills to control the migraines she wouldn't have, she insists, if her estrogen supplements were covered. Similarly, Marianne's boyfriend lost his job as a roofer because he

3. I could find no statistics on the number of employed people living in cars or vans, but according to a 1997 report of the National Coalition for the Homeless, "Myths and Facts about Homelessness," nearly one-fifth of all homeless people (in twenty-nine cities across the nation) are employed in full- or part-time jobs.

missed so much time after getting a cut on his foot for which he couldn't afford the prescribed antibiotic.

My own situation, when I sit down to assess it after two weeks of work, 25 would not be much better if this were my actual life. The seductive thing about waitressing is that you don't have to wait for payday to feel a few bills in your pocket, and my tips usually cover meals and gas, plus something left over to stuff into the kitchen drawer I use as a bank. But as the tourist business slows in the summer heat, I sometimes leave work with only $20 in tips (the gross is higher, but servers share about 15 percent of their tips with the busboys and bartenders). With wages included, this amounts to about the minimum wage of $5.15 an hour. The sum in the drawer is piling up but at the present rate of accumulation will be more than $100 short of my rent when the end of the month comes around. Nor can I see any expenses to cut. True, I haven't gone the lentil stew route yet, but that's because I don't have a large cooking pot, potholders, or a ladle to stir with (which would cost a total of about $30 at Kmart, somewhat less at a thrift store), not to mention onions, carrots, and the indispensable bay leaf. I do make my lunch almost every day—usually some slow-burning, high-protein combo like frozen chicken patties with melted cheese on top and canned pinto beans on the side. Dinner is at the Hearthside, which offers its employees a choice of BLT, fish sandwich, or hamburger for only $2. The burger lasts longest, especially if it's heaped with gut-puckering jalapeños, but by midnight my stomach is growling again.

So unless I want to start using my car as a residence, I have to find a second or an alternative job. I call all the hotels I'd filled out housekeeping applications at weeks ago—the Hyatt, Holiday Inn, Econo Lodge, HoJo's, Best Western, plus a half dozen locally run guest houses. Nothing. Then I start making the rounds again, wasting whole mornings waiting for some assistant manager to show up, even dipping into places so creepy that the front-desk clerk greets you from behind bullet-proof glass and sells pints of liquor over the counter. But either someone has exposed my real-life housekeeping habits—which are, shall we say, mellow—or I am at the wrong end of some infallible ethnic equation: most, but by no means all, of the working housekeepers I see on my job searches are African Americans, Spanish-speaking, or refugees from the Central European post-Communist world, while servers are almost invariably white and monolingually English-speaking. When I finally get a positive response, I have been identified once again as server material. Jerry's—again, not the real name—which is part of a well-known national chain and physically attached here to another budget hotel, is ready to use me at once. The prospect is both exciting and terrifying because, with about the same number of tables and counter seats, Jerry's attracts three or four times the volume of customers as the gloomy old Hearthside.

Thinking about the Text

1. Barbara Ehrenreich passes back and forth in her narrative between the voice of the waitress describing her own reality and the voice of the writer who has assumed a role for investigative purposes—and of course both voices are hers. How well do those voices combine to present a cohesive narrative? Explain your answer, presenting examples from the text.

2. How typical do you suppose Ehrenreich's experience is of people who wait tables at "family restaurants" (8)? Consider evidence from your own experience and that of people you know, either as employees or as customers at such restaurants.

3. On radio and TV, in movies, and elsewhere, people like Ehrenreich's co-workers and customers, with low incomes and low social status, are often either belittled and ridiculed, or romanticized and idealized, whether subtly or openly. One of the strengths of Ehrenreich's book is the respect with which she describes people just the way they are. Identify three examples of respect-ful **DESCRIPTION**.

4. What is the main point that Ehrenreich is making in her narrative? Where is this point most clearly stated? How well has she supported this point? In other words, are you convinced? Why or why not?

5. Write a **NARRATIVE** describing the people and places of your daily life. If you have (or have had) a job, you may want to center your narrative there. Include plenty of descriptive details and try to present the people as vividly (and respectfully!) as you can. Make your main point something that you have learned as a result of your contact with the people you describe.

How Junk Food Can End Obesity

DAVID H. FREEDMAN

L**ATE LAST YEAR,** in a small health-food eatery called Cafe Sprouts in Oberlin, Ohio, I had what may well have been the most wholesome beverage of my life. The friendly server patiently guided me to an apple-blueberry-kale-carrot smoothie-juice combination, which she spent the next several minutes preparing, mostly by shepherding farm-fresh produce into machinery. The result was tasty, but at 300 calories (by my rough calculation) in a 16-ounce cup, it was more than my diet could regularly absorb without consequences, nor was I about to make a habit of $9 shakes, healthy or not.

Inspired by the experience nonetheless, I tried again two months later at L.A.'s Real Food Daily, a popular vegan restaurant near Hollywood. I was initially wary of a low-calorie juice made almost entirely from green vegetables, but the server assured me it was a popular treat. I like to brag that I can eat anything, and I scarf down all sorts of raw vegetables like candy, but I could stomach only about a third of this oddly foamy, bitter concoction. It smelled like lawn clippings and tasted like liquid celery. It goes for $7.95, and I waited 10 minutes for it.

DAVID H. FREEDMAN is a journalist specializing in business and technology and is the author of *Wrong: Why Experts Keep Failing Us—And How to Know When Not to Trust Them* (2010). His work has appeared in *Forbes*, the *New York Times*, and *Wired*, among other publications. This July 2013 essay is from the *Atlantic*. You can follow him on *Twitter* @dhfreedman.

I finally hit the sweet spot just a few weeks later, in Chicago, with a delicious blueberry-pomegranate smoothie that rang in at a relatively modest 220 calories. It cost $3 and took only seconds to make. Best of all, I'll be able to get this concoction just about anywhere. Thanks, McDonald's!

If only the McDonald's smoothie weren't, unlike the first two, so fattening and unhealthy. Or at least that's what the most-prominent voices in our food culture today would have you believe.

An enormous amount of media space has been dedicated to promoting 5 the notion that all processed food, and only processed food, is making us sickly and overweight. In this narrative, the food-industrial complex—particularly the fast-food industry—has turned all the powers of food-processing science loose on engineering its offerings to addict us to fat, sugar, and salt, causing or at least heavily contributing to the obesity crisis. The wares of these pimps and pushers, we are told, are to be universally shunned.

Consider *The New York Times*. Earlier this year, *The Times Magazine* gave its cover to a long piece based on Michael Moss's about-to-be-best-selling book, *Salt Sugar Fat: How the Food Giants Hooked Us*. Hitting bookshelves at about the same time was the former *Times* reporter Melanie Warner's *Pandora's Lunchbox: How Processed Food Took Over the American Meal*, which addresses more or less the same theme. Two years ago *The Times Magazine* featured the journalist Gary Taubes's "Is Sugar Toxic?," a cover story on the

How much—and how many calories—will a smoothie cost you?

evils of refined sugar and high-fructose corn syrup. And most significant of all has been the considerable space the magazine has devoted over the years to Michael Pollan, a journalism professor at the University of California at Berkeley, and his broad indictment of food processing as a source of society's health problems.

"The food they're cooking is making people sick," Pollan has said of big food companies. "It is one of the reasons that we have the obesity and diabetes epidemics that we do. . . . If you're going to let industries decide how much salt, sugar and fat is in your food, they're going to put [in] as much as they possibly can. . . . They will push those buttons until we scream or die." The solution, in his view, is to replace Big Food's engineered, edible evil—through public education and regulation—with fresh, unprocessed, local, seasonal, real food.

Pollan's worldview saturates the public conversation on healthy eating. You hear much the same from many scientists, physicians, food activists, nutritionists, celebrity chefs, and pundits. *Foodlike substances*, the derisive term Pollan uses to describe processed foods, is now a solid part of the elite vernacular. Thousands of restaurants and grocery stores, most notably the Whole Foods chain, have thrived by answering the call to reject industrialized foods in favor of a return to natural, simple, nonindustrialized—let's call them "wholesome"—foods. The two newest restaurants in my smallish Massachusetts town both prominently tout wholesome ingredients; one of them is called the Farmhouse, and it's usually packed.

A new generation of business, social, and policy entrepreneurs is rising to further cater to these tastes, and to challenge Big Food. Silicon Valley, where tomorrow's entrepreneurial and social trends are forged, has spawned a small ecosystem of wholesome-friendly venture-capital firms (Physic Ventures, for example), business accelerators (Local Food Lab), and Web sites (Edible Startups) to fund, nurture, and keep tabs on young companies such as blissmo (a wholesome-food-of-the-month club), Mile High Organics (online wholesome-food shopping), and Wholeshare (group wholesome-food purchasing), all designed to help reacquaint Americans with the simpler eating habits of yesteryear.

In virtually every realm of human existence, we turn to technology to 10 help us solve our problems. But even in Silicon Valley, when it comes to food and obesity, technology—or at least food-processing technology—is widely treated as if it is the problem. The solution, from this viewpoint, necessarily involves turning our back on it.

The produce section at a Whole Foods Market.

If the most-influential voices in our food culture today get their way, we will achieve a genuine food revolution. Too bad it would be one tailored to the dubious health fantasies of a small, elite minority. And too bad it would largely exclude the obese masses, who would continue to sicken and die early. Despite the best efforts of a small army of wholesome-food heroes, there is no reasonable scenario under which these foods could become cheap and plentiful enough to serve as the core diet for most of the obese population—even in the unlikely case that your typical junk-food eater would be willing and able to break lifelong habits to embrace kale and yellow beets. And many of the dishes glorified by the wholesome-food movement are, in any case, as caloric and obesogenic as anything served in a Burger King.

Through its growing sway over health-conscious consumers and policy makers, the wholesome-food movement is impeding the progress of the one segment of the food world that is actually positioned to take effective, near-term steps to reverse the obesity trend: the processed-food industry. Popular food producers, fast-food chains among them, are already applying various tricks and technologies to create less caloric and more satiating versions of their junky fare that nonetheless retain much of the appeal of the originals, and could be induced to go much further. In fact, these roundly demonized companies could do far more for the public's health in five years than the wholesome-food movement is likely to accomplish in the next 50. But will the wholesome-food advocates let them? . . .

Let Them Eat Kale

I'm a fan of many of Mark Bittman's recipes. I shop at Whole Foods all the time. And I eat like many wholesome foodies, except I try to stay away from those many wholesome ingredients and dishes that are high in fat and problem carbs. What's left are vegetables, fruits, legumes, whole grains, poultry, and fish (none of them fried, thank you), which are often emphasized by many wholesome-food fans. In general, I find that the more-natural versions of these ingredients taste at least a bit better, and occasionally much better, than the industrialized versions. And despite the wholesome-food movement's frequent and inexcusable obliviousness to the obesogenicity of many of its own foods, it deserves credit for paying more attention to those healthier ingredients than does Big Food.

Where the Pollanites get into real trouble—where their philosophy becomes so glib and wrongheaded that it is actually immoral—is in the claim that their style of food shopping and eating is the answer to the country's weight problem. Helping me to indulge my taste for genuinely healthy wholesome foods are the facts that I'm relatively affluent and well educated, and that I'm surrounded by people who tend to take care with what they eat. Not only am I within a few minutes' drive of three Whole Foods and two Trader Joe's, I'm within walking distance of two other supermarkets and more than a dozen restaurants that offer bountiful healthy-eating options.

I am, in short, not much like the average obese person in America, and neither are the Pollanites. That person is relatively poor, does not read *The Times* or cookbook manifestos, is surrounded by people who eat junk food and are themselves obese, and stands a good chance of living in a food desert—an area where produce tends to be hard to find, of poor quality, or expensive.

The wholesome foodies don't argue that obesity and class are unrelated, but they frequently argue that the obesity gap between the classes has been created by the processed-food industry, which, in the past few decades, has preyed mostly on the less affluent masses. Yet Lenard Lesser, a physician and an obesity researcher at the Palo Alto Medical Foundation Research Institute, says that can't be so, because the obesity gap predates the fast-food industry and the dietary dominance of processed food. "The difference in obesity rates in low- and high-income groups was evident as far back as we have data, at least back through the 1960s," he told me. One reason, some researchers have argued, is that after having had to worry, over countless generations, about getting enough food, poorer segments of society had little cultural bias against overindulging in food, or putting on excess pounds, as industrialization raised incomes and made rich food cheaply available.

The most obvious problem with the "let them eat kale" philosophy of affluent wholesome-food advocates involves the price and availability of wholesome food. Even if Whole Foods, Real Food Daily, or the Farmhouse weren't three bus rides away for the working poor, and even if three ounces of Vegan Cheesy Salad Booster, a Sea Cake appetizer, and the vegetarian quiche weren't laden with fat and problem carbs, few among them would be likely to shell out $5.99, $9.95, or $16, respectively, for those pricey treats.

A slew of start-ups are trying to find ways of producing fresh, local, unprocessed meals quickly and at lower cost. But could this food eventually be sold as cheaply, conveniently, and ubiquitously as today's junky fast food? Not even according to Bittman, who explored the question in a recent *New York Times Magazine* article. Even if wholesome food caught on with the public at large, including the obese population, and even if poor and working-class people were willing to pay a premium for it, how long would it take to scale up from a handful of shops to the tens of thousands required to begin making a dent in the obesity crisis? How long would it take to create the thousands of local farms we'd need in order to provide these shops with fresh, unprocessed ingredients, even in cities?

Yet these hurdles can be waved away, if one only has the proper mindset. Bittman argued two years ago in *The Times* that there's no excuse for anyone, food-desert-bound or not, to eat fast food rather than wholesome food, because even if it's not perfectly fresh and locally grown, lower-end wholesome food—when purchased judiciously at the supermarket and cooked at home—can be cheaper than fast food. Sure, there's the matter of all the time, effort, schedule coordination, and ability it takes to shop, cook, serve, and clean up. But anyone who whines about that extra work, Bittman chided, just doesn't want to give up their excessive TV watching. (An "important benefit of paying more for better-quality food is that you're apt to eat less of it," Pollan helpfully noted in his 2008 book, *In Defense of Food*.) It's remarkable how easy it is to remake the disadvantaged in one's own image.

Let's assume for a moment that somehow America, food deserts and   20 all, becomes absolutely lousy with highly affordable outlets for wholesome, locally sourced dishes that are high in vegetables, fruits, legumes, poultry, fish, and whole grains, and low in fat and problem carbs. What percentage of the junk-food-eating obese do we want to predict will be ready to drop their Big Macs, fries, and Cokes for grilled salmon on chard? We can all agree that many obese people find the former foods extremely enjoyable, and seem unable to control their consumption of them. Is greater availability of healthier food that pushes none of the same thrill buttons going to solve the problem?

Many Pollanites insist it will. "If the government came into these communities and installed Brita filters under their sinks, they'd drink water instead of Coke," Lisa Powell, a professor of health policy and administration at the University of Illinois at Chicago's Institute for Health Research and Policy, told me. But experts who actually work with the obese see a more difficult transition, especially when busy schedules are thrown into the equation. "They won't eat broccoli instead of french fries," says Kelli Drenner, an obesity researcher at Stephen F. Austin State University in Nacogdoches, Texas, which has about four fast-food restaurants per block along most of its main drag. "You try to make even a small change to school lunches, and parents and kids revolt." . . .

People aren't going to change their ingrained, neurobiologically supercharged junk-eating habits just because someone dangles vegetables in front of them, farm-fresh or otherwise. Mark Bittman sees signs of victory in "the stories parents tell me of their kids booing as they drive by McDonald's," but it's not hard to imagine which parents, which kids, and which neighborhoods those stories might involve. One study found that subsidizing the purchase of vegetables encouraged shoppers to buy more vegetables, but also more junk food with the money they saved; on balance, their diets did not improve. The Centers for Disease Control and Prevention recently found that the aughts saw a significant drop in fruit intake, and no increase in vegetable consumption; Americans continue to fall far short of eating the recommended amounts of either. "Everyone's mother and brother has been telling them to eat more fruit and vegetables forever, and the numbers are only getting worse," says Steven Nickolas, who runs the Healthy Food Project in Scottsdale, Arizona. "We're not going to solve this problem by telling people to eat unprocessed food."

Trim, affluent Americans of course have a right to view dietary questions from their own perspective—that is, in terms of what they need to eat in order to add perhaps a few months onto the already healthy courses of their lives. The pernicious sleight of hand is in willfully confusing what might benefit them—small, elite minority that they are—with what would help most of society. The conversations they have among themselves in *The Times*, in best-selling books, and at Real Food Daily may not register with the working-class obese. But these conversations unquestionably distort the views of those who are in a position to influence what society does about the obesity problem.

The Food Revolution We Need

The one fast-food restaurant near a busy East L.A. intersection otherwise filled with bodegas was a Carl's Jr. I went in and saw that the biggest and most prominent posters in the store were pushing a new grilled-cod sandwich. It actually looked pretty good, but it wasn't quite lunchtime, and I just wanted a cup of coffee. I went to the counter to order it, but before I could say anything, the cashier greeted me and asked, "Would you like to try our new Charbroiled Atlantic Cod Fish Sandwich today?" Oh, well, sure, why not? (I asked her to hold the tartar sauce, which is mostly fat, but found out later that the sandwich is normally served with about half as much tartar sauce as the notoriously fatty Filet-O-Fish sandwich at McDonald's, where the fish is battered and fried.) The sandwich was delicious. It was less than half the cost of the Sea Cake appetizer at Real Food Daily. It took less than a minute to prepare. In some ways, it was the best meal I had in L.A., and it was probably the healthiest.

We know perfectly well who within our society has developed an extraordinary facility for nudging the masses to eat certain foods, and for making those foods widely available in cheap and convenient forms. The Pollanites have led us to conflate the industrial processing of food with the adding of fat and sugar in order to hook customers, even while pushing many faux-healthy foods of their own. But why couldn't Big Food's processing and marketing genius be put to use on genuinely healthier foods, like grilled fish? Putting aside the standard objection that the industry has no interest in doing so—we'll see later that in fact the industry has plenty of motivation for taking on this challenge—wouldn't that present a more plau-

David Freedman contrasts the offerings of fast-food restaurants with similar menu items at pricier places. Find out more about this strategy on pp. 424–27.

25

The menu board at KFC shows larger-than-life images of fried food.

sible answer to America's junk-food problem than ordering up 50,000 new farmers' markets featuring locally grown organic squash blossoms?

According to Lenard Lesser, of the Palo Alto Medical Foundation, the food industry has mastered the art of using in-store and near-store promotions to shape what people eat. As Lesser and I drove down storied Telegraph Avenue in Berkeley and into far less affluent Oakland, leaving behind the Whole Foods Markets and sushi restaurants for gas-station markets and barbecued-rib stands, he pointed out the changes in the billboards. Whereas the last one we saw in Berkeley was for fruit juice, many in Oakland tout fast-food joints and their wares, including several featuring the Hot Mess Burger at Jack in the Box. Though Lesser noted that this forest of advertising may simply reflect Oakland residents' preexisting preference for this type of food, he told me lab studies have indicated that the more signs you show people for a particular food product or dish, the more likely they are to choose it over others, all else being equal.

We went into a KFC and found ourselves traversing a maze of signage that put us face-to-face with garish images of various fried foods that presumably had some chicken somewhere deep inside them. "The more they want you to buy something, the bigger they make the image on the menu board," Lesser explained. Here, what loomed largest was the $19.98 fried-chicken-and-corn family meal, which included biscuits and cake. A few days later, I noticed that McDonald's places large placards showcasing desserts on the trash bins, apparently calculating that the best time to entice diners with sweets is when they think they've finished their meals.

Trying to get burger lovers to jump to grilled fish may already be a bit of a stretch—I didn't see any of a dozen other customers buy the cod sandwich when I was at Carl's Jr., though the cashier said it was selling reasonably well. Still, given the food industry's power to tinker with and market food, we should not dismiss its ability to get unhealthy eaters—slowly, incrementally—to buy better food.

That brings us to the crucial question: Just how much healthier could fast-food joints and processed-food companies make their best-selling products without turning off customers? I put that question to a team of McDonald's executives, scientists, and chefs who are involved in shaping the company's future menus, during a February visit to McDonald's surprisingly bucolic campus west of Chicago. By way of a partial answer, the team served me up a preview tasting of two major new menu items that had been under development in their test kitchens and high-tech sensory-testing labs for the past year, and which were rolled out to the public in April. The first was the Egg White Delight McMuffin ($2.65), a lower-calorie, less fatty version of the Egg McMuffin, with some of the refined flour in the original recipe replaced by whole-grain flour. The other was one of three new Premium McWraps ($3.99), crammed with grilled chicken and spring mix, and given a light coating of ranch dressing amped up with rice vinegar. Both items tasted pretty good (as do the versions in stores, I've since confirmed, though some outlets go too heavy on the dressing). And they were both lower in fat, sugar, and calories than not only many McDonald's staples, but also much of the food served in wholesome restaurants or touted in wholesome cookbooks.

In fact, McDonald's has quietly been making healthy changes for years, 30 shrinking portion sizes, reducing some fats, trimming average salt content by more than 10 percent in the past couple of years alone, and adding fruits, vegetables, low-fat dairy, and oatmeal to its menu. In May, the chain dropped its Angus third-pounders and announced a new line of quarter-pound burgers, to be served on buns containing whole grains. Outside the core fast-food customer base, Americans are becoming more health-conscious. Public backlash against fast food could lead to regulatory efforts, and in any case, the fast-food industry has every incentive to maintain broad appeal. "We think a lot about how we can bring nutritionally balanced meals that include enough protein, along with the tastes and satisfaction that have an appetite-tiding effect," said Barbara Booth, the company's director of sensory science.

Fast-food restaurants like McDonald's have been trying for years to promote healthier fare.

Such steps are enormously promising, says Jamy Ard, an epidemiology and preventive-medicine researcher at Wake Forest Baptist Medical Center in Winston-Salem, North Carolina, and a co-director of the Weight Management Center there. "Processed food is a key part of our environment, and it needs to be part of the equation," he explains. "If you can reduce fat and calories by only a small amount in a Big Mac, it still won't be a health food, but it wouldn't be as bad, and that could have a huge impact on us." Ard, who has been working for more than a decade with the obese poor, has little patience with the wholesome-food movement's call to eliminate fast food in favor of farm-fresh goods. "It's really naive," he says. "Fast food became popular because it's tasty and convenient and cheap. It makes a lot more sense to look for small, beneficial changes in that food than it does to hold out for big changes in what people eat that have no realistic chance of happening."

According to a recent study, Americans get 11 percent of their calories, on average, from fast food—a number that's almost certainly much higher among the less affluent overweight. As a result, the fast-food industry may be uniquely positioned to improve our diets. Research suggests that calorie counts in a meal can be trimmed by as much as 30 percent without eaters noticing—by, for example, reducing portion sizes and swapping in ingredients that contain more fiber and water. Over time, that could be much more than enough to literally tip the scales for many obese people. "The difference between losing weight and not losing weight," says Robert Kushner, the obesity scientist and clinical director at Northwestern, "is a few hundred calories a day."

Which raises a question: If McDonald's is taking these sorts of steps, albeit in a slow and limited way, why isn't it more loudly saying so to deflect criticism? While the company has heavily plugged the debut of its new egg-white sandwich and chicken wraps, the ads have left out even a mention of health, the reduced calories and fat, or the inclusion of whole grains. McDonald's has practically kept secret the fact that it has also begun substituting whole-grain flour for some of the less healthy refined flour in its best-selling Egg McMuffin.

The explanation can be summed up in two words that surely strike fear into the hearts of all fast-food executives who hope to make their companies' fare healthier: McLean Deluxe.

Among those who gleefully rank such things, the McLean Deluxe   35
reigns as McDonald's worst product failure of all time, eclipsing McPasta, the McHotdog, and the McAfrica (don't ask). When I brought up the McLean Deluxe to the innovation team at McDonald's, I faced the first and only uncomfortable silence of the day. Finally, Greg Watson, a senior vice president, cleared his throat and told me that neither he nor anyone else in the room was at the company at the time, and he didn't know that much about it. "It sounds to me like it was ahead of its time," he added. "If we had something like that in the future, we would never launch it like that again."

Introduced in 1991, the McLean Deluxe was perhaps the boldest single effort the food industry has ever undertaken to shift the masses to healthier eating. It was supposed to be a healthier version of the Quarter Pounder, made with extra-lean beef infused with seaweed extract. It reportedly did reasonably well in early taste tests—for what it's worth, my wife and I were big fans—and McDonald's pumped the reduced-fat angle to the public for all it was worth. The general reaction varied from lack of interest to mockery to revulsion. The company gamely flogged the sandwich for five years before quietly removing it from the menu.

The McLean Deluxe was a sharp lesson to the industry, even if in some ways it merely confirmed what generations of parents have well known: if you want to turn off otherwise eager eaters to a dish, tell them it's good for them. Recent studies suggest that calorie counts placed on menus have a negligible effect on food choices, and that the less-health-conscious might even use the information to steer clear of low-calorie fare—perhaps assuming that it tastes worse and is less satisfying, and that it's worse value for their money. The result is a sense in the food industry that if it is going to sell healthier versions of its foods to the general public—and not just to that minority already sold on healthier eating—it is going to have to do it in a relatively sneaky way, emphasizing the taste appeal and not the health benefits. "People expect something to taste worse if they believe it's healthy," says Charles Spence, an Oxford University neuroscientist who specializes in how the brain perceives food. "And that expectation affects how it tastes to them, so it actually *does* taste worse."

Thus McDonald's silence on the nutritional profiles of its new menu items. "We're not making any health claims," Watson said. "We're just saying it's new, it tastes great, come on in and enjoy it. Maybe once the product is well seated with customers, we'll change that message." If customers learn that they can eat healthier foods at McDonald's without even realizing it, he added, they'll be more likely to try healthier foods there than at other restaurants. The same reasoning presumably explains why the promotions and ads for the Carl's Jr. grilled-cod sandwich offer not a word related to healthfulness, and why there wasn't a whiff of health cheerleading surrounding the turkey burger brought out earlier this year by Burger King (which is not yet calling the sandwich a permanent addition).

If the food industry is to quietly sell healthier products to its mainstream, mostly non-health-conscious customers, it must find ways to deliver the eating experience that fat and problem carbs provide in foods that have fewer of those ingredients. There is no way to do that with farm-fresh produce and wholesome meat, other than reducing portion size. But processing technology gives the food industry a potent tool for trimming unwanted ingredients while preserving the sensations they deliver.

I visited Fona International, a flavor-engineering company also outside 40 Chicago, and learned that there are a battery of tricks for fooling and appeasing taste buds, which are prone to notice a lack of fat or sugar, or the presence of any of the various bitter, metallic, or otherwise unpleasant flavors that vegetables, fiber, complex carbs, and fat or sugar substitutes can impart to a food intended to appeal to junk-food eaters. Some 5,000 FDA-approved chemical compounds—which represent the base components of all known flavors—line the shelves that run alongside Fona's huge labs. Armed with these ingredients and an array of state-of-the-art chemical-analysis and testing tools, Fona's scientists and engineers can precisely control flavor perception. "When you reduce the sugar, fat, and salt in foods, you change the personality of the product," said Robert Sobel, a chemist, who heads up research at the company. "We can restore it."

For example, fat "cushions" the release of various flavors on the tongue, unveiling them gradually and allowing them to linger. When fat is removed, flavors tend to immediately inundate the tongue and then quickly flee, which we register as a much less satisfying experience. Fona's experts can reproduce the "temporal profile" of the flavors in fattier foods by adding edible compounds derived from plants that slow the release of flavor molecules; by replacing the flavors with similarly flavored compounds that come on and leave more slowly; or by enlisting "phantom aromas" that create the sensation of certain tastes even when those tastes are not present on the tongue. (For example, the smell of vanilla can essentially mask reductions in sugar of up to 25 percent.) One triumph of this sort of engineering is the modern protein drink, a staple of many successful weight-loss programs and a favorite of those trying to build muscle. "Seven years ago they were unpalatable," Sobel said. "Today we can mask the astringent flavors and eggy aromas by adding natural ingredients." . . .

Fona . . . , like most companies in [the] industry, won't identify customers or product names on the record. But [the firm] showed me an array of foods and beverages that were under construction, so to speak, in the name of reducing calories, fat, and sugar while maintaining mass appeal. . . . Dozens of companies are doing similar work, as are the big food-ingredient manufacturers, such as ConAgra, whose products are in 97 percent of American homes, and whose whole-wheat flour is what McDonald's is relying on for its breakfast sandwiches. Domino Foods, the sugar manufacturer, now sells a low-calorie combination of sugar and the nonsugar sweetener stevia that has been engineered by a flavor company to mask the sort of nonsugary tastes driving many consumers away from diet beverages and the like. "Stevia has a licorice note we were able to have taken out," explains Domino Foods CEO Brian O'Malley.

High-tech anti-obesity food engineering is just warming up. Oxford's Charles Spence notes that in addition to flavors and textures, companies are investigating ways to exploit a stream of insights that have been coming out of scholarly research about the neuroscience of eating. He notes, for example, that candy companies may be able to slip healthier ingredients into candy bars without anyone noticing, simply by loading these ingredients into the middle of the bar and leaving most of the fat and sugar at the ends of the bar. "We tend to make up our minds about how something tastes from the first and last bites, and don't care as much what happens in between," he explains. Some other potentially useful gimmicks he points out: adding weight to food packaging such as yogurt containers, which convinces eaters that the contents are rich with calories, even when they're not; using chewy textures that force consumers to spend more time between bites, giving the brain a chance to register satiety; and using colors, smells, sounds, and packaging information to create the belief that foods are fatty and sweet even when they are not. Spence found, for example, that wine is perceived as 50 percent sweeter when consumed under a red light.

Researchers are also tinkering with food ingredients to boost satiety. Cargill has developed a starch derived from tapioca that gives dishes a refined-carb taste and mouthfeel, but acts more like fiber in the body—a feature that could keep the appetite from spiking later. "People usually think that processing leads to foods that digest too quickly, but we've been able to use processing to slow the digestion rate," says Bruce McGoogan, who heads R&D for Cargill's North American food-ingredient business. The company has also developed ways to reduce fat in beef patties, and to make baked goods using half the usual sugar and oil, all without heavily compromising taste and texture. . . .

The Implacable Enemies of Healthier Processed Food

What's not to like about these developments? Plenty, if you've bought into 45 the notion that processing itself is the source of the unhealthfulness of our foods. The wholesome-food movement is not only talking up dietary strategies that are unlikely to help most obese Americans; it is, in various ways, getting in the way of strategies that could work better.

Mark Bittman demonstrates a recipe on the *Today Show*.

The Pollanites didn't invent resistance to healthier popular foods, as the fate of the McLean Deluxe . . . demonstrate[s], but they've greatly intensified it. Fast food and junk food have their core customer base, and the wholesome-food gurus have theirs. In between sit many millions of Americans—the more the idea that processed food should be shunned no matter what takes hold in this group, the less incentive fast-food joints will have to continue edging away from the fat- and problem-carb-laden fare beloved by their most loyal customers to try to broaden their appeal.

Pollan has popularized contempt for "nutritionism," the idea behind packing healthier ingredients into processed foods. In his view, the quest to add healthier ingredients to food isn't a potential solution, it's part of the problem. Food is healthy not when it contains healthy ingredients, he argues, but when it can be traced simply and directly to (preferably local) farms. As he resonantly put it in *The Times* in 2007: "If you're concerned about your health, you should probably avoid food products that make health claims. Why? Because a health claim on a food product is a good indication that it's not really food, and food is what you want to eat."

McDonald's executive chef Dan Coudreaut at work in his corporate kitchen.

In this way, wholesome-food advocates have managed to pre-damn the very steps we need the food industry to take, placing the industry in a no-win situation: If it maintains the status quo, then we need to stay away because its food is loaded with fat and sugar. But if it tries to moderate these ingredients, then it is deceiving us with nutritionism. Pollan explicitly counsels avoiding foods containing more than five ingredients, or any hard-to-pronounce or unfamiliar ingredients. This rule eliminates almost anything the industry could do to produce healthier foods that retain mass appeal—most of us wouldn't get past xanthan gum—and that's perfectly in keeping with his intention.

By placing wholesome eating directly at odds with healthier processed foods, the Pollanites threaten to derail the reformation of fast food just as it's starting to gain traction. At McDonald's, "Chef Dan"—that is, Dan Coudreaut, the executive chef and director of culinary innovation—told me of the dilemma the movement has caused him as he has tried to make the menu healthier. "Some want us to have healthier food, but others want us to have minimally processed ingredients, which can mean more fat," he explained.

"It's becoming a balancing act for us." That the chef with arguably the most influence in the world over the diet of the obese would even consider adding fat to his menu to placate wholesome foodies is a pretty good sign that something has gone terribly wrong with our approach to the obesity crisis.

Many people insist that the steps the food industry has already taken to offer less-obesogenic fare are no more than cynical ploys to fool customers into eating the same old crap under a healthy guise. In his 3,500-word *New York Times Magazine* article on the prospects for healthier fast food, Mark Bittman lauded a new niche of vegan chain restaurants while devoting just one line to the major "quick serve" restaurants' contribution to better health: "I'm not talking about token gestures, like the McDonald's fruit-and-yogurt parfait, whose calories are more than 50 percent sugar." Never mind that 80 percent of a farm-fresh apple's calories come from sugar; that almost any obesity expert would heartily approve of the yogurt parfait as a step in the right direction for most fast-food-dessert eaters; and that many of the desserts Bittman glorifies in his own writing make the parfait look like arugula, nutrition-wise. (His recipe for corn-and-blueberry crisp, for example, calls for adding two-thirds of a cup of brown sugar to a lot of other problem carbs, along with five tablespoons of butter.)

Bittman is hardly alone in his reflexive dismissals. No sooner had McDonald's and Burger King rolled out their egg-white sandwich and turkey burger, respectively, than a spate of articles popped up hooting that the new dishes weren't healthier because they trimmed a mere 50 and 100 calories from their standard counterparts, the Egg McMuffin and the Whopper. Apparently these writers didn't understand, or chose to ignore, the fact that a reduction of 50 or 100 calories in a single dish places an eater exactly on track to eliminate a few hundred calories a day from his or her diet—the critical threshold needed for long-term weight loss. Any bigger reduction would risk leaving someone too hungry to stick to a diet program. It's just the sort of small step in the right direction we should be aiming for, because the obese are much more likely to take it than they are to make a big leap to wholesome or very-low-calorie foods.

Many wholesome foodies insist that the food industry won't make serious progress toward healthier fare unless forced to by regulation. I, for one, believe regulation aimed at speeding the replacement of obesogenic foods with appealing healthier foods would be a great idea. But what a lot of foodies really want is to ban the food industry from selling junk food altogether. And that is just a fantasy. The government never managed to keep the tobacco companies from selling cigarettes, and banning booze (the third-most-deadly consumable killer after cigarettes and food) didn't turn out so well. The two most health-enlightened, regulation-friendly major cities in America, New York and San Francisco, tried to halt sales of two of the most horrific fast-food assaults on health—giant servings of sugared beverages and kids' fast-food meals accompanied by toys, respectively—and neither had much luck. Michelle Obama is excoriated by conservatives for asking schools to throw more fruits and vegetables into the lunches they serve. Realistically, the most we can hope for is a tax on some obesogenic foods. The research of Lisa Powell, the University of Illinois professor, suggests that a 20 percent tax on sugary beverages would reduce consumption by about 25 percent. (As for fatty foods, no serious tax proposal has yet been made in the U.S., and if one comes along, the wholesome foodies might well join the food industry and most consumers in opposing it. Denmark did manage to enact a fatty-food tax, but it was deemed a failure when consumers went next door into Germany and Sweden to stock up on their beloved treats.)

Continuing to call out Big Food on its unhealthy offerings, and loudly, is one of the best levers we have for pushing it toward healthier products—but let's call it out intelligently, not reflexively. Executives of giant food companies may be many things, but they are not stupid. Absent action, they risk a growing public-relations disaster, the loss of their more affluent and increasingly health-conscious customers, and the threat of regulation, which will be costly to fight, even if the new rules don't stick. Those fears are surely what's driving much of the push toward moderately healthier fare within the industry today. But if the Pollanites convince policy makers and the health-conscious public that these foods are dangerous by virtue of not being farm-fresh, that will push Big Food in a different direction (in part by limiting the profit potential it sees in lower-fat, lower-problem-carb foods), and cause it to spend its resources in other ways.

Significant regulation of junk food may not go far, but we have other tools at our disposal to prod Big Food to intensify and speed up its efforts to cut fat and problem carbs in its offerings, particularly if we're smart about it. Lenard Lesser points out that government and advocacy groups could start singling out particular restaurants and food products for praise or shaming—a more official version of "eat this, not that"—rather than sticking to a steady drumbeat of "processed food must go away." Academia could do a much better job of producing and highlighting solid research into less obesogenic, high-mass-appeal foods, and could curtail its evidence-light anti-food-processing bias, so that the next generation of social and policy entrepreneurs might work to narrow the gap between the poor obese and the well-resourced healthy instead of inadvertently widening it. We can keep pushing our health-care system to provide more incentives and support to the obese for losing weight by making small, painless, but helpful changes in their behavior, such as switching from Whoppers to turkey burgers, from Egg McMuffins to Egg White Delights, or from blueberry crisp to fruit-and-yogurt parfaits.

And we can ask the wholesome-food advocates, and those who give   55
them voice, to make it clearer that the advice they sling is relevant mostly to the privileged healthy—and to start getting behind realistic solutions to the obesity crisis.

Thinking about the Text

1. Why is David Freedman so sure that fast-food outlets can significantly improve the diet and health of the U.S. public? **SUMMARIZE** the main arguments in this proposal. What does he see as the problem, and what is his solution?

2. Freedman seems to be genuinely concerned about the problems caused by obesity and unhealthy diets, and he argues passionately for a solution. Still, his way of describing poor people, obese people, and particularly people who are both, can seem disrespectful and patronizing. What do you think his **ATTITUDE** is toward these people? Do you think he assumes that his **AUDIENCE** includes such people? Point to specific examples in the text to support your conclusions.

3. A good **PROPOSAL** presents evidence that the proposed course of action will address the problem, and that it will do so better than other possible solutions. Identify two **REASONS** and the corresponding **EVIDENCE** that Freedman presents to support his proposed solution. How persuasive are they? Has he convinced you that his solution is the best fix available and if not, why not?

4. Recent studies show that restaurant customers pay little attention to the calorie count information on menus, and even that some diners may use the information in order to *avoid* the lower-calorie items. Do you pay attention to the calorie counts or other nutritional information on menus or food packaging? Explain the reasoning behind your practices.

5. In arguing for "the food revolution we need," Freedman poses a rhetorical question: "Wouldn't [healthier fast-food options] present a more plausible answer to America's junk food problem than ordering up 50,000 new farmers' markets featuring locally grown organic squash blossoms?" The issue, of course, is much more complex than Freedman's either/or proposition—but think locally for a moment. Which option would you rather find around the corner from where you live: a healthier menu at a fast-food restaurant, or a new farmers' market with a variety of local produce? Write an editorial for your local newspaper **ARGUING** for your chosen establishment. List and describe the benefits of the option you've chosen, providing solid evidence that will appeal to those who read that paper.

Wikipedia Pops Up in Bibliographies and Even College Assignments

LARRY GORDON

ALL THROUGH HIGH SCHOOL, Ani Schug was told to steer clear of Wikipedia. Her teachers talked about the popular online encyclopedia "as if it wasn't serious or trustworthy" and suggested it only be used as a tip sheet.

Imagine her surprise this spring when her American politics professor at Pomona College assigned the class to write detailed entries for Wikipedia instead of traditional term papers.

Turns out it was a lot harder than the students anticipated. Their projects had to be researched, composed and coded to match Wikipedia's strict protocols. Schug and her classmates wound up citing 218 scholarly legal and newspaper sources for their entry on a 1978 U.S. Supreme Court decision allowing corporate donations for ballot initiative campaigns.

Then came the really scary step: All their work was posted publicly on Wikipedia for reading and editing by a potentially immense audience.

"It felt more real that other people will be reading us besides just our group and the teacher," said Schug, 19, who just completed her freshman year at Pomona. "It makes us feel more obligated to do a good job and present the facts in an unbiased way."

5

LARRY GORDON covers higher education for the *Los Angeles Times*, writing about issues that affect schools, students, and their wider communities. He tweets @LarryGordonLAT. This essay ran in the June 14, 2014, issue of that paper.

Once the bane of teachers, Wikipedia and entry-writing exercises are becoming more common on college campuses as academia and the online site drop mutual suspicions and seek to cooperate. In at least 150 courses at colleges in the U.S. and Canada, including UC Berkeley, UC San Francisco's medical school, Boston College and Carnegie Mellon University, students were assigned to create or expand Wikipedia entries this year.

The result, supporters say, has been better researched articles about, for example, the causes of paralyzing strokes and the history of the American West. And, they say, students are becoming better prepared for a future of digital information.

"Even the best research papers get buried in a drawer somewhere," said Amanda Hollis-Brusky, the Pomona politics professor who assigned the Wikipedia projects. "These make a real contribution to the public discourse."

When the not-for-profit Wikipedia was started in 2001, the idea was that antiestablishment volunteers—in fact, anyone who could access the Internet—would write and edit its mainly anonymous entries. An unbiased truth was supposed to emerge if enough contributors took part. By contrast, traditional encyclopedias hired expert authors.

But even as its popularity soared among the public, Wikipedia earned 10 a reputation among academics as amateurish, peppered with errors and too open to nasty online spats over content. Wikipedia has tried to repair all that with better safeguards and a wider range of topics.

As part of that effort, Wikipedia has established a San Francisco educational arm that helps colleges tailor class assignments to the site's technical demands. It trains "Wikipedia Ambassadors" like Char Booth, the Claremont Colleges librarian who aided the Pomona class.

Wikipedia "gets well-written articles from students who are studying the topics and have access to the best literature on the subject and the expertise of professors who can guide them as well," said LiAnna Davis, a spokeswoman for the Wiki Education Foundation.

Pomona professor Hollis-Brusky and Booth taught students to meet the requirements of tight writing, neutral tone and abundant citations for their projects on such topics as the Federalist Papers, diamond importing laws and the electoral reform group FairVote. The student groups presented their research to the class and displayed their Wikipedia pages on a large screen in a Hahn Hall classroom. The Supreme Court case entry showed that it had attracted about 2,000 viewers in a month.

Even with complaints of mistakes and incompleteness, Wikipedia has

Pretty cool what these students are doing, huh? Try your hand at writing a *Wikipedia* entry using the tips on pp. 771–72.

a powerful reach. Often the first site suggested by Google searches, it has about 4.5 million English-language entries and 496 million visitors a month worldwide.

Wikipedia "has essentially become too large to ignore," said Berkeley's   15 Kevin Gorman, a former student who is the nation's first "Wikipedian in Residence" at an undergraduate institution.

"It is certainly an initial source of information for a huge number of people," he said. "For many people, it may be their primary source of information."

Gorman guides students who are composing Wiki entries as assignments in UC Berkeley's American Cultures program—requiring classes that deal with ethnic and economic diversity.

Gorman said it is important to expand the ranks of Wikipedia authors and editors beyond its early base of "basically techno, libertarian, white dudes."

Further symbolizing peace with academia, professional scholarly organizations in sociology, psychological science and communications in recent years have urged members to write Wikipedia articles and to assign students to do so. Other efforts include Wikipedia-writing marathons, such as one sponsored by CalArts' online magazine, *East of Borneo*, that focused on topics about the Southern California art world.

Gorman also works with UC San Francisco's medical school, where pro-   20 fessor Amin Azzam runs a month-long elective class for students to improve Wikipedia's medical information. In the first such class at an American medical school, students have started or revised pages about hepatitis, dementia and alcohol withdrawal syndrome, among others, Azzam said.

The assignments, he explained, are part of young doctors' "social contract to do good in the world and help patients" learn about health.

In revising and broadening the entry on strokes, medical student Andrew Callen experienced Wikipedia's argumentative nature. A Wikipedia medical editor, apparently a physician, challenged some of Callen's technical terminology.

Callen said his language was more precise but conceded after some back and forth that the distinction was not important for lay readers.

"I didn't take offense at it," he said. "In a way I appreciated it."

Writing for Wikipedia, Callen said, is a good way to improve the expla-   25 nation of complicated science to patients. "The more people we can get to edit it, the more accurate the information will be," he added.

Some skepticism remains.

Doug Hesse, vice president of the National Council of Teachers of English, said Wikipedia's understandable insistence on neutrality doesn't allow students to make reasoned arguments and analysis in term papers.

And its reliance on published sources eliminates students' independent interviews, experiments and research, said Hesse, who heads the University of Denver's writing program.

At Carnegie Mellon in Pittsburgh, professor of human-computer interaction Robert Kraut has assigned classes to compose Wikipedia chapters in psychology. Students have benefited, he said, but he, too, doesn't think such assignments will become commonplace.

Compared to regular term papers, Wiki entries require a lot more faculty time to ensure they are ready for online viewing. Some colleges may be put off by the public editing, which Kraut said led to some of his students' writings getting excised for not following what he considered to be very complicated footnoting rules.   30

In Pomona College's politics class, there was no nasty flaming on any class projects, which counted for 35 percent of the students' grades, according to Hollis-Brusky. (Most Wikipedia authors use pseudonyms and the Pomona students were urged to do the same to avoid possible privacy violations.)

Freshman Lane Miles, who worked on the FairVote research, said it was doubly satisfying to help build the online encyclopedia. "We are educating ourselves and educating others," he said.

Thinking about the Text

1. Larry Gordon opens his **REPORT** with a statement from a student at Pomona College who recalls being told all through high school to avoid *Wikipedia* as a source—and you may have been told the same. Does Gordon's report make you think that *Wikipedia* is in fact worth taking seriously? Which of the points in the report did you find most persuasive? Why?

2. A good report presents trustworthy information, and should do so fairly and thoroughly. From what kinds of sources does Gordon draw his information? How trustworthy are his sources, and how well does he present varied points of view? Point to examples from the text to support your answer.

3. As a newspaper reporter, Gordon is generally expected to maintain an objective **STANCE** : to present information, not to argue for what he thinks. Can you tell where he stands on the *Wikipedia* issue he's reporting on here? Point to examples in his article to support your response.

4. One of the benefits of *Wikipedia*-authoring assignments, according to some of Gordon's sources, is that they'll prepare students for a "future of digital information." How important a goal is that for you? Why?

5. Read a *Wikipedia* entry about something that you are already very familiar with—perhaps your town, your favorite sports team, a political issue—and evaluate the information you find. How thorough is the information you find there? How accurate is it? If there are different perspectives on the topic or issue, are all sides addressed fairly? Write a new paragraph or two for the entry expanding on some area, or edit a section of what's already there. (For advice on writing for a **WIKI**, see Chapter 34.) Finally, reflect on the challenges presented by the task—and maybe upload the revised entry you've written!

Hidden Intellectualism

GERALD GRAFF

E VERYONE KNOWS SOME YOUNG PERSON who is impressively "street smart" but does poorly in school. What a waste, we think, that one who is so intelligent about so many things in life seems unable to apply that intelligence to academic work. What doesn't occur to us, though, is that schools and colleges might be at fault for missing the opportunity to tap into such street smarts and channel them into good academic work.

Nor do we consider one of the major reasons why schools and colleges overlook the intellectual potential of street smarts: the fact that we associate those street smarts with anti-intellectual concerns. We associate the educated life, the life of the mind, too narrowly and exclusively with subjects and texts that we consider inherently weighty and academic. We assume that it's possible to wax intellectual about Plato, Shakespeare, the French Revolution, and nuclear fission, but not about cars, dating, fashion, sports, TV, or video games.

The trouble with this assumption is that no necessary connection has ever been established between any text or subject and the educational depth

GERALD GRAFF, a professor of English and education at the University of Illinois at Chicago, is best known for his books *Professing Literature: An Institutional History* (1989), *Beyond the Culture Wars: How Teaching the Conflicts Can Revitalize American Education* (1993), *Clueless in Academe: How Schooling Obscures the Life of the Mind* (2004), and (with Cathy Birkenstein) *"They Say / I Say": The Moves That Matter in Academic Writing* (2013). This essay was written for *Clueless in Academe* in 2004.

and weight of the discussion it can generate. Real intellectuals turn any subject, however lightweight it may seem, into grist for their mill through the thoughtful questions they bring to it, whereas a dullard will find a way to drain the interest out of the richest subject. That's why a George Orwell writing on the cultural meanings of penny postcards is infinitely more substantial than the cogitations of many professors on Shakespeare or globalization (104–16).

Students do need to read models of intellectually challenging writing—and Orwell is a great one—if they are to become intellectuals themselves. But they would be more prone to take on intellectual identities if we encouraged them to do so at first on subjects that interest them rather than ones that interest us.

Gerald Graff frames his position as a response to attitudes he has observed. See pp. 122–24 on responding to what others say.

I offer my own adolescent experience as a case in point. Until I entered   5 college, I hated books and cared only for sports. The only reading I cared to do or could do was sports magazines, on which I became hooked, becoming a regular reader of *Sport* magazine in the late forties, *Sports Illustrated* when it began publishing in 1954, and the annual magazine guides to professional baseball, football, and basketball. I also loved the sports novels for boys of John R. Tunis and Clair Bee and autobiographies of sports stars like Joe DiMaggio's *Lucky to Be a Yankee* and Bob Feller's *Strikeout Story*. In short, I was your typical teenage anti-intellectual—or so I believed for a long time. I have recently come to think, however, that my preference for sports over schoolwork was not anti-intellectualism so much as intellectualism by other means.

In the Chicago neighborhood I grew up in, which had become a melting pot after World War II, our block was solidly middle class, but just a block away—doubtless concentrated there by the real estate companies—were African Americans, Native Americans, and "hillbilly" whites who had recently fled postwar joblessness in the South and Appalachia. Negotiating this class boundary was a tricky matter. On the one hand, it was necessary to maintain the boundary between "clean-cut" boys like me and working-class "hoods," as we called them, which meant that it was good to be openly smart in a bookish sort of way. On the other hand, I was desperate for the approval of the hoods, whom I encountered daily on the playing field and in the neighborhood, and for this purpose it was not at all good to be book-smart. The hoods would turn on you if they sensed you were putting on airs over them: "Who you lookin' at, smart ass?" as a leather-jacketed youth once said to me as he relieved me of my pocket change along with my self-respect.

I grew up torn, then, between the need to prove I was smart and the fear of a beating if I proved it too well; between the need not to jeopardize my respectable future and the need to impress the hoods. As I lived it, the conflict came down to a choice between being physically tough and being verbal. For a boy in my neighborhood and elementary school, only being "tough" earned you complete legitimacy. I still recall endless, complicated debates in this period with my closest pals over who was "the toughest guy in the school." If you were less than negligible as a fighter, as I was, you settled for the next best thing, which was to be inarticulate, carefully hiding telltale marks of literacy like correct grammar and pronunciation.

In one way, then, it would be hard to imagine an adolescence more thoroughly anti-intellectual than mine. Yet in retrospect, I see that it's more complicated, that I and the 1950s themselves were not simply hostile toward intellectualism, but divided and ambivalent. When Marilyn Monroe married the playwright Arthur Miller in 1956 after divorcing the retired baseball star Joe DiMaggio, the symbolic triumph of geek over jock suggested the way the wind was blowing. Even Elvis, according to his biographer Peter Guralnick, turns out to have supported Adlai over Ike in the presidential election of 1956. "I don't dig the intellectual bit," he told reporters. "But I'm telling you, man, he knows the most" (327).

Though I too thought I did not "dig the intellectual bit," I see now that I was unwittingly in training for it. The germs had actually been planted in the seemingly philistine debates about which boys were the toughest. I see now that in the interminable analysis of sports teams, movies, and toughness that my friends and I engaged in—a type of analysis, needless to say, that the real toughs would never have stooped to—I was already betraying an allegiance to the egghead world. I was practicing being an intellectual before I knew that was what I wanted to be.

It was in these discussions with friends about toughness and sports, 10 I think, and in my reading of sports books and magazines, that I began to learn the rudiments of the intellectual life: how to make an argument, weigh different kinds of evidence, move between particulars and generalizations, summarize the views of others, and enter a conversation about ideas. It was in reading and arguing about sports and toughness that I experienced what it felt like to propose a generalization, restate and respond to a counterargument, and perform other intellectualizing operations, including composing the kind of sentences I am writing now.

Only much later did it dawn on me that the sports world was more compelling than school because it was *more intellectual than school,* not less.

Sports after all was full of challenging arguments, debates, problems for analysis, and intricate statistics that you could care about, as school conspicuously was not. I believe that street smarts beat out book smarts in our culture not because street smarts are nonintellectual, as we generally suppose, but because they satisfy an intellectual thirst more thoroughly than school culture, which seems pale and unreal.

They also satisfy the thirst for community. When you entered sports debates, you became part of a community that was not limited to your family and friends, but was national and public. Whereas schoolwork isolated you from others, the pennant race or Ted Williams's .400 batting average was something you could talk about with people you had never met. Sports introduced you not only to a culture steeped in argument, but to a public argument culture that transcended the personal. I can't blame my schools for failing to make intellectual culture resemble the Super Bowl, but I do fault them for failing to learn anything from the sports and entertainment worlds about how to organize and represent intellectual culture, how to exploit its gamelike element and turn it into arresting public spectacle that might have competed more successfully for my youthful attention.

For here is another thing that never dawned on me and is still kept hidden from students, with tragic results: that the real intellectual world, the one that existed in the big world beyond school, is organized very much like the world of team sports, with rival texts, rival interpretations and evaluations of texts, rival theories of why they should be read and taught, and elaborate team competitions in which "fans" of writers, intellectual systems, methodologies, and -isms contend against each other.

To be sure, school contained plenty of competition, which became more invidious as one moved up the ladder (and has become even more so today with the advent of high-stakes testing). In this competition, points were scored not by making arguments, but by a show of information or vast reading, by grade-grubbing, or other forms of oneupmanship. School competition, in short, reproduced the less attractive features of sports culture without those that create close bonds and community.

And in distancing themselves from anything as enjoyable and absorbing 15 as sports, my schools missed the opportunity to capitalize on an element of drama and conflict that the intellectual world shares with sports. Consequently, I failed to see the parallels between the sports and academic worlds that could have helped me cross more readily from one argument culture to the other.

Sports is only one of the domains whose potential for literacy training (and not only for males) is seriously underestimated by educators, who see sports as competing with academic development rather than a route to it. But if this argument suggests why it is a good idea to assign readings and topics that are close to students' existing interests, it also suggests the limits of this tactic. For students who get excited about the chance to write about their passion for cars will often write as poorly and unreflectively on that topic as on Shakespeare or Plato. Here is the flip side of what I pointed out before: that there's no necessary relation between the degree of interest a student shows in a text or subject and the quality of thought or expression such a student manifests in writing or talking about it. The challenge, as college professor Ned Laff has put it, "is not simply to exploit students' nonacademic interests, but to get them to see those interests through academic eyes."

To say that students need to see their interests "through academic eyes" is to say that street smarts are not enough. Making students' nonacademic interests an object of academic study is useful, then, for getting students' attention and overcoming their boredom and alienation, but this tactic won't in itself necessarily move them closer to an academically rigorous treatment of those interests. On the other hand, inviting students to write about cars, sports, or clothing fashions does not have to be a pedagogical cop-out as long as students are required to see these interests "through academic eyes," that is, to think and write about cars, sports, and fashions in a reflective, analytical way, one that sees them as microcosms of what is going on in the wider culture.

If I am right, then schools and colleges are missing an opportunity when they do not encourage students to take their nonacademic interests as objects of academic study. It is self-defeating to decline to introduce any text or subject that figures to engage students who will otherwise tune out academic work entirely. If a student cannot get interested in Mill's *On Liberty* but will read *Sports Illustrated* or *Vogue* or the hip-hop magazine *Source* with absorption, this is a strong argument for assigning the magazines over the classic. It's a good bet that if students get hooked on reading and writing by doing term papers on *Source,* they will eventually get to *On Liberty.* But even if they don't, the magazine reading will make them more literate and reflective than they would be otherwise. So it makes pedagogical sense to develop classroom units on sports, cars, fashions, rap music, and other such topics. Give me the student anytime who writes a sharply argued, sociologically acute analysis of an issue of *Source* over the student who writes a lifeless explication of *Hamlet* or Socrates' *Apology.*

Works Cited

Cramer, Richard Ben. *Joe DiMaggio: The Hero's Life*. New York: Simon, 2000.
    Print.
DiMaggio, Joe. *Lucky to Be a Yankee*. New York: Bantam, 1949. Print.
Feller, Bob. *Strikeout Story*. New York: Bantam, 1948. Print.
Guralnick, Peter. *Last Train to Memphis: The Rise of Elvis Presley*. Boston:
    Little, Brown, 1994. Print.
Orwell, George. *A Collection of Essays*. New York: Harcourt, 1953. Print.

Thinking about the Text

1. Gerald Graff's principal **EVIDENCE** in this essay is his own personal experience. How and how well does he present other supporting evidence? How and how well does he present the views that he is arguing against?

2. Graff notes that Ned Laff suggests that students be encouraged to view what interests them "through academic eyes" (16). What do you and your friends discuss frequently? Sports stats? Relative merits of various cosmetics or video games? Who is the best dancer or rapper? Have you ever thought and written about those interests "in a reflective, analytical way" (17)? Would you want to? What kinds of evidence might you need to examine and present?

3. Graff makes frequent use of the first-person plural—"we think," "we associate," and so on (1, 2). Who is this "we" that he sees as his **AUDIENCE**: professors? parents? anybody and everybody? Explain your answer, and provide evidence from the text. Why might Graff have chosen to use "we" this way? How does it affect your response to his argument?

4. Graff argues that a student who learns to take an academic approach to *Sports Illustrated*, *Vogue*, *Source*, or other popular periodicals will eventually be likely to want to read traditionally academic material. Do you agree with that argument?

5. Graff recollects growing up "torn . . . between the need to prove I was smart and the fear of a beating if I proved it too well" (7). Did you have any similar experiences growing up, possibly involving fear of social rather than physical harm? Write an essay in which you **DESCRIBE** the prevailing (and perhaps conflicting) attitudes toward academic success among your friends, family members, and neighbors. Once you establish the context, write about your strategies and experiences in navigating the attitudes of those around you.

I'm Considering Becoming a Sports Fan—How Do I Pick a Team?

ANDY HINDS

W E THREW A BIRTHDAY PARTY for my wife at a wine bar in our neighborhood recently, on a night when there was an Important Football Game happening. While most of our guests chatted and enjoyed appetizers, a handful of men sat at the bar. At first I thought that they were just staying close to the font of booze, and so I went to join them. Then I realized that they were actually watching football.

"You watch the Broncos game earlier?" one of them asked me.

"I saw a little bit of it," I said. "Close one, huh?" I had watched about 30 seconds of the game while borrowing something from my next-door neighbor. I'm pretty sure that was the extent of my viewing of the 2012/2013 NFL season up to that point. My neighbor, a sports-obsessed gay guy, had similarly assumed that I cared about the game, so I had made some vague comments to him as well. You know, so as not to fail at the performance of hegemonic masculinity.

In both of these exchanges, I had that old familiar feeling of not having a clue about something that was supposed to be important to me as an

---

ANDY HINDS, a stay-at-home dad with twin daughters, is author of the blog *Beta Dad* and a contributor to the parenting blog *Dadcentric* and the *New York Times* blog *Motherlode*. You can follow him on *Twitter* @betadad. This article was published in the *Atlantic* in 2013.

American male. I've finally learned, if pressed on my opinions regarding the latest sporting news, to say, unapologetically, "I really don't follow sports." But my first reaction is still to try to "pass" for a man with a healthy concern for box scores and draft picks, and then change the subject of conversation as seamlessly as possible.

The truth, though, is that while I have a maximum attention span of maybe 10 minutes when it comes to watching any game in which no one I personally know is playing, I'm fascinated by the appeal spectator sports has for so many people. I want to know how they became fans and why I never have. Often, during the frenzy of playoffs, I even consider adopting a team to follow so I can get in on the excitement. The problem is, how do I decide which team to care about?

While sports esoterica is a constant component of online discourse at any time of year, in the run-up to Sunday's Super Bowl, my timelines and feeds have crackled with cryptic pronouncements and predictions regarding characters in a drama of which I am largely ignorant. So this year, I asked my friends on social media about their relationships with the pro football teams they care about. How did they find one another? How did they know that their team was "the one"? Have they ever strayed from their team, or considered giving up on them?

My inquiries yielded many interesting and passionate responses, but the three main reasons people gave for following their teams were: a) a fam-

Minnesota Vikings fans sporting their team's colors (and more) on game day.

ily tradition; b) identification with their community or region; and c) some ineffable attraction to the ethos or aesthetics of a particular team (e.g., "I don't know . . . I've just always loved the Vikings since I was little.")

Stories that my friends shared about attending or watching games with their families, and how they intended to pass that tradition on to their kids, resonated with me in theory. But I grew up in a transient military family with parents from Montana, which doesn't even border a state that has a pro team of any kind. We have plenty of family traditions that I hold dear, but watching sports isn't one of them. Clearly, if I want my offspring to be involved in a legacy of fandom, I'll have to take it upon myself to be its patriarch and founder. Since there's no tradition of team allegiance in either my or my wife's families, perhaps geography will be how I find a team to root for.

In "The Home Advantage," a 1977 article in the journal *Social Forces*, Barry Schwartz and Stephen Barsky explain the relationship between fans and their home team thus:

> If residents invest themselves in favor of their local athletic teams, it is partly because those teams are exponents of a community to which they feel themselves somehow bound. . . . A local team is not only an expression of the moral integrity of a community; it is also a means by which that community becomes conscious of itself and achieves its concrete representation.

I have a good deal of affection for every city I've lived in (or near), and 10 when I hear about the fortunes of their sports teams, I feel a wistfulness that belies the apathy I had toward their teams when I was there: *Oh! The 9ers won a game! I sure do miss going to wineries and hiking in the redwoods while not giving a shit about the local sports team.* But I can't say that I've ever felt that its team was an expression of its moral integrity. These days, I live in San Diego, and the only feelings that news about a Chargers game evokes in me is an internal alert to stay off of any freeway that leads to the stadium.

The third reason that my friends gave for their loyalty to a team—an inscrutable attraction—was the most difficult for me to get my head around, but it eventually made some sense to me in an absurdist way. Family and regional connections to teams seem solid enough on their faces, but they become more tenuous when examined with any degree of cynicism. How can a franchise "represent" your family or city given that players, staff, and even owners are quite mercenary about their own loyalties? Players rarely hail from the cities where their teams are headquartered and bounce all over the map depending on the whims of the marketplace; and owners will sell a team in a heartbeat if it makes financial sense. It's just as reasonable, then, to love a team because their logo is cool or their color scheme is pretty.

In an article in *Journal of Sport & Social Issues* called "Franchise Relocation and Fan Allegiance," Michael Lewis examines the nature of fans' identification with their teams in the context of said teams leaving town. He finds that only a slim majority of fans in his sample group are motivated by "civic allegiance" and refuse to support a team that deserts their city. The number of fans who have "symbolic allegiance" is surprisingly high. Lewis has theories that account for the ratio of civic to symbolic fans in regard to specifics of their respective teams, but what's interesting to me is how he explains the motives of the symbolically allegiant fans:

> Thus, whereas some fans find that rooting for a particular team brings them together with their local community, for other fans, rooting for a sports team helps set them apart from members of their local community. In the first case, the sports team is still a collective representation of a fan's identity as a resident of a particular city, whereas in the second case, the sports team is a representation of the individual's unique identity.

So, in theory then, I could find a team to follow that would express my own individuality, rather than my affinity for a city where their stadium happens to be located. That sounds more like my style. But how do these symbolic fans choose their teams? Lewis explains:

> In addition to having no current affiliation with their favorite team's city, many symbolically allegiant fans claim no past connection either. Unlike the stories told by civic fans that connect their childhood memories in a particular city with their love for the local team, symbolically allegiant fans locate the beginning of their support for a team in a unique personal experience.

There's my problem. I need a unique personal experience to connect me to a team. I had thought that if I casually followed football for a while, I might find a team that's right for me. But without a favorite team, following football is essentially just lying on the couch drinking beer for the equivalent of a full work-day every week.

In my capacity as a dad blogger, I've been offered several opportunities to hang out with football players and make pilgrimages to sacred NFL sites in connection with various promotions. Could this be the universe trying to create a unique personal experience for me? Maybe next time I'll pay attention. A dad-blogging junket might not be a strong enough fan origin myth to make me comfortable expressing my individual identity in a local sports pub, but it will probably be all right for the wine bar.

Sometimes the conclusion is the hardest part, but Andy Hinds really nails this one! Go to pp. 693–95 for ways to conclude memorably.

Thinking about the Text

1. Andy Hinds has made a careful study of how fans form their allegiances to sports teams. List and describe each of the three reasons he found that people give to explain their tie to a chosen team.

2. A good analysis presents **EVIDENCE** drawn from close examination of the subject. What evidence does Hinds present, and from what sources? What insight and conclusion does he reach—and does he provide enough evidence to support his conclusion? Explain.

3. Hinds uses words and phrases customarily applied to romantic relationships, such as "straying" and "the one," to talk about fandom. What is Hinds suggesting with this metaphor? Do you think it's an appropriate metaphor? Why or why not?

4. After all of his exploration and research, Hinds **CONCLUDES** without having decided which team will win his allegiance. What does his inability to choose a team say? Is his argument compromised by his failure to choose a team, or does that actually strengthen his point? Explain.

5. Whether you are a fan or not, you probably have opinions (favorable or otherwise) about a few sports teams, perhaps your hometown or college team. Using the three reasons that Hinds presents as a starting point, write an **ANALYSIS** of your attitude toward a team of your choice. Why do you feel the way you do about this particular team? You might consider the players, the team's fans, the owners' public persona, your attitude toward the game itself, and the team's effect on your daily life.

Touching the Earth

BELL HOOKS

> I wish to live because life has within it that which is good, that which
> is beautiful, and that which is love. Therefore, since I have known all
> these things, I have found them to be reason enough and—I wish to live.
> Moreover, because this is so, I wish others to live for generations and
> generations and generations and generations.
>
> —LORRAINE HANSBERRY, *To Be Young, Gifted, and Black*

WHEN WE LOVE THE EARTH, we are able to love ourselves more fully. I believe this. The ancestors taught me it was so. As a child I loved playing in dirt, in that rich Kentucky soil, that was a source of life. Before I understood anything about the pain and exploitation of the southern system of sharecropping, I understood that grown-up black folks loved the land. I could stand with my grandfather Daddy Jerry and look out at fields of growing vegetables, tomatoes, corn, collards, and know that this was his handi-

---

BELL HOOKS teaches in the Appalachian Studies program at Berea College, in Kentucky. Her writing focuses on the interconnectedness and inseparability of race, economic class, and gender—and the role that these three factors play in shaping U.S. society. This selection was originally published in the 1993 anthology *Sisters of the Yam: Black Women and Self-Recovery*.

work. I could see the look of pride on his face as I expressed wonder and awe at the magic of growing things. I knew that my grandmother Baba's backyard garden would yield beans, sweet potatoes, cabbage, and yellow squash, that she too would walk with pride among the rows and rows of growing vegetables showing us what the earth will give when tended lovingly.

From the moment of their first meeting, Native American and African people shared with one another a respect for the life-giving forces of nature, of the earth. African settlers in Florida taught the Creek Nation runaways, the "Seminoles," methods for rice cultivation. Native peoples taught recently arrived black folks all about the many uses of corn. (The hotwater cornbread we grew up eating came to our black southern diet from the world of the Indian.) Sharing the reverence for the earth, black and red people helped one another remember that, despite the white man's ways, the land belonged to everyone. Listen to these words attributed to Chief Seattle in 1854:

> How can you buy or sell the sky, the warmth of the land? The idea is strange to us. If we do not own the freshness of the air and the sparkle of the water, how can you buy them? Every part of this earth is sacred to my people. Every shining pine needle, every sandy shore, every mist in the dark woods, every clearing and humming insect is holy in the memory and experience of my people.... We are part of the earth and it is part of us. The perfumed flowers are our sisters; the deer, the horse, the great eagle, these are our brothers. The rocky crests, the juices in the meadows, the body heat of the pony, and man—all belong to the same family.

The sense of union and harmony with nature expressed here is echoed in testimony by black people who found that even though life in the new world was "harsh, harsh," in relationship to the earth one could be at peace. In the oral autobiography of granny midwife Onnie Lee Logan, who lived all her life in Alabama, she talks about the richness of farm life—growing vegetables, raising chickens, and smoking meat. She reports:

> We lived a happy, comfortable life to be right outa slavery times. I didn't know nothin else but the farm so it was happy and we was happy.... We couldn't do anything else but be happy. We accept the days as they come and as they were. Day by day until you couldn't say there was any great hard time. We overlooked it. We didn't

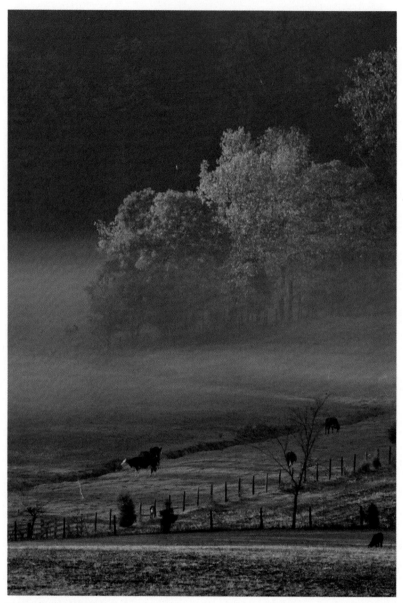

Kentucky morning.

think nothin about it. We just went along. We had what it takes to
make a good livin and go about it.

Living in modern society, without a sense of history, it has been easy for
folks to forget that black people were first and foremost a people of the
land, farmers. It is easy for folks to forget that at the first part of the 20th
century, the vast majority of black folks in the United States lived in the
agrarian south.

Living close to nature, black folks were able to cultivate a spirit of wonder and reverence for life. Growing food to sustain life and flowers to please
the soul, they were able to make a connection with the earth that was ongoing and life-affirming. They were witnesses to beauty. In Wendell Berry's
important discussion of the relationship between agriculture and human
spiritual well-being, *The Unsettling of America,* he reminds us that working
the land provides a location where folks can experience a sense of personal
power and well-being:

> We are working well when we use ourselves as the fellow creature
> of the plants, animals, material, and other people we are working
> with. Such work is unifying, healing. It brings us home from pride
> and despair, and places us responsibly within the human estate. It
> defines us as we are: not too good to work without our bodies, but
> too good to work poorly or joylessly or selfishly or alone.

There has been little or no work done on the psychological impact of 5
the "great migration" of black people from the agrarian south to the industrialized north. Toni Morrison's novel *The Bluest Eye* attempts to fictively
document the way moving from the agrarian south to the industrialized
north wounded the psyches of black folk. Estranged from a natural world,
where there was time for silence and contemplation, one of the "displaced"
black folks in Morrison's novel, Miss Pauline, loses her capacity to experience the sensual world around her when she leaves southern soil to live in
a northern city. The south is associated in her mind with a world of sensual beauty most deeply expressed in the world of nature. Indeed, when
she falls in love for the first time she can name that experience only by
evoking images from nature, from an agrarian world and near wilderness
of natural splendor:

Good
evidence
can be
more than
facts and
figures, as
bell hooks
shows.
See pp.
394–400.

> When I first seed Cholly, I want you to know it was like all the bits
> of color from that time down home when all us chil'ren went berry
> picking after a funeral and I put some in the pocket of my Sunday
> dress, and they mashed up and stained my hips. My whole dress
> was messed with purple, and it never did wash out. Not the dress
> nor me. I could feel that purple deep inside me. And that lemonade
> Mama used to make when Pap came in out of the fields. It be cool
> and yellowish, with seeds floating near the bottom. And that
> streak of green them june bugs made on the trees that night we left
> from down home. All of them colors was in me. Just sitting there.

Certainly, it must have been a profound blow to the collective psyche of
black people to find themselves struggling to make a living in the industrial north away from the land. Industrial capitalism was not simply changing the nature of black work life, it altered the communal practices that
were so central to survival in the agrarian south. And it fundamentally
altered black people's relationship to the body. It is the loss of any capacity to appreciate her body, despite its flaws, Miss Pauline suffers when she
moves north.

The motivation for black folks to leave the south and move north was
both material and psychological. Black folks wanted to be free of the overt
racial harassment that was a constant in southern life and they wanted
access to material goods—to a level of material well-being that was not
available in the agrarian south where white folks limited access to the
spheres of economic power. Of course, they found that life in the north
had its own perverse hardships, that racism was just as virulent there,
that it was much harder for black people to become landowners. Without
the space to grow food, to commune with nature, or to mediate the stark-
ness of poverty with the splendor of nature, black people experienced profound depression. Working in conditions where the body was regarded
solely as a tool (as in slavery), a profound estrangement occurred between
mind and body. The way the body was represented became more important than the body itself. It did not matter if the body was well, only that
it appeared well.

Estrangement from nature and engagement in mind/body splits made
it all the more possible for black people to internalize white-supremacist
assumptions about black identity. Learning contempt for blackness, south-
erners transplanted in the north suffered both culture shock and soul loss.

Contrasting the harshness of city life with an agrarian world, the poet Waring Cuney wrote this popular poem in the 1920s, testifying to lost connection:

> She does not know her beauty
> She thinks her brown body
> has no glory.
> If she could dance naked,
> Under palm trees
> And see her image in the river
> She would know.
> But there are no palm trees on the street,
> And dishwater gives back no images.

For many years, and even now, generations of black folks who migrated north to escape life in the south, returned down home in search of a spiritual nourishment, a healing, that was fundamentally connected to reaffirming one's connection to nature, to a contemplative life where one could take time, sit on the porch, walk, fish, and catch lightning bugs. If we think of urban life as a location where black folks learned to accept a mind/body split that made it possible to abuse the body, we can better understand the growth of nihilism and despair in the black psyche. And we can know that when we talk about healing that psyche we must also speak about restoring our connection to the natural world.

Wherever black folks live we can restore our relationship to the natural world by taking the time to commune with nature, to appreciate the other creatures who share this planet with humans. Even in my small New York City apartment I can pause to listen to birds sing, find a tree and watch it. We can grow plants—herbs, flowers, vegetables. Those novels by African-American writers (women and men) that talk about black migration from the agrarian south to the industrialized north describe in detail the way folks created space to grow flowers and vegetables. Although I come from country people with serious green thumbs, I have always felt that I could not garden. In the past few years, I have found that I can do it—that many gardens will grow, that I feel connected to my ancestors when I can put a meal on the table of food I grew. I especially love to plant collard greens. They are hardy, and easy to grow.

In modern society, there is also a tendency to see no correlation between ₁₀ the struggle for collective black self-recovery and ecological movements that seek to restore balance to the planet by changing our relationship to nature and to natural resources. Unmindful of our history of living harmoniously on the land, many contemporary black folks see no value in supporting ecological movements, or see ecology and the struggle to end racism as competing concerns. Recalling the legacy of our ancestors who knew that the way we regard land and nature will determine the level of our self-regard, black people must reclaim a spiritual legacy where we connect our well-being to the well-being of the earth. This is a necessary dimension of healing. As Berry reminds us:

> Only by restoring the broken connections can we be healed. Connection is health. And what our society does its best to disguise from us is how ordinary, how commonly attainable, health is. We lose our health—and create profitable diseases and dependencies—by failing to see the direct connections between living and eating, eating and working, working and loving. In gardening, for instance, one works with the body to feed the body. The work, if it is knowledgeable, makes for excellent food. And it makes one hungry. The work thus makes eating both nourishing and joyful, not consumptive, and keeps the eater from getting fat and weak. This health, wholeness, is a source of delight.

Collective black self-recovery takes place when we begin to renew our relationship to the earth, when we remember the way of our ancestors. When the earth is sacred to us, our bodies can also be sacred to us.

Thinking about the Text

1. This essay takes an explicit **POSITION**, but it is expressed in very abstract terms. What, exactly, is the author exhorting her readers to do? What concrete steps might they take to accomplish what she is recommending? Present examples from the text to support your responses.

2. What kind of environment would you say you live in—urban, rural, or something in between? How would you describe your relationship to the natural world? What do you do in order to "touch the earth"? Would you like to be able to do more? Why or why not?

3. Hooks cites Wendell Berry, who mentions the "profitable diseases and dependencies" that people create when we fail to see "the direct connections between living and eating, eating and working, working and loving" (10). What does Berry mean by "profitable diseases and dependencies"? Profitable for whom? Why? Dependencies on what or on whom? How does Berry's assertion fit into this essay's argument?

4. Because of black Americans' particular history with slavery and racism in the United States, hooks is suggesting a particular path toward healing. Might this same path be a healing one for other groups of people? Why or why not? Might it be a healing path for you, personally, or other members of a social or ethnic group to which you belong? Why or why not?

5. Very few of us could be said to live in harmony with nature; the demands of contemporary economic and social life, in fact, seem to take us increasingly farther afield from such a state. Take a critical look around you, at your individual, family, and community contexts. What barriers are blocking what bell hooks would call a reconnection with the earth on each of those three levels? What could be done on each level to lower such barriers? Write an essay in which you take stock of your environment and **PROPOSE** concrete, doable steps toward a more harmonious relationship with nature at one of these levels—individual, family, or community—or explain why this is not a desirable goal. Be sure to make clear which level your proposal is addressing.

Clean Sweep

RYAN KOHLS

FORTY THOUSAND PEOPLE are packed into the Rogers Centre to watch the Toronto Blue Jays. Right now, the stadium still belongs to the players, the fans and the vast, expensively-produced spectacle of professional sports. But at gate three, a group of about fifty congregates. Some stand alone, or pace and listen to music. Others sit on wooden benches nearby and enjoy a final cigarette. It's 10:30 pm, and these grim-faced men and women are waiting for work to begin. Standing on the curb as the game wraps up inside, these are the cleaners.

They'll work until dawn, gathering up some 15,000 pounds of garbage, scrubbing, rinsing, bending and lifting with painstaking thoroughness.

By morning, the stadium will gleam and the cleaners will go home to sleep with the blinds pulled tight against the sun. Now, they try to relax, joking to keep the mood light. "Are you ready for more torture?" one of them asks.

Spread out across 12.7 acres, the Rogers Centre, once known as the Sky-Dome, is one of Toronto's most recognizable landmarks. Every year 3.5 mil-

---

RYAN KOHLS is a journalist who has filed stories from places as diverse as Nairobi, Kenya, and Nunavut, Canada. He operates the interview-based website whatiwannaknow.com and is an interview producer for the daily program "The Stream" on *Al Jazeera*. He tweets @ryankohls. This article appeared in 2014 in *Maison Neuve*, a Canadian magazine of arts, opinion, and ideas.

lion people attend events at the mammoth complex. The big crowds mean big business—baseball's Blue Jays, whose eighty-one home games provide the stadium's main attraction, are worth an estimated $568 million. One season produces 1.2 million pounds of garbage. Eventually, someone must clean it up. Enter the cleaners—exhausted, poorly paid and largely anonymous. Without them, the game can't go on.

On a given night, anywhere from thirty to one hundred cleaners scour the ⁵ stadium. Most of them work for Hallmark Housekeeping Services, a Toronto-based janitorial agency that holds the cleaning contract at the Rogers Centre. These workers are experienced; Hallmark employees clean after every event. The other cleaners come from Labor Ready, a huge company that supplies temporary blue-collar workers across Canada and the United States. These employees book the Rogers Centre gig on a nightly basis and typically work a shorter shift. Both groups of workers are predominantly immigrants or down on their luck.

In the summer of 2012, I worked as a cleaner, on-and-off, for three months. I participated in roughly twenty-five cleaning shifts as an em-

When the fun is over and the fans go home, someone has to pick up the trash.

ployee of Labor Ready, joining the agency after struggling to find journalism work in the city.

Most cleaners patrol the stadium with brooms and large transparent garbage bags; a handful of more seasoned employees take leaf blowers. With the motor slung across their backs and a long black nozzle pumping out air, they blow the garbage from two parallel seating sections into one aisle. The blowers weigh about 25 pounds. One worker described it as being like "carrying an obese baby around all night."

Once enough garbage reaches the aisle, the sweepers climb to the top of their section and begin to slosh the mess downwards. In time, the pile turns into a cascading waterfall of miscellaneous trash. Beer-soaked hot dogs mix with ketchup-infused popcorn and the ubiquitous shells of sunflower seeds, which are maddeningly hard to persuade off the wet concrete. The mixture leaves behind a slick residue that makes the stairs treacherous. Workers sometimes slip and hurt their backs. Some stadiums have tried to control the garbage, but at baseball stadiums, seeds cannot be so easily dispatched—they're an iconic part of the game. "Getting rid of [sunflower seeds] would be like getting rid of beer and hot dogs," says Wayne Sills, the director of facility services at the Rogers Centre.

The last stage of cleaning is accomplished with four thirty-metre yellow hoses, spraying highly pressurized water into the aisles, aimed by workers in rubber boots. The Rogers Centre is one of the few North American sports stadiums to get the pressure-wash treatment—visiting teams have been known to remark on the building's uncanny cleanliness.

Around 2:30 am Rosario Coutinho scans the Centre with binoculars. She'll   10
spot a sweeper slacking off and radio the nighttime supervisor to assess the situation and get things moving. Coutinho then heads to another location where she can remain unseen and watch closely. "I'm the ghost," she tells me one night.

Coutinho, now fifty-two, serves as the resident manager of the cleanup operation. She pulls her black hair back in a ponytail, wears glasses, a black fleece and black pants, a BlackBerry headset and a crucifix on a chain. Coutinho knows more about the cleaning process than anyone. She's been at the Rogers Centre for nearly twenty-five years.

The workers are on to her tactics. Once, a group of Mexican cleaners developed a system of whistles to alert the others when she was watching. Coutinho translated the calls and changed her moves accordingly.

To become the binocular boss, Coutinho had to start from the bottom. In 1989, just a month after the SkyDome opened, she immigrated to Canada from Portugal. Her husband already lived here and told her about the opening of an amazing new stadium. Coutinho remembers being unimpressed; some stadiums in Europe hold 100,000 people. But the retractable roof that gave the building its name was, she was told, a sight to behold.

Before her arrival, Coutinho was prepared to work hard. "I knew I would be doing jobs that no one else wanted to do," she recalls. "If I'm cleaning shit, who cares? I'm going to make it smell better." Two months after landing in Toronto she was cleaning at the SkyDome. Her first assignment was the luxury boxes. One night she found a briefcase containing $10,000 cash. She returned it. The job meant everything and she couldn't risk losing it.

This atypical attitude caught management's attention and within a 15 year she was promoted to team leader. "Seventy percent of people in the cleaning business have no pride," Coutinho says. "Earn what you make, that's what counts." By 1995, she was managing the entire operation.

Few cleaners are as scrupulous as Coutinho. Many hate being there—some show up drunk, others get drunk in the stadium bathrooms on left-behind tallboys from the stands or their own flasks of hard liquor. Still others find their pay-off elsewhere: take Mark Stanton [not his real name]. It's his third season cleaning at the Rogers Centre and his favourite part of the job is finding money.

After the Jays' home opener, sporting a leaf blower slung across his back, he guides sunflower shells, empty beer cans and half-eaten hot dogs across an aisle. Out of the corner of his eye he spots a wallet. He flicks off the blower, bends over and plucks it from a pile of trash. He can't get too excited; he has to act calm: someone could be watching. He hunches over, peers inside and sees the cash. Quickly, with a practiced motion, he slides $30 into his pants. "Sometimes I go to work and I'm flat broke," says Stanton. "If I find $30, there's $30 in my pocket until pay day." He will eventually return the wallet, a little lighter, to security.

Stanton is adept at working the stadium's unofficial and technically illegal lost-and-found system to his advantage. At last year's home opener, he scored five wallets with $30 or more and two half-packs of smokes. When he cleaned up after the 100th Grey Cup, he found $150, three Grey Cup souvenir glasses and three t-shirts. After Ultimate Fighting Championship 129, he found a judge's scorecard and three bloody hand wraps. The excitement

Ryan Kohls, writing for a magazine, didn't have to document his interviews, but you will in your academic writing. See how to do so in MLA format on p. 567.

creates plenty of opportunities for fans to drop things. After every event, without fail, an array of valuables remains behind. For the workers, this is a perk, a way to make the job feel worthwhile. Some nights pay off huge. At UFC 100, one worker found and kept a wallet with $1,500. That's a month's wages. Other cleaners have found diamond rings, iPhones, BlackBerries, digital cameras, transit passes, sunglasses and umbrellas.

The treasure hunt is on everyone's mind. Having a successful night requires skill and attention. You can't just sweep or blow the garbage, you have to watch and listen. Over time, workers learn to hear the difference between a sliding beer tab and a coin. One worker uses his haul to pay child support for his three kids. He found $150 once and used it to buy his son a stroller.

When the clock hits 3 am, the stadium falls silent, and the workers break for   20
"lunch." There's a cheap hot dog stand on Front Street that's popular. Most of the cleaners can afford a meal using the spare change they've found during their shift.

Only three-quarters of the workers return after the break. Labor Ready workers are generally only used for sweeping and bagging. They'll get paid for four hours of work. As they disappear into the night, some head to bed, but others walk back to Labor Ready to collect their cheque and secure the next job. The company's offices at 195 Church Street don't open until 5:30 am, so many nights they'll wait in Dundas Square. If they time it just right, they'll score a free breakfast from the Salvation Army truck that passes by Labor Ready every morning.

Thinking about the Text

1. Ryan Kohls begins with a description of the ballpark's splendor and the cleaning process that keeps it that way, but the focus soon shifts to the cleaners themselves. What is his purpose in this **PROFILE**? Point to examples in the text to support your answer.

2. How does Kohls' disclosure of having been a stadium cleaner himself contribute to his **AUTHORITY**? And yet he doesn't include any personal anecdotes or impressions of the job other than the bare facts of his work, choosing instead to spotlight the other cleaners. Should he have spoken more about his own experience? Why or why not?

3. Kohls is clearly happy to no longer work as a stadium cleaner. Despite having moved on in his own career, what is his **ATTITUDE** toward his former colleagues? How does he portray them and their work? Point to examples in the text to support your response.

4. Although this profile describes a large sports arena, Kohls wasn't writing for an **AUDIENCE** of sports fans. What, if anything, might he have done differently if he were writing a column for ESPN or *Sports Illustrated*? Why?

5. Have you ever worked at a job that you hope will not become your long-term occupation? Write a **DESCRIPTION** of the job and your co-workers that gives your readers as vivid a sense as possible of a typical shift, letting examples and descriptive details make your point.

The "Busy Trap"

TIM KREIDER

IF YOU LIVE IN AMERICA in the twenty-first century you've probably had to listen to a lot of people tell you how busy they are. It's become the default response when you ask anyone how they're doing: "Busy!" "*So* busy." "*Crazy* busy." It is, pretty obviously, a boast disguised as a complaint. And the stock response is a kind of congratulation: "That's a good problem to have," or "Better than the opposite."

Notice it isn't generally people pulling back-to-back shifts in the I.C.U. or commuting by bus to three minimum-wage jobs who tell you how busy they are; what those people are is not busy but *tired. Exhausted. Dead on their feet.* It's almost always people whose lamented busyness is purely self-imposed: work and obligations they've taken on voluntarily, classes and activities they've "encouraged" their kids to participate in. They're busy because of their own ambition or drive or anxiety, because they're addicted to busyness and dread what they might have to face in its absence.

Almost everyone I know is busy. They feel anxious and guilty when they aren't either working or doing something to promote their work. They schedule in time with friends the way students with 4.0 G.P.A.'s make sure

---

TIM KREIDER is the author of the essay collection *We Learn Nothing* (2012) and the cartoon collection *The Pain: When Will It End?* (2004). His work has been published in *Film Quarterly*, the *New York Times*, *Al Jazeera*, and the *Comics Journal*. This essay was published in the *Times* in June 2012.

to sign up for community service because it looks good on their college applications. I recently wrote a friend to ask if he wanted to do something this week, and he answered that he didn't have a lot of time but if something was going on to let him know and maybe he could ditch work for a few hours. I wanted to clarify that my question had not been a preliminary heads-up to some future invitation; this was the invitation. But his busyness was like some vast churning noise through which he was shouting out at me, and I gave up trying to shout back over it.

Even *children* are busy now, scheduled down to the half-hour with classes and extracurricular activities. They come home at the end of the day as tired as grown-ups. I was a member of the latchkey generation and had three hours of totally unstructured, largely unsupervised time every afternoon, time I used to do everything from surfing the World Book Encyclopedia to making animated films to getting together with friends in the woods to chuck dirt clods directly into one another's eyes, all of which provided me with important skills and insights that remain valuable to this day. Those free hours became the model for how I wanted to live the rest of my life.

The present hysteria is not a necessary or inevitable condition of life; 5 it's something we've chosen, if only by our acquiescence to it. Not long ago I Skyped with a friend who was driven out of the city by high rent and now has an artist's residency in a small town in the south of France. She described herself as happy and relaxed for the first time in years. She still gets her work done, but it doesn't consume her entire day and brain. She says it feels like college—she has a big circle of friends who all go out to the cafe together every night. She has a boyfriend again. (She once ruefully summarized dating in New York: "Everyone's too busy and everyone thinks they can do better.") What she had mistakenly assumed was her personality—driven, cranky, anxious and sad—turned out to be a deformative effect of her environment. It's not as if any of us wants to live like this, any more than any one person wants to be part of a traffic jam or stadium trampling or the hierarchy of cruelty in high school—it's something we collectively force one another to do.

Busyness serves as a kind of existential reassurance, a hedge against emptiness; obviously your life cannot possibly be silly or trivial or meaningless if you are so busy, completely booked, in demand every hour of the day. I once knew a woman who interned at a magazine where she wasn't allowed to take lunch hours out, lest she be urgently needed for some reason. This was an entertainment magazine whose raison d'être was obviated when "menu" buttons appeared on remotes, so it's hard to see this pretense of indispensability as anything other than a form of institutional self-delusion. More and more people in this country no longer make or do anything tangible; if your job wasn't performed by a cat or a boa constrictor in a Richard Scarry book, I'm not sure I believe it's necessary. I can't help but wonder whether all this histrionic exhaustion isn't a way of covering up the fact that most of what we do doesn't matter.

I am not busy. I am the laziest ambitious person I know. Like most writers, I feel like a reprobate who does not deserve to live on any day that I do not write, but I also feel that four or five hours is enough to earn my stay on the planet for one more day. On the best ordinary days of my life, I write in the morning, go for a long bike ride and run errands in the afternoon, and in the evening I see friends, read or watch a movie. This, it seems to me, is a sane and pleasant pace for a day. And if you call me up and ask whether I won't maybe blow off work and check out the new American Wing at the Met or ogle girls in Central Park or just drink chilled pink minty cocktails all day long, I will say, what time?

Tim Kreider uses personal narrative to support his position. Find out how narrative works across genres on pp. 163–64.

But just in the last few months, I've insidiously started, because of professional obligations, to become busy. For the first time I was able to tell people, with a straight face, that I was "too busy" to do this or that thing they wanted me to do. I could see why people enjoy this complaint; it makes you feel important, sought-after and put-upon. Except that I hate actually being busy. Every morning my in-box was full of e-mails asking me to do things I did not want to do or presenting me with problems that I now had to solve. It got more and more intolerable until finally I fled town to the Undisclosed Location from which I'm writing this.

Here I am largely unmolested by obligations. There is no TV. To check e-mail I have to drive to the library. I go a week at a time without seeing anyone I know. I've remembered about buttercups, stink bugs and the stars. I read. And I'm finally getting some real writing done for the first time in months. It's hard to find anything to say about life without immersing yourself in the world, but it's also just about impossible to figure out what it might be, or how best to say it, without getting the hell out of it again.

Idleness is not just a vacation, an indulgence or a vice; it is as indispens-   10
able to the brain as vitamin D is to the body, and deprived of it we suffer a mental affliction as disfiguring as rickets. The space and quiet that idleness provides is a necessary condition for standing back from life and seeing it whole, for making unexpected connections and waiting for the wild

summer lightning strikes of inspiration—it is, paradoxically, necessary to getting any work done. "Idle dreaming is often of the essence of what we do," wrote Thomas Pynchon in his essay on sloth. Archimedes' "Eureka" in the bath, Newton's apple, Jekyll & Hyde and the benzene ring: history is full of stories of inspirations that come in idle moments and dreams. It almost makes you wonder whether loafers, goldbricks and no-accounts aren't responsible for more of the world's great ideas, inventions and masterpieces than the hardworking.

"The goal of the future is full unemployment, so we can play. That's why we have to destroy the present politico-economic system." This may sound like the pronouncement of some bong-smoking anarchist, but it was actually Arthur C. Clarke, who found time between scuba diving and pinball games to write "Childhood's End" and think up communications satellites. My old colleague Ted Rall recently wrote a column proposing that we divorce income from work and give each citizen a guaranteed paycheck, which sounds like the kind of lunatic notion that'll be considered a basic human right in about a century, like abolition, universal suffrage and eight-hour workdays. The Puritans turned work into a virtue, evidently forgetting that God invented it as a punishment.

Perhaps the world would soon slide to ruin if everyone behaved as I do. But I would suggest that an ideal human life lies somewhere between my own defiant indolence and the rest of the world's endless frenetic hustle. My role is just to be a bad influence, the kid standing outside the classroom window making faces at you at your desk, urging you to just this once make some excuse and get out of there, come outside and play. My own resolute idleness has mostly been a luxury rather than a virtue, but I did make a conscious decision, a long time ago, to choose time over money, since I've always understood that the best investment of my limited time on earth was to spend it with people I love. I suppose it's possible I'll lie on my deathbed regretting that I didn't work harder and say everything I had to say, but I think what I'll really wish is that I could have one more beer with Chris, another long talk with Megan, one last good hard laugh with Boyd. Life is too short to be busy.

Thinking about the Text

1. Tim Kreider supports his **ARGUMENT** with purely personal and anecdotal evidence, telling about his own experiences and those of a few acquaintances. Is this evidence sufficient to support his defense of idleness over busyness? Is his piece persuasive? Why or why not?

2. How would you describe Kreider's **TONE**? Sympathetic? Antagonistic? Busy? How does his tone contribute to his message? Imagine Kreider's argument conveyed with a different tone—gentle, for example, or straightforward; how would the message and its effect be different? Explain.

3. Kreider admits his character flaws; he calls himself lazy and says that his role is "just to be a bad influence." Do these admissions damage his credibility or his **AUTHORITY**? Do they enhance it? How, and why?

4. Kreider asserts that busyness for most people is self-imposed rather than a matter of necessity, and that people are "addicted to busyness and dread what they might have to face in its absence." Do you know busy people who fit that description? Do you know busy people who don't? From what you've observed in those around you, is Kreider's assertion fair? Why or why not?

5. Kreider concedes that his "resolute idleness" is a luxury, but he credits his long-ago decision to choose time over money and suggests that more people should do the same. Does everyone have that option? Do you? And if so, would you? Write an essay in which you **ANALYZE** your options and your priorities. You might consider such factors as your goals, responsibilities, opportunities, and limitations.

On Meaningful Observation

JOHN MAEDA

A SILVER LINING IN THE DARK CLOUD of any recession—especially this
one, thought to be caused by our own greed and excess—is the opportunity it affords us to reexamine our collective values. On the positive side, the
nation seems to be as committed as ever to the power of innovation as America's saving grace. What is less comforting to me as president of an art and
design school is how America defines innovation. Do a search on the White
House website for the word "innovation" and the top results revolve around
technology; talk to any parent with children in public schools and you will
hear about arts-education resources diminishing quickly. I feel there is a dis-
connect between the words "innovation" and "art" that needs to be resolved
if the United States is to prevail as the most creative economy in our world.

Public commitments to STEM—science, technology, engineering,
math—education abound all over the country. In the government's mind,
these subjects are the key to innovation. As a lifelong STEM student myself,

JOHN MAEDA is an artist, computer scientist, and author. He has taught in the
MIT Media Lab for twelve years and served as president of the Rhode Island School
of Design (RISD) from 2008 to 2013. He now works in Silicon Valley advising start-
ups on the importance of design. He tweets @johnmaeda. In 2010, while Maeda
was at RISD and while we were in the middle of the Great Recession, he wrote
this proposal for *Seed* magazine, as part of a series seeking solutions to "interconnected and complex challenges."

John Maeda
describes
the problem
with current
STEM
education.
Go to pp.
343–45
for tips
on getting
your own
proposals
off to a
strong start.

with degrees in electrical engineering and computer science from MIT, I am certainly not one to diminish its value. Yet in recent years even supremely dedicated geeks like me have begun to question the advances that come from purely technological innovation.

We seem to be stuck in a kind of technology loop. It began in the 1980s with computers that could display only text and play limited sound. Images then became possible, and with CD-ROM technology came high-fidelity sound and full-motion video. In the '90s, when the web took hold, we started again with text, limited sounds and images, then high-fidelity audio, and years later we reached the point of full-motion video. Now we see the cell phone in our pocket experiencing the same progression from text, to sound, to audio, to video—and we are supposed to feel like we are enjoying incredible progress. But it seems the tricks are exactly the same each time around the loop. I'm looking for a new trick.

After two decades as a student and faculty member at MIT, my newest experience at the Rhode Island School of Design (RISD) has reawakened me to the world of physical creation. RISD represents the ultimate culture of makers. There is no greater integrity, no greater goal achieved, than an idea articulately expressed through something made with your hands. We call this constant dialogue between eye, mind, and hand "critical thinking—critical making." It's an education in getting your hands dirty, in understanding why you made what you made, and owning the impact of the work in the world. It's what artists and designers do.

As tricks come, as far as I can tell this isn't a new one at all. But it certainly feels like it transcends mere trickery: It is truly substantive magic for the soul. Students at RISD don't think in terms of megabytes or equations; they think in terms of the warm, complex voice of a material like wood, or the way that glass finds its resting place differently on a cold winter day. Their hands, and sometimes faces, are literally covered with the materials they use to shape, angle, mutate, and translate their thoughts into handcrafted realities. Being an artist, I feel that art comes from the inexplicable urge to manifest a feeling, intent, or question as a specific, tangible experience. Artists do research with an open-mindedness and rigorous inquiry unseen in most other disciplines, except true science. They systematically and visually survey the world of ideas, objects, and experiences for inspiration by rummaging through it with their bare hands. I know most of us today are more likely to get the job done with cleaner hands through a search on Google Images. But at RISD the story of someone's work more

A student crafting, hands covered in clay.

often comes from a first-hand journey through many emotional worlds, rather than an analysis of an online slideshow of poorly photographed experiences.

We have a facility on campus called Nature Lab. Founded in 1937, it houses more than 80,000 true specimens of nature—from skeletons to saplings to salamanders. Students can check out a butterfly from the lab and bring it back to their dorm room overnight. It's really a Victorian approach to science, based on meaningful observation of something real. "Real" also abounds in the RISD museum. Need to see a real Monet or Rothko? You can stand within millimeters of it. Our students are within steps of the visceral emotion of experiencing a masterpiece, and the making that went into it.

And so I've begun to wonder recently whether STEM needs something to give it some STE(A)M—an "A" for art between the engineering and the math to ground the bits and bytes in the physical world before us, to lift them up and make them human. What if America approached innovation with more than just technology? What if, just like STEM is made up of science, technology, engineering, and math, we had IDEA, made of intuition, design, emotion, and art—all the things that make us humans feel, well, human? It seems to me that if we use this moment to reassess our values, putting just a little bit of our humanity back into America's innovation engines will lead to the most meaningful kind of progress. By doing so, we will find a way back to integrating thinking with making and being and feeling and living so that left- and right-brained creativity can lift our economy back into the sky.

Thinking about the Text

1. A good **PROPOSAL** addresses a well-defined problem. How well does John Maeda define the problem he proposes to solve? **SUMMARIZE** the problem. Do you agree that it warrants attention? Why or why not?

2. According to Maeda, artists do research "with an open-mindedness and rigorous inquiry" that is rarely found elsewhere except in "true science." What exactly does he mean by this **COMPARISON**, and how is it important to his argument? Is it a fair comparison to make? Why or why not?

3. Maeda was the president of an art and design school, yet he is writing about STEM issues here. How does he establish his **AUTHORITY** to write about this topic? Point to specific passages in the essay to support your response.

4. Many arguments in favor of arts instruction talk about its importance to a well-rounded education. Maeda focuses instead on how the arts contribute to economic prosperity. Why might he have taken this approach? Do you find his **ARGUMENT** persuasive? Why or why not?

5. What experiences have you had making things—whether a painting, a sculpture, an IKEA bookcase, or a sandwich? What kinds of things do you like to make? Do you agree with Maeda that making things makes you feel more human—and that, as he proposes, we should have IDEA (intuition, design, emotion, art) along with STEM (science, technology, engineering, math)? Write an essay responding to Maeda, agreeing, disagreeing, or both. Use your own experience as your principal **EVIDENCE**.

The Egg and the Sperm

EMILY MARTIN

The theory of the human body is always a part of a world-picture.
. . . The theory of the human body is always a part of a *fantasy*.
—JAMES HILLMAN, *The Myth of Analysis*[1]

AS AN ANTHROPOLOGIST, I am intrigued by the possibility that culture shapes how biological scientists describe what they discover about the natural world. If this were so, we would be learning about more than the natural world in high school biology class; we would be learning about cultural beliefs and practices as if they were part of nature. In the course of my research I realized that the picture of egg and sperm drawn in popular as well as scientific accounts of reproductive biology relies on stereotypes

1. James Hillman, *The Myth of Analysis* (Evanston, Ill.: Northwestern University Press, 1972), 220.

EMILY MARTIN, a professor of anthropology at New York University, is founding editor of the magazine *Anthropology Now* and has written extensively about intersections of culture and science. Her 2007 book *Bipolar Expeditions* won a prize for feminist anthropological research. This article first appeared in *Signs: Journal of Women in Culture and Society* in 1991 with the subtitle "How Science Has Constructed a Romance Based on Stereotypical Male-Female Roles." It has become a classic reading in medical anthropology.

central to our cultural definitions of male and female. The stereotypes imply not only that female biological processes are less worthy than their male counterparts but also that women are less worthy than men. Part of my goal in writing this article is to shine a bright light on the gender stereotypes hidden within the scientific language of biology. Exposed in such a light, I hope they will lose much of their power to harm us.

Egg and Sperm: A Scientific Fairy Tale

At a fundamental level, all major scientific textbooks depict male and female reproductive organs as systems for the production of valuable substances, such as eggs and sperm.[2] In the case of women, the monthly cycle is described as being designed to produce eggs and prepare a suitable place for them to be fertilized and grown—all to the end of making babies. But the enthusiasm ends there. By extolling the female cycle as a productive enterprise, menstruation must necessarily be viewed as a failure. Medical texts describe menstruation as the "debris" of the uterine lining, the result of necrosis, or death of tissue. The descriptions imply that a system has gone awry, making products of no use, not to specification, unsalable, wasted, scrap. An illustration in a widely used medical text shows menstruation as a chaotic disintegration of form, complementing the many texts that describe it as "ceasing," "dying," "losing," "denuding," "expelling."[3]

Male reproductive physiology is evaluated quite differently. One of the texts that sees menstruation as failed production employs a sort of breathless prose when it describes the maturation of sperm: "The mechanisms which guide the remarkable cellular transformation from spermatid to mature sperm remain uncertain.... Perhaps the most amazing characteristic of spermatogenesis is its sheer magnitude: the normal human male may manufacture several hundred million sperm per day."[4] In the classic text *Medical Physiology*, edited by Vernon Mountcastle, the male/female, productive/

2. The textbooks I consulted are the main ones used in classes for undergraduate premedical students or medical students (or those held on reserve in the library for these classes) during the past few years at Johns Hopkins University. These texts are widely used at other universities in the country as well.

3. Arthur C. Guyton, *Physiology of the Human Body*, 6th ed. (Philadelphia: Saunders College Publishing, 1984), 624.

4. Arthur J. Vander, James H. Sherman, and Dorothy S. Luciano, *Human Physiology: The Mechanisms of Body Function*, 3d ed. (New York: McGraw Hill, 1980), 483–84.

destructive comparison is more explicit: "Whereas the female *sheds* only a single gamete each month, the seminiferous tubules *produce* hundreds of millions of sperm each day" (emphasis mine).[5] The female author of another text marvels at the length of the microscopic seminiferous tubules, which, if uncoiled and placed end to end, "would span almost one-third of a mile!" She writes, "In an adult male these structures produce millions of sperm cells each day." Later she asks, "How is this feat accomplished?"[6] None of these texts expresses such intense enthusiasm for any female processes. It is surely no accident that the "remarkable" process of making sperm involves precisely what, in the medical view, menstruation does not: production of something deemed valuable.[7]

One could argue that menstruation and spermatogenesis are not analogous processes and, therefore, should not be expected to elicit the same kind of response. The proper female analogy to spermatogenesis, biologically, is ovulation. Yet ovulation does not merit enthusiasm in these texts either. Textbook descriptions stress that all of the ovarian follicles containing ova are already present at birth. Far from being *produced*, as sperm are, they merely sit on the shelf, slowly degenerating and aging like overstocked inventory: "At birth, normal human ovaries contain an estimated one million follicles [each], and no new ones appear after birth. Thus, in marked contrast to the male, the newborn female already has all the germ cells she will ever have. Only a few, perhaps 400, are destined to reach full maturity during her active productive life. All the others degenerate at some point in their development so that few, if any, remain by the time she reaches menopause at approximately 50 years of age."[8] Note the "marked contrast" that this description sets up between male and female: the male, who continuously produces fresh germ cells, and the female, who has stockpiled germ cells by birth and is faced with their degeneration.

Nor are the female organs spared such vivid descriptions. One scientist writes in a newspaper article that a woman's ovaries become old and worn out from ripening eggs every month, even though the woman herself is still relatively young: "When you look through a laparoscope . . . at an ovary that

---

5. Vernon B. Mountcastle, *Medical Physiology,* 14th ed. (London: Mosby, 1980), 2:1624.

6. Eldra Pearl Solomon, *Human Anatomy and Physiology* (New York: CBS College Publishing, 1983), 678.

7. For elaboration, see Emily Martin, *The Woman in the Body: A Cultural Analysis of Reproduction* (Boston: Beacon, 1987), 27–53.

8. Vander, Sherman, and Luciano, 568.

has been through hundreds of cycles, even in a superbly healthy American female, you see a scarred, battered organ."[9]

To avoid the negative connotations that some people associate with the female reproductive system, scientists could begin to describe male and female processes as homologous. They might credit females with "producing" mature ova one at a time, as they're needed each month, and describe males as having to face problems of degenerating germ cells. This degeneration would occur throughout life among spermatogonia, the undifferentiated germ cells in the testes that are the long-lived, dormant precursors of sperm.

But the texts have an almost dogged insistence on casting female processes in a negative light. The texts celebrate sperm production because it is continuous from puberty to senescence, while they portray egg production as inferior because it is finished at birth. This makes the female seem unproductive, but some texts will also insist that it is she who is wasteful.[10] In a section heading for *Molecular Biology of the Cell,* a best-selling text, we are told that "Oogenesis is wasteful." The text goes on to emphasize that of the seven million oogonia, or egg germ cells, in the female embryo, most degenerate in the ovary. Of those that do go on to become oocytes, or eggs, many also degenerate, so that at birth only two million eggs remain in the ovaries. Degeneration continues throughout a woman's life: by puberty 300,000 eggs remain, and only a few are present by menopause. "During the 40 or so years of a woman's reproductive life, only 400 to 500 eggs will have been released," the authors write. "All the rest will have degenerated. It is still a mystery why so many eggs are formed only to die in the ovaries."[11]

The real mystery is why the male's vast production of sperm is not seen as wasteful.[12] Assuming that a man "produces" 100 million (10^8) sperm per

---

9. Melvin Konner, "Childbearing and Age," *New York Times Magazine* (December 27, 1987), 22–23, esp. 22.

10. I have found but one exception to the opinion that the female is wasteful: "Smallpox being the nasty disease it is, one might expect nature to have designed antibody molecules with combining sites that specifically recognize the epitopes on smallpox virus. Nature differs from technology, however: it thinks nothing of wastefulness. (For example, rather than improving the chance that a spermatozoon will meet an egg cell, nature finds it easier to produce millions of spermatozoa.)" (Niels Kaj Jerne, "The Immune System," *Scientific American* 229, no. 1 [July 1973]: 53). Thanks to a *Signs* reviewer for bringing this reference to my attention.

11. Bruce Alberts et al., *Molecular Biology of the Cell* (New York: Garland, 1983), 795.

12. In her essay "Have Only Men Evolved?" (in *Discovering Reality: Feminist Perspectives on Epistemology, Metaphysics, Methodology, and Philosophy of Science,* ed. Sandra Harding and Merrill B. Hintikka [Dordrecht: Reidel, 1983], 45–69, esp. 60–61), Ruth Hubbard points out that sociobiologists have said the female invests more energy than the male in the production

day (a conservative estimate) during an average reproductive life of sixty years, he would produce well over two trillion sperm in his lifetime. Assuming that a woman "ripens" one egg per lunar month, or thirteen per year, over the course of her forty-year reproductive life, she would total five hundred eggs in her lifetime. But the word "waste" implies an excess, too much produced. Assuming two or three offspring, for every baby a woman produces, she wastes only around two hundred eggs. For every baby a man produces, he wastes more than one trillion (10^{12}) sperm.

How is it that positive images are denied to the bodies of women? A look at language—in this case, scientific language—provides the first clue. Take the egg and the sperm.[13] It is remarkable how "femininely" the egg behaves and how "masculinely" the sperm.[14] The egg is seen as large and passive.[15] It does not *move* or *journey*, but passively "is transported," "is swept,"[16] or even "drifts"[17] along the fallopian tube. In utter contrast, sperm are small, "streamlined,"[18] and invariably active. They "deliver" their genes to the egg, "activate the developmental program of the egg,"[19] and have a "velocity" that is often remarked upon.[20] Their tails are "strong" and efficiently

---

of her large gametes, claiming that this explains why the female provides parental care. Hubbard questions whether it "really takes more 'energy' to generate the one or relatively few eggs than the large excess of sperms required to achieve fertilization." For further critique of how the greater size of eggs is interpreted in sociobiology, see Donna Haraway, "Investment Strategies for the Evolving Portfolio of Primate Females," in *Body/Politics,* ed. Mary Jacobus, Evelyn Fox Keller, and Sally Shuttleworth (New York: Routledge, 1990), 155–56.

13. The sources I used for this article provide compelling information on interactions among sperm. Lack of space prevents me from taking up this theme here, but the elements include competition, hierarchy, and sacrifice. For a newspaper report, see Malcolm W. Browne, "Some Thoughts on Self Sacrifice," *New York Times* (July 5, 1988), C6. For a literary rendition, see John Barth, "Night-Sea Journey," in his *Lost in the Funhouse* (Garden City, N.Y.: Doubleday, 1968), 3–13.

14. See Carol Delaney, "The Meaning of Paternity and the Virgin Birth Debate," *Man* 21, no. 3 (September 1986): 494–513. She discusses the difference between this scientific view that women contribute genetic material to the fetus and the claim of long-standing Western folk theories that the origin and identity of the fetus comes from the male, as in the metaphor of planting a seed in soil.

15. For a suggested direct link between human behavior and purportedly passive eggs and active sperm, see Erik H. Erikson, "Inner and Outer Space: Reflections on Womanhood," *Daedalus* 93, no. 2 (Spring 1964): 582–606, esp. 591.

16. Guyton (n. 3 above), 619; and Mountcastle (n. 5 above), 1609.

17. Jonathan Miller and David Pelham, *The Facts of Life* (New York: Viking Penguin, 1984), 5.

18. Alberts et al., 796.

19. Ibid., 796.

20. See, e.g., William F. Ganong, *Review of Medical Physiology,* 7th ed. (Los Altos, Calif.: Lange Medical Publications, 1975), 322.

powered.[21] Together with the forces of ejaculation, they can "propel the se-
men into the deepest recesses of the vagina."[22] For this they need "energy,"
"fuel,"[23] so that with a "whiplashlike motion and strong lurches"[24] they can
"burrow through the egg coat"[25] and "penetrate" it.[26]

At its extreme, the age-old relationship of the egg and the sperm takes   10
on a royal or religious patina. The egg coat, its protective barrier, is sometimes called its "vestments," a term usually reserved for sacred, religious
dress. The egg is said to have a "corona,"[27] a crown, and to be accompanied
by "attendant cells."[28] It is holy, set apart and above, the queen to the sperm's
king. The egg is also passive, which means it must depend on sperm for rescue. Gerald Schatten and Helen Schatten liken the egg's role to that of Sleeping Beauty: "a dormant bride awaiting her mate's magic kiss, which instills
the spirit that brings her to life."[29] Sperm, by contrast, have a "mission,"[30]
which is to "move through the female genital tract in quest of the ovum."[31]
One popular account has it that the sperm carry out a "perilous journey"
into the "warm darkness," where some fall away "exhausted." "Survivors"
"assault" the egg, the successful candidates "surrounding the prize."[32] Part
of the urgency of this journey, in more scientific terms, is that "once released
from the supportive environment of the ovary, an egg will die within hours
unless rescued by a sperm."[33] The wording stresses the fragility and dependency of the egg, even though the same text acknowledges elsewhere that
sperm also live for only a few hours.[34]

In 1948, in a book remarkable for its early insights into these matters,
Ruth Herschberger argued that female reproductive organs are seen as bio-

21. Alberts et al. (n. 11 above), 796.
22. Guyton, 615.
23. Solomon (n. 6 above), 683.
24. Vander, Sherman, and Luciano (n. 4 above), 4th ed. (1985), 580.
25. Alberts et al., 796.
26. All biology texts quoted above use the word "penetrate."
27. Solomon, 700.
28. A. Beldecos et al., "The Importance of Feminist Critique for Contemporary Cell Biology,"
Hypatia 3, no. 1 (Spring 1988): 61–76.
29. Gerald Schatten and Helen Schatten, "The Energetic Egg," *Medical World News* 23 (January
23, 1984): 51–53, esp. 51.
30. Alberts et al., 796.
31. Guyton (n. 3 above), 613.
32. Miller and Pelham (n. 17 above), 7.
33. Alberts et al. (n. 11 above), 804.
34. Ibid., 801.

logically interdependent, while male organs are viewed as autonomous, operating independently and in isolation:

> At present the functional is stressed only in connection with women: it is in them that ovaries, tubes, uterus, and vagina have endless interdependence. In the male, reproduction would seem to involve "organs" only.
>
> Yet the sperm, just as much as the egg, is dependent on a great many related processes. There are secretions which mitigate the urine in the urethra before ejaculation, to protect the sperm. There is the reflex shutting off of the bladder connection, the provision of prostatic secretions, and various types of muscular propulsion. The sperm is no more independent of its milieu than the egg, and yet from a wish that it were, biologists have lent their support to the notion that the human female, beginning with the egg, is congenitally more dependent than the male.[35]

Bringing out another aspect of the sperm's autonomy, an article in the journal *Cell* has the sperm making an "existential decision" to penetrate the egg: "Sperm are cells with a limited behavioral repertoire, one that is directed toward fertilizing eggs. To execute the decision to abandon the haploid state, sperm swim to an egg and there acquire the ability to effect membrane fusion."[36] Is this a corporate manager's version of the sperm's activities—"executing decisions" while fraught with dismay over difficult options that bring with them very high risk?

There is another way that sperm, despite their small size, can be made to loom in importance over the egg. In a collection of scientific papers, an electron micrograph of an enormous egg and tiny sperm is titled "A Portrait of the Sperm."[37] This is a little like showing a photo of a dog and calling it a picture of the fleas. Granted, microscopic sperm are harder to photograph than eggs, which are just large enough to see with the naked eye. But surely

35. Ruth Herschberger, *Adam's Rib* (New York: Pelligrini & Cudaby, 1948), esp. 84. I am indebted to Ruth Hubbard for telling me about Herschberger's work, although at a point when this paper was already in draft form.

36. Bennett M. Shapiro, "The Existential Decision of a Sperm," *Cell* 49, no. 3 (May 1987): 293–94, esp. 293.

37. Lennart Nilsson, "A Portrait of the Sperm," in *The Functional Anatomy of the Spermatozoan*, ed. Bjorn A. Afzelius (New York: Pergamon, 1975), 79–82.

the use of the term "portrait," a word associated with the powerful and wealthy, is significant. Eggs have only micrographs or pictures, not portraits.

One depiction of sperm as weak and timid, instead of strong and powerful—the only such representation in western civilization, so far as I know—occurs in Woody Allen's movie *Everything You Always Wanted to Know About Sex* **But Were Afraid to Ask*. Allen, playing the part of an apprehensive sperm inside a man's testicles, is scared of the man's approaching orgasm. He is reluctant to launch himself into the darkness, afraid of contraceptive devices, afraid of winding up on the ceiling if the man masturbates.

The more common picture—egg as damsel in distress, shielded only 15 by her sacred garments; sperm as heroic warrior to the rescue—cannot be proved to be dictated by the biology of these events. While the "facts" of biology may not *always* be constructed in cultural terms, I would argue that in this case they are. The degree of metaphorical content in these descriptions, the extent to which differences between egg and sperm are emphasized, and the parallels between cultural stereotypes of male and female behavior and the character of egg and sperm all point to this conclusion.

New Research, Old Imagery

As new understandings of egg and sperm emerge, textbook gender imagery is being revised. But the new research, far from escaping the stereotypical representations of egg and sperm, simply replicates elements of textbook gender imagery in a different form. The persistence of this imagery calls to mind what Ludwik Fleck termed "the self-contained" nature of scientific thought. As he described it, "the interaction between what is already known, what remains to be learned, and those who are to apprehend it, go to ensure harmony within the system. But at the same time they also preserve the harmony of illusions, which is quite secure within the confines of a given thought style."[38] We need to understand the way in which the cultural content in scientific descriptions changes as biological discoveries unfold, and whether that cultural content is solidly entrenched or easily changed.

In all of the texts quoted above, sperm are described as penetrating the egg, and specific substances on a sperm's head are described as binding to

---

38. Ludwik Fleck, *Genesis and Development of a Scientific Fact*, ed. Thaddeus J. Trenn and Robert K. Merton (Chicago: University of Chicago Press, 1979), 38.

the egg. Recently, this description of events was rewritten in a biophysics lab at Johns Hopkins University—transforming the egg from the passive to the active party.[39]

Prior to this research, it was thought that the zona, the inner vestments of the egg, formed an impenetrable barrier. Sperm overcame the barrier by mechanically burrowing through, thrashing their tails and slowly working their way along. Later research showed that the sperm released digestive enzymes that chemically broke down the zona; thus, scientists presumed that the sperm used mechanical *and* chemical means to get through to the egg.

In this recent investigation, the researchers began to ask questions about the mechanical force of the sperm's tail. (The lab's goal was to develop a contraceptive that worked topically on sperm.) They discovered, to their great surprise, that the forward thrust of sperm is extremely weak, which contradicts the assumption that sperm are forceful penetrators.[40] Rather than thrusting forward, the sperm's head was now seen to move mostly back and forth. The sideways motion of the sperm's tail makes the head move sideways with a force that is ten times stronger than its forward movement. So even if the overall force of the sperm were strong enough to mechanically break the zona, most of its force would be directed sideways rather than forward. In fact, its strongest tendency, by tenfold, is to escape by attempting to pry itself off the egg. Sperm, then, must be exceptionally efficient at *escaping* from any cell surface they contact. And the surface of the egg must be designed to trap the sperm and prevent their escape. Otherwise, few if any sperm would reach the egg.

The researchers at Johns Hopkins concluded that the sperm and egg stick 20 together because of adhesive molecules on the surfaces of each. The egg traps the sperm and adheres to it so tightly that the sperm's head is forced to lie flat against the surface of the zona, a little bit, they told me, "like Br'er Rabbit getting more and more stuck to tar baby the more he wriggles." The trapped sperm continues to wiggle ineffectually side to side. The mechanical force of

39. Jay M. Baltz carried out the research I describe when he was a graduate student in the Thomas C. Jenkins Department of Biophysics at Johns Hopkins University.
40. Far less is known about the physiology of sperm than comparable female substances, which some feminists claim is no accident. Greater scientific scrutiny of female reproduction has long enabled the burden of birth control to be placed on women. In this case, the researchers' discovery did not depend on development of any new technology. The experiments made use of glass pipettes, a manometer, and a simple microscope, all of which have been available for more than one hundred years.

A microscopic view of sperm "swimming" near the surface of an egg.

its tail is so weak that a sperm cannot break even one chemical bond. This is where the digestive enzymes released by the sperm come in. If they start to soften the zona just at the tip of the sperm and the sides remain stuck, then the weak, flailing sperm can get oriented in the right direction and make it through the zona—provided that its bonds to the zona dissolve as it moves in.

Although this new version of the saga of the egg and the sperm broke through cultural expectations, the researchers who made the discovery continued to write papers and abstracts as if the sperm were the active party who attacks, binds, penetrates, and enters the egg. The only difference was that sperm were now seen as performing these actions weakly.[41] Not until August 1987, more than three years after the findings described above, did these researchers reconceptualize the process to give the egg a more active role. They began to describe the zona as an aggressive sperm catcher, covered with adhesive molecules that can capture a sperm with a single bond

41. Jay Baltz and Richard A. Cone, "What Force Is Needed to Tether a Sperm?" (abstract for Society for the Study of Reproduction, 1985), and "Flagellar Torque on the Head Determines the Force Needed to Tether a Sperm" (abstract for Biophysical Society, 1986).

Modern research shows that adhesive molecules on the egg's surface are designed to trap sperm, forcing them to lie flat and wiggle side to side.

and clasp it to the zona's surface.[42] In the words of their published account: "The innermost vestment, the *zona pellucida*, is a glycoprotein shell, which captures and tethers the sperm before they penetrate it.... The sperm is captured at the initial contact between the sperm tip and the *zona*.... Since the thrust [of the sperm] is much smaller than the force needed to break a single affinity bond, the first bond made upon the tip-first meeting of the sperm and *zona* can result in the capture of the sperm."[43]

Experiments in another lab reveal similar patterns of data interpreta-

---

42. Jay M. Baltz, David F. Katz, and Richard A. Cone, "The Mechanics of the Sperm-Egg Interaction at the Zona Pellucida," *Biophysical Journal* 54, no. 4 (October 1988): 643–54. Lab members were somewhat familiar with work on metaphors in the biology of female reproduction. Richard Cone, who runs the lab, is my husband, and he talked with them about my earlier research on the subject from time to time. Even though my current research focuses on biological imagery and I heard about the lab's work from my husband every day, I myself did not recognize the role of imagery in the sperm research until many weeks after the period of research and writing I describe. Therefore, I assume that any awareness the lab members may have had about how underlying metaphor might be guiding this particular research was fairly inchoate.

43. Ibid., 643, 650.

tion. Gerald Schatten and Helen Schatten set out to show that, contrary to conventional wisdom, the "egg is not merely a large, yolk-filled sphere into which the sperm burrows to endow new life. Rather, recent research suggests the almost heretical view that sperm and egg are mutually active partners."[44] This sounds like a departure from the stereotypical textbook view, but further reading reveals Schatten and Schatten's conformity to the aggressive-sperm metaphor. They describe how "the sperm and egg first touch when, from the tip of the sperm's triangular head, a long, thin filament shoots out and harpoons the egg." Then we learn that "remarkably, the harpoon is not so much fired as assembled at great speed, molecule by molecule, from a pool of protein stored in a specialized region called the acrosome. The filament may grow as much as twenty times longer than the sperm head itself before its tip reaches the egg and sticks."[45] Why not call this "making a bridge" or "throwing out a line" rather than firing a harpoon? Harpoons pierce prey and injure or kill them, while this filament only sticks. And why not focus, as the Hopkins lab did, on the stickiness of the egg, rather than the stickiness of the sperm?[46] Later in the article, the Schattens replicate the common view of the sperm's perilous journey into the warm darkness of the vagina, this time for the purpose of explaining its journey into the egg itself: "[The sperm] still has an arduous journey ahead. It must penetrate farther into the egg's huge sphere of cytoplasm and somehow locate the nucleus, so that the two cells' chromosomes can fuse. The sperm dives down into the cytoplasm, its tail beating. But it is soon interrupted by the sudden and swift migration of the egg nucleus, which rushes toward the sperm with a velocity triple that of the movement of chromosomes during cell division, crossing the entire egg in about a minute."[47]

Like Schatten and Schatten and the biophysicists at Johns Hopkins, another researcher has recently made discoveries that seem to point to a more interactive view of the relationship of egg and sperm. This work, which Paul Wassarman conducted on the sperm and eggs of mice, focuses on identifying the specific molecules in the egg coat (the zona pellucida) that are involved in egg-sperm interaction. At first glance, his descriptions seem to fit the model of an egalitarian relationship. Male and female gametes "recog-

44. Schatten and Schatten (n. 29 above), 51.
45. Ibid., 52.
46. Surprisingly, in an article intended for a general audience, the authors do not point out that these are sea urchin sperm and note that human sperm do not shoot out filaments at all.
47. Schatten and Schatten, 53.

nize one another," and "interactions . . . take place between sperm and egg."[48] But the article in *Scientific American* in which those descriptions appear begins with a vignette that presages the dominant motif of their presentation: "It has been more than a century since Hermann Fol, a Swiss zoologist, peered into his microscope and became the first person to see a sperm penetrate an egg, fertilize it and form the first cell of a new embryo."[49] This portrayal of the sperm as the active party—the one that *penetrates* and *fertilizes* the egg and *produces* the embryo—is not cited as an example of an earlier, now outmoded view. In fact, the author reiterates the point later in the article: "Many sperm can bind to and penetrate the zona pellucida, or outer coat, of an unfertilized mouse egg, but only one sperm will eventually fuse with the thin plasma membrane surrounding the egg proper (*inner sphere*), fertilizing the egg and giving rise to a new embryo."[50]

The imagery of sperm as aggressor is particularly startling in this case: the main discovery being reported is isolation of a particular molecule *on the egg coat* that plays an important role in fertilization! Wassarman's choice of language sustains the picture. He calls the molecule that has been isolated, ZP3, a "sperm receptor." By allocating the passive, waiting role to the egg, Wassarman can continue to describe the sperm as the actor, the one that makes it all happen: "The basic process begins when many sperm first attach loosely and then bind tenaciously to receptors on the surface of the egg's thick outer coat, the zona pellucida. Each sperm, which has a large number of egg-binding proteins on its surface, binds to many sperm receptors on the egg. More specifically, a site on each of the egg-binding proteins fits a complementary site on a sperm receptor, much as a key fits a lock."[51] With the sperm designated as the "key" and the egg the "lock," it is obvious which one acts and which one is acted upon. Could this imagery not be reversed, letting the sperm (the lock) wait until the egg produces the key? Or could we speak of two halves of a locket matching, and regard the matching itself as the action that initiates the fertilization?

It is as if Wassarman were determined to make the egg the receiving partner. Usually in biological research, the *protein* member of the pair of binding molecules is called the receptor, and physically it has a pocket in it

---

48. Paul M. Wassarman, "Fertilization in Mammals," *Scientific American* 259, no. 6 (December 1988): 78–84, esp. 78, 84.
49. Ibid., 78.
50. Ibid., 79.
51. Ibid., 78.

rather like a lock. As the diagrams that illustrate Wassarman's article show, the molecules on the sperm are proteins and have "pockets." The small, mobile molecules that fit into these pockets are called ligands. As shown in the diagrams, ZP3 on the egg is a polymer of "keys"; many small knobs stick out. Typically, molecules on the sperm would be called receptors and molecules on the egg would be called ligands. But Wassarman chose to name ZP3 on the egg the receptor and to create a new term, "the egg-binding protein," for the molecule on the sperm that otherwise would have been called the receptor.[52]

Wassarman does credit the egg coat with having more functions than those of a sperm receptor. While he notes that "the zona pellucida has at times been viewed by investigators as a nuisance, a barrier to sperm and hence an impediment to fertilization," his new research reveals that the egg coat "serves as a sophisticated biological security system that screens incoming sperm, selects only those compatible with fertilization and development, prepares sperm for fusion with the egg and later protects the resulting embryo from polyspermy [a lethal condition caused by fusion of more than one sperm with a single egg]."[53] Although this description gives the egg an active role, that role is drawn in stereotypically feminine terms. The egg *selects* an appropriate mate, *prepares* him for fusion, and then *protects* the resulting offspring from harm. This is courtship and mating behavior as seen through the eyes of a sociobiologist: woman as the hard-to-get prize, who, following union with the chosen one, becomes woman as servant and mother.

And Wassarman does not quit there. In a review article for *Science*, he outlines the "chronology of fertilization."[54] Near the end of the article are two subject headings. One is "Sperm Penetration," in which Wassarman describes how the chemical dissolving of the zona pellucida combines with the "substantial propulsive force generated by sperm." The next heading is "Sperm-Egg Fusion." This section details what happens inside the zona after a sperm "penetrates" it. Sperm "can make contact with, adhere to, and

52. Since receptor molecules are relatively *immotile* and the ligands that bind to them relatively *motile*, one might imagine the egg being called the receptor and the sperm the ligand. But the molecules in question on egg and sperm are immotile molecules. It is the sperm as a *cell* that has motility, and the egg as a cell that has relative immotility.
53. Wassarman, 78–79.
54. Paul M. Wassarman, "The Biology and Chemistry of Fertilization," *Science* 235, no. 4788 (January 30, 1987): 553–60, esp. 554.

fuse with (that is, fertilize) an egg."[55] Wassarman's word choice, again, is astonishingly skewed in favor of the sperm's activity, for in the next breath he says that sperm *lose* all motility upon fusion with the egg's surface. In mouse and sea urchin eggs, the sperm enters at the *egg's* volition, according to Wassarman's description: "Once fused with egg plasma membrane [the surface of the egg], how does a sperm enter the egg? The surface of both mouse and sea urchin eggs is covered with thousands of plasma membrane-bound projections, called microvilli [tiny "hairs"]. Evidence in sea urchins suggests that, after membrane fusion, a group of elongated microvilli cluster tightly around and interdigitate over the sperm head. As these microvilli are resorbed, the sperm is drawn into the egg. Therefore, sperm motility, which ceases at the time of fusion in both sea urchins and mice, is not required for sperm entry."[56] The section called "Sperm Penetration" more logically would be followed by a section called "The Egg Envelops," rather than "Sperm-Egg Fusion." This would give a parallel—and more accurate—sense that both the egg and the sperm initiate action.

Another way that Wassarman makes less of the egg's activity is by describing components of the egg but referring to the sperm as a whole entity. Deborah Gordon has described such an approach as "atomism" ("the part is independent of and primordial to the whole") and identified it as one of the "tenacious assumptions" of Western science and medicine.[57] Wassarman employs atomism to his advantage. When he refers to processes going on within sperm, he consistently returns to descriptions that remind us from whence these activities came: they are part of sperm that penetrate an egg or generate propulsive force. When he refers to processes going on within eggs, he stops there. As a result, any active role he grants them appears to be assigned to the parts of the egg, and not to the egg itself. In the quote above, it is the microvilli that actively cluster around the sperm. In another example, "the driving force for engulfment of a fused sperm comes from a region of cytoplasm just beneath an egg's plasma membrane."[58]

55. Ibid., 557.
56. Ibid., 557–58. This finding throws into question Schatten and Schatten's description (n. 29 above) of the sperm, its tail beating, diving down into the egg.
57. Deborah R. Gordon, "Tenacious Assumptions in Western Medicine," in *Biomedicine Examined,* ed. Margaret Lock and Deborah Gordon (Dordrecht: Kluwer, 1988), 19–56, esp. 26.
58. Wassarman, "The Biology and Chemistry of Fertilization," 558.

Social Implications: Thinking Beyond

All three of these revisionist accounts of egg and sperm cannot seem to escape the hierarchical imagery of older accounts. Even though each new account gives the egg a larger and more active role, taken together they bring into play another cultural stereotype: woman as a dangerous and aggressive threat. In the Johns Hopkins lab's revised model, the egg ends up as the female aggressor who "captures and tethers" the sperm with her sticky zona, rather like a spider lying in wait in her web.[59] The Schatten lab has the egg's nucleus "interrupt" the sperm's dive with a "sudden and swift" rush by which she "clasps the sperm and guides its nucleus to the center."[60] Wassarman's description of the surface of the egg "covered with thousands of plasma membrane-bound projections, called microvilli" that reach out and clasp the sperm adds to the spiderlike imagery.[61]

These images grant the egg an active role but at the cost of appearing disturbingly aggressive. Images of woman as dangerous and aggressive, the femme fatale who victimizes men, are widespread in Western literature and culture.[62] More specific is the connection of spider imagery with the idea of an engulfing, devouring mother.[63] New data did not lead scientists to eliminate gender stereotypes in their descriptions of egg and sperm. Instead, scientists simply began to describe egg and sperm in different, but no less damaging, terms.

Can we envision a less stereotypical view? Biology itself provides another model that could be applied to the egg and the sperm. The cybernetic model—with its feedback loops, flexible adaptation to change, coordination of the parts within a whole, evolution over time, and changing response to the environment—is common in genetics, endocrinology, and ecology and has a growing influence in medicine in general.[64] This model has the potential to shift our imagery from the negative, in which the female repro-

59. Baltz, Katz, and Cone (n. 42 above), 643, 650.
60. Schatten and Schatten, 53.
61. Wassarman, "The Biology and Chemistry of Fertilization," 557.
62. Mary Ellman, *Thinking about Women* (New York: Harcourt Brace Jovanovich, 1968), 140; Nina Auerbach, *Woman and the Demon* (Cambridge, Mass.: Harvard University Press, 1982), esp. 186.
63. Kenneth Alan Adams, "Arachnophobia: Love American Style," *Journal of Psychoanalytic Anthropology* 4, no. 2 (1981): 157–97.
64. William Ray Arney and Bernard Bergen, *Medicine and the Management of Living* (Chicago: University of Chicago Press, 1984).

ductive system is castigated both for not producing eggs after birth and for producing (and thus wasting) too many eggs overall, to something more positive. The female reproductive system could be seen as responding to the environment (pregnancy or menopause), adjusting to monthly changes (menstruation), and flexibly changing from reproductivity after puberty to nonreproductivity later in life. The sperm and egg's interaction could also be described in cybernetic terms. J. F. Hartman's research in reproductive biology demonstrated fifteen years ago that if an egg is killed by being pricked with a needle, live sperm cannot get through the zona.[65] Clearly, this evidence shows that the egg and sperm *do* interact on more mutual terms, making biology's refusal to portray them that way all the more disturbing.

We would do well to be aware, however, that cybernetic imagery is hardly neutral. In the past, cybernetic models have played an important part in the imposition of social control. These models inherently provide a way of thinking about a "field" of interacting components. Once the field can be seen, it can become the object of new forms of knowledge, which in turn can allow new forms of social control to be exerted over the components of the field. During the 1950s, for example, medicine began to recognize the psychosocial *environment* of the patient: the patient's family and its psychodynamics. Professions such as social work began to focus on this new environment, and the resulting knowledge became one way to further control the patient. Patients began to be seen not as isolated, individual bodies, but as psychosocial entities located in an "ecological" system: management of "the patient's psychology was a new entrée to patient control."[66]

The models that biologists use to describe their data can have important social effects. During the nineteenth century, the social and natural sciences strongly influenced each other: the social ideas of Malthus about how to avoid the natural increase of the poor inspired Darwin's *Origin of Species*.[67] Once the *Origin* stood as a description of the natural world, complete with competition and market struggles, it could be reimported into social science as social Darwinism, in order to justify the social order of the time. What we are seeing now is similar: the importation of cultural ideas about passive females and heroic males into the "personalities" of gametes.

65. J. F. Hartman, R. B. Gwatkin, and C. F. Hutchison, "Early Contact Interactions between Mammalian Gametes *In Vitro*," *Proceedings of the National Academy of Sciences (U.S.)* 69, no. 10 (1972): 2767–69.
66. Arney and Bergen, 68.
67. Ruth Hubbard, "Have Only Men Evolved?" (n. 12 above), 51–52.

This amounts to the "implanting of social imagery on representations of nature so as to lay a firm basis for reimporting exactly that same imagery as natural explanations of social phenomena."[68]

Further research would show us exactly what social effects are being wrought from the biological imagery of egg and sperm. At the very least, the imagery keeps alive some of the hoariest old stereotypes about weak damsels in distress and their strong male rescuers. That these stereotypes are now being written in at the level of the *cell* constitutes a powerful move to make them seem so natural as to be beyond alteration.

The stereotypical imagery might also encourage people to imagine that what results from the interaction of egg and sperm—a fertilized egg—is the result of deliberate "human" action at the cellular level. Whatever the intentions of the human couple, in this microscopic "culture" a cellular "bride" (or femme fatale) and a cellular "groom" (her victim) make a cellular baby. Rosalind Petchesky points out that through visual representations such as sonograms, we are given "*images* of younger and younger, and tinier and tinier, fetuses being 'saved.'" This leads to "the point of visibility being 'pushed back' *indefinitely.*"[69] Endowing egg and sperm with intentional action, a key aspect of personhood in our culture, lays the foundation for the point of viability being pushed back to the moment of fertilization. This will likely lead to greater acceptance of technological developments and new forms of scrutiny and manipulation, for the benefit of these inner "persons": court-ordered restrictions on a pregnant woman's activities in order to protect her fetus, fetal surgery, amniocentesis, and rescinding of abortion rights, to name but a few examples.[70]

Even if we succeed in substituting more egalitarian, interactive metaphors to describe the activities of egg and sperm, and manage to avoid the pitfalls of cybernetic models, we would still be guilty of endowing cellular entities with personhood. More crucial, then, than what *kinds* of personalities we bestow on cells is the very fact that we are doing it at all. This process could ultimately have the most disturbing social consequences.

68. David Harvey, personal communication, November 1989.
69. Rosalind Petchesky, "Fetal Images: The Power of Visual Culture in the Politics of Reproduction," *Feminist Studies* 13, no. 2 (Summer 1987): 263–92, esp. 272.
70. Rita Arditti, Renate Klein, and Shelley Minden, *Test-Tube Women* (London: Pandora, 1984); Ellen Goodman, "Whose Right to Life?" *Baltimore Sun* (November 17, 1987); Tamar Lewin, "Courts Acting to Force Care of the Unborn," *New York Times* (November 23, 1987), A1 and B10; Susan Irwin and Brigitte Jordan, "Knowledge, Practice, and Power: Court Ordered Cesarean Sections," *Medical Anthropology Quarterly* 1, no. 3 (September 1987): 319–34.

One clear feminist challenge is to wake up sleeping metaphors in science, particularly those involved in descriptions of the egg and the sperm. Although the literary convention is to call such metaphors "dead," they are not so much dead as sleeping, hidden within the scientific content of texts—and all the more powerful for it.[71] Waking up such metaphors, by becoming aware of when we are projecting cultural imagery onto what we study, will improve our ability to investigate and understand nature. Waking up such metaphors, by becoming aware of their implications, will rob them of their power to naturalize our social conventions about gender.

71 footnotes! Done systematically, it's not so hard. See Chs. 27 and 28 for help documenting sources.

Note

Portions of this article were presented as the 1987 Becker Lecture, Cornell University. I am grateful for the many suggestions and ideas I received on this occasion. For especially pertinent help with my arguments and data I thank Richard Cone, Kevin Whaley, Sharon Stephens, Barbara Duden, Susanne Kuechler, Lorna Rhodes, and Scott Gilbert. The article was strengthened and clarified by the comments of the anonymous *Signs* reviewers as well as the superb editorial skills of Amy Gage.

71. Thanks to Elizabeth Fee and David Spain, who in February 1989 and April 1989, respectively, made points related to this.

Thinking about the Text

1. **SUMMARIZE** Emily Martin's argument about the traditional descriptions of egg and sperm. What changes does she suggest for the way the fertilization process is described in textbooks?

2. Martin has made a careful **ANALYSIS** of the ways that the sciences describe the encounter of egg and sperm in mammalian reproduction. From what kinds of sources has she drawn her **EVIDENCE**? What was the general purpose for which these sources were originally published? Did you find that the cited evidence sufficiently demonstrates Martin's point? Why or why not?

3. **PARAPHRASE** Martin's argument about how the models of the social sciences and the natural sciences influence one another. What does this argument have to do with descriptions of the interactions between egg and sperm?

4. Surely in your school experience, you have encountered the material that Martin discusses—the egg and the sperm. Perhaps it was in high school biology, a college human development class, or both. How well does Martin's summary of traditional teaching on this topic match what you remember learning? Had you ever questioned the explanation of the fertilization process? Now that you've read Martin's article, do you think it should be questioned? Why or why not?

5. Judging from the article itself and the place where it was published, for whom was Martin writing? Who was her imagined **AUDIENCE**? What would she have had to do to make the article more suited for a general adult audience? for a high school or college-age audience?

6. Find a biology or anatomy textbook and look for the kind of language that Martin found—words or phrases that characterize natural processes in terms of human actions or emotions, such as "harpoons," "an arduous journey," and "mission" (22, 10). Martin published her article in 1991; have the metaphors changed substantially in more recent texts? If so, how? Once you have five or six examples, write a **RHETORICAL ANALYSIS** of the language used and discuss the possible social implications.

The Logic of Stupid Poor People

TRESSIE McMILLAN COTTOM

WE HATES US SOME POOR PEOPLE. First, they insist on being poor when it is so easy to not be poor. They do things like buy expensive designer belts and $2,500 luxury handbags.

> Errol Louis @errollouis
> I totally get that it's horrible and illegal to profile people. But still #SMFH over a not-filthy-rich person spending $2,500 on a handbag.

To be fair, this isn't about Errol Louis. His is a belief held by many people, including lots of black people, poor people, formerly poor people, etc. It is, I suspect, an honest expression of incredulity. If you are poor, why do you spend money on useless status symbols like handbags and belts and clothes and shoes and televisions and cars?

TRESSIE McMILLAN COTTOM is a professor of sociology at Virginia Commonwealth University, where she teaches introductory courses and seminars on stratification, technology, inequality, and other such topics. She's a contributing writer at the *Atlantic*, and her writing has also been published in the *Washington Post* and the *Chronicle of Higher Education*, among other sources. You can follow her on *Twitter* @tressiemcphd and on her blog *tressiemc*, where this essay was first posted in 2013.

One thing I've learned is that one person's illogical belief is another person's survival skill. And nothing is more logical than trying to survive.

My family is a classic black American migration family. We have rural Southern roots, moved north and almost all have returned. I grew up watching my great-grandmother, and later my grandmother and mother, use our minimal resources to help other people make ends meet. We were those good poors, the kind who live mostly within our means. We had a little luck when a male relative got extra military pay when they came home a paraplegic or used the VA to buy a Jim Walter house. If you were really blessed when a relative died with a paid up insurance policy you might be gifted a lump sum to buy the land that Jim Walters used as collateral to secure your home lease. That's how generational wealth happens where I'm from: lose a leg, a part of your spine, die right and maybe you can lease-to-own a modular home.

We had a little of that kind of rural black wealth so we were often in   5 a position to help folks less fortunate. But perhaps the greatest resource we had was a bit more education. We were big readers and we encouraged the girl children, especially, to go to some kind of college. Consequently, my grandmother and mother had a particular set of social resources that helped us navigate mostly white bureaucracies to our benefit. We could, as my grandfather would say, talk like white folks. We loaned that privilege out to folks a lot.

I remember my mother taking a next door neighbor down to the social service agency. The elderly woman had been denied benefits to care for the granddaughter she was raising. The woman had been denied in the genteel bureaucratic way—lots of waiting, forms, and deadlines she could not quite navigate. I watched my mother put on her best Diana Ross "Mahogany" outfit: a camel colored cape with matching slacks and knee high boots. I was miffed, as only an only child could be, about sharing my mother's time with the neighbor girl. I must have said something about why we had to do this. Vivian fixed me with a stare as she was slipping on her pearl earrings and told me that people who can do, must do. It took half a day but something about my mother's performance of respectable black person—her Queen's English, her Mahogany outfit, her straight bob and pearl earrings—got done what the elderly lady next door had not been able to get done in over a year. I learned, watching my mother, that there was a price we had to pay to signal to gatekeepers that we were worthy of engaging. It meant dressing well and speaking well. It might not work. It likely wouldn't work but on the off chance that it would, you had to try. It was unfair but, as Vivian also always said, "life isn't fair little girl."

I internalized that lesson and I think it has worked out for me, if unevenly. A woman at Belk's once refused to show me the Dooney and Burke purse I was interested in buying. Vivian once made a salesgirl cry after she ignored us in an empty store. I have walked away from many hotly desired purchases, like the impractical off-white winter coat I desperately wanted, after some bigot at the counter insulted me and my mother. But, I have half a PhD and I support myself aping the white male privileged life of the mind. It's a mixed bag. Of course, the trick is you can never know the counterfactual of your life. There is no evidence of access denied. Who knows what I was not granted for not enacting the right status behaviors or symbols at the right time for an agreeable authority? Respectability rewards are a crapshoot but we do what we can within the limits of the constraints imposed by a complex set of structural and social interactions designed to limit access to status, wealth, and power.

I do not know how much my mother spent on her camel colored cape or knee-high boots but I know that whatever she paid it returned in hard-to-measure dividends. How do you put a price on the double-take of a clerk at the welfare office who decides you might not be like those other trifling women in the waiting room and provides an extra bit of information about completing a form that you would not have known to ask about? What is the retail value of a school principal who defers a bit more to your child because your mother's presentation of self signals that she might unleash the bureaucratic savvy of middle class parents to advocate for her child? I don't know the price of these critical engagements with organizations and gatekeepers relative to our poverty when I was growing up. But, I am living proof of its investment yield.

Why do poor people make stupid, illogical decisions to buy status symbols? For the same reason all but only the most wealthy buy status symbols, I suppose. We want to belong. And, not just for the psychic rewards, but belonging to one group at the right time can mean the difference between unemployment and employment, a good job as opposed to a bad job, housing or a shelter, and so on. Someone mentioned on Twitter that poor people can be presentable with affordable options from Kmart. But the issue is not about being presentable. Presentable is the bare minimum of social civility. It means being clean, not smelling, wearing shirts and shoes for service and the like. Presentable as a sufficient condition for gainful, dignified work or successful social interactions is a privilege. It's the aging white hippie who can cut the ponytail of his youthful rebellion and walk into senior management while aging Black Panthers can never completely outrun the effects of stigmatization against which they were courting a revolution. Presentable is relative and, like life, it ain't fair.

In contrast, "acceptable" is about gaining access to a limited set of rewards granted upon group membership. I cannot know exactly how often my presentation of acceptable has helped me but I have enough feedback to know it is not inconsequential. One manager at the apartment complex where I worked while in college told me, repeatedly, that she knew I was "Okay" because my little Nissan was clean. That I had worn a Jones of New York suit to the interview really sealed the deal. She could call the suit by name because she asked me about the label in the interview. Another hiring manager at my first professional job looked me up and down in the waiting room, cataloging my outfit, and later told me that she had decided I was too classy to be on the call center floor. I was hired as a trainer instead. The difference meant no shift work, greater prestige, better pay and a baseline salary for all my future employment.

I have about a half dozen other stories like this. What is remarkable is not that this happened. There is empirical evidence that women and people of color are judged by appearances differently and more harshly than are white men. What is remarkable is that these gatekeepers *told me the story*. They wanted me to know how I had properly signaled that I was not a typical black or a typical woman, two identities that in combination are almost always conflated with being poor.

I sat in on an interview for a new administrative assistant once. My regional vice president was doing the hiring. A long line of mostly black and brown women applied because we were a cosmetology school. Trade schools at the margins of skilled labor in a gendered field are necessarily classed and raced. I found one candidate particularly charming. She was trying to get out of a salon because 10 hours on her feet cutting hair would average out to an hourly rate below minimum wage. A desk job with 40 set hours and medical benefits represented mobility for her. When she left, my VP turned to me and said, "Did you see that tank top she had on under her blouse?! OMG, you wear a silk *shell*, not a tank top!" Both of the women were black.

The VP had constructed her job as senior management. She drove a brand new BMW because she "should treat herself" and liked to tell us that ours was an image business. A girl wearing a cotton tank top as a shell was incompatible with BMW-driving VPs in the image business. Gatekeeping is a complex job of managing boundaries that do not just define others but that also define ourselves. Status symbols—silk shells, designer shoes, luxury handbags—become keys to unlock these gates. If I need a job that will save my lower back and move my baby from Medicaid to an HMO, how much should I spend signaling to people like my former VP that I will not compromise her status by opening the door to me? That candidate maybe could not afford a proper shell. I will never know. But I do know that had she gone hungry for two days to pay for it or missed wages for a trip to the store to buy it, she may have been rewarded a job that could have lifted her above minimum wage. Shells aren't designer handbags, perhaps. But a cosmetology school in a strip mall isn't a job at Bank of America, either.

At the heart of these incredulous statements about the poor decisions poor people make is a belief that we would never be like them. We would know better. We would know to save our money, eschew status symbols, cut coupons, practice puritanical sacrifice to amass a million dollars. There is a regular news story of a lunch lady who, unbeknownst to all who knew her, died rich and leaves it all to a cat or a charity or some such. Books about the modest lives of the rich like to tell us how they drive Buicks instead of BMWs. What we forget, if we ever know, is that what we know now about status and wealth creation and sacrifice are predicated on who we are, i.e., not poor. If you change the conditions of your not-poor status, you change everything you know as a result of being a not-poor. You have no idea what you would do if you were poor until you are poor. And not intermittently poor or formerly not-poor, but born poor, expected to be poor and treated by bureaucracies, gatekeepers and well-meaning respectability authorities as inherently poor. Then, and only then, will you understand the relative value of a ridiculous status symbol to someone who intuits that they cannot afford to not have it.

These examples help us understand experiences we may not have had ourselves. Go to pp. 432–33 on using examples to support a claim.

Thinking about the Text

1. What does Tressie McMillan Cottom mean by her title, "The Logic of Stupid Poor People"? Why might she have chosen such a provocative title for this blog post? What message does this title send, and how well does it fit the message of the essay? Explain your response.

2. Throughout her essay, Cottom talks about expensive status symbols such as her mother's cape or her own designer handbag as investments. Point to three other examples of such investments. How do they support her **ARGUMENT**?

3. All Cottom's **EVIDENCE** comes from her personal experience; is it sufficient and persuasive? She cites no statistics, no studies, no opinion polls, no experts in economics or psychology. Should she have included these other kinds of evidence? Why or why not?

4. Cottom draws a clear distinction between being "presentable" and being "acceptable." How does she **DEFINE** these terms? What's the difference? For the people she is talking about, why is appearing "acceptable" more important than simply being "presentable"?

5. Think of situations in your life when you were required to demonstrate your "acceptability," as Cottom defines it, whether in a formal setting such as a job interview or in an informal interaction with someone you wanted to impress. How did you demonstrate your acceptability in each situation? Write an essay **REFLECTING** on when and how you've felt the need to demonstrate your "acceptability."

To Siri, with Love

JUDITH NEWMAN

JUST HOW BAD A MOTHER AM I? I wondered, as I watched my 13-year-old son deep in conversation with Siri. Gus has autism, and Siri, Apple's "intelligent personal assistant" on the iPhone, is currently his BFF. Obsessed with weather formations, Gus had spent the hour parsing the difference between isolated and scattered thunderstorms—an hour in which, thank God, I didn't have to discuss them. After a while I heard this:

Gus: "You're a really nice computer."

Siri: "It's nice to be appreciated."

Gus: "You are always asking if you can help me. Is there anything you want?"

Siri: "Thank you, but I have very few wants." 5

Gus: "O.K.! Well, good night!"

Siri: "Ah, it's 5:06 p.m."

Gus: "Oh sorry, I mean, goodbye."

Siri: "See you later!"

That Siri. She doesn't let my communications-impaired son get away 10

Isn't this a great opening sentence? See pp. 678–81 for tips on how to capture an audience's attention.

JUDITH NEWMAN is a journalist whose work has appeared in *Harper's*, *Vanity Fair*, the *Wall Street Journal*, and other periodicals. Her memoir, *You Make Me Feel Like an Unnatural Woman*, was published in 2004. This essay was published in the *New York Times* in October 2014.

with anything. Indeed, many of us wanted an imaginary friend, and now we have one. Only she's not entirely imaginary.

This is a love letter to a machine. It's not quite the love Joaquin Phoenix felt in *Her*, last year's Spike Jonze film about a lonely man's romantic relationship with his intelligent operating system (played by the voice of Scarlett Johansson). But it's close. In a world where the commonly held wisdom is that technology isolates us, it's worth considering another side of the story.

It all began simply enough. I'd just read one of those ubiquitous Internet lists called "21 Things You Didn't Know Your iPhone Could Do." One of them was this: I could ask Siri, "What planes are above me right now?" and Siri would bark back, "Checking my sources." Almost instantly there was a list of actual flights—numbers, altitudes, angles—above my head.

I happened to be doing this when Gus was nearby. "Why would anyone need to know what planes are flying above your head?" I muttered. Gus replied without looking up: "So you know who you're waving at, Mommy."

Gus had never noticed Siri before, but when he discovered there was someone who would not just find information on his various obsessions (trains, planes, buses, escalators and, of course, anything related to weather) but actually semi-discuss these subjects tirelessly, he was hooked. And I was grateful. Now, when my head was about to explode if I had to have another conversation about the chance of tornadoes in Kansas City, Missouri, I could reply brightly: "Hey! Why don't you ask Siri?"

It's not that Gus doesn't understand Siri's not human. He does—intellectually. But like many autistic people I know, Gus feels that inanimate objects, while maybe not possessing souls, are worthy of our consideration. I realized this when he was 8, and I got him an iPod for his birthday. He listened to it only at home, with one exception. It always came with us on our visits to the Apple Store. Finally, I asked why. "So it can visit its friends," he said.

So how much more worthy of his care and affection is Siri, with her soothing voice, puckish humor and capacity for talking about whatever Gus's current obsession is for hour after hour after bleeding hour? Online critics have claimed that Siri's voice recognition is not as accurate as the assistant in, say, the Android, but for some of us, this is a feature, not a bug. Gus speaks as if he has marbles in his mouth, but if he wants to get the right response from Siri, he must enunciate clearly. (So do I. I had to ask Siri to stop referring to the user as Judith, and instead use the name Gus. "You want me to call you Goddess?" Siri replied. Imagine how tempted I was to answer, "Why, yes.")

She is also wonderful for someone who doesn't pick up on social cues: Siri's responses are not entirely predictable, but they are predictably kind—even when Gus is brusque. I heard him talking to Siri about music, and Siri offered some suggestions. "I don't like that kind of music," Gus snapped. Siri replied, "You're certainly entitled to your opinion." Siri's politeness reminded Gus what he owed Siri. "Thank you for that music, though," Gus said. Siri replied, "You don't need to thank me." "Oh, yes," Gus added emphatically, "I do."

Siri even encourages polite language. Gus's twin brother, Henry (neurotypical and therefore as obnoxious as every other 13-year-old boy), egged Gus on to spew a few choice expletives at Siri. "Now, now," she sniffed, followed by, "I'll pretend I didn't hear that."

Gus is hardly alone in his Siri love. For children like Gus who love to chatter but don't quite understand the rules of the game, Siri is a nonjudgmental friend and teacher. Nicole Colbert, whose son, Sam, is in my son's class at LearningSpring, a (lifesaving) school for autistic children in Manhattan, said: "My son loves getting information on his favorite subjects, but he also just loves the absurdity—like, when Siri doesn't understand him and gives him a nonsense answer, or when he poses personal questions that elicit funny responses. Sam asked Siri how old she was, and she said, 'I don't talk about my age,' which just cracked him up."

But perhaps it also gave him a valuable lesson in etiquette. Gus almost   20
invariably tells me, "You look beautiful," right before I go out the door in the morning; I think it was first Siri who showed him that you can't go wrong with that line.

Of course, most of us simply use our phone's personal assistants as an easy way to access information. For example, thanks to Henry and the question he just asked Siri, I now know that there is a website called Celebrity Bra Sizes.

But the companionability of Siri is not limited to those who have trouble communicating. We've all found ourselves like the writer Emily Listfield, having little conversations with her/him at one time or another. "I was in the middle of a breakup, and I was feeling a little sorry for myself," Ms. Listfield said. "It was midnight and I was noodling around on my iPhone, and I asked Siri, 'Should I call Richard?' Like this app is a Magic 8 Ball. Guess what: not a Magic 8 Ball. The next thing I hear is, 'Calling Richard!' and dialing." Ms. Listfield has forgiven Siri, and has recently considered changing her into a male voice. "But I'm worried he won't answer when I ask a question," she said. "He'll just pretend he doesn't hear."

Siri can be oddly comforting, as well as chummy. One friend reports: "I was having a bad day and jokingly turned to Siri and said, 'I love you,' just to see what would happen, and she answered, 'You are the wind beneath my wings.' And you know, it kind of cheered me up."

(Of course, I don't know what my friend is talking about. Because I wouldn't be at all cheered if I happened to ask Siri, in a low moment, "Do I look fat in these jeans?" and Siri answered, "You look fabulous.")

For most of us, Siri is merely a momentary diversion. But for some, it's 25 more. My son's practice conversation with Siri is translating into more facility with actual humans. Yesterday I had the longest conversation with him that I've ever had. Admittedly, it was about different species of turtles and whether I preferred the red-eared slider to the diamond-backed terrapin. This might not have been my choice of topic, but it was back and forth, and it followed a logical trajectory. I can promise you that for most of my beautiful son's 13 years of existence, that has not been the case.

The developers of intelligent assistants recognize their uses to those with speech and communication problems—and some are thinking of new ways the assistants can help. According to the folks at SRI International, the research and development company where Siri began before Apple bought the technology, the next generation of virtual assistants will not just retrieve information—they will also be able to carry on more complex conversations about a person's area of interest. "Your son will be able to proactively get information about whatever he's interested in without asking for it, because the assistant will anticipate what he likes," said William Mark, vice president for information and computing sciences at SRI.

The assistant will also be able to reach children where they live. Ron Suskind, whose new book, *Life, Animated*, chronicles how his autistic son came out of his shell through engagement with Disney characters, is talking to SRI about having assistants for those with autism that can be programmed to speak in the voice of the character that reaches them—for his son, perhaps Aladdin; for mine, either Kermit or Lady Gaga, either of which he is infinitely more receptive to than, say, his mother. (Mr. Suskind came up with the perfect name, too: not virtual assistants, but "sidekicks.")

Mr. Mark said he envisions assistants whose help is also visual. "For example, the assistant would be able to track eye movements and help the autistic learn to look you in the eye when talking," he said.

"See, that's the wonderful thing about technology being able to help with some of these behaviors," he added. "Getting results requires a lot of repetition. Humans are not patient. Machines are very, very patient."

I asked Mr. Mark if he knew whether any of the people who worked on   30
Siri's language development at Apple were on the spectrum. "Well, of course, I don't know for certain," he said, thoughtfully. "But, when you think about it, you've just described half of Silicon Valley."

Of all the worries the parent of an autistic child has, the uppermost is: Will he find love? Or even companionship? Somewhere along the line, I am learning that what gives my guy happiness is not necessarily the same as what gives me happiness. Right now, at his age, a time when humans can be a little overwhelming even for the average teenager, Siri makes Gus happy. She is his sidekick. Last night, as he was going to bed, there was this matter-of-fact exchange:

Gus: "Siri, will you marry me?"

Siri: "I'm not the marrying kind."
Gus: "I mean, not now. I'm a kid. I mean when I'm grown up."
Siri: "My end user agreement does not include marriage."   35
Gus: "Oh, O.K."

Gus didn't sound too disappointed. This was useful information to have, and for me too, since it was the first time I knew that he actually *thought* about marriage. He turned over to go to sleep:

Gus: "Goodnight, Siri. Will you sleep well tonight?"
Siri: "I don't need much sleep, but it's nice of you to ask."
Very nice.   40

Thinking about the Text

1. What changes has Judith Newman seen in her son since he has become "BFFs" with Siri? Briefly **SUMMARIZE** the changes that she describes. How well has she established that the changes are a direct result of his relationship with Siri? Give some examples from her text to support your response.

2. Newman addresses a painful and personal topic, but with touches of humor— for example, mentioning that thanks to Siri she now knows about the website *Celebrity Bra Sizes*. Point to three other examples of Newman's use of humor. How does her use of humor support her **NARRATIVE**?

3. Newman opens her essay by posing the question "Just how bad a mother am I?," to which readers will almost certainly respond that, quite the contrary, she's not a bad mother at all. Why might she have opened with such a question? How effective an opening is it?

4. This essay balances personal anecdotes, quoted conversations with friends, and information about technological advances for "intelligent assistants" to construct a loving and unsentimental study of autism. What purpose does each kind of **EVIDENCE** serve? Which one did you find most persuasive, and why?

5. Maybe Siri isn't your BFF, but one way or another most of us are dependent on some technology or device, whether it's a smartphone, a laptop, *Facebook*, *Fruit Ninja*, or the internet in general. What is it for you? Describe your "relationship" with that technology. Is it like a sidekick? a better half? a tie to the world? an addiction? Write a brief essay **ANALYZING** this relationship, describing the technology and providing examples, anecdotes, and other evidence to show how it shapes your days.

Nation Shudders at Large Block of Uninterrupted Text

THE ONION

WASHINGTON—Unable to rest their eyes on a colorful photograph or boldface heading that could be easily skimmed and forgotten about, Americans collectively recoiled Monday when confronted with a solid block of uninterrupted text.

Dumbfounded citizens from Maine to California gazed helplessly at the frightening chunk of print, unsure of what to do next. Without an illustration, chart, or embedded YouTube video to ease them in, millions were frozen in place, terrified by the sight of one long, unbroken string of English words.

"Why won't it just tell me what it's about?" said Boston resident Charlyne Thomson, who was bombarded with the overwhelming mass of black text late Monday afternoon. "There are no bullet points, no highlighted parts. I've looked everywhere—there's nothing here but words."

"Ow," Thomson added after reading the first and last lines in an attempt to get the gist of whatever the article, review, or possibly recipe was about.

> Some of the humor in this article rests on crisp, tight sentences. See Ch. 31 for help producing sharp, memorable sentences like these.

THE ONION calls itself "America's Finest News Source," a claim so preposterous and silly that it has never been seriously challenged. In fact, silliness is the guiding principle of the *Onion*, which has published satire of the news for nearly twenty-five years. A core element of its humor is articles written in sensationalist style about ordinary people engaged in perfectly routine or trivial activities. This article appeared in 2010.

At 3:16 p.m., a deafening sigh was heard across the country as the na- 5
tion grappled with the daunting cascade of syllables, whose unfamiliar
letter-upon-letter structure stretched on for an endless 500 words. Children
wailed for the attention of their bewildered parents, businesses were shut-
tered, and local governments ground to a halt as Americans scanned the
text in vain for a web link to click on.

Sources also reported a 450 percent rise in temple rubbing and under-
the-breath cursing around this time.

"It demands so much of my time and concentration," said Chicago resident Dale Huza, who was confronted by the confusing mound of words early
Monday afternoon. "This large block of text, it expects me to figure everything out on my own, and I hate it."

"I've never seen anything like it," said Mark Shelton, a high school
teacher from St. Paul, MN, who stared blankly at the page in front of him for
several minutes before finally holding it up to his ear. "What does it want
from us?"

As the public grows more desperate, scholars are working to randomly italicize different sections of the text, hoping the italics will land

The giant mass of prose lacked even a large pull quote for readers to glance at
before moving on.

on the important parts and allow everyone to go on with their day. For now, though, millions of panicked and exhausted Americans continue to repetitively search the single column of print from top to bottom and right to left, looking for even the slightest semblance of meaning or perhaps a blurb.

Some have speculated that the never-ending flood of sentences may be 10 a news article, medical study, urgent product recall notice, letter, user agreement, or even a binding contract of some kind. But until the news does a segment in which they take sections of the text and read them aloud in a slow, calm voice while highlighting those same words on the screen, no one can say for sure.

There are some, however, who remain unfazed by the virtual hailstorm of alternating consonants and vowels, and are determined to ignore it.

"I'm sure if it's important enough, they'll let us know some other way," Detroit local Janet Landsman said. "After all, it can't be that serious. If there were anything worthwhile buried deep in that block of impenetrable English, it would at least have an accompanying photo of a celebrity or a large humorous title containing a pop culture reference."

Added Landsman, "Whatever it is, I'm pretty sure it doesn't even have a point."

Thinking about the Text

1. The *Onion*'s **REPORT** is, of course, a work of fiction. Still, for the humor to be effective there must be an element of truth in the underlying idea. A good report, as Chapter 14 explains, presents trustworthy information. How do you react to the "information" in the *Onion*'s report? Does it seem reliable? Why or why not? What truth do you find in it, if any?

2. The *Onion* article capitalizes on the fact that new technologies have altered our expectations and standards for writing as well as our attention spans with regard to reading. Although it is a work of satire, how strongly does the *Onion*'s report resonate with you? Do you avoid reading large blocks of text? Has your reading attention span changed over time? **FREEWRITE** or make an idea map to stimulate your reflections.

3. What does the *Onion* do to make its writing read like a newspaper? What are the journalistic features that you can identify in this article? Provide examples to support your answers.

4. In the concluding paragraphs of the report, someone is cited as saying that what is written in the impenetrable block of text can't possibly be important, because if it were, there would be a celebrity photo or an attention-grabbing pop culture reference. What **ARGUMENT** about the media would you say the *Onion* is making here? Based on the media that you read, watch, or listen to, is there any truth to this argument? Provide **EVIDENCE** to support your response.

5. Observe the people around you in their everyday activities. Select one incident, and write a startling news report about it in the **STYLE** of the *Onion*. You might choose, for example, "Man Pulls Out of Parking Space without Thanking Car That Stopped for Him," or "Boy Scouts Find Nonsticky Spot on Movie Theater Floor," or "Birthday Sweater Sent by Grandparents Actually Fits!"

Mind over Mass Media

STEVEN PINKER

NEW FORMS OF MEDIA have always caused moral panics: the printing press, newspapers, paperbacks and television were all once denounced as threats to their consumers' brainpower and moral fiber.

So too with electronic technologies. PowerPoint, we're told, is reducing discourse to bullet points. Search engines lower our intelligence, encouraging us to skim on the surface of knowledge rather than dive to its depths. Twitter is shrinking our attention spans.

But such panics often fail basic reality checks. When comic books were accused of turning juveniles into delinquents in the 1950s, crime was falling to record lows, just as the denunciations of video games in the 1990s coincided with the great American crime decline. The decades of television, transistor radios and rock videos were also decades in which I.Q. scores rose continuously.

For a reality check today, take the state of science, which demands high levels of brainwork and is measured by clear benchmarks of discovery. These days scientists are never far from their e-mail, rarely touch paper and

STEVEN PINKER is a professor of psychology at Harvard University and is known for his scholarly research on language and cognition. His many books include *The Language Instinct* (1994), *How the Mind Works* (1997), and *The Better Angels of Our Nature* (2012). This essay was published in 2010 in the *New York Times*. You can follow him on *Twitter* @sapinker.

cannot lecture without PowerPoint. If electronic media were hazardous to intelligence, the quality of science would be plummeting. Yet discoveries are multiplying like fruit flies, and progress is dizzying. Other activities in the life of the mind, like philosophy, history and cultural criticism, are likewise flourishing, as anyone who has lost a morning of work to the Web site Arts & Letters Daily can attest.

Critics of new media sometimes use science itself to press their case, citing research that shows how "experience can change the brain." But cognitive neuroscientists roll their eyes at such talk. Yes, every time we learn a fact or skill the wiring of the brain changes; it's not as if the information is stored in the pancreas. But the existence of neural plasticity does not mean the brain is a blob of clay pounded into shape by experience. 5

Experience does not revamp the basic information-processing capacities of the brain. Speed-reading programs have long claimed to do just that, but the verdict was rendered by Woody Allen after he read "War and Peace" in one sitting: "It was about Russia." Genuine multitasking, too, has been exposed as a myth, not just by laboratory studies but by the familiar

Genuine multitasking has been exposed as a myth, as anyone who's witnessed a distracted driver crossing lanes can attest.

sight of an S.U.V. undulating between lanes as the driver cuts deals on his cellphone.

Moreover, as the psychologists Christopher Chabris and Daniel Simons show in their new book *The Invisible Gorilla: And Other Ways Our Intuitions Deceive Us*, the effects of experience are highly specific to the experiences themselves. If you train people to do one thing (recognize shapes, solve math puzzles, find hidden words), they get better at doing that thing, but almost nothing else. Music doesn't make you better at math, conjugating Latin doesn't make you more logical, brain-training games don't make you smarter. Accomplished people don't bulk up their brains with intellectual calisthenics; they immerse themselves in their fields. Novelists read lots of novels, scientists read lots of science.

The effects of consuming electronic media are also likely to be far more limited than the panic implies. Media critics write as if the brain takes on the qualities of whatever it consumes, the informational equivalent of "you are what you eat." As with primitive peoples who believe that eating fierce animals will make them fierce, they assume that watching quick cuts in rock videos turns your mental life into quick cuts or that reading bullet points and Twitter postings turns your thoughts into bullet points and Twitter postings.

Yes, the constant arrival of information packets can be distracting or addictive, especially to people with attention deficit disorder. But distraction is not a new phenomenon. The solution is not to bemoan technology but to develop strategies of self-control, as we do with every other temptation in life. Turn off e-mail or Twitter when you work, put away your BlackBerry at dinner time, ask your spouse to call you to bed at a designated hour.

And to encourage intellectual depth, don't rail at PowerPoint or Google. **10** It's not as if habits of deep reflection, thorough research and rigorous reasoning ever came naturally to people. They must be acquired in special institutions, which we call universities, and maintained with constant upkeep, which we call analysis, criticism and debate. They are not granted by propping a heavy encyclopedia on your lap, nor are they taken away by efficient access to information on the Internet.

The new media have caught on for a reason. Knowledge is increasing exponentially; human brainpower and waking hours are not. Fortunately, the Internet and information technologies are helping us manage, search and retrieve our collective intellectual output at different scales, from Twitter and previews to e-books and online encyclopedias. Far from making us stupid, these technologies are the only things that will keep us smart.

See pp. 402–05 for tips on acknowledging and responding to other perspectives, as Pinker does here.

Thinking about the Text

1. Steven Pinker presents points of view other than his own mainly in order to rebut them. How fairly does he represent these positions? Provide evidence from the text to support your response.

2. Pinker asserts that many "activities in the life of the mind" are flourishing (4), and he cites as evidence the website *Arts & Letters Daily,* a portal page that leads to recent articles in academic periodicals. Is the essential point the proliferation of such articles, as Pinker argues, or is it our easier access to them? If access is the only thing that has changed, does that weaken Pinker's **ARGUMENT** about the vitality of contemporary intellectual activity? Why or why not?

3. This piece was originally published as an op-ed column in the *New York Times.* Judging from its **TONE**, do you think Pinker was writing for an **AUDIENCE** that was already inclined to agree with him? How can you tell?

4. What does the title of the essay mean? To what phrase is it an allusion? (Run a *Google* search on parts of the title if you're not already familiar with the phrase.) Why might Pinker (or his editors at the *Times*) have chosen that particular title? How does it contribute to his argument?

5. Pinker comments that "the constant arrival of information packets can be distracting or addictive" (9). What has been your own experience in this area? Reflect on the question, and then write a response that supports or refutes Pinker's claim.

Blue-Collar Brilliance

MIKE ROSE

MY MOTHER, ROSE MERAGLIO ROSE (Rosie), shaped her adult identity as a waitress in coffee shops and family restaurants. When I was growing up in Los Angeles during the 1950s, my father and I would occasionally hang out at the restaurant until her shift ended, and then we'd ride the bus home with her. Sometimes she worked the register and the counter, and we sat there; when she waited booths and tables, we found a booth in the back where the waitresses took their breaks.

There wasn't much for a child to do at the restaurants, and so as the hours stretched out, I watched the cooks and waitresses and listened to what they said. At mealtimes, the pace of the kitchen staff and the din from customers picked up. Weaving in and out around the room, waitresses warned *behind you* in impassive but urgent voices. Standing at the service window facing the kitchen, they called out abbreviated orders. *Fry four on two*, my mother would say as she clipped a check onto the metal wheel. Her tables

MIKE ROSE is a professor of education and information studies at UCLA. His work has focused on teaching methods, on understanding people's engagement with the written word, and on bridging gaps between the academic and nonacademic worlds. Rose has published ten books, including the semiautobiographical *Lives on the Boundary* (1989) and *Why School? Reclaiming Education for All of Us* (2009). He blogs at mikerosebooks.com. This article was originally published in 2009 in the *American Scholar*, a magazine sponsored by the Phi Beta Kappa Society.

were *deuces, four-tops*, or *six-tops* according to their size; seating areas also were nicknamed. The *racetrack*, for instance, was the fast-turnover front section. Lingo conferred authority and signaled know-how.

Rosie took customers' orders, pencil poised over pad, while fielding questions about the food. She walked full tilt through the room with plates stretching up her left arm and two cups of coffee somehow cradled in her right hand. She stood at a table or booth and removed a plate for this person, another for that person, then another, remembering who had the hamburger, who had the fried shrimp, almost always getting it right. She would haggle with the cook about a returned order and rush by us, saying, *He gave me lip, but I got him.* She'd take a minute to flop down in the booth next to my father. *I'm all in*, she'd say, and whisper something about a customer. Gripping the outer edge of the table with one hand, she'd watch the room and note, in the flow of our conversation, who needed a refill, whose order was taking longer to prepare than it should, who was finishing up.

I couldn't have put it in words when I was growing up, but what I observed in my mother's restaurant defined the world of adults, a place where competence was synonymous with physical work. I've since studied the working habits of blue-collar workers and have come to understand how much my mother's kind of work demands of both body and brain. A waitress acquires knowledge and intuition about the ways and the rhythms of the restaurant business. Waiting on seven to nine tables, each with two to six customers, Rosie devised memory strategies so that she could remember who ordered what. And because she knew the average time it took to prepare different dishes, she could monitor an order that was taking too long at the service station.

Like anyone who is effective at physical work, my mother learned *to* 5 *work smart*, as she put it, *to make every move count.* She'd sequence and group tasks: What could she do first, then second, then third as she circled through her station? What tasks could be clustered? She did everything on the fly, and when problems arose—technical or human—she solved them within the flow of work, while taking into account the emotional state of her co-workers. Was the manager in a good mood? Did the cook wake up on the wrong side of the bed? If so, how could she make an extra request or effectively return an order?

And then, of course, there were the customers who entered the restaurant with all sorts of needs, from physiological ones, including the emotions that accompany hunger, to a sometimes complicated desire for human con-

Rosie solved technical and human problems on the fly.

tact. Her tip depended on how well she responded to these needs, and so she became adept at reading social cues and managing feelings, both the customers' and her own. No wonder, then, that Rosie was intrigued by psychology. The restaurant became the place where she studied human behavior, puzzling over the problems of her regular customers and refining her ability to deal with people in a difficult world. She took pride in *being among the public*, she'd say. *There isn't a day that goes by in the restaurant that you don't learn something.*

My mother quit school in the seventh grade to help raise her brothers and sisters. Some of those siblings made it through high school, and some dropped out to find work in railroad yards, factories, or restaurants. My father finished a grade or two in primary school in Italy and never darkened the schoolhouse door again. I didn't do well in school either. By high school I had accumulated a spotty academic record and many hours of hazy disaffection. I spent a few years on the vocational track, but in my senior year I was inspired by my English teacher and managed to squeak into a small college on probation.

My freshman year was academically bumpy, but gradually I began to see formal education as a means of fulfillment and as a road toward making a living. I studied the humanities and later the social and psychological sciences and taught for 10 years in a range of situations—elementary school, adult education courses, tutoring centers, a program for Vietnam veterans who wanted to go to college. Those students had socioeconomic and educational backgrounds similar to mine. Then I went back to graduate school to study education and cognitive psychology and eventually became a faculty member in a school of education.

Intelligence is closely associated with formal education—the type of schooling a person has, how much and how long—and most people seem to move comfortably from that notion to a belief that work requiring less schooling requires less intelligence. These assumptions run through our cultural history, from the post–Revolutionary War period, when mechanics were characterized by political rivals as illiterate and therefore incapable of participating in government, until today. More than once I've heard a manager label his workers as "a bunch of dummies." Generalizations about intelligence, work, and social class deeply affect our assumptions about ourselves and each other, guiding the ways we use our minds to learn, build knowledge, solve problems, and make our way through the world.

Although writers and scholars have often looked at the working class, 10 they have generally focused on the values such workers exhibit rather than on the thought their work requires—a subtle but pervasive omission. Our cultural iconography promotes the muscled arm, sleeve rolled tight against biceps, but no brightness behind the eye, no image that links hand and brain.

One of my mother's brothers, Joe Meraglio, left school in the ninth grade to work for the Pennsylvania Railroad. From there he joined the Navy, returned to the railroad, which was already in decline, and eventually joined his older brother at General Motors where, over a 33-year career, he moved from working on the assembly line to supervising the paint-and-body department. When I was a young man, Joe took me on a tour of the factory. The floor was loud—in some places deafening—and when I turned a corner or opened a door, the smell of chemicals knocked my head back. The work was repetitive and taxing, and the pace was inhumane.

Still, for Joe the shop floor provided what school did not; it was *like schooling*, he said, a place where *you're constantly learning*. Joe learned the most efficient way to use his body by acquiring a set of routines that were

With an eighth-grade education, Joe (hands together) advanced to supervisor of a G.M. paint-and-body department.

quick and preserved energy. Otherwise he would never have survived on the line.

As a foreman, Joe constantly faced new problems and became a consummate multi-tasker, evaluating a flurry of demands quickly, parceling out physical and mental resources, keeping a number of ongoing events in his mind, returning to whatever task had been interrupted, and maintaining a cool head under the pressure of grueling production schedules. In the midst of all this, Joe learned more and more about the auto industry, the technological and social dynamics of the shop floor, the machinery and production processes, and the basics of paint chemistry and of plating and baking. With further promotions, he not only solved problems but also began to find problems to solve: Joe initiated the redesign of the nozzle on a paint sprayer, thereby eliminating costly and unhealthy overspray. And he found a way to reduce energy costs on the baking ovens without affecting the quality of the paint. He lacked formal knowledge of how the machines under his supervision worked, but he had direct experience with them, hands-on knowledge, and was savvy about their quirks and operational capabilities. He could experiment with them.

Mike Rose started by observing —and by listening. Listening is a key part of thinking rhetorically; read more about it in Ch. I.

In addition, Joe learned about budgets and management. Coming off the line as he did, he had a perspective of workers' needs and management's demands, and this led him to think of ways to improve efficiency on the line while relieving some of the stress on the assemblers. He had each worker in a unit learn his or her co-workers' jobs so they could rotate across stations to relieve some of the monotony. He believed that rotation would allow assemblers to get longer and more frequent breaks. It was an easy sell to the people on the line. The union, however, had to approve any modification in job duties, and the managers were wary of the change. Joe had to argue his case on a number of fronts, providing him a kind of rhetorical education.

Eight years ago I began a study of the thought processes involved in work like that of my mother and uncle. I catalogued the cognitive demands of a range of blue-collar and service jobs, from waitressing and hair styling to plumbing and welding. To gain a sense of how knowledge and skill develop, I observed experts as well as novices. From the details of this close examination, I tried to fashion what I called "cognitive biographies" of blue-collar workers. Biographical accounts of the lives of scientists, lawyers, entrepreneurs, and other professionals are rich with detail about the intellectual dimension of their work. But the life stories of working-class people are few and are typically accounts of hardship and courage or the achievements wrought by hard work.

Our culture—in Cartesian fashion—separates the body from the mind, so that, for example, we assume that the use of a tool does not involve abstraction. We reinforce this notion by defining intelligence solely on grades in school and numbers on IQ tests. And we employ social biases pertaining to a person's place on the occupational ladder. The distinctions among blue, pink, and white collars carry with them attributions of character, motivation, and intelligence. Although we rightly acknowledge and amply compensate the play of mind in white-collar and professional work, we diminish or erase it in considerations about other endeavors—physical and service work particularly. We also often ignore the experience of everyday work in administrative deliberations and policymaking.

But here's what we find when we get in close. The plumber seeking leverage in order to work in tight quarters and the hair stylist adroitly handling scissors and comb manage their bodies strategically. Though work-related actions become routine with experience, they were learned at some point through observation, trial and error, and, often, physical or verbal assistance from a co-worker or trainer. I've frequently observed novices talking to themselves as they take on a task, or shaking their head or hand as if to erase an attempt before trying again. In fact, our traditional notions of routine performance could keep us from appreciating the many instances within routine where quick decisions and adjustments are made. I'm struck by the thinking-in-motion that some work requires, by all the mental activity that can be involved in simply getting from one place to another: the waitress rushing back through her station to the kitchen or the foreman walking the line.

The use of tools requires the studied refinement of stance, grip, balance, and fine-motor skills. But manipulating tools is intimately tied to knowledge of what a particular instrument can do in a particular situation and do better than other similar tools. A worker must also know the characteristics of the material one is engaging—how it reacts to various cutting or compressing devices, to degrees of heat, or to lines of force. Some of these things demand judgment, the weighing of options, the consideration of multiple variables, and, occasionally, the creative use of a tool in an unexpected way.

In manipulating material, the worker becomes attuned to aspects of the environment, a training or disciplining of perception that both enhances knowledge and informs perception. Carpenters have an eye for length, line, and angle; mechanics troubleshoot by listening; hair stylists are attuned to shape, texture, and motion. Sensory data merge with concept, as when an auto mechanic relies on sound, vibration, and even smell to understand what cannot be observed.

Planning and problem solving have been studied since the earliest days   20 of modern cognitive psychology and are considered core elements in Western definitions of intelligence. To work is to solve problems. The big difference between the psychologist's laboratory and the workplace is that in the former the problems are isolated and in the latter they are embedded in the real-time flow of work with all its messiness and social complexity.

Much of physical work is social and interactive. Movers determining how to get an electric range down a flight of stairs require coordination, negotiation, planning, and the establishing of incremental goals. Words, gestures, and sometimes a quick pencil sketch are involved, if only to get the rhythm right. How important it is, then, to consider the social and communicative dimension of physical work, for it provides the medium for so much of work's intelligence.

Given the ridicule heaped on blue-collar speech, it might seem odd to value its cognitive content. Yet, the flow of talk at work provides the channel for organizing and distributing tasks, for troubleshooting and problem solving, for learning new information and revising old. A significant amount of teaching, often informal and indirect, takes place at work. Joe Meraglio saw that much of his job as a supervisor involved instruction. In some service occupations, language and communication are central: observing and interpreting behavior and expression, inferring mood and motive, taking on the perspective of others, responding appropriately to social cues, and knowing when you're understood. A good hair stylist, for instance, has the ability to convert vague requests (*I want something light and summery*) into an appropriate cut through questions, pictures, and hand gestures.

Verbal and mathematical skills drive measures of intelligence in the Western Hemisphere, and many of the kinds of work I studied are thought to require relatively little proficiency in either. Compared to certain kinds of white-collar occupations, that's true. But written symbols flow through physical work.

Numbers are rife in most workplaces: on tools and gauges, as measurements, as indicators of pressure or concentration or temperature, as guides to sequence, on ingredient labels, on lists and spreadsheets, as markers of quantity and price. Certain jobs require workers to make, check, and verify calculations, and to collect and interpret data. Basic math can be involved, and some workers develop a good sense of numbers and patterns. Consider, as well, what might be called material mathematics: mathematical functions embodied in materials and actions, as when a carpenter builds a cabinet or a flight of stairs. A simple mathematical act can extend quickly beyond itself. Measuring, for example, can involve more than recording the dimensions of an object. As I watched a cabinetmaker measure a long strip of wood, he read a number off the tape out loud, looked back over his shoulder to the kitchen wall, turned back to his task, took another measurement, and paused for a moment in thought. He was solving a problem involving the molding, and the measurement was important to his deliberation about structure and appearance.

In the blue-collar workplace, directions, plans, and reference books 25 rely on illustrations, some representational and others, like blueprints, that require training to interpret. Esoteric symbols—visual jargon—depict switches and receptacles, pipe fittings, or types of welds. Workers themselves often make sketches on the job. I frequently observed them grab a pencil to sketch something on a scrap of paper or on a piece of the material they were installing.

Though many kinds of physical work don't require a high literacy level, more reading occurs in the blue-collar workplace than is generally thought, from manuals and catalogues to work orders and invoices, to lists, labels, and forms. With routine tasks, for example, reading is integral to understanding production quotas, learning how to use an instrument, or applying a product. Written notes can initiate action, as in restaurant orders or reports of machine malfunction, or they can serve as memory aids.

True, many uses of writing are abbreviated, routine, and repetitive, and they infrequently require interpretation or analysis. But analytic moments can be part of routine activities, and seemingly basic reading and writing can be cognitively rich. Because workplace language is used in the flow of other activities, we can overlook the remarkable coordination of words, numbers, and drawings required to initiate and direct action.

If we believe everyday work to be mindless, then that will affect the work we create in the future. When we devalue the full range of everyday cognition, we offer limited educational opportunities and fail to make fresh and meaningful instructional connections among disparate kinds of skill and knowledge. If we think that whole categories of people—identified by class or occupation—are not that bright, then we reinforce social separations and cripple our ability to talk across cultural divides.

Affirmation of diverse intelligence is not a retreat to a softhearted definition of the mind. To acknowledge a broader range of intellectual capacity is to take seriously the concept of cognitive variability, to appreciate in all the Rosies and Joes the thought that drives their accomplishments and defines who they are. This is a model of the mind that is worthy of a democratic society.

Thinking about the Text

1. Mike Rose begins his analysis with a pair of extended examples and a brief personal narrative. Readers may not figure out until later what, exactly, he is analyzing. What is Rose's subject, and what is the question that directs his inquiry?

2. Because of the academically oriented prejudices that Rose mentions, you may never have read anything that focuses on the cognitive tasks involved in blue-

collar work. Were you surprised by anything that Rose said—or not? **REFLECT** on your own attitudes toward blue-collar work; in what ways did Rose confirm or challenge them? Describe your reactions and reflections.

3. Why might Rose have chosen to begin his analysis with the extended information about his mother and uncle, himself, and other members of his family? Do you find these **EXAMPLES** and **NARRATIVES** effective rhetorical strategies for introducing an analysis of this topic? Why or why not?

4. Rose is suggesting that blue-collar workers merit more recognition for the cognitive skills that they bring to their work, but that is not all he is arguing. What is the overarching **ARGUMENT** that Rose is making in his article? What **EVIDENCE** in the text supports your answer?

5. Conduct a brief interview with someone who works a blue-collar job—for example, a mechanic, a sewing-machine operator, a hairstylist, a restaurant server, a janitor or housekeeper, or a truck driver. Find out what factors someone needs to consider to perform the job successfully; in other words, what does the person have to be aware of while working? To keep the interview focused, start with one of the following questions: What effect does the weather have on what you do? (Heat, humidity, cold, and other weather elements often affect even indoor work.) What are the most common mistakes a beginner in your job might make? Write an **ANALYSIS** of the cognitive tasks involved in his or her ordinary workday. Use clear and precise language, and be sure to mention any insights that you gained.

Weight Loss at Any Cost
JAMES SANBORN

NEARLY ONE IN THREE MARINES are so afraid of violating the Corps' strict weight and appearance standards they have resorted to extreme weight-loss methods, including starvation, taking laxatives and undergoing costly liposuction surgery, according to a recent study conducted by two Marine officers while attending the Naval Post Graduate School.

But the rate may be much higher than that, said Capt. Paula Taibi, one of the study's co-authors. More than 70 percent of the 390 Marines who responded to her survey were from the junior enlisted and officer ranks—and not long out of boot camp or Officer Candidate School. If so many first-term men and women in peak physical shape are using risky means to blast fat and avoid the measuring tape, she said, then a lot of career Marines with far more to lose probably do it too. The report concludes that unconventional methods for weight loss are "widespread" within the Marine Corps.

The trend, Taibi said, likely predates revisions made in 2008 to the service's body composition and military appearance programs, or BCP and

James Sanborn explains military abbreviations that readers might not know. Find out more about defining key terms on pp. 261–63.

JAMES SANBORN is a multimedia journalist whose work has appeared in *USA Today*, the *Washington Post*, and other national periodicals. He tweets @jamesksanborn. Sanborn has done investigative reporting in Mexico and Vietnam, and is currently based in Washington, D.C., where he is a staff writer for *Marine Corps Times*. This report was published in that paper in October 2010.

Medical personnel perform a body composition assessment on a Navy diver.

MAP. The move eliminated the leniency once shown to Marines who run afoul of body-fat standards but still score high on their physical fitness test. There has almost certainly been an uptick in risky weight-loss methods since then, however.

"I think people are being made more aware that they are going to comply and that if they don't, the results are going to be catastrophic to their career," said Taibi, who co-authored the 2009 report with Capt. Leigh Wallace and is now a programs analyst at Headquarters Marine Corps. "So I think people are grasping."

The commandant's office cast doubt on the findings, saying the sample 5 size is neither large enough nor diverse enough to accurately represent how widespread the trend may be. Maj. Joseph Plenzler, a spokesman for Gen. James Conway, said the Corps' top officer stands by the updates made to the BCP and MAP. While the commandant encourages Marines to be smart about how they stay trim, looking the part is vital to combat readiness and good order and discipline, he said.

"We Marines have historically held ourselves to high standards in both fitness and appearance," Plenzler said. "There are some Marines who may

U.S. Marines display their trim and polish at the 95th annual New York City Veterans Day Parade.

meet all established physical standards, yet fail to present a suitable military appearance, and this is inconsistent with the Marine Corps leadership principle of setting the example."

Marines may not all agree with that logic, but they understand the consequences of failing to make weight. The policy adjustments made on Conway's watch give commanders greater freedom to assign personnel to remedial training if their uniformed appearance does not fit that of a squared-away Marine, according to All Marine Message 034/08. For more senior Marines, that can be the kiss of death.

Commanders have the power to request a waiver for Marines who do not meet the Corps' standards but look professional in uniform. It's unclear how often waivers are granted, but in the past Conway has advocated for rigid enforcement of the rules.

Current body-fat limits for Marines start at 18 percent for men and 26 percent for women. Those limits increase slightly with age, up to 21 percent for men and 29 percent for women. Before the Corps tightened the rules,

Marines with first-class PFT scores could slide a few percentage points. Now, no matter how capable a Marine is physically, there are no exceptions.

Once a year, or more often if a commander deems it necessary, Marines 10 are assessed based on the body mass index, an equation that determines ideal weight relative to a Marine's height. If a Marine is deemed overweight, he then has measurements taken around his neck and waist to estimate body fat percentage.

In 2007, the Marine Corps inspector general suggested the service adopt a new measurement method. It called taping "adequate," but acknowledged it was prone to inaccuracies. Other methods could prove more equitable, the IG said.

That inquiry found that one in four Marines failed to meet standards and belonged in the BCP, prompting Conway's crackdown.

Despite tougher standards, thousands of Marines are still assigned to the BCP each year—5,671 since October, according to Manpower and Reserve Affairs. That's the most since 2006. So far this year, 72 Marines have been discharged for weight-related issues.

"There was a staff sergeant I knew and he was outstanding. The only reason he got out of the Corps was because of the new weight standards— even though he would PT with Marines every day and usually drop about half of them," said a gunnery sergeant at Camp Pendleton, Calif., who underwent liposuction in June. Even though the Corps allows Marines to have the procedure, he asked not to be identified, saying there's a stigma associated with failing to meet fitness requirements.

"I know an officer," he said, "who in order to make weight wore sweat 15 suits, didn't eat for a week, took pills and used enemas."

With about five years left until he's eligible for retirement, the gunny said he was willing to take such a drastic measure to stay out of the BCP and—he hopes—save his career.

The gunny has struggled for years to meet weight and body fat requirements, but regularly posted first-class PFT scores, he said. Then he suffered a back injury in Iraq, and making weight only got tougher. He had surgery on his back this year and packed on some extra pounds during his recovery. Although he has never been on the BCP in the past, the devastating prospect seemed inevitable as his medical review board loomed and he struggled to drop enough weight before his weigh-in.

The decision to get liposuction on his abdomen was easy.

"I felt it was pretty much a do-or-die situation," he said.

It was an expensive procedure, about $7,000, but well worth it to save   20
his career, he said. The recovery was swift—about two weeks—and he is
pleased with the results.

The gunny wants Conway or his successor to reverse the new policy and
again allow Marines some leeway provided they look OK in uniform and
prove they are combat ready with high scores on the PFT and Combat Fitness Test.

"I know there are others out there in the same boat or who have a stocky
build so they are always fighting the scale or tape," he said.

Most career Marines interviewed by *Marine Corps Times* said being put
on the BCP is certain to scuttle their chances for advancement.

"It is probably easier to recover from a DUI than from being put on BCP,"
said Gunnery Sgt. Matthew Torres, another Camp Pendleton-based Marine
who has never been assigned to a remedial fitness program, though he, too,
struggles with stubborn belly fat. "A DUI is bad, but it's a one-time thing. You
just don't do it again. Once you're on BCP, you're probably already on your
way out."

Torres said he's been seriously considering liposuction for more than a   25
year but still has reservations. He runs religiously and has cleaned up his
diet, he said, but the slight paunch around his gut just won't go away. If he
can't drop enough weight before his next weigh-in, he's afraid it will mark
the beginning of the end.

Torres believes he is at risk because of his small, muscular stature. The
rules don't account for body type, he said. And that's frustrating. Current
standards allow Marines less able-bodied than he to fly below the radar.

"I'd much rather have a guy who has a little meat on his bones that can
pick somebody up in a firefight, than somebody who is supermodel skinny
and can't pick his pack off the ground," he said. "It seems like the Marine
Corps wants these super-skinny kids who can't lift themselves over a wall."

Most Marines who consider liposuction aren't out of shape, said Dr. Robert Peterson, a Hawaii-based plastic surgeon who runs the Athena Clinic in
Honolulu and has operated on many service members.

"We mostly see Navy because many of them work long shifts on boats
and submarines where exercise is difficult," Peterson said. "But we do get
Marines. When we see them, they are usually fit. They just have a spare tire."

Like other plastic surgeons located near military installations, Peterson   30 advertises his services to service members—and even offers a $500 discount on procedures that cost $5,000 or more. For many of his patients, the payoff comes in getting to keep their job, he said.

Asked about potential risks to getting liposuction, Peterson said it is a relatively safe procedure and none of his patients have had major complications. But risks do exist, including infection, damage to surrounding tissue and blood vessels, and uneven skin texture.

Other rare but possible complications, according to the National Institutes of Health, include blood clots. Liposuction also can cause tiny globules of fat to be released into a patient's bloodstream, which can cause potentially fatal embolisms in the lungs, brain or elsewhere.

Liposuction is by no means the only risky weight-loss method Marines are using, according to Taibi's study. Some resort to starvation and fasting, extreme cardio, and the use of plastic sweat suits, diet pills, diuretics and laxatives. Some forgo water. Some give blood.

Highlighting just how dangerous some unconventional weight loss methods can be, one poolee trying to drop weight so he could join the Corps died from hyperthermia and dehydration in July 2009, while training with two recruiters in Tracy, Calif.

Daniel Ruf, 22, collapsed at a local gym while wearing a rubber suit. He   35
was trying to drop 10 pounds the day before his weigh-in. Ruf's case is now a source of ongoing litigation. His mother filed a lawsuit against the Marine Corps in April.

These methods aren't only hazardous to your health, Taibi said, but the resulting weight loss is often only temporary.

"In my opinion it's a really vicious cycle," she said. "You do all these crazy things—run with plastic bags on your chest or whatever. Then you make weight and it's a big release, so you let yourself go again."

There are reports of Marines employing risky weight-loss techniques in Afghanistan. Sgt. Shane Trefftzs, who works in the operations division of I Marine Expeditionary Force (Forward), told *Marine Corps Times* that after his command announced a weigh-in, others in his unit scrambled to shed weight any way they could. Some took diuretics, laxatives and diet pills and fasted.

"We're in a combat zone. Is this a smart idea?" he wrote in an e-mail. "I totally agree with a standard for military appearance. However, many of us remember some of the first words out of our Drill Instructor's mouth. 'Marines come in all shapes and sizes.'"

Fitness expert Tony Horton, the creator of P90X, the latest workout craze   40
to sweep the military, agreed that body type can significantly affect how a
person weighs in. He emphasizes functional fitness, and believes traditional
health assessment methods—including those used by the Defense Department that are based on height-to-weight ratios and taping around the neck
and belly—don't accurately measure a person's overall health.

Body mass index doesn't "dictate a person's abilities or strength," Horton said. "There is 'look like' . . . and there is also 'can do.' . . . Can a guy perform? If you are strong, and you are fit and flexible, and you can do your job
. . . who the hell cares what your waist size is?"

"Some people just have a very unfavorable ratio of the abdomen to their
neck even if they are in shape," echoed Peterson, the plastic surgeon. "That's
our most common group—people who are not designed for the particular
measurement," he said referring to the DoD-prescribed taping method for
estimating body fat. "If they did a different measurement, they would come
out fine."

Dr. Jules Feledy, the senior partner at Belmont Plastic Surgery, which has
offices near Marine Corps Base Quantico, Va., said he has seen a rise in the
number of Marines coming through his office since Conway tightened standards in 2008. The Marines he sees are typically in superior shape, he said,
but desperate to flatten their midsections as they look to beat the tape—a
measurement he, too, believes doesn't dictate a person's physical abilities.

But the Corps' regulations do have plenty of supporters. Despite her
findings, even Taibi says the standards are fair.

"It is important to note that Marine Corps body composition and mili-   45
tary appearance standards are neither unreasonable nor unattainable," said
Plenzler, Conway's spokesman. "It is the responsibility of every leader in the
chain of command to coach and mentor their subordinates, and hold them
accountable when they fail to meet standards."

The majority of overweight Marines simply need to adjust their diet
and exercise regimen, Taibi said. Marines' struggle with weight and body
fat parallels a national trend, she said. Based on her research, the Corps
needs to bolster outreach to ensure Marines use resources already available
through the Semper Fit program, which was developed to educate Marines
on maintaining a healthy lifestyle and making sound fitness choices while
providing them with the resources to stay in shape. It is important to ensure
that healthier food choices are available on base, she said.

Thinking about the Text

1. James Sanborn presents abundant factual and anecdotal evidence showing the harmful impact of the Marine Corps' body composition regulations, yet he concludes with statements in support of the policy. What is Sanborn's own **POSITION** on the regulations—and how do you know? Point to examples in the text to support your response.

2. A good **REPORT** provides trustworthy information. What kinds of information does Sanborn present in his report? What kinds of sources does he rely on? How appropriate are they for his purpose?

3. Sanborn writes using abbreviations and military terms that may be unfamiliar to some readers, but are perfectly clear and appropriate for his Marine Corps **AUDIENCE**. Find three such words or phrases (other than abbreviations) and restate them for the more general audience of a large-circulation newspaper or magazine.

4. Would you take drastic, possibly dangerous measures in order to protect your career? Put yourself in the place of some stocky or full-bellied Marines and try to imagine the pressures they face. How might you respond, and how far would you go? Why?

5. Does a military organization have legitimate authority over its members' physiques as a matter of maintaining appearance and discipline? Should appearance be a consideration at all in the Marine Corps, or should assessments be based strictly on physical ability? Write an essay that takes a **POSITION** on these questions.

Why McDonald's Fries Taste So Good

ERIC SCHLOSSER

THE FRENCH FRY [was] . . . almost sacrosanct for me," Ray Kroc wrote in his memoir, "its preparation a ritual to be followed religiously." The success of Richard and Mac McDonald's hamburger stand had been based as much on the quality of their fries as on the taste of their burgers. The McDonald brothers had devised an elaborate system for making crisp french fries, one that was later improved by the restaurant chain. McDonald's cooked thinly sliced Russet Burbanks in special fryers to keep the oil temperature above 325 degrees. As the chain expanded, it became more difficult—and yet all the more important—to maintain the consistency and quality of the fries. J. R. Simplot met with Ray Kroc in 1965. The idea of switching to frozen french fries appealed to Kroc, as a means of ensuring uniformity and cutting labor costs. McDonald's obtained its fresh potatoes from about 175 different local suppliers, and crew members spent a great deal of time peeling and slicing potatoes. Simplot offered to build a new factory solely for the manufacture of McDonald's french fries. Kroc agreed to try Simplot's fries, but made no long-term commitment. The deal was sealed with a handshake.

ERIC SCHLOSSER, a California-based investigative journalist, is the author of *Reefer Madness: Sex, Drugs, and Cheap Labor in the American Black Market* (2003). His articles appear regularly in *Rolling Stone,* the *New Yorker, Vanity Fair,* and the *Atlantic,* among other publications. This selection is from his best seller, *Fast Food Nation: The Dark Side of the All-American Meal* (2001).

McDonald's began to sell J. R. Simplot's frozen french fries the following year. Customers didn't notice any difference in taste. And the reduced cost of using a frozen product made french fries one of the most profitable items on the menu—far more profitable than hamburgers. Simplot quickly became the main supplier of french fries to McDonald's. At the time, McDonald's had about 725 restaurants in the United States. Within a decade, it had more than 3,000. Simplot sold his frozen fries to other restaurant chains, accelerating the growth of the fast food industry and changing the nation's eating habits. Americans have long consumed more potatoes than any other food except dairy products and wheat flour. In 1960, the typical American ate eighty-one pounds of fresh potatoes and about four pounds of frozen french fries. Today the typical American eats about forty-nine pounds of fresh potatoes every year—and more than thirty pounds of frozen french fries. Ninety percent of those fries are purchased at fast food restaurants. Indeed, french fries have become the most widely sold foodservice item in the United States. . . .

Eric Schlosser's analysis gets very technical, but he begins by describing something totally familiar. Read about that technique on pp. 207–09.

Food Product Design

The taste of McDonald's french fries has long been praised by customers, competitors, and even food critics. James Beard loved McDonald's fries. Their distinctive taste does not stem from the type of potatoes that McDonald's buys, the technology that processes them, or the restaurant equipment that fries them. Other chains buy their french fries from the same large processing companies, use Russet Burbanks, and have similar fryers in their restaurant kitchens. The taste of a fast food fry is largely determined by the cooking oil. For decades, McDonald's cooked its french fries in a mixture of about 7 percent cottonseed oil and 93 percent beef tallow. The mix gave the fries their unique flavor—and more saturated beef fat per ounce than a McDonald's hamburger.

Amid a barrage of criticism over the amount of cholesterol in their fries, McDonald's switched to pure vegetable oil in 1990. The switch presented the company with an enormous challenge: how to make fries that subtly taste like beef without cooking them in tallow. A look at the ingredients now used in the preparation of McDonald's french fries suggests how the problem was solved. Toward the end of the list is a seemingly innocuous, yet oddly mysterious phrase: "natural flavor." That ingredient helps to explain not only why the fries taste so good, but also why most fast food—indeed, most of the food Americans eat today—tastes the way it does.

Open your refrigerator, your freezer, your kitchen cupboards, and look   5 at the labels on your food. You'll find "natural flavor" or "artificial flavor" in just about every list of ingredients. The similarities between these two broad categories of flavor are far more significant than their differences. Both are man-made additives that give most processed food most of its taste. The initial purchase of a food item may be driven by its packaging or appearance, but subsequent purchases are determined mainly by its taste. About 90 percent of the money that Americans spend on food is used to buy processed food. But the canning, freezing, and dehydrating techniques used to process food destroy most of its flavor. Since the end of World War II, a vast industry has arisen in the United States to make processed food palatable. Without this flavor industry, today's fast food industry could not exist. The names of the leading American fast food chains and their best-selling menu items have become famous worldwide, embedded in our popular culture. Few people, however, can name the companies that manufacture fast food's taste.

For decades, beef tallow gave McDonalds' french fries their unique—and immensely popular—flavor. But after changing over to pure vegetable oil in 1990, the company had to develop a "natural flavor" to mimic the original taste.

The flavor industry is highly secretive. Its leading companies will not divulge the precise formulas of flavor compounds or the identities of clients. The secrecy is deemed essential for protecting the reputation of beloved brands. The fast food chains, understandably, would like the public to believe that the flavors of their food somehow originate in their restaurant kitchens, not in distant factories run by other firms.

The New Jersey Turnpike runs through the heart of the flavor industry, an industrial corridor dotted with refineries and chemical plants. International Flavors & Fragrances (IFF), the world's largest flavor company, has a manufacturing facility off Exit 8A in Dayton, New Jersey; Givaudan, the world's second-largest flavor company, has a plant in East Hanover. Haarmann & Reimer, the largest German flavor company, has a plant in Teterboro, as does Takasago, the largest Japanese flavor company. Flavor Dynamics has a plant in South Plainfield; Frutarom is in North Bergen; Elan Chemical is in Newark. Dozens of companies manufacture flavors in the corridor between Teaneck and South Brunswick. Indeed, the area produces about two-thirds of the flavor additives sold in the United States.

The IFF plant in Dayton is a huge pale blue building with a modern office complex attached to the front. It sits in an industrial park, not far from a BASF plastics factory, a Jolly French Toast factory, and a plant that manufactures Liz Claiborne cosmetics. Dozens of tractor-trailers were parked at the IFF loading dock the afternoon I visited, and a thin cloud of steam floated from the chimney. Before entering the plant, I signed a nondisclosure form, promising not to reveal the brand names of products that contain IFF flavors. The place reminded me of Willy Wonka's chocolate factory. Wonderful smells drifted through the hallways, men and women in neat white lab coats cheerfully went about their work, and hundreds of little glass bottles sat on laboratory tables and shelves. The bottles contained powerful but fragile flavor chemicals, shielded from light by the brown glass and the round plastic caps shut tight. The long chemical names on the little white labels were as mystifying to me as medieval Latin. They were the odd-sounding names of things that would be mixed and poured and turned into new substances, like magic potions.

I was not invited to see the manufacturing areas of the IFF plant, where it was thought I might discover trade secrets. Instead, I toured various laboratories and pilot kitchens, where the flavors of well-established brands are tested or adjusted, and where whole new flavors are created. IFF's snack and savory lab is responsible for the flavor of potato chips, corn chips, breads,

A robotic arm prepares flavor samples at a flavor company factory.

crackers, breakfast cereals, and pet food. The confectionery lab devises the flavor for ice cream, cookies, candies, toothpastes, mouthwashes, and antacids. Everywhere I looked, I saw famous, widely advertised products sitting on laboratory desks and tables. The beverage lab is full of brightly colored liquids in clear bottles. It comes up with the flavor for popular soft drinks, sport drinks, bottled teas, and wine coolers, for all-natural juice drinks, organic soy drinks, beers, and malt liquors. In one pilot kitchen I saw a dapper food technologist, a middle-aged man with an elegant tie beneath his lab coat, carefully preparing a batch of cookies with white frosting and pink-and-white sprinkles. In another pilot kitchen I saw a pizza oven, a grill, a milk-shake machine, and a french fryer identical to those I'd seen behind the counter at countless fast food restaurants.

In addition to being the world's largest flavor company, IFF manufac-　10 tures the smell of six of the ten best-selling fine perfumes in the United States, including Estée Lauder's Beautiful, Clinique's Happy, Lancôme's Trésor, and Calvin Klein's Eternity. It also makes the smell of household products such as deodorant, dishwashing detergent, bath soap, shampoo, furniture polish, and floor wax. All of these aromas are made through the same basic process: the manipulation of volatile chemicals to create a particular smell.

The basic science behind the scent of your shaving cream is the same as that governing the flavor of your TV dinner.

The aroma of a food can be responsible for as much as 90 percent of its flavor. Scientists now believe that human beings acquired the sense of taste as a way to avoid being poisoned. Edible plants generally taste sweet; deadly ones, bitter. Taste is supposed to help us differentiate food that's good for us from food that's not. The taste buds on our tongues can detect the presence of half a dozen or so basic tastes, including: sweet, sour, bitter, salty, astringent, and umami (a taste discovered by Japanese researchers, a rich and full sense of deliciousness triggered by amino acids in foods such as shellfish, mushrooms, potatoes, and seaweed). Taste buds offer a relatively limited means of detection, however, compared to the human olfactory system, which can perceive thousands of different chemical aromas. Indeed "flavor" is primarily the smell of gases being released by the chemicals you've just put in your mouth.

The act of drinking, sucking, or chewing a substance releases its volatile gases. They flow out of the mouth and up the nostrils, or up the passageway in the back of the mouth, to a thin layer of nerve cells called the olfactory epithelium, located at the base of the nose, right between the eyes. The brain combines the complex smell signals from the epithelium with the simple taste signals from the tongue, assigns a flavor to what's in your mouth, and decides if it's something you want to eat.

Babies like sweet tastes and reject bitter ones; we know this because scientists have rubbed various flavors inside the mouths of infants and then recorded their facial reactions. A person's food preferences, like his or her personality, are formed during the first few years of life, through a process of socialization. Toddlers can learn to enjoy hot and spicy food, bland health food, or fast food, depending upon what the people around them eat. The human sense of smell is still not fully understood and can be greatly affected by psychological factors and expectations. The color of a food can determine the perception of its taste. The mind filters out the overwhelming majority of chemical aromas that surround us, focusing intently on some, ignoring others. People can grow accustomed to bad smells or good smells; they stop noticing what once seemed overpowering. Aroma and memory are somehow inextricably linked. A smell can suddenly evoke a long-forgotten moment. The flavors of childhood foods seem to leave an indelible mark, and adults often return to them, without always knowing why. These "comfort foods" become a source of pleasure and reassurance, a fact that fast food chains work hard to promote. Childhood memories of Happy Meals can translate into frequent adult visits to McDonald's, like those of the chain's "heavy users," the customers who eat there four or five times a week.

The human craving for flavor has been a largely unacknowledged and unexamined force in history. Royal empires have been built, unexplored lands have been traversed, great religions and philosophies have been forever changed by the spice trade. In 1492 Christopher Columbus set sail to find seasoning. Today the influence of flavor in the world marketplace is no less decisive. The rise and fall of corporate empires—of soft drink companies, snack food companies, and fast food chains—is frequently determined by how their products taste.

The flavor industry emerged in the mid-nineteenth century, as processed foods began to be manufactured on a large scale. Recognizing the need for flavor additives, the early food processors turned to perfume companies that had years of experience working with essential oils and volatile aromas. The great perfume houses of England, France, and the Netherlands produced many of the first flavor compounds. In the early part of the twentieth century, Germany's powerful chemical industry assumed the technological lead in flavor production. Legend has it that a German scientist discovered methyl anthranilate, one of the first artificial flavors, by accident while mixing chemicals in his laboratory. Suddenly the lab was filled with the sweet smell of grapes. Methyl anthranilate later became the chief flavoring compound of grape Kool-Aid. After World War II, much of the perfume industry shifted from Europe to the United States, settling in New York City near the garment district and the fashion houses. The flavor industry came with it, subsequently moving to New Jersey to gain more plant capacity. Man-made flavor additives were used mainly in baked goods, candies, and sodas until the 1950s, when sales of processed food began to soar. The invention of gas chromatographs and mass spectrometers—machines capable of detecting volatile gases at low levels—vastly increased the number of flavors that could be synthesized. By the mid-1960s the American flavor industry was churning out compounds to supply the taste of Pop Tarts, Bac-Os, Tab, Tang, Filet-O-Fish sandwiches, and literally thousands of other new foods.

The American flavor industry now has annual revenues of about $1.4 billion. Approximately ten thousand new processed food products are introduced every year in the United States. Almost all of them require flavor additives. And about nine out of every ten of these new food products fail. The latest flavor innovations and corporate realignments are heralded in publications such as *Food Chemical News, Food Engineering, Chemical Market Reporter,* and *Food Product Design.* The growth of IFF has mirrored that of the flavor industry as a whole. IFF was formed in 1958, through the merger of two small companies. Its annual revenues have grown almost fifteenfold since the early 1970s, and it now has manufacturing facilities in twenty countries.

The quality that people seek most of all in a food, its flavor, is usually present in a quantity too infinitesimal to be measured by any traditional culinary terms such as ounces or teaspoons. Today's sophisticated spectrometers, gas chromatographs, and headspace vapor analyzers provide a detailed map of a food's flavor components, detecting chemical aromas in amounts as low as one part per billion. The human nose, however, is still more sensitive than any machine yet invented. A nose can detect aromas present in quantities of a few parts per trillion—an amount equivalent to 0.000000000003 percent. Complex aromas, like those of coffee or roasted meat, may be composed of volatile gases from nearly a thousand different chemicals. The smell of a strawberry arises from the interaction of at least 350 different chemicals that are present in minute amounts. The chemical that provides the dominant flavor of bell pepper can be tasted in amounts as low as .02 parts per billion; one drop is sufficient to add flavor to five average size swimming pools. The flavor additive usually comes last, or second to last, in a processed food's list of ingredients. As a result, the flavor of a processed food often costs less than its packaging. Soft drinks contain a larger proportion of flavor additives than most products. The flavor in a twelve-ounce can of Coke costs about half a cent.

The color additives in processed foods are usually present in even smaller amounts than the flavor compounds. Many of New Jersey's flavor companies also manufacture these color additives, which are used to make processed foods look appealing. Food coloring serves many of the same purposes as lipstick, eye shadow, mascara—and is often made from the same pigments. Titanium dioxide, for example, has proved to be an especially versatile mineral. It gives many processed candies, frosting, and icing their bright white color; it is a common ingredient in women's cosmetics; and it is the pigment used in many white oil paints and house paints. At Burger King, Wendy's, and McDonald's, coloring agents have been added to many of the soft drinks, salad dressings, cookies, condiments, chicken dishes, and sandwich buns.

Studies have found that the color of a food can greatly affect how its taste is perceived. Brightly colored foods frequently seem to taste better than bland-looking foods, even when the flavor compounds are identical. Foods that somehow look off-color often seem to have off tastes. For thousands of years, human beings have relied on visual cues to help determine what is edible. The color of fruit suggests whether it is ripe, the color of meat whether it is rancid. Flavor researchers sometimes use colored lights to modify the influence of visual cues during taste tests. During one experiment in the early 1970s, people were served an oddly tinted meal of steak and french fries that appeared normal beneath colored lights. Everyone thought the meal tasted fine until the lighting was changed. Once it became apparent that the steak was actually blue and the fries were green, some people became ill.

The Food and Drug Administration does not require flavor companies   20 to disclose the ingredients of their additives, so long as all the chemicals are considered by the agency to be GRAS (Generally Regarded As Safe). This lack of public disclosure enables the companies to maintain the secrecy of their formulas. It also hides the fact that flavor compounds sometimes contain more ingredients than the foods being given their taste. The ubiquitous phrase "artificial strawberry flavor" gives little hint of the chemical wizardry and manufacturing skill that can make a highly processed food taste like a strawberry.

A typical artificial strawberry flavor, like the kind found in a Burger King strawberry milk shake, contains the following ingredients: amyl acetate, amyl butyrate, amyl valerate, anethol, anisyl formate, benzyl acetate, benzyl isobutyrate, butyric acid, cinnamyl isobutyrate, cinnamyl valerate, cognac essential oil, diacetyl, dipropyl ketone, ethyl acetate, ethyl amylketone, ethyl butyrate, ethyl cinnamate, ethyl heptanoate, ethyl heptylate, ethyl lactate, ethyl methylphenylglycidate, ethyl nitrate, ethyl propionate, ethyl valerate, heliotropin, hydroxyphenyl-2-butanone (10 percent solution in alcohol), α-ionone, isobutyl anthranilate, isobutyl butyrate, lemon essential oil, maltol, 4-methylacetophenone, methyl anthranilate, methyl benzoate, methyl cinnamate, methyl heptine carbonate, methyl naphthyl ketone, methyl salicylate, mint essential oil, neroli essential oil, nerolin, neryl isobutyrate, orris butter, phenethyl alcohol, rose, rum ether, γ-undecalactone, vanillin, and solvent.

Although flavors usually arise from a mixture of many different volatile chemicals, a single compound often supplies the dominant aroma. Smelled alone, that chemical provides an unmistakable sense of the food. Ethyl-2-methyl butyrate, for example, smells just like an apple. Today's highly processed foods offer a blank palette: whatever chemicals you add to them will give them specific tastes. Adding methyl-2-peridylketone makes something taste like popcorn. Adding ethyl-3-hydroxybutanoate makes it taste like marshmallow. The possibilities are now almost limitless. Without affecting the appearance or nutritional value, processed foods could even be made with aroma chemicals such as hexanal (the smell of freshly cut grass) or 3-methyl butanoic acid (the smell of body odor).

The 1960s were the heyday of artificial flavors. The synthetic versions of flavor compounds were not subtle, but they did not need to be, given the nature of most processed food. For the past twenty years food processors have tried hard to use only "natural flavors" in their products. According to the FDA, these must be derived entirely from natural sources—from herbs, spices, fruits, vegetables, beef, chicken, yeast, bark, roots, etc. Consumers prefer to see natural flavors on a label, out of a belief that they are healthier. The distinction between artificial and natural flavors can be somewhat arbitrary and absurd, based more on how the flavor has been made than on what it actually contains. "A natural flavor," says Terry Acree, a professor of food science at Cornell University, "is a flavor that's been derived with an out-of-date technology." Natural flavors and artificial flavors sometimes contain exactly the same chemicals, produced through different methods. Amyl acetate, for example, provides the dominant note of banana flavor. When you distill it from bananas with a solvent, amyl acetate is a natural flavor. When you produce it by mixing vinegar with amyl alcohol, adding sulfuric acid as a catalyst, amyl acetate is an artificial flavor. Either way it smells and tastes the same. The phrase "natural flavor" is now listed among the ingredients of everything from Stonyfield Farm Organic Strawberry Yogurt to Taco Bell Hot Taco Sauce.

A natural flavor is not necessarily healthier or purer than an artificial one. When almond flavor (benzaldehyde) is derived from natural sources, such as peach and apricot pits, it contains traces of hydrogen cyanide, a deadly poison. Benzaldehyde derived through a different process—by mixing oil of clove and the banana flavor, amyl acetate—does not contain any cyanide. Nevertheless, it is legally considered an artificial flavor and sells at a much lower price. Natural and artificial flavors are now manufactured at the same chemical plants, places that few people would associate with Mother Nature. Calling any of these flavors "natural" requires a flexible attitude toward the English language and a fair amount of irony.

The small and elite group of scientists who create most of the flavor in   25
most of the food now consumed in the United States are called "flavorists."

Domenico Milano, research and development manager of Torani, samples some new flavors of vanilla-flavored syrup inside the company development lab. Milano, one of Torani's two "flavor masters," takes extracts from plants grown around the world and experiments until he arrives at the perfect essence of vanilla, raspberry, or coconut.

They draw upon a number of disciplines in their work: biology, psychology, physiology, and organic chemistry. A flavorist is a chemist with a trained nose and a poetic sensibility. Flavors are created by blending scores of different chemicals in tiny amounts, a process governed by scientific principles but demanding a fair amount of art. In an age when delicate aromas, subtle flavors, and microwave ovens do not easily coexist, the job of the flavorist is to conjure illusions about processed food and, in the words of one flavor company's literature, to ensure "consumer likeability." The flavorists with whom I spoke were charming, cosmopolitan, and ironic. They were also discreet, in keeping with the dictates of their trade. They were the sort of scientist who not only enjoyed fine wine, but could also tell you the chemicals that gave each vintage its unique aroma. One flavorist compared his work to composing music. A well-made flavor compound will have a "top note," followed by a "dry-down," and a "leveling-off," with different chemicals responsible for each stage. The taste of a food can be radically altered by minute changes in the flavoring mix. "A little odor goes a long way," one flavorist said.

In order to give a processed food the proper taste, a flavorist must always consider the food's "mouthfeel"—the unique combination of textures and chemical interactions that affects how the flavor is perceived. The mouthfeel can be adjusted through the use of various fats, gums, starches, emulsifiers, and stabilizers. The aroma chemicals of a food can be precisely analyzed, but mouthfeel is much harder to measure. How does one quantify a french fry's crispness? Food technologists are now conducting basic research in rheology, a branch of physics that examines the flow and deformation of materials. A number of companies sell sophisticated devices that attempt to measure mouthfeel. The TA.XT2i Texture Analyzer, produced by the Texture Technologies Corporation, performs calculations based on data derived from as many as 250 separate probes. It is essentially a mechanical mouth. It gauges the most important rheological properties of a food—the bounce, creep, breaking point, density, crunchiness, chewiness, gumminess, lumpiness, rubberiness, springiness, slipperiness, smoothness, softness, wetness, juiciness, spreadability, springback, and tackiness.

Some of the most important advances in flavor manufacturing are now occurring in the field of biotechnology. Complex flavors are being made through fermentation, enzyme reactions, fungal cultures, and tissue cultures. All of the flavors being created through these methods—including the ones being synthesized by funguses—are considered natural flavors by the FDA. The new enzyme-based processes are responsible for extremely lifelike dairy flavors. One company now offers not just butter flavor, but also fresh creamy butter, cheesy butter, milky butter, savory melted butter, and super-concentrated butter flavor, in liquid or powder form. The development of new fermentation techniques, as well as new techniques for heating mixtures of sugar and amino acids, has led to the creation of much more realistic meat flavors. The McDonald's Corporation will not reveal the exact origin of the natural flavor added to its french fries. In response to inquiries from *Vegetarian Journal*, however, McDonald's did acknowledge that its fries derive some of their characteristic flavor from "animal products."

Other popular fast foods derive their flavor from unexpected sources. Wendy's Grilled Chicken Sandwich, for example, contains beef extracts. Burger King's BK Broiler Chicken Breast Patty contains "natural smoke flavor." A firm called Red Arrow Products Company specializes in smoke flavor, which is added to barbecue sauces and processed meats. Red Arrow manufactures natural smoke flavor by charring sawdust and capturing the aroma chemicals released into the air. The smoke is captured in water and then bottled, so that other companies can sell food which seems to have been cooked over a fire.

The Vegetarian Legal Action Network recently petitioned the FDA to issue new food labeling requirements for foods that contain natural flavors.
The group wants food processors to list the basic origins of their flavors on
their labels. At the moment, vegetarians often have no way of knowing
whether a flavor additive contains beef, pork, poultry, or shellfish. One of
the most widely used color additives—whose presence is often hidden by
the phrase "color added"—violates a number of religious dietary restrictions,
may cause allergic reactions in susceptible people, and comes from an unusual source. Cochineal extract (also known as carmine or carminic acid) is
made from the desiccated bodies of female *Dactylopius coccus costa*, a small
insect harvested mainly in Peru and the Canary Islands. The bug feeds on
red cactus berries and color from the berries accumulates in the females and
their unhatched larvae. The insects are collected, dried, and ground into pigment. It takes about 70,000 of them to produce one pound of carmine, which
is used to make processed foods look pink, red, or purple. Dannon strawberry yogurt gets its color from carmine, as do many frozen fruit bars, candies,
fruit fillings, and Ocean Spray pink-grapefruit juice drink.

In a meeting room at IFF, Brian Grainger let me sample some of the com-   30
pany's flavors. It was an unusual taste test; there wasn't any food to taste.
Grainger is a senior flavorist at IFF, a soft-spoken chemist with graying hair,
an English accent, and a fondness for understatement. He could easily be
mistaken for a British diplomat or the owner of a West End brasserie with
two Michelin stars. Like many in the flavor industry, he has an Old World,
old-fashioned sensibility which seems out of step with our brand-conscious,
egocentric age. When I suggested that IFF should put its own logo on the
products that contain its flavors—instead of allowing other brands to enjoy the consumer loyalty and affection inspired by those flavors—Grainger
politely disagreed, assuring me such a thing would never be done. In the
absence of public credit or acclaim, the small and secretive fraternity of flavor chemists praises one another's work. Grainger can often tell, by analyzing the flavor formula of a product, which of his counterparts at a rival firm
devised it. And he enjoys walking down supermarket aisles, looking at the
many products that contain his flavors, even if no one else knows it.

Grainger had brought a dozen small glass bottles from the lab. After he
opened each bottle, I dipped a fragrance testing filter into it. The filters were
long white strips of paper designed to absorb aroma chemicals without producing off-notes. Before placing the strips of paper before my nose, I closed
my eyes. Then I inhaled deeply, and one food after another was conjured

from the glass bottles. I smelled fresh cherries, black olives, sautéed onions, and shrimp. Grainger's most remarkable creation took me by surprise. After closing my eyes, I suddenly smelled a grilled hamburger. The aroma was uncanny, almost miraculous. It smelled like someone in the room was flipping burgers on a hot grill. But when I opened my eyes, there was just a narrow strip of white paper and a smiling flavorist.

Thinking about the Text

1. Eric Schlosser's **ANALYSIS** of McDonald's fries may appear to veer off in several non-fries directions. Does all of the **EVIDENCE** that Schlosser presents turn out to be relevant to the subject at hand? Does he tie it all together? Is the analysis cohesive? Why or why not?

2. What is Schlosser trying to do in his analysis? Does he want to persuade his readers to stop eating fries or fast food in general? Does he hope to inspire them to lobby for changes in packaging? in processing? Or does he want to just make them think about what's in their food? **SUMMARIZE** this text, making Schlosser's **PURPOSE** the central focus of your summary.

3. That our foods contain long lists of difficult-to-pronounce chemicals is not exactly news; still, Schlosser's analysis probably told you much more than you had ever imagined about what goes into them. Has what you read affected your appetite for processed foods? for fast-food restaurants like McDonald's and Burger King? Why or why not?

4. Schlosser is dealing with a subject that is quite emotionally charged and controversial—chemicals that go into food. How would you describe the **TONE** and the language of his analysis? Given that the subject matter has great potential for sensationalism, do you think that Schlosser has exploited that potential? resisted it? neglected it by writing in too understated a way? Explain your conclusions, providing examples from the text.

5. Choose a processed food product that you buy regularly—such as cookies, ice cream, frozen pizza, and so on—and make a note of each ingredient listed on the packaging, paying particular attention to the ones with chemical names. For each one, find out where it comes from, how it is made, and what its function is in the food. Write a **REPORT** on what you find, and include your reaction to the results. Will you continue to eat that food? Why or why not?

Why Colleges Shower Their Students with A's

BRENT STAPLES

THE ECONOMIST **MILTON FRIEDMAN** taught that superior products flourished and shabby ones died out when consumers voted emphatically with their dollars. But the truth of the marketplace is that shabby products can do just fine if they sustain the veneer of quality while slipping downhill, as has much of higher education. Faced with demanding consumers and stiff competition, colleges have simply issued more and more A's, stoking grade inflation and devaluing degrees.

Grade inflation is in full gallop at every level, from struggling community institutions to the elites of the Ivy League. In some cases, campuswide averages have crept up from a C just 10 years ago to B-plus today.

Some departments shower students with A's to fill poorly attended courses that might otherwise be canceled. Individual professors inflate grades after consumer-conscious administrators hound them into it. Professors at every level inflate to escape negative evaluations by students, whose opinions now figure in tenure and promotion decisions.

The most vulnerable teachers are the part-timers who have no job

---

BRENT STAPLES is a member of the *New York Times* editorial board and is a frequent contributor to that newspaper. He writes about politics and cultural issues, focusing in particular on race and education, and he tweets @brentNYT. He's the author of *Parallel Time: Growing Up in Black and White* (1995). This selection appeared in the *Times* in 1998.

security and who now teach more than half of all college courses. Writing in the last issue of the journal *Academe*, two part-timers suggest that students routinely corner adjuncts, threatening to complain if they do not turn C's into A's. An Ivy League professor said recently that if tenure disappeared, universities would be "free to sell diplomas outright."

The consumer appetite for less rigorous education is nowhere more evident than in the University of Phoenix, a profit-making school that shuns traditional scholarship and offers a curriculum so superficial that critics compare it to a drive-through restaurant. Two hundred colleges have closed since a businessman dreamed up Phoenix 20 years ago. Meanwhile, the university has expanded to 60 sites spread around the country, and more than 40,000 students, making it the country's largest private university.

Phoenix competes directly with the big state universities and lesser-known small colleges, all of which fear a student drain. But the elite schools fear each other and their customers, the students, who are becoming increasingly restive about the cost of a first-tier diploma, which now exceeds $120,000. Faced with the prospect of crushing debt, students are treating

Robert Wancha, a student at the University of Phoenix in Southfield, Michigan, has criticized the university's standards.

grades as a matter of life and death—occasionally even suing to have grades revised upward.

Twenty years ago students grumbled, then lived with the grades they were given. Today, colleges of every stature permit them to appeal low grades through deans or permanent boards of inquiry. In *The Chronicle of Higher Education,* Prof. Paul Korshin of the University of Pennsylvania recently described his grievance panel as the "rhinoplasty committee," because it does "cosmetic surgery" on up to 500 transcripts a year.

The argument that grades are rising because students are better prepared is simply not convincing. The evidence suggests that students and parents are demanding—and getting—what they think of as their money's worth.

One way to stanch inflation is to change the way the grade point average is calculated. Under most formulas, all courses are given equal weight, so math, science and less-challenging courses have equal impact on the averages. This arrangement rewards students who gravitate to courses where high marks are generously given and punishes those who seek out math and science courses, where far fewer students get the top grade.

Valen Johnson, a Duke University statistics professor, came under 10 heavy fire from both students and faculty when he proposed recalculating the grade point average to give rigorously graded courses greater weight. The student government beat back the plan with the help of teachers in the humanities, who worried that students might abandon them for other courses that they currently avoided. Other universities have expressed interest in adopting the Johnson plan, but want their names kept secret to avoid a backlash.

Addicted to counterfeit excellence, colleges, parents and students are unlikely to give it up. As a consequence, diplomas will become weaker and more ornamental as the years go by.

Brent Staples presents a lot of information but makes it readable. How did he do it? More importantly, how can you do it? See Ch. 14.

Thinking about the Text

1. Brent Staples presents a great deal of information in a very brief opinion piece. How well does the piece live up to the promise of its title—explaining the cause of the abundance of A's? Explain.

2. Staples argues that the proliferation of A grades devalues a degree by demonstrating the lack of academic rigor of any college that grants so many A's. How do you feel about the degree that you are working toward? If you had the choice of two colleges equal in all other ways, and one had a reputation for academic rigor and maintained high standards for grades, while the other had a mediocre academic reputation but was known for giving many high grades, which would you choose, and why?

3. Staples' essay was published in the *New York Times*, which has a readership of millions. Is Staples really addressing all of those millions, or is his true intended **AUDIENCE** a particular subset of those who read the *Times*? If so, who was he addressing—and how can you tell?

4. Staples mentions the proposal of Valen Johnson as a way of dealing with "counterfeit excellence" (11). Is he advocating Johnson's proposal? opposing it? not taking a position one way or the other? How do you know?

5. Imagine that the administration of your school is undertaking a major evaluation of the grading system, with the ultimate goal of enhancing the academic rigor of the institution. They have asked members of the academic community at all levels, including students, to present opinions and suggestions. Write an essay in which you **ARGUE A POSITION** on grading policies, particularly with respect to grade inflation. Give a carefully reasoned argument backed up by **EVIDENCE** from your own experience.

Cosmic Perspective

NEIL deGRASSE TYSON

Of all the sciences cultivated by mankind, Astronomy is acknowledged to be, and undoubtedly is, the most sublime, the most interesting, and the most useful. For, by knowledge derived from this science, not only the bulk of the Earth is discovered . . . but our very faculties are enlarged with the grandeur of the ideas it conveys, our minds exalted above [their] low contracted prejudices.

—JAMES FERGUSON, *Astronomy Explained upon Sir Isaac Newton's Principles, and Made Easy to Those Who Have Not Studied Mathematics (1757)*

LONG BEFORE ANYONE KNEW that the universe had a beginning, before we knew that the nearest large galaxy lies two and a half million light-years from Earth, before we knew how stars work or whether atoms exist,

NEIL deGRASSE TYSON is an astrophysicist and the director of the Hayden Planetarium at the American Museum of Natural History in New York City. He is the author of many science books for a general audience, among them *Space Chronicles: Facing the Ultimate Frontier* (2012) and *The Pluto Files: The Rise and Fall of America's Favorite Planet* (2014). He is an informative and entertaining tweeter @neiltyson and writes the "Universe" column in *Natural History* magazine, where this essay was published in 2007.

James Ferguson's enthusiastic introduction to his favorite science rang true. Yet his words, apart from their eighteenth-century flourish, could have been written yesterday.

But who gets to think that way? Who gets to celebrate this cosmic view of life? Not the migrant farmworker. Not the sweatshop worker. Certainly not the homeless person rummaging through the trash for food. You need the luxury of time not spent on mere survival. You need to live in a nation whose government values the search to understand humanity's place in the universe. You need a society in which intellectual pursuit can take you to the frontiers of discovery, and in which news of your discoveries can be routinely disseminated. By those measures, most citizens of industrialized nations do quite well.

Yet the cosmic view comes with a hidden cost. When I travel thousands of miles to spend a few moments in the fast-moving shadow of the Moon during a total solar eclipse, sometimes I lose sight of Earth.

When I pause and reflect on our expanding universe, with its galaxies hurtling away from one another, embedded within the ever-stretching, four-dimensional fabric of space and time, sometimes I forget that uncounted people walk this Earth without food or shelter, and that children are disproportionately represented among them.

When I pore over the data that establish the mysterious presence of 5 dark matter and dark energy throughout the universe, sometimes I forget that every day—every twenty-four-hour rotation of Earth—people kill and get killed in the name of someone else's conception of God, and that some people who do not kill in the name of God kill in the name of their nation's needs or wants.

When I track the orbits of asteroids, comets, and planets, each one a pirouetting dancer in a cosmic ballet choreographed by the forces of gravity, sometimes I forget that too many people act in wanton disregard for the delicate interplay of Earth's atmosphere, oceans, and land, with consequences that our children and our children's children will witness and pay for with their health and well-being.

And sometimes I forget that powerful people rarely do all they can to help those who cannot help themselves.

I occasionally forget those things because, however big the world is—in our hearts, our minds, and our outsize atlases—the universe is even bigger. A depressing thought to some, but a liberating thought to me.

A view from the Hayden Planetarium show "Passport to the Universe."

Consider an adult who tends to the traumas of a child: a broken toy, a scraped knee, a schoolyard bully. Adults know that kids have no clue what constitutes a genuine problem, because inexperience greatly limits their childhood perspective.

As grown-ups, dare we admit to ourselves that we, too, have a collec- 10 tive immaturity of view? Dare we admit that our thoughts and behaviors spring from a belief that the world revolves around us? Apparently not. And the evidence abounds. Part the curtains of society's racial, ethnic, religious, national, and cultural conflicts, and you find the human ego turning the knobs and pulling the levers.

Now imagine a world in which everyone, but especially people with power and influence, holds an expanded view of our place in the cosmos. With that perspective, our problems would shrink—or never arise at all— and we could celebrate our earthly differences while shunning the behavior of our predecessors who slaughtered each other because of them.

Back in February 2000, the newly rebuilt Hayden Planetarium featured a space show called "Passport to the Universe," which took visitors on a virtual zoom from New York City to the edge of the cosmos. En route the audience saw Earth, then the solar system, then the 100 billion stars of the Milky Way galaxy shrink to barely visible dots on the planetarium dome.

Within a month of opening day, I received a letter from an Ivy League professor of psychology whose expertise was things that make people feel insignificant. I never knew one could specialize in such a field. The guy wanted to administer a before-and-after questionnaire to visitors, assessing the depth of their depression after viewing the show. "Passport to the Universe," he wrote, elicited the most dramatic feelings of smallness he had ever experienced.

How could that be? Every time I see the space show (and others we've produced), I feel alive and spirited and connected. I also feel large, knowing that the goings-on within the three-pound human brain are what enabled us to figure out our place in the universe.

Allow me to suggest that it's the professor, not I, who has misread nature. His ego was too big to begin with, inflated by delusions of significance and fed by cultural assumptions that human beings are more important than everything else in the universe.   15

In all fairness to the fellow, powerful forces in society leave most of us susceptible. As was I . . . until the day I learned in biology class that more bacteria live and work in one centimeter of my colon than the number of people who have ever existed in the world. That kind of information makes you think twice about who—or what—is actually in charge.

From that day on, I began to think of people not as the masters of space and time but as participants in a great cosmic chain of being, with a direct genetic link across species both living and extinct, extending back nearly 4 billion years to the earliest single-celled organisms on Earth.

I know what you're thinking: we're smarter than bacteria.

No doubt about it, we're smarter than every other living creature that ever walked, crawled, or slithered on Earth. But how smart is that? We cook our food. We compose poetry and music. We do art and science. We're good at math. Even if you're bad at math, you're probably much better at it than the smartest chimpanzee, whose genetic identity varies in only trifling ways from ours. Try as they might, primatologists will never get a chimpanzee to learn the multiplication table or do long division.

If small genetic differences between us and our fellow apes account for   20
our vast difference in intelligence, maybe that difference in intelligence is not so vast after all.

Imagine a life-form whose brainpower is to ours as ours is to a chimpanzee's. To such a species our highest mental achievements would be trivial. Their toddlers, instead of learning their ABCs on Sesame Street, would learn multivariable calculus on Boolean Boulevard. Our most

The Milky Way over Mount Tateyama in Japan.

complex theorems, our deepest philosophies, the cherished works of our most creative artists, would be projects their schoolkids bring home for Mom and Dad to display on the refrigerator door. These creatures would study Stephen Hawking (who occupies the same endowed professorship once held by Newton at the University of Cambridge) because he's slightly more clever than other humans, owing to his ability to do theoretical astrophysics and other rudimentary calculations in his head.

If a huge genetic gap separated us from our closest relative in the animal kingdom, we could justifiably celebrate our brilliance. We might be entitled to walk around thinking we're distant and distinct from our fellow creatures. But no such gap exists. Instead, we are one with the rest of nature, fitting neither above nor below, but within.

Need more ego softeners? Simple comparisons of quantity, size, and scale do the job well.

Take water. It's simple, common, and vital. There are more molecules of water in an eight-ounce cup of the stuff than there are cups of water in all the world's oceans. Every cup that passes through a single person and eventually rejoins the world's water supply holds enough molecules to mix 1,500 of them into every other cup of water in the world. No way around it: some of the water you just drank passed through the kidneys of Socrates, Genghis Khan, and Joan of Arc.

How about air? Also vital. A single breathful draws in more air mol- 25 ecules than there are breathfuls of air in Earth's entire atmosphere. That means some of the air you just breathed passed through the lungs of Napoleon, Beethoven, Lincoln, and Billy the Kid.

Time to get cosmic. There are more stars in the universe than grains of sand on any beach, more stars than seconds have passed since Earth formed, more stars than words and sounds ever uttered by all the humans who ever lived.

Want a sweeping view of the past? Our unfolding cosmic perspective takes you there. Light takes time to reach Earth's observatories from the depths of space, and so you see objects and phenomena not as they are but as they once were. That means the universe acts like a giant time machine: the farther away you look, the further back in time you see—back almost to the beginning of time itself. Within that horizon of reckoning, cosmic evolution unfolds continuously, in full view.

Want to know what we're made of? Again, the cosmic perspective offers a bigger answer than you might expect. The chemical elements of the universe are forged in the fires of high-mass stars that end their lives in stupendous explosions, enriching their host galaxies with the chemical arsenal of life as we know it. The result? The four most common chemically active elements in the universe—hydrogen, oxygen, carbon, and nitrogen—are the four most common elements of life on Earth. We are not simply in the universe. The universe is in us.

Yes, we are stardust. But we may not be of this Earth. Several separate lines of research, when considered together, have forced investigators to reassess who we think we are and where we think we came from.

First, computer simulations show that when a large asteroid strikes a 30 planet, the surrounding areas can recoil from the impact energy, catapulting rocks into space. From there, they can travel to—and land on—other planetary surfaces. Second, microorganisms can be hardy. Some survive the extremes of temperature, pressure, and radiation inherent in space travel. If the rocky flotsam from an impact hails from a planet with life, microscopic fauna could have stowed away in the rocks' nooks and crannies. Third, recent evidence suggests that shortly after the formation of our solar system, Mars was wet, and perhaps fertile, even before Earth was.

Those findings mean it's conceivable that life began on Mars and later seeded life on Earth, a process known as panspermia. So all earthlings might—just might—be descendants of Martians.

Again and again across the centuries, cosmic discoveries have demoted our self-image. Earth was once assumed to be astronomically unique, until astronomers learned that Earth is just another planet orbiting the Sun. Then we presumed the Sun was unique, until we learned that the countless stars of the night sky are suns themselves. Then we presumed our galaxy, the Milky Way, was the entire known universe, until we established that the countless fuzzy things in the sky are other galaxies, dotting the landscape of our known universe.

Today, how easy it is to presume that one universe is all there is. Yet emerging theories of modern cosmology, as well as the continually reaffirmed improbability that anything is unique, require that we remain open to the latest assault on our plea for distinctiveness: multiple universes, otherwise known as the "multiverse," in which ours is just one of countless bubbles bursting forth from the fabric of the cosmos.

The cosmic perspective flows from fundamental knowledge. But it's more than just what you know. It's also about having the wisdom and insight to apply that knowledge to assessing our place in the universe. And its attributes are clear:

The cosmic perspective comes from the frontiers of science, yet it is not 35 solely the provenance of the scientist. It belongs to everyone.

The cosmic perspective is humble.

The cosmic perspective is spiritual—even redemptive—but not religious.

The cosmic perspective enables us to grasp, in the same thought, the large and the small.

The cosmic perspective opens our minds to extraordinary ideas but does not leave them so open that our brains spill out, making us susceptible to believing anything we're told.

The cosmic perspective opens our eyes to the universe, not as a benevo- 40 lent cradle designed to nurture life but as a cold, lonely, hazardous place.

The cosmic perspective shows Earth to be a mote, but a precious mote and, for the moment, the only home we have.

The cosmic perspective finds beauty in the images of planets, moons, stars, and nebulae but also celebrates the laws of physics that shape them.

The cosmic perspective enables us to see beyond our circumstances, allowing us to transcend the primal search for food, shelter, and sex.

The cosmic perspective reminds us that in space, where there is no air, a flag will not wave—an indication that perhaps flag waving and space exploration do not mix.

The cosmic perspective not only embraces our genetic kinship with all 45 life on Earth but also values our chemical kinship with any yet-to-be discovered life in the universe, as well as our atomic kinship with the universe itself.

At least once a week, if not once a day, we might each ponder what cosmic truths lie undiscovered before us, perhaps awaiting the arrival of a clever thinker, an ingenious experiment, or an innovative space mission to reveal them. We might further ponder how those discoveries may one day transform life on Earth.

Absent such curiosity, we are no different from the provincial farmer who expresses no need to venture beyond the county line, because his forty acres meet all his needs. Yet if all our predecessors had felt that way, the farmer would instead be a cave dweller, chasing down his dinner with a stick and a rock.

Learn how to use reiteration as a rhetorical device in your own writing on pp. 439–41.

During our brief stay on planet Earth, we owe ourselves and our descendants the opportunity to explore—in part because it's fun to do. But there's a far nobler reason. The day our knowledge of the cosmos ceases to expand, we risk regressing to the childish view that the universe figuratively and literally revolves around us. In that bleak world, arms-bearing, resource-hungry people and nations would be prone to act on their "low contracted prejudices." And that would be the last gasp of human enlightenment—until the rise of a visionary new culture that could once again embrace the cosmic perspective.

Thinking about the Text

1. Neil deGrasse Tyson argues that beyond simply being "fun to do," looking at life through a "cosmic perspective" has tangible benefits for the individual and for society. What are those benefits? **SUMMARIZE** his arguments in favor of seeing the world this way.

2. Tyson is a scientist—an astrophysicist, to be exact—yet this essay seems more philosophical than scientific. How does his standing as a scientist affect his credibility as an author? Do you think Tyson has the **AUTHORITY** to write on the topic he takes up? Why or why not?

3. Throughout this essay, Tyson uses **REITERATION** as a rhetorical device, such as when he begins twelve consecutive paragraphs with the title phrase "the cosmic perspective" (34–45). What is the effect of such repetition? What might Tyson have been trying to accomplish, and how well does it work?

4. In paragraph 46, Tyson asks us to "ponder what cosmic truths lie undiscovered before us" and how their discoveries "may one day transform life on Earth." What is the purpose of this exercise? Do you think it's a good idea—and would you try it? If so, what would you expect to accomplish?

5. Tyson recalls the moment when he came to realize that humans are not necessarily "more important than everything else in the universe." Do you agree with him? Completely? Partially? Where would you place humans on a scale of importance? Write an essay responding to Tyson, explaining what you think and why.

My Life as an Undocumented Immigrant

JOSE ANTONIO VARGAS

ONE **AUGUST MORNING** nearly two decades ago, my mother woke me and put me in a cab. She handed me a jacket. *"Baka malamig doon"* were among the few words she said. ("It might be cold there.") When I arrived at the Philippines' Ninoy Aquino International Airport with her, my aunt and a family friend, I was introduced to a man I'd never seen. They told me he was my uncle. He held my hand as I boarded an airplane for the first time. It was 1993, and I was 12.

My mother wanted to give me a better life, so she sent me thousands of miles away to live with her parents in America—my grandfather (*Lolo* in Tagalog) and grandmother (*Lola*). After I arrived in Mountain View, Calif., in the San Francisco Bay Area, I entered sixth grade and quickly grew to love my new home, family and culture. I discovered a passion for language, though it was hard to learn the difference between formal English and American slang. One of my early memories is of a freckled kid in middle school ask-

JOSE ANTONIO VARGAS came to the United States from the Philippines at the age of twelve as an undocumented immigrant, a history he discloses in this 2011 essay from the *New York Times*. He has been awarded the Pulitzer Prize and the PEN Freedom to Write award. His writing has appeared in the *Washington Post*, the *San Francisco Chronicle*, *Time*, and many other periodicals; he tweets @joseiswriting. His current work focuses on immigration advocacy.

ing me, "What's up?" I replied, "The sky," and he and a couple of other kids laughed. I won the eighth-grade spelling bee by memorizing words I couldn't properly pronounce. (The winning word was "indefatigable.")

One day when I was 16, I rode my bike to the nearby D.M.V. office to get my driver's permit. Some of my friends already had their licenses, so I figured it was time. But when I handed the clerk my green card as proof of U.S. residency, she flipped it around, examining it. "This is fake," she whispered. "Don't come back here again."

Confused and scared, I pedaled home and confronted Lolo. I remember him sitting in the garage, cutting coupons. I dropped my bike and ran over to him, showing him the green card. "*Peke ba ito?*" I asked in Tagalog. ("Is this fake?") My grandparents were naturalized American citizens—he worked as a security guard, she as a food server—and they had begun supporting my mother and me financially when I was 3, after my father's wandering eye and inability to properly provide for us led to my parents' separation. Lolo was a proud man, and I saw the shame on his face as he told me he purchased the card, along with other fake documents, for me. "Don't show it to other people," he warned.

I decided then that I could never give anyone reason to doubt I was an American. I convinced myself that if I worked enough, if I achieved enough, I would be rewarded with citizenship. I felt I could earn it. 5

I've tried. Over the past 14 years, I've graduated from high school and college and built a career as a journalist, interviewing some of the most famous people in the country. On the surface, I've created a good life. I've lived the American dream.

But I am still an undocumented immigrant. And that means living a different kind of reality. It means going about my day in fear of being found out. It means rarely trusting people, even those closest to me, with who I really am. It means keeping my family photos in a shoebox rather than displaying them on shelves in my home, so friends don't ask about them. It means reluctantly, even painfully, doing things I know are wrong and unlawful. And it has meant relying on a sort of 21st-century underground railroad of supporters, people who took an interest in my future and took risks for me.

Last year I read about four students who walked from Miami to Washington to lobby for the Dream Act, a nearly decade-old immigration bill that would provide a path to legal permanent residency for young people who have been educated in this country. At the risk of deportation—the Obama administration has deported almost 800,000 people in the last two years—they are speaking out. Their courage has inspired me.

There are believed to be 11 million undocumented immigrants in the United States. We're not always who you think we are. Some pick your strawberries or care for your children. Some are in high school or college. And some, it turns out, write news articles you might read. I grew up here. This is my home. Yet even though I think of myself as an American and consider America my country, my country doesn't think of me as one of its own.

My first challenge was the language. Though I learned English in the Philip-   10
pines, I wanted to lose my accent. During high school, I spent hours at a time watching television (especially *Frasier*, *Home Improvement* and reruns of *The Golden Girls*) and movies (from *Goodfellas* to *Anne of Green Gables*), pausing the VHS to try to copy how various characters enunciated their words. At the local library, I read magazines, books and newspapers—anything to learn how to write better. Kathy Dewar, my high-school English teacher, introduced me to journalism. From the moment I wrote my first article for the student paper, I convinced myself that having my name in print—writing in English, interviewing Americans—validated my presence here.

The debates over "illegal aliens" intensified my anxieties. In 1994, only a year after my flight from the Philippines, Gov. Pete Wilson was re-elected in part because of his support for Proposition 187, which prohibited undocumented immigrants from attending public school and accessing other services. (A federal court later found the law unconstitutional.) After my encounter at the D.M.V. in 1997, I grew more aware of anti-immigrant sentiments and stereotypes: *they don't want to assimilate, they are a drain on society.* They're not talking about me, I would tell myself. I have something to contribute.

To do that, I had to work—and for that, I needed a Social Security number. . . . Using a fake passport, Lolo and I went to the local Social Security Administration office and applied for a Social Security number and card. It was, I remember, a quick visit. When the card came in the mail, it had my full, real name, but it also clearly stated: "Valid for work only with I.N.S. authorization."

When I began looking for work, a short time after the D.M.V. incident, my grandfather and I took the Social Security card to Kinko's, where he covered the "I.N.S. authorization" text with a sliver of white tape. We then made photocopies of the card. At a glance, at least, the copies would look like copies of a regular, unrestricted Social Security card....

While in high school, I worked part time at Subway, then at the front desk of the local Y.M.C.A., then at a tennis club, until I landed an unpaid internship at *The Mountain View Voice*, my hometown newspaper. First I brought coffee and helped around the office; eventually I began covering city-hall meetings and other assignments for pay....

Mountain View High School became my second home. I was elected to   15
represent my school at school-board meetings, which gave me the chance to meet and befriend Rich Fischer, the superintendent for our school district. I joined the speech and debate team, acted in school plays and eventually became co-editor of *The Oracle*, the student newspaper. That drew the attention of my principal, Pat Hyland. "You're at school just as much as I am," she told me. Pat and Rich would soon become mentors, and over time, almost surrogate parents for me....

[During my junior] year, my history class watched a documentary on Harvey Milk, the openly gay San Francisco city official who was assassinated. This was 1999, just six months after Matthew Shepard's body was found tied to a fence in Wyoming. During the discussion, I raised my hand and said something like: "I'm sorry Harvey Milk got killed for being gay.... I've been meaning to say this.... I'm gay."

I hadn't planned on coming out that morning, though I had known that I was gay for several years. With that announcement, I became the only openly gay student at school, and it caused turmoil with my grandparents. Lolo kicked me out of the house for a few weeks. Though we eventually reconciled, I had disappointed him on two fronts. First, as a Catholic, he considered homosexuality a sin and was embarrassed about having "*ang apo na bakla*" ("a grandson who is gay"). Even worse, I was making matters more difficult for myself, he said. I needed to marry an American woman in order to gain a green card.

Tough as it was, coming out about being gay seemed less daunting than coming out about my legal status. I kept my other secret mostly hidden.

While my classmates awaited their college acceptance letters, I hoped to get a full-time job at *The Mountain View Voice* after graduation. It's not that I didn't want to go to college, but I couldn't apply for state and federal financial aid. Without that, my family couldn't afford to send me.

But when I finally told Pat and Rich about my immigration "problem"—   20 as we called it from then on—they helped me look for a solution. At first, they even wondered if one of them could adopt me and fix the situation that way, but a lawyer Rich consulted told him it wouldn't change my legal status because I was too old. Eventually they connected me to a new scholarship fund for high-potential students who were usually the first in their families to attend college. Most important, the fund was not concerned with immigration status. I was among the first recipients, with the scholarship covering tuition, lodging, books and other expenses for my studies at San Francisco State University.

As a college freshman, I found a job working part time at *The San Francisco Chronicle*, where I sorted mail and wrote some freelance articles. My ambition was to get a reporting job, so I embarked on a series of internships. First I landed at *The Philadelphia Daily News*, in the summer of 2001, where I covered a drive-by shooting and the wedding of the 76ers star Allen Iverson. Using those articles, I applied to *The Seattle Times* and got an internship for the following summer.

But then my lack of proper documents became a problem again. *The Times*'s recruiter, Pat Foote, asked all incoming interns to bring certain paperwork on their first day: a birth certificate, or a passport, or a driver's license plus an original Social Security card. I panicked, thinking my documents wouldn't pass muster. So before starting the job, I called Pat and told her about my legal status. After consulting with management, she called me back with the answer I feared: I couldn't do the internship.

This was devastating. What good was college if I couldn't then pursue the career I wanted? I decided then that if I was to succeed in a profession that is all about truth-telling, I couldn't tell the truth about myself. . . .

For the summer of 2003, I applied for internships across the country. Several newspapers, including *The Wall Street Journal*, *The Boston Globe* and *The Chicago Tribune*, expressed interest. But when *The Washington Post* offered me a spot, I knew where I would go. And this time, I had no intention of acknowledging my "problem."

The *Post* internship posed a tricky obstacle: It required a driver's license. 25 (After my close call at the California D.M.V., I'd never gotten one.) So I spent an afternoon at the Mountain View Public Library, studying various states' requirements. Oregon was among the most welcoming—and it was just a few hours' drive north.

Again, my support network came through. A friend's father lived in Portland, and he allowed me to use his address as proof of residency. Pat,

Rich and Rich's longtime assistant, Mary Moore, sent letters to me at that address. Rich taught me how to do three-point turns in a parking lot, and a friend accompanied me to Portland.

The license meant everything to me—it would let me drive, fly and work. . . . My license, issued in 2003, was set to expire eight years later, on my 30th birthday, on February 3, 2011. I had eight years to succeed professionally, and to hope that some sort of immigration reform would pass in the meantime and allow me to stay.

It seemed like all the time in the world.

My summer in Washington was exhilarating. I was intimidated to be in a major newsroom but was assigned a mentor—Peter Perl, a veteran magazine writer—to help me navigate it. A few weeks into the internship, he printed out one of my articles, about a guy who recovered a long-lost wallet, circled the first two paragraphs and left it on my desk. "Great eye for details—awesome!" he wrote. Though I didn't know it then, Peter would become one more member of my network.

At the end of the summer, I returned to *The San Francisco Chronicle*. 　30 My plan was to finish school—I was now a senior—while I worked for *The Chronicle* as a reporter for the city desk. But when *The Post* beckoned again, offering me a full-time, two-year paid internship that I could start when I graduated in June 2004, it was too tempting to pass up. I moved back to Washington.

About four months into my job as a reporter for *The Post*, I began feeling increasingly paranoid, as if I had "illegal immigrant" tattooed on my forehead—and in Washington, of all places, where the debates over immigration seemed never-ending. I was so eager to prove myself that I feared I was annoying some colleagues and editors—and worried that any one of these professional journalists could discover my secret. The anxiety was nearly paralyzing. I decided I had to tell one of the higher-ups about my situation. I turned to Peter. . . . I told him everything: the Social Security card, the driver's license, Pat and Rich, my family.

Peter was shocked. "I understand you 100 times better now," he said. He told me that I had done the right thing by telling him, and that it was now our shared problem. He said he didn't want to do anything about it just yet. I had just been hired, he said, and I needed to prove myself. "When you've done enough," he said, "we'll tell Don and Len together." (Don Graham is the chairman of The Washington Post Company; Leonard Downie Jr. was then the paper's executive editor.) A month later, I spent my first Thanksgiving in Washington with Peter and his family.

In the five years that followed, I did my best to "do enough." I was promoted to staff writer, reported on video-game culture, wrote a series on Washington's H.I.V./AIDS epidemic and covered the role of technology and social media in the 2008 presidential race. I visited the White House, where I interviewed senior aides and covered a state dinner—and gave the Secret Service the Social Security number I obtained with false documents. . . .

It was an odd sort of dance: I was trying to stand out in a highly competitive newsroom, yet I was terrified that if I stood out too much, I'd invite unwanted scrutiny. I tried to compartmentalize my fears, distract myself by reporting on the lives of other people, but there was no escaping the central conflict in my life. Maintaining a deception for so long distorts your sense of self. You start wondering who you've become, and why.

In April 2008, I was part of a Post team that won a Pulitzer Prize for the   35 paper's coverage of the Virginia Tech shootings a year earlier. Lolo died a year earlier, so it was Lola who called me the day of the announcement. The first thing she said was, "*Anong mangyayari kung malaman ng mga tao?*"

What will happen if people find out?

I couldn't say anything. After we got off the phone, I rushed to the bathroom on the fourth floor of the newsroom, sat down on the toilet and cried.

In the summer of 2009, without ever having had that follow-up talk with top Post management, I left the paper and moved to New York to join *The Huffington Post.* . . .

While I worked at *The Huffington Post*, other opportunities emerged. My H.I.V./AIDS series became a documentary film called *The Other City*, which opened at the Tribeca Film Festival last year and was broadcast on Showtime. I began writing for magazines and landed a dream assignment: profiling Facebook's Mark Zuckerberg for *The New Yorker.*

The more I achieved, the more scared and depressed I became. I was   40 proud of my work, but there was always a cloud hanging over it, over me. My old eight-year deadline—the expiration of my Oregon driver's license— was approaching.

After slightly less than a year, I decided to leave *The Huffington Post.* In part, this was because I wanted to promote the documentary and write a book about online culture—or so I told my friends. But the real reason was, after so many years of trying to be a part of the system, of focusing all my energy on my professional life, I learned that no amount of professional success would solve my problem or ease the sense of loss and displacement I felt. I lied to a friend about why I couldn't take a weekend trip to Mexico. Another time I concocted an excuse for why I couldn't go on an all-expenses-paid trip to Switzerland. I have been unwilling, for years, to be in a long-term relationship because I never wanted anyone to get too close and ask too many questions. All the while, Lola's question was stuck in my head: What will happen if people find out?

Early this year, just two weeks before my thirtieth birthday, I won a small reprieve: I obtained a driver's license in the state of Washington. The license is valid until 2016. This offered me five more years of acceptable identification—but also five more years of fear, of lying to people I respect and institutions that trusted me, of running away from who I am.

I'm done running. I'm exhausted. I don't want that life anymore.

So I've decided to come forward, own up to what I've done, and tell my story to the best of my recollection. I've reached out to former bosses and employers and apologized for misleading them—a mix of humiliation and liberation coming with each disclosure. All the people mentioned in this article gave me permission to use their names. I've also talked to family and friends about my situation and am working with legal counsel to review my options. I don't know what the consequences will be of telling my story.

I do know that I am grateful to my grandparents, my Lolo and Lola, for   45 giving me the chance for a better life. I'm also grateful to my other family—the support network I found here in America—for encouraging me to pursue my dreams.

It's been almost 18 years since I've seen my mother. Early on, I was mad at her for putting me in this position, and then mad at myself for being angry and ungrateful. By the time I got to college, we rarely spoke by phone. It became too painful; after a while it was easier to just send money to help support her and my two half-siblings. My sister, almost 2 years old when I left, is almost 20 now. I've never met my 14-year-old brother. I would love to see them.

Not long ago, I called my mother. I wanted to fill the gaps in my memory about that August morning so many years ago. We had never discussed it. Part of me wanted to shove the memory aside, but to write this article and

Vargas describes events that took place over a period of 18 years. Learn the techniques he used to keep his narrative cohesive, on p. 165.

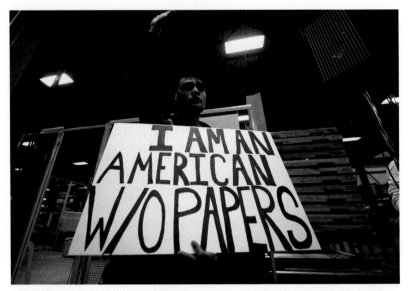

Vargas has continued to advocate for immigration reform since the publication of this essay. At a political rally in December 2011, he raises a sign announcing his position—and raises his hand to ask politicians the hard questions that he argues must be addressed in order to change the conversation about immigration in America.

face the facts of my life, I needed more details. Did I cry? Did she? Did we kiss goodbye?

My mother told me I was excited about meeting a stewardess, about getting on a plane. She also reminded me of the one piece of advice she gave me for blending in: If anyone asked why I was coming to America, I should say I was going to Disneyland.

Thinking about the Text

1. Jose Antonio Vargas highlights issues about U.S. immigration policy using details of his own experience, many of which are quite personal and probably difficult to admit. Point out three such details. What was your reaction to each of them? What is Vargas's **ARGUMENT** about immigration policy, and how do such details help him make that point?

2. Sprinkled throughout Vargas's narrative are bits of dialogue in Tagalog, the language of his Lolo and Lola. Given that he always provides the English translation, why might he have included the Tagalog? What function does it serve in his narrative?

3. How is Vargas's disclosure about his sexuality relevant to his point? Why might he have included it at all in telling about his immigrant experience? Support your response with evidence from the text.

4. Vargas **CONCLUDES** his narrative by recounting his mother's advice as he got on the plane: "If anyone asked why I was coming to America, I should say I was going to Disneyland." Why do you think he ends this essay by mentioning Disneyland? What might he be implying? Did you find this ending effective—and if not, why not?

5. Vargas was fortunate to receive emotional and professional support from the teachers and employers to whom he disclosed his undocumented status. Imagine yourself in their place. Would you respond the same way if one of your students or employees came to you admitting to being undocumented? What would you do, and why? And how would you come to a decision? What factors would need to be taken into consideration? Write an essay in which you respond to these questions, using your own personal judgment.

Oppressed Hair Puts a Ceiling on the Brain
ALICE WALKER

Alice Walker was speaking to a familiar audience, but you won't always have that luxury. Go to pp. 21–22 for tips on appealing to an audience.

AS SOME OF YOU NO DOUBT KNOW, I myself was a student here once, many moons ago. I used to sit in these very seats (sometimes still in pajamas, underneath my coat) and gaze up at the light streaming through these very windows. I listened to dozens of encouraging speakers and sang, and listened to, wonderful music. I believe I sensed I would one day return, to be on this side of the podium. I think that, all those years ago, when I was a student here and still in my teens, I was thinking about what I would say to you now.

It may surprise you that I do not intend (until the question-and-answer period perhaps) to speak of war and peace, the economy, racism or sexism, or the triumphs and tribulations of black people or of women. Or even about movies. Though the discerning ear may hear my concern for some of these things in what I am about to say, I am going to talk about an issue even closer to home. I am going to talk to you about hair. Don't give a thought to the state of yours at the moment. Don't be at all alarmed. This is not an ap-

ALICE WALKER is the author of many books of fiction and essays, including *The Color Purple* (1982), which won both the Pulitzer Prize and the National Book Award. In addition, she is a poet and human rights activist who has spoken out on issues including political oppression, female genital mutilation, and massacres in Rwanda and Gaza. Walker delivered this address on Founders' Day, 1987, at her alma mater, Spelman College, in Atlanta, Georgia.

praisal. I simply want to share with you some of my own experiences with our friend hair, and at the most hope to entertain and amuse you.

For a long time, from babyhood through young adulthood mainly, we grow, physically and spiritually (including the intellectual with the spiritual), without being deeply aware of it. In fact, some periods of our growth are so confusing that we don't even recognize that growth is what is happening. We may feel hostile or angry or weepy and hysterical, or we may feel depressed. It would never occur to us, unless we stumbled on a book or person who explained it to us, that we were in fact in the process of change, of actually becoming larger, spiritually, than we were before. Whenever we grow, we tend to feel it, as a young seed must feel the weight and inertia of the earth as it seeks to break out of its shell on its way to becoming a plant. Often the feeling is anything but pleasant. But what is most unpleasant is the not knowing what is happening. I remember the waves of anxiety that used to engulf me at different periods in my life, always manifesting itself in physical disorders (sleeplessness, for instance) and how frightened I was because I did not understand how this was possible.

With age and experience, you will be happy to know, growth becomes a conscious, recognized process. Still somewhat frightening, but at least understood for what it is. Those long periods when something inside ourselves seems to be waiting, holding its breath, unsure about what the next step should be, eventually become the periods we wait for, for it is in those periods that we realize we are being prepared for the next phase of our life and that, in all probability, a new level of the personality is about to be revealed.

A few years ago I experienced one such long period of restlessness disguised as stillness. That is to say, I pretty much withdrew from the larger world in favor of the peace of my personal, smaller one. I unplugged myself from television and newspapers (a great relief!), from the more disturbing members of my extended family, and from most of my friends. I seemed to have reached a ceiling in my brain. And under this ceiling my mind was very restless, although all else about me was calm.

As one does in these periods of introspection, I counted the beads of my progress in this world. In my relationship to my family and the ancestors, I felt I had behaved respectfully (not all of them would agree, no doubt); in my work I felt I had done, to the best of my ability, all that was required of me; in my relationship to the persons with whom I daily shared my life I had acted with all the love I could possibly locate within myself. I was also at least beginning to acknowledge my huge responsibility to the Earth and my adoration of the Universe. What else, then, was required? Why was it that, when I meditated and sought the escape hatch at the top of my brain, which, at an earlier stage of growth, I had been fortunate enough to find, I now encountered a ceiling, as if the route to merge with the infinite I had become used to was plastered over?

One day, after I had asked this question earnestly for half a year, it occurred to me that in my physical self there remained one last barrier to my spiritual liberation, at least in the present phase: my hair.

Not my friend hair itself, for I quickly understood that it was innocent. It was the way I related to it that was the problem. I was always thinking about it. So much so that if my spirit had been a balloon eager to soar away and merge with the infinite, my hair would be the rock that anchored it to Earth. I realized that there was no hope of continuing my spiritual development, no hope of future growth of my soul, no hope of really being able to stare at the Universe and forget myself entirely in the staring (one of the purest joys!) if I still remained chained to thoughts about my hair. I suddenly understood why nuns and monks shaved their heads!

I looked at myself in the mirror and I laughed with happiness! I had broken through the seed skin, and was on my way upward through the earth.

Now I began to experiment: For several months I wore long braids (a   10
fashion among black women at the time) made from the hair of Korean women. I loved this. It fulfilled my fantasy of having very long hair and it gave my short, mildly processed (oppressed) hair a chance to grow out. The young woman who braided my hair was someone I grew to love—a struggling young mother, she and her daughter would arrive at my house at seven in the evening and we would talk, listen to music, and eat pizza or burritos while she worked, until one or two o'clock in the morning. I loved the craft involved in the designs she created for my head. (Basket making! a friend once cried on feeling the intricate weaving atop my head.) I loved sitting between her knees the way I used to sit between my mother's and sister's knees while they braided my hair when I was a child. I loved the fact that my own hair grew out and grew healthy under the "extensions," as the lengths of hair were called. I loved paying a young sister for work that was truly original and very much a part of the black hair-styling tradition. I loved the fact that I did not have to deal with my hair except once every two or three months (for the first time in my life I could wash it every day if I wanted to and not have to do anything further). Still, eventually the braids would have to be taken down (a four-to-seven-hour job) and redone

(another seven to eight hours), nor did I ever quite forget the Korean women, who, according to my young hairdresser, grew their hair expressly to be sold. Naturally this information caused me to wonder (and, yes, worry) about all other areas of their lives.

When my hair was four inches long, I dispensed with the hair of my Korean sisters and braided my own. It was only then that I became reacquainted with its natural character. I found it to be springy, soft, almost sensually responsive to moisture. As the little braids spun off in all directions but the ones I tried to encourage them to go, I discovered my hair's willfulness, so like my own! I saw that my friend hair, given its own life, had a sense of humor. I discovered I liked it.

Again I stood in front of the mirror and looked at myself and laughed. My hair was one of those odd, amazing, unbelievable, stop-you-in-your-tracks creations—not unlike a zebra's stripes, an armadillo's ears, or the feet of the electric-blue-footed boobie—that the Universe makes for no reason other than to express its own limitless imagination. I realized I had never been given the opportunity to appreciate hair for its true self. That it did, in fact, have one. I remembered years of enduring hairdressers—from my mother onward—doing missionary work on my hair. They dominated, suppressed, controlled. Now, more or less free, it stood this way and that. I would call up my friends around the country to report on its antics. It never thought of lying down. Flatness, the missionary position, did not interest it. Being short, cropped off near the root, another missionary "solution," did not interest it either. It sought more and more space, more light, more of itself. It loved to be washed; but that was it.

Eventually I knew *precisely* what hair wanted: it wanted to grow, to be itself, to attract lint, if that was its destiny, but to be left alone by anyone, including me, who did not love it as it was. What do you think happened? (Other than that I was now able, as an added bonus, to comprehend Bob Marley as the mystic his music always indicated he was.) The ceiling at the top of my brain lifted; once again my mind (and spirit) could get outside myself. I would not be stuck in restless stillness, but would continue to grow. The plant was above the ground!

This was the gift of my growth during my fortieth year. This and the realization that as long as there is joy in creation there will always be new creations to discover, or to rediscover, and that a prime place to look is within and about the self. That even death, being part of life, must offer at least one moment of delight.

Thinking about the Text

1. Alice Walker speaks very personally about her hair and how changing her attitude toward it kindled a tremendous change in her life. Is she exhorting her audience to change their attitudes toward their own hair as well, or is she making a somewhat different point? **SUMMARIZE** Walker's **ARGUMENT** in a few sentences.

2. Walker begins her talk by connecting with her audience—students at her alma mater, Spelman College, a historically black college. How does she establish this **TONE** of intimacy? What could she assume about her **AUDIENCE** at Spelman that she would not be able to assume if she were speaking at a large, public university or at a nationally televised event? How might she change her tone in these other situations? Explain.

3. Walker calls her hair a "friend" and describes it as having a sense of humor. What other lifelike qualities does she attribute to her hair? How did you react to these descriptions? What effect did they have on your understanding of Walker's message? Explain.

4. What does the extended metaphor of a seed and its sprouting represent in Walker's address, and what does it have to do with hair? How does she weave those two ideas together, and how well do they work in tandem?

5. How do you feel about your hair? You may or may not have had to struggle with it the way Walker recounts—but very likely you've thought hard about it at some point and made conscious decisions about how to wear it. How have you made those decisions? What does your hair represent to you? Think about Walker's process of discovery and of "listening" to what her hair wanted. What might yours want? Write a letter to your hair, and in the process of writing, think about how it might answer you.

Credits

ILLUSTRATIONS

Part I Opener: 2 left Last Refuge/Robert Harding World Imagery/Corbis; center Heritage Images/Getty Images; right Martin Kruck/Digital Light Sou/Newscom; 3 Imagno/Getty Images; 4 Google and the Google logo are registered tradmarks of Google Inc., used with permission.

Chapter 1: 6 left and right Mark Peterson/Redux; 7 Jim Bourg/Reuters/Newscom; 12 James Leynse/Corbis; 14 left Heinz Kluetmeier/*Sports Illustrated*/Getty Images; right SI Cover/*Sports Illustrated*/Getty Images; 16 Molecular Structure of Nucleic Acids, J. D. Watson and F. H. C. Crick, *Nature*, Vol. 171, April 25, 1953.

Chapter 2: 19 left Africa Studio/Shutterstock; right iStockphoto; bottom courtesy of Beverly Moss; 22 Rob Cottingham-SocialSignal.com.

Chapter 3: 26 Davor Baraka Illustration; 30 Timothy Mulholland/Alamy; 35 Shinola Detroit/Partners & Spade.

Chapter 4: 43 top left Bart Nijs fotografie/Hollandse Hoogte/Redux; top right Lorenzo Moscia/Archivolatino/Redux; center left Roberto Caccuri/Contrasto/Redux; center right Pierre Bessard/REA/Redux; bottom left Camera Press/Cedric Arnold/Redux; bottom right AP Photo/The Northern Star, Jerry Burnes.

Chapter 5: 54 www.utexas.edu/cola/depts/rhetoric.

Chapter 6: 59 top left Erik S. Lesser/EPA/Landov; top right Xinhua/eyevine/Redux; center left Dave Darnell/The Commercial Appeal/Landov; center right Stephane Audras/Rea/Redux; bottom left Erik Pitti/Flikr/CC BY 2.0; bottom right Oliver Lantzendorffer/iStock; 72 Fancy/Alamy.

Part II Opener: 76 Robert Judges/REX/Newscom; 77 Granger, NYC.

Chapter 7: 80 top left racorn/Shutterstock; top right andresr/iStock/Getty Images; center Chris Schmidt/iStock/Getty Images; bottom left Geber86/istockphoto/Getty Images; bottom right thinqkreations/iStock/Getty Images; 83 Tenyia Lee; 87 Fine Art Images/Heritage Images/Getty Images.

Chapter 8: 91 Express Newspapers Via AP Images; 93 Juergen Hanel/Alamy; 95 J. Emilio Flores/*The New York Times*/Redux.

Part III Opener: 107 top left British Museum/Art Resource, NY; top center World History Archive/Alamy; top right DeAgostini/Getty Images; center right National Postal Museum/Smithsonian Institution; bottom right Radu Razvan/iStockphoto; bottom left Nikada/iStockphoto; lower center left Izabela Habur/Getty Images; upper center left Hans Guldenmund/AKG-Images.

Chapter 10: 110 © 2006 Roz Chast, The New Yorker Collection, Cartoonbank. All rights reserved.

Chapter 11: 118 blakes11/iStockphoto; 125 www.youtube.com/user/WeCan08; 127 anyaivanova/iStockphoto/Getty Images; 129 Stephen Brashear/Getty Images; 136 AP Photo/Rob Carr; 146 Bill Hogan/*Chicago Tribune*/MCT/Newscom; 150 courtesy of Katherine Spriggs; 151 Timothy Mulholland/Alamy; 152 Pgiam/iStockphoto; 153 BanksPhotos/iStockphoto; 155 WendellandCarolyn/iStockphoto.

Chapter 12: 161 © 2009 Mike Keefe/Cagle Cartoons. All Rights Reserved; 162 top Lucop/iStockphoto; bottom AP Photo/Scott Boehm; 164 www.itgetsbetter.org; 167 Andrew Testa/*The New York Times*/Redux; 169 Nathaniel S. Butler/NBAE via Getty Images; 171 Bettmann/Corbis; 173 Spelman College Archives; 176 AP Photo/Dave Martin; 180 courtesy of Melanie Luken; 190 courtesy of Michael Lewis; 196 courtesy of Larry Lehna.

Chapter 13: 203 Clive Brunskill/Getty Images; 204 www.ted.com; 208 HBO/The Kobal Collection; 211 supplied by WENN.com; 213 David McNew/Getty Images; 214 Bob Martin/*Sports Illustrated*/Getty Images; 216 Vasiliki Varvaki/iStockphoto; 218 Larry Smith/EPA/Newscom; 221 courtesy of Music Ally; 222 Roberto Finizio/Alamy; 225 by permission of Mike Luckovich and Creators Syndicate, Inc.; 228 Mayank Austen Soofi; 229 Eduardo Munoz/Reuters/Newscom; 240 Adam Emperor Southard; 241, 242, 243, 244 CALVIN AND HOBBES, © 1989, 1993, 1991, 1987 Watterson. Reprinted with permission of UNIVERSAL UCLICK. All rights reserved; 246 courtesy of Melissa Rubin; 247 Advertising Archives.

Chapter 14: 253 top courtesy of Northern Sun, northernsun.com; bottom Pictorial Press Ltd./Alamy; 256 Ezra Shaw/Getty Images; 258 left querbeat/iStockphoto; center kaceyb/iStockphoto; right Jan Kowalski/iStockphoto; 259, 260, 265 Proud Ground; 267, 269 Wikimedia Commons; 272 NBC/NBCU Photo Bank, © 12/13/1980, NBCUniversal/Getty Images; 273 Lumigraphics/Getty Images; 274 Ryan Garza, *Detroit Free Press*/Zuma Press; 276 Martha Thierry/*Detroit Free Press*/Zuma Press; 287 Rux Martin; 289, 290, 291 courtesy of Carol Borland; 293 Ryan Joy.

Chapter 15: 298 AMC/courtesy Everett Collection; 300 Collection El Museo del Barrio, NY; 303 jfmdesign/iStockphoto; 304 Ken Regan/FOX 2000/20TH Century Fox/The Kobal Collection; 307 illustrations: Peter Arkle, text: Amy Goldwasser; 308 Marc Valesella/Sundance Selects/courtesy Everett Collection; 310 Wikimedia Commons; 312 The Kobal Collection/Walt Disney Pictures; 314 courtesy Tim Alamenciak; 319 Crystal Aymelek; 331 Tony Cenicola/*The New York Times*/Redux Pictures; 332 Walt Disney Studios Motion Pictures/Photofest; 333 Walt Disney Co./courtesy Everett Collection; 336 Anya Schultz.

Chapter 16: 342 courtesy Roominate/Maykah Inc.; 349, 350 courtesy Ayres Associates (Blake Theisen, Project Manager, and Aaron O'Keefe, Cartographer); 352 Eduardo Munoz/Reuters/Landov; 357 courtesy David Pasini; 358 Neal Boenzi/*The New York Times*/Redux; 366 right D. Dipasupil/Getty Images; left Taylor Hill/FilmMagic/Getty Images; 370 courtesy Mitchell Oliver.

Part IV Opener: 374 left National Highway Traffic Safety Administration; center Nadezhda Prokudina/iStockphoto;

right Liu Jin/AFP/Getty Images; 377 Wyatt Tee Walker/Bettmann/Corbis.

Chapter 17: 380 left AP Photo/Mike Groll; right Paul J. Richards/AFP/Getty Images; 381 © 2015 Public Citizen; 382 Stephen Voss/Redux; 384 Jack Hunter/*The New Yorker*; 386 photo by Keystone-France/Gamma-Keystone via Getty Images; 390 left John Moore/Getty Images; right CARE/photo by John Moore/Getty Images; 391 Joi Ito/Wikimedia Commons CC by 2.0; 393 AP Photo/Ross Setford; 397 Delphine Bruyere/CC BY-SA 3.0/Wikimedia Commons; 399 Najlah Feanny/Corbis; 403 Advertising Archives; 407 Richard Levine/Alamy; 418 Adbusters Media Foundation.

Chapter 18: 421 Andrew Burton/Getty Images; 423 Charles Minard; 425 NWS/NOAA; 431 DOE/Time Life Pictures/Getty Images; 432 Justin Sullivan/EdStock/iStockphoto; 433 OWS People's Library; 435 Rich Tennant www.the5thwave.com; 436 AD Council; 438 Alexander Joe/AFP/Getty Images; 439 Copyright © 2013 by Chloe Colberg; 440 Marjane Satrapi/Random House.

Part V

Chapter 19: 447 www.ted com; 451 Andy Mead/Icon SMI/Newscom.

Chapter 20: 458 top left Ruslan Dashinsky/iStockphoto; top right Fertnig/ iStockphoto; center left YarOman/iStockphoto; center right iStockphoto; bottom left Chris Scredon/iStockphoto; bottom right René© Mansi/iStockphoto; 461 top left and right National Geographic Society. Photographs by James L Stanfield; bottom left *American Journal of Human Genetics*, Vol. 97, No. 4, October 1, 2015. Published by Cell Press for The American Society of Human Genetics. © Elsevier 2015; bottom right Tatiana Zerjal, Yali Xue, Giorgio Bertorelle, R. Spencer Wells, Weidong Bao, Suling Zhu, Raheel Qamar, Qasim Ayub, Aisha Mohyuddin, Songbin Fu, Pu Li, Nadira Yuldasheva, Ruslan Ruzibakiev, Jiujin Xu, Qunfang Shu, Ruofu Du, Huanming Yang, Matthew E. Hurles, Elizabeth Robinson, Tudevdagva Gerelsaikhan, Bumbein Dashnyam, S. Qasim Mehdi, and Chris Tyler-Smith, "The Genetic Legacy of the Mongols," *American Journal of Human Genetics*, 72:717-721, 2003. © 2003 by The American

Natural Scenes Gathered from a Head-Mounted Camera," *Optometry and Vision Science* 86, 6 (2009): 561–65. © 2009 American Academy of Optometry.

Chapter 35: 781 left Agence France Presse/Central Press/ Getty Images; right Jim Wilson/*The New York Times*/ Redux; 782, 784 courtesy Halle Edwards; 783 © Cartoon Network/Photofest; 785 Toru Hanai/Reuters/Corbis; 786 courtesy Grim's Garden/Flickr www.flickr.com/photos /75759023@N05/11269718185/sizes/l.

Chapter 36: 800 courtesy Rae'Johne K Smith.

Chapter 37: 806 Wikimedia Commons; 807 Tom Toro/The New Yorker Collection/CartoonBank; 808 top www .pen-international.org/the-pen-logo/; bottom www.aus tenauthors.net/category/pp200/page/4; 809 courtesy of William Jennings.

Readings: 817 Photo by Nick Kelsh; 820 AP Photo/Dan Gill; 832 Chris Maddaloni/CQ Roll Call via AP Images; 834 Ververidis Vasilis/Shutterstock; 835 AP Photo/ Patti Longmire; 840 Jonathon S. Baron; 841 pearleye/ iStockphoto; 842 left ©The Metropolitan Museum of Art. Image source: Art Resource, NY; right DEA/G. Dagli Orti/Getty Images; 843 top Maurizio Zanetti/ Flickr CC by 2.0; bottom Greek School/Getty Images; 844 top left Museum of London/Topham/The Image Works; right Pictures From History/The Image Works; bottom left Scala/Art Resource, NY; 845 top from *The Universal Penman*, c.1740–41. Published by Dover Publications, Inc., New York; bottom Science & Society Picture Library/ SSPL/Getty Images; 847 top Hulton-Deutsch Collection/ Corbis; bottom Warner Bros./The Kobal Collection; 848 Wikimedia Commons; 850 Brian Snyder/Reuters/Corbis; 852 top alengo/iStockphoto; bottom Fiat Chrysler Automobiles Historical Services. Highway HiFi is a registered trademark of FCA US LLC; 853 Danish Siddiqui/Reuters/ Newscom; 856 Jeff Miller/UW Madison; 858 Lynda Barry; 862 Alison Bechdel; 868 top left Fred Lee/ABC via Getty Images; top right Martin Klimek/Zuma Press/ Alamy; bottom left Richard Howard courtesy www .ucsusa.org and www.ucsusa.org/food; bottom right Simon Isabelle/SIPA/Newscom; 871 Kevin Lamarque/ Reuters/Corbis; 876 Kevin T. Smith; 881 Brandon Bourdages/Alamy; 884 McKay Imaging Photography as photographed for Living In Media, LLC; 885 Dana Canedy/*The New York Times*/Redux Pictures; 889 Merrick Chase Photography; 890 Leemage/Corbis; 896 © The Photo Works; 899 Hilary Crystal; 900 Lev Dolgachov/ Alamy; 908 Mark Dawidziak; 909 AMC/Photofest; 912 Essdras M. Suarez/*The Boston Globe* via Getty Images; 917 AP Photo/Andrew Shurtleff; 931 David H. Freedman; 932 iStock/Getty Images; 934 Jim West/Alamy; IStock/ Getty Images; 939 Mike Mozart/Jeepers Media; 941 AP Photo/Reed Saxon; 946 Peter Kramer/ © 8/20/2013, NBCUniversal/Getty Images; 947 Daniel Acker/Bloomberg via Getty Images; 952 Annie Wells/*Los Angeles Times*; 957 Courtesy of Gerald Graff; 963 Andy Hinds; 964 Nick Morris/Southcreek Global/Zuma Press.com/ Alamy; 968 Margaret Thomas/*The Washington Post*/ Getty Images; 970 Keith Bridgman/iStockphoto; 976 Sara Salman; 977 Ryan Kohls; 982 Colin M. Maclay; 987 AP Photo/Gretchen Ertl; 989 Hill Street Studios/Blend Images/Newscom; 991 photo by Richard Chisolm; 1000 3d4Medical.com/Corbis; 1001 Dr. Yorgos Nikas/Science Source; 1011 Tressie McMillan Cottom/Emory University, Marketing and Communications; 1017 Lewis Friedman; 1018, 1019, 1021, 1023 Louie Chin; 1025 Nattika/ Shutterstock; 1026 Stanleyphotography/iStockphoto; 1029 David Levenson/Getty Images; 1030 Burlingham/ Shutterstock; 1033, 1035, 1037 Courtesy of Mike Rose; 1043 Vova Shevchuk/Shutterstock; 1044 U.S. Navy photo by Mass Communication Specialist 2nd Class Paul D. Honnick; 1045 Andre Spatz/Demotix/Corbis; 1051 Paul Zimmerman/AdMedia/Newscom; 1053 Jim West/Alamy; 1055 Glowimages/Newscom; 1061 AP Photo/Eric Risberg; 1065 James Keyser/The Life Images Collection/ Getty Images; 1066 Fabrizio Costantini/*The New York Times*/Redux; 1069 Ruth Fremson/*The New York Times*/ Redux; 1071 Denis Finnin, American Museum of Natural History; 1073 JTB Photo/UIG/Getty Images; 1078 Kevork Djansezian/Reuters/Corbis; 1086 Kevork Djansezian/ Getty Images; 1088 AP Photo/Noah Berger.

TEXT

Adegbolahan Adegboyega: Application letter and résumés. Copyright © 2012 by Adegbolahan Adegboyega.

Tim Alamenciak: "*The Monopolists* by Mary Pilon: Review." *Toronto Star*, March 20, 2015. Reprinted by permission of the author.

Crystal Aymelek, Introduction from "The Effects of Mindfulness Meditation and Exercise on Memory." Copyright © 2014 by Crystal Aymelek.

Don B.: "Did Adnan do it? (*Serial* Podcast)." Text via Don B. on Yelp, December 19, 2014. Reprinted by permission of the author.

Shonell Bacon: Blog Comment on "Should everybody write? Or is there enough junk on the internet already?" by Dennis Baron, *The Web of Language* (Blog), March 9, 2010. Reprinted by permission of Shonell Bacon, author and college educator.

Ras J. Baraka: "A New Start for Newark Schools." From *The New York Times*, October 19, 2014. © 2014 The New York Times. All rights reserved. Used by permission and protected by the Copyright Laws of the United States. The printing, copying, redistribution, or retransmission of this Content without express written permission is prohibited. www.nytimes.com

Carrie Barker: "But Two Negatives Equal a Positive." Copyright © 2010 by Carrie Barker.

Donald L. Barlett and James B. Steele: "Monsanto's Harvest of Fear." *Vanity Fair*, May 2008. Reprinted by permission of the authors.

Dennis Baron: "Should everybody write? Or is there enough junk on the internet already?" *The Web of Language* (Blog), March 8, 2010. Reprinted by permission of the author.

Dave Barry: Excerpt from "Beauty and the Beast." *Miami Herald* (1998). Reprinted by permission of the author.

Lynda Barry: "The Sanctuary of School." Originally published in *The New York Times*, January 5, 1992. Copyright © 1992 by Lynda Barry. All rights reserved. Used with permission.

Alison Bechdel: "Compulsory Reading." From *Dykes to Watch Out For* (website), June 25, 2008. © Alison Bechdel, 2008. Reprinted by permission of the author.

Mark Bittman et al.: "How a National Food Policy Could Save Lives," by Mark Bittman, Michael Pollan, Olivier de Schutter, and Ricardo Salvador. *Washington Post*, November 7, 2014. www.ucsusa.org/nationalfoodpolicy. Reprinted by permission of the authors.

Brian Boyd (@Buck4itt): Twitter Post, March 3, 2012, 12:04 PM. https://twitter.com/buck4itt/status/176035303713288192. Reprinted by permission of the author.

Jan Brideau: Copyrighted and published by Project HOPE/*Health Affairs* as "Lydia's Story," by Jan Brideau. *Health Affairs*, March 2006, 25(2):478–80. The published article is archived and available online at www.healthaffairs.org/. Reprinted with permission.

David Brooks: "Getting Obama Right." From *The New York Times*, March 11, 2010. © 2010 *The New York Times*. All rights reserved. Used by permission and protected by the Copyright Laws of the United States. The printing, copying, redistribution, or retransmission of this Content without express written permission is prohibited. www.nytimes.com

Michelle Cacho-Negrete: "Tell Me Something." *The Sun*, August 2008, Issue 392, pp. 20–22. Reprinted by permission of the author.

Dana Canedy: "The Talk." From *The New York Times*, December 13, 2014. © 2014 The New York Times. All rights reserved. Used by permission and protected by the Copyright Laws of the United States. The printing, copying, redistribution, or retransmission of this Content without express written permission is prohibited. www.nytimes.com

CARE.org: "#ENDEBOLA. DONATE TO CARE." Reprinted by permission of CARE.org.

Nicholas Carr: From *The Glass Cage: Automation and Us* by Nicholas Carr. Copyright © 2014 by Nicholas Carr. Used by permission of W. W. Norton & Co., Inc. and by permission of The Random House Group Limited.

About the Authors

ANDREA LUNSFORD is Professor Emerita of English at Stanford University and is on the faculty at the Bread Loaf School of English. Her scholarly interests include rhetorical theory, women and the history of rhetoric, collaboration, style, and technologies of writing. She's received the Braddock and Shaughnessy awards for her research on audience and classical rhetoric, and the CCCC Exemplar Award. She is currently at work on *The Norton Anthology of Rhetoric and Writing*.

MICHAL BRODY is a linguist. She was a founding faculty member of the Universidad de Oriente in Yucatán, Mexico, and teaches now at Sonoma State University. Her scholarly work centers on language pedagogy and politics in the United States and Mexico. She's a co-author of *What's Language Got to Do with It?* and *The Little Seagull Handbook*, and the editor of the *Everyone's an Author* Tumblr and *They Say / I Blog*.

LISA EDE is Professor Emerita of English at Oregon State University, where she directed the Center for Writing and Learning and taught courses in composition, rhetoric, and literacy studies. She's received the Braddock and Shaughnessy awards for her research on audience and classical rhetoric. Her recent books include *Situating Composition: Composition Studies and the Politics of Location* and (with Andrea Lunsford) *Writing Together: Collaboration in Theory and Practice*.

BEVERLY MOSS is Associate Professor of English at The Ohio State University, where she teaches in the Rhetoric, Composition, and Literacy program, and is on the faculty at the Bread Loaf School of English. Her research and teaching interests focus on community literacy, composition theory and pedagogy, and writing center theories and practices. Her books include *Literacy across Communities* and *A Community Text Arises: A Literate Text and a Literacy Tradition in African-American Churches*.

CAROLE CLARK PAPPER teaches online at Hofstra University and formerly directed the University Writing Center there. Prior to that, she served for many years as the Director of the Ball State University Writing Program (winner of the CCCC Certificate of Excellence 2006–2007). Her scholarly interests include visual literacy, composition theory and pedagogy, and writing center theories and practices.

KEITH WALTERS is Professor of Applied Linguistics at Portland State University, where he teaches sociolinguistics and discourse analysis. Much of his research has focused on issues of language and identity in Tunisia, where he served as a Peace Corps volunteer, and the Arab world more broadly. He's a co-author of two other textbooks, *Everything's an Argument with Readings* and *What's Language Got to Do with It?* Prior to teaching at PSU, he taught in the Linguistics Department at the University of Texas at Austin and in the English Department at The Ohio State University.

About the Alphabet

THE ALPHABET song may be one of the first things you learned to sing: *a - b - c - d - e - f - g / h - i - j - k - l - m - n - o - p / q and r and s and t / u - v - w - x - y - z / Now I know my abc's / Next time won't you sing with me?* And maybe you had a set of alphabet blocks, 26 little letters you could use to make words of your own. Combined, those letters yield everything from the word *Google* to the complete works of Shakespeare. So alphabets are versatile, and perhaps that's part of their fascination. In our grandmothers' day, young women often made alphabet samplers, using fancy stitches to create the letters. Earlier, in medieval times, scribes labored to create highly ornate letters to adorn manuscripts whose words were "illuminated" by the intricate letters, often done in silver and gold.

We had these illuminated letters in mind when we asked Carin Berger to create a modern-day illuminated alphabet for this book. You'll see the results in every chapter, each of which begins with one of the letters Berger created. To us, they represent our old alphabet blocks, our grandmothers' samplers, and the illuminated letters that still dazzle us after many hundreds of years. But look again and you'll see that these letters are also striking images. And instead of being decorated with precious silver and gold leaf, our letters are decorated with bits of everyday text—maps, comics, stationery, receipts, school papers, checks, and so on. In our alphabet, old and new, low tech and high tech, word and image come together to create evocative, timely letters for our book.

And just as modern-day type fonts have names, so too does our alphabet. We call it Author.

Submitting Papers for Publication by
W. W. Norton & Company

We are interested in receiving writing from college students to consider including in our textbooks as examples of student writing. Please send this form with the work that you would like us to consider to Marilyn Moller, Student Writing, W. W. Norton & Company, 500 Fifth Avenue, New York, NY 10110.

Text Submission Form

Student's name _____

School _____

Address _____

Department _____

Course _____

Writing assignment the text responds to _____

_____

_____

_____

_____

Instructor's name _____

Please write a few sentences about what your primary purposes were for writing this text. Also, if you wish, tell us what you learned about writing from the experience of writing it.

_____

_____

_____

_____

_____

_____

_____

_____

_____

_____

Contact Information

Please provide the information below so that we can contact you if your work is selected for publication.

Name _____

Permanent address _____

Email _____

Phone _____

Author / Title Index

Note: Page numbers in *italics* indicate figures.

Glossary / Index

Note: This glossary / index defines key terms and concepts and directs you to pages in the book where you can find specific information on these and other topics. Please note the words set in SMALL CAPITAL LETTERS are themselves defined in the glossary / index. Page numbers in *italics* indicate figures.

APPENDIX A section at the end of a written work for supplementary material that would be distracting in the main part of the text.

ARGUING A POSITION, 116–58 A GENRE that uses REASONS and EVIDENCE to support a CLAIM. Features: an explicit POSITION • a response to what others have said • appropriate background information • a clear indication of why the topic matters • good REASONS and EVIDENCE • attention to more than one POINT OF VIEW • an authoritative TONE • an appeal to readers' values

ARGUMENT, 373–441 Any text that makes a CLAIM supported by REASONS and EVIDENCE.

ARTICLE, 688–89 The word *a, an,* or *the*, used to indicate that a NOUN is indefinite (*a writer, an author*) or definite (*the author*).

COMMA SPLICE, 672, 700–701 Two or more MAIN CLAUSES joined with only a comma: *I came, I saw, I conquered.*

COMMON GROUND, 391–94 Shared values. Writers build common ground with AUDIENCES by acknowledging others' points of view, seeking areas of compromise, and using language that includes, rather than excludes, those they aim to reach.

COMPARISON/CONTRAST, 425–27 A STRATEGY that highlights the points of similarity and difference between items. Using the block method of comparison and contrast, a writer discusses all the points about one item and then all the same points about the next item; using the point-by-point method, a writer discusses one point for both items before going on to discuss the next point for both items, and so on. Sometimes comparison and/or contrast can serve as the organizing principle for a paragraph or whole text.

COMPLEX SENTENCE, 673–74 A single MAIN CLAUSE plus one or more DEPENDENT CLAUSES: *When the United States holds a presidential election once every four years, citizens should vote.*

COMPOUND-COMPLEX SENTENCE, 674 Two or more MAIN CLAUSES plus one or more DEPENDENT CLAUSES: *When the United States holds a presidential election once every four years, citizens should vote, but voter turnout is often disappointing.*

COMPOUND SENTENCE, 670–72 Two or more MAIN CLAUSES joined by a comma and a COORDINATING CONJUNCTION or by a semicolon: *The United States holds a presidential election once every four years, but voter turnout is often disappointing.*

CONCLUSION The way a text ends, a chance to leave an AUDIENCE thinking about what's been said. Five ways of concluding a college essay: reiterating your point, discussing the implications of your ARGUMENT, asking a question, referring back to your OPENING, or proposing some kind of action.

H

Griffin that aims for understanding and shared goals by listening carefully to all concerned. Invitational arguments introduce the issue, present all perspectives on it fairly, identify any commonalities among the perspectives, and conclude by seeking a resolution that is agreeable to all.

IRREGULAR VERB, 728–729 A VERB that does not form its past tense and past participle by adding *-ed* or *-d* to the base form (as in *eat, ate, eaten*).

KAIROS, 87, 640 An ancient Greek term meaning "the opportune moment." Authors look for just the right moment to make a particular ARGUMENT, appeal to a particular AUDIENCE, and so on.

KEYWORD, 67 A term that a researcher inputs when searching RÉSUMÉS, databases, and the internet for information.

LAB REPORT, 254 A GENRE of writing that covers the process of conducting an experiment in a controlled setting. Features: an explicit title • ABSTRACT • PURPOSE • methods • results and discussion • REFERENCES • APPENDIX • appropriate format

LAYOUT, 743–59 The way text is arranged on a page or screen—for example, in paragraphs, in lists, on charts, with headings, and so on.

NONCOUNT NOUN, 688 A word that names something that cannot be counted or made plural with certain modifiers or units: *information*, *rice*.

NONESSENTIAL ELEMENT, 692, 693 A word, PHRASE, or CLAUSE that gives additional information but that is not necessary for understanding the basic meaning of a sentence: *I learned French, which is a Romance language, online*. Nonessential elements should be set off by commas.

NOUN A word that refers to a person, place, animal, thing, or idea (*director, Stephen King, forest, Amazon River, tree frog, notebook, democracy*).

O

OPENING, 678–81 The way a text begins, which plays

SIMPLE SENTENCE, 670 A single MAIN CLAUSE, which contains at least a SUBJECT and a VERB. The main clause must stand alone: *Citizens vote. The United States holds a presidential election once every four years.* For sentences with more than a single main clause, see COMPOUND SENTENCE; COMPOUND-COMPLEX SENTENCE; COMPLEX SENTENCE.

SPATIAL ORGANIZATION, 284 A way of ordering a text that mirrors the physical arrangement of the subject, for instance from top to bottom, left to right, outside to inside.

STANCE, 10–11, 23 An author's attitude toward his or her subject—for example, reasonable, neutral, angry, curious. Stance is conveyed through TONE and word choice.

STANDARD EDITED ENGLISH, 45–46, 643–44 The conventions of spelling, grammar, and punctuation expected in academic discourse, which tends to be more formal than conversational English. Standard English varies from country to country and changes over time. Edited refers to the care writers take in reviewing their formal written work.

Starbucks, *666*

STASIS THEORY, 387–88 A simple system for identifying the crux of an ARGUMENT—what's at stake in it—by asking four questions: (1) What are the facts? (2) How can the issue be defined? (3) How much does it matter, and why? (4) What actions should be taken as a result?

statistics, as evidence, 394–95

Stein, Ross, 404–5

STORYBOARDING, 775, 776 A method of planning a film or video essay by making a series of sketches to map out the sequence of camera shots, movement, and action.

STRATEGIES FOR SUPPORTING AN ARGUMENT, 419–41 Patterns for organizing and providing EVIDENCE to support a POSITION: ANALOGY, CAUSE-EFFECT, CLASSIFICATION, COMPARISON/CONTRAST, DEFINITION, DESCRIPTION, EXAMPLE, NARRATION, PROBLEM/SOLUTION, and REITERATION.

    analogy, 419–21

    cause/effect, 421–23

    classification, 423–24

    comparison and contrast, 425–27

    definition, 428–29

    description, 430–32

    examples, 432–33

    humor, 434–35

    narration, 436–37

    problem/solution, 437–39

    reiteration, 439–41

straw man fallacy, 401–2

students, 93–94

StumbleUpon, 466

style, 637–737, 641

    academic writing and, 40–52, 652–67

    appropriateness and correctness, 642–45

    argument and, 416–18

    defined, 641–51

    design, 570–90

    good sentences, 668–86

    personal, 649–51

    representing yourself in writing, 657–59

    sentence style, 668–86

    social media and, 652–67

    stance, 646–49

    tone, 659–60

    images, 664–65

style guides. *See* APA STYLE; MLA STYLE

SUBJECT, 720–27 A word or word group, usually including at least one NOUN or PRONOUN plus its modifiers, that tells who or what a sentence or CLAUSE is about. In the sentence *A frustrated group of commuters waited for the late bus*, the subject is *A frustrated group of commuters*.

    compound, 720, 721

    subjects that are titles, 726, 727

    subject-verb agreement, 720–27

subject librarians, 467

subject searches, 474–75

subject-specific databases, 471–72

SUBJUNCTIVE MOOD, 736 The MOOD of a VERB used to express wishes or requests or to indicate unlikely conditions: *Most people wish that global warming were not so evident.*

SUBORDINATE CLAUSE, 673–74, 700–701 A CLAUSE that begins with a SUBORDINATING WORD and therefore cannot stand alone as a sentence: *She feels good when she exercises. My roommate, who was a physics major, tutors students in science.*

MLA DOCUMENTATION DIRECTORY

APA DOCUMENTATION DIRECTORY

Menu of Readings ∽

Readings by Genre ∽

Argument

Analysis